Industry Canada
Research Publications Program

PERSPECTIVES ON NORTH AMERICAN FREE TRADE

THE CHANGING INDUSTRY AND SKILL MIX OF CANADA'S INTERNATIONAL TRADE

By Peter Dungan and Steve Murphy
University of Toronto

Aussi disponible en français

Canadian Cataloguing in Publication Data

Dungan, D. Peter

The changing industry and skill mix of Canada's international trade

(Perspectives on North American free trade)
Text in English and French on inverted pages.
Title on added t.p.: Évolution du profil sectoriel et professionnel du commerce international du Canada.
Includes bibliographical references.
ISBN 0-662-64211-2
Cat. no. C21-28/4-1999

1. Foreign trade and employment – Canada.
2. Labor supply – Canada.
3. International trade.
I. Murphy, Steven.
II. Canada. Industry Canada.
III. Title.
IV. Series.

HD5710.75C3D86 1999   382.0971   C99-980165-1E

The list of titles available in the Research Publications Program and details on how to obtain copies can be found at the end of this document. Abstracts of research volumes and papers published in Industry Canada's various series, and the full text of our quarterly newsletter, *MICRO*, are available on *STRATEGIS*, the Department's online business information site, at http://strategis.ic.gc.ca.

Comments should be addressed to:

Someshwar Rao
Director
Strategic Investment Analysis
Micro-Economic Policy Analysis
Industry Canada
5th Floor, West Tower
235 Queen Street
Ottawa, Ontario
K1A 0H5

Tel.: (613) 941-8187
Fax: (613) 991-1261
E-mail: rao.someshwar@ic.gc.ca

Acknowledgments

The authors would like to express their appreciation to Frank Lee, Surendra Gera and participants at an Industry Canada workshop for numerous excellent suggestions on an earlier version of this study. They are also grateful for the insightful comments of two anonymous referees. Any remaining errors are, of course, our own.

TABLE OF CONTENTS

PREFACE

Toward the mid-1980s, as international markets and production were becoming more global in scope and outlook, Canada was in danger of being pushed to the margin of the world economy. We were not equipped to expand our participation in global markets, and we were in danger of losing our own markets. Moreover, with over two-thirds of our exports destined for the United States and the share steadily climbing, we were highly exposed to rising U.S. protectionist sentiments. In essence, our past prosperity had made us complacent about the precarious position we faced as a trading nation.

It was in such a climate that the government undertook the steps necessary to renew and strengthen the economy, rather than resist the forces of global change. The government's approach was to make the private sector the driving force of this economic renewal. Policies were adopted to encourage and reward entrepreneurship and facilitate adaptation to the changing economic environment.

As a trading nation, getting our trade relations with the United States right was an obvious goal. It was decided that a free trade agreement was needed in order to forestall protectionist tendencies in the United States, enhance Canada's security of access to the American market and improve the predictability of trade relations with our neighbour to the south.

The Canada-United States Free Trade Agreement (FTA) was implemented in 1989. Five years later, in 1994, the North American Free Trade Agreement (NAFTA) came into effect and basically extended the FTA to the fast-growing Mexican market.

These free trade agreements were expected to increase prosperity in Canada by raising the efficiency and productivity of Canadian businesses. Such agreements are known to be mutually beneficial to the economies of the parties involved, and are particularly beneficial to the relatively small economies, such as that of Canada. They first expose domestically protected firms to international competition. Second, they reward innovative and productive firms by giving them access to larger markets. This increases trade flows between participating countries and improves the overall efficiency of their economies. The FTA and NAFTA were no exception; they were signed in the hope of obtaining those benefits for the Canadian economy after an initial adjustment period. Yet concomitantly, there were legitimate concerns about possible plant closures and job losses in Canada.

More than ten years have passed since the implementation of the FTA — enough time to reliably assess the implications of the agreement for the Canadian economy. In this context, the Micro-Economic Policy Analysis Branch has asked a group of experts to examine the Canadian economy in light of the FTA. The six papers coming out of this exercise are now being published under the general heading of *Perspectives on North American Free Trade*. These papers analyse a broad spectrum of issues ranging from the impact of the FTA on interprovincial trade flows to its impact on the productivity performance of the Canadian economy. In addition, the viability of the Canadian manufacturing sector is assessed, as is the relationship between outward foreign direct investment and trade flows. The papers also explore the implications of trade for the evolution of Canada's industrial structure and skill mix along with an assessment of Canada's migration patterns with the United States.

Peter Dungan and Steve Murphy set out to examine the changing industry and skill mix of Canadian exports and imports over the past three decades. The primary technique they use is input-output (I/O) analysis. This is supplemented by detailed sectoral education (skill) data from the Canadian occupational Projection System (COPS).

With these data, the authors estimate how much of Canada's employment is associated with exports and imports and whether changes in the industrial composition of our trade have affected the employment and skill mix of jobs over time. A key finding is that despite the rising importance of exports in overall economic activity, the growth in the share of employment attributable to exports has been much less pronounced. The major reason for this, according to the authors, is that exports now have a much higher import content in intermediate inputs than in the past. Likewise, if our imports were to be produced in Canada, our technology would produced them with much more imported intermediate inputs than was the case in the past.

The authors also find that changes in the employment mix are directly related to the composition of exports, along with the degree of import penetration for intermediate inputs. However, relative labour productivity and technical change were found to be less important.

EXECUTIVE SUMMARY

The intention of the project is to examine in detail the industry and skill mix of Canadian exports and imports as they stood in 1997 and to ask how this mix has changed since 1961. Some important and timely questions underlie the study: How much of Canada's employment is associated with exporting, and how much has this changed over the last three decades? To what extent do Canadian exports and export employment still depend upon raw materials, and how much have our exports moved to being made up of tertiary manufacturing and services? Even if such a movement has occurred, the skill mix implications are not clear: at least some primary sector jobs require considerable skill and are very well paid, while many manufacturing and services jobs require little skill and are poorly rewarded. How has the education/skill mix of Canadian export employment changed over time, and in relation to employment in the entire economy? On the import side there is the widely-held conception that a more open economy and heavier reliance on imports has pushed aside low-skill jobs in Canada and has led to lower incomes for the less skilled. To what extent can we identify such a trend from 1961 through 1997?

The study uses Input-Output (I/O) techniques to address these questions, supplemented by detailed sectoral education data from the Canadian Occupational Projection System (COPS). We build upon earlier studies at Industry Canada and elsewhere by using annual I/O tables for 1961 through 1992 and supplementary detail to extend the analysis through 1997, and by using a somewhat greater industrial disaggregation. Results are presented in both aggregated and disaggregated form together with a variety of sensitivity tests and with decompositions of the sources of change in export and "import replacement" employment over 1961–97.

Main Findings

- While exports and imports have grown strongly as shares of the Canadian economy since 1961 — and massively so in the 1990s — the growth in the share of employment attributable to exports (or "displaced" by imports) has been *much less rapid*. The major reason is import penetration: Exports today have a much higher import content in intermediate inputs that in the past. As for imports, if they too were to be produced in Canada, today's technology would have them produced with much more imported intermediate inputs than was true in the 1960s.

- When our detailed sectoral results are aggregated, Canadian exports have always been *above the average* for total business output in labour productivity — especially when the effect of agriculture in the 1960s is netted out. However, this relatively high labour productivity of exports has shown almost *no tendency to increase* over time. Along with higher labour productivity comes higher returns to labour in exports — but again, this relative performance in exports shows almost no trend over time. However, since the share of employment attributable to exports has been growing over time, it can be concluded that exports are helping to lift both the *overall level* of Canadian labour productivity and returns to labour.

- The sources of change in the employment mix of Canadian exports are primarily the final export mix itself and the degree of import penetration for intermediate inputs. Generally less important are changes among sectors in relative labour productivity or "technical change" as embodied in changes in Input-Output coefficients. The same observation applies for the most part also to changes in the employment mix of Canadian imports.

- Changes in export employment shares have occurred across a wider range of industries than might be imagined. Of the ten industry groups that increased their share of export employment by over one percentage point from 1961 to 1997, four are service industries (Personal and other services, Business services, Trade, and Finance), but the other six are various manufacturing categories, some of which might have been expected given the Auto Pact and changing technology — like Motor vehicles, Electrical and electronic products and Rubber and plastic products — and some that are surprising — like Leather, textile and clothing products. Of the four industries with declines in export employment shares of over one percentage point, the two largest declines are in primary production (Mining excluding oil and gas; and Agriculture, forestry and fishing), one is in raw material processing and manufacturing (Paper and allied products and printing) and the fourth is Transportation.

- Combining the I/O results with data on education mix by industry leads to the conclusion that since 1961 the mix of Canadian export employment (both direct and indirect) has continually evolved to emphasize industries with more highly-educated workers. However, this also turns out to be true of business-sector employment *as a whole*. If exports are compared to the total business sector in relative uses of different education mixes, the conclusion is that employment from exports is "bi-polar" in distribution. Exports *exceed* the economy-wide average in employing workers with low education, and also in employing workers with relatively advanced education. The relative ratios have changed only a little over the last three decades.

- The labour productivity of employment "displaced" by imports (if it were to be produced with Canadian technology) is invariably *lower* than that of exports — although it is still *above* the business-sector average for most years. The ratio has fallen to about the economy-wide average in recent years indicating some new inroads into replacing lower-productivity employment. Nonetheless, the evidence is that imports, on the whole, are not replacing exceptionally low-productivity employment (which is probably concentrated in non-tradable services in any event). However, imports are displacing "relatively" more jobs than exports are adding. If macro policies can keep the economy near full employment, and the pace of change is not too fast, this means that Canada is replacing low-productivity employment with high-productivity employment through expanded international trade, and is thereby made better off.

- Comparing changes in employment shares of exports and imports, it is remarkable that the largest increases and decreases occur, in many cases, in the *same* sectors. Personal and business services, and Trade show among the largest increases in employment shares for both exports and imports, while Mining, Agriculture and Forestry show among the largest decreases in employment shares for both exports and imports. *Both* Canadian exports and Canadian imports have become more intensive in service employment and less intensive in employment for the production of raw materials.

- The education mix calculations show that, at least by Canadian technology and education shares by sector, Canadian imports have been above the business-sector average in overall education content. In recent years, however, this discrepancy has been narrowing, indicating some increased competition from imports in sectors using lower-skill workers. Nonetheless, Canadian imports remain above the business sector average in education content. This result may seem at odds with the previous point about labour productivity and labour returns. However, it should be noted that we found productivity and returns to labour in imports also to be *above* the business-sector average, although they were also *lower* than for exports. Finding that the education mix is above the business-sector average is not inconsistent with this. The anomaly, perhaps, is that *export* productivity and returns are so high when at least part of the education mix is low. The anomaly can, however, be better understood if it is recalled that education, as broadly measured, is not the sole determinant of either productivity or returns to labour; high capital or natural-resource endowments also matter.

1. INTRODUCTION

This project seeks to examine, in some detail, the industry and skill mix of Canadian exports and imports as they stood in 1997 and to ask how this mix has changed over the past three decades. Obviously, there are some important and very timely questions that will underlie this study: Canada, at least at one time, had the reputation of being a "hewer of wood and drawer of water" — that is, of being primarily an exporter of raw materials and an importer of finished goods. To what extent is this still true? Or how much have our exports moved to being made up of tertiary manufacturing and services? Even if such a movement has occurred, the skill mix implications are not clear: at least some primary sector jobs require considerable skill and are very well paid, while many manufacturing and services jobs require little skill and are poorly rewarded. On the import side there is the widely-held conception that a more open economy and heavier reliance on imports has pushed aside low-skill jobs in Canada and has led to lower incomes for the less skilled.

The primary method we use is Input-Output (I/O) analysis — a technique employed in a number of recent studies conducted at Industry Canada and by several other Canadian researchers. However, we are able to extend the time frame from some earlier studies by using a complete time series of I/O tables from 1961 through 1992 and by using supplementary industrial detail to extend the analysis through 1997. The I/O analysis also proceeds on a highly disaggregated basis, with over 150 industries being distinguished in the calculations. Finally, we are able to supplement the I/O work with detailed industry skill data from the Canadian Occupational Projection System (COPS) for 1986 and 1991; these data are used to make estimates of the changing educational skill mix of exports and imports over time, insofar as skill mix changes are due to changes in the industrial mix.

Three cautions on the methods and results should be noted up front: First, it is important to note at the outset that, while the industry and skill mix of exports is a fairly straightforward concept, by the industry and skill mix of imports we mean the industry and skill mix of equivalent or competitive production in Canada, not the industry and skill mix of the foreign country from which the imports originated. Second, Input-Output analysis and the associated skill calculations done here can establish important descriptions and associations but not necessarily "causality". For example, while exports may be found to be associated with a certain number of jobs at a particular time, they did not necessarily create or "cause" these jobs, nor would the workers so employed have necessarily remained unemployed in the absence of the exports. The third caution is that the description and analysis is based on input-output relationships that occurred, at least in part, only because relative prices and scarcities were what they were in any given year, although we assume them to be "fixed" ("Leontief technology"). Had relative prices been different — say because of different monetary or exchange-rate policies — then different technologies might have been adopted and different I/O coefficients would have been observed. All in all, the primary purpose of the analysis presented in this study is to give an initial description of what has happened, preparatory to deeper analysis of causality, and, possibly, policy prescriptions.

The paper is organized as follows: Section 2 describes the data and calculation methods we have used in greater detail. Section 3 reviews some of the underlying literature and points out differences and advances in the present study relative to earlier Canadian work. Section 4 examines how the place of exports has changed in the Canadian economy since 1961, and how the industrial output and employment mix of exports has altered over that time. Changes in the employment mix are decomposed into four main sub-components. Then, adding industry skill-mix data, we discuss the education/skill mix of Canadian exports in recent years and, to the extent possible, determine what changes may have occurred in this mix over time. Section 5 repeats the analysis for Section 4, but for imports. Finally, Section 6 reports on our conclusions and main findings. Several appendices present details of the calculations, sensitivity tests and more detailed industrial results.

2. DATA AND METHODS

In studying the employment and skill mix of Canadian exports and imports from 1961 to 1997, two primary data sources will be exploited. The first is the time series of detailed Input-Output (I/O) tables produced by Statistics Canada. The Institute for Policy Analysis has collected this data set over the years and prepared a variety of software tools for exploiting it. Our I/O calculations proceed at what is termed by Statistics Canada the "L" ("Large") disaggregation level, which permits us to examine over 160 industries. The data set covers the period 1961 through 1992 with annual tables.

Unfortunately, at the time this study was prepared, I/O tables beyond 1992 were unavailable. In an effort to bring the analysis up through 1997, we have collected data on aggregate domestic product, exports, imports and employment and have matched them as closely as possible to the I/O "L" disaggregation categories. We have combined these data with the 1992 I/O tables to extend our analysis of exports and imports through 1997. However, the results for 1993–97 must be taken cautiously, both because only the 1992 tables were used, and because our matching of published data for output, employment, etc. with I/O categories can only be approximate.

Why use Input-Output data? Why not simply examine "export" or "import-competing" industries and count up their employment? The answer to both questions lies in the multi-industry structure of production or, as the phrase goes, in "the production of commodities by means of commodities". If Canada exports so many dollars worth of automobiles, and the auto industry employed so many workers, that is worth knowing — but it is not the whole story. Included in the exported autos may have been steel produced in Canada, and that steel may have in turn been produced from Canadian iron ore. Some of the employees of the steel and mining industries were also therefore involved *indirectly* in exporting the automobile, and it will be important in properly accounting for employment generated by exports to take this indirect input into account. In addition, a great deal of the exported auto may have been produced with *imported* parts — which would have no effect on Canadian employment —, whereas exports of another product or service, apparently smaller in dollar value, might have much greater Canadian content and a greater total impact on Canadian employment. Therefore, it will also be important to take into account the relative *import* contents of indirect inputs into production.

Fortunately, the annual Input-Output system provides, for each year, a picture of all these inter-industry interactions and, with appropriate manipulations, the entire backward chain of production inputs to produce exports (or to have replaced imports) can be derived from the system. Thus the importance of the I/O database for this study. The estimates of employment generated by exports (or, speaking loosely, replaced by imports) that are derived are not sums of the observed employment of what are deemed to be "export oriented" industries, but instead the employees involved in those shares of all industries producing for export either directly or indirectly at all stages back down the production sequence.

For each year between 1961 and 1997 our initial industrial-mix calculations proceed as follows:[1] We begin with the matrix of final demands by final-demand category and by industry. The export or import columns of this matrix tell us the industrial breakdown of exports or imports in that year. (From here on we will refer only to export impacts, but the determination of import effects is very similar).[2] The column is then multiplied by the "Leontief inverse" of the matrix of input-output coefficients to yield an estimate of the gross output in each of the 161 industries that is being used to supply exports in that year *together with* all intermediate inputs back along the production chain. For those not familiar with I/O terms, the "Leontief inverse" is simply the end result of the manipulations of the I/O data needed to extract the impacts of particular expenditures (like exports) on industrial production including all intermediate processing stages. Note too that the calculation we use also includes automatically the average "leakage" into imports for demands from each industry as reflected in the data for that year. Coefficients derived from I/O data are then applied to the gross output impacts thus calculated to determine impacts on domestic product at factor cost ("domestic product" hereafter), employment, and wages and salaries earned — and consequently the average remuneration per employee in sectors supplying exports. These results are presented and examined both in absolute form and as relative shares of total domestic product and employment for the year.

By comparing our calculations annually and over different intervals, we see how output and employment mixes changed over time in providing Canadian exports. While the full 161-industry detail is presented, so also is a smaller 24-industry aggregation in order to determine broad trends in shifts of export production.

The Canadian I/O database is available in both current-dollar (or nominal) form and constant-dollar (or real) form. The constant-dollar data maintained by Statistics Canada use different base years for different sub-intervals and these must be spliced together by the user if a full time series from 1961 through 1992 is required. We have conducted our calculations using primarily the nominal tables, for several reasons: First, because we are primarily interested in changing *shares* of output and employment mixes, there is no inflationary distortion as such that enters calculations based on nominal data. We are simply examining changes in relative dollar earnings or relative employment in different export or import categories. Second, deflation of the massive amount of detail in the I/O tables is very difficult, and the possibility of deflation error has to be considered. The nominal data are the raw data in this case, and less likely to suffer from judgmental distortion. As noted above, to obtain a full time series of real I/O data several sub-periods with different base years must be spliced, further increasing the danger of distortion. And third, extension of the data from 1992 through 1997 is not possible in *real* terms for exports and imports for the type and level of detail required to match with the I/O 160-industry disaggregation — at least not with the resources available to us. If we wished to have consistent series from 1961 through 1997, then use of the nominal I/O data was required.

To check for sensitivity to the choice of nominal vs. real I/O series, we have conducted some of the calculations presented below with *both* data sets for 1961–92 and have compared the results. On the whole, the nominal data, in our judgement, yield results that are generally equivalent to those obtained from the real data, and, where they differ, the nominal series are smoother on a year-to-year basis and more intuitively appealing. As changes are observed across the entire 1961–97 period or ten-year spans within it, it is important to investigate their source. There are two possible contributors to a changing output mix from exports: The first is that the sectoral components of Canadian exports are themselves changing (as is shown in changing coefficients in the export vector in the final-demand matrix); and the second is that the industrial processes used to produce the export goods are changing (as is shown in changes in various coefficients from the input-output system). We decompose these two components by, for example, running the 1961 export mix on the 1971 input-output coefficients, or vice-versa. Within the I/O system we further differentiate between changes in the I/O "technical" coefficients (those describing how one industry uses products from others as inputs), and changes in import coefficients (reflecting the changing mix of imports and domestic production in satisfying both final and intermediate demand for products). For employment shifts from exports an additional source of change is alterations in the relative labour productivity of different industries between comparison years. Once again, this source is separately identified by examining changes in employment/output coefficients between comparison periods. A total of four sources of change in export or import employment shifts are thus examined: (1) changes in the export or import mix, (2) changes in "technical" I/O coefficients, (3) changes in import requirements for intermediate or final demand, and (4) changes in relative labour productivity among sectors.[3]

The second primary data source used in this study is the database of industry employment by occupation and by educational (or skill) level maintained by the Canadian Occupational Projection System (COPS) group at Human Resources Development Canada. In coordinating this database with the I/O database, and making allowance for some "Unassigned" components in the COPS data, we can obtain a disaggregation of 112 industries. Unfortunately, only two years of data are available: 1991 and 1986.[4] This means that we can only examine education-mix changes *within industries* between these two dates. We examine changes in the educational mix between 1986 and 1991, but for all years before 1986 we had to use the 1986 educational mix, and for the years 1992–97 we used the 1991 educational mix. However, using the 1986 or 1991 educational mix, together with I/O information on how the industry mix of exports and imports have changed from 1961–86 and from 1991–97 we are at least able to gain valuable insight into overall skill mix changes in these periods that are the result of changes in the *industrial* mix. Moreover, from the I/O industry data we not only are able to determine industrial employment mix changes but also changes in labour productivity and aggregate returns to labour (in effect, wage impacts).

The application of the COPS data is relatively straightforward. As noted above, the I/O calculations provide us with the employment by industry associated with exports in each of the years to be examined on a 161-industry disaggregation. First we aggregate up to the 112-industry aggregation available from COPS. Then we simply apportion these total employment estimates using shares from the COPS data for the appropriate educational (or occupational, if used) breakdown that we desire. Once the calculations are complete, we can state something like: In 1961, exports accounted for x percent of total employment in that year. These jobs were distributed among the following educational groups: no secondary, secondary, trade school, university and college, post-graduate, etc. (but recall that we must use 1986 education weights for 1961!) We can then present the same figures for 1997 and selected intervening years and compare them with 1961 to show changes in proportions and shares. As noted in the I/O discussion above, we are able to break down the employment impacts between changes in the export mix, changes in technical and import coefficients (or the structure of production), and changes in relative labour productivity among sectors. Further, between 1986 and 1991, we are able to measure the contribution of a changing skill or occupational mix *within* industries.

3. BACKGROUND AND RELATED STUDIES

While the primary intent of this study was to produce new empirical work, we have examined the relevant literature to determine if comparable studies have been done for Canada or for other industrialized nations. There is, not surprisingly, a very broad literature on the question of how changes in the levels and conditions of foreign trade have changed employment and wages, both in particular industries and in economies overall. The underlying policy concern is that increased trade with developing, low-wage countries will be hurting low-wage and low-skill industries in industrialized countries, leading to higher unemployment amongst the low skilled and diminished relative earning power (and hence, perhaps, a growing gap between high-skill and low-skill earnings in such countries). The primary analytical underpinning is the Heckscher-Ohlin theory or principle, "...whose central insight is that countries export goods that use intensively the factors of production with which they are relatively abundantly endowed.." (Wood, 1995, p.58). There are numerous papers on this subject — especially for the United States. Examples include the papers by Freeman, Richardson and Wood in a special issue of the *Journal of Economic Perspectives* in 1995, and papers by Sachs and Shatz, and Feenstra and Hanson in the *AEA Papers and Proceedings* of 1996. An earlier summary of the U.S. record can be found in Levy and Murnane (1992). In addition there are numerous studies examining some or all of the OECD countries, often together with the less developed countries (LDC's). Examples include Lawrence (1996) and Thygesen, Kosai and Lawrence (1996).

However, while there is a wide literature on the basic trade-and-wages question for the United States (and also for the United Kingdom), so far we have found much less empirical work in this general area for Canada. For example, only one relevant article has appeared in *Canadian Public Policy* in recent years (Gera and Mang, 1998), and in the *Canadian Journal of Economics* the sole major recent contribution has been Gaston and Trefler (1997) — which is really confined to the impacts of the Canada-United States Free Trade Agreement. The most recent study closest to our own in intention and methods is Betts and McCurdy (1993). These authors use I/O tables for 1961, 1971 and 1981 to determine sources of total employment change over the two subperiods in a 39-industry disaggregation. The sources of employment change examined include changes in the five major categories of final demand, and changes in I/O technical coefficients, labour productivity and hours per worker. In addition, they examine impacts on a detailed occupational breakdown.

Moreover, while the literature — at least for the United States and United Kingdom — on this general topic is vast, relatively little that we can find makes use of anything like the empirical approaches used here. Almost all the studies use panel-type data on wages or particular employer or employee groups, or confine their attention to particular economic sectors, whether narrow or broad (e.g., Manufacturing — see Betts, 1997). We use Input-Output techniques as the foundation of our approach, and have found only two good and immediate references to I/O based studies outside Canada: the first is by Gregory and Greenhalgh (1997) for the United Kingdom and the second is a reference in Tyson and Zysman (1988) to an I/O study for the United States by the Office of Technology Assessment (1987), which would have been based on much earlier I/O data and so is now quite dated.

Gregory and Greenhalgh (1997) use current-dollar I/O tables for 1979, 1985 and 1990 to examine the changes in labour demand in the United Kingdom in the 1980s and, in particular, to look for evidence of "deindustrialization" and the impact of changing international trade on both the level of employment and its sectoral distribution and on aggregate employment income. Changes in sectoral output and employment are decomposed into components based on domestic final demand, exports, import penetration and changes in inter-industry purchases (technical change) and in technical change as it affects labour demand per unit of output. While the study's results — as with most studies of this sort — are primarily in the details, a few general conclusions could be drawn: No one source of "deindustrialization" could be found. Import penetration, the splitting off of services from goods producing sectors, and labour-saving technical change all were found to contribute. Import penetration was found to be important and large, but was balanced by export growth. Labour-saving technical change was more important than loss of markets in reducing labour demand — but this effect was apparent in all sectors in the 1980s. The study found some evidence of structural shifts from international competition pushing the economy in the direction of higher value-added or high-technology sectors, but there was also evidence in some sectors that this was not so, as there were rising imports and low value added in some high-technology products.

For Canada, the closest studies in approach to the work we have done, aside from Betts and McCurdy (1993), are Industry Canada reports by Gera and Mang (1997) (published subsequently as Gera and Mang, 1998) and Gera and Massé (1996), each a considerable extension of earlier work by the OECD (1992) that covered only the period 1981–86 and a small number of aggregated industries. Gera and Mang (1998 and 1997) and Gera and Massé (1996) all use constant-dollar I/O tables for 1971, 1981, 1986 and 1991 at the highest level of disaggregation available (over 200 industries and over 600 commodities). In the final report, however, data on 111 industries are reported, still well beyond the 33 identified in the OECD study. Because the Statistics Canada constant-dollar tables are not on comparable bases, three sub-periods are examined: 1971–81, 1981–86 and 1986–91. A very detailed decomposition of the sources of changes in output and employment between the reference years is calculated. Finally, a division of industries into high, medium and low knowledge categories developed by Lee and Has (1996) is used to examine the relative performance of industries and employment according to knowledge intensity over the periods studied.[5]

These studies resulted in a wide range of conclusions that cannot be completely summarized here. Widespread structural change was identified but, more surprisingly, the pace of change between 1971 and 1991 was found not to have accelerated, and the growth leaders were largely the same over the entire span. There was, of course, a relative shift in employment towards services. Skill intensity was found to be increasing in Manufacturing *and* in Services — but most jobs were still concentrated in the low and medium knowledge categories. International trade was found to play an increasingly important role in determining the relative growth rates of industries, including in the natural resource sector (where domestic effects were often negative), and services were also becoming more exposed to international trade. Trade expansion was also found to have a definite "knowledge bias" (at least using the categories of Lee and Has (1996)): "High-knowledge industries in the tradable sector seem to have benefitted the most from export performance; low-knowledge industries have seen their relative decline hastened by import competition." (Gera and Mang, 1998, p.149).

In many ways, the most recent study closest to our own in intention and methods is Betts and McCurdy (1993). These authors use I/O tables for 1961, 1971 and 1981 to determine sources of total employment change over the two subperiods by a 39-industry disaggregation. The sources of employment change examined include changes in the five major categories of final demand, and changes in I/O technical coefficients, labour productivity and hours per worker. In addition, they examined impacts on a detailed occupational breakdown. Among other findings, they determined that the higher rate of private-sector employment growth in the 1970s over the 1960s was associated primarily with lower growth in labour productivity, since final-demand growth actually fell in the 1970s relative to the 1960s, especially in exports. They also found that the primary source of intersectoral variation in employment growth in the 1960s was different rates of labour productivity growth, while the primary source in the 1970s was different rates of growth of final demand sectors.

Our own study builds upon this earlier work. Its special features include calculations brought up to the more recent past, a broader industrial disaggregation, a concentration on the special features of exports and imports in employment growth, and the use of relatively recent disaggregated data on the educational and skill mix of industries.

As with the other I/O based studies reviewed briefly above, the primary intention is *description* of the economy and its changes over time, as an ingredient to understanding and, eventually, useful policy. As Betts and McCurdy note (1993, p.289) ".. input-output analysis remains useful as a way of assessing the relative importance of various factors which have contributed to changes in an economic aggregate such as employment." But it is important not to lose sight of the fact that description and association do not necessarily imply full causation. For example, while exports may be found to be associated with a certain number of jobs, they did not necessarily create or "cause" these jobs, nor would the workers so employed have remained unemployed in the absence of exports (a functioning labour market would have eventually seen them employed in some other fashion — but perhaps not earning as much).[6] A related caution is that the description and analysis is based on input-output relationships that occurred, at least in part, only because relative prices and scarcities were what they were in any given year, although we assume them to be "fixed" ("Leontief technology"). Had relative prices been different — say because of different monetary or exchange-rate policies — then different technologies might have been adopted and different I/O coefficients would have been observed. Again, the primary purpose of the analysis is initial description of what has happened, preparatory to deeper analysis of causality, and, possibly, policy prescriptions.

4. CHANGES IN THE INDUSTRY
AND SKILL MIX OF CANADIAN EXPORTS

In this section we examine, with the aid of National Accounts data and calculations based on a time-series of Input-Output tables, how the place of exports has changed in the Canadian economy since 1961, and how the industrial output and employment mix of exports has altered over that time. Then, adding industry skill-mix data, we discuss the education/skill mix of Canadian exports in recent years and, to the extent possible, determine what changes may have occurred in this mix over time.

Exports in the Canadian Economy, 1961–97: National Accounts Perspective

We begin by reviewing aggregate data for the place of exports in the Canadian economy. These data are from the National Accounts and will be the most familiar to readers. A series of key ratios or indicators is presented for 1961–97 in Table 1.

Columns 1 and 2 of Table 1 (plotted in Figure 1) show the growth of exports as a share of GDP since 1961. Measured in 1992 dollars, exports have grown from 12.5 percent of GDP in 1961 to just over 37 percent in 1997. Measured in current dollars, exports grew from 17.7 percent of GDP in 1961 to just over 40 percent in 1997. By either measure, Canada's economy has, since 1961, moved massively into world markets, and section 5 shows a corresponding growth in imports, as Canadian markets have opened up to the world. Especially impressive is the growth of exports (and imports) in the 1990s.

Note that for 1992, which is the last year available for I/O analysis, the shares of exports in GDP are identical at 27 percent since this is the base year for the National Accounts. The difference in the growth shares between real and nominal measures can be explained by the movement of the relative price of exports over the last 36 years. (By relative price we mean the price of exports relative to the prices of all the goods included in GDP (which includes exports) as measured by the GDP deflator). As seen in column 3 of Table 1, the relative price of exports declined significantly from 1961 through 1992, with most of the decline evident in the 1980s as relative energy prices weakened. However, there has been a modest rise in the relative price of exports since 1992.

This relative price increase has made the constant dollar (1992 dollars) share of exports rise less than the current dollar share since 1992 — although both increases are enormous for a five-year period by historical standards. Since our I/O work will concentrate primarily on relative *current* dollar shares or ratios, the distinction should be kept in mind.

It is interesting to ask if the rise in export share (both in recent years and since 1961) has been more attributable to changes in the shares of exports of goods or exports of services. National Accounts data (columns 4 and 5 in Table 1 and Figure 2) indicate that while the share of both goods and services exports have risen in GDP, the major part of the overall increase in export share is due to a rise in the share of exports of *goods*. This is true both for the 1961–92 period for which we have I/O data, and for the subsequent 1992–97 period.

Finally, column 6 of Table 1 shows exports as a share, not of GDP but of private-sector GDP at factor cost. The latter concept excludes government "production" (largely in the form of wages and salaries of government employees and government capital consumption allowances — neither of which has any important export component), and also excludes indirect taxes (less subsidies) which are included in the "market price" concept of aggregate GDP. Most of the I/O work below concentrates on comparisons or changes in ratios of exports to this "private-sector at factor cost" concept, which is most readily accessible within the tables, and also the more meaningful concept for comparison. Column 6 presents the National Accounts equivalent and, as can be seen, the increase in share of exports is from 21.7 percent in 1961 to 34.0 percent in 1992 — and finally to almost 50 percent by 1997. The fact that the share of exports in total GDP (in current dollars) does not rise as much (only from 17.7 percent to 27.2 percent over1961–92) reflects the growth of the government sector in this period and an increase in average indirect taxation.

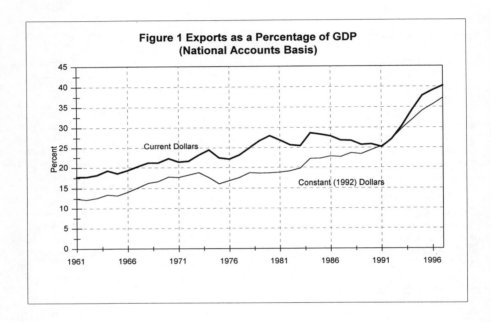

Figure 1 Exports as a Percentage of GDP
(National Accounts Basis)

	(1) Exports as a % of GDP ($92)	(2) Exports as a % of GDP (Current Dollars)	(3) Ratio: Export Deflator to GDP Deflator	(4) Goods Exports as a % of GDP (Current Dollars)	(5) Services Exports as a % of GDP (Current Dollars)	(6) Exports as a % of Private-Sector GDP at Factor Cost
1961	12.5	17.7	1.42	15.2	2.5	21.7
1962	12.2	17.8	1.46	15.2	2.6	21.8
1963	12.6	18.2	1.44	15.5	2.6	22.2
1964	13.5	19.3	1.43	16.6	2.6	23.6
1965	13.2	18.6	1.40	15.9	2.6	22.8
1966	14.1	19.4	1.37	16.6	2.7	23.8
1967	15.2	20.3	1.34	16.9	3.4	25.1
1968	16.2	21.2	1.31	18.5	2.6	26.2
1969	16.6	21.2	1.27	18.4	2.8	26.3
1970	17.7	22.3	1.26	19.3	2.9	27.5
1971	17.6	21.4	1.21	18.6	2.8	26.5
1972	18.2	21.6	1.19	19.0	2.6	26.8
1973	18.8	23.1	1.23	20.5	2.6	28.5
1974	17.5	24.5	1.40	21.7	2.7	30.0
1975	16.0	22.4	1.40	19.8	2.6	27.0
1976	16.8	22.1	1.31	19.5	2.6	26.8
1977	17.5	23.1	1.32	20.6	2.5	28.1
1978	18.7	25.0	1.34	22.3	2.7	30.2
1979	18.6	26.8	1.44	23.9	2.9	32.0
1980	18.7	28.0	1.50	25.1	2.9	33.2
1981	18.8	26.9	1.43	23.9	3.0	32.5
1982	19.1	25.7	1.34	22.8	2.9	31.3
1983	19.8	25.5	1.29	22.6	2.9	30.8
1984	22.2	28.7	1.29	25.7	2.9	34.5
1985	22.2	28.3	1.27	25.3	3.0	34.0
1986	22.8	27.9	1.22	24.5	3.4	33.9
1987	22.6	26.9	1.19	23.6	3.3	32.7
1988	23.6	26.8	1.13	23.5	3.3	32.7
1989	23.3	25.7	1.10	22.4	3.3	31.6
1990	24.4	25.9	1.06	22.4	3.5	32.0
1991	25.4	25.2	0.99	21.6	3.6	31.3
1992	27.2	27.2	1.00	23.4	3.8	34.0
1993	29.7	30.4	1.02	26.3	4.1	38.0
1994	31.9	34.3	1.07	29.9	4.4	42.7
1995	34.2	37.8	1.11	33.2	4.7	46.8
1996	35.7	39.1	1.10	34.2	4.9	48.3
1997	37.3	40.2	1.08	35.2	5.0	49.5

Table 1 Aggregate Exports in the National Accounts, 1961–97

Exports in the Canadian Economy: Aggregate Results from the I/O Analysis

The I/O calculations to determine the impact of exports on Canadian output (domestic product) and employment have been conducted for each year from 1961 through 1997.[7] Individual industry impacts have been aggregated across all industries to derive economy-wide impacts, and these are summarized by year in Table 2 and the accompanying figures (Figures 3–8). Note again that these results are not simply sums of the outputs or employment levels of particular industries that are deemed to be primarily "exporters"; instead they are estimates of the direct and *all indirect* output and employment required to produce the exports observed in each year.

Column 1 of Table 2 provides something of a bridge between the more familiar National Accounts data and I/O calculations and concepts. This column shows exports (from the I/O database) as a share of business-sector domestic product, or value added, (also from the I/O database). This is the closest equivalent in the I/O data to column 6 of Table 1 and, as can be seen, both the estimated shares and their changes between 1961 and 1997 are quite close. (The differences are attributable to different classification schemes and to different definitions of the government sector.) Note that the I/O data show a slightly larger increase in export share from 1961–92 than do the National Accounts data, although through 1997 the changes in share are almost identical between the two measures.

Proceeding to column 4 of Table 2 (and Figure 3), we come to the central theme of this report — the impact of exports on employment.[8] As can be seen, the share of export employment in total business-sector employment has indeed risen: from 17.1 percent in 1961 to 23.1 percent in 1992, and finally to 28.3 percent in 1997 — but the increase in the share of employment is much less than the increase in the share of exports relative to business-sector product. This is the first major insight that the I/O calculations have yielded (at least to the authors of this report): namely, that the impact of export growth on employment has been positive, but considerably less than might be imagined from looking purely at the shares of exports to GDP.

The search for the cause of the lower increase in the export *employment* share begins with productivity: A first thought might be that the lower share increase is the result of rising relative labour productivity in export production: The idea here would be that Canada has tended to export more in those sectors in which labour-productivity gains are especially large. However, the I/O calculations quickly put this possibility to rest: Column 5 of Table 2 (shown in Figure 6), shows that, while relative labour productivity in producing (directly or indirectly) for exports has always been above the business sector average (the ratio is above 1.0), the growth in *relative* labour productivity has been uneven and has, in fact, declined back almost to mid-1960s levels by 1997. Canada exports relatively high labour-productivity goods and services, therefore, but there has been no relentless climb in relative export labour productivity from the 1960s through the 1990s that would explain why the employment share of exports has not grown at the same pace as the share of exports in GDP.

While on the subject of export relative productivity, a caution should be noted: The drop-off in relative labour productivity after 1988/89 coincides with the 1990–92 recession period. The phenomenon of "labour hoarding" tends to reduce labour productivity in all sectors during a recession, but since exports were especially hard hit in the 1990–91 recession under the impact of an over-valued dollar, it is possible that labour hoarding was proportionally greater in the export sectors and that their relative labour productivity accordingly suffered. Since 1992 I/O coefficients have been used in the calculations for 1993–97, then any lingering relative labour hoarding effects by sector from that year would be holding down our measures of relative labour productivity performance for exports in these years.

Since relative labour productivity in exports has risen little since the 1960s then it should be the case that the increase in the export share of business-sector domestic product should have risen much like that of employment — and column 2 of Table 2 confirms this point. The difference in columns 1 and 2 is important to understand: The denominator is the same in each case (total business sector domestic product). For column 1, the numerator is observed export sales (from the I/O database, plus extension past 1992) while for column 2 the numerator is the *impact* (via I/O Leontief calculations) of these exports on individual industry domestic products (which are then summed). While exports *sales* have risen as a share of domestic product since 1961, the impact that a dollar of export sales has on stimulating domestic product (whether directly or indirectly) has *fallen*. As a result, the ratio of export sales to total business domestic product has grown more than the ratio of domestic product *stimulated by* exports to total business domestic product (see Figure 4).

The reason for this reduction in the impact of exports is simply imports: Column 3 of Table 2 shows the imports required to produce exports as a percentage of the domestic product stimulated by exports. As the table shows, in 1961 for every dollar of domestic product attributable to exports, just over 12 cents of imports were required. By 1992 this figure had risen to 40 cents, and by 1997 our less-complete estimates suggest it was just under 50 cents. As Figure 5 shows, some of this increase in the import content of exports is clearly attributable to the implementation of the Canada-United States. Auto Pact from 1966 through the early 1970s. However, the import impact of exports has risen steadily since then, meaning that the output (and employment) shares of exports have risen considerably less rapidly than the overall share of export sales in GDP.

Given that the import share of exports has increased, we might have expected that the *indirect* impacts of exports on output and employment had risen relative to direct impacts — reflecting a greater share of more complex or manufactured exports requiring more intermediate production. This is partly the case: From 1961 through the late 1980s, column 7 of Table 2 and Figure 7 show that the ratio of direct to total employment impacts for exports declined slowly, reflecting greater indirect impacts. Still, the rate of decline is very gradual. From the late 1980s through 1992, however, the ratio increased again, indicating a reduction in relative indirect impacts. For 1993–97, a large increase in the relative impact of directly over indirectly induced employment is indicated, but it must be recalled that we are using the 1992 I/O technical coefficients throughout this period. The shift in the *mix* of exports and imports in the 1990s is such that greater direct, rather than indirect, impacts on export-generated employment would have resulted, but whether this has been offset by changes in the structure of production we cannot tell until I/O tables past 1992 can be used.

Finally, the I/O system permits us to calculate the impacts of exports on total remuneration to labour. (We have aggregated wages and salaries, supplementary labour income and the income of unincorporated business into this category). The returns to labour can be expressed as a ratio to employment generated to determine the relative returns to labour in exporting. As column 8 of Table 2 and Figure 8 show, this ratio climbed steadily from 1961 through the mid 1970s and has then remained relatively constant through 1992 — but at a value greater than 1.0 (calculations past 1992 are not available.) Some of the increase in the ratio from 1961 to the early 1970s has to do with the relative decline of agriculture in exports and export employment.

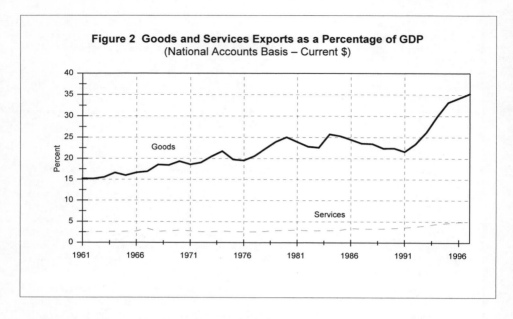

Figure 2 Goods and Services Exports as a Percentage of GDP
(National Accounts Basis – Current $)

        Before proceeding to more disaggregated results, two sensitivity tests on the aggregate calculations should be noted: The aggregate calculations were also performed for 1961–92 using real, rather than nominal I/O tables, and the nominal calculations were repeated excluding agricultural exports because this sector underwent major structural change, especially in the 1960s. Details of each sensitivity test are presented in Appendix 2. Briefly, neither alternative results in any major change in the broad conclusions drawn above. However, use of the real calculations does reduce the relative labour productivity drop-off for exports in 1990–92, and exclusion of Agriculture shows relative labour earnings in exports to be above the economy-wide average in *all* decades, not just since the 1960s.

Table 2 Aggregate Comparisons from I/O Calculations – Exports – 1961–97

	(1) Exports as a % of Business Sector Domestic Product	(2) Domestic Product in Exports as a % of Business Domestic Product	(3) Imports from Exports as a % of Domestic Product from Exports	(4) Employment in Exports as a % of Total Business Employment	(5) Labour Productivity in Exports Relative to Business Sector	(6) Direct Employment in Exports as a % of Total Employment	(7) Ratio: Direct to Total Employment in Exports	(8) Ratio: Returns to Labour in Exports vs. Business Sector
1961	20.82	17.83	12.29	17.20	1.04	9.46	0.55	0.92
1962	20.72	17.70	12.33	16.12	1.10	8.55	0.53	0.97
1963	21.32	18.19	12.52	16.74	1.09	8.94	0.53	0.97
1964	22.68	19.19	13.13	17.77	1.08	9.54	0.54	0.95
1965	21.76	18.35	13.40	16.61	1.10	8.74	0.53	0.98
1966	22.96	19.04	16.04	17.19	1.11	8.94	0.52	1.01
1967	23.90	19.32	18.82	17.47	1.11	8.83	0.51	1.01
1968	26.35	20.61	22.67	18.26	1.13	9.11	0.50	1.03
1969	26.47	20.50	23.86	17.66	1.16	8.69	0.49	1.06
1970	28.31	21.86	24.14	19.62	1.11	9.88	0.50	1.04
1971	27.46	21.06	24.81	19.38	1.09	9.78	0.50	1.03
1972	27.83	21.35	24.72	19.13	1.12	9.75	0.51	1.04
1973	29.33	22.80	23.60	19.27	1.18	9.81	0.51	1.06
1974	29.79	23.15	25.54	18.99	1.22	9.76	0.51	1.07
1975	27.28	21.01	27.47	17.83	1.18	9.13	0.51	1.07
1976	27.84	21.23	27.33	18.25	1.16	9.24	0.51	1.08
1977	29.70	22.26	29.28	19.17	1.16	9.59	0.50	1.08
1978	32.10	23.76	31.00	20.06	1.18	10.09	0.50	1.10
1979	33.66	25.57	28.20	20.58	1.24	10.45	0.51	1.11
1980	34.63	26.27	29.04	21.37	1.23	10.78	0.50	1.09
1981	33.63	24.76	30.95	20.91	1.18	10.52	0.50	1.10
1982	32.48	23.83	30.71	21.04	1.13	10.35	0.49	1.10
1983	32.16	23.97	29.78	20.98	1.14	10.42	0.50	1.08
1984	35.40	26.05	32.16	21.97	1.19	10.96	0.50	1.09
1985	35.16	25.43	34.55	20.99	1.21	10.28	0.49	1.11
1986	34.14	23.96	37.55	20.56	1.17	10.07	0.49	1.12
1987	32.85	23.75	33.60	20.24	1.17	9.86	0.49	1.10
1988	32.80	23.63	33.73	19.95	1.18	9.57	0.48	1.10
1989	31.82	22.76	34.45	19.55	1.16	9.32	0.48	1.10
1990	33.12	23.42	35.80	21.41	1.09	10.80	0.50	1.06

Table 2 (cont'd)

	(1) Exports as a % of Business Sector Domestic Product	(2) Domestic Product in Exports as a % of Business Domestic Product	(3) Imports from Exports as a % of Domestic Product from Exports	(4) Employment in Exports as a % of Total Business Employment	(5) Labour Productivity in Exports Relative to Business Sector	(6) Direct Employment in Exports as a % of Total Employment	(7) Ratio: Direct to Total Employment in Exports	(8) Ratio: Returns to Labour in Exports vs. Business Sector
1991	32.28	22.82	36.69	21.75	1.05	10.99	0.51	1.06
1992	35.24	24.28	40.19	23.07	1.05	11.82	0.51	1.06
1993	38.39	25.75	44.00	23.60	1.09	13.13	0.56	n.a.
1994	42.34	28.07	45.74	25.40	1.11	15.48	0.61	n.a.
1995	45.63	30.28	45.58	26.90	1.13	17.44	0.65	n.a.
1996	46.44	30.80	45.75	27.86	1.11	18.55	0.67	n.a.
1997	47.66	31.17	47.97	28.31	1.10	19.28	0.68	n.a.

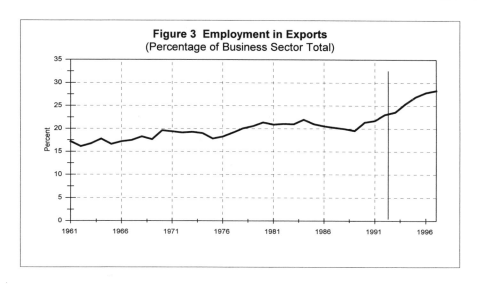

Figure 3 Employment in Exports
(Percentage of Business Sector Total)

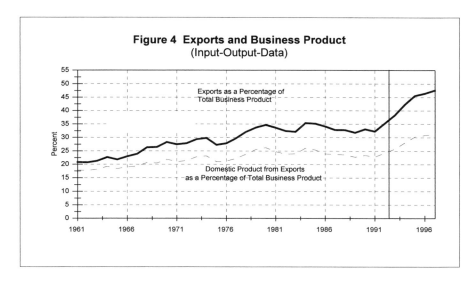

Figure 4 Exports and Business Product
(Input-Output-Data)

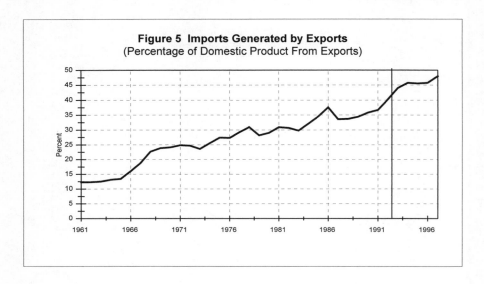

Figure 5 Imports Generated by Exports
(Percentage of Domestic Product From Exports)

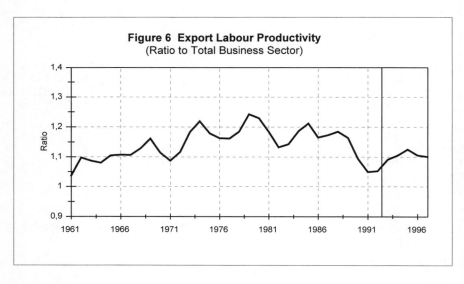

Figure 6 Export Labour Productivity
(Ratio to Total Business Sector)

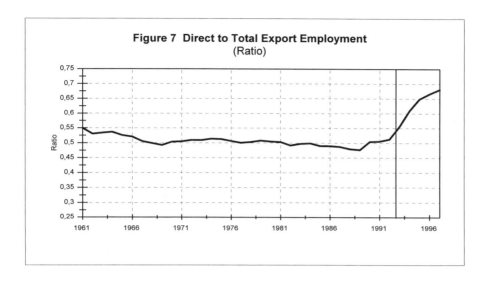

Figure 7 Direct to Total Export Employment
(Ratio)

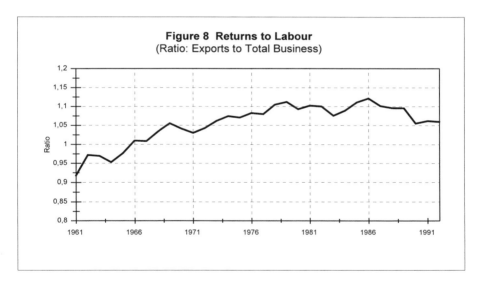

Figure 8 Returns to Labour
(Ratio: Exports to Total Business)

The Changing Industrial Mix of Exports: 24-Industry Aggregation

We move now from examining aggregate to more disaggregated results. Tables 3A and 3B show, at a special 24-industry 'Small (S)' disaggregation developed for this paper, the employment attributable to exports as a share both of total export employment and of total employment, for both 1961 and 1997.[10] The table also shows the change in each share between the two years. Table 3A shows these shares in order by industry — where the industries are arranged in the customary order of primary, manufacturing, construction and tertiary (or services). Table 3B shows the same impacts, but sorted in order from largest increase in share of export employment to largest decrease. Table 3C again shows the same impacts, but this time sorted from largest to smallest in terms of 1997 export employment as a percentage of total employment.

The figures in Tables 3A, 3B and 3C are interesting both in their absolute sizes in each year and changes over the 1961–97 period. Export employment (both direct and indirect) in Agriculture, forestry and fishing (AFF), for example, constituted 2.3 percent of all business sector employment in 1997 — a healthy share of the 28.3 percent of total business employment accounted for by *all* export employment. In fact, of the 24 industry groups in this aggregation only 3, all in services, accounted for larger shares of total business employment. Nonetheless, the weight of Agriculture, forestry and fishing has changed markedly since 1961: In that year, AFF export employment accounted for 5.8 percent of all business sector employment — about a third of the 17.2 percent of business-sector employment accounted for by *all* exports. The decline of 3.5 percentage points is the largest, in absolute value, of the 24 sectors in the aggregation.

Examining the 1961–97 changes more closely, we can see in Table 3B that, of the ten industry groups that increased their share of export employment by over one percentage point, four are service industries (Personal and other services, Business services, Trade, and Finance). The other six are various Manufacturing categories, including some that might be expected given the Auto Pact and changing technology since 1961 — like Motor vehicles, Electrical and electronic products, and Rubber and plastic products — and some that are surprising — like Leather, textile, and clothing products. Of the four industries with declines in export employment shares of over one percentage point, the two largest declines are in primary production (Mining excluding oil and gas, and Agriculture, forestry and fishing), one is in raw material processing and manufacturing (Paper and allied products and printing) and the fourth is Transportation.

Equivalent tables for the full 161-industry disaggregation are provided in Appendix 4, together with discussion of the results.

Table 3A Employment Shares: 1961 to 1997 – 24 Industry Groups

24-Industry Aggregation	1961 Export Employment as a % of Total Export Employment	1961 Export Employment as a % of Total Employment	1997 Export Employment as a % of Total Export Employment	1997 Export Employment as a % of Total Employment	Change 1961–97 Export Employment as a % of Total Export Employment	Change 1961–97 Export Employment as a % of Total Employment
S1. Agriculture, Forestry, Fishing and Trapping	33.72	5.80	8.19	2.32	-25.53	-3.48
S2. Mining excluding Oil and Gas	7.80	1.34	2.11	0.60	-5.69	-0.74
S3. Crude Petroleum and Natural Gas	0.60	0.10	0.87	0.24	0.27	0.14
S4. Food. Beverages and Tobacco	3.14	0.54	2.45	0.69	-0.69	0.15
S5. Rubber and Plastic Products	0.42	0.07	2.42	0.68	1.99	0.61
S6. Leather. Textile and Clothing Products	1.40	0.24	2.84	0.80	1.44	0.56
S7. Wood and Furniture Products	4.83	0.83	4.07	1.15	-0.76	0.32
S8. Paper and Allied Products and Printing	7.09	1.22	3.30	0.93	-3.79	-0.29
S9. Primary Metals and Metal Fabricating	6.46	1.11	5.64	1.60	-0.82	0.48
S10. Machinery	1.39	0.24	2.45	0.69	1.06	0.45
S11. Motor Vehicles and Parts	0.53	0.09	5.26	1.49	4.74	1.40
S12. Other Transportation Equipment	1.57	0.27	1.98	0.56	0.41	0.29
S13. Electrical and Electronic Products	1.34	0.23	3.60	1.02	2.26	0.79
S14. Refined Petrol.. Chemicals and Non-met.	2.73	0.47	2.39	0.68	-0.35	0.21
S15. Other Manufactured Products	0.82	0.14	1.84	0.52	1.02	0.38
S16. Construction	2.12	0.36	1.42	0.40	-0.70	0.04
S17. Transportation and Pipelines	10.61	1.82	7.53	2.13	-3.08	0.31
S18. Storage	0.78	0.13	0.64	0.18	-0.14	0.05
S19. Utilities	2.14	0.37	2.72	0.77	0.58	0.40
S20. Trade	5.97	1.03	12.68	3.59	6.71	2.56
S21. Finance. Insurance and Real Estate	1.64	0.28	3.87	1.10	2.23	0.81
S22. Gov't Royalties and Owner Occ. Dwell.	0.00	0.00	0.00	0.00	0.00	0.00
S23. Business Services	1.57	0.27	10.65	3.02	9.08	2.74
S24. Personal and Other Services	1.32	0.23	11.11	3.15	9.79	2.92
TOTAL	100.00	17.20	100.00	28.31	0.00	11.11

Table 3B Employment Shares: 1961 to 1997 – 24 Industry Groups – Sorted by Size of Change

24-Industry Aggregation	1961 Export Employment as a % of Total Export Employment	1961 Export Employment as a % of Total Employment	1997 Export Employment as a % of Total Export Employment	1997 Export Employment as a % of Total Employment	Change 1961–97 Export Employment as a % of Total Export Employment	Change 1961–97 Export Employment as a % of Total Employment
S24. Personal and Other Services	1.32	0.23	11.11	3.15	9.79	2.92
S23. Business Services	1.57	0.27	10.65	3.02	9.08	2.74
S20. Trade	5.97	1.03	12.68	3.59	6.71	2.56
S11. Motor Vehicles and Parts	0.53	0.09	5.26	1.49	4.74	1.40
S13. Electrical and Electronic Products	1.34	0.23	3.60	1.02	2.26	0.79
S21. Finance, Insurance and Real Estate	1.64	0.28	3.87	1.10	2.23	0.81
S5. Rubber and Plastic Products	0.42	0.07	2.42	0.68	1.99	0.61
S6. Leather, Textile and Clothing Products	1.40	0.24	2.84	0.80	1.44	0.56
S10. Machinery	1.39	0.24	2.45	0.69	1.06	0.45
S15. Other Manufactured Products	0.82	0.14	1.84	0.52	1.02	0.38
S19. Utilities	2.14	0.37	2.72	0.77	0.58	0.40
S12. Other Transportation Equipment	1.57	0.27	1.98	0.56	0.41	0.29
S3. Crude Petroleum and Natural Gas	0.60	0.10	0.87	0.24	0.27	0.14
S22. Gov't Royalties and Owner Occ. Dwell.	0.00	0.00	0.00	0.00	0.00	0.00
S18. Storage	0.78	0.13	0.64	0.18	-0.14	0.05
S14. Refined Petrol., Chemicals and Non-met.	2.73	0.47	2.39	0.68	-0.35	0.21
S4. Food, Beverages and Tobacco	3.14	0.54	2.45	0.69	-0.69	0.15
S16. Construction	2.12	0.36	1.42	0.40	-0.70	0.04
S7. Wood and Furniture Products	4.83	0.83	4.07	1.15	-0.76	0.32
S9. Primary Metals and Metal Fabricating	6.46	1.11	5.64	1.60	-0.82	0.48
S17. Transportation and Pipelines	10.61	1.82	7.53	2.13	-3.08	0.31
S8. Paper and Allied Products and Printing	7.09	1.22	3.30	0.93	-3.79	-0.29
S2. Mining excluding Oil and Gas	7.80	1.34	2.11	0.60	-5.69	-0.74
S1. Agriculture, Forestry, Fishing and Trapping	33.72	5.80	8.19	2.32	-25.53	-3.48
TOTAL	100.00	17.20	100.00	28.31	0.00	11.11

Table 3C Employment Shares: 1961 to 1997 – 24 Industry Groups –
Sorted by Export Employment as a Percentage of Total Employment

24-Industry Aggregation	1961		1997		Change 1961–97	
	Export Employment as a % of Total Export Employment	Export Employment as a % of Total Employment	Export Employment as a % of Total Export Employment	Export Employment as a % of Total Employment	Export Employment as a % of Total Export Employment	Export Employment as a % of Total Employment
S20. Trade	5.97	1.03	12.68	3.59	6.71	2.56
S24. Personal and Other Services	1.32	0.23	11.11	3.15	9.79	2.92
S23. Business Services	1.57	0.27	10.65	3.02	9.08	2.74
S1. Agriculture, Forestry, Fishing and Trapping	33.72	5.80	8.19	2.32	-25.53	-3.48
S17. Transportation and Pipelines	10.61	1.82	7.53	2.13	-3.08	0.31
S9. Primary Metals and Metal Fabricating	6.46	1.11	5.64	1.60	-0.82	0.48
S11. Motor Vehicles and Parts	0.53	0.09	5.26	1.49	4.74	1.40
S7. Wood and Furniture Products	4.83	0.83	4.07	1.15	-0.76	0.32
S21. Finance, Insurance and Real Estate	1.64	0.28	3.87	1.10	2.23	0.81
S13. Electrical and Electronic Products	1.34	0.23	3.60	1.02	2.26	0.79
S8. Paper and Allied Products and Printing	7.09	1.22	3.30	0.93	-3.79	-0.29
S6. Leather, Textile and Clothing Products	1.40	0.24	2.84	0.80	1.44	0.56
S19. Utilities	2.14	0.37	2.72	0.77	0.58	0.40
S4. Food, Beverages and Tobacco	3.14	0.54	2.45	0.69	-0.69	0.15
S10. Machinery	1.39	0.24	2.45	0.69	1.06	0.45
S5. Rubber and Plastic Products	0.42	0.07	2.42	0.68	1.99	0.61
S14. Refined Petrol., Chemicals and Non-met.	2.73	0.47	2.39	0.68	-0.35	0.21
S2. Mining excluding Oil and Gas	7.80	1.34	2.11	0.60	-5.69	-0.74
S12. Other Transportation Equipment	1.57	0.27	1.98	0.56	0.41	0.29
S15. Other Manufactured Products	0.82	0.14	1.84	0.52	1.02	0.38
S16. Construction	2.12	0.36	1.42	0.40	-0.70	0.04
S3. Crude Petroleum and Natural Gas	0.60	0.10	0.87	0.24	0.27	0.14
S18. Storage	0.78	0.13	0.64	0.18	-0.14	0.05
S22. Gov't Royalties and Owner Occ. Dwell.	0.00	0.00	0.00	0.00	0.00	0.00
TOTAL	100.00	17.20	100.00	28.31	0.00	11.11

Changes in Export Employment Impacts over Selected Sub-Periods

The summary tables presented above cover a very long time span. It is also useful to examine employment impacts over various sub-periods. These results are presented in Tables 4A-4D for the periods 1961–71, 1971–81, 1981–91, and 1991–97. The tables present only the 24-industry aggregation, and are sorted by changes in export employment as a percentage of total export employment. Finally, a summary of the period-to-period changes only is presented in Table 5.

Turning to the summary of period-to-period changes in Table 5, a number of observations are forthcoming: Agriculture, forestry and fishing, for example, has lost "share" of export employment in all sub-periods, but by far the biggest decline actually occurred in the 1960s. Thereafter, the pace of decline in this sector has been smaller and steadier. Mining, on the other hand, has declined in share of export employment in all sub-periods, while Food, beverages and tobacco has seen periods of both decline and increase, with the former predominating.

Of special note are Leather, textiles and clothing, and Wood and furniture: If not too badly distorted by using the 1992 I/O tables for 1993–97, the figures in Table 11 indicate an interesting turnaround in shares of export employment over 1991–97, when previous declines (Wood) or steady performance (Leather, etc.) were replaced by significant increases in export employment share. While we cannot tell in the framework of this study, the timing of this reversal just after the United States-Canada Free Trade Agreement (FTA) is suggestive. [Gaston and Trefler (1997) also found positive employment impacts of the FTA on the clothing and wood industries].

Like Mining, Paper and allied products has lost export employment share in all sub-periods, and Primary metals and metal fabricating in all periods after the 1960s. Machinery, however, gained in all but the 1980s.

For Motor vehicles and parts, all the gain in export employment share was over 1961–71 as the Auto Pact was implemented. Thereafter, there has actually been a small net decline in share. Other transportation equipment (rail, ships and aircraft and parts) also gained in the earliest subperiod and lost net export employment share subsequently. Perhaps surprisingly, Electrical products also made its largest gain in export employment share in the 1961–71 period. However, it also gained considerably in the 1980s as well.

Transportation and pipelines lost export employment share in all sub-periods, reflecting perhaps a lower transportation-intensity of Canadian exports over time, as well as greater productivity gains in the sectors.

For Trade, Finance, Business services, and Personal services, there have been gains in export employment shares in all subperiods. It is interesting to note that this "shift to services" in export employment is not a recent phenomenon: share gains in Trade, Finance, and Business services were as large in the 1960s as in later periods. Only for Personal and other services can it be seen that the bulk of the increased export employment share occurred after 1980.

Table 4A Employment Shares: 1961 to 1971 – 24 Industry Groups – Sorted by Size of Change

24-Industry Aggregation	1961		1971		Change 1961-71	
	Export Employment as a % of Total Export Employment	Export Employment as a % of Total Employment	Export Employment as a % of Total Export Employment	Export Employment as a % of Total Employment	Export Employment as a % of Total Export Employment	Export Employment as a % of Total Employment
S11. Motor Vehicles and Parts	0.53	0.09	6.54	1.27	6.01	1.18
S20. Trade	5.97	1.03	8.67	1.68	2.70	0.65
S23. Business Services	1.57	0.27	3.78	0.73	2.21	0.46
S9. Primary Metals and Metal Fabricating	6.46	1.11	8.44	1.63	1.97	0.52
S13. Electrical and Electronic Products	1.34	0.23	3.17	0.61	1.83	0.38
S24. Personal and Other Services	1.32	0.23	2.25	0.44	0.93	0.21
S12. Other Transportation Equipment	1.57	0.27	2.39	0.46	0.83	0.19
S10. Machinery	1.39	0.24	2.12	0.41	0.73	0.17
S5. Rubber and Plastic Products	0.42	0.07	1.04	0.20	0.62	0.13
S21. Finance, Insurance and Real Estate	1.64	0.28	2.26	0.44	0.61	0.15
S15. Other Manufactured Products	0.82	0.14	1.20	0.23	0.38	0.09
S14. Refined Petrol.. Chemicals and Non-met.	2.73	0.47	3.08	0.60	0.35	0.13
S19. Utilities	2.14	0.37	2.49	0.48	0.35	0.11
S6. Leather, Textile and Clothing Products	1.40	0.24	1.70	0.33	0.30	0.09
S3. Crude Petroleum and Natural Gas	0.60	0.10	0.87	0.17	0.28	0.07
S22. Gov't Royalties and Owner Occ. Dwell.	0.00	0.00	0.00	0.00	0.00	0.00
S18. Storage	0.78	0.13	0.58	0.11	-0.21	-0.02
S4. Food, Beverages and Tobacco	3.14	0.54	2.80	0.54	-0.34	0.00
S16. Construction	2.12	0.36	1.61	0.31	-0.51	-0.05
S7. Wood and Furniture Products	4.83	0.83	4.23	0.82	-0.60	-0.01
S8. Paper and Allied Products and Printing	7.09	1.22	6.38	1.24	-0.70	0.02
S2. Mining excluding Oil and Gas	7.80	1.34	6.95	1.35	-0.84	0.01
S17. Transportation and Pipelines	10.61	1.82	9.37	1.82	-1.24	-0.01
S1. Agriculture, Forestry, Fishing and Trapping	33.72	5.80	18.07	3.50	-15.65	-2.30
TOTAL	100.00	17.20	100.00	19.38	0.00	2.18

Table 4B Employment Shares: 1971 to 1981 – 24 Industry Groups – Sorted by Size of Change

24-Industry Aggregation	1971		1981		Change 1971-81	
	Export Employment as a % of Total Export Employment	Export Employment as a % of Total Employment	Export Employment as a % of Total Export Employment	Export Employment as a % of Total Employment	Export Employment as a % of Total Export Employment	Export Employment as a % of Total Employment
S23. Business Services	3.78	0.73	6.76	1.41	2.98	0.68
S20. Trade	8.67	1.68	10.31	2.16	1.64	0.48
S24. Personal and Other Services	2.25	0.44	3.32	0.69	1.06	0.26
S21. Finance. Insurance and Real Estate	2.26	0.44	3.24	0.68	0.98	0.24
S19. Utilities	2.49	0.48	3.21	0.67	0.72	0.19
S10. Machinery	2.12	0.41	2.76	0.58	0.64	0.17
S5. Rubber and Plastic Products	1.04	0.20	1.31	0.27	0.27	0.07
S3. Crude Petroleum and Natural Gas	0.87	0.17	1.05	0.22	0.18	0.05
S4. Food. Beverages and Tobacco	2.80	0.54	2.89	0.60	0.09	0.06
S15. Other Manufactured Products	1.20	0.23	1.29	0.27	0.08	0.04
S13. Electrical and Electronic Products	3.17	0.61	3.20	0.67	0.03	0.06
S22. Gov't Royalties and Owner Occ. Dwell.	0.00	0.00	0.00	0.00	0.00	-0.00
S18. Storage	0.58	0.11	0.52	0.11	-0.06	-0.00
S16. Construction	1.61	0.31	1.55	0.32	-0.06	0.01
S7. Wood and Furniture Products	4.23	0.82	4.09	0.86	-0.14	0.04
S12. Other Transportation Equipment	2.39	0.46	2.21	0.46	-0.18	-0.00
S14. Refined Petrol.. Chemicals and Non-met.	3.08	0.60	2.88	0.60	-0.20	0.00
S6. Leather. Textile and Clothing Products	1.70	0.33	1.40	0.29	-0.30	-0.04
S17. Transportation and Pipelines	9.37	1.82	8.96	1.87	-0.41	0.06
S9. Primary Metals and Metal Fabricating	8.44	1.63	7.69	1.61	-0.75	-0.03
S8. Paper and Allied Products and Printing	6.38	1.24	5.47	1.14	-0.91	-0.09
S11. Motor Vehicles and Parts	6.54	1.27	5.41	1.13	-1.13	-0.14
S2. Mining excluding Oil and Gas	6.95	1.35	4.95	1.03	-2.01	-0.31
S1. Agriculture. Forestry. Fishing and Trapping	18.07	3.50	15.52	3.25	-2.55	-0.26
TOTAL	100.00	19.38	100.00	20.91	0.00	1.53

Table 4C Employment Shares: 1981 to 1991 – 24 Industry Groups – Sorted by Size of Change

24-Industry Aggregation	1981 Export Employment as a % of Total Export Employment	1981 Export Employment as a % of Total Employment	1991 Export Employment as a % of Total Export Employment	1991 Export Employment as a % of Total Employment	Change 1981–91 Export Employment as a % of Total Export Employment	Change 1981–91 Export Employment as a % of Total Employment
S24. Personal and Other Services	3.32	0.69	10.03	2.18	6.72	1.49
S23. Business Services	6.76	1.41	8.91	1.94	2.15	0.52
S20. Trade	10.31	2.16	11.61	2.52	1.30	0.37
S11. Motor Vehicles and Parts	5.41	1.13	6.11	1.33	0.70	0.20
S21. Finance, Insurance and Real Estate	3.24	0.68	3.83	0.83	0.59	0.16
S13. Electrical and Electronic Products	3.20	0.67	3.72	0.81	0.52	0.14
S5. Rubber and Plastic Products	1.31	0.27	1.72	0.37	0.41	0.10
S6. Leather, Textile and Clothing Products	1.40	0.29	1.64	0.36	0.24	0.06
S15. Other Manufactured Products	1.29	0.27	1.46	0.32	0.18	0.05
S3. Crude Petroleum and Natural Gas	1.05	0.22	1.15	0.25	0.09	0.03
S18. Storage	0.52	0.11	0.54	0.12	0.02	0.01
S22. Gov't Royalties and Owner Occ. Dwell.	0.00	0.00	0.00	0.00	0.00	0.00
S12. Other Transportation Equipment	2.21	0.46	2.11	0.46	-0.10	-0.00
S16. Construction	1.55	0.32	1.30	0.28	-0.25	-0.04
S14. Refined Petrol., Chemicals and Non-met.	2.88	0.60	2.62	0.57	-0.26	-0.03
S19. Utilities	3.21	0.67	2.79	0.61	-0.43	-0.07
S4. Food, Beverages and Tobacco	2.89	0.60	2.38	0.52	-0.51	-0.09
S10. Machinery	2.76	0.58	1.99	0.43	-0.78	-0.15
S8. Paper and Allied Products and Printing	5.47	1.14	4.60	1.00	-0.88	-0.14
S7. Wood and Furniture Products	4.09	0.86	3.12	0.68	-0.97	-0.18
S17. Transportation and Pipelines	8.96	1.87	7.74	1.68	-1.21	-0.19
S9. Primary Metals and Metal Fabricating	7.69	1.61	6.47	1.41	-1.22	-0.20
S2. Mining excluding Oil and Gas	4.95	1.03	3.00	0.65	-1.95	-0.38
S1. Agriculture, Forestry, Fishing and Trapping	15.52	3.25	11.16	2.43	-4.36	-0.82
TOTAL	100.00	20.91	100.00	21.75	-0.00	0.84

Table 4D Employment Shares: 1991 to 1997 – 24 Industry Groups – Sorted by Size of Change

24-Industry Aggregation	1991 Export Employment as a % of Total Export Employment	1991 Export Employment as a % of Total Employment	1997 Export Employment as a % of Total Export Employment	1997 Export Employment as a % of Total Employment	Change 1991–97 Export Employment as a % of Total Export Employment	Change 1991–97 Export Employment as a % of Total Employment
S23. Business Services	8.91	1.94	10.65	3.02	1.74	1.08
S6. Leather, Textile and Clothing Products	1.64	0.36	2.84	0.80	1.20	0.45
S24. Personal and Other Services	10.03	2.18	11.11	3.15	1.08	0.96
S20. Trade	11.61	2.52	12.68	3.59	1.07	1.06
S7. Wood and Furniture Products	3.12	0.68	4.07	1.15	0.94	0.47
S5. Rubber and Plastic Products	1.72	0.37	2.42	0.68	0.70	0.31
S10. Machinery	1.99	0.43	2.45	0.69	0.46	0.26
S15. Other Manufactured Products	1.46	0.32	1.84	0.52	0.38	0.20
S16. Construction	1.30	0.28	1.42	0.40	0.12	0.12
S18. Storage	0.54	0.12	0.64	0.18	0.10	0.06
S4. Food, Beverages and Tobacco	2.38	0.52	2.45	0.69	0.07	0.18
S21. Finance, Insurance and Real Estate	3.83	0.83	3.87	1.10	0.04	0.26
S22. Gov't Royalties and Owner Occ. Dwell.	0.00	0.00	0.00	0.00	0.00	0.00
S19. Utilities	2.79	0.61	2.72	0.77	-0.07	0.16
S13. Electrical and Electronic Products	3.72	0.81	3.60	1.02	-0.12	0.21
S12. Other Transportation Equipment	2.11	0.46	1.98	0.56	-0.13	0.10
S17. Transportation and Pipelines	7.74	1.68	7.53	2.13	-0.22	0.45
S14. Refined Petrol.. Chemicals and Non-met.	2.62	0.57	2.39	0.68	-0.23	0.11
S3. Crude Petroleum and Natural Gas	1.15	0.25	0.87	0.24	-0.28	0.00
S9. Primary Metals and Metal Fabricating	6.47	1.41	5.64	1.60	-0.83	0.19
S11. Motor Vehicles and Parts	6.11	1.33	5.26	1.49	-0.85	0.16
S2. Mining excluding Oil and Gas	3.00	0.65	2.11	0.60	-0.89	-0.06
S8. Paper and Allied Products and Printing	4.60	1.00	3.30	0.93	-1.30	-0.07
S1. Agriculture, Forestry, Fishing and Trapping	11.16	2.43	8.19	2.32	-2.97	-0.11
TOTAL	100.00	21.75	100.00	28.31	0.00	6.57

Table 5 Employment Shares: Changes from 1961 to 1997 – 24 Industry Groups					
Export Employment as a Percentage of Total Export Employment					
24-Industry Aggregation	**1961–97**	**1961–71**	**1971–81**	**1981–91**	**1991–97**
S1. Agriculture, Forestry, Fishing and Trapping	-25.5	-15.7	-2.5	-4.4	-3.0
S2. Mining excluding Oil and Gas	-5.7	-0.8	-2.0	-1.9	-0.9
S3. Crude Petroleum and Natural Gas	0.3	0.3	0.2	0.1	-0.3
S4. Food. Beverages and Tobacco	-0.7	-0.3	0.1	-0.5	0.1
S5. Rubber and Plastic Products	2.0	0.6	0.3	0.4	0.7
S6. Leather. Textile and Clothing Products	1.4	0.3	-0.3	0.2	1.2
S7. Wood and Furniture Products	-0.8	-0.6	-0.1	-1.0	0.9
S8. Paper and Allied Products and Printing	-3.8	-0.7	-0.9	-0.9	-1.3
S9. Primary Metals and Metal Fabricating	-0.8	2.0	-0.7	-1.2	-0.8
S10. Machinery	1.1	0.7	0.6	-0.8	0.5
S11. Motor Vehicles and Parts	4.7	6.0	-1.1	0.7	-0.8
S12. Other Transportation Equipment	0.4	0.8	-0.2	-0.1	-0.1
S13. Electrical and Electronic Products	2.3	1.8	0.0	0.5	-0.1
S14. Refined Petrol.. Chemicals and Non-met.	-0.3	0.4	-0.2	-0.3	-0.2
S15. Other Manufactured Products	1.0	0.4	0.1	0.2	0.4
S16. Construction	-0.7	-0.5	-0.1	-0.3	0.1
S17. Transportation and Pipelines	-3.1	-1.2	-0.4	-1.2	-0.2
S18. Storage	-0.1	-0.2	-0.1	0.0	0.1
S19. Utilities	0.6	0.4	0.7	-0.4	-0.1
S20. Trade	6.7	2.7	1.6	1.3	1.1
S21. Finance. Insurance and Real Estate	2.2	0.6	1.0	0.6	0.0
S22. Gov't Royalties and Owner Occupied Dwellings	0.0	0.0	0.0	0.0	0.0
S23. Business Services	9.1	2.2	3.0	2.2	1.7
S24. Personal and Other Services	9.8	0.9	1.1	6.7	1.1

Decomposing Changes in the Employment Mix of Exports, 1961–97

As noted above in Section 2 on methods, it is possible to decompose changes in export employment shares between two years into a number of components. While the decomposition is exhaustive (in the sense that if all the components considered are changed simultaneously from the base year to the comparison year they exactly explain all changes between the years), they interact with each other such that the sum of the individual impacts do not equal the total, leaving a residual/interaction term.

With this in mind, the following components of changes in export shares between two years are considered: (1) Changes in export shares: These are the weights of the 161 industries used for the I/O calculation in exports as they change from the base year to the comparison year; (2) Changes in employment/output ratio, that is the ratio of employment (in persons) to output (in total sales) for each of the 161 industries in the I/O calculations; (3) Changes in input/output coefficients — the "technical coefficients" that describe the shares of the 161 possible industrial inputs to each of the 161 producing industries; and (4) Changes in import coefficients: These are the shares of any new demand (other than exports) from an industry that goes to imports rather than being satisfied from domestic production.

The decompositions have been performed over a number of different time spans and at both the 24-industry and 161-industry aggregations. Table 6A shows the decomposition of changes from 1961 through 1997 for the 24-industry aggregation, in numerical order, while Table 6B presents the same data, but sorted in order from largest positive to largest negative changes. Tables A.4A and A.4B in Appendix 4 present the decompositions from 1961 through 1992, but at the 161-industry disaggregation. Finally, Tables 7A through 7D show 24-industry decompositions for the sub-periods 1961–71, 1971–81, 1981–91 and 1991–97, respectively.

We will discuss primarily the results in Table 6B, for 1961–97 at the 24-industry aggregation. Personal and other services is the industry with the largest positive change in share of export employment over the 1961–97 period. As can be seen, the increase is primarily due to two factors: an increase in the relative export share of the industry itself or of industries that use this sector intensively, and a decrease in *relative* import content — which acts positively on the sector's employment share and so takes a positive sign. For Business services, the next in size of employment share gain, these two factors are also at work, but are supplemented by a relative *loss* in labour productivity (which adds to employment share and therefore takes a positive sign) and by increased use of these services by other exporting sectors (as shown by the 1.17 under "Change in input/output coefficients". For Trade, on the other hand, which has the third-largest employment share gain, the source is overwhelmingly a decrease in relative import content. There is also some positive contribution from changes in the export mix, while Trade has actually improved its relative labour productivity, leading to a negative contribution from the employment/output ratio.

Motor vehicles and parts, and Electrical and electronic products are similar in that both have gained export employment share primarily from changes in Canada's export mix — with a large offset for each in import content. Rubber and plastic products (largely the latter) and Leather, textiles and clothing, however, have gained in export employment share *both* due to gains in the export mix *and* due to a reduction in relative import content.

Turning to those sectors with large export employment-share losses, again several different patterns emerge. Transportation and pipelines lost share primarily due to the export mix: in 1997, Canada is exporting relatively more types of goods and services that are less transport intensive than in 1961. The decline is not due to the fact that some export-type goods require less transport than before (which would have shown up as a negative under input-output coefficients), although the mix among transport types has changed, nor to improved relative labour productivity in transport, which would have shown up in the employment/output ratio column.

Paper and allied products and printing is somewhat more diverse in the causes for loss of export employment share: Changes in the export mix are still the prime cause, but are supplemented by improved relative labour productivity (the -0.74 under employment/output ratio) and by greater relative import penetration as a provider of intermediate inputs to exports (-0.42). Mining, and Agriculture and forestry have also lost export employment share both due to changes in the export mix and to increased import penetration for intermediate inputs. Agriculture and forestry also had a small negative contribution from improved labour productivity, and a positive offset from greater intermediate inputs of Agricultural and forestry inputs to other exports (the 0.82 under "Change in input/output coefficients").

Examining all the sector decompositions in Table 6A or 6B, it can be seen that the primary contributors to changes in export employment shares are the export mix itself, followed in many cases by changes in relative import penetration in the supply of intermediate inputs. Changes in relative labour productivity are, with one or two exceptions, much less important, while changes in the I/O technical coefficients are least important of all. However, the last statement is qualified by the fact that for 1993–97, within the 1961–97 period under examination, I/O technical coefficients are fixed due to the use of the 1992 coefficients for each of these years.

Table 6A Decomposition of Changes in Employment Shares: 1961 to 1997 – 24 Industries

	1961	1997	Change 1961–97	Due to:				
	Export Employ't as a % of Total Export Employ't	Export Employ't as a % of Total Export Employ't	Export Employ't as a % of Total Export Employ't	Change in Export Shares	Change in Employ't /Output Ratio	Change in Input/ Output Coeff's	Change in Import Coeff's	Residual /Inter-action
S1. Agriculture, Forestry, Fishing and Trapping	33.72	8.19	-25.53	-14.83	-0.64	0.82	-5.56	-5.33
S2. Mining excluding Oil and Gas	7.80	2.11	-5.69	-4.69	-0.23	-0.01	-1.38	0.61
S3. Crude Petroleum and Natural Gas	0.60	0.87	0.27	0.36	-0.03	0.07	-0.39	0.26
S4. Food, Beverages and Tobacco	3.14	2.45	-0.69	-1.10	-0.27	0.15	0.15	0.39
S5. Rubber and Plastic Products	0.42	2.42	1.99	1.86	-0.02	-0.40	0.52	0.04
S6. Leather, Textile and Clothing Products	1.40	2.84	1.44	1.76	-0.39	-0.20	0.47	-0.21
S7. Wood and Furniture Products	4.83	4.07	-0.76	0.06	-0.45	0.36	-1.46	0.72
S8. Paper and Allied Products and Printing	7.09	3.30	-3.79	-2.71	-0.74	0.02	-0.42	0.06
S9. Primary Metals and Metal Fabricating	6.46	5.64	-0.82	0.46	-0.78	-0.92	-0.23	0.64
S10. Machinery	1.39	2.45	1.06	1.17	-0.23	-0.09	-0.01	0.21
S11. Motor Vehicles and Parts	0.53	5.26	4.74	4.93	-0.23	-0.60	-3.29	3.92
S12. Other Transportation Equipment	1.57	1.98	0.41	0.71	-0.21	-0.13	-0.32	0.37
S13. Electrical and Electronic Products	1.34	3.60	2.26	2.80	0.16	-0.47	-2.11	1.87
S14. Refined Petrol.. Chemicals and Non-met.	2.73	2.39	-0.35	0.58	-0.23	-0.29	-1.06	0.66
S15. Other Manufactured Products	0.82	1.84	1.02	1.02	-0.11	-0.09	0.33	-0.13
S16. Construction	2.12	1.42	-0.70	-0.67	-0.56	0.00	0.01	0.51
S17. Transportation and Pipelines	10.61	7.53	-3.08	-2.43	0.20	0.09	0.01	-0.96
S18. Storage	0.78	0.64	-0.14	-0.83	-0.26	0.09	0.31	0.57
S19. Utilities	2.14	2.72	0.58	-0.20	0.65	0.06	-0.72	0.86
S20. Trade	5.97	12.68	6.71	0.91	-0.48	0.19	4.05	2.03
S21. Finance, Insurance and Real Estate	1.64	3.87	2.23	0.38	0.83	-0.03	0.58	0.47
S22. Gov't Royalties and Owner Occ. Dwell.	0.00	0.00	0.00	0.00	0.00	0.00	0.00	0.00
S23. Business Services	1.57	10.65	9.08	4.71	3.54	1.17	4.21	-4.56
S24. Personal and Other Services	1.32	11.11	9.79	5.72	0.48	0.29	6.30	-3.00
TOTAL	100.00	100.00	0.00	0.00	0.00	0.00	0.00	0.00

Table 6B Decomposition of Changes in Employment Shares: 1961 to 1997 – 24 Industries

Sorted by Size of Change	1961 Export Employ't as a % of Total Export Employ't	1997 Export Employ't as a % of Total Export Employ't	Change 1961-97 Export Employ't as a % of Total Export Employ't	Due to: Change in Export Shares	Change in Employ't /Output Ratio	Change in Input/ Output Coeff's	Change in Import Coeff's	Residual /Inter- action
S24. Personal and Other Services	1.32	11.11	9.79	5.72	0.48	0.29	6.30	-3.00
S23. Business Services	1.57	10.65	9.08	4.71	3.54	1.17	4.21	-4.56
S20. Trade	5.97	12.68	6.71	0.91	-0.48	0.19	4.05	2.03
S11. Motor Vehicles and Parts	0.53	5.26	4.74	4.93	-0.23	-0.60	-3.29	3.92
S13. Electrical and Electronic Products	1.34	3.60	2.26	2.80	0.16	-0.47	-2.11	1.87
S21. Finance. Insurance and Real Estate	1.64	3.87	2.23	0.38	0.83	-0.03	0.58	0.47
S5. Rubber and Plastic Products	0.42	2.42	1.99	1.86	-0.02	-0.40	0.52	0.04
S6. Leather. Textile and Clothing Products	1.40	2.84	1.44	1.76	-0.39	-0.20	0.47	-0.21
S10. Machinery	1.39	2.45	1.06	1.17	-0.23	-0.09	-0.01	0.21
S15. Other Manufactured Products	0.82	1.84	1.02	1.02	-0.11	-0.09	0.33	-0.13
S19. Utilities	2.14	2.72	0.58	-0.20	0.65	-0.02	-0.72	0.86
S12. Other Transportation Equipment	1.57	1.98	0.41	0.71	-0.21	-0.13	-0.32	0.37
S3. Crude Petroleum and Natural Gas	0.60	0.87	0.27	0.36	-0.03	0.07	-0.39	0.26
S22. Gov't Royalties and Owner Occ. Dwell.	0.00	0.00	0.00	0.00	0.00	0.00	0.00	0.00
S18. Storage	0.78	0.64	-0.14	-0.83	-0.26	0.06	0.31	0.57
S14. Refined Petrol.. Chemicals and Non-met.	2.73	2.39	-0.35	0.58	-0.23	-0.29	-1.06	0.66
S4. Food. Beverages and Tobacco	3.14	2.45	-0.69	-1.10	-0.27	0.15	0.15	0.39
S16. Construction	2.12	1.42	-0.70	-0.67	-0.56	0.00	0.01	0.51
S7. Wood and Furniture Products	4.83	4.07	-0.76	0.06	-0.45	0.36	-1.46	0.72
S9. Primary Metals and Metal Fabricating	6.46	5.64	-0.82	0.46	-0.78	-0.92	-0.23	0.64
S17. Transportation and Pipelines	10.61	7.53	-3.08	-2.43	0.20	0.09	0.01	-0.96
S8. Paper and Allied Products and Printing	7.09	3.30	-3.79	-2.71	-0.74	0.02	-0.42	0.06
S2. Mining excluding Oil and Gas	7.80	2.11	-5.69	-4.69	-0.23	-0.01	-1.38	0.61
S1. Agriculture. Forestry. Fishing and Trapping	33.72	8.19	-25.53	-14.83	-0.64	0.82	-5.56	-5.33
TOTAL	100.00	100.00	0.00	0.00	0.00	0.00	0.00	0.00

Table 7A Decomposition of Changes in Employment Shares: 1961 to 1971 – 24 Industries

Sorted by Size of Change	1961 — Export Employ't as a % of Total Export Employ't	1971 — Export Employ't as a % of Total Export Employ't	Change 1961–71 — Export Employ't as a % of Total Export Employ't	Due to: Change in Export Shares	Due to: Change in Employ't /Output Ratio	Due to: Change in Input/Output Coeff's	Due to: Change in Import Coeff's	Due to: Residual /Inter-action
S11. Motor Vehicles and Parts	0.53	6.54	6.01	6.12	-0.01	-0.84	-1.52	2.25
S20. Trade	5.97	8.67	2.70	0.99	0.23	-0.01	1.22	0.27
S23. Business Services	1.57	3.78	2.21	1.28	1.12	0.21	0.72	-1.13
S9. Primary Metals and Metal Fabricating	6.46	8.44	1.97	1.37	-0.11	-0.24	0.74	0.21
S13. Electrical and Electronic Products	1.34	3.17	1.83	1.72	-0.00	-0.12	0.32	-0.09
S24. Personal and Other Services	1.32	2.25	0.93	0.39	0.09	-0.00	0.56	-0.11
S12. Other Transportation Equipment	1.57	2.39	0.83	0.82	-0.05	-0.02	-0.13	0.21
S10. Machinery	1.39	2.12	0.73	0.77	0.06	0.00	-0.08	-0.02
S5. Rubber and Plastic Products	0.42	1.04	0.62	0.53	0.14	-0.05	0.05	-0.05
S21. Finance, Insurance and Real Estate	1.64	2.26	0.61	0.13	0.19	-0.00	0.29	0.00
S15. Other Manufactured Products	0.82	1.20	0.38	0.38	0.02	-0.03	0.05	-0.04
S14. Refined Petrol., Chemicals and Non-met.	2.73	3.08	0.35	0.05	-0.11	0.00	0.32	0.09
S19. Utilities	2.14	2.49	0.35	-0.04	0.15	0.01	0.18	0.04
S6. Leather, Textile and Clothing Products	1.40	1.70	0.30	0.34	-0.11	-0.01	0.10	-0.01
S3. Crude Petroleum and Natural Gas	0.60	0.87	0.28	0.34	0.00	0.03	-0.15	0.06
S22. Gov't Royalties and Owner Occ. Dwell.	0.00	0.00	0.00	0.00	0.00	0.00	0.00	0.00
S18. Storage	0.78	0.58	-0.21	-0.19	-0.07	0.01	0.04	0.00
S4. Food, Beverages and Tobacco	3.14	2.80	-0.34	-0.44	-0.11	0.07	0.16	-0.02
S16. Construction	2.12	1.61	-0.51	-0.01	-0.24	0.02	-0.23	-0.05
S7. Wood and Furniture Products	4.83	4.23	-0.60	-0.35	0.03	0.13	-0.36	-0.05
S8. Paper and Allied Products and Printing	7.09	6.38	-0.70	-2.07	-0.41	0.12	1.14	0.51
S2. Mining excluding Oil and Gas	7.80	6.95	-0.84	-2.34	0.22	0.02	0.60	0.66
S17. Transportation and Pipelines	10.61	9.37	-1.24	-0.38	-0.07	0.18	-0.86	-0.11
S1. Agriculture, Forestry, Fishing and Trapping	33.72	18.07	-15.65	-9.44	-0.96	0.52	-3.14	-2.63

Table 7B Decomposition of Changes in Employment Shares: 1971 to 1981 – 24 Industries

Sorted by Size of Change	1971 Export Employ't as a % of Total Export Employ't	1981 Export Employ't as a % of Total Export Employ't	Change 1971–81 Export Employ't as a % of Total Export Employ't	Change in Export Shares	Due to: Change in Employ't/Output Ratio	Change in Input/Output Coeff's	Change in Import Coeff's	Residual /Inter-action
S23. Business Services	3.78	6.76	2.98	0.75	0.58	0.03	1.87	-0.24
S20. Trade	8.67	10.31	1.64	0.42	-0.62	0.02	1.93	-0.12
S24. Personal and Other Services	2.25	3.32	1.06	-0.24	0.21	0.04	1.07	-0.02
S21. Finance. Insurance and Real Estate	2.26	3.24	0.98	0.16	0.11	-0.01	0.81	-0.09
S19. Utilities	2.49	3.21	0.72	0.50	0.06	0.03	0.08	0.04
S10. Machinery	2.12	2.76	0.64	0.64	0.06	-0.01	0.04	-0.08
S5. Rubber and Plastic Products	1.04	1.31	0.27	0.24	0.01	-0.02	0.11	-0.07
S3. Crude Petroleum and Natural Gas	0.87	1.05	0.18	0.38	0.16	0.03	-0.66	0.27
S4. Food. Beverages and Tobacco	2.80	2.89	0.09	0.01	0.07	0.05	0.01	-0.06
S15. Other Manufactured Products	1.20	1.29	0.08	0.20	-0.04	-0.02	-0.09	0.03
S13. Electrical and Electronic Products	3.17	3.20	0.03	0.33	0.03	-0.12	-0.21	0.00
S22. Gov't Royalties and Owner Occ. Dwell.	0.00	0.00	0.00	0.00	0.00	0.00	0.00	0.00
S18. Storage	0.58	0.52	-0.06	-0.19	-0.06	0.01	0.13	0.05
S16. Construction	1.61	1.55	-0.06	0.06	-0.12	0.02	-0.13	0.12
S7. Wood and Furniture Products	4.23	4.09	-0.14	-0.34	0.13	0.06	0.11	-0.10
S12. Other Transportation Equipment	2.39	2.21	-0.18	-0.15	0.02	0.03	-0.20	0.13
S14. Refined Petrol.. Chemicals and Non-met.	3.08	2.88	-0.20	0.28	0.27	0.08	-1.35	0.52
S6. Leather. Textile and Clothing Products	1.70	1.40	-0.30	-0.13	-0.11	-0.03	0.01	-0.05
S17. Transportation and Pipelines	9.37	8.96	-0.41	-0.91	-0.16	0.13	0.79	-0.26
S9. Primary Metals and Metal Fabricating	8.44	7.69	-0.75	-0.19	-0.02	-0.38	-0.07	-0.09
S8. Paper and Allied Products and Printing	6.38	5.47	-0.91	0.05	-0.06	0.09	-0.81	-0.18
S11. Motor Vehicles and Parts	6.54	5.41	-1.13	-1.99	0.01	-0.21	0.92	0.15
S2. Mining excluding Oil and Gas	6.95	4.95	-2.01	-0.22	-0.37	-0.14	-1.77	0.50
S1. Agriculture. Forestry. Fishing and Trapping	18.07	15.52	-2.55	0.33	-0.16	0.30	-2.58	-0.44

Table 7C Decomposition of Changes in Employment Shares: 1981 to 1991 – 24 Industries

Sorted by Size of Change	1981 Export Employ't as a % of Total Export Employ't	1991 Export Employ't as a % of Total Export Employ't	Change 1981–91 Export Employ't as a % of Total Export Employ't	Due to: Change in Export Shares	Change in Employ't /Output Ratio	Change in Input/Output Coeff's	Change in Import Coeff's	Residual /Interaction
S24. Personal and Other Services	3.32	10.03	6.72	5.68	0.29	-0.26	1.05	-0.03
S23. Business Services	6.76	8.91	2.15	1.69	0.66	0.25	-0.71	0.27
S20. Trade	10.31	11.61	1.30	0.17	0.88	0.08	0.35	-0.19
S11. Motor Vehicles and Parts	5.41	6.11	0.70	1.31	-0.34	0.56	-0.61	-0.22
S21. Finance, Insurance and Real Estate	3.24	3.83	0.59	0.31	0.83	-0.02	-0.90	0.37
S13. Electrical and Electronic Products	3.20	3.72	0.52	1.49	-0.01	-0.30	-1.28	0.62
S5. Rubber and Plastic Products	1.31	1.72	0.41	0.37	-0.02	-0.15	0.27	-0.07
S6. Leather, Textile and Clothing Products	1.40	1.64	0.24	0.34	-0.10	-0.11	0.14	-0.03
S15. Other Manufactured Products	1.29	1.46	0.18	0.06	-0.09	-0.05	0.18	0.08
S3. Crude Petroleum and Natural Gas	1.05	1.15	0.09	-0.44	-0.28	0.05	0.52	0.24
S18. Storage	0.52	0.54	0.02	0.01	-0.04	0.00	0.07	-0.02
S22. Gov't Royalties and Owner Occ Dwellings	0.00	0.00	0.00	0.00	0.00	0.00	0.00	0.00
S12. Other Transportation Equipment	2.21	2.11	-0.10	0.19	-0.08	0.05	-0.09	-0.17
S16. Construction	1.55	1.30	-0.25	-0.22	-0.20	-0.01	0.20	-0.02
S14. Refined Petrol., Chemicals and Non-met.	2.88	2.62	-0.26	0.05	-0.24	-0.21	0.21	-0.06
S19. Utilities	3.21	2.79	-0.43	-0.21	0.49	-0.02	-0.78	0.10
S4. Food, Beverages and Tobacco	2.89	2.38	-0.51	-0.27	-0.20	-0.02	0.08	-0.09
S10. Machinery	2.76	1.99	-0.78	-0.97	-0.19	-0.02	0.33	0.08
S8. Paper and Allied Products and Printing	5.47	4.60	-0.88	-0.57	-0.26	-0.08	0.23	-0.20
S7. Wood and Furniture Products	4.09	3.12	-0.97	-0.24	-0.20	0.02	-0.23	-0.32
S17. Transportation and Pipelines	8.96	7.74	-1.21	0.15	-0.22	-0.17	-0.63	-0.34
S9. Primary Metals and Metal Fabricating	7.69	6.47	-1.22	-0.88	-0.67	-0.03	0.64	-0.28
S2. Mining excluding Oil and Gas	4.95	3.00	-1.95	-1.55	-0.25	0.17	-0.07	-0.25
S1. Agriculture, Forestry, Fishing and Trapping	15.52	11.16	-4.36	-6.46	0.25	0.27	1.03	0.55

Table 7D Decomposition of Changes in Employment Shares: 1991 to 1997 – 24 Industries

Sorted by Size of Change	1991 Export Employ't as a % of Total Export Employ't	1997 Export Employ't as a % of Total Export Employ't	Change 1991–97 Export Employ't as a % of Total Export Employ't	Due to:				
				Change in Export Shares	Change in Employ't /Output Ratio	Change in Input/ Output Coeff's	Change in Import Coeff's	Residual /Inter-action
S23. Business Services	8.91	10.65	1.74	0.00	0.19	0.01	1.46	0.08
S6. Leather. Textile and Clothing Products	1.64	2.84	1.20	1.19	-0.02	-0.12	0.30	-0.15
S24. Personal and Other Services	10.03	11.11	1.08	-1.36	0.03	0.24	1.84	0.33
S20. Trade	11.61	12.68	1.07	-0.18	-0.28	0.11	1.23	0.18
S7. Wood and Furniture Products	3.12	4.07	0.94	1.16	-0.03	0.13	-0.50	0.20
S5. Rubber and Plastic Products	1.72	2.42	0.70	0.79	-0.00	-0.22	0.16	-0.03
S10. Machinery	1.99	2.45	0.46	0.66	-0.00	-0.08	-0.19	0.07
S15. Other Manufactured Products	1.46	1.84	0.38	0.38	0.09	0.01	0.18	-0.28
S16. Construction	1.30	1.42	0.12	-0.13	-0.01	-0.01	0.22	0.04
S18. Storage	0.54	0.64	0.10	-0.11	0.00	0.02	0.15	0.03
S4. Food. Beverages and Tobacco	2.38	2.45	0.07	-0.15	0.02	0.06	0.15	-0.01
S21. Finance. Insurance and Real Estate	3.83	3.87	0.04	-0.01	-0.20	-0.02	0.22	0.06
S22. Gov't Royalties and Owner Occ. Dwell.	0.00	0.00	0.00	0.00	0.00	0.00	0.00	0.00
S19. Utilities	2.79	2.72	-0.07	-0.07	0.05	-0.01	-0.07	0.03
S13. Electrical and Electronic Products	3.72	3.60	-0.12	0.64	0.35	0.20	-0.28	-1.04
S12. Other Transportation Equipment	2.11	1.98	-0.13	-0.08	-0.01	-0.14	0.05	0.04
S17. Transportation and Pipelines	7.74	7.53	-0.22	-1.00	-0.03	0.06	0.55	0.21
S14. Refined Petrol.. Chemicals and Non-met.	2.62	2.39	-0.23	0.31	0.01	-0.18	-0.40	0.02
S3. Crude Petroleum and Natural Gas	1.15	0.87	-0.28	-0.02	0.01	-0.03	-0.23	-0.00
S9. Primary Metals and Metal Fabricating	6.47	5.64	-0.83	0.45	-0.08	-0.32	-0.90	0.02
S11. Motor Vehicles and Parts	6.11	5.26	-0.85	0.35	0.02	0.09	-1.51	0.20
S2. Mining excluding Oil and Gas	3.00	2.11	-0.89	-0.95	-0.01	-0.09	0.02	0.15
S8. Paper and Allied Products and Printing	4.60	3.30	-1.30	-0.66	-0.05	0.01	-0.46	-0.15
S1. Agriculture. Forestry. Fishing and Trapping	11.16	8.19	-2.97	-1.21	-0.07	0.29	-1.98	0.01

The Changing Skill Mix of Canadian Exports

Use of the COPS data for 1986 and 1991 permits us to identify the "skill" or "educational" mix of employment for a total of 112 industries — all of which are single industries within the 161 I/O industry disaggregation or are sums of several 161-industry components.

The six educational categories divide employed individuals into categories by the highest degree or certificate obtained. These are: (1) No secondary school, (2) Secondary school only, (3) Trade certificate or diploma, (4) Post-secondary, non-university certificate or diploma, (5) University certificate or diploma below or up to Bachelor's, and (6) All post-graduate degrees. Table 8A shows shares of employment by the 112-industry disaggregation for 1991, while Table 8B shows shares for 1986. Table 8C shows the 1991 share less the 1986 share: it therefore indicates how much shares have changed both in aggregate and by industry between 1986 and 1991. These tables also indicate the concordance between the 112 industries available from the COPS data and the 161 industry I/O large disaggregation. For convenience, we have also aggregated the 112 industries into our small 24-industry categories using export employment weights. The shares for 1991 and for 1986 are presented in Tables 9A and 9B respectively, while the differences between the two years are reported in Table 9C.

The totals from Table 9A show that, in 1991, 34 percent of non-government employment had not completed secondary school, and a further 26 percent had completed only secondary school. Another 27 percent had either a trade certificate or diploma or some kind of post-secondary non-university degree. Finally, 13 percent had either a Bachelor's or some kind of post-graduate degree. Within industries, variation around these aggregate shares is considerable: In Agriculture, forestry, etc. 53 percent of the workforce had not finished secondary school, followed by Leather, textile and clothing at 52 percent, and Food, beverages and tobacco at 50 percent. Some other manufacturing sectors also have rather high proportions of low-education workers, including Wood and furniture at 48 percent, Rubber and plastic products at 41 percent, and Motor vehicles and parts at 41 percent. At the low end for shares of no-secondary school workers are Business services at 12 percent, Crude petroleum at 14 percent, Finance etc. at 16 percent, and Utilities at 19 percent.

Trade certificates are prominent in Mining, Paper and printing, Primary metals, Machinery and Other transportation equipment in Manufacturing, together with Construction. Post-secondary non-university degrees have a higher share in Other transport equipment, Electrical and electronic products, Utilities, Finance and real estate, and Business services.

University degrees, whether Bachelor's or graduate, have the highest shares in Crude petroleum, and Business services, followed by Other transport equipment, Electrical and electronic products, Refined petroleum products and chemicals, Utilities, and Finance.

From Table 9C it can be seen that there was an increase in overall education levels of the workforce, even in the five-year span between 1986 and 1991.[10] The share of employed persons with no secondary school diploma dropped by 4 percent, with one or two percentage point improvements in all the categories above Secondary school. The improvement occurred generally across all sectors, the one exception being Personal and other services, in which the share of the workforce with no secondary school actually increased by 4 percentage points. However, it must be recalled that this figure is a weighted average of a number of components, with the weights being export employment in the relevant year. A quick glance at Table 8C will show that most components within this sector displayed at least some reduction in share of workers with no secondary education. The rise in this category for the aggregate therefore reflects a shift within the export mix of the components to sectors with higher shares of workers with no secondary diploma.

By applying these education shares to the employment results discussed above, we can obtain the educational shares of both total non-government employment and employment resulting from exports for each year from 1961 through 1997. As noted above, the 1986 educational mix must be used for 1961–86, while the 1991 mix is used for 1992–97. Years between 1991 and 1986 are calculated using simple weighted averages of the two base years. We caution readers most strongly that the results presented for 1961–85 and for 1992–97 are suggestive only: they represent how *aggregate* skill mixes would have changed during these periods due to changes in total business-sector or export employment *if the education levels of the individual industries had remained the same.*[11]

Table 10A reports on the calculated educational shares for exports, while Table 10B shows the corresponding educational shares for the business sector as a whole. The series in each of these tables are plotted in Figures 9 and 10. The ratios of export education shares to those of the total business sector are shown in Table 10C and the series in that table are plotted in Figures 11 and 12.

From Table 10A it will be observed that the industry mix of exports in Canada has changed since 1961 so as to increase the share of employment with post-secondary (and secondary) education and to reduce the share of employment in the 'No-secondary' category. Recall that, up to 1986, this shift *only* reflects a changing industrial mix, since the educational mix within each industry is (of necessity) held at the 1986 level. In addition, the industry mix of exports continued to change after 1991 so as to emphasize sectors with higher educational needs. Again, after 1991, the educational share shifts in Table 10A only reflect changes in the industry mix of exports, since the educational mix within each industry is held at 1991 levels. Only between 1986 and 1991 do changes in the education mix of exports include improvements in the educational mixes of individual industries themselves. Close perusal of Table 10A, and especially a glance at Figure 9 (where results from 1986 through 1991 are demarcated by vertical bars), shows that the improvement in educational mix is calculated to have been more rapid from 1986 to 1991.

Briefly, then, the calculations show that since 1961 the mix of Canadian exports (considering both direct and indirect employment) has continually evolved so as to emphasize industries that have more highly educated workers. If the improvement in industrial education levels between 1986 and 1991 is, as likely, indicative of more longer-term improvements in education levels by industry, then export-oriented employment from 1961 through 1997 may have become even more education intensive than the results in Table 10A and Figure 9 suggest.

However, while indeed Table 10A indicates that Canadian exports have become more "educationally intensive" since 1961, an examination of Table 10B and Figure 10 shows that the same is largely true of the business sector of the economy *as a whole*. This raises the question of whether exports have become relatively more or less educationally intensive than total business output over the 1961–97 period.

The question is addressed in Table 10C and Figures 11 and 12 which show the *ratios* of education shares in exports relative to the total business economy — in other words, the figures in Table 10A divided by the Figures in Table 10B, by year and education level. The figure 1.074 in column 1 and row 1 of Table 10C thus indicates that in 1961 the share in total export employment of those who had not finished secondary school was 1.074 times the share of those who had not finished secondary school in the entire business-sector work force. Similarly, in 1961 the share of those in export employment who had a post-graduate degree was 0.99 of the share of those who had a post-graduate degree among all business-sector employees.

Table 10C and Figures 11 and 12 indicate that the education of employment resulting from exports is "bi-polar" in distribution — and generally always has been. Export employment is more concentrated in "No-secondary" education than is total employment, and also, less surprisingly, in Trade school education. It uses less than the economy-wide amount of "Secondary only" education levels, but is above the economy-wide average in Post-graduate employment and, more recently, in University at Bachelor's level. It is almost exactly at the economy average for Post-secondary, non-university education.

As can be seen from the charts, these ratios have changed relatively little over three decades. The ratio for the proportion of those employed with Secondary education only has gradually risen towards the business-wide level since 1980, while the ratio for Post-graduate education fell off sometime in the later 1980s, although it remains above the business-wide average. As noted, there has been a gradual rise in the University to Bachelor's ratio from a position at or below the business-wide total in the 1960s and 1970s to just above this level in the 1990s. While it may be an excessive generalization, and our data limitations must be kept in mind, it appears that Canada almost has two separate export sectors: one that uses more unskilled and trade-oriented workers than the economy as a whole (in sectors as diverse as Agriculture and forestry, Motor vehicles, and Food and accommodation), and one that uses more educated workers than the economy as a whole (again in diverse sectors like Crude petroleum, Other transport equipment (aircraft especially), Electrical and electronic products, Petroleum refining and chemicals, Finance, and Business services). Put too simply, the split may reflect the bi-polar nature of the customers for Canadian exports: Exports, according to theory, should embody factors of production in which the exporting country has a relative abundance. Compared to the United States, Canada has a relative "abundance" of a somewhat less-educated workforce (often combined with relative abundance in raw materials production). On the other hand, compared to many of its trading partners beyond the United States, Canada has a relative abundance of highly-educated workers, and exports accordingly.

Table 8A Education/Skill Shares: 1991 – 112 Industries (COPS Data)

	No Secondary School	Secondary School Only	Trade Certificate or Diploma	Post-Sec. Non-Univ. Degree	University up to Bachelor's Degree	All Post-Graduate Degrees	Equivalent 161 Industry No's
001 Agriculture and Related	0.54	0.21	0.10	0.08	0.05	0.02	1
002 Fishing and Trapping	0.60	0.16	0.13	0.06	0.04	0.01	2
003 Logging and Forestry	0.43	0.24	0.14	0.11	0.07	0.01	3
004 Metal Mines	0.36	0.19	0.24	0.12	0.07	0.02	4-6
005 Non-Metal Mines	0.37	0.20	0.25	0.10	0.06	0.02	7-9
006 Coal Mines	0.35	0.19	0.30	0.11	0.04	0.01	10
007 Crude Petroleum and Natural Gas	0.14	0.21	0.17	0.18	0.23	0.07	11
008 Quarries and Sand Pits	0.54	0.22	0.13	0.06	0.04	0.00	12
009 Services Related to Mineral Extraction	0.39	0.22	0.18	0.12	0.07	0.02	13
010 Meat and Poultry	0.51	0.25	0.11	0.07	0.04	0.01	14-15
011 Fish Products Industry	0.63	0.17	0.11	0.05	0.03	0.01	16
012 Fruit and Vegetable Processing	0.46	0.25	0.12	0.09	0.07	0.01	17
013 Dairy Products	0.38	0.29	0.13	0.12	0.06	0.01	18
014 Vegetable Oil Mills (excluding Corn)	0.30	0.17	0.19	0.17	0.13	0.04	20
015 Bread, Biscuit and Other Bakery	0.47	0.27	0.12	0.08	0.05	0.01	21-22
016 Cane and Beet Sugar Industry	0.43	0.28	0.10	0.10	0.08	0.01	23
017 Miscellaneous Food Industries	0.39	0.27	0.11	0.11	0.10	0.02	19+24
018 Soft Drink Industry	0.38	0.31	0.13	0.08	0.08	0.02	25
019 Distillery Products Industry	0.28	0.30	0.14	0.13	0.11	0.04	26
020 Brewery Products Industry	0.28	0.33	0.14	0.12	0.10	0.03	27
021 Wine Industry	0.24	0.34	0.11	0.11	0.16	0.04	28
022 Tobacco Products Industries	0.31	0.28	0.12	0.17	0.10	0.02	29
023 Rubber Products Industries	0.40	0.25	0.16	0.12	0.06	0.01	30
024 Plastic Products Industries	0.42	0.28	0.12	0.10	0.06	0.02	31
025 Leather and Footwear	0.58	0.24	0.08	0.06	0.03	0.01	32-34
026 Primary Textiles	0.45	0.26	0.13	0.09	0.05	0.02	35-37
027 Textile Products (including Carpet)	0.49	0.25	0.09	0.09	0.06	0.02	38-40
028 Clothing and Hosiery	0.56	0.24	0.08	0.06	0.05	0.01	41-42
029 Sawmills, Planing and Shingle Mills	0.50	0.21	0.18	0.07	0.03	0.01	43
030 Veneer and Plywood Industries	0.50	0.26	0.13	0.08	0.03	0.01	44
031 Sash, Door and Other Millwork Industries	0.41	0.29	0.16	0.10	0.04	0.01	45

Table 8A (cont'd)

	No Secondary School	Secondary School Only	Trade Certificate or Diploma	Post-Sec. Non-Univ. Degree	University up to Bachelor's Degree	All Post-Grad Degrees	Equivalent 161 Industry No's
032 Wooden Box and Coffin Industries	0.46	0.32	0.08	0.09	0.05	0.01	46
033 Other Wood Industries	0.45	0.25	0.15	0.10	0.04	0.01	47
034 Furniture and Fixtures	0.45	0.25	0.15	0.09	0.05	0.01	48-50
035 Pulp and Paper Industries	0.27	0.27	0.24	0.13	0.08	0.02	51
036 Other Paper Products	0.40	0.29	0.11	0.11	0.07	0.02	52-54
037 Printing and Publishing Industries	0.27	0.30	0.13	0.15	0.12	0.03	55
038 Plate making. Typesetting and Bindery	0.31	0.32	0.14	0.14	0.08	0.01	56
039 Primary Steel Industries	0.36	0.24	0.21	0.11	0.06	0.01	57
040 Steel Pipe and Tube Industry	0.39	0.22	0.21	0.11	0.06	0.01	58
041 Iron Foundries	0.47	0.20	0.20	0.09	0.04	0.01	59
042 Non-Ferrous Smelting and Refining	0.27	0.21	0.26	0.15	0.09	0.02	60
043 Alum. Rolling. Casting and Extruding	0.30	0.26	0.18	0.14	0.09	0.03	61
044 Copper Rolling. Casting and Extruding	0.34	0.32	0.14	0.13	0.05	0.01	62
045 Other Metal Rolling. Casting, etc.	0.40	0.21	0.17	0.11	0.07	0.03	63
046 Power Boiler and Struct. Metal Industries	0.31	0.19	0.29	0.13	0.06	0.02	64
047 Ornamental and Arch. Metal Products	0.40	0.27	0.17	0.09	0.05	0.01	65
048 Stamped. Pressed and Coated Metals	0.37	0.25	0.18	0.11	0.07	0.01	66
049 Wire and Wire Products Industries	0.40	0.26	0.16	0.10	0.06	0.02	67
050 Hardware Tool and Cutlery Industries	0.31	0.24	0.26	0.13	0.05	0.01	68
051 Heating Equipment Industry	0.34	0.23	0.21	0.14	0.07	0.01	69
052 Machine Shops Industry	0.25	0.20	0.38	0.13	0.03	0.01	70
053 Other Metal Fabricating Industries	0.36	0.25	0.19	0.12	0.06	0.02	71
054 Agricultural Implement Industry	0.40	0.24	0.17	0.12	0.06	0.01	72
055 Commercial Refrigeration Equipment	0.30	0.26	0.23	0.12	0.07	0.02	73
056 Other Machinery and Equip. Industries	0.27	0.22	0.23	0.17	0.09	0.02	74
057 Aircraft and Aircraft Parts Industries	0.19	0.21	0.22	0.21	0.13	0.04	75
058 Motor Vehicle Industry	0.36	0.28	0.17	0.10	0.07	0.02	76
059 Truck. Bus Body and Trailer Industries	0.42	0.25	0.19	0.09	0.05	0.01	77
060 Motor Vehicle Parts and Accessories	0.43	0.26	0.14	0.10	0.05	0.01	78
061 Railroad Rolling Stock Industry	0.30	0.24	0.23	0.15	0.06	0.01	79
062 Shipbuilding and Repair Industry	0.26	0.13	0.37	0.17	0.05	0.01	80
063 Misc. Transport. Equip. Industries	0.39	0.23	0.19	0.10	0.07	0.02	81
064 Small Electrical Appliance Industry	0.41	0.27	0.12	0.13	0.06	0.00	82
065 Major Appliances (Elec. and Non-Elec.)	0.42	0.27	0.15	0.11	0.05	0.01	83

Table 8A (cont'd)

	No Secondary School	Secondary School Only	Trade Certificate or Diploma	Post-Sec. Non-Univ. Degree	University up to Bachelor's Degree	All Post-Grad Degrees	Equivalent 161 Industry No's
066 Record Players, Radio and TV Receivers	0.30	0.28	0.09	0.16	0.14	0.02	84
067 Electronic Equipment Industries	0.19	0.23	0.11	0.23	0.18	0.06	85
068 Office, Store and Business Machines	0.14	0.24	0.11	0.22	0.21	0.08	86
069 Other Elect. and Electronic Products	0.33	0.24	0.14	0.16	0.11	0.03	87-89
070 Clay Products Industries	0.38	0.26	0.13	0.11	0.08	0.03	90
071 Cement Industry	0.40	0.23	0.17	0.10	0.09	0.01	91
072 Concrete Products Industry	0.47	0.24	0.14	0.09	0.06	0.01	92
073 Ready-Mix Concrete Industry	0.51	0.21	0.14	0.09	0.04	0.01	93
074 Glass and Glass Products Industries	0.44	0.26	0.14	0.09	0.05	0.01	94
075 Non-Metallic Mineral Products n.e.c.	0.40	0.24	0.15	0.11	0.08	0.02	95
076 Refined Petroleum and Coal Products	0.19	0.27	0.21	0.18	0.11	0.04	96
077 Industrial Chemicals Industries n.e.c.	0.18	0.25	0.19	0.19	0.15	0.05	97
078 Plastic and Synthetic Resin Industries	0.24	0.30	0.16	0.14	0.13	0.04	98
079 Pharmaceutical and Medicine Industry	0.15	0.24	0.08	0.17	0.25	0.10	99
080 Paint and Varnish Industry	0.30	0.33	0.11	0.13	0.11	0.02	100
081 Soap and Cleaning Compounds Industry	0.24	0.32	0.09	0.13	0.17	0.04	101
082 Toilet Preparations Industry	0.29	0.28	0.10	0.16	0.13	0.04	102
083 Chemicals and Chemical Products	0.27	0.27	0.13	0.15	0.14	0.04	103
084 Jewelry and Precious Metals Industry	0.39	0.28	0.13	0.12	0.07	0.01	104
085 Sporting Goods and Toys Industries	0.42	0.28	0.11	0.10	0.08	0.01	105
086 Sign and Display Industry	0.29	0.31	0.15	0.16	0.07	0.02	106
087 Other Manufacturing Industry	0.31	0.27	0.13	0.17	0.10	0.03	107-108
088 Construction	0.37	0.23	0.25	0.10	0.05	0.01	109-117
089 Air Transport and Incidental Services	0.14	0.31	0.19	0.23	0.11	0.02	118
090 Railway and Transport and Rel. Services	0.35	0.27	0.21	0.10	0.06	0.01	119
091 Water Transport and Related Services	0.31	0.22	0.21	0.17	0.07	0.02	120
092 Truck Transport Industries	0.51	0.25	0.14	0.07	0.03	0.00	121
093 Public Transit	0.40	0.29	0.15	0.10	0.04	0.01	122-123
094 Other Transport and Services to Transport	0.47	0.25	0.13	0.08	0.05	0.02	124-126
095 Pipeline Transport Industries	0.15	0.24	0.18	0.22	0.16	0.05	127
096 Storage and Warehousing Industries	0.38	0.33	0.12	0.09	0.05	0.02	128
097 Telecomm. Broadcasting Industry	0.12	0.25	0.11	0.29	0.18	0.05	129
098 Telecommunication Carriers and Other	0.15	0.36	0.13	0.20	0.13	0.03	130

Table 8A (cont'd)

	No Secondary School	Secondary School Only	Trade Certificate or Diploma	Post-Sec. Non-Univ. Degree	University up to Bachelor's Degree	All Post-Graduate Degrees	Equivalent 161 Industry No's
		38	10	11			
099 Postal Service Industry	0.32	0.22	0.24	0.23	0.07	0.01	131
100 Electric Power Systems Industry	0.12	0.29	0.18	0.17	0.14	0.05	132
101 Gas Distribution Systems Industry	0.18	0.23	0.16	0.12	0.14	0.03	133
102 Other Utility Industries n.e.c.	0.39	0.31	0.14	0.14	0.07	0.02	134
103 Wholesale Trade Industries	0.30	0.34	0.13	0.10	0.10	0.02	135
104 Retail Trade Industries	0.36	0.34	0.10	0.10	0.06	0.01	136
105 Finance. Insurance and Real Estate	0.16	0.22	0.09	0.19	0.17	0.04	137-139
106 Other Business Services Industries	0.12	0.13	0.06	0.20	0.26	0.11	142-144
107 Educational Services Industries	0.10	0.16	0.12	0.11	0.35	0.25	145
108 Hospitals and Health Services	0.17	0.32	0.08	0.31	0.15	0.10	146-147
109 Accommodation and Food Services Industry	0.46	0.32	0.08	0.09	0.05	0.01	148
110 Motion Picture. Amusement and Recreation	0.30	0.23	0.26	0.13	0.13	0.03	149-150
111 Personal and Household Services	0.34	0.25	0.13	0.11	0.05	0.01	151-152
112 Other Services and Organizations	0.30	0.26	0.13	0.14	0.12	0.07	153-154
TOTAL NON-GOVERNMENT	0.30			0.14	0.12	0.05	1-154

Table 8B Education/Skill Shares: 1986 – 112 Industries (COPS Data)

	No Secondary School	Secondary School Only	Trade Certificate or Diploma	Post-Sec. Non-Univ. Degree	University up to Bachelor's Degree	All Post-Graduate Degrees	No Secondary School
001 Agriculture and Related	0.58	0.21	0.08	0.07	0.06	0.01	1
002 Fishing and Trapping	0.65	0.15	0.11	0.05	0.03	0.01	2
003 Logging and Forestry	0.49	0.22	0.12	0.10	0.06	0.01	3
004 Metal Mines	0.41	0.20	0.23	0.09	0.06	0.01	4-6
005 Non-Metal Mines	0.39	0.20	0.23	0.11	0.05	0.01	7-9
006 Coal Mines	0.36	0.18	0.28	0.10	0.06	0.01	10
007 Crude Petroleum and Natural Gas	0.16	0.23	0.14	0.17	0.24	0.06	11
008 Quarries and Sand and Pits	0.57	0.22	0.13	0.05	0.02	0.00	12
009 Services Related to Mineral Extraction	0.42	0.23	0.15	0.09	0.08	0.02	13
010 Meat and Poultry	0.54	0.25	0.10	0.06	0.04	0.01	14-15
011 Fish Products Industry	0.68	0.15	0.11	0.04	0.02	0.00	16
012 Fruit and Vegetable Processing	0.51	0.22	0.10	0.09	0.07	0.01	17
013 Dairy Products	0.43	0.28	0.12	0.10	0.05	0.01	18
014 Vegetable Oil Mills (excluding Corn)	0.34	0.17	0.18	0.17	0.10	0.03	20
015 Bread, Biscuit and Other Bakery	0.52	0.27	0.10	0.07	0.04	0.01	21-22
016 Cane and Beet Sugar Industry	0.52	0.23	0.10	0.08	0.06	0.01	23
017 Miscellaneous Food Industries	0.41	0.28	0.09	0.10	0.09	0.02	19+24
018 Soft Drink Industry	0.41	0.33	0.10	0.08	0.06	0.01	25
019 Distillery Products Industry	0.31	0.30	0.13	0.10	0.13	0.04	26
020 Brewery Products Industry	0.32	0.33	0.14	0.10	0.10	0.02	27
021 Wine Industry	0.32	0.30	0.11	0.12	0.12	0.02	28
022 Tobacco Products Industries	0.40	0.26	0.11	0.14	0.08	0.02	29
023 Rubber Products Industries	0.42	0.27	0.15	0.09	0.05	0.01	30
024 Plastic Products Industries	0.45	0.28	0.11	0.09	0.06	0.01	31
025 Leather and Footwear	0.63	0.22	0.06	0.05	0.03	0.01	32-34
026 Primary Textiles	0.50	0.26	0.11	0.08	0.04	0.01	35-37
027 Textile Products (including Carpet)	0.50	0.27	0.09	0.08	0.05	0.01	38-40
028 Clothing and Hosiery	0.62	0.22	0.07	0.05	0.03	0.01	41-42
029 Sawmills, Planing and Shingle Mills	0.53	0.21	0.17	0.06	0.03	0.00	43
030 Veneer and Plywood Industries	0.55	0.23	0.14	0.06	0.03	0.01	44
031 Sash, Door and Other Millwork Industries	0.47	0.28	0.14	0.08	0.03	0.00	45
032 Wooden Box and Coffin Industries	0.56	0.27	0.10	0.05	0.02	0.01	46
033 Other Wood Industries	0.49	0.23	0.16	0.07	0.04	0.01	47
034 Furniture and Fixtures	0.48	0.26	0.13	0.08	0.04	0.01	48-50
035 Pulp and Paper Industries	0.33	0.28	0.21	0.11	0.06	0.01	51

Table 8B (cont'd)

	No Secondary School	Secondary School Only	Trade Certificate or Diploma	Post-Sec. Non-Univ. Degree	University up to Bachelor's Degree	All Post-Graduate Degrees	No Secondary School
036 Other Paper Products	0.46	0.28	0.10	0.09	0.05	0.01	52-54
037 Printing and Publishing Industries	0.29	0.33	0.13	0.13	0.10	0.02	55
038 Plate making, Typesetting and Bindery	0.30	0.33	0.14	0.14	0.07	0.01	56
039 Primary Steel Industries	0.39	0.25	0.19	0.10	0.05	0.01	57
040 Steel Pipe and Tube Industry	0.44	0.25	0.17	0.09	0.05	0.01	58
041 Iron Foundries	0.51	0.21	0.14	0.08	0.05	0.01	59
042 Non-Ferrous Smelting and Refining	0.34	0.23	0.22	0.12	0.07	0.02	60
043 Alum. Rolling. Casting and Extruding	0.33	0.31	0.15	0.11	0.07	0.02	61
044 Copper Rolling. Casting and Extruding	0.44	0.27	0.14	0.11	0.03	0.01	62
045 Other Metal Rolling. Casting, etc.	0.43	0.22	0.16	0.12	0.06	0.01	63
046 Power Boiler and Struct. Metal Industries	0.32	0.21	0.28	0.12	0.06	0.02	64
047 Ornamental and Arch. Metal Products	0.43	0.27	0.15	0.10	0.05	0.01	65
048 Stamped, Pressed and Coated Metals	0.41	0.26	0.16	0.09	0.06	0.01	66
049 Wire and Wire Products Industries	0.45	0.26	0.14	0.10	0.05	0.01	67
050 Hardware Tool and Cutlery Industries	0.35	0.26	0.23	0.12	0.04	0.01	68
051 Heating Equipment Industry	0.37	0.25	0.16	0.13	0.07	0.02	69
052 Machine Shops Industry	0.27	0.23	0.35	0.11	0.03	0.00	70
053 Other Metal Fabricating Industries	0.41	0.25	0.18	0.10	0.05	0.01	71
054 Agricultural Implement Industry	0.38	0.24	0.19	0.12	0.06	0.02	72
055 Commercial Refrigeration Equipment	0.33	0.27	0.19	0.12	0.07	0.01	73
056 Other Machinery and Equip. Industries	0.28	0.25	0.23	0.15	0.07	0.02	74
057 Aircraft and Aircraft Parts Industries	0.23	0.26	0.19	0.17	0.11	0.03	75
058 Motor Vehicle Industry	0.44	0.27	0.15	0.08	0.05	0.01	76
059 Truck, Bus Body and Trailer Industries	0.43	0.25	0.20	0.09	0.03	0.00	77
060 Motor Vehicle Parts and Accessories	0.46	0.26	0.13	0.09	0.04	0.01	78
061 Railroad Rolling Stock Industry	0.33	0.20	0.25	0.14	0.6	0.02	79
062 Shipbuilding and Repair Industry	0.32	0.17	0.33	0.13	0.05	0.01	80
063 Misc. Transport. Equipment Industries	0.40	0.24	0.21	0.10	0.04	0.01	81
064 Small Electrical Appliance Industry	0.43	0.28	0.13	0.10	0.05	0.01	82
065 Major Appliances (Elec. and Non-Elec.)	0.45	0.28	0.12	0.10	0.04	0.01	83
066 Record Players, Radio and TV Receivers	0.39	0.25	0.12	0.14	0.10	0.02	84
067 Electronic Equipment Industries	0.25	0.24	0.11	0.21	0.15	0.05	85
068 Office, Store and Business Machines	0.13	0.28	0.09	0.24	0.21	0.05	86
069 Other Elect. and Electronic Products	0.38	0.26	0.13	0.12	0.08	0.02	87-89
070 Clay Products Industries	0.48	0.25	0.09	0.09	0.07	0.02	90

Table 8B (cont'd)

	No Secondary School	Secondary School Only	Trade Certificate or Diploma	Post-Sec. Non-Univ. Degree	University up to Bachelor's Degree	All Post-Graduate Degrees	No Secondary School
071 Cement Industry	0.36	0.25	0.20	0.10	0.08	0.02	91
072 Concrete Products Industry	0.50	0.24	0.12	0.09	0.05	0.01	92
073 Ready-Mix Concrete Industry	0.53	0.22	0.14	0.08	0.03	0.01	93
074 Glass and Glass Products Industries	0.48	0.26	0.12	0.09	0.05	0.01	94
075 Non-Metallic Mineral Products n.e.c.	0.43	0.25	0.12	0.10	0.08	0.02	95
076 Refined Petroleum and Coal Products	0.17	0.29	0.17	0.16	0.16	0.05	96
077 Industrial Chemicals Industries n.e.c.	0.20	0.26	0.18	0.15	0.16	0.05	97
078 Plastic and Synthetic Resin Industries	0.24	0.31	0.14	0.15	0.12	0.04	98
079 Pharmaceutical and Medicine Industry	0.22	0.27	0.07	0.14	0.24	0.06	99
080 Paint and Varnish Industry	0.33	0.32	0.10	0.12	0.12	0.02	100
081 Soap and Cleaning Compounds Industry	0.30	0.28	0.09	0.14	0.15	0.04	101
082 Toilet Preparations Industry	0.32	0.31	0.09	0.13	0.12	0.03	102
083 Chemicals and Chemical Products	0.30	0.27	0.13	0.14	0.13	0.03	103
084 Jewelry and Precious Metals Industry	0.43	0.29	0.10	0.10	0.07	0.02	104
085 Sorting Goods and Toys Industries	0.46	0.29	0.10	0.09	0.05	0.01	105
086 Sign and Display Industry	0.36	0.30	0.16	0.12	0.06	0.01	106
087 Other Manufacturing Industry	0.35	0.28	0.12	0.14	0.08	0.02	107-108
088 Construction	0.41	0.23	0.24	0.08	0.04	0.01	109-117
089 Air Transport and Incidental Services	0.17	0.34	0.17	0.20	0.10	0.02	118
090 Railway and Transport and Rel. Services	0.40	0.28	0.18	0.08	0.05	0.01	119
091 Water Transport and Related Services	0.36	0.22	0.20	0.15	0.06	0.01	120
092 Truck Transport Industries	0.56	0.24	0.12	0.05	0.02	0.00	121
093 Public Transit	0.44	0.29	0.14	0.08	0.04	0.01	122-123
094 Other Transport and Services to Transport	0.51	0.25	0.12	0.07	0.04	0.01	124-126
095 Pipeline Transport Industries	0.17	0.28	0.16	0.19	0.16	0.04	127
096 Storage and Warehousing Industries	0.46	0.31	0.11	0.08	0.04	0.01	128
097 Telecomm. Broadcasting Industry	0.13	0.30	0.10	0.26	0.17	0.04	129
098 Telecommunication Carriers and Other	0.19	0.40	0.12	0.17	0.10	0.02	130
099 Postal Service Industry	0.38	0.38	0.08	0.09	0.05	0.01	131
100 Electric Power Systems Industry	0.15	0.25	0.23	0.19	0.12	0.05	132
101 Gas Distribution Systems Industry	0.22	0.29	0.19	0.15	0.12	0.02	133
102 Other Utility Industries n.e.c.	0.49	0.23	0.14	0.09	0.04	0.01	134
103 Wholesale Trade Industries	0.33	0.32	0.13	0.13	0.08	0.01	135
104 Retail Trade Industries	0.38	0.34	0.13	0.09	0.06	0.01	136
105 Finance, Insurance and Real Estate	0.19	0.37	0.10	0.16	0.14	0.03	137-139

Table 8B (cont'd)

	No Secondary School	Secondary School Only	Trade Certificate or Diploma	Post-Sec. Non-Univ. Degree	University up to Bachelor's Degree	All Post-Graduate Degrees	No Secondary School
106 Other Business Services Industries	0.13	0.24	0.08	0.20	0.25	0.10	142-144
107 Educational Services Industries	0.11	0.13	0.05	0.11	0.37	0.23	145
108 Hospitals and Health Services	0.18	0.17	0.11	0.31	0.19	0.04	146-147
109 Accommodation and Food Services Industry	0.49	0.31	0.08	0.07	0.04	0.01	148
110 Motion Picture, Amusement and Recreation	0.32	0.34	0.08	0.12	0.12	0.03	149-150
111 Personal and Household Services	0.37	0.23	0.27	0.09	0.03	0.00	151-152
112 Other Services and Organizations	0.30	0.26	0.12	0.13	0.12	0.06	153-154
TOTAL NON-GOVERNMENT	0.33	0.26	0.13	0.13	0.11	0.04	1-154

Table 8C Education/Skill Shares: Changes: 1986–91 (COPS Data)

	No Secondary School	Secondary School Only	Trade Certificate or Diploma	Post-Sec. Non-Univ. Degree	University up to Bachelor's Degree	All Post-Graduate Degrees	Equivalent 161 Industry No's
001 Agriculture and Related	-0.04	0.01	0.02	0.01	0.00	0.01	1
002 Fishing and Trapping	-0.05	0.01	0.02	0.01	0.00	0.00	2
003 Logging and Forestry	-0.05	0.03	0.01	0.01	0.00	0.00	3
004 Metal Mines	-0.05	-0.00	0.01	0.02	0.01	0.01	4-6
005 Non-Metal Mines	-0.02	-0.00	0.01	-0.01	0.01	0.00	7-9
006 Coal Mines	-0.02	0.01	0.01	0.01	0.01	0.00	10
007 Crude Petroleum and Natural Gas	-0.01	-0.01	0.03	0.01	-0.02	0.00	11
008 Quarries and Sand Pits	-0.03	-0.00	0.01	0.01	-0.01	-0.00	12
009 Services Related to Mineral Extraction	-0.03	-0.02	0.03	0.02	0.02	0.00	13
010 Meat and Poultry	-0.03	0.00	0.01	0.01	-0.01	0.00	14-15
011 Fish Products Industry	-0.05	0.02	0.01	0.01	0.00	0.00	16
012 Fruit and Vegetable Processing	-0.05	0.02	0.02	0.01	0.01	0.00	17
013 Dairy Products	-0.05	0.01	0.01	0.02	-0.00	-0.00	18
014 Vegetable Oil Mills (excluding Corn)	-0.04	-0.00	0.01	-0.00	0.03	0.01	20
015 Bread. Biscuit and Other Bakery	-0.05	0.00	0.02	0.01	0.01	0.00	21-22
016 Cane and Beet Sugar Industry	-0.09	0.05	0.00	0.02	0.02	-0.00	23
017 Miscellaneous Food Industries	-0.03	-0.01	0.01	0.01	0.01	0.01	19+24
018 Soft Drink Industry	-0.03	-0.02	0.03	-0.01	0.03	0.01	25
019 Distillery Products Industry	-0.04	0.00	0.01	0.03	-0.01	0.01	26
020 Brewery Products Industry	-0.03	-0.00	0.00	0.02	0.01	0.00	27
021 Wine Industry	-0.08	0.04	-0.00	-0.01	0.03	0.02	28
022 Tobacco Products Industries	-0.09	0.02	0.02	0.03	0.02	0.00	29
023 Rubber Products Industries	-0.02	-0.01	0.01	0.02	0.01	0.00	30
024 Plastic Products Industries	-0.04	-0.01	0.02	0.02	0.01	0.01	31
025 Leather and Footwear	-0.05	0.02	0.02	0.01	0.00	0.00	32-34
026 Primary Textiles	-0.05	0.00	0.02	0.01	0.01	0.01	35-37
027 Textile Products (including Carpet)	-0.01	-0.02	0.01	0.01	0.01	0.01	38-40
028 Clothing and Hosiery	-0.05	0.02	0.00	0.01	0.01	0.00	41-42
029 Sawmills. Planing and Shingle Mills	-0.04	0.00	0.02	0.02	0.00	0.00	43
030 Veneer and Plywood Industries	-0.05	0.03	-0.01	0.02	0.01	-0.00	44
031 Sash. Door and Other Millwork Industries	-0.06	0.01	0.01	0.02	0.01	0.00	45
032 Wooden Box and Coffin Industries	-0.10	0.05	-0.02	0.03	0.03	-0.00	46
033 Other Wood Industries	-0.04	0.02	-0.01	0.03	0.00	-0.00	47
034 Furniture and Fixtures	-0.03	-0.00	0.02	0.01	0.01	0.00	48-50

Table 8C (cont'd)

	No Secondary School	Secondary School Only	Trade Certificate or Diploma	Post-Sec. Non-Univ. Degree	University up to Bachelor's Degree	All Post-Graduate Degrees	Equivalent 161 Industry No's
035 Pulp and Paper Industries	-0.06	-0.01	0.03	0.02	0.02	0.01	51
036 Other Paper Products	-0.07	0.01	0.01	0.03	0.02	0.01	52-54
037 Printing and Publishing Industries	-0.02	-0.03	-0.00	0.02	0.02	0.01	55
038 Plate making, Typesetting and Bindery	0.01	-0.01	-0.00	0.00	0.00	0.00	56
039 Primary Steel Industries	-0.03	-0.01	0.02	0.01	0.01	0.00	57
040 Steel Pipe and Tube Industry	-0.04	-0.02	0.04	0.02	0.02	-0.00	58
041 Iron Foundries	-0.04	-0.01	0.06	0.01	-0.01	-0.00	59
042 Non-Ferrous Smelting and Refining	-0.07	-0.01	0.04	0.02	0.01	0.00	60
043 Alum. Rolling, Casting and Extruding	-0.03	-0.05	0.02	0.03	0.02	0.01	61
044 Copper Rolling, Casting and Extruding	-0.10	0.06	0.00	0.02	0.02	0.00	62
045 Other Metal Rolling, Casting, etc.	-0.02	-0.01	0.01	-0.00	0.01	0.02	63
046 Power Boiler and Struct. Metal Industries	-0.01	-0.02	0.01	0.02	-0.00	0.00	64
047 Ornamental and Arch. Metal Products	-0.02	-0.00	0.02	-0.00	0.01	0.00	65
048 Stamped, Pressed and Coated Metals	-0.05	-0.01	0.02	0.02	0.02	0.00	66
049 Wire and Wire Products Industries	-0.04	0.01	0.02	-0.00	0.01	0.01	67
050 Hardware Tool and Cutlery Industries	-0.04	-0.02	0.03	0.01	0.01	0.01	68
051 Heating Equipment Industry	-0.03	-0.03	0.05	0.01	0.00	-0.01	69
052 Machine Shops Industry	-0.02	-0.03	0.03	0.01	0.00	0.00	70
053 Other Metal Fabricating Industries	-0.05	0.00	0.01	0.02	0.01	0.01	71
054 Agricultural Implement Industry	0.02	0.00	-0.02	0.00	-0.00	-0.00	72
055 Commercial Refrigeration Equipment	-0.03	-0.01	0.04	-0.00	0.00	0.01	73
056 Other Machinery and Equip. Industries	-0.01	-0.03	0.00	0.01	0.02	0.00	74
057 Aircraft and Aircraft Parts Industries	-0.05	-0.05	0.03	0.04	0.02	0.01	75
058 Motor Vehicle Industry	-0.07	0.01	0.02	0.02	0.01	0.01	76
059 Truck, Bus Body and Trailer Industries	-0.01	0.00	-0.01	0.00	0.02	0.00	77
060 Motor Vehicle Parts and Accessories	-0.03	0.00	0.00	0.01	0.01	0.00	78
061 Railroad Rolling Stock Industry	-0.02	0.04	-0.02	0.01	-0.00	-0.00	79
062 Shipbuilding and Repair Industry	-0.06	-0.04	0.05	0.04	0.01	0.01	80
063 Misc. Transport. Equip. Industries	-0.01	-0.01	-0.02	-0.00	0.02	0.01	81
064 Small Electrical Appliance Industry	-0.03	-0.01	-0.00	0.03	0.02	-0.01	82
065 Major Appliances (Elec. and Non-Elec.)	-0.03	-0.02	0.03	0.01	0.02	-0.00	83
066 Record Players, Radio and TV Receivers	-0.08	0.04	-0.02	0.02	0.04	-0.00	84
067 Electronic Equipment Industries	-0.05	-0.01	-0.00	0.02	0.03	0.01	85

Table 8C (cont'd)

	No Secondary School	Secondary School Only	Trade Certificate or Diploma	Post-Sec. Non-Univ. Degree	University up to Bachelor's Degree	All Post-Graduate Degrees	Equivalent 161 Industry No's
068 Office, Store and Business Machines	0.01	-0.04	0.02	-0.02	-0.00	0.03	86
069 Other Elect. and Electronic Products	-0.05	-0.02	0.01	0.03	0.02	0.01	87-89
070 Clay Products Industries	-0.10	0.02	0.05	0.02	0.01	0.01	90
071 Cement Industry	0.03	-0.02	-0.03	0.01	0.01	-0.01	91
072 Concrete Products Industry	-0.03	-0.00	0.01	0.01	0.01	0.00	92
073 Ready-Mix Concrete Industry	-0.02	-0.01	0.00	0.02	0.01	0.00	93
074 Glass and Glass Products Industries	-0.04	0.00	0.02	0.01	0.01	-0.00	94
075 Non-Metallic Mineral Products n.e.c.	-0.04	-0.01	0.04	0.01	0.00	0.00	95
076 Refined Petroleum and Coal Products	0.02	-0.02	0.04	0.02	-0.05	-0.00	96
077 Industrial Chemicals Industries n.e.c.	-0.03	-0.01	0.01	0.04	-0.01	-0.00	97
078 Plastic and Synthetic Resin Industries	-0.01	-0.00	0.02	-0.01	0.00	-0.00	98
079 Pharmaceutical and Medicine Industry	-0.06	-0.02	0.01	0.03	0.01	0.04	99
080 Paint and Varnish Industry	-0.03	0.01	0.01	0.01	-0.01	0.00	100
081 Soap and Cleaning Compounds Industry	-0.06	0.04	0.00	-0.00	0.02	0.00	101
082 Toilet Preparations Industry	-0.03	-0.03	0.01	0.03	0.01	0.01	102
083 Chemicals and Chemical Products	-0.03	-0.01	0.00	0.01	0.01	0.01	103
084 Jewelry and Precious Metals Industry	-0.05	-0.01	0.03	0.02	0.00	-0.00	104
085 Sporting Goods and Toys Industries	-0.04	-0.01	0.00	0.01	0.03	0.00	105
086 Sign and Display Industry	-0.06	0.01	-0.01	0.04	0.01	0.01	106
087 Other Manufacturing Industry	-0.04	-0.02	0.01	0.02	0.02	0.01	107-108
088 Construction	-0.04	0.00	0.01	0.02	0.01	0.00	109-117
089 Air Transport and Incidental Services	-0.03	-0.04	0.02	0.03	0.01	0.00	118
090 Railway and Transport and Rel. Services	-0.06	-0.00	0.04	0.01	0.01	0.00	119
091 Water Transport and Related Services	-0.05	0.00	0.01	0.02	0.01	0.00	120
092 Truck Transport Industries	-0.05	0.01	0.02	0.02	0.00	0.00	121
093 Public Transit	-0.04	0.00	0.01	0.02	0.00	0.00	122-123
094 Other Transport and Services to Transport	-0.04	-0.00	0.02	0.01	0.01	0.01	124-126
095 Pipeline Transport Industries	-0.02	-0.04	0.01	0.03	-0.00	0.02	127
096 Storage and Warehousing Industries	-0.07	0.02	0.01	0.02	0.01	0.01	128
097 Telecomm. Broadcasting Industry	-0.01	-0.05	0.01	0.03	0.01	0.01	129
098 Telecommunication Carriers and Other	-0.04	-0.04	0.01	0.04	0.03	0.01	130
099 Postal Service Industry	-0.05	-0.01	0.02	0.02	0.02	0.01	131
100 Electric Power Systems Industry	-0.04	-0.03	0.01	0.03	0.02	0.01	132

Table 8C (cont'd)

	No Secondary School	Secondary School Only	Trade Certificate or Diploma	Post-Sec. Non-Univ. Degree	University up to Bachelor's Degree	All Post-Graduate Degrees	Equivalent 161 Industry No's
101 Gas Distribution Systems Industry	-0.04	0.00	-0.01	0.02	0.02	0.01	133
102 Other Utility Industries n.e.c.	-0.09	0.00	0.02	0.03	0.03	0.01	134
103 Wholesale Trade Industries	-0.03	-0.02	0.01	0.02	0.01	0.01	135
104 Retail Trade Industries	-0.03	0.01	0.00	0.01	0.01	0.00	136
105 Finance. Insurance and Real Estate	-0.03	-0.03	0.00	0.02	0.02	0.01	137-139
106 Other Business Services Industries	-0.01	-0.02	0.00	0.01	0.01	0.01	142-144
107 Educational Services Industries	-0.01	0.00	0.00	-0.00	-0.02	0.02	145
108 Hospitals and Health Services	-0.01	-0.00	0.00	-0.00	-0.04	0.06	146-147
109 Accomm. and Food Services Industry	-0.03	0.00	0.00	0.01	0.01	0.00	148
110 Motion Picture. Amusement and Recreation	-0.01	-0.02	0.01	0.01	0.01	0.00	149-150
111 Personal and Household Services	-0.03	0.00	-0.01	0.02	0.02	0.00	151-152
112 Other Services and Organizations	-0.00	-0.01	0.01	0.01	-0.00	0.00	153-154
TOTAL NON-GOVERNMENT	-0.04	-0.01	0.01	0.02	0.01	0.01	1-154

24-Industry Aggregation	No Secondary School	Secondary School Only	Trade Certificate or Diploma	Post-Sec. Non-Univ. Degree	University up to Bachelor's Degree	All Post-Graduate Degrees
S1. Agriculture, Forestry, Fishing and Trapping	0.53	0.21	0.11	0.08	0.05	0.02
S2. Mining excluding Oil and Gas	0.37	0.20	0.24	0.11	0.06	0.02
S3. Crude Petroleum and Natural Gas	0.14	0.21	0.17	0.18	0.23	0.07
S4. Food. Beverages and Tobacco	0.50	0.23	0.12	0.08	0.06	0.01
S5. Rubber and Plastic Products	0.41	0.27	0.14	0.11	0.06	0.02
S6. Leather. Textile and Clothing Products	0.52	0.25	0.10	0.08	0.05	0.01
S7. Wood and Furniture Products	0.48	0.23	0.17	0.08	0.04	0.01
S8. Paper and Allied Products and Printing	0.28	0.28	0.20	0.13	0.09	0.02
S9. Primary Metals and Metal Fabricating	0.33	0.23	0.24	0.12	0.06	0.02
S10. Machinery	0.29	0.22	0.22	0.16	0.08	0.02
S11. Motor Vehicles and Parts	0.41	0.27	0.15	0.10	0.06	0.01
S12. Other Transportation Equipment	0.21	0.21	0.23	0.20	0.12	0.04
S13. Electrical and Electronic Products	0.23	0.24	0.12	0.20	0.16	0.05
S14. Refined Petrol.. Chemicals and Non-met.	0.27	0.27	0.15	0.15	0.13	0.04
S15. Other Manufactured Products	0.33	0.27	0.13	0.16	0.09	0.02
S16. Construction	0.37	0.23	0.25	0.10	0.05	0.01
S17. Transportation and Pipelines	0.42	0.26	0.16	0.10	0.05	0.01
S18. Storage	0.38	0.33	0.12	0.09	0.05	0.02
S19. Utilities	0.19	0.29	0.17	0.19	0.12	0.03
S20. Trade	0.32	0.32	0.14	0.13	0.08	0.02
S21. Finance. Insurance and Real Estate	0.16	0.34	0.10	0.19	0.17	0.04
S22. Gov't Royalties and Owner Occ. Dwell.	0.00	0.00	0.00	0.00	0.00	0.00
S23. Business Services	0.12	0.22	0.09	0.20	0.26	0.11
S24. Personal and Other Services	0.39	0.29	0.10	0.11	0.08	0.03
TOTAL	0.34	0.26	0.14	0.13	0.10	0.03

Table 9B Export Education/Skill Shares: 1986 – 24 Industries (Export Employment Weights)

24-Industry Aggregation	No Secondary School	Secondary School Only	Trade Certificate or Diploma	Post-Sec. Non-Univ. Degree	University up to Bachelor's Degree	All Post-Graduate Degrees
S1. Agriculture, Forestry, Fishing and Trapping	0.57	0.20	0.09	0.08	0.05	0.01
S2. Mining excluding Oil and Gas	0.41	0.20	0.22	0.09	0.06	0.01
S3. Crude Petroleum and Natural Gas	0.16	0.23	0.14	0.17	0.24	0.06
S4. Food. Beverages and Tobacco	0.56	0.21	0.11	0.06	0.05	0.01
S5. Rubber and Plastic Products	0.44	0.28	0.13	0.09	0.06	0.01
S6. Leather. Textile and Clothing Products	0.56	0.24	0.08	0.06	0.04	0.01
S7. Wood and Furniture Products	0.52	0.22	0.16	0.06	0.03	0.01
S8. Paper and Allied Products and Printing	0.33	0.29	0.18	0.11	0.07	0.01
S9. Primary Metals and Metal Fabricating	0.38	0.24	0.20	0.11	0.06	0.01
S10. Machinery	0.30	0.25	0.22	0.15	0.07	0.02
S11. Motor Vehicles and Parts	0.45	0.26	0.14	0.09	0.05	0.01
S12. Other Transportation Equipment	0.26	0.25	0.21	0.16	0.09	0.03
S13. Electrical and Electronic Products	0.27	0.26	0.11	0.19	0.14	0.04
S14. Refined Petrol.. Chemicals and Non-met.	0.30	0.27	0.14	0.13	0.12	0.03
S15. Other Manufactured Products	0.37	0.28	0.12	0.13	0.07	0.02
S16. Construction	0.41	0.23	0.24	0.08	0.04	0.01
S17. Transportation and Pipelines	0.48	0.25	0.14	0.08	0.04	0.01
S18. Storage	0.46	0.31	0.11	0.08	0.04	0.01
S19. Utilities	0.23	0.32	0.16	0.17	0.10	0.03
S20. Trade	0.34	0.33	0.13	0.12	0.07	0.01
S21. Finance. Insurance and Real Estate	0.19	0.37	0.10	0.16	0.14	0.03
S22. Gov't Royalties and Owner Occ. Dwell.	0.00	0.00	0.00	0.00	0.00	0.00
S23. Business Services	0.13	0.24	0.08	0.20	0.25	0.10
S24. Personal and Other Services	0.35	0.27	0.11	0.12	0.11	0.05
TOTAL	0.38	0.26	0.14	0.11	0.09	0.02

Table 9C Export Education/Skill Shares: Changes 1986–91 – 24 Industries

24-Industry Aggregation	No Secondary School	Secondary School Only	Trade Certificate or Diploma	Post-Sec. Non-Univ. Degree	University up to Bachelor's Degree	All Post-Graduate Degrees
S1. Agriculture, Forestry, Fishing and Trapping	-0.04	0.01	0.02	0.01	-0.00	0.01
S2. Mining excluding Oil and Gas	-0.04	-0.00	0.01	0.02	0.00	0.01
S3. Crude Petroleum and Natural Gas	-0.01	-0.01	0.03	0.01	-0.01	0.00
S4. Food. Beverages and Tobacco	-0.06	0.02	0.01	0.01	0.01	0.00
S5. Rubber and Plastic Products	-0.03	-0.01	0.01	0.02	0.01	0.00
S6. Leather. Textile and Clothing Products	-0.04	0.01	0.01	0.01	0.01	0.00
S7. Wood and Furniture Products	-0.04	0.01	0.01	0.02	0.00	0.00
S8. Paper and Allied Products and Printing	-0.05	-0.01	0.02	0.02	0.02	0.01
S9. Primary Metals and Metal Fabricating	-0.04	-0.01	0.03	0.02	0.01	0.00
S10. Machinery	-0.01	-0.02	0.00	0.01	0.01	0.00
S11. Motor Vehicles and Parts	-0.05	0.00	0.01	0.02	0.01	0.00
S12. Other Transportation Equipment	-0.05	-0.04	0.01	0.04	0.02	0.01
S13. Electrical and Electronic Products	-0.04	-0.02	0.00	0.02	0.02	0.01
S14. Refined Petrol.. Chemicals and Non-met.	-0.03	-0.01	0.01	0.02	0.00	0.01
S15. Other Manufactured Products	-0.05	-0.01	0.01	0.03	0.02	0.01
S16. Construction	-0.04	0.00	0.01	0.02	0.01	0.00
S17. Transportation and Pipelines	-0.06	0.00	0.02	0.02	0.01	0.00
S18. Storage	-0.07	0.02	0.01	0.02	0.01	0.01
S19. Utilities	-0.04	-0.02	0.01	0.03	0.02	0.01
S20. Trade	-0.03	-0.01	0.01	0.01	0.01	0.01
S21. Finance. Insurance and Real Estate	-0.03	-0.03	0.00	0.02	0.02	0.01
S22. Gov't Royalties and Owner Occ. Dwell.	0.00	0.00	0.00	0.00	0.00	0.00
S23. Business Services	-0.01	-0.02	0.00	0.01	0.01	0.01
S24. Personal and Other Services	0.04	0.02	-0.01	-0.01	-0.02	-0.02
TOTAL	-0.04	-0.00	0.01	0.02	0.01	0.01

Table 10A Education/Skill Shares of Exports, 1961–97					
	No Secondary School	Secondary School Only	Trade Certificate or Diploma	Post-Sec. Non-Univ. Degree	University up to Bachelor's Degree	All Post-Graduate Degrees
1961	0.441	0.240	0.140	0.098	0.066	0.014
1962	0.430	0.242	0.144	0.100	0.068	0.015
1963	0.431	0.242	0.143	0.100	0.068	0.015
1964	0.434	0.242	0.140	0.100	0.068	0.015
1965	0.428	0.244	0.142	0.101	0.069	0.016
1966	0.420	0.247	0.144	0.103	0.070	0.016
1967	0.411	0.249	0.146	0.105	0.072	0.017
1968	0.406	0.251	0.147	0.106	0.072	0.018
1969	0.397	0.254	0.148	0.108	0.074	0.019
1970	0.401	0.253	0.147	0.107	0.074	0.018
1971	0.405	0.252	0.145	0.106	0.074	0.018
1972	0.403	0.252	0.145	0.107	0.074	0.018
1973	0.403	0.253	0.144	0.107	0.074	0.018
1974	0.402	0.253	0.144	0.107	0.075	0.019
1975	0.399	0.254	0.144	0.108	0.076	0.019
1976	0.395	0.255	0.145	0.109	0.077	0.019
1977	0.396	0.255	0.144	0.108	0.077	0.020
1978	0.393	0.256	0.143	0.109	0.078	0.020
1979	0.390	0.256	0.143	0.110	0.080	0.021
1980	0.391	0.255	0.141	0.111	0.081	0.021
1981	0.388	0.256	0.141	0.112	0.082	0.022
1982	0.386	0.257	0.140	0.112	0.083	0.022
1983	0.389	0.257	0.137	0.112	0.083	0.022
1984	0.386	0.258	0.136	0.113	0.084	0.022
1985	0.379	0.260	0.136	0.114	0.086	0.023
1986	0.378	0.260	0.138	0.114	0.086	0.023
1987	0.373	0.259	0.139	0.117	0.088	0.024
1988	0.364	0.258	0.141	0.121	0.090	0.026
1989	0.352	0.257	0.145	0.125	0.093	0.028
1990	0.350	0.259	0.143	0.126	0.093	0.028
1991	0.341	0.258	0.144	0.130	0.097	0.030
1992	0.343	0.258	0.143	0.130	0.097	0.030
1993	0.339	0.260	0.142	0.130	0.098	0.030
1994	0.337	0.260	0.142	0.131	0.099	0.031
1995	0.336	0.261	0.142	0.131	0.099	0.031
1996	0.335	0.261	0.141	0.132	0.100	0.031
1997	0.338	0.260	0.140	0.131	0.100	0.031

	No Secondary School	Secondary School Only	Trade Certificate or Diploma	Post-Sec. Non-Univ. Degree	University up to Bachelor's Degree	All Post-Graduate Degrees
Table 10B Education/Skill Shares of Business Sector Employment, 1961–97						
1961	0.411	0.269	0.136	0.102	0.068	0.015
1962	0.408	0.270	0.136	0.102	0.069	0.015
1963	0.406	0.270	0.136	0.103	0.069	0.015
1964	0.404	0.271	0.137	0.103	0.070	0.015
1965	0.402	0.271	0.138	0.104	0.070	0.016
1966	0.398	0.272	0.139	0.105	0.071	0.016
1967	0.396	0.273	0.138	0.105	0.071	0.016
1968	0.395	0.273	0.138	0.106	0.072	0.016
1969	0.393	0.274	0.137	0.106	0.073	0.017
1970	0.390	0.275	0.137	0.107	0.073	0.017
1971	0.389	0.275	0.137	0.107	0.074	0.017
1972	0.387	0.277	0.137	0.108	0.075	0.017
1973	0.385	0.277	0.137	0.108	0.075	0.018
1974	0.383	0.278	0.137	0.109	0.076	0.018
1975	0.381	0.279	0.136	0.109	0.077	0.018
1976	0.381	0.279	0.136	0.109	0.077	0.018
1977	0.378	0.279	0.136	0.110	0.078	0.019
1978	0.378	0.280	0.135	0.110	0.079	0.019
1979	0.377	0.280	0.135	0.111	0.079	0.019
1980	0.375	0.280	0.134	0.111	0.080	0.020
1981	0.374	0.280	0.134	0.112	0.081	0.020
1982	0.370	0.281	0.133	0.113	0.082	0.021
1983	0.370	0.281	0.131	0.113	0.083	0.021
1984	0.370	0.282	0.131	0.113	0.084	0.021
1985	0.368	0.282	0.131	0.114	0.084	0.021
1986	0.368	0.282	0.131	0.114	0.084	0.021
1987	0.361	0.281	0.133	0.117	0.086	0.022
1988	0.353	0.280	0.135	0.120	0.088	0.024
1989	0.346	0.278	0.137	0.123	0.090	0.025
1990	0.338	0.277	0.138	0.127	0.093	0.027
1991	0.330	0.276	0.140	0.131	0.096	0.029
1992	0.329	0.276	0.139	0.131	0.096	0.029
1993	0.330	0.276	0.138	0.131	0.096	0.029
1994	0.330	0.276	0.138	0.131	0.096	0.029
1995	0.328	0.276	0.138	0.131	0.097	0.030
1996	0.328	0.275	0.138	0.131	0.098	0.030
1997	0.326	0.275	0.137	0.132	0.099	0.030

Table 10C Ratio: Education/Skill Shares of Exports/Total Business Sector Employment, 1961–97						
	No Secondary School	Secondary School Only	Trade Certificate or Diploma	Post-Sec. Non-Univ. Degree	University up to Bachelor's Degree	All Post-Graduate Degrees
1961	1.074	0.892	1.029	0.966	0.976	0.990
1962	1.054	0.898	1.057	0.981	0.990	1.031
1963	1.061	0.897	1.046	0.976	0.983	1.020
1964	1.073	0.896	1.025	0.969	0.978	1.004
1965	1.064	0.901	1.029	0.975	0.988	1.027
1966	1.056	0.907	1.036	0.981	0.991	1.037
1967	1.038	0.913	1.056	0.998	1.003	1.071
1968	1.027	0.918	1.069	1.004	1.006	1.088
1969	1.012	0.925	1.076	1.015	1.025	1.127
1970	1.028	0.918	1.067	1.003	1.009	1.087
1971	1.040	0.913	1.058	0.994	1.000	1.066
1972	1.042	0.913	1.060	0.991	0.995	1.058
1973	1.046	0.914	1.056	0.987	0.989	1.045
1974	1.049	0.912	1.051	0.986	0.992	1.044
1975	1.045	0.911	1.062	0.988	0.993	1.046
1976	1.038	0.914	1.068	0.992	0.999	1.063
1977	1.046	0.913	1.062	0.987	0.991	1.051
1978	1.040	0.915	1.064	0.991	0.997	1.066
1979	1.036	0.916	1.058	0.999	1.009	1.079
1980	1.043	0.912	1.052	0.995	1.008	1.074
1981	1.038	0.912	1.054	1.001	1.016	1.087
1982	1.042	0.913	1.053	0.996	1.011	1.076
1983	1.050	0.913	1.043	0.989	1.002	1.059
1984	1.043	0.917	1.041	0.995	1.011	1.075
1985	1.031	0.923	1.042	1.006	1.027	1.098
1986	1.026	0.923	1.052	1.007	1.026	1.106
1987	1.033	0.923	1.044	1.002	1.021	1.088
1988	1.029	0.922	1.046	1.005	1.027	1.089
1989	1.019	0.924	1.058	1.012	1.034	1.087
1990	1.038	0.937	1.031	0.994	1.004	1.027
1991	1.035	0.935	1.035	0.995	1.013	1.033
1992	1.042	0.934	1.027	0.991	1.011	1.030
1993	1.027	0.941	1.030	1.000	1.023	1.041
1994	1.023	0.943	1.024	1.003	1.031	1.052
1995	1.023	0.947	1.027	1.001	1.023	1.038
1996	1.022	0.949	1.026	1.002	1.022	1.032
1997	1.035	0.946	1.016	0.994	1.012	1.023

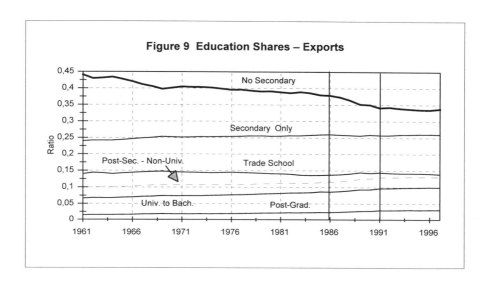

Figure 9 Education Shares – Exports

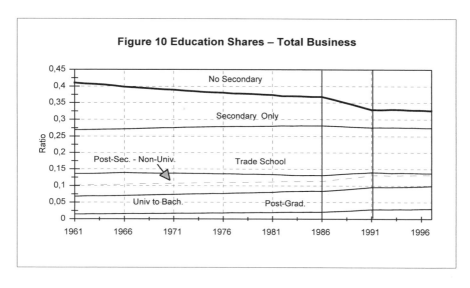

Figure 10 Education Shares – Total Business

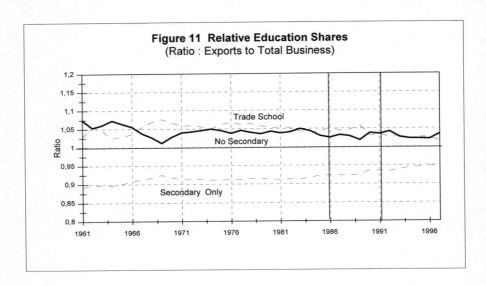

Figure 11 Relative Education Shares
(Ratio : Exports to Total Business)

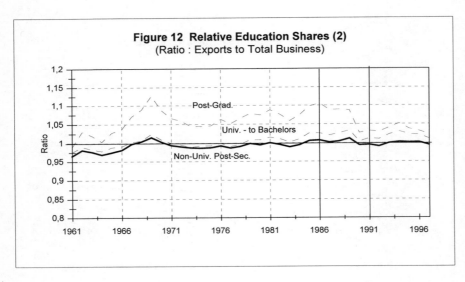

Figure 12 Relative Education Shares (2)
(Ratio : Exports to Total Business)

5. CHANGES IN THE INDUSTRY
AND SKILL MIX OF CANADIAN IMPORTS

The section above examined the place of exports in the Canadian economy and how the industrial output and employment mix of exports had changed over time. This section repeats these calculations and analysis, but for Canadian imports. Of necessity, the results here are somewhat more speculative than in the previous section. While in Section 4 we were examining, subject to data limitations, what industrial and skill mix was *actually used* to produce Canadian exports, in this section we will be asking what industrial and skill mix *would have been used* to produce Canadian imports in Canada, instead of abroad, with the existing Canadian industrial technology and workforce. Given that these goods were, indeed, imported, it is probable that different technologies and skill mixes were used to produce them abroad. Nevertheless, the exercise is useful to see, as imports have grown in the Canadian economy, what the equivalent Canadian industry and skill mix would have been and, likely, where import pressures have been felt the most.

As explained in Section 2 (Methods and Data) above, there is a question of where this hypothetical substitution of domestic production for imports should end. According to the technology reflected in the Canadian I/O tables, producing domestically some or all of the goods that were historically imported would have required other imports as intermediate inputs. Rather than try to replace imports all the way back along the production chain — which would have taken us further and further from the reality of the structure of Canadian production — we have chosen to model domestic production of observed imports only. Any further imports that might be required to "produce" these imports domestically are permitted to occur and are not satisfied by further domestic production. For this reason, and for the others listed above, when we refer to "import-replaced" output or employment in describing the results of our calculations below, much caution must be used in interpreting both the term and the results.

Imports in the Canadian Economy, 1961–97: National Accounts Perspective

As was the case for exports, we begin by reviewing aggregate data for the place of imports in the Canadian economy from the National Accounts. A series of key ratios or indicators is presented for 1961–97 in Table 11 and plotted in Figures 13 and 14.

Columns 1 and 2 of Table 11 (plotted in Figure 13) show the growth of imports as a share of GDP since 1961. Measured in 1992 dollars, imports have grown from 10.8 percent of GDP in 1961 to just over 36 percent in 1997. Measured in current dollars, imports grew from 18.2 percent of GDP in 1961 to 38.5 percent in 1997. Note that for 1992, the last year for which data are available for I/O analysis, the shares of imports in GDP are identical at 27.5 percent since this is the base year for the National Accounts.

The difference in the growth shares can be explained by the movement of the relative price of imports over the last 36 years. (By relative price we mean the price of imports relative to the prices of all the goods included in GDP as measured by the GDP deflator). As seen in column 3 of Table 11, the relative price of imports declined significantly from 1961 through 1992, with much of the decline evident in the 1980s as relative energy and other commodity prices weakened. There has, however, been a modest rise in the relative price of imports since 1992.

This relative price increase for imports has made the constant dollar (1992 dollar) share of imports rise less than the current-dollar share since 1992 — although both increases, as for exports, are very large for a five-year period by historical standards.

As for exports, it is interesting to ask if the rise in share (both in recent years and since 1961) has been more attributable to changes in the shares of imports of goods or imports of services. National Accounts data (columns 4 and 5 in Table 11 and Figure 14) indicate that while the share of both goods and services imports have risen in GDP, the major part of the overall increase in import share is due to a rise in the share of imports of *goods*. This is true both for the 1961–92 period for which we have I/O data, and for the subsequent 1992–97 period.

Finally, column 6 of Table 11 shows imports as a share, not of GDP but of private-sector GDP at factor cost. The latter concept excludes government "production" and indirect taxes less subsidies, which are included in the "market price" concept of aggregate GDP. Most of the I/O work below concentrates on comparisons or changes in ratios of imports to this "private-sector at factor cost" concept. Column 6 presents the National Accounts equivalent and, as can be seen, the increase in share of imports is from 22.3 percent in 1961 to 34.5 percent in 1992 — and finally to just over 47 percent by 1997. As for exports, the fact that the share of imports in total GDP (in current dollars) does not rise as much (only from 18.2 percent to 27.5 percent over 1961–92) reflects the growth of the government sector in this period and an increase in average indirect taxation.

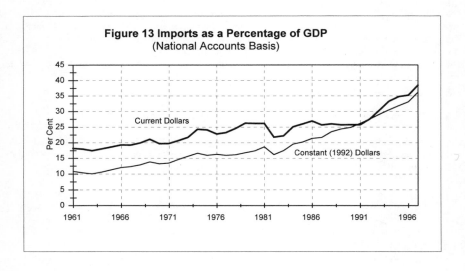

Figure 13 Imports as a Percentage of GDP (National Accounts Basis)

		Table 11 Aggregate Imports in the National Accounts, 1961–97				
	(1)	(2)	(3)	(4)	(5)	(6)
	Imports as a % of GDP ($92)	Imports as a % of GDP (Current Dollars)	Ratio: Import Deflator to GDP Deflator	Goods Imports as a % of GDP (Current Dollars)	Services Imports as a % of GDP (Current Dollars)	Imports as a % of Private-Sector GDP at Factor Cost
1961	10.8	18.2	1.68	14.5	3.7	22.3
1962	10.4	18.0	1.73	14.5	3.5	22.1
1963	10.0	17.5	1.74	14.2	3.3	21.4
1964	10.6	18.1	1.70	14.7	3.4	22.2
1965	11.3	18.7	1.65	15.4	3.3	23.0
1966	12.0	19.3	1.60	16.0	3.3	23.7
1967	12.3	19.3	1.56	15.9	3.4	23.8
1968	12.9	20.0	1.55	16.6	3.4	24.7
1969	13.9	21.1	1.52	17.3	3.8	26.1
1970	13.3	19.7	1.49	15.8	3.9	24.4
1971	13.5	19.8	1.47	16.0	3.8	24.5
1972	14.6	20.7	1.42	17.1	3.6	25.7
1973	15.6	21.7	1.39	18.1	3.7	26.7
1974	16.7	24.3	1.46	20.6	3.7	29.8
1975	16.0	24.1	1.51	20.1	4.0	29.1
1976	16.3	22.8	1.40	18.8	4.1	27.7
1977	15.9	23.3	1.46	19.2	4.1	28.3
1978	16.2	24.6	1.52	20.4	4.2	29.8
1979	16.8	26.3	1.56	22.3	3.9	31.4
1980	17.4	26.2	1.50	22.1	4.0	31.0
1981	18.7	26.2	1.40	22.1	4.1	31.6
1982	16.2	21.8	1.34	17.9	3.9	26.6
1983	17.5	22.2	1.27	18.3	3.9	26.9
1984	19.6	25.1	1.28	21.2	3.9	30.3
1985	20.2	26.0	1.29	22.0	4.0	31.2
1986	21.4	26.9	1.26	22.5	4.4	32.7
1987	21.7	25.7	1.18	21.4	4.3	31.3
1988	23.5	26.0	1.11	21.7	4.3	31.7
1989	24.4	25.7	1.05	21.2	4.5	31.6
1990	24.9	25.8	1.04	20.8	5.0	31.8
1991	26.2	25.8	0.99	20.6	5.2	32.1
1992	27.5	27.5	1.00	22.1	5.4	34.5
1993	29.1	30.4	1.05	24.5	5.9	38.0
1994	30.5	33.3	1.09	27.4	5.9	41.4
1995	31.9	34.8	1.09	28.9	5.9	43.1
1996	33.1	35.3	1.06	29.2	6.1	43.6
1997	36.2	38.5	1.06	32.5	6.0	47.4

Imports in the Canadian Economy: Aggregate Results from the I/O Analysis

I/O calculations to determine the impact of replacing historical imports (at least the first "round") on Canadian output (domestic product) and employment have been conducted for each year from 1961 through 1997.[12] Individual industry impacts have been aggregated across all industries to derive economy-wide impacts, and these are summarized by year in Table 12 and the accompanying figures (Figures 15-20). As with the export calculations, these aggregate results present fully worked-out impacts on output and employment — in this case, of hypothetical import replacement. They are not simply sums of the outputs or employment levels of particular industries which are deemed to be primarily "import competitors"; instead they are estimates of the direct and all indirect output and employment required to produce domestically the first round of imports actually observed in each year.

Column 1 of Table 12 bridges between the more familiar National Accounts data and I/O calculations and concepts. This column shows imports (from the I/O database) as a share of business-sector domestic product, or value added, (also from the I/O database). This is the closest equivalent in the I/O data to column 6 of Table 11. The differences are larger than for exports but again are attributable to different classification schemes and to different definitions of the government sector. They also reflect possible discrepancies from our own updating of the I/O aggregate data on imports after 1992.

Proceeding to column 4 of Table 12 (and Figure 21), we come again to the central theme of this report — the impact on employment. As can be seen, the share of "import replaced" employment in total business-sector employment has indeed risen: from 16.4 percent in 1961 to 26.0 percent in 1992, and finally to 32.7 percent in 1997 — but, just as for exports, the increase in share of employment is much less than the increase in share of imports relative to business-sector product. The reason is also the same: increased "import penetration": From column 3 of Table 12 it can be seen that in 1961, if Canada had tried to produce what it imported, it would have required additional imports representing about 20 percent of the domestic product that would have been generated to produce the first round of imports. By 1997, this figure had risen to over 50 percent. Thus, while there has been considerable growth in employment and domestic product (see column 2) "displaced" by imports, the growth has not been nearly as large as that of the share of imports in GDP itself (see Figure 16).

Comparing the employment impacts of exports and "import replacement" is interesting: (see column 4 in Tables 2 and 12, and Figures 3 and 15). Employment "displaced" by imports in 1961, at 16.4 percent of total business employment, was just under the 17.2 percent of employment attributable to exports. (Both measures, it should be recalled, include employment for all intermediate inputs as well.) By 1992, however, the figure had reached to 26 percent for imports against 23.1 percent for exports, and by 1997 32.7 percent for imports against 28.3 percent for exports. That is, imports appear to have replaced more jobs than exports have provided. Why is this so? And, as might first appear, is this a bad thing? The answers to these two questions are closely related.

The principal insight comes from comparing calculated average labour productivity in exports and "import replacement" — see column 5 in each of Tables 2 and 12, and Figures 6 and 18. As can be seen, labour productivity in "import replacement" is invariably lower than in exports (it is at, or slightly above, the average for the economy as a whole), and in fact has fallen relatively in recent years. Thus, even though imports have actually grown slightly less than exports as a share of GDP, because it is lower

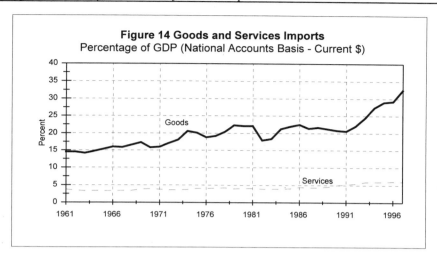

Figure 14 Goods and Services Imports
Percentage of GDP (National Accounts Basis - Current $)

productivity output (at least by Canadian technology) it has tended to "displace" more jobs. However, if we subscribe to the mainstream macroeconomic principle that economies tend to full employment in the longer-run, whatever their output mix, then the result of increased international trade has not been any permanent loss of jobs, but rather the replacement of lower-productivity output (which we import instead) with higher-productivity output (which we export) — leaving the Canadian economy earning more than it otherwise would. Moreover, this result is what mainstream international trade theory would also lead us to expect. Only to the extent that trade changes have occurred too fast for the labour force to respond in full has increased international trade "cost jobs" by increasing structural unemployment (workers displaced by imports who cannot be employed elsewhere in the economy) and the full-employment unemployment rate.

Another element requiring discussion in Table 12 is the relative importance of direct and indirect employment in "import replacement" (see columns 6 and 7, and Figure 19). As can be seen, the ratio of direct to total employment in "import replacement" hovers just under 60 percent through 1992 and then rises rapidly thereafter. The rise after 1992, which is also seen for exports, must be taken cautiously because I/O tables after 1992 are not available. Before the 1990s, the constancy of the ratio is notable, indicating no "deepening" of inter-industry technology in "import replacement" over this long span. Also notable is the fact that the ratio for import replacement is higher than that for exports (compare Figures 7 and 19). Thus, the Canadian import mix, if it were to be produced with Canadian technology, would involve fewer intermediate inputs (and more imported inputs) than the Canadian export mix.

Finally, as for exports, the I/O system permits us to calculate impacts of "import replacement" on the total remuneration to labour (aggregating wages and salaries, supplementary labour income and the income of unincorporated businesses into this category). The returns to labour can be expressed as a ratio to employment generated to determine the relative returns to labour in import replacement. As column 8 of Table 12 and Figure 20 show, this ratio remained relatively steady from 1961 to 1976, it rose to a slightly higher plateau in the late-1970s and fell after 1988. At all times, however, it has been above 1.0,

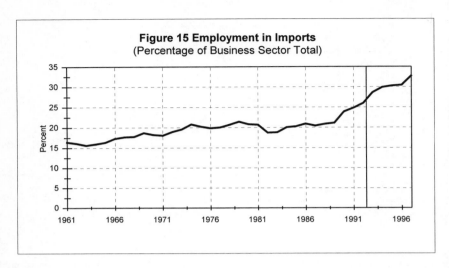

Figure 15 Employment in Imports
(Percentage of Business Sector Total)

indicating returns to labour above the business-sector average. When compared to returns to labour in exports, however (see Table 2 and Figure 8), the returns to labour in import replacement have been uniformly lower since the early 1970s (when the effect of Agriculture had been reduced). This might have been expected given that labour productivity in "import replacement" was also found to be lower than for exports. Again, the implication is that international trade has permitted Canada to substitute somewhat higher-paying jobs for relatively lower-paying ones. However, it should be kept in mind that even import-replacement labour returns are above the business-sector average. This indicates, not surprisingly, that there is a sizeable part of the economy which is relatively low paid and not much subject to international competition — some services, construction and some localized manufacturing (like cement) would be examples. While Canada is deriving net benefits from trade, on average it is not importing goods that, at least by its own technology, would be produced by very low-paid and low-productivity workers.

Table 12 Aggregate Comparisons from I/O Calculations – Imports – 1961–97

	(1) Imports as a % of Business Sector Domestic Product	(2) Domestic Product in Imports as a % of Business Domestic Product	(3) "Imports" from Imports as a % of Domestic Product from Imports	(4) Employment in Imports as a % of Total Business Employment	(5) Labour Productivity in Imports Relative to Business Sector	(6) Direct Employment in Imports as a % of Total Employment	(7) Ratio: Direct to Total Employment in Imports	(8) Ratio: Returns to Labour in Imports vs. Business Sector
1961	21.31	17.03	20.01	16.44	1.04	9.55	0.58	1.01
1962	21.37	17.15	19.66	16.10	1.06	9.33	0.58	1.01
1963	20.77	16.75	19.31	15.60	1.07	8.97	0.57	1.01
1964	21.45	17.15	20.18	15.94	1.08	9.21	0.58	1.02
1965	22.14	17.67	20.78	16.34	1.08	9.39	0.57	1.03
1966	23.29	18.42	22.34	17.30	1.06	9.92	0.57	1.02
1967	23.83	18.60	23.82	17.72	1.05	10.19	0.58	1.02
1968	24.93	18.99	26.48	17.78	1.07	10.21	0.57	1.03
1969	26.43	19.96	27.32	18.71	1.07	10.74	0.57	1.04
1970	24.91	18.76	27.41	18.24	1.03	10.52	0.58	1.04
1971	25.39	18.98	28.37	18.07	1.05	10.29	0.57	1.04
1972	27.02	20.05	29.35	18.98	1.06	10.83	0.57	1.03
1973	27.83	20.64	29.69	19.60	1.05	11.23	0.57	1.03
1974	31.29	23.14	31.15	20.81	1.11	11.86	0.57	1.03
1975	30.15	22.31	31.85	20.24	1.10	11.44	0.57	1.03
1976	28.94	21.38	31.12	19.89	1.08	11.34	0.57	1.03
1977	29.71	21.58	33.17	20.05	1.08	11.36	0.57	1.04
1978	31.47	22.54	35.07	20.70	1.09	11.79	0.57	1.06
1979	33.39	23.89	35.80	21.44	1.11	12.23	0.57	1.08
1980	32.55	23.53	34.83	20.82	1.13	11.92	0.57	1.08
1981	32.82	23.41	35.32	20.69	1.13	11.88	0.57	1.09
1982	27.65	20.15	31.94	18.74	1.08	10.68	0.57	1.09
1983	27.57	19.94	33.62	18.83	1.06	10.69	0.57	1.07
1984	30.86	22.02	36.13	20.09	1.10	11.42	0.57	1.07
1985	32.05	22.41	39.12	20.27	1.11	11.45	0.56	1.09
1986	33.08	22.57	41.68	20.92	1.08	11.88	0.57	1.08
1987	31.62	21.74	40.58	20.43	1.06	11.47	0.56	1.07
1988	32.09	22.20	39.33	20.85	1.06	11.77	0.56	1.07
1989	32.10	22.26	39.00	21.11	1.05	11.96	0.57	1.05
1990	34.14	23.83	37.87	23.92	1.00	14.20	0.59	1.01

Table 12 (cont'd)

	(1) Imports as a % of Business Sector Domestic Product	(2) Domestic Product in Imports as a % of Business Domestic Product	(3) "Imports" from Imports as a % of Domestic Product from Imports	(4) Employment in Imports as a % of Total Business Employment	(5) Labour Productivity in Imports Relative to Business Sector	(6) Direct Employment in Imports as a % of Total Employment	(7) Ratio: Direct to Total Employment in Imports	(8) Ratio: Returns to Labour in Imports vs. Business Sector
1991	34.54	23.99	39.38	24.84	0.97	14.75	0.59	1.01
1992	37.15	25.25	42.27	25.99	0.97	15.60	0.60	1.01
1993	42.59	28.45	44.89	28.64	0.99	18.51	0.65	n.a.
1994	46.32	30.46	47.25	29.91	1.02	21.06	0.70	n.a.
1995	47.72	31.24	47.94	30.30	1.03	22.40	0.74	n.a.
1996	47.54	30.93	48.87	30.47	1.01	22.78	0.75	n.a.
1997	52.37	33.51	51.50	32.69	1.03	24.90	0.76	n.a.

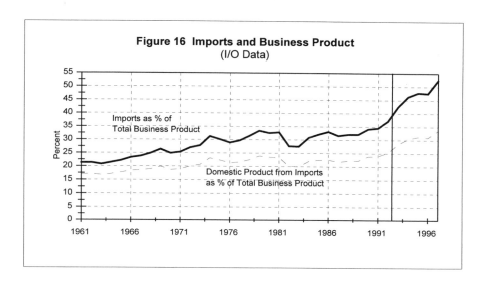

Figure 16 Imports and Business Product
(I/O Data)

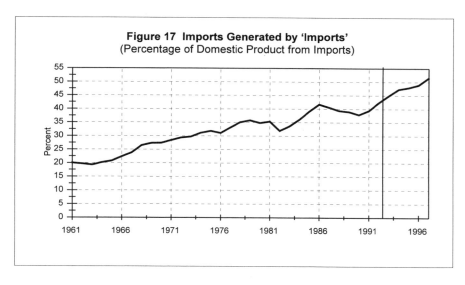

Figure 17 Imports Generated by 'Imports'
(Percentage of Domestic Product from Imports)

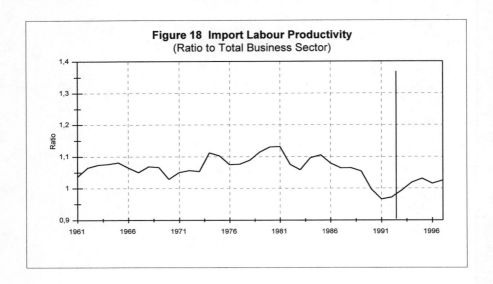

Figure 18 Import Labour Productivity
(Ratio to Total Business Sector)

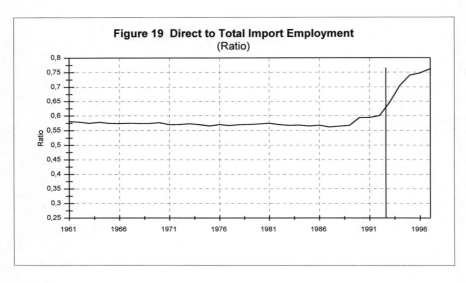

Figure 19 Direct to Total Import Employment
(Ratio)

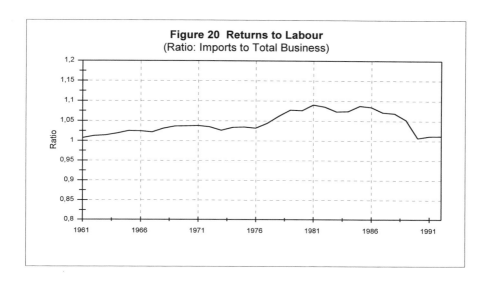

Figure 20 Returns to Labour
(Ratio: Imports to Total Business)

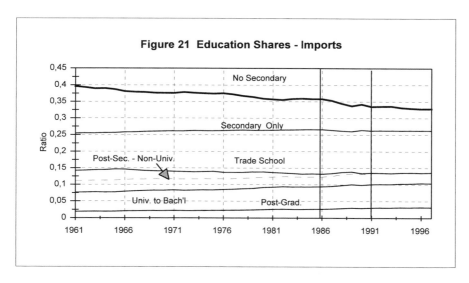

Figure 21 Education Shares - Imports

The Changing Industrial Mix of Imports: 24-Industry Aggregation

As with exports, we move now from examining aggregate to more disaggregated results and changes over time. Tables 13A and 13B show, at the 24-industry aggregation level, the employment attributable to imports as a share both of total import employment and of total employment, for 1961 and 1997. The table also shows the change in shares between the two years. Table 13A shows these shares in order by industry, while Table 13B shows the impacts sorted in order from largest increase in share of import employment to largest decrease. Table 13C shows the same impacts, but this time sorted from largest to smallest in terms of 1997 import employment as a percentage of total employment.

The figures in Tables 13A, B and C are interesting both in their absolute sizes in each year, and for changes over the 1961–97 period. In 1997, the first three industries in terms of share of total employment represented by "import replacement" employment were all in the services sector: Personal and other services, Business services, and Trade. Given that imports of services are not themselves a huge component of total imports, it can be seen that much, though not all, of the impact of these services is coming through indirect inputs into "import replacement". The other industries accounting in their import replacement impacts for between 2 and 3 percent of total business sector employment are: Primary metals and metal fabricating (2.4 percent), Motor vehicles and parts (2.0 percent), and Electrical and electronic products (2.6 percent). Each of these industries, and the three service types mentioned, figure strongly in 1997 export employment also, indicating trade specialization within these industries leading to heavy two-way trade.

Examining changes from 1961 to 1997 more closely, we can see in Table 13B that, of the seven industry groups that increased their share of import employment by over one percentage point, four are service industries (Personal and other services, Business services, Trade, and Finance). The other three are various Manufacturing categories that might be expected given the Auto Pact and changing technology: Motor vehicles, Electrical and electronic products, and Rubber and plastic products. There are eight industries with declines in import employment shares of over one percentage point: the two largest are in primary production (Mining excluding oil and gas, and Agriculture, forestry and fishing). The others are all in manufacturing, and many indicate by their presence that the Canadian economy has increased its own domestic processing of raw materials over the years since 1961 — such as Primary metal, Refined petroleum products and chemicals, and Paper and allied products. Others also indicate a maturing of Canadian domestic manufacturing over the period that was able to (in relative terms) supplant imports — such as Machinery, and Other transport equipment.

Comparing the equivalent tables for exports and imports (Tables 3B and 13B), it is perhaps remarkable that the sectors with the largest increases and decreases in employment shares are virtually the same in each case: Personal and business services, and Trade at the top, and Mining and Agriculture and forestry at the bottom. *Both* Canadian exports and Canadian imports have become more intensive in service employment and less intensive in employment in production of raw materials.

An analysis of the changing industrial mix of imports at the disaggregated 161-industry classification level is provided in Appendix 5.

Table 13A Employment Shares, 1961 to 1997 – 24 Industry Groups

24-Industry Aggregation	1961		1997		Change 1961–97	
	Import Employment as a % of Total Import Employment	Import Employment as a % of Total Employment	Import Employment as a % of Total Import Employment	Import Employment as a % of Total Employment	Import Employment as a % of Total Import Employment	Import Employment as a % of Total Employment
S1. Agriculture, Forestry, Fishing and Trapping	13.92	2.29	3.69	1.21	-10.22	-1.08
S2. Mining excluding Oil and Gas	5.18	0.85	1.08	0.35	-4.10	-0.50
S3. Crude Petroleum and Natural Gas	1.12	0.18	0.48	0.16	-0.64	-0.03
S4. Food, Beverages and Tobacco	2.83	0.47	2.13	0.70	-0.70	0.23
S5. Rubber and Plastic Products	1.44	0.24	3.03	0.99	1.58	0.75
S6. Leather, Textile and Clothing Products	7.88	1.30	5.81	1.90	-2.07	0.60
S7. Wood and Furniture Products	1.78	0.29	1.49	0.49	-0.29	0.19
S8. Paper and Allied Products and Printing	4.45	0.73	3.12	1.02	-1.32	0.29
S9. Primary Metals and Metal Fabricating	10.49	1.72	7.26	2.37	-3.23	0.65
S10. Machinery	6.31	1.04	5.16	1.69	-1.14	0.65
S11. Motor Vehicles and Parts	4.67	0.77	6.22	2.03	1.55	1.26
S12. Other Transportation Equipment	3.15	0.52	1.75	0.57	-1.40	0.06
S13. Electrical and Electronic Products	6.02	0.99	8.05	2.63	2.03	1.64
S14. Refined Petrol.. Chemicals and Non-met.	5.61	0.92	3.36	1.10	-2.25	0.18
S15. Other Manufactured Products	3.95	0.65	4.40	1.44	0.46	0.79
S16. Construction	1.47	0.24	1.02	0.33	-0.45	0.09
S17. Transportation and Pipelines	4.51	0.74	4.26	1.39	-0.25	0.65
S18. Storage	0.17	0.03	0.13	0.04	-0.03	0.02
S19. Utilities	2.07	0.34	2.35	0.77	0.28	0.43
S20. Trade	5.85	0.96	8.85	2.89	2.99	1.93
S21. Finance, Insurance and Real Estate	2.03	0.33	4.13	1.35	2.11	1.02
S22. Gov't Royalties and Owner Occ. Dwell.	0.00	0.00	0.00	0.00	0.00	0.00
S23. Business Services	3.13	0.51	10.33	3.38	7.20	2.86
S24. Personal and Other Services	1.97	0.32	11.88	3.88	9.90	3.56
TOTAL	100.00	16.44	100.00	32.69	-0.00	16.25

Table 13B Employment Shares, 1961 to 1997 – 24 Industry Groups – Sorted by Size of Change

24-Industry Aggregation	1961 Import Employment as a % of Total Import Employment	1961 Import Employment as a % of Total Employment	1997 Import Employment as a % of Total Import Employment	1997 Import Employment as a % of Total Employment	Change 1961–97 Import Employment as a % of Total Import Employment	Change 1961–97 Import Employment as a % of Total Employment
S24. Personal and Other Services	1.97	0.32	11.88	3.88	9.90	35.60
S23. Business Services	3.13	0.51	10.33	3.38	7.20	2.86
S20. Trade	5.85	0.96	8.85	2.89	2.99	1.93
S21. Finance, Insurance and Real Estate	2.03	0.33	4.13	1.35	2.11	1.02
S13. Electrical and Electronic Products	6.02	0.99	8.05	2.63	2.03	1.64
S5. Rubber and Plastic Products	1.44	0.24	3.03	0.99	1.58	0.75
S11. Motor Vehicles and Parts	4.67	0.77	6.22	2.03	1.55	1.26
S15. Other Manufactured Products	3.95	0.65	4.40	1.44	0.46	0.79
S19. Utilities	2.07	0.34	2.35	0.77	0.28	0.43
S22. Gov't Royalties and Owner Occ. Dwell.	0.00	0.00	0.00	0.00	0.00	0.00
S18. Storage	0.17	0.03	0.13	0.04	-0.03	0.02
S17. Transportation and Pipelines	4.51	0.74	4.26	1.39	-0.25	0.65
S7. Wood and Furniture Products	1.78	0.29	1.49	0.49	-0.29	0.19
S16. Construction	1.47	0.24	1.02	0.33	-0.45	0.09
S3. Crude Petroleum and Natural Gas	1.12	0.18	0.48	0.16	-0.64	-0.03
S4. Food, Beverages and Tobacco	2.83	0.47	2.13	0.70	-0.70	0.23
S10. Machinery	6.31	1.04	5.16	1.69	-1.14	0.65
S8. Paper and Allied Products and Printing	4.45	0.73	3.12	1.02	-1.32	0.29
S12. Other Transportation Equipment	3.15	0.52	1.75	0.57	-1.40	0.06
S6. Leather, Textile and Clothing Products	7.88	1.30	5.81	1.90	-2.07	0.60
S14. Refined Petrol.. Chemicals and Non-met.	5.61	0.92	3.36	1.10	-2.25	0.18
S9. Primary Metals and Metal Fabricating	10.49	1.72	7.26	2.37	-3.23	0.65
S2. Mining excluding Oil and Gas	5.18	0.85	1.08	0.35	-4.10	-0.50
S1. Agriculture, Forestry, Fishing and Trapping	13.92	2.29	3.69	1.21	-10.22	-1.08
TOTAL	100.00	16.44	100.00	32.69	0.00	16.25

Table 13C Employment Shares: 1961 to 1997 – 24 Industry Groups – Sorted by Import Employment as a % of Total Employment

24-Industry Aggregation	1961		1997		Change 1961–97	
	Import Employment as a % of Total Import Employment	Import Employment as a % of Total Employment	Import Employment as a % of Total Import Employment	Import Employment as a % of Total Employment	Import Employment as a % of Total Import Employment	Import Employment as a % of Total Employment
S24. Personal and Other Services	1.97	0.32	11.88	3.88	9.90	3.56
S23. Business Services	3.13	0.51	10.33	3.38	7.20	2.86
S20. Trade	5.85	0.96	8.85	2.89	2.99	1.93
S13. Electrical and Electronic Products	6.02	0.99	8.05	2.63	2.03	1.64
S9. Primary Metals and Metal Fabricating	10.49	1.72	7.26	2.37	-3.23	0.65
S11. Motor Vehicles and Parts	4.67	0.77	6.22	2.03	1.55	1.26
S6. Leather, Textile and Clothing Products	7.88	1.30	5.81	1.90	-2.07	0.60
S10. Machinery	6.31	1.04	5.16	1.69	-1.14	0.65
S15. Other Manufactured Products	3.95	0.65	4.40	1.44	0.46	0.79
S17. Transportation and Pipelines	4.51	0.74	4.26	1.39	-0.25	0.65
S21. Finance, Insurance and Real Estate	2.03	0.33	4.13	1.35	2.11	1.02
S1. Agriculture, Forestry, Fishing and Trapping	13.92	2.29	3.69	1.21	-10.22	-1.08
S14. Refined Petrol., Chemicals and Non-met.	5.61	0.92	3.36	1.10	-2.25	0.18
S8. Paper and Allied Products and Printing	4.45	0.73	3.12	1.02	-1.32	0.29
S5. Rubber and Plastic Products	1.44	0.24	3.03	0.99	1.58	0.75
S19. Utilities	2.07	0.34	2.35	0.77	0.28	0.43
S4. Food, Beverages and Tobacco	2.83	0.47	2.13	0.70	-0.70	0.23
S12. Other Transportation Equipment	3.15	0.52	1.75	0.57	-1.40	0.06
S7. Wood and Furniture Products	1.78	0.29	1.49	0.49	-0.29	0.19
S2. Mining excluding Oil and Gas	5.18	0.85	1.08	0.35	-4.10	-0.50
S16. Construction	1.47	0.24	1.02	0.33	-0.45	0.09
S3. Crude Petroleum and Natural Gas	1.12	0.18	0.48	0.16	-0.64	-0.03
S18. Storage	0.17	0.03	0.13	0.04	-0.03	0.02
S22. Gov't Royalties and Owner Occ. Dwell.	0.00	0.00	0.00	0.00	0.00	0.00
TOTAL	100.00	16.44	100.00	32.69	-0.00	16.25

Changes in Import Employment Impacts over Selected Sub-Periods

The summary and detail tables presented above cover very long time spans — either 1961–97 or 1961–92. It is also useful to select intermediate years and to examine import employment impacts in these years, noting how these impacts have changed over sub-periods. These results are presented in Tables 14A-D for the periods 1961–71, 1971–81, 1981–91, and 1991–97. The tables contain only the 24-industry aggregation, and are sorted by changes in import employment as a percentage of total import employment. Finally, a summary of the period-to-period changes is presented in Table 15.

Turning to the summary of period-to-period changes in Table 15, a number of observations are forthcoming: Agriculture, forestry and fishing, as was the case for exports, has lost "share" of import replacement employment in all sub-periods, but by far the biggest decline occurred in the 1960s. Thereafter, the pace of decline in this sector has been smaller and steadier but it apparently increased in the 1990s. Mining, on the other hand, has seen its share of import employment decline primarily in the 1960s and the 1990s. Relative import penetration in Food, beverages and tobacco occurred primarily in the 1960s, while the decline in import penetration for Leather, textile and clothing products happened through the 1960s and 1970s.

In Metals and machinery, there was a strong period of decline of relative import penetration in the 1980s. In the 1990s imports of Machinery have rebounded, partly fueled by very strong Machinery investment demand. In Motor vehicles and parts there was a large increase in import employment share in the 1960s under the Auto Pact. Since then the increase has been gradually whittled away by about half.

Interestingly, the increase in import employment share for Electrical and electronic products is not simply a recent phenomenon. Half of the share increase occurred in the 1960s and the share actually declined in the 1980s before rising again in the 1990s.

Finally, as noted before, the biggest increases in employment shares for imports are for the major services. However, this is not simply a recent development. The primary increases in import employment shares for Business services, for example, occurred in the 1960s and 1970s, and for Finance in the 1970s. For Trade (primarily wholesale trade) again the largest share gains were made in the 1960s and 1970s. For Personal services, however, there was a massive share increase in the 1980s, with some decline in the 1990s.

Decomposing Changes in the Employment Mix of Imports, 1961–97

As with exports, it is possible to decompose changes in import employment shares between two years into a number of components: (1) Changes in import shares, (2) Changes in the employment/output ratio, (3) Changes in input/output coefficients, and (4) Changes in import coefficients.

The decompositions have been performed over a number of different time spans and at both the 24-industry and 161-industry aggregations. Table 16A shows the decomposition of changes from 1961 through 1997 for the 24-industry aggregation, in numerical order, while Table 16B presents the same data, but sorted in order from largest positive to largest negative changes. The 161-industry decompositions are provided in Appendix 5. Finally, Tables 17A through 17D show 24-industry decompositions for the sub-periods 1961–71, 1971–81, 1981–91 and 1991–97 respectively.

Table 14A Employment Shares: 1961 to 1971 – 24 Industry Groups – Sorted by Size of Change

24-Industry Aggregation	1961		1971		Change 1961–71	
	Import Employment as a % of Total Import Employment	Import Employment as a % of Total Employment	Import Employment as a % of Total Import Employment	Import Employment as a % of Total Employment	Import Employment as a % of Total Import Employment	Import Employment as a % of Total Employment
S11. Motor Vehicles and Parts	4.67	0.77	8.39	1.52	3.72	0.75
S23. Business Services	3.13	0.51	5.76	1.04	2.63	0.53
S20. Trade	5.85	0.96	7.23	1.31	1.37	0.34
S13. Electrical and Electronic Products	6.02	0.99	7.27	1.31	1.25	0.32
S9. Primary Metals and Metal Fabricating	10.49	1.72	11.69	2.11	1.20	0.39
S21. Finance. Insurance and Real Estate	2.03	0.33	2.93	0.53	0.90	0.20
S24. Personal and Other Services	1.97	0.32	2.78	0.50	0.81	0.18
S5. Rubber and Plastic Products	1.44	0.24	2.07	0.37	0.63	0.14
S19. Utilities	2.07	0.34	2.39	0.43	0.32	0.09
S15. Other Manufactured Products	3.95	0.65	4.19	0.76	0.24	0.11
S22. Gov't Royalties and Owner Occ. Dwell.	0.00	0.00	0.00	0.00	0.00	0.00
S18. Storage	0.17	0.03	0.13	0.02	-0.04	-0.00
S10. Machinery	6.31	1.04	6.15	1.11	-0.16	0.07
S16. Construction	1.47	0.24	1.15	0.21	-0.32	-0.03
S8. Paper and Allied Products and Printing	4.45	0.73	4.09	0.74	-0.36	0.01
S3. Crude Petroleum and Natural Gas	1.12	0.18	0.74	0.13	-0.38	-0.05
S14. Refined Petrol.. Chemicals and Non-met.	5.61	0.92	5.21	0.94	-0.40	0.02
S7. Wood and Furniture Products	1.78	0.29	1.37	0.25	-0.41	-0.05
S6. Leather. Textile and Clothing Products	7.88	1.30	7.38	1.33	-0.50	0.04
S17. Transportation and Pipelines	4.51	0.74	3.95	0.71	-0.55	-0.03
S4. Food. Beverages and Tobacco	2.83	0.47	2.13	0.39	-0.70	-0.08
S12. Other Transportation Equipment	3.15	0.52	2.12	0.38	-1.03	-0.13
S2. Mining excluding Oil and Gas	5.18	0.85	3.06	0.55	-2.12	-0.30
S1. Agriculture. Forestry. Fishing and Trapping	13.92	2.29	7.81	1.41	-6.11	-0.88
TOTAL	100.00	16.44	100.00	18.07	-0.00	1.63

Table 14B Employment Shares: 1971 to 1981 – 24 Industry Groups – Sorted by Size of Change

24-Industry Aggregation	1971		1981		Change 1971–81	
	Import Employment as a % of Total Import Employment	Import Employment as a % of Total Employment	Import Employment as a % of Total Import Employment	Import Employment as a % of Total Employment	Import Employment as a % of Total Import Employment	Import Employment as a % of Total Employment
S23. Business Services	5.76	1.04	9.24	1.91	3.48	0.87
S21. Finance. Insurance and Real Estate	2.93	0.53	4.21	0.87	1.28	0.34
S24. Personal and Other Services	2.78	0.50	4.06	0.84	1.28	0.34
S20. Trade	7.23	1.31	8.23	1.70	1.00	0.40
S12. Other Transportation Equipment	2.12	0.38	2.66	0.55	0.54	0.17
S3. Crude Petroleum and Natural Gas	0.74	0.13	1.07	0.22	0.33	0.09
S10. Machinery	6.15	1.11	6.44	1.33	0.29	0.22
S13. Electrical and Electronic Products	7.27	1.31	7.54	1.56	0.27	0.25
S19. Utilities	2.39	0.43	2.59	0.54	0.21	0.11
S7. Wood and Furniture Products	1.37	0.25	1.46	0.30	0.10	0.06
S22. Gov't Royalties and Owner Occ. Dwell.	0.00	0.00	0.00	0.00	0.00	0.00
S18. Storage	0.13	0.02	0.13	0.03	-0.00	0.00
S5. Rubber and Plastic Products	2.07	0.37	2.05	0.42	-0.02	0.05
S16. Construction	1.15	0.21	1.10	0.23	-0.05	0.02
S4. Food. Beverages and Tobacco	2.13	0.39	2.00	0.41	-0.14	0.03
S17. Transportation and Pipelines	3.95	0.71	3.68	0.76	-0.28	0.05
S15. Other Manufactured Products	4.19	0.76	3.85	0.80	-0.34	0.04
S11. Motor Vehicles and Parts	8.39	1.52	7.77	1.61	-0.62	0.09
S2. Mining excluding Oil and Gas	3.06	0.55	2.37	0.49	-0.69	-0.06
S8. Paper and Allied Products and Printing	4.09	0.74	3.35	0.69	-0.74	-0.05
S14. Refined Petrol.. Chemicals and Non-met.	5.21	0.94	4.05	0.84	-1.16	-0.10
S9. Primary Metals and Metal Fabricating	11.69	2.11	10.29	2.13	-1.40	0.02
S6. Leather. Textile and Clothing Products	7.38	1.33	5.73	1.18	-1.66	-0.15
S1. Agriculture. Forestry. Fishing and Trapping	7.81	1.41	6.12	1.27	-1.69	-0.14
TOTAL	100.00	18.07	100.00	20.69	0.00	2.62

Table 14C Employment Shares: 1981 to 1991 – 24 Industry Groups – Sorted by Size of Change

24-Industry Aggregation	1981		1991		Change 1981–91	
	Import Employment as a % of Total Import Employment	Import Employment as a % of Total Employment	Import Employment as a % of Total Import Employment	Import Employment as a % of Total Employment	Import Employment as a % of Total Import Employment	Import Employment as a % of Total Employment
S24. Personal and Other Services	4.06	0.84	13.18	3.27	9.12	2.43
S17. Transportation and Pipelines	3.68	0.76	4.12	1.02	0.44	0.26
S5. Rubber and Plastic Products	2.05	0.42	2.40	0.60	0.35	0.17
S7. Wood and Furniture Products	1.46	0.30	1.73	0.43	0.27	0.13
S21. Finance. Insurance and Real Estate	4.21	0.87	4.47	1.11	0.26	0.24
S8. Paper and Allied Products and Printing	3.35	0.69	3.54	0.88	0.20	0.19
S4. Food. Beverages and Tobacco	2.00	0.41	2.17	0.54	0.18	0.13
S6. Leather. Textile and Clothing Products	5.73	1.18	5.86	1.46	0.13	0.27
S23. Business Services	9.24	1.91	9.25	2.30	0.01	0.39
S20. Trade	8.23	1.70	8.24	2.05	0.01	0.34
S22. Gov't Royalties and Owner Occ. Dwell.	0.00	0.00	0.00	0.00	0.00	0.00
S18. Storage	0.13	0.03	0.10	0.03	-0.02	-0.00
S15. Other Manufactured Products	3.85	0.80	3.76	0.93	-0.09	0.14
S19. Utilities	2.59	0.54	2.40	0.60	-0.20	0.06
S16. Construction	1.10	0.23	0.90	0.22	-0.21	-0.01
S3. Crude Petroleum and Natural Gas	1.07	0.22	0.64	0.16	-0.43	-0.06
S14. Refined Petrol.. Chemicals and Non-met.	4.05	0.84	3.60	0.90	-0.45	0.06
S1. Agriculture. Forestry. Fishing and Trapping	6.12	1.27	5.49	1.36	-0.63	0.10
S13. Electrical and Electronic Products	7.54	1.56	6.77	1.68	-0.76	0.12
S12. Other Transportation Equipment	2.66	0.55	1.56	0.39	-1.10	-0.16
S11. Motor Vehicles and Parts	7.77	1.61	6.67	1.66	-1.10	0.05
S2. Mining excluding Oil and Gas	2.37	0.49	1.15	0.29	-1.22	-0.21
S10. Machinery	6.44	1.33	4.11	1.02	-2.33	-0.31
S9. Primary Metals and Metal Fabricating	10.29	2.13	7.87	1.95	-2.42	-0.17
TOTAL	100.00	20.69	100.00	24.84	0.00	4.15

Table 14D Employment Shares: 1991 to 1997 – 24 Industry Groups – Sorted by Size of Change

24-Industry Aggregation	1991 Import Employment as a % of Total Import Employment	1991 Import Employment as a % of Total Employment	1997 Import Employment as a % of Total Import Employment	1997 Import Employment as a % of Total Employment	Change 1991–97 Import Employment as a % of Total Import Employment	Change 1991–97 Import Employment as a % of Total Employment
S13. Electrical and Electronic Products	6.77	1.68	8.05	2.63	1.28	0.95
S23. Business Services	9.25	2.30	10.33	3.38	1.08	1.08
S10. Machinery	4.11	1.02	5.16	1.69	1.05	0.67
S15. Other Manufactured Products	3.76	0.93	4.40	1.44	0.65	0.51
S5. Rubber and Plastic Products	2.40	0.60	3.03	0.99	0.63	0.39
S20. Trade	8.24	2.05	8.85	2.89	0.61	0.85
S12. Other Transportation Equipment	1.56	0.39	1.75	0.57	0.19	0.18
S17. Transportation and Pipelines	4.12	1.02	4.26	1.39	0.14	0.37
S16. Construction	0.90	0.22	1.02	0.33	0.13	0.11
S18. Storage	0.10	0.03	0.13	0.04	0.03	0.02
S22. Gov't Royalties and Owner Occ. Dwell.	0.00	0.00	0.00	0.00	0.00	0.00
S4. Food. Beverages and Tobacco	2.17	0.54	2.13	0.70	-0.04	0.16
S6. Leather. Textile and Clothing Products	5.86	1.46	5.81	1.90	-0.04	0.45
S19. Utilities	2.40	0.60	2.35	0.77	-0.05	0.17
S2. Mining excluding Oil and Gas	1.15	0.29	1.08	0.35	-0.07	0.07
S3. Crude Petroleum and Natural Gas	0.64	0.16	0.48	0.16	-0.17	-0.00
S7. Wood and Furniture Products	1.73	0.43	1.49	0.49	-0.24	0.06
S14. Refined Petrol.. Chemicals and Non-met.	3.60	0.90	3.36	1.10	-0.25	0.20
S21. Finance. Insurance and Real Estate	4.47	1.11	4.13	1.35	-0.34	0.24
S8. Paper and Allied Products and Printing	3.54	0.88	3.12	1.02	-0.42	0.14
S11. Motor Vehicles and Parts	6.67	1.66	6.22	2.03	-0.45	0.38
S9. Primary Metals and Metal Fabricating	7.87	1.95	7.26	2.37	-0.61	0.42
S24. Personal and Other Services	13.18	3.27	11.88	3.88	-1.30	0.61
S1. Agriculture. Forestry. Fishing and Trapping	5.49	1.36	3.69	1.21	-1.80	-0.16
TOTAL	100.00	24.84	100.00	32.69	-0.00	7.85

Table 15 Employment Shares: Changes from 1961 to 1997 – 24 Industry Groups

Import Employment as a % of Total Import Employment

24-Industry Aggregation	1961–97	1961–71	1971–81	1981–91	1991–97
S1. Agriculture, Forestry, Fishing and Trapping	-10.2	-6.1	-1.7	-0.6	-1.8
S2. Mining excluding Oil and Gas	-4.1	-2.1	-0.7	-1.2	-0.1
S3. Crude Petroleum and Natural Gas	-0.6	-0.4	0.3	-0.4	-0.2
S4. Food, Beverages and Tobacco	-0.7	-0.7	-0.1	0.2	-0.0
S5. Rubber and Plastic Products	1.6	0.6	-0.0	0.3	0.6
S6. Leather, Textile and Clothing Products	-2.1	-0.5	-1.7	0.1	-0.0
S7. Wood and Furniture Products	-0.3	-0.4	0.1	0.3	-0.2
S8. Paper and Allied Products and Printing	-1.3	-0.4	-0.7	0.2	-0.4
S9. Primary Metals and Metal Fabricating	-3.2	1.2	-1.4	-2.4	-0.6
S10. Machinery	-1.1	-0.2	0.3	-2.3	1.1
S11. Motor Vehicles and Parts	1.5	3.7	-0.6	-1.1	-0.5
S12. Other Transportation Equipment	-1.4	-1.0	0.5	-1.1	0.2
S13. Electrical and Electronic Products	2.0	1.3	0.3	-0.8	1.3
S14. Refined Petrol.. Chemicals and Non-met.	-2.2	-0.4	-1.2	-0.4	-0.2
S15. Other Manufactured Products	0.5	0.2	-0.3	-0.1	0.6
S16. Construction	-0.4	-0.3	-0.0	-0.2	0.1
S17. Transportation and Pipelines	-0.3	-0.6	-0.3	0.4	0.1
S18. Storage	-0.0	-0.0	-0.0	-0.0	0.0
S19. Utilities	0.3	0.3	0.2	-0.2	-0.1
S20. Trade	3.0	1.4	1.0	0.0	0.6
S21. Finance, Insurance and Real Estate	2.1	0.9	1.3	0.3	-0.3
S22. Gov't Royalties and Owner Occ. Dwell.	0.0	0	0	0.0	0.0
S23. Business Services	7.2	2.6	3.5	0.0	1.1
S24. Personal and Other Services	9.9	0.8	1.3	9.1	-1.3

Table 16A Decomposition of Changes in Employment Shares: 1961 to 1997 – 24 Industries

	1961	1997	Change 1961–97	Change in Import Shares	Due to: Change in Employ't /Output Ratio	Due to: Change in Input/ Output Coeff's	Due to: Change in Import Coeff's	Residual /Inter-action
	Import Employ't as a % of Total Import Employ't	Import Employ't as a % of Total Import Employ't	Import Employ't as a % of Total Import Employ't					
S1. Agriculture, Forestry, Fishing and Trapping	13.92	3.69	-10.22	-5.10	-0.64	0.30	-3.08	-1.70
S2. Mining excluding Oil and Gas	5.18	1.08	-4.10	-1.22	-0.09	-0.10	-0.89	-1.80
S3. Crude Petroleum and Natural Gas	1.12	0.48	-0.64	-0.42	0.01	0.03	-0.26	-0.00
S4. Food, Beverages and Tobacco	2.83	2.13	-0.70	-1.19	-0.21	0.11	-0.01	0.60
S5. Rubber and Plastic Products	1.44	3.03	1.58	1.20	0.03	-0.29	0.46	0.18
S6. Leather, Textile and Clothing Products	7.88	5.81	-2.07	-1.72	-0.58	-0.02	0.64	-0.38
S7. Wood and Furniture Products	1.78	1.49	-0.29	-0.05	-0.19	0.06	-0.18	0.06
S8. Paper and Allied Products and Printing	4.45	3.12	-1.32	-0.82	-0.79	-0.04	-0.20	0.53
S9. Primary Metals and Metal Fabricating	10.49	7.26	-3.23	-2.00	-0.88	-0.90	-0.56	1.11
S10. Machinery	6.31	5.16	-1.14	-1.33	-0.39	0.19	-0.28	0.67
S11. Motor Vehicles and Parts	4.67	6.22	1.55	2.71	-0.33	-0.02	-2.92	2.11
S12. Other Transportation Equipment	3.15	1.75	-1.40	-0.83	-0.15	-0.15	-0.46	0.19
S13. Electrical and Electronic Products	6.02	8.05	2.03	3.73	1.18	0.37	-3.41	0.16
S14. Refined Petrol.. Chemicals and Non-met.	5.61	3.36	-2.25	-0.83	-0.26	-0.20	-1.46	0.50
S15. Other Manufactured Products	3.95	4.40	0.46	-0.16	-0.17	0.09	0.48	0.22
S16. Construction	1.47	1.02	-0.45	-0.20	-0.40	-0.04	-0.05	0.25
S17. Transportation and Pipelines	4.51	4.26	-0.25	0.71	-0.31	-0.22	0.11	-0.54
S18. Storage	0.17	0.13	-0.03	-0.05	-0.15	-0.00	0.06	0.11
S19. Utilities	2.07	2.35	0.28	-0.06	0.60	-0.10	-0.88	0.71
S20. Trade	5.85	8.85	2.99	-0.64	-0.19	-0.37	2.48	1.72
S21. Finance, Insurance and Real Estate	2.03	4.13	2.11	0.51	0.67	-0.01	0.41	0.54
S22. Gov't Royalties and Owner Occ. Dwell.	0.00	0.00	0.00	0.00	0.00	0.00	0.00	0.00
S23. Business Services	3.13	10.33	7.20	1.47	3.04	1.02	3.61	-1.94
S24. Personal and Other Services	1.97	11.88	9.90	6.31	0.18	0.31	6.39	-3.29
TOTAL	100.00	100.00	-0.00	0.00	-0.00	-0.00	0.00	0.00

Table 16B Decomposition of Changes in Employment Shares: 1961 to 1997 – 24 Industries

Sorted by Size of Change	1961 Import Employ't as a % of Total Import Employ't	1997 Import Employ't as a % of Total Import Employ't	Change 1961–97 Import Employ't as a % of Total Import Employ't	Change in Import Shares	Change in Employ't /Output Ratio	Change in Input/ Output Coeff's	Change in Import Coeff's	Residual /Inter- action
S24. Personal and Other Services	1.97	11.88	9.90	6.31	0.18	0.31	6.39	-3.29
S23. Business Services	3.13	10.33	7.20	1.47	3.04	1.02	3.61	-1.94
S20. Trade	5.85	8.85	2.99	-0.64	-0.19	-0.37	2.48	1.72
S21. Finance. Insurance and Real Estate	2.03	4.13	2.11	0.51	0.67	-0.01	0.41	0.54
S13. Electrical and Electronic Products	6.02	8.05	2.03	3.73	1.18	0.37	-3.41	0.16
S5. Rubber and Plastic Products	1.44	3.03	1.58	1.20	0.03	-0.29	0.46	0.18
S11. Motor Vehicles and Parts	4.67	6.22	1.55	2.71	-0.33	-0.02	-2.92	2.11
S15. Other Manufactured Products	3.95	4.40	0.46	-0.16	-0.17	0.09	0.48	0.22
S19. Utilities	2.07	2.35	0.28	-0.06	0.60	-0.10	-0.88	0.71
S22. Gov't Royalties and Owner Occ. Dwell.	0.00	0.00	0.00	0.00	0.00	0.00	0.00	0.00
S18. Storage	0.17	0.13	-0.03	-0.05	-0.15	-0.00	0.06	0.11
S17. Transportation and Pipelines	4.51	4.26	-0.25	0.71	-0.31	-0.22	0.11	-0.54
S7. Wood and Furniture Products	1.78	1.49	-0.29	-0.05	-0.19	0.06	-0.18	0.06
S16. Construction	1.47	1.02	-0.45	-0.20	-0.40	-0.04	-0.05	0.25
S3. Crude Petroleum and Natural Gas	1.12	0.48	-0.64	-0.42	0.01	0.03	-0.26	-0.00
S4. Food. Beverages and Tobacco	2.83	2.13	-0.70	-1.19	-0.21	0.11	-0.01	0.60
S10. Machinery	6.31	5.16	-1.14	-1.33	-0.39	0.19	-0.28	0.67
S8. Paper and Allied Products and Printing	4.45	3.12	-1.32	-0.82	-0.79	-0.04	-0.20	0.53
S12. Other Transportation Equipment	3.15	1.75	-1.40	-0.83	-0.15	-0.15	-0.46	0.19
S6. Leather. Textile and Clothing Products	7.88	5.81	-2.07	-1.72	-0.58	-0.02	0.64	-0.38
S14. Refined Petrol... Chemicals and Non-met.	5.61	3.36	-2.25	-0.83	-0.26	-0.20	-1.46	0.50
S9. Primary Metals and Metal Fabricating	10.49	7.26	-3.23	-2.00	-0.88	-0.90	-0.56	1.11
S2. Mining excluding Oil and Gas	5.18	1.08	-4.10	-1.22	-0.09	-0.10	-0.89	-1.80
S1. Agriculture. Forestry. Fishing and Trapping	13.92	3.69	-10.22	-5.10	-0.64	0.30	-3.08	-1.70
TOTAL	100.00	100.00	-0.00	0.00	-0.00	-0.00	0.00	0.00

Table 17A Decomposition of Changes in Employment Shares: 1961 to 1971 – 24 Industries

Sorted by Size of Change	1961 Import Employ't as a % of Total Import Employ't	1971 Import Employ't as a % of Total Import Employ't	Change 1961–71 Import Employ't as a % of Total Import Employ't	Change in Import Shares	Due to: Change in Employ't /Output Ratio	Change in Input/ Output Coeff's	Change in Import Coeff's	Residual /Inter- action
S11. Motor Vehicles and Parts	4.67	8.39	3.72	4.76	0.03	-0.63	-1.87	1.42
S23. Business Services	3.13	5.76	2.63	0.97	1.09	0.30	0.99	-0.72
S20. Trade	5.85	7.23	1.37	0.43	-0.09	-0.05	0.90	0.19
S13. Electrical and Electronic Products	6.02	7.27	1.25	0.80	0.02	-0.18	0.59	0.02
S9. Primary Metals and Metal Fabricating	10.49	11.69	1.20	0.43	0.04	-0.19	0.74	0.18
S21. Finance, Insurance and Real Estate	2.03	2.93	0.90	0.37	0.22	0.01	0.36	-0.07
S24. Personal and Other Services	1.97	2.78	0.81	0.21	-0.01	0.02	0.65	-0.06
S5. Rubber and Plastic Products	1.44	2.07	0.63	0.51	0.12	-0.02	0.05	-0.04
S19. Utilities	2.07	2.39	0.32	0.06	0.11	0.01	0.07	0.06
S15. Other Manufactured Products	3.95	4.19	0.24	0.18	0.02	0.04	0.05	-0.05
S22. Gov't Royalties and Owner Occ. Dwell.	0.00	0.00	0.00	0.00	0.00	0.00	0.00	0.00
S18. Storage	0.17	0.13	-0.04	-0.02	-0.03	0.00	0.01	0.01
S10. Machinery	6.31	6.15	-0.16	0.09	0.05	0.11	-0.37	-0.04
S16. Construction	1.47	1.15	-0.32	-0.11	-0.13	0.02	-0.19	0.09
S8. Paper and Allied Products and Printing	4.45	4.09	-0.36	-0.50	-0.45	0.06	0.39	0.14
S3. Crude Petroleum and Natural Gas	1.12	0.74	-0.38	-0.24	0.01	0.03	-0.15	-0.03
S14. Refined Petrol.. Chemicals and Non-met.	5.61	5.21	-0.40	-0.69	-0.20	0.07	0.34	0.09
S7. Wood and Furniture Products	1.78	1.37	-0.41	-0.35	-0.03	0.04	-0.06	-0.00
S6. Leather, Textile and Clothing Products	7.88	7.38	-0.50	-0.80	-0.13	0.09	0.25	0.10
S17. Transportation and Pipelines	4.51	3.95	-0.55	-0.06	-0.16	0.02	-0.40	0.04
S4. Food, Beverages and Tobacco	2.83	2.13	-0.70	-0.92	-0.04	0.06	0.11	0.09
S12. Other Transportation Equipment	3.15	2.12	-1.03	-1.00	-0.03	-0.04	-0.07	0.11
S2. Mining excluding Oil and Gas	5.18	3.06	-2.12	-0.87	0.12	0.00	-0.71	-0.66
S1. Agriculture. Forestry. Fishing and Trapping	13.92	7.81	-6.11	-3.27	-0.53	0.24	-1.68	-0.87

Table 17B Decomposition of Changes in Employment Shares: 1971 to 1981 – 24 Industries

Sorted by Size of Change	1971 Import Employ't as a % of Total Import Employ't	1981 Import Employ't as a % of Total Import Employ't	Change 1971–81 Import Employ't as a % of Total Import Employ't	Change in Import Shares	Due to: Change in Employ't /Output Ratio	Change in Input/ Output Coeff's	Change in Import Coeff's	Residual /Inter-action
S23. Business Services	5.76	9.24	3.48	0.81	0.53	0.15	2.26	-0.27
S21. Finance. Insurance and Real Estate	2.93	4.21	1.28	0.33	0.10	0.03	0.94	-0.12
S24. Personal and Other Services	2.78	4.06	1.28	-0.09	0.21	0.06	1.19	-0.10
S20. Trade	7.23	8.23	1.00	0.32	-0.52	-0.05	1.31	-0.07
S12. Other Transportation Equipment	2.12	2.66	0.54	0.68	0.02	0.06	-0.36	0.14
S3. Crude Petroleum and Natural Gas	0.74	1.07	0.33	0.51	0.12	0.04	-0.74	0.40
S10. Machinery	6.15	6.44	0.29	0.37	0.11	0.11	-0.19	-0.10
S13. Electrical and Electronic Products	7.27	7.54	0.27	0.94	0.04	-0.13	-0.63	0.04
S19. Utilities	2.39	2.59	0.21	0.06	0.04	0.01	0.07	0.03
S7. Wood and Furniture Products	1.37	1.46	0.10	0.16	-0.01	0.01	-0.02	-0.04
S22. Gov't Royalties and Owner Occ. Dwell.	0.00	0.00	0.00	0.00	0.00	0.00	0.00	0.00
S18. Storage	0.13	0.13	-0.00	-0.00	-0.04	0.00	0.03	0.01
S5. Rubber and Plastic Products	2.07	2.05	-0.02	-0.10	0.03	0.00	0.04	0.01
S16. Construction	1.15	1.10	-0.05	0.15	-0.17	0.00	-0.14	0.12
S4. Food. Beverages and Tobacco	2.13	2.00	-0.14	-0.09	0.05	0.04	-0.10	-0.03
S17. Transportation and Pipelines	3.95	3.68	-0.28	-0.09	-0.31	-0.01	0.25	-0.12
S15. Other Manufactured Products	4.19	3.85	-0.34	-0.45	0.05	0.03	-0.02	0.03
S11. Motor Vehicles and Parts	8.39	7.77	-0.62	-1.96	0.01	-0.08	1.25	0.15
S2. Mining excluding Oil and Gas	3.06	2.37	-0.69	0.56	-0.19	-0.19	-1.40	0.54
S8. Paper and Allied Products and Printing	4.09	3.35	-0.74	-0.35	-0.09	0.03	-0.29	-0.03
S14. Refined Petrol.. Chemicals and Non-met.	5.21	4.05	-1.16	-0.34	0.31	0.13	-1.49	0.24
S9. Primary Metals and Metal Fabricating	11.69	10.29	-1.40	-0.05	-0.15	-0.43	-0.49	-0.28
S6. Leather. Textile and Clothing Products	7.38	5.73	-1.66	-1.09	-0.21	0.09	-0.14	-0.31
S1. Agriculture. Forestry. Fishing and Trapping	7.81	6.12	-1.69	-0.28	0.06	0.10	-1.32	-0.24

Table 17C Decomposition of Changes in Employment Shares: 1981 to 1991 – 24 Industries

Sorted by Size of Change	1981 — Import Employ't as a % of Total Import Employ't	1991 — Import Employ't as a % of Total Import Employ't	Change 1981–91 — Import Employ't as a % of Total Import Employ't	Due to: Change in Import Shares	Change in Employ't /Output Ratio	Change in Input/ Output Coeff's	Change in Import Coeff's	Residual /Inter- action
S24. Personal and Other Services	4.06	13.18	9.12	8.40	0.08	-0.12	1.19	-0.43
S17. Transportation and Pipelines	3.68	4.12	0.44	1.03	-0.15	-0.13	-0.30	-0.02
S5. Rubber and Plastic Products	2.05	2.40	0.35	0.19	0.02	-0.11	0.38	-0.12
S7. Wood and Furniture Products	1.46	1.73	0.27	0.35	-0.08	-0.00	0.15	-0.15
S21. Finance. Insurance and Real Estate	4.21	4.47	0.26	0.30	0.71	0.01	-1.09	0.34
S8. Paper and Allied Products and Printing	3.35	3.54	0.20	0.54	-0.17	-0.10	0.05	-0.12
S4. Food. Beverages and Tobacco	2.00	2.17	0.18	0.30	-0.15	-0.01	0.05	-0.01
S6. Leather. Textile and Clothing Products	5.73	5.86	0.13	0.35	-0.28	-0.14	0.44	-0.25
S23. Business Services	9.24	9.25	0.01	-0.25	0.83	0.28	-0.78	-0.06
S20. Trade	8.23	8.24	0.01	-1.18	0.94	0.04	0.14	0.07
S22. Gov't Royalties and Owner Occ. Dwell.	0.00	0.00	0.00	0.00	0.00	0.00	0.00	0.00
S18. Storage	0.13	0.10	-0.02	-0.01	-0.02	-0.00	0.01	-0.00
S15. Other Manufactured Products	3.85	3.76	-0.09	-0.18	-0.18	-0.02	0.39	-0.10
S19. Utilities	2.59	2.40	-0.20	-0.03	0.40	-0.02	-0.70	0.16
S16. Construction	1.10	0.90	-0.21	-0.18	-0.11	-0.00	0.13	-0.05
S3. Crude Petroleum and Natural Gas	1.07	0.64	-0.43	-1.08	-0.17	0.04	0.29	0.50
S14. Refined Petrol.. Chemicals and Non-met.	4.05	3.60	-0.45	-0.01	-0.27	-0.19	0.11	-0.09
S1. Agriculture. Forestry. Fishing and Trapping	6.12	5.49	-0.63	-1.38	-0.25	0.10	0.68	0.22
S13. Electrical and Electronic Products	7.54	6.77	-0.76	1.28	0.01	-0.34	-2.08	0.36
S12. Other Transportation Equipment	2.66	1.56	-1.10	-0.82	-0.03	0.05	-0.08	-0.21
S11. Motor Vehicles and Parts	7.77	6.67	-1.10	-0.34	-0.19	0.48	-0.67	-0.39
S2. Mining excluding Oil and Gas	2.37	1.15	-1.22	-1.32	-0.10	0.14	0.01	0.05
S10. Machinery	6.44	4.11	-2.33	-3.22	-0.23	0.04	0.65	0.43
S9. Primary Metals and Metal Fabricating	10.29	7.87	-2.42	-2.74	-0.58	0.01	1.03	-0.14

Table 17D Decomposition of Changes in Employment Shares: 1991 to 1997 – 24 Industries

Sorted by Size of Change	1991 Import Employ't as a % of Total Import Employ't	1997 Import Employ't as a % of Total Import Employ't	Change 1991-97 Import Employ't as a % of Total Import Employ't	Change in Import Shares	Due to: Change in Employ't /Output Ratio	Change in Input/ Output Coeff's	Change in Import Coeff's	Residual /Interaction
S13. Electrical and Electronic Products	6.77	8.05	1.28	2.44	1.39	1.30	0.18	-4.03
S23. Business Services	9.25	10.33	1.08	-0.30	-0.00	-0.07	1.06	0.39
S10. Machinery	4.11	5.16	1.05	1.34	-0.09	-0.02	-0.48	0.30
S15. Other Manufactured Products	3.76	4.40	0.65	0.58	0.10	0.07	0.29	-0.39
S5. Rubber and Plastic Products	2.40	3.03	0.63	0.66	-0.04	-0.23	0.17	0.06
S20. Trade	8.24	8.85	0.61	0.00	-0.27	-0.17	0.67	0.37
S12. Other Transportation Equipment	1.56	1.75	0.19	0.29	-0.03	-0.15	-0.02	0.10
S17. Transportation and Pipelines	4.12	4.26	0.14	-0.32	-0.06	-0.10	0.38	0.24
S16. Construction	0.90	1.02	0.13	-0.01	-0.01	-0.04	0.14	0.05
S18. Storage	0.10	0.13	0.03	-0.00	-0.00	-0.00	0.03	0.01
S22. Gov't Royalties and Owner Occ. Dwell.	0.00	0.00	0.00	0.00	0.00	0.00	0.00	0.00
S4. Food, Beverages and Tobacco	2.17	2.13	-0.04	-0.23	-0.01	0.03	0.08	0.09
S6. Leather, Textile and Clothing Products	5.86	5.81	-0.04	-0.52	-0.12	-0.11	0.43	0.26
S19. Utilities	2.40	2.35	-0.05	0.02	0.02	-0.06	-0.13	0.09
S2. Mining excluding Oil and Gas	1.15	1.08	-0.07	0.07	-0.02	-0.12	-0.05	0.05
S3. Crude Petroleum and Natural Gas	0.64	0.48	-0.17	0.00	-0.00	-0.04	-0.14	0.02
S7. Wood and Furniture Products	1.73	1.49	-0.24	-0.09	-0.04	0.01	-0.15	0.03
S14. Refined Petrol., Chemicals and Non-met.	3.60	3.36	-0.25	0.26	-0.04	-0.17	-0.50	0.21
S21. Finance, Insurance and Real Estate	4.47	4.13	-0.34	-0.37	-0.26	-0.05	0.13	0.21
S8. Paper and Allied Products and Printing	3.54	3.12	-0.42	-0.33	-0.12	-0.04	-0.08	0.16
S11. Motor Vehicles and Parts	6.67	6.22	-0.45	0.57	-0.09	0.14	-1.37	0.29
S9. Primary Metals and Metal Fabricating	7.87	7.26	-0.61	0.80	-0.14	-0.43	-1.28	0.45
S24. Personal and Other Services	13.18	11.88	-1.30	-4.20	-0.11	0.17	1.73	1.10
S1. Agriculture, Forestry, Fishing and Trapping	5.49	3.69	-1.80	-0.67	-0.07	0.08	-1.10	-0.03

We will discuss primarily the results in Table 16B, for 1961–97 at the 24-industry aggregation. Not surprisingly, there are many similarities between this table and the equivalent one for export employment shares (Table 6B). This is partly because 1961–97 changes in employment/output ratios, input/output coefficients and Import coefficients are the same between these two years, whether we are analyzing exports or imports. Only the first component of the decomposition — the import share in this case — will differ. Of course, the numerical results are not identical for the other columns because of different aggregation weights and different interactions with the export or import shares.

For the sectors showing large changes in employment share the primary sources, as for exports, are the import shares themselves and the import coefficients. Changes in relative employment/output ratios and in input/output coefficients are generally much less important.

There are, however, several exceptions: Changes in the employment/output ratio are important components of overall import employment shares for Business services, Electrical and electronic products, and Paper and primary metals. Changes in I/O coefficients are important for Business services again, and Primary metals.

For the remaining sectors there are a variety of patterns of influence. Sometimes the import shares and import coefficients reinforce each other in effect and sometimes they offset.

The Changing Skill Mix of Canadian Imports

As for exports, we can now apply educational shares by industry to the employment impacts generated above to get some idea of the (Canadian) educational mix of the employment that imports are "displacing". Also as for exports, the results for years outside the range 1986–91 must be considered as illustrative only, and reflect only changes in the mix of employment by sector and not any changes in educational mix within industries themselves.

See the section entitled The Changing Skill Mix of Canadian Exports above for a further description of the basic COPS data and for listing of educational shares by the 112 industries available at the most detailed disaggregation. These data have been aggregated to the 24-industry level using import employment weights in Tables 18A and 18B for 1991 and 1986 respectively.

Table 19A reports on the calculated educational shares for imports, while Table 10B above in Section 4 shows the corresponding educational shares for the business sector as a whole. The series in Table 19A are plotted in Figure 21.

As with exports, the critical concern is not with the absolute educational shares of imports over 1961–97, but with how these compare to the economy as a whole. The ratios of import education shares to those of the total business sector are shown in Table 19B and the series in that table are plotted in Figures 22 and 23. These will be reviewed on their own and compared with the results for exports as presented in Table 10C and Figures 11 and 12.

Table 19B and Figures 22 and 23 are fairly unequivocal in showing that, over the entire time span, Canadian imports have been — at least by Canadian technology and education shares by sector — *above* the business-sector average in overall education content. In recent years, however, there are strong signs that the discrepancy with respect to the average education level of Canadian output is narrowing. This indicates relatively greater displacement of lower skill Canadian employment by imports in more recent years, but the average for imports remains above Canadian average skill levels.

As can be seen from Figure 22, import employment has had a share of employees having only secondary education that is only about .95 of the business sector total almost continually since 1961. During most of the period since 1961 the share of "import" employees having no secondary diploma has also been somewhat below that of the total business sector; however, in about 1990 this ratio shifted such that "import" employees had just above the total business sector average share of no secondary. In the same year this a shift in the relative share of trade school education — with import employment moving from just above to just below the business-sector average. As can be seen from Figures 23, import employment has invariably had shares of post-secondary education of all kinds above the total business-sector average. However, each type has converged toward the business sector average starting in the late 1980s.

Table 18A Import Education/Skill Shares, 1991 – 24 Industries (Import Employment Weights)

24-Industry Aggregation	No Secondary School	Secondary School Only	Trade Certificate or Diploma	Post-Sec. Non-Univ. Degree	University up to Bachelor's Degree	All Post-Graduate Degrees
S1. Agriculture, Forestry, Fishing and Trapping	0.53	0.21	0.10	0.08	0.05	0.02
S2. Mining excluding Oil and Gas	0.38	0.20	0.23	0.11	0.06	0.02
S3. Crude Petroleum and Natural Gas	0.14	0.21	0.17	0.18	0.23	0.07
S4. Food. Beverages and Tobacco	0.44	0.26	0.12	0.09	0.07	0.02
S5. Rubber and Plastic Products	0.41	0.27	0.14	0.11	0.06	0.02
S6. Leather. Textile and Clothing Products	0.53	0.25	0.09	0.07	0.05	0.01
S7. Wood and Furniture Products	0.45	0.25	0.15	0.09	0.04	0.01
S8. Paper and Allied Products and Printing	0.30	0.30	0.15	0.14	0.10	0.02
S9. Primary Metals and Metal Fabricating	0.34	0.23	0.23	0.12	0.06	0.01
S10. Machinery	0.29	0.23	0.22	0.16	0.08	0.02
S11. Motor Vehicles and Parts	0.42	0.26	0.14	0.10	0.06	0.01
S12. Other Transportation Equipment	0.22	0.21	0.23	0.19	0.11	0.03
S13. Electrical and Electronic Products	0.25	0.24	0.12	0.19	0.15	0.05
S14. Refined Petrol.. Chemicals and Non-met.	0.28	0.27	0.14	0.14	0.13	0.04
S15. Other Manufactured Products	0.33	0.27	0.13	0.15	0.09	0.02
S16. Construction	0.37	0.23	0.25	0.10	0.05	0.01
S17. Transportation and Pipelines	0.38	0.26	0.16	0.12	0.06	0.01
S18. Storage	0.38	0.33	0.12	0.09	0.05	0.02
S19. Utilities	0.19	0.30	0.16	0.19	0.12	0.03
S20. Trade	0.32	0.32	0.13	0.13	0.08	0.02
S21. Finance. Insurance and Real Estate	0.16	0.34	0.10	0.19	0.17	0.04
S22. Gov't Royalties and Owner Occ. Dwell.	0.00	0.00	0.00	0.00	0.00	0.00
S23. Business Services	0.12	0.22	0.09	0.20	0.26	0.11
S24. Personal and Other Services	0.40	0.30	0.09	0.11	0.08	0.03
TOTAL	0.33	0.26	0.14	0.13	0.10	0.03

Table 18B Import Education/Skill Shares: 1986 – 24 Industries (Import Employment Weights)

24-Industry Aggregation	No Secondary School	Secondary School Only	Trade Certificate or Diploma	Post-Sec. Non-Univ. Degree	University up to Bachelor's Degree	All Post-Graduate Degrees
S1. Agriculture, Forestry, Fishing and Trapping	0.58	0.20	0.08	0.07	0.05	0.01
S2. Mining excluding Oil and Gas	0.41	0.20	0.22	0.09	0.06	0.01
S3. Crude Petroleum and Natural Gas	0.16	0.23	0.14	0.17	0.24	0.06
S4. Food. Beverages and Tobacco	0.49	0.24	0.10	0.08	0.07	0.01
S5. Rubber and Plastic Products	0.44	0.28	0.13	0.09	0.06	0.01
S6. Leather. Textile and Clothing Products	0.57	0.24	0.08	0.06	0.04	0.01
S7. Wood and Furniture Products	0.51	0.24	0.14	0.07	0.03	0.01
S8. Paper and Allied Products and Printing	0.33	0.31	0.15	0.12	0.08	0.02
S9. Primary Metals and Metal Fabricating	0.38	0.25	0.20	0.11	0.05	0.01
S10. Machinery	0.30	0.25	0.22	0.15	0.07	0.02
S11. Motor Vehicles and Parts	0.45	0.26	0.14	0.09	0.05	0.01
S12. Other Transportation Equipment	0.26	0.25	0.21	0.16	0.09	0.03
S13. Electrical and Electronic Products	0.28	0.26	0.11	0.18	0.13	0.04
S14. Refined Petrol.. Chemicals and Non-met.	0.31	0.27	0.13	0.13	0.13	0.03
S15. Other Manufactured Products	0.37	0.28	0.12	0.13	0.08	0.02
S16. Construction	0.41	0.23	0.24	0.08	0.04	0.01
S17. Transportation and Pipelines	0.46	0.26	0.14	0.09	0.05	0.01
S18. Storage	0.46	0.31	0.11	0.08	0.04	0.01
S19. Utilities	0.23	0.33	0.14	0.16	0.10	0.03
S20. Trade	0.35	0.33	0.13	0.11	0.07	0.01
S21. Finance. Insurance and Real Estate	0.19	0.37	0.10	0.16	0.14	0.03
S22. Gov't Royalties and Owner Occ. Dwell.	0.00	0.00	0.00	0.00	0.00	0.00
S23. Business Services	0.13	0.24	0.08	0.20	0.25	0.10
S24. Personal and Other Services	0.36	0.28	0.10	0.12	0.10	0.04
TOTAL	0.36	0.27	0.13	0.12	0.09	0.03

	No Secondary School	Secondary School Only	Trade Certificate or Diploma	Post-Sec. Non-Univ. Degree	University up to Bachelor's Degree	All Post-Graduate Degrees
Table 19A Education/Skill Shares of Imports, 1961–97						
1961	0.396	0.255	0.142	0.111	0.076	0.019
1962	0.394	0.255	0.143	0.112	0.077	0.019
1963	0.390	0.256	0.145	0.113	0.078	0.019
1964	0.390	0.256	0.145	0.113	0.077	0.019
1965	0.387	0.257	0.146	0.113	0.077	0.019
1966	0.381	0.258	0.146	0.115	0.079	0.021
1967	0.379	0.259	0.144	0.116	0.081	0.021
1968	0.378	0.260	0.142	0.116	0.082	0.021
1969	0.377	0.261	0.141	0.117	0.083	0.022
1970	0.376	0.261	0.141	0.117	0.083	0.022
1971	0.376	0.262	0.140	0.117	0.083	0.022
1972	0.378	0.262	0.139	0.116	0.083	0.022
1973	0.377	0.263	0.138	0.117	0.083	0.022
1974	0.375	0.263	0.139	0.117	0.084	0.022
1975	0.374	0.263	0.140	0.117	0.084	0.022
1976	0.375	0.263	0.137	0.117	0.085	0.023
1977	0.371	0.264	0.137	0.118	0.086	0.023
1978	0.367	0.265	0.137	0.119	0.088	0.024
1979	0.364	0.264	0.138	0.120	0.089	0.024
1980	0.359	0.264	0.138	0.122	0.091	0.025
1981	0.357	0.265	0.137	0.123	0.093	0.026
1982	0.355	0.265	0.135	0.124	0.094	0.026
1983	0.358	0.266	0.134	0.123	0.093	0.026
1984	0.359	0.266	0.132	0.123	0.093	0.026
1985	0.358	0.266	0.133	0.123	0.094	0.026
1986	0.358	0.266	0.132	0.123	0.094	0.026
1987	0.353	0.264	0.134	0.126	0.096	0.027
1988	0.344	0.262	0.137	0.130	0.098	0.029
1989	0.337	0.261	0.138	0.133	0.101	0.030
1990	0.342	0.265	0.134	0.131	0.099	0.030
1991	0.335	0.263	0.136	0.134	0.101	0.031
1992	0.336	0.263	0.135	0.134	0.101	0.031
1993	0.336	0.263	0.134	0.134	0.101	0.031
1994	0.331	0.263	0.136	0.135	0.103	0.032
1995	0.330	0.263	0.136	0.136	0.103	0.032
1996	0.328	0.263	0.135	0.136	0.104	0.032
1997	0.329	0.263	0.136	0.137	0.104	0.032

	No Secondary School	Secondary School Only	Trade Certificate or Diploma	Post-Sec. Non-Univ. Degree	University up to Bachelor's Degree	All Post-Graduate Degrees
Table 19B Ratio: Education/Skill Shares of Imports/ Total Business-Sector Employment, 1961–97						
1961	0.965	0.948	1.044	1.097	1.123	1.284
1962	0.965	0.948	1.050	1.094	1.115	1.271
1963	0.959	0.947	1.061	1.100	1.120	1.283
1964	0.965	0.947	1.057	1.092	1.107	1.257
1965	0.963	0.948	1.060	1.092	1.104	1.248
1966	0.957	0.949	1.051	1.100	1.126	1.294
1967	0.956	0.949	1.043	1.105	1.133	1.310
1968	0.958	0.950	1.034	1.100	1.134	1.319
1969	0.959	0.950	1.028	1.101	1.139	1.323
1970	0.964	0.949	1.025	1.097	1.128	1.295
1971	0.966	0.951	1.017	1.095	1.128	1.293
1972	0.978	0.947	1.015	1.081	1.108	1.257
1973	0.978	0.949	1.012	1.082	1.105	1.249
1974	0.979	0.945	1.016	1.077	1.106	1.250
1975	0.980	0.943	1.030	1.072	1.094	1.233
1976	0.985	0.944	1.008	1.072	1.104	1.247
1977	0.982	0.946	1.010	1.074	1.105	1.243
1978	0.972	0.947	1.020	1.083	1.114	1.257
1979	0.966	0.945	1.027	1.089	1.123	1.272
1980	0.957	0.944	1.030	1.098	1.140	1.293
1981	0.955	0.944	1.023	1.104	1.150	1.302
1982	0.958	0.943	1.021	1.100	1.141	1.277
1983	0.967	0.945	1.020	1.091	1.118	1.240
1984	0.972	0.944	1.009	1.087	1.118	1.243
1985	0.973	0.945	1.012	1.085	1.114	1.234
1986	0.971	0.944	1.009	1.085	1.122	1.250
1987	0.977	0.941	1.009	1.076	1.112	1.218
1988	0.973	0.938	1.019	1.080	1.110	1.201
1989	0.974	0.937	1.011	1.076	1.116	1.191
1990	1.012	0.956	0.970	1.033	1.060	1.088
1991	1.016	0.954	0.973	1.028	1.057	1.074
1992	1.020	0.953	0.970	1.023	1.056	1.070
1993	1.016	0.953	0.975	1.027	1.058	1.067
1994	1.005	0.953	0.980	1.035	1.071	1.085
1995	1.004	0.955	0.984	1.037	1.066	1.072
1996	1.000	0.958	0.984	1.038	1.068	1.071
1997	1.007	0.955	0.989	1.036	1.054	1.048

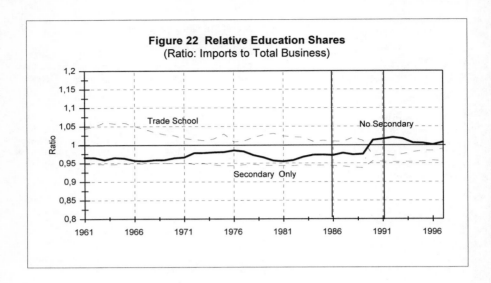

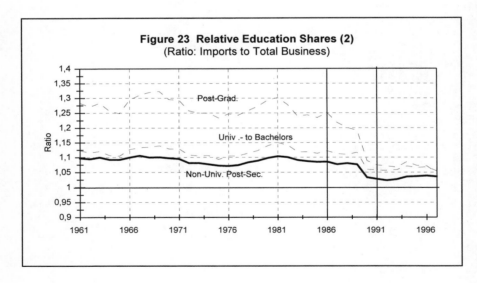

6. CONCLUSIONS

The value of a detailed study such as ours partly resides in the detailed calculation results presented, in that they are somewhat more up to date and comprehensive than those of similar past studies. With luck, they may permit other researchers in the field and readers to answer their own specific questions in various areas, and perhaps to suggest new questions.

Nonetheless, we also attempt to draw some broad conclusions of our own. Some have already been touched upon in the discussions above.

1) While exports and imports have grown strongly as a proportion of the Canadian economy since 1961 — especially in the 1990s — the growth in the share of employment attributable to exports (or "displaced" by imports) has been *much less rapid*. The major reason is import penetration: Exports today have a much higher import content in intermediate inputs that in the past. As for imports, if they were to be produced in Canada, today's technology would have them produced with much more imported intermediate inputs than in the 1960s.

2) When our detailed sectoral results are aggregated, Canadian exports are always above the average for total business output in labour productivity — especially when the effect of Agriculture in the 1960s is netted out. However, this relatively high labour productivity of exports has shown almost *no tendency to increase* over time. Along with higher labour productivity comes higher returns to labour in exports — but again, this relative performance in exports shows almost no trend over time. However, since the share of employment attributable to exports has been steadily growing, it could be concluded that exports are helping to lift both the *overall level* of Canadian labour productivity and returns to labour.

3) The sources of change in the employment mix of Canadian exports are primarily the final export mix itself and the degree of import penetration for intermediate inputs. Generally less important are changes among sectors in relative labour productivity or "technical change" as embodied in changes in input-output coefficients — although for particular industries they may still be crucial (e.g., Rail transport). The same observation essentially applies to changes in the employment mix of Canadian imports.

4) Changes in export employment shares have occurred across a wider range of industries than might be imagined. Of the ten industry groups that increased their share of export employment by over one percent point from 1961 to 1997, four are service industries (Personal and other services, Business services, Trade, and Finance), but the other six are various manufacturing categories, some of which might have been expected given the Auto Pact and changing technology — like Motor vehicles, Electrical and electronic products, and Rubber and plastic products — and some that are surprising — like Leather, textile and clothing products. Of the four industries with declines in export employment shares of over one percentage point, the two largest declines are in primary production (Mining excluding oil and gas, and Agriculture, forestry and fishing), one is in raw material processing and manufacturing (Paper and allied products and printing) and the fourth is Transportation. The timing of changes is also sometimes surprising: For example, the Motor vehicle industry gained almost all of its increase in export employment share from 1961 to 1971 and share gains in Trade, Finance, and Business services were as large in the 1960s as in other periods. In short, the individual industrial detailed results are important.

5)   Combining the input-output results with data on education mix by industry leads to the
     conclusion that since 1961 the mix of Canadian export employment (both direct and indirect) has
     continually evolved to emphasize industries with more highly-educated workers. However, this
     also turns out to be true of business-sector employment as a whole. If exports are compared to
     the total business sector in relative uses of different education profiles, the conclusion is that
     employment from exports is "bi-polar" in distribution. Exports exceed the economy-wide average
     in employing workers with low education, and also in employing workers with relatively
     advanced education. The relative ratios have changed only a little over the last three decades.

6)   The labour productivity of employment "displaced" by imports (if it were to be produced with
     Canadian technology) is invariably lower than that of exports — although it is still above the
     business-sector average for most years. The ratio has fallen to about the economy-wide average
     in recent years. Thus, there is evidence that imports, on the whole, are not replacing
     exceptionally low-productivity employment (which is probably concentrated in non-tradable
     services in any event). However, imports are displacing "relatively" more jobs than exports are
     adding. If macro policies can keep the economy near full employment, and the pace of change is
     not too fast, this means that Canada is replacing low-productivity employment with high-
     productivity employment through expanded international trade, and is thereby better off.

7)   Comparing changes in employment shares of exports and imports, it is remarkable that the
     largest increases and decreases occur, in many cases, in the *same* sectors. Personal and Business
     services, and Trade have among the largest increases in employment shares for both exports and
     imports, and Mining, Agriculture and Forestry have among the largest decreases in employment
     shares for both exports and imports. *Both* Canadian exports and Canadian imports have become
     more intensive in service employment and less intensive in raw materials production
     employment.

8)   The education mix calculations show that, at least for Canadian technology and education shares
     by sector, Canadian imports have been above the business-sector average in overall education
     content. In recent years, however, this discrepancy has been narrowing, indicating some
     increased competition from imports in sectors using lower-skill workers. Nonetheless, Canadian
     imports remain above the business sector average in education content. This result may seem at
     odds with the previous point about labour productivity and labour returns. However, it should be
     noted that we found productivity and returns to labour in imports to be *above* the business-sector
     average, although they were also *lower* than for exports. Finding that the education mix is above
     the business-sector average is not inconsistent with this. This anomaly, perhaps, is that export
     productivity and returns are so high when at least part of the education mix is low. The anomaly
     can, however, be better understood if it is recalled that education, as broadly measured, is not the
     sole determinant of either productivity or returns to labour. High capital or natural resource
     endowments can make even relatively uneducated labour highly productive and highly rewarded,
     and that seems to be the case for such Canadian exports sectors as Motor vehicles and Metal
     products.

NOTES

1   For greater detail, see Appendix 1.

2   Note also that all references to imports should be taken to be mean imports net of any re-exports.

3   Courakis, Maskus and Webster (1997) point out that trying to "assign blame" between globalization (increased trade) and technical change in examining employment losses (or changes) may be something of a false dichotomy and is at variance with trade theory, since both effects will be driven by underlying changes in technology and tastes. The point may be valid in terms of assessing causality or formulating policy, but the intention in our study is simply to find out first what the data say in terms of the relative contributions of various factors.

4   The 1986 and 1991 data sets are not on a completely comparable basis and some judgement was required to reconcile the two.

5   An alternative method of examining impacts of imports and technology on employment and wages without using I/O techniques is found in Lee (1996).

6   We are grateful to an anonymous referee for emphasizing this point and providing this particular example.

7   Recall that for 1993–97, the 1992 I/O coefficients are used, while exports, employment shares and import coefficients have been estimated for the actual year.

8   Note that here and at all other times in this report employment is measured in terms of number of persons employed, and not hours worked. Employment can include part-time employment, as is the practice, for example, in the Labour Force Survey. Conclusions regarding employment shares and labour productivity can be skewed sometimes by failing to consider changes in hours worked per employee.

9   Details of the aggregation and of the SIC codes of the 161 most-disaggregated industries are given in Appendix 3.

10   Unfortunately, we cannot be sure that higher educational attainment actually reflects improved skills or abilities of the workforce. It may, in the succinct phrase offered by an anonymous referee, simply represent "creeping credentialism": a job may be no more demanding of skill than in the past, but now requires a university degree (perhaps since many graduates are now available) when formerly a high school diploma was considered adequate.

11   In light of the problem of "creeping credentialism" (see footnote above), the use of relatively fixed education requirements by industry may actually offer some advantages in identifying how the changing industrial mix of exports has affected skill demands over time.

12   As for the export analysis, of course, the 1992 I/O coefficients are used for 1993–97, while import levels, employment shares and import coefficients have been estimated for the actual year.

BIBLIOGRAPHY

Betts, Julian R. (1997), "The Skill Bias of Technological Change in Canadian Manufacturing Industries", *Review of Economics and Statistics*, February, LXXIX:1, 146-150.

_____ (1989), "Two Exact, Non-Arbitrary and General Methods of Decomposing Temporal Change", *Economics Letters*, 30 , 151-156.

Betts, Julian R. and Thomas McCurdy (1993), "Sources of Employment Growth by Occupation and Industry in Canada", *Relations Industrielles*, 48:2, 285-304.

Courakis, Anthony, Keith E. Maskus and Allan Webster (1997), "Occupational Employment and Wage Changes in the UK: Trade and Technology Effects", in *International Trade and Labour Markets*, Jitendralal Borkakoti and Chris Milner (eds.), New York: St. Martin's Press.

Feenstra, Robert C. and Gordon H. Hanson (1996), "Globalization, Outsourcing and Wage Inequality", *American Economic Review - Papers and Proceedings*, May, 86:2, 240-245.

Freeman, Richard B. (1995), "Are Your Wages Set in Beijing?", *Journal of Economic Perspectives*, 9:3 (Summer), 15-32.

Gaston, Noel and Daniel Trefler (1997), "The Labour-Market Consequences of the Canada-U.S. Free Trade Agreement", *Canadian Journal of Economics*, February, XXX:1, 18-41.

Gera, Surendra and Kurt Mang (1998), "The Knowledge-Based Economy: Shifts in Industrial Output", *Canadian Public Policy/Analyse de Politiques*, June, XXIV:2, 149-184.

_____ (1997), *The Knowledge-Based Economy: Shifts in Industrial Output*, Industry Canada, Working Paper Number 15, January.

_____ , and Philippe Massé (1996), *Employment Performance in the Knowledge-Based Economy*, Industry Canada, Working Paper Number 14, December.

Gregory, Mary and Christine Greenhalgh(1997), "International Trade, Deindustrialization and Labour Demand: An Input-Output Study for the UK (1979–90)" in *International Trade and Labour Markets*, Jitendralal Borkakoti and Chris Milner (eds.), New York: St. Martin's Press.

Lawrence, Robert Z. (1996) *Single World, Divided Nations*, Washington: Brookings Institution Press and Paris: OECD Development Centre.

Lee, Frank (1996) *Implications of Technology and Imports on Employment and Wages in Canada*, Industry Canada, Working Paper Number 12, July.

Lee, Frank and H. Has. (1996), "A Quantitative Assessment of High-Knowledge Industries versus Low-Knowledge Industries", in *The Implications of Knowledge-Based Growth for Micro-Economic Policies,* P. Howitt (ed.), The Industry Canada Research Series, Calgary: University of Calgary Press.

Levy, Frank and Richard J. Murnane (1992), "U.S. Earnings Levels and Earnings Inequality: A Review of Recent Trends and Proposed Explanations", *Journal of Economic Literature*, XXX:3, September.

Organization for Economic Cooperation and Development (1992), *Structural Change and Industrial Performance: A Seven-Country Growth Decomposition Study*, Paris: OECD.

Richardson, J. David (1995), "Income Inequality and Trade: How to Think, What to Conclude", *Journal of Economic Perspectives*, 9:3 (Summer), 33-55.

Sachs, Jeffrey D. and Howard J. Shatz (1996), "U.S. Trade with Developing Countries and Wage Inequality", *American Economic Review - Papers and Proceedings*, May, 86:2, 234-239.

Thygesen, Niels, Yutaka Kosai and Robert Z. Lawrence (1996), *Globalization and Trilateral Labor Markets*, A Report to the Trilateral Commission: 49, New York: The Trilateral Commission.

Tyson, Laura D'Andrea and John Zysman (1988), "Trade and Employment: An Overview of the Issues and Evidence", in *The Dynamics of Trade and Employment*, Laura D'Andrea Tyson, William T. Dickens and John Zysman (eds.), Cambridge: Ballinger.

Wood, Adrian (1995), "How Trade Hurt Unskilled Workers, *Journal of Economic Perspectives*, 9:3 Summer, 57–80.

APPENDIX 1
A MORE DETAILED DESCRIPTION OF THE CALCULATIONS

This appendix describes the calculations behind the paper's results in somewhat greater detail and in more algebraic form. Very roughly, the notation follows that of Gera and Mang (1997, pp 69–70).

To begin, consider the calculations for only one year (say, 1992) and recall that there are 161 industries in the "L" aggregation employed.

The basic I/O relationship for this or any other year is as follows:

$$g = Bg + fo + fx + fm \tag{1}$$

where
- g: the 1x161 vector of total gross output for each industry
- B: matrix of direct input coefficients b_{ij} — the direct input requirements from industry i to produce one unit of output for industry j
- fo: 1x161 vector of all final demands other than exports and imports less re-exports
- fx: 1x161 vector of all exports
- fm: 1x161 vector of all imports less re-exports (defined as negative values)

Note that Bg constitutes all intermediate demands upon the output of any industrial sector, while the sum of $fo + fx + fm$ constitutes all net final demand on the output of any sector. These two groups must identically equal the total output of a sector (g) since inventory changes, whether intended or unintended, are a part of fo.

To determine the impact on g of any change in one of the f final demand components, some behavioural judgements must be made with respect to "leakages" of demand out of the backward chain of production. In the standard Statistics Canada I/O model, and in the work of Gera and Mang (1997), three leakages are assumed: through imports, through provision of demand from inventories, and through provision of demand from "government production", i.e. the provision of government services and infrastructure. We take the simpler alternative of permitting only leakages from consumption. In our judgement, the provision of government services are largely fixed in any one year and would vary little even with relatively large changes in demand. The term is, in any event, very small. How much even major changes in demand would be met from inventories is also, in our view, an open question, but more to the point is the fact that inventory "ratios", from which the leakage would have to be calculated, can vary drastically for some sectors from year to year, yielding, in our experience, wild and unreasonable swings in results and impacts. We therefore restrict ourselves to leakages from imports, where average import leakage in any sector in a given year is defined as the ratio of imports over domestic production *less exports* for that sector in the given year. Exports are not included in calculating the average import leakage, since re-exports have already been netted out, and exports will only be supplied from domestic production.

Thus we assume an equation for imports as follows:

$$fm = \quad M \cdot (Bg + fo) = M \cdot (g - fx) \tag{2}$$

where M is a matrix with zeros off the diagonals and diagonal elements for row and column i defined as:

$$M_{ii} = fm_i / (g_i - fx_i) \tag{3}$$

Therefore, equation (1) may be re-written as

$$g = Bg + fo + fx + M(g\text{-}fx) \tag{3}$$

Solving for *g* we proceed as follows:

$$g - Bg - Mg = fo + fx - Mfx$$

$$(I - B - M) g = fo + (I - M) fx$$

$$g = (I - B - M)^{-1} \cdot (fo + (I - M) fx). \tag{4}$$

Solving for *changes* in *fx* we get:

$$\Delta g = (I - B - M)^{-1} \cdot (I - M) \cdot \Delta fx \tag{5}$$

Equation 5 is therefore the equation used to obtain the change in output by sector (the change in *g*) for a given change in *fx*. In our case, the amount we enter for the change in *fx* is the actual level of *fx* in the year being examined.

From the I/O data in each year, supplementary ratios for domestic product (or value added) per unit of total output, employment per unit of total output and returns to labour per unit of total output can all be calculated. These ratios are then applied to the Δg as calculated above in order to obtain impacts of exports in that year on domestic product, employment and returns to labour for each industry:

$$rdp_i = dp_i / g_i \text{, where } rdp \text{ and } dp \text{ are ratios and levels of domestic product}$$

$$re_i = e_i / g_i \text{, where } re \text{ and } e \text{ are ratios and levels of employment in persons}$$

$$rw_i = w_i / g_i \text{, where } rw \text{ and } w \text{ are ratios and levels of returns to labour}$$

Then:

$$\Delta dp = rdp \cdot \Delta g$$

$$\Delta e = re \cdot \Delta g$$

$$\Delta w = rw \cdot \Delta g$$

Decomposition:

For any two years, say 1961 and 1992, the employment attributable to the exports of that year can be calculated as:

$$\Delta e_{92} = re_{92} \cdot (I - B_{92} - M_{92})^{-1} \cdot (I - M_{92}) \cdot fx_{92} \text{, and} \tag{6}$$

$$\Delta e_{61} = re_{61} \cdot (I - B_{61} - M_{61})^{-1} \cdot (I - M_{61}) \cdot fx_{61} \tag{7}$$

To determine the independent contributions, the Δe_{92} calculation is repeated successively using re_{61}, B_{61}, M_{61}, and fx_{61} instead. Since it is ratios of employees in different industries to total employment that is reported, we use shares of industries in fx_{61}, rather than levels, but the alternative calculation gives the same result.

This decomposition is less elaborate than the growth decomposition used by Gera and Mang (1997, pp. 71–74); but it serves the primary purpose of displaying the major contributors to changes in employment share between two years. The decomposition is exhaustive in the sense that if all four elements for 1961 (fx_{61}, re_{61}, etc.) were to be entered together in equation (6) then obviously the result would be equation (7), and all the difference between the two years would be explained. However, because of interaction between the terms, the sum of the individual items will not equal the total change, and thus a residual/interaction term is reported in the decomposition tables. As far as we can see, any attempt to "distribute" the interaction term will be somewhat arbitrary. If the interaction term were to be distributed proportionally, there would of course be no change in the relative weights of the contributing items. (For an alternative decomposition approach that removes the residual term, see Betts, 1989.

APPENDIX 2
TESTING FOR SENSITIVITY IN THE
AGGREGATE CALCULATIONS FOR EXPORTS

This appendix presents detailed results for two alternative sets of export calculations. The first set uses real or constant dollar, rather than nominal, I/O tables and data, and the second excludes Agriculture from the calculations.

Use of Constant Dollar Data

As noted in Section 2 above, we have done most of the calculations in this paper using nominal data, either from the I/O system or from other sources. Use of nominal data permits us to extend some of the calculations into 1993–97 and avoids potential re-basing difficulties between the different series of real I/O tables. Nonetheless, it has been possible to perform some of the calculations described above using constant dollar (or real) data instead and to test whether this alternative leads to major differences in results and implications.

Table A.1 reports aggregate results identical in concept to those of Table 2 in Section 4, except that our chained series of real I/O tables has been used. Data cannot be extended past 1992 and the calculation of returns to labour is not possible. The columns of Tables 2 and A.1 can be compared directly to determine differences from using real and nominal concepts; several of these comparisons are shown in Figures A.1-A.3.

Figure A.1 compares employment in exports, as a percentage of the total business sector, under the two calculations. Both series show a pattern of gradual increase after 1961, with somewhat stronger increases for the real calculations in the 1960s. In each there is a decline in export's employment share after 1984, but the drop is much more abrupt in the real calculations — and somewhat difficult to understand. After 1984, results from the two series are nearly identical. Both series therefore show that the share of Canadian employment due to exports has risen only gradually from 1961 through 1992. The real calculations show that the share is more pronounced in movement, and with a puzzling drop after 1984 that had not be recouped even by 1992.

Figure A.2 compares domestic product due to exports as a share of total business product, using both the nominal and real series. The pattern is somewhat the same as for employment, showing a gradual upward trend, with the real calculations being more volatile. Note that from the late 1980s, the real data suggest a slightly stronger increase in GDP share of exports than do the nominal data.

Finally, the two different calculations for labour productivity in exports are compared in Figure A.3. Both calculations suggest that there has been no strong trend in this term: it has always been greater than the economy-wide average (it is always above 1.0), but there has been no pronounced trend. The real calculations suggest a significant decline in relative productivity in the mid-1970s, most of which has been gradually recouped. Unlike the nominal data, the real data show little relative decline after the late 1980s, suggesting that the decline in the nominal series is due to a relative valuation of exports rather than to a decline in relative physical productivity.

Excluding Agricultural Exports

Because Agriculture is a major contributor to exports, and because the sector underwent major structural change, especially in the 1960s, we have calculated the aggregate, nominal measures of Table 2 in Section 4 *excluding* agricultural exports for comparison. (Note that it is exports of agricultural products we have excluded from the calculation; there may be some indirect impact through the Agricultural sector if it needs to produce indirect inputs for other types of exports). This calculation also shows an example of how other exclusions could be done in the calculations, although such variations (which could be quite voluminous) have not been included in the present paper.

Table A.2 summarizes the aggregate annual calculations excluding agricultural exports; results here should be compared with the equivalent aggregate nominal calculations including exports as shown in Table 2 of Section 4. Figures A.4-A.6 compare the two calculations for three key indicators.

Figure A.4 shows employment attributable to exports as a ratio to total business-sector employment both in total (from Table 2) and with agricultural exports excluded. As can be seen, agricultural exports did indeed matter more in the 1960s, although their impact, on a dollar basis, was also substantial in the 1980s. Inclusion or exclusion of agricultural exports does not affect any judgements with respect to trends.

Figure A.5 plots labour productivity in exports both with and without agricultural exports. As can be seen, excluding agricultural exports flattens the trend all the more and clearly makes export labour productivity rank ahead of average labour productivity in all decades.

Finally, Figure A.6 plots returns to labour (including unincorporated business income) in exports relative to the total business sector. If agricultural exports are excluded, then export-related employment has enjoyed returns above the business-sector average in all decades. However, the basic story of a rising trend through the mid-1980s and a slight fall-off thereafter is unchanged.

Table A.1 Aggregate Comparisons from I/O Calculations – Exports
REAL – 1961–92

	(1) Exports as a % of Business Sector Domestic Product	(2) Domestic Product in Exports as a % of Business Domestic Product	(3) Imports from Exports as a % of Domestic Product from Exports	(4) Employment in Exports as a % of Total Business Employment	(5) Labour Productivity in Exports Relative to Business Sector	(6) Direct Employment in Exports as a % of Total Empl.	(7) Ratio: Direct to Total Employment in Exports
1961	25.39	20.66	18.48	17.62	1.17	9.59	0.54
1962	25.38	20.79	17.64	16.90	1.23	8.92	0.53
1963	25.96	21.25	17.90	17.67	1.20	9.34	0.53
1964	27.51	22.52	17.76	18.68	1.21	9.77	0.52
1965	26.71	21.66	18.82	18.10	1.20	9.53	0.53
1966	28.81	22.50	23.48	19.08	1.18	10.08	0.53
1967	31.51	23.54	28.95	19.82	1.19	10.40	0.52
1968	35.73	26.08	32.29	21.39	1.22	11.13	0.52
1969	37.77	26.72	36.64	21.45	1.25	11.25	0.52
1970	40.57	28.39	38.33	23.30	1.22	12.66	0.54
1971	40.50	28.45	38.13	22.98	1.24	12.34	0.54
1972	41.96	29.45	38.33	22.87	1.29	12.53	0.55
1973	43.23	30.40	38.07	22.63	1.34	12.32	0.54
1974	40.08	28.02	38.74	21.41	1.31	11.45	0.53
1975	37.19	25.38	41.85	20.41	1.24	10.96	0.54
1976	37.93	25.27	45.56	21.28	1.19	11.52	0.54
1977	39.25	25.51	49.28	22.40	1.14	11.97	0.53
1978	41.78	25.21	60.93	22.80	1.11	12.85	0.56
1979	40.32	26.65	46.35	23.65	1.13	12.87	0.54
1980	39.59	25.95	47.15	24.05	1.08	12.92	0.54
1981	39.81	26.33	46.05	24.41	1.08	13.08	0.54
1982	40.99	26.21	51.02	24.66	1.06	13.15	0.53
1983	43.29	27.27	53.58	24.90	1.10	13.43	0.54
1984	49.22	30.46	56.48	26.75	1.14	14.51	0.54
1985	36.17	25.48	36.92	21.83	1.17	11.05	0.51
1986	34.14	23.96	37.55	20.85	1.15	10.21	0.49
1987	33.85	24.16	35.43	20.46	1.18	10.00	0.49
1988	34.79	24.28	38.56	20.20	1.20	9.71	0.48
1989	34.35	23.74	40.09	19.70	1.20	9.44	0.48
1990	37.02	25.29	41.91	21.85	1.16	11.09	0.51
1991	38.44	26.19	42.21	22.62	1.16	11.61	0.51
1992	41.37	27.64	45.01	23.63	1.17	12.27	0.52

Table A.2 Aggregate Comparisons from I/O Calculations – Exports – 1961–97

Excluding the Agriculture Industry

	(1) Exports as a % of Business Sector Domestic Product	(2) Domestic Product in Exports as a % of Business Sector Domestic Product	(3) Imports from Exports as a % of Domestic Product from Exports	(4) Employment in Exports as a % of Total Business Employment	(5) Labour Productivity in Exports Relative to Business Sector	(6) Direct Employment in Exports as a % of Total Employment	(7) Ratio: Direct to Total Employment in Exports	(8) Ratio: Returns to Labour in Exports vs. Business Sector
1961	19.34	17.01	13.15	14.61	1.16	6.68	0.46	1.01
1962	19.77	17.09	13.28	14.53	1.18	6.65	0.46	1.02
1963	20.12	17.43	13.67	14.95	1.17	6.82	0.46	1.02
1964	21.12	18.22	14.22	15.34	1.19	6.98	0.45	1.02
1965	20.56	17.56	14.45	14.76	1.19	6.75	0.46	1.03
1966	21.77	18.17	17.58	15.62	1.16	7.17	0.46	1.04
1967	23.32	18.96	19.82	16.49	1.15	7.63	0.46	1.04
1968	26.13	20.46	23.73	17.69	1.16	8.22	0.46	1.05
1969	26.69	20.60	24.68	17.58	1.17	8.30	0.47	1.06
1970	28.02	21.60	25.19	18.84	1.15	8.89	0.47	1.07
1971	26.88	20.66	26.07	18.32	1.13	8.54	0.47	1.06
1972	27.22	20.95	25.87	18.07	1.16	8.57	0.47	1.08
1973	28.72	22.26	25.08	18.23	1.22	8.66	0.47	1.08
1974	28.83	22.37	27.46	17.62	1.27	8.28	0.47	1.10
1975	26.51	20.38	29.53	16.66	1.22	7.80	0.47	1.10
1976	27.29	20.81	28.85	17.34	1.20	8.16	0.47	1.11
1977	29.10	21.84	30.69	18.15	1.20	8.46	0.47	1.12
1978	31.75	23.45	32.43	19.25	1.22	9.16	0.48	1.13
1979	33.27	25.22	29.49	19.65	1.28	9.46	0.48	1.14
1980	33.77	25.68	30.57	20.06	1.28	9.43	0.47	1.13
1981	32.87	24.18	32.65	19.75	1.22	9.30	0.47	1.14
1982	31.58	23.21	32.42	19.84	1.17	9.08	0.46	1.14
1983	31.12	23.40	31.16	19.55	1.20	8.93	0.46	1.13
1984	34.65	25.55	33.56	20.67	1.24	9.61	0.46	1.13
1985	34.78	25.15	35.68	20.10	1.25	9.33	0.46	1.15
1986	34.09	23.78	38.73	20.00	1.19	9.44	0.47	1.14
1987	32.56	23.50	34.44	19.48	1.21	9.28	0.48	1.13
1988	32.47	23.34	34.71	19.18	1.22	8.94	0.47	1.12

Table A.2 (cont'd)

Excluding the Agriculture Industry

	(1) Exports as a % of Business Sector Domestic Product	(2) Domestic Product in Exports as a % of Business Domestic Product	(3) Imports from Exports as a % of Domestic Product from Exports	(4) Employment in Exports as a % of Total Business Employment	(5) Labour Productivity in Exports Relative to Business Sector	(6) Direct Employment in Exports as a % of Total Employment	(7) Ratio: Direct to Total Employment in Exports	(8) Ratio: Returns to Labour in Exports vs. Business Sector
1989	31.63	22.60	35.20	19.04	1.19	8.87	0.47	1.12
1990	32.77	23.19	36.58	20.78	1.12	10.31	0.50	1.08
1991	31.93	22.59	37.47	21.12	1.07	10.52	0.50	1.09
1992	34.74	23.95	41.14	22.17	1.08	11.16	0.50	1.09
1993	38.36	25.64	44.79	23.22	1.10	12.88	0.55	n.a.
1994	42.47	28.06	46.61	25.24	1.11	15.18	0.60	n.a.
1995	45.91	30.35	46.48	26.86	1.13	17.11	0.64	n.a.
1996	47.01	31.04	46.84	28.04	1.11	18.13	0.65	n.a.
1997	47.74	31.08	49.04	28.03	1.11	18.71	0.67	n.a.

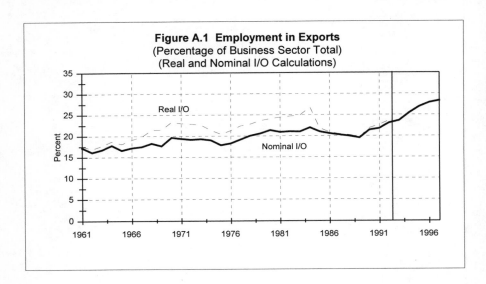

Figure A.1 Employment in Exports
(Percentage of Business Sector Total)
(Real and Nominal I/O Calculations)

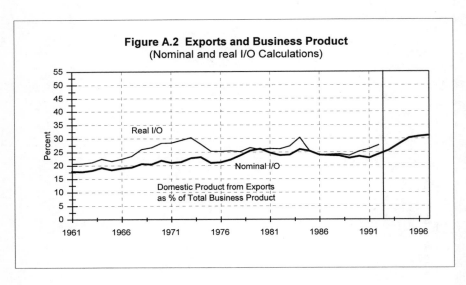

Figure A.2 Exports and Business Product
(Nominal and real I/O Calculations)

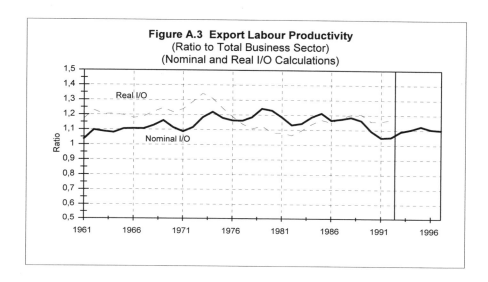

Figure A.3 Export Labour Productivity
(Ratio to Total Business Sector)
(Nominal and Real I/O Calculations)

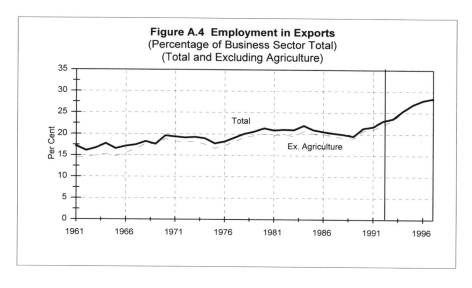

Figure A.4 Employment in Exports
(Percentage of Business Sector Total)
(Total and Excluding Agriculture)

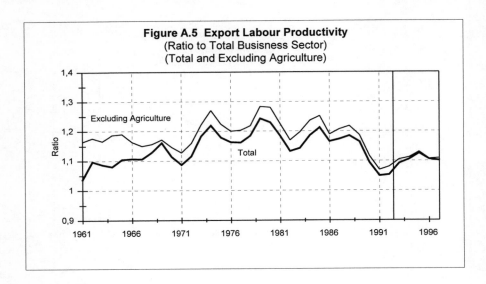

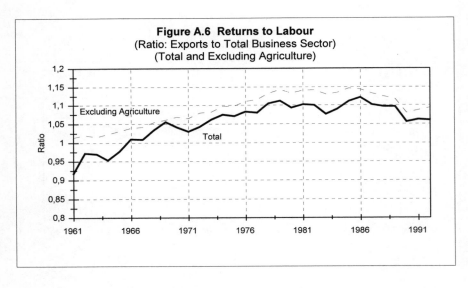

APPENDIX 3
24-INDUSTRY AGGREGATION – AGGREGATION PARAMETERS

24-Industry Aggregation	Input/Output 161-Industry 'L' Components	COPS 112-Industry Components	SIC Group
S1. Agriculture, Forestry, Fishing and Trapping	1-3	1-3	01-05
S2. Mining excluding Oil and Gas	4-10, 12-13	4-6, 8–9	06, 08, 09
S3. Crude Petroleum and Natural Gas	11	7	7
S4. Food, Beverages and Tobacco	14-29	36454	36444
S5. Rubber and Plastic Products	30, 31	23, 24	15, 16
S6. Leather, Textile and Clothing Products	32-42	25-28	17-19, 24
S7. Wood and Furniture Products	43-50	29-34	25, 26
S8. Paper and Allied Products and Printing	51-56	35-38	27, 28
S9. Primary Metals and Metal Fabricating	57-71	39-53	29, 30
S10. Machinery	72-74	54-56	31
S11. Motor Vehicles and Parts	76-78	58-60	323-325
S12. Other Transportation Equipment	75, 79-81	57, 61-63	321, 326-329
S13. Electrical and Electronic Products	82-89	64-69	33
S14. Refined Petrol., Chemicals and Non-met.	90-103	70-83	· 35-37
S15. Other Manufactured Products	104-108	84-87	39
S16. Construction	109-117	88	40-44
S17. Transportation and Pipelines	118-127	89-95	45, 46
S18. Storage	128	96	47
S19. Utilities	129-134	97-102	48, 49
S20. Trade	135, 136	103, 104	50-69
S21. Finance, Insurance and Real Estate	137-139	105	70-74
S22. Gov't Royalties and Owner Occ. Dwell.	140, 141	none	75, 76
S23. Business Services	142-144	106	77
S24. Personal and Other Services	145-154	107-112	85-99

APPENDIX 4

THE CHANGING INDUSTRIAL MIX OF EXPORTS
161-INDUSTRY AGGREGATION

Tables A.3A and A.3B show the detailed results behind the aggregates in Tables 3A and 3B in Section 4, using the full 161-industry calculations. In these tables the years 1961 and 1992 are shown, representing the span of our complete I/O data. In Table A.3A the industries are listed in standard or numerical order from primary production through manufacturing and services. In Table A.3B the sectors are sorted from largest increase in export employment shares to largest decrease.

Those industries showing the largest increase in share of export employment tend to be of three major types[1]: The first, and most numerous are service industries of all types, from Accommodation and Food services, through Business and professional services, Trade, and Banking. How much this increase in Services employment is due to an expansion of direct exports in these industries and how much is due to other industries using more services as inputs (or to changing relative labour productivity among sectors) is analyzed in the decompositions section below. For now, the fact that exports of services in aggregate did not rise significantly relative to exports of goods from 1961 through 1992 (as we observed in Table 1) suggests that it is largely a change in intermediate inputs for exporting or relative sector productivity that is responsible for this shift.

The second group of industries increasing their employment share is Motor vehicles and Motor vehicle parts, and Accessories. This might be expected from the Auto Pact and from the continued expansion and integration of the North American auto industry. Note that the third major element in the expansion of export employment shares is, gratifyingly, Electronic equipment industries, indicating that Canada has been able to find important export opportunities in this rising worldwide sector.

At the bottom of the table are the sectors which have seen the largest declines in share of export employment. As can be seen, these are primary production sectors like Agriculture, Forestry and some of the Mines, together with associated sectors like Non-ferrous smelting and refining, Pulp and paper, and Sawmills. Also noteworthy is the decline in the share of Rail transport since 1961; as exports have grown they have tended to be shipped much less by rail.

Finally, this appendix also presents the 161-industry decompositions of changes in employment shares from 1961 to 1992 in Tables A.4A and A.4B.

---

[1]The ranking tends to be the same for export employment as a percentage of *total* employment as well, but there can be small differences due to the fact that export employment has itself changed as a share of total employment over the same time period.

Table A.3A Employment Shares: 1961 to 1992 – 161 Industries

	1961		1992		Change 1961–92	
	Export Employment as a % of Total Export Employment	Export Employment as a % of Total Employment	Export Employment as a % of Total Export Employment	Export Employment as a % of Total Employment	Export Employment as a % of Total Export Employment	Export Employment as a % of Total Employment
001 Agriculture and Related	26.93	4.63	8.69	2.01	-18.24	-2.63
002 Fishing and Trapping	1.24	0.21	1.38	0.32	0.14	0.11
003 Logging and Forestry	5.55	0.95	1.77	0.41	-3.78	-0.55
004 Gold Mines	1.81	0.31	0.35	0.08	-1.46	-0.23
005 Other Metal Mines	3.35	0.58	0.87	0.20	-2.48	-0.38
006 Iron Mines	0.79	0.14	0.22	0.05	-0.58	-0.09
007 Asbestos Mines	0.72	0.12	0.10	0.02	-0.62	-0.10
008 Non-Metal excl. Coal and Asbestos	0.28	0.05	0.25	0.06	-0.03	0.01
009 Salt Mines	0.04	0.01	0.02	0.00	-0.02	-0.00
010 Coal Mines	0.52	0.09	0.25	0.06	-0.27	-0.03
011 Crude Petroleum and Natural Gas	0.60	0.10	1.09	0.25	0.50	0.15
012 Quarries and Sand Pits	0.13	0.02	0.09	0.02	-0.04	-0.00
013 Services Related to Mineral Extraction	0.16	0.03	0.51	0.12	0.35	0.09
014 Meat and Meat Prod. (excl. Poultry)	0.28	0.05	0.37	0.09	0.09	0.04
015 Poultry Products	0.01	0.00	0.04	0.01	0.02	0.01
016 Fish Products Industry	1.11	0.19	0.87	0.20	-0.25	0.01
017 Fruit and Vegetable Processing	0.08	0.01	0.15	0.04	0.07	0.02
018 Dairy Products	0.17	0.03	0.09	0.02	-0.08	-0.01
019 Feed Industry	0.34	0.06	0.16	0.04	-0.18	-0.02
020 Vegetable Oil Mills (excluding Corn)	0.03	0.00	0.02	0.00	-0.01	0.00
021 Biscuit Industry	0.02	0.00	0.04	0.01	0.02	0.01
022 Bread and Other Bakery Prod. Industries	0.04	0.01	0.11	0.02	0.06	0.02
023 Cane and Beet Sugar Industry	0.02	0.00	0.01	0.00	-0.00	0.00
024 Miscellaneous Food Industries	0.53	0.09	0.34	0.08	-0.19	-0.01
025 Soft Drink Industry	0.01	0.00	0.07	0.02	0.06	0.01
026 Distillery Products Industry	0.31	0.05	0.09	0.02	-0.22	-0.03
027 Brewery Products Industry	0.04	0.01	0.06	0.01	0.02	0.01
028 Wine Industry	0.00	0.00	0.01	0.00	0.01	0.00
029 Tobacco Products Industries	0.13	0.02	0.06	0.01	-0.07	-0.01
030 Rubber Products Industries	0.29	0.05	0.77	0.18	0.48	0.13

Table A.3A (cont'd)

	1961		1992		Change 1961–92	
	Export Employment as a % of Total Export Employment	Export Employment as a % of Total Employment	Export Employment as a % of Total Export Employment	Export Employment as a % of Total Employment	Export Employment as a % of Total Export Employment	Export Employment as a % of Total Employment
031 Plastic Products Industries	0.13	0.02	0.98	0.23	0.84	0.20
032 Leather Tanneries	0.09	0.02	0.02	0.01	-0.07	-0.01
033 Footwear Industry	0.07	0.01	0.09	0.02	0.02	0.01
034 Misc. Leather and Allied Prod. Ind.	0.04	0.01	0.04	0.01	0.00	0.00
035 Man-Made Fibre Yarn and Woven Cloth	0.51	0.09	0.34	0.08	-0.17	-0.01
036 Wool Yarn and Woven Cloth Industry	0.14	0.02	0.07	0.02	-0.07	-0.01
037 Broad Knitted Fabric Industry	0.01	0.00	0.03	0.01	0.02	0.00
038 Misc. Textile Products Industries	0.25	0.04	0.29	0.07	0.04	0.02
039 Contract Textile Dyeing and Finishing	0.02	0.00	0.06	0.01	0.04	0.01
040 Carpet. Mat and Rug Industry	0.00	0.00	0.04	0.01	0.04	0.01
041 Clothing Industry excl. Hosiery	0.25	0.04	0.66	0.15	0.41	0.11
042 Hosiery Industry	0.02	0.00	0.01	0.00	-0.01	-0.00
043 Sawmills. Planing and Shingle Mills	3.85	0.66	1.99	0.46	-1.86	-0.20
044 Veneer and Plywood Industries	0.36	0.06	0.16	0.04	-0.20	-0.03
045 Sash. Door and Other Millwork Industries	0.23	0.04	0.30	0.07	0.07	0.03
046 Wooden Box and Coffin Industries	0.10	0.02	0.06	0.01	-0.04	-0.00
047 Other Wood Industries	0.22	0.04	0.25	0.06	0.03	0.02
048 Household Furniture Industries	0.04	0.01	0.33	0.08	0.29	0.07
049 Office Furniture Industry	0.00	0.00	0.14	0.03	0.13	0.03
050 Other Furniture and Fixture Industries	0.03	0.01	0.13	0.03	0.10	0.02
051 Pulp and Paper Industries	5.92	1.02	2.64	0.61	-3.27	-0.41
052 Asphalt Roofing Industry	0.02	0.00	0.02	0.01	0.01	0.00
053 Paper Box and Bag Industries	0.27	0.05	0.30	0.07	0.03	0.02
054 Other Converted Paper Prod. Industries	0.15	0.03	0.26	0.06	0.11	0.03
055 Printing and Publishing Industries	0.65	0.11	0.93	0.22	0.29	0.10
056 Plate making. Typesetting and Bindery	0.08	0.01	0.15	0.03	0.07	0.02
057 Primary Steel Industries	1.10	0.19	1.24	0.29	0.14	0.10
058 Steel Pipe and Tube Industry	0.03	0.00	0.11	0.02	0.08	0.02
059 Iron Foundries	0.16	0.03	0.23	0.05	0.08	0.03
060 Non-Ferrous Smelting and Refining	3.18	0.55	1.20	0.28	-1.98	-0.27

Table A.3A (cont'd)

	1961		1992		Change 1961-92	
	Export Employment as a % of Total Export Employment	Export Employment as a % of Total Employment	Export Employment as a % of Total Export Employment	Export Employment as a % of Total Employment	Export Employment as a % of Total Export Employment	Export Employment as a % of Total Employment
061 Alum. Rolling, Casting and Extruding	0.24	0.04	0.20	0.05	-0.04	0.01
062 Copper Rolling, Casting and Extruding	0.11	0.02	0.07	0.02	-0.04	-0.00
063 Other Metal Rolling, Casting, etc.	0.15	0.03	0.20	0.05	0.05	0.02
064 Power Boiler and Struct. Metal Industries	0.19	0.03	0.24	0.06	0.05	0.02
065 Ornamental and Arch. Metal Products	0.06	0.01	0.15	0.04	0.09	0.02
066 Stamped. Pressed and Coated Metals	0.29	0.05	0.59	0.14	0.31	0.09
067 Wire and Wire Products Industries	0.31	0.05	0.30	0.07	-0.00	0.02
068 Hardware Tool and Cutlery Industries	0.19	0.03	0.39	0.09	0.20	0.06
069 Heating Equipment Industry	0.03	0.01	0.05	0.01	0.02	0.01
070 Machine Shops Industry	0.15	0.03	0.69	0.16	0.55	0.13
071 Other Metal Fabricating Industries	0.28	0.05	0.39	0.09	0.11	0.04
072 Agricultural Implement Industry	0.72	0.12	0.21	0.05	-0.51	-0.07
073 Commercial Refrigeration Equipment	0.02	0.00	0.11	0.03	0.10	0.02
074 Other Machinery and Equip. Industries	0.65	0.11	1.70	0.39	1.05	0.28
075 Aircraft and Aircraft Parts Industries	1.17	0.20	1.62	0.37	0.44	0.17
076 Motor Vehicle Industry	0.11	0.02	2.32	0.54	2.21	0.52
077 Truck. Bus Body and Trailer Industries	0.04	0.01	0.16	0.04	0.12	0.03
078 Motor Vehicle Parts and Accessories	0.37	0.06	3.72	0.86	3.35	0.79
079 Railroad Rolling Stock Industry	0.11	0.02	0.20	0.05	0.09	0.03
080 Shipbuilding and Repair Industry	0.25	0.04	0.11	0.03	-0.14	-0.02
081 Misc. Transport. Equip. Industries	0.03	0.01	0.11	0.02	0.07	0.02
082 Small Electrical Appliance Industry	0.02	0.00	0.05	0.01	0.03	0.01
083 Major Appliances (Elec. and Non-Elec.)	0.08	0.01	0.09	0.02	0.01	0.01
084 Record Players. Radio and TV Receivers	0.05	0.01	0.09	0.02	0.05	0.01
085 Electronic Equipment Industries	0.40	0.07	1.82	0.42	1.42	0.35
086 Office. Store and Business Machines	0.26	0.04	0.71	0.16	0.45	0.12
087 Communic... Energy Wire and Cable	0.13	0.02	0.15	0.03	0.02	0.01
088 Battery Industry	0.03	0.01	0.04	0.01	0.01	0.00
089 Other Elect. and Electronic Products	0.38	0.07	0.79	0.18	0.40	0.12
090 Clay Products Industries	0.06	0.01	0.01	0.00	-0.05	-0.01

Table A.3A (cont'd)

	1961		1992		Change 1961–92	
	Export Employment as a % of Total Export Employment	Export Employment as a % of Total Employment	Export Employment as a % of Total Export Employment	Export Employment as a % of Total Employment	Export Employment as a % of Total Export Employment	Export Employment as a % of Total Employment
091 Cement Industry	0.03	0.00	0.03	0.01	0.00	0.00
092 Concrete Products Industry	0.02	0.00	0.03	0.01	0.00	0.00
093 Ready-Mix Concrete Industry	0.01	0.00	0.02	0.00	0.01	0.00
094 Glass and Glass Products Industries	0.10	0.02	0.21	0.05	0.11	0.03
095 Non-Metallic Mineral Products n.e.c.	0.38	0.07	0.27	0.06	-0.11	-0.00
096 Refined Petroleum and Coal Products	0.21	0.04	0.21	0.05	-0.00	0.01
097 Industrial Chemicals Industries n.e.c.	1.05	0.18	0.63	0.15	-0.42	-0.04
098 Plastic and Synthetic Resin Industries	0.16	0.03	0.26	0.06	0.10	0.03
099 Pharmaceutical and Medicine Industry	0.09	0.02	0.14	0.03	0.05	0.02
100 Paint and Varnish Industry	0.11	0.02	0.13	0.03	0.03	0.01
101 Soap and Cleaning Compounds Industry	0.07	0.01	0.10	0.02	0.03	0.01
102 Toilet Preparations Industry	0.01	0.00	0.06	0.01	0.06	0.01
103 Chemicals and Chemical Products	0.43	0.07	0.52	0.12	0.09	0.05
104 Jewelry and Precious Metals Industry	0.14	0.02	0.15	0.03	0.01	0.01
105 Sporting Goods and Toys Industries	0.06	0.01	0.15	0.03	0.08	0.02
106 Sign and Display Industry	0.05	0.01	0.09	0.02	0.04	0.01
107 Floor Tile. Linoleum. Coated Fabrics	0.03	0.00	0.06	0.01	0.03	0.01
108 Other Manufacturing Industry n.e.c.	0.54	0.09	1.04	0.24	0.50	0.15
109 Repair Construction	2.11	0.36	1.28	0.30	-0.83	-0.07
110 Residential Construction	0.00	0.00	0.00	0.00	0.00	0.00
111 Non-Residential Bldg Construction	0.00	0.00	0.00	0.00	0.00	0.00
112 Road. Highway and Airstrip Constr.	0.00	0.00	0.00	0.00	0.00	0.00
113 Gas and Oil Facility Construction	0.00	0.00	0.00	0.00	0.00	0.00
114 Dams and Irrigation Projects	0.00	0.00	0.00	0.00	0.00	0.00
115 Railway and Telephone Teleg. Constr.	0.00	0.00	0.00	0.00	0.00	0.00
116 Other Engineering Construction	0.00	0.00	0.00	0.00	0.00	0.00
117 Construction. Other Activities	0.01	0.00	0.02	0.00	0.00	0.00
118 Air Transport and Incidental Services	0.16	0.03	0.62	0.14	0.46	0.11
119 Railway and Transport and Rel. Services	5.07	0.87	1.30	0.30	-3.77	-0.57
120 Water Transport and Related Services	2.10	0.36	0.62	0.14	-1.48	-0.22

Table A.3A (cont'd)

	1961		1992		Change 1961–92	
	Export Employment as a % of Total Export Employment	Export Employment as a % of Total Employment	Export Employment as a % of Total Export Employment	Export Employment as a % of Total Employment	Export Employment as a % of Total Export Employment	Export Employment as a % of Total Employment
121 Truck Transport Industries	2.92	0.50	3.13	0.72	0.21	0.22
122 Urban Transit System Industry	0.01	0.00	0.10	0.02	0.08	0.02
123 Interurban and Rural Transit Systems	0.01	0.00	0.06	0.01	0.04	0.01
124 Taxicab Industry	0.15	0.03	0.41	0.10	0.26	0.07
125 Other Transport and Services to Transport	0.07	0.01	1.10	0.25	1.03	0.24
126 Highway and Bridge Maintenance Ind.	0.01	0.00	0.01	0.00	-0.01	-0.00
127 Pipeline Transport Industries	0.11	0.02	0.18	0.04	0.07	0.02
128 Storage and Warehousing Industries	0.78	0.13	0.49	0.11	-0.29	-0.02
129 Telecomm. Broadcasting Industry	0.42	0.07	0.21	0.05	-0.20	-0.02
130 Telecommunication Carriers and Other	0.53	0.09	0.74	0.17	0.21	0.08
131 Postal Service Industry	0.26	0.04	0.52	0.12	0.26	0.08
132 Electric Power Systems Industry	0.77	0.13	1.00	0.23	0.23	0.10
133 Gas Distribution Systems Industry	0.12	0.02	0.10	0.02	-0.02	0.00
134 Other Utility Industries n.e.c.	0.05	0.01	0.25	0.06	0.20	0.05
135 Wholesale Trade Industries	3.63	0.63	7.96	1.84	4.33	1.21
136 Retail Trade Industries	2.34	0.40	3.74	0.86	1.40	0.46
137 Banks, Credit Union and Oth. Dep. Inst.	0.46	0.08	1.55	0.36	1.09	0.28
138 Trust, Other Finance and Real Estate	0.51	0.09	1.59	0.37	1.09	0.28
139 Insurance Industries	0.67	0.12	0.70	0.16	0.03	0.05
140 Govt. Royalties on Nat. Resources	0.00	0.00	0.00	0.00	0.00	0.00
141 Owner Occupied Dwellings	0.00	0.00	0.00	0.00	0.00	0.00
142 Other Business Services Industries	0.45	0.08	4.60	1.06	4.15	0.98
143 Professional Business Services	0.94	0.16	4.03	0.93	3.10	0.77
144 Advertising Services	0.18	0.03	0.41	0.09	0.23	0.06
145 Educational Services Industries	0.08	0.01	0.21	0.05	0.13	0.03
146 Hospitals	0.02	0.00	0.05	0.01	0.03	0.01
147 Other Health Services	0.00	0.00	0.01	0.00	0.01	0.00
148 Accomm. and Food Services Industry	0.46	0.08	5.74	1.32	5.28	1.25
149 Motion Picture and Video Industries	0.05	0.01	0.20	0.05	0.15	0.04
150 Other Amusement and Recreational Serv.	0.03	0.01	0.59	0.14	0.56	0.13

Table A.3A (cont'd)

	1961		1992		Change 1961–92	
	Export Employment as a % of Total Export Employment	Export Employment as a % of Total Employment	Export Employment as a % of Total Export Employment	Export Employment as a % of Total Employment	Export Employment as a % of Total Export Employment	Export Employment as a % of Total Employment
151 Laundries and Cleaners	0.04	0.01	0.09	0.02	0.04	0.01
152 Other Personal Services	0.00	0.00	0.01	0.00	0.01	0.00
153 Photographers	0.01	0.00	0.03	0.01	0.02	0.01
154 Misc. Service Industries	0.62	0.11	3.02	0.70	2.39	0.59
TOTAL	100.00	17.20	100.00	23.07	0.00	5.87

Table A.3B Employment Shares: 1961 to 1992 – 161 Industries – Sorted by Size of Change

	1961		1992		Change 1961–92	
	Export Employment as a % of Total Export Employment	Export Employment as a % of Total Employment	Export Employment as a % of Total Export Employment	Export Employment as a % of Total Employment	Export Employment as a % of Total Export Employment	Export Employment as a % of Total Employment
148 Accomm. and Food Services Industry	0.46	0.08	5.74	1.32	5.28	1.25
135 Wholesale Trade Industries	3.63	0.63	7.96	1.84	4.33	1.21
142 Other Business Services Industries	0.45	0.08	4.60	1.06	4.15	0.98
078 Motor Vehicle Parts and Accessories	0.37	0.06	3.72	0.86	3.35	0.79
143 Professional Business Services	0.94	0.16	4.03	0.93	3.10	0.77
154 Misc. Service Industries	0.62	0.11	3.02	0.70	2.39	0.59
076 Motor Vehicle Industry	0.11	0.02	2.32	0.54	2.21	0.52
085 Electronic Equipment Industries	0.40	0.07	1.82	0.42	1.42	0.35
136 Retail Trade Industries	2.34	0.40	3.74	0.86	1.40	0.46
137 Banks, Credit Union and Oth. Dep. Inst.	0.46	0.08	1.55	0.36	1.09	0.28
138 Trust. Other Finance and Real Estate	0.51	0.09	1.59	0.37	1.09	0.28
074 Other Machinery and Equip. Industries	0.65	0.11	1.70	0.39	1.05	0.28
125 Other Transport and Services to Transp.	0.07	0.01	1.10	0.25	1.03	0.24
031 Plastic Products Industries	0.13	0.02	0.98	0.23	0.84	0.20
150 Other Amusement and Recr. Services	0.03	0.01	0.59	0.14	0.56	0.13
070 Machine Shops Industry	0.15	0.03	0.69	0.16	0.55	0.13
108 Other Manufacturing Industry n.e.c.	0.54	0.09	1.04	0.24	0.50	0.15
011 Crude Petroleum and Natural Gas	0.60	0.10	1.09	0.25	0.50	0.15
030 Rubber Products Industries	0.29	0.05	0.77	0.18	0.48	0.13
118 Air Transport and Incidental Services	0.16	0.03	0.62	0.14	0.46	0.11
086 Office, Store and Business Machines	0.26	0.04	0.71	0.16	0.45	0.12
075 Aircraft and Aircraft Parts Industries	1.17	0.20	1.62	0.37	0.44	0.17
041 Clothing Industry excluding Hosiery	0.25	0.04	0.66	0.15	0.41	0.11
089 Other Elect. and Electronic Products	0.38	0.07	0.79	0.18	0.40	0.12
013 Services Related to Mineral Extraction	0.16	0.03	0.51	0.12	0.35	0.09
066 Stamped. Pressed and Coated Metals	0.29	0.05	0.59	0.14	0.31	0.09
055 Printing and Publishing Industries	0.65	0.11	0.93	0.22	0.29	0.10
048 Household Furniture Industries	0.04	0.01	0.33	0.08	0.29	0.07
131 Postal Service Industry	0.26	0.04	0.52	0.12	0.26	0.08
124 Taxicab Industry	0.15	0.03	0.41	0.10	0.26	0.07
144 Advertising Services	0.18	0.03	0.41	0.09	0.23	0.06
132 Electric Power Systems Industry	0.77	0.13	1.00	0.23	0.23	0.10

Table A.3B (cont'd)

	1961		1992		Change 1961–92	
	Export Employment as a % of Total Export Employment	Export Employment as a % of Total Employment	Export Employment as a % of Total Export Employment	Export Employment as a % of Total Employment	Export Employment as a % of Total Export Employment	Export Employment as a % of Total Employment
121 Truck Transport Industries	2.92	0.50	3.13	0.72	0.21	0.22
130 Telecommunication Carriers and Other	0.53	0.09	0.74	0.17	0.21	0.08
068 Hardware Tool and Cutlery Industries	0.19	0.03	0.39	0.09	0.20	0.06
134 Other Utility Industries n.e.c.	0.05	0.01	0.25	0.06	0.20	0.05
149 Motion Picture and Video Industries	0.05	0.01	0.20	0.05	0.15	0.04
002 Fishing and Trapping	1.24	0.21	1.38	0.32	0.14	0.11
057 Primary Steel Industries	1.10	0.19	1.24	0.29	0.14	0.10
049 Office Furniture Industry	0.00	0.00	0.14	0.03	0.13	0.03
145 Educational Services Industries	0.08	0.01	0.21	0.05	0.13	0.03
077 Truck, Bus Body and Trailer Industries	0.04	0.01	0.16	0.04	0.12	0.03
071 Other Metal Fabricating Industries	0.28	0.05	0.39	0.09	0.11	0.04
094 Glass and Glass Products Industries	0.10	0.02	0.21	0.05	0.11	0.03
054 Other Converted Paper Prod. Industries	0.15	0.03	0.26	0.06	0.11	0.03
098 Plastic and Synthetic Resin Industries	0.16	0.03	0.26	0.06	0.10	0.03
050 Other Furniture and Fixture Industries	0.03	0.01	0.13	0.03	0.10	0.02
073 Commercial Refrigeration Equipment	0.02	0.00	0.11	0.03	0.10	0.02
103 Chemicals and Chemical Products	0.43	0.07	0.52	0.12	0.09	0.05
065 Ornamental and Arch. Metal Products	0.06	0.01	0.15	0.04	0.09	0.02
014 Meat and Meat Prod. (excl. Poultry)	0.28	0.05	0.37	0.09	0.09	0.04
079 Railroad Rolling Stock Industry	0.11	0.02	0.20	0.05	0.09	0.03
122 Urban Transit System Industry	0.01	0.00	0.10	0.02	0.08	0.02
105 Sporting Goods and Toys Industries	0.06	0.01	0.15	0.03	0.08	0.02
058 Steel Pipe and Tube Industry	0.03	0.00	0.11	0.02	0.08	0.02
059 Iron Foundries	0.16	0.03	0.23	0.05	0.08	0.03
017 Fruit and Vegetable Processing	0.08	0.01	0.15	0.04	0.07	0.02
081 Misc. Transport. Equip. Industries	0.03	0.01	0.11	0.02	0.07	0.02
127 Pipeline Transport Industries	0.11	0.02	0.18	0.04	0.07	0.02
045 Sash. Door and Other Millwork Ind.	0.23	0.04	0.30	0.07	0.07	0.03
056 Plate making. Typesetting and Bindery	0.08	0.01	0.15	0.03	0.07	0.02
022 Bread and Other Bakery Prod. Ind.	0.04	0.01	0.11	0.02	0.06	0.02
025 Soft Drink Industry	0.01	0.00	0.07	0.02	0.06	0.01

Table A.3B (cont'd)

	1961		1992		Change 1961–92	
	Export Employment as a % of Total Export Employment	Export Employment as a % of Total Employment	Export Employment as a % of Total Export Employment	Export Employment as a % of Total Employment	Export Employment as a % of Total Export Employment	Export Employment as a % of Total Employment
102 Toilet Preparations Industry	0.01	0.00	0.06	0.01	0.06	0.01
099 Pharmaceutical and Medicine Industry	0.09	0.02	0.14	0.03	0.05	0.02
064 Power Boiler and Struct. Metal Ind.	0.19	0.03	0.24	0.06	0.05	0.02
063 Other Metal Rolling. Casting. etc.	0.15	0.03	0.20	0.05	0.05	0.02
084 Record Players. Radio and TV Receivers	0.05	0.01	0.09	0.02	0.05	0.01
151 Laundries and Cleaners	0.04	0.01	0.09	0.02	0.04	0.01
123 Interurban and Rural Transit Systems	0.01	0.00	0.06	0.01	0.04	0.01
040 Carpet. Mat and Rug Industry	0.00	0.00	0.04	0.01	0.04	0.01
038 Misc. Textile Products Industries	0.25	0.04	0.29	0.07	0.04	0.02
106 Sign and Display Industry	0.05	0.01	0.09	0.02	0.04	0.01
039 Contract Textile Dyeing and Finishing	0.02	0.00	0.06	0.01	0.04	0.01
146 Hospitals	0.02	0.00	0.05	0.01	0.03	0.01
101 Soap and Cleaning Compounds Industry	0.07	0.01	0.10	0.02	0.03	0.01
047 Other Wood Industries	0.22	0.04	0.25	0.06	0.03	0.02
107 Floor Tile. Linoleum. Coated Fabrics	0.03	0.00	0.06	0.01	0.03	0.01
100 Paint and Varnish Industry	0.11	0.02	0.13	0.03	0.03	0.01
139 Insurance Industries	0.67	0.12	0.70	0.16	0.03	0.05
053 Paper Box and Bag Industries	0.27	0.05	0.30	0.07	0.03	0.02
082 Small Electrical Appliance Industry	0.02	0.00	0.05	0.01	0.03	0.01
087 Communic.. Energy Wire and Cable	0.13	0.02	0.15	0.03	0.02	0.01
153 Photographers	0.01	0.00	0.03	0.01	0.02	0.01
015 Poultry Products	0.01	0.00	0.04	0.01	0.02	0.01
027 Brewery Products Industry	0.04	0.01	0.06	0.01	0.02	0.01
069 Heating Equipment Industry	0.03	0.01	0.05	0.01	0.02	0.01
033 Footwear Industry	0.07	0.01	0.09	0.02	0.02	0.01
021 Biscuit Industry	0.02	0.00	0.04	0.01	0.02	0.01
037 Broad Knitted Fabric Industry	0.01	0.00	0.03	0.01	0.01	0.00
147 Other Health Services	0.00	0.00	0.01	0.00	0.01	0.00
083 Major Appliances (Elec. and Non-Elec.)	0.08	0.01	0.09	0.02	0.01	0.01
152 Other Personal Services	0.00	0.00	0.01	0.00	0.01	0.00
104 Jewelry and Precious Metals Industry	0.14	0.02	0.15	0.03	0.01	0.01

Table A.3B (cont'd)

	1961		1992		Change 1961–92	
	Export Employment as a % of Total Export Employment	Export Employment as a % of Total Employment	Export Employment as a % of Total Export Employment	Export Employment as a % of Total Employment	Export Employment as a % of Total Export Employment	Export Employment as a % of Total Employment
093 Ready-Mix Concrete Industry	0.01	0.00	0.00	0.00	0.01	0.00
028 Wine Industry	0.00	0.00	0.00	0.00	0.01	0.00
052 Asphalt Roofing Industry	0.02	0.00	0.01	0.01	0.01	0.00
088 Battery Industry	0.03	0.01	0.04	0.01	0.01	0.00
092 Concrete Products Industry	0.02	0.00	0.03	0.01	0.00	0.00
091 Cement Industry	0.03	0.00	0.03	0.01	0.00	0.00
117 Construction. Other Activities	0.01	0.00	0.02	0.00	0.00	0.00
034 Misc. Leather and Allied Prod. Ind.	0.04	0.01	0.04	0.01	0.00	0.00
113 Gas and Oil Facility Construction	0.00	0.00	0.00	0.00	0.00	0.00
111 Non-Residential Bldg Construction	0.00	0.00	0.00	0.00	0.00	0.00
112 Road. Highway and Airstrip Constr.	0.00	0.00	0.00	0.00	0.00	0.00
114 Dams and Irrigation Projects	0.00	0.00	0.00	0.00	0.00	0.00
141 Owner Occupied Dwellings	0.00	0.00	0.00	0.00	0.00	0.00
116 Other Engineering Construction	0.00	0.00	0.00	0.00	0.00	0.00
115 Railway and Telephone Teleg. Constr.	0.00	0.00	0.00	0.00	0.00	0.00
110 Residential Construction	0.00	0.00	0.00	0.00	0.00	0.00
140 Govt. Royalties on Nat. Resources	0.00	0.00	0.00	0.00	0.00	0.00
096 Refined Petroleum and Coal Products	0.21	0.04	0.21	0.05	-0.00	0.01
067 Wire and Wire Products Industries	0.31	0.05	0.30	0.07	-0.00	0.02
023 Cane and Beer Sugar Industry	0.02	0.00	0.01	0.00	-0.00	0.00
126 Highway and Bridge Maintenance Ind.	0.01	0.00	0.01	0.00	-0.01	-0.00
020 Vegetable Oil Mills (excluding Corn)	0.03	0.00	0.02	0.00	-0.01	0.00
042 Hosiery Industry	0.02	0.00	0.01	0.00	-0.01	-0.00
133 Gas Distribution Systems Industry	0.12	0.02	0.10	0.02	-0.02	0.00
009 Salt Mines	0.04	0.01	0.02	0.00	-0.02	-0.00
008 Non-Metal excl. Coal and Asbestos	0.28	0.05	0.25	0.06	-0.03	0.01
012 Quarries and Sand Pits	0.13	0.02	0.09	0.02	-0.04	-0.00
061 Alum. Rolling. Casting and Extruding	0.24	0.04	0.20	0.05	-0.04	0.01
046 Wooden Box and Coffin Industries	0.10	0.02	0.06	0.01	-0.04	0.00
062 Copper Rolling. Casting and Extruding	0.11	0.02	0.07	0.02	-0.04	-0.00
090 Clay Products Industries	0.06	0.01	0.01	0.00	-0.05	-0.01

Table A.3B (cont'd)

	1961		1992		Change 1961–92	
	Export Employment as a % of Total Export Employment	Export Employment as a % of Total Employment	Export Employment as a % of Total Export Employment	Export Employment as a % of Total Employment	Export Employment as a % of Total Export Employment	Export Employment as a % of Total Employment
036 Wool Yarn and Woven Cloth Industry	0.14	0.02	0.07	0.02	-0.07	-0.01
032 Leather Tanneries	0.09	0.02	0.02	0.01	-0.07	-0.01
029 Tobacco Products Industries	0.13	0.02	0.06	0.01	-0.07	-0.01
018 Dairy Products	0.17	0.03	0.09	0.02	-0.08	-0.01
095 Non-Metallic Mineral Products n.e.c.	0.38	0.07	0.27	0.06	-0.11	-0.00
080 Shipbuilding and Repair Industry	0.25	0.04	0.11	0.03	-0.14	-0.02
035 Man-Made Fibre Yarn and Woven Cloth	0.51	0.09	0.34	0.08	-0.17	-0.01
019 Feed Industry	0.34	0.06	0.16	0.04	-0.18	-0.02
024 Miscellaneous Food Industries	0.53	0.09	0.34	0.08	-0.19	-0.01
044 Veneer and Plywood Industries	0.36	0.06	0.16	0.04	-0.20	-0.03
129 Telecomm. Broadcasting Industry	0.42	0.07	0.21	0.05	-0.20	-0.02
026 Distillery Products Industry	0.31	0.05	0.09	0.02	-0.22	-0.03
016 Fish Products Industry	1.11	0.19	0.87	0.20	-0.25	0.01
010 Coal Mines	0.52	0.09	0.25	0.06	-0.27	-0.03
128 Storage and Warehousing Industries	0.78	0.13	0.49	0.11	-0.29	-0.02
097 Industrial Chemicals Industries n.e.c.	1.05	0.18	0.63	0.15	-0.42	-0.04
072 Agricultural Implement Industry	0.72	0.12	0.21	0.05	-0.51	-0.07
006 Iron Mines	0.79	0.14	0.22	0.05	-0.58	-0.09
007 Asbestos Mines	0.72	0.12	0.10	0.02	-0.62	-0.10
109 Repair Construction	2.11	0.36	1.28	0.30	-0.83	-0.07
004 Gold Mines	1.81	0.31	0.35	0.08	-1.46	-0.23
120 Water Transport and Related Services	2.10	0.36	0.62	0.14	-1.48	-0.22
043 Sawmills. Planing and Shingle Mills	3.85	0.66	1.99	0.46	-1.86	-0.20
060 Non-Ferrous Smelting and Refining	3.18	0.55	1.20	0.28	-1.98	-0.27
005 Other Metal Mines	3.35	0.58	0.87	0.20	-2.48	-0.38
051 Pulp and Paper Industries	5.92	1.02	2.64	0.61	-3.27	-0.41
119 Railway and Transport and Rel. Services	5.07	0.87	1.30	0.30	-3.77	-0.57
003 Logging and Forestry	5.55	0.95	1.77	0.41	-3.78	-0.55
001 Agriculture and Related	26.93	4.63	8.69	2.01	-18.24	-2.63
TOTAL	100.00	17.20	100.00	23.07	0.00	5.87

	1961	1992	Change 1961–92	Due to:				
	Export Employ't as a % of Total Export Employ't	Export Employ't as a % of Total Export Employ't	Export Employ't as a % of Total Export Employ't	Change in Export Shares	Change in Employ't /Output Ratio	Change in Input/ Output Coeff's	Change in Import Coeff's	Residual /Interaction
001 Agriculture and Related	26.93	8.69	-18.24	-13.16	-3.23	-0.30	0.55	-2.09
002 Fishing and Trapping	1.24	1.38	0.14	-0.64	0.46	-0.14	0.22	0.24
003 Logging and Forestry	5.55	1.77	-3.78	-1.36	-1.17	-0.21	0.11	-1.15
004 Gold Mines	1.81	0.35	-1.46	-0.31	-0.64	-0.02	0.02	-0.50
005 Other Metal Mines	3.35	0.87	-2.48	-1.31	-0.14	-0.26	-0.05	-0.72
006 Iron Mines	0.79	0.22	-0.58	-0.48	-0.04	-0.03	0.03	-0.06
007 Asbestos Mines	0.72	0.10	-0.62	-1.06	0.04	-0.02	0.01	0.41
008 Non-Metal excl Coal and Asbestos	0.28	0.25	-0.03	0.01	-0.26	-0.00	0.05	0.17
009 Salt Mines	0.04	0.02	-0.02	-0.01	-0.00	-0.01	0.00	-0.00
010 Coal Mines	0.52	0.25	-0.27	0.18	-0.89	-0.05	0.01	0.47
011 Crude Petroleum and Natural Gas	0.60	1.09	0.50	0.47	-0.25	-0.01	0.14	0.14
012 Quarries and Sand Pits	0.13	0.09	-0.04	-0.06	0.00	-0.01	0.00	0.03
013 Services Related to Mineral Extraction	0.16	0.51	0.35	0.04	0.24	0.22	0.06	-0.21
014 Meat and Meat Prod (excl. Poultry)	0.28	0.37	0.09	0.02	0.09	-0.06	0.01	0.03
015 Poultry Products	0.01	0.04	0.02	0.01	0.01	-0.00	0.00	-0.00
016 Fish Products Industry	1.11	0.87	-0.25	-0.31	0.07	-0.08	0.05	0.04
017 Fruit and Vegetable Processing	0.08	0.15	0.07	0.08	-0.01	-0.01	0.01	0.02
018 Dairy Products	0.17	0.09	-0.08	-0.05	-0.02	-0.01	0.00	-0.00
019 Feed Industry	0.34	0.16	-0.18	-0.16	-0.00	-0.01	-0.01	0.00
020 Vegetable Oil Mills (excluding Corn)	0.03	0.02	-0.01	-0.01	-0.00	-0.00	0.00	0.00
021 Biscuit Industry	0.02	0.04	0.02	0.02	-0.01	0.00	0.00	0.00
022 Bread and Other Bakery Prod. Industries	0.04	0.11	0.06	0.07	0.00	-0.01	0.00	0.01
023 Cane and Beer Sugar Industry	0.02	0.01	-0.00	0.00	0.00	-0.01	0.00	0.00
024 Miscellaneous Food Industries	0.53	0.34	-0.19	-0.20	0.04	-0.06	0.01	0.01
025 Soft Drink Industry	0.01	0.07	0.06	0.05	-0.05	0.01	0.01	0.05
026 Distillery Products Industry	0.31	0.09	-0.22	-0.25	0.01	-0.01	0.00	0.02
027 Brewery Products Industry	0.04	0.06	0.02	0.02	-0.00	-0.01	0.01	0.00
028 Wine Industry	0.00	0.01	0.01	0.01	-0.00	-0.00	0.00	0.00
029 Tobacco Products Industries	0.13	0.06	-0.07	-0.02	-0.03	-0.00	-0.00	-0.02
030 Rubber Products Industries	0.29	0.77	0.48	0.55	0.13	-0.13	-0.15	0.08

Table A.4A (cont'd)

	1961 Export Employ't as a % of Total Export Employ't	1992 Export Employ't as a % of Total Export Employ't	Change 1961-92 Export Employ't as a % of Total Export Employ't	Due to: Change in Export Shares	Change in Employ't/Output Ratio	Change in Input/Output Coeff's	Change in Import Coeff's	Residual/Interaction
031 Plastic Products Industries	0.13	0.98	0.84	0.59	0.06	0.21	-0.04	0.03
032 Leather Tanneries	0.09	0.02	-0.07	-0.07	0.00	0.00	-0.02	0.02
033 Footwear Industry	0.07	0.09	0.02	0.02	0.01	-0.01	-0.01	0.01
034 Misc. Leather and Allied Prod. Ind.	0.04	0.04	0.00	0.01	0.01	-0.00	-0.01	0.00
035 Man-Made Fibre Yarn and Woven Cloth	0.51	0.34	-0.17	0.05	-0.05	-0.14	-0.06	0.03
036 Wool Yarn and Woven Cloth Industry	0.14	0.07	-0.07	-0.03	0.00	-0.04	-0.02	0.02
037 Broad Knitted Fabric Industry	0.01	0.03	0.02	0.02	-0.00	0.01	-0.00	-0.00
038 Misc. Textile Products Industries	0.25	0.29	0.04	0.06	0.05	-0.05	-0.02	0.00
039 Contract Textile Dyeing and Finishing	0.02	0.06	0.04	0.04	0.01	0.01	-0.01	-0.02
040 Carpet. Mat and Rug Industry	0.00	0.04	0.04	0.04	-0.01	-0.00	-0.00	0.01
041 Clothing Industry excl. Hosiery	0.25	0.66	0.41	0.45	0.05	-0.07	-0.01	-0.01
042 Hosiery Industry	0.02	0.01	-0.01	-0.01	0.00	-0.00	0.00	0.00
043 Sawmills. Planing and Shingle Mills	3.85	1.99	-1.86	-0.98	-0.98	-0.08	0.17	0.02
044 Veneer and Plywood Industries	0.36	0.16	-0.20	-0.17	-0.02	-0.03	0.01	0.01
045 Sash. Door and Other Millwork Ind.	0.23	0.30	0.07	0.06	0.04	-0.05	0.02	-0.00
046 Wooden Box and Coffin Industries	0.10	0.06	-0.04	-0.01	-0.01	-0.01	-0.01	-0.00
047 Other Wood Industries	0.22	0.25	0.03	0.12	-0.15	-0.03	0.02	0.07
048 Household Furniture Industries	0.04	0.33	0.29	0.30	0.03	-0.03	0.01	-0.02
049 Office Furniture Industry	0.00	0.14	0.13	0.13	0.00	-0.01	0.01	0.00
050 Other Furniture and Fixture Industries	0.03	0.13	0.10	0.09	0.03	-0.01	0.00	-0.01
051 Pulp and Paper Industries	5.92	2.64	-3.27	-3.27	0.02	-0.33	0.14	0.17
052 Asphalt Roofing Industry	0.02	0.02	0.01	0.01	-0.01	-0.01	0.00	0.01
053 Paper Box and Bag Industries	0.27	0.30	0.03	0.06	0.03	-0.11	-0.02	0.06
054 Other Converted Paper Prod. Industries	0.15	0.26	0.11	0.11	0.03	-0.08	-0.01	0.05
055 Printing and Publishing Industries	0.65	0.93	0.29	0.33	-0.01	-0.23	-0.04	0.23
056 Plate making. Typesetting and Bindery	0.08	0.15	0.07	0.06	0.02	-0.04	-0.00	0.02
057 Primary Steel Industries	1.10	1.24	0.14	0.30	-0.03	-0.15	-0.19	0.21
058 Steel Pipe and Tube Industry	0.03	0.11	0.08	0.05	0.04	-0.01	-0.00	0.00
059 Iron Foundries	0.16	0.23	0.08	0.08	-0.05	-0.00	-0.02	0.08

Table A.4A (cont'd)

	1961	1992	Change 1961–92	Due to:				
	Export Employ't as a % of Total Export Employ't	Export Employ't as a % of Total Export Employ't	Export Employ't as a % of Total Export Employ't	Change in Export Shares	Change in Employ't /Output Ratio	Change in Input/ Output Coeff's	Change in Import Coeff's	Residual /Interaction
060 Non-Ferrous Smelting and Refining	3.18	1.20	-1.98	-1.79	-0.04	-0.10	-0.02	-0.03
061 Alum. Rolling. Casting and Extruding	0.24	0.20	-0.04	0.04	-0.13	0.03	-0.08	0.10
062 Copper Rolling. Casting and Extruding	0.11	0.07	-0.04	-0.07	0.03	-0.06	-0.04	0.10
063 Other Metal Rolling. Casting, etc.	0.15	0.20	0.05	-0.02	0.07	-0.05	-0.02	0.07
064 Power Boiler and Struct. Metal Ind.	0.19	0.24	0.05	0.07	0.04	-0.10	0.01	0.04
065 Ornamental and Arch. Metal Products	0.06	0.15	0.09	0.08	0.01	0.00	0.00	-0.01
066 Stamped. Pressed and Coated Metals	0.29	0.59	0.31	0.30	0.09	-0.09	-0.07	0.06
067 Wire and Wire Products Industries	0.31	0.30	-0.00	0.16	0.04	-0.23	-0.07	0.09
068 Hardware Tool and Cutlery Industries	0.19	0.39	0.20	0.17	0.10	-0.04	-0.02	-0.00
069 Heating Equipment Industry	0.03	0.05	0.02	0.02	0.01	-0.01	-0.00	-0.00
070 Machine Shops Industry	0.15	0.69	0.55	0.49	0.16	0.05	-0.16	-0.00
071 Other Metal Fabricating Industries	0.28	0.39	0.11	0.15	0.03	-0.08	-0.06	0.07
072 Agricultural Implement Industry	0.72	0.21	-0.51	-0.57	0.02	-0.04	0.02	0.06
073 Commercial Refrigeration Equipment	0.02	0.11	0.10	0.09	0.02	0.03	-0.04	-0.00
074 Other Machinery and Equip. Industries	0.65	1.70	1.05	1.05	0.11	-0.12	-0.05	0.05
075 Aircraft and Aircraft Parts Industries	1.17	1.62	0.44	0.56	-0.10	-0.14	0.04	0.09
076 Motor Vehicle Industry	0.11	2.32	2.21	2.26	-1.56	-0.28	0.18	1.59
077 Truck. Bus Body and Trailer Industries	0.04	0.16	0.12	0.12	0.02	0.01	-0.00	-0.02
078 Motor Vehicle Parts and Accessories	0.37	3.72	3.35	3.47	-0.31	-0.03	-1.06	1.27
079 Railroad Rolling Stock Industry	0.11	0.20	0.09	0.14	-0.06	-0.02	-0.01	0.03
080 Shipbuilding and Repair Industry	0.25	0.11	-0.14	-0.14	-0.02	-0.00	0.01	0.01
081 Misc. Transport. Equip. Industries	0.03	0.11	0.07	0.08	-0.06	-0.00	0.01	0.05
082 Small Electrical Appliance Industry	0.02	0.05	0.03	0.03	0.01	-0.01	-0.00	0.00
083 Major Appliances (Elec. and Non-Elec.)	0.08	0.09	0.01	0.02	-0.00	-0.01	-0.01	0.00
084 Record Players. Radio and TV Receivers	0.05	0.09	0.05	0.07	-0.03	-0.01	-0.05	0.07
085 Electronic Equipment Industries	0.40	1.82	1.42	1.58	-1.62	0.09	-0.39	1.75
086 Office. Store and Business Machines	0.26	0.71	0.45	0.55	-0.16	-0.07	-0.16	0.29
087 Communic... Energy Wire and Cable	0.13	0.15	0.02	0.03	0.01	-0.03	-0.02	0.03
088 Battery Industry	0.03	0.04	0.01	0.01	0.01	-0.01	-0.01	0.01

Table A.4A (cont'd)

	1961	1992	Change 1961–92	Due to:				
	Export Employ't as a % of Total Export Employ't	Export Employ't as a % of Total Export Employ't	Export Employ't as a % of Total Export Employ't	Change in Export Shares	Change in Employ't /Output Ratio	Change in Input/ Output Coeff's	Change in Import Coeff's	Residual /Interaction
089 Other Elect. and Electronic Products	0.38	0.79	0.40	0.40	0.07	-0.06	-0.16	0.16
090 Clay Products Industries	0.06	0.01	-0.05	-0.02	-0.00	-0.01	-0.00	-0.01
091 Cement Industry	0.03	0.03	0.00	0.01	0.00	-0.01	0.00	-0.00
092 Concrete Products Industry	0.02	0.03	0.00	0.01	0.00	-0.01	0.00	0.00
093 Ready-Mix Concrete Industry	0.01	0.02	0.01	-0.00	0.01	0.00	0.00	0.00
094 Glass and Glass Products Industries	0.10	0.21	0.11	0.13	-0.02	-0.11	-0.01	0.12
095 Non-Metallic Mineral Products n.e.c.	0.38	0.27	-0.11	-0.08	0.00	-0.06	-0.03	0.06
096 Refined Petroleum and Coal Products	0.21	0.21	-0.00	0.05	-0.10	-0.00	-0.00	0.05
097 Industrial Chemicals Industries n.e.c.	1.05	0.63	-0.42	-0.09	-0.37	0.03	-0.05	0.05
098 Plastic and Synthetic Resin Industries	0.16	0.26	0.10	0.13	-0.08	0.01	-0.03	0.07
099 Pharmaceutical and Medicine Industry	0.09	0.14	0.05	0.06	-0.04	0.01	0.00	0.03
100 Paint and Varnish Industry	0.11	0.13	0.03	0.05	-0.01	-0.00	-0.03	0.02
101 Soap and Cleaning Compounds Industry	0.07	0.10	0.03	0.02	0.03	-0.02	-0.01	0.01
102 Toilet Preparations Industry	0.01	0.06	0.06	0.05	0.01	-0.00	-0.00	0.01
103 Chemicals and Chemical Products	0.43	0.52	0.09	0.08	-0.07	0.03	-0.07	0.12
104 Jewelry and Precious Metals Industry	0.14	0.15	0.01	0.01	0.02	-0.02	-0.00	0.00
105 Sporting Goods and Toys Industries	0.06	0.15	0.08	0.09	-0.01	-0.02	0.00	0.01
106 Sign and Display Industry	0.05	0.09	0.04	0.03	0.03	-0.03	-0.00	0.01
107 Floor Tile. Linoleum. Coated Fabrics	0.03	0.06	0.03	0.04	0.00	-0.01	-0.01	0.01
108 Other Manufacturing Industry n.e.c.	0.54	1.04	0.50	0.52	0.12	-0.10	-0.09	0.06
109 Repair Construction	2.11	1.28	-0.83	-0.41	-0.19	-0.43	0.02	0.19
110 Residential Construction	0.00	0.00	0.00	0.00	0.00	0.00	0.00	0.00
111 Non-Residential Bldg Construction	0.00	0.00	0.00	0.00	0.00	0.00	0.00	0.00
112 Road. Highway and Airstrip Constr.	0.00	0.00	0.00	0.00	0.00	0.00	0.00	0.00
113 Gas and Oil Facility Construction	0.00	0.00	0.00	0.00	0.00	0.00	0.00	0.00
114 Dams and Irrigation Projects	0.00	0.00	0.00	0.00	0.00	0.00	0.00	0.00
115 Railway and Telephone Teleg. Constr.	0.00	0.00	0.00	0.00	0.00	0.00	0.00	0.00
116 Other Engineering Construction	0.00	0.00	0.00	0.00	0.00	0.00	0.00	0.00
117 Construction. Other Activities	0.01	0.02	0.00	0.00	0.01	-0.01	-0.00	0.01
118 Air Transport and Incidental Services	0.16	0.62	0.46	0.41	-0.04	0.03	-0.04	0.11

	1961	1992	Change 1961–92	Due to:				
	Export Employ't as a % of Total Export Employ't	Export Employ't as a % of Total Export Employ't	Export Employ't as a % of Total Export Employ't	Change in Export Shares	Change in Employ't /Output Ratio	Change in Input/ Output Coeff's	Change in Import Coeff's	Residual /Interaction
119 Railway and Transport and Rel. Services	5.07	1.30	-3.77	-0.66	-0.37	-1.80	0.01	-0.94
120 Water Transport and Related Services	2.10	0.62	-1.48	-0.79	-0.18	-0.23	0.03	-0.30
121 Truck Transport Industries	2.92	3.13	0.21	-0.95	-0.56	0.99	0.10	0.64
122 Urban Transit System Industry	0.01	0.10	0.08	0.07	0.05	-0.01	0.00	-0.03
123 Interurban and Rural Transit Systems.	0.01	0.06	0.04	0.05	-0.01	-0.01	-0.00	0.02
124 Taxicab Industry	0.15	0.41	0.26	0.17	0.08	0.04	-0.04	0.01
125 Other Transport and Services to Transp.	0.07	1.10	1.03	0.13	0.56	0.66	0.03	-0.35
126 Highway and Bridge Maintenance Ind.	0.01	0.01	-0.01	-0.00	-0.00	-0.00	0.00	0.00
127 Pipeline Transport Industries	0.11	0.18	0.07	0.01	0.04	-0.01	0.01	0.01
128 Storage and Warehousing Industries	0.78	0.49	-0.29	-0.56	0.17	-0.19	0.03	0.26
129 Telecomm. Broadcasting Industry	0.42	0.21	-0.20	-0.08	-0.19	0.05	-0.00	0.01
130 Telecommunication Carriers and Other	0.53	0.74	0.21	0.20	-0.21	0.04	-0.01	0.19
131 Postal Service Industry	0.26	0.52	0.26	0.17	0.01	0.03	0.01	0.05
132 Electric Power Systems Industry	0.77	1.00	0.23	-0.33	-0.21	0.39	0.00	0.38
133 Gas Distribution Systems Industry	0.12	0.10	-0.02	-0.00	-0.05	0.01	0.00	0.02
134 Other Utility Industries n.e.c.	0.05	0.25	0.20	-0.00	0.01	0.19	-0.00	0.01
135 Wholesale Trade Industries	3.63	7.96	4.33	1.37	1.95	0.66	0.11	0.23
136 Retail Trade Industries	2.34	3.74	1.40	-0.03	1.22	-0.79	0.03	0.96
137 Banks. Credit Union and Oth. Dep. Inst.	0.46	1.55	1.09	0.15	-0.01	0.80	-0.00	0.16
138 Trust. Other Finance and Real Estate	0.51	1.59	1.09	0.22	0.62	0.25	0.02	-0.03
139 Insurance Industries	0.67	0.70	0.03	0.17	-0.10	-0.11	0.01	0.05
140 Govt. Royalties on Nat. Resources	0.00	0.00	0.00	0.00	0.00	0.00	0.00	0.00
141 Owner Occupied Dwellings	0.00	0.00	0.00	0.00	0.00	0.00	0.00	0.00
142 Other Business Services Industries	0.45	4.60	4.15	2.15	1.68	1.85	0.91	-2.45
143 Professional Business Services	0.94	4.03	3.10	1.98	0.94	1.15	0.18	-1.15
144 Advertising Services	0.18	0.41	0.23	0.01	0.07	0.17	0.01	-0.02
145 Educational Services Industries	0.08	0.21	0.13	0.11	0.03	-0.02	0.02	-0.01
146 Hospitals	0.02	0.05	0.03	0.04	-0.01	-0.01	0.00	-0.01
147 Other Health Services	0.00	0.01	0.01	0.00	0.00	0.01	0.00	-0.01
148 Accomm. and Food Services Industry	0.46	5.74	5.28	4.73	2.95	-0.42	0.03	-2.01

Table A.4A (cont'd)

	1961	1992	Change 1961–92	Change in Export Shares	Change in Employ't /Output Ratio	Due to: Change in Input/ Output Coeff's	Change in Import Coeff's	Residual /Interaction
	Export Employ't as a % of Total Export Employ't	Export Employ't as a % of Total Export Employ't	Export Employ't as a % of Total Export Employ't					
149 Motion Picture and Video Industries	0.05	0.20	0.15	0.10	0.01	0.02	0.01	0.01
150 Other Amusement and Recreat. Serv.	0.03	0.59	0.56	0.56	0.16	-0.06	0.04	-0.14
151 Laundries and Cleaners	0.04	0.09	0.04	0.02	0.02	-0.01	-0.00	0.02
152 Other Personal Services	0.00	0.01	0.01	0.00	0.00	-0.00	0.00	0.00
153 Photographers	0.01	0.03	0.02	0.01	0.02	0.01	0.00	-0.00
154 Misc. Service Industries	0.62	3.02	2.39	-0.02	1.77	1.03	0.07	-0.46

Table A.4B Decomposition of Changes in Employment Shares: 1961 to 1992 – 161 Industries

Sorted by Size of Change	1961	1992	Change 1961–92	Due to:			
	Export Employ't as a % of Total Export Employ't	Export Employ't as a % of Total Export Employ't	Export Employ't as a % of Total Export Employ't	Change in Export Shares	Change in Employ't /Output Ratio	Change in Input/ Output Coeff's	Change in Import Coeff's	Residual /Interaction
148 Accomm. and Food Services Industry	0.46	5.74	5.28	4.73	2.95	-0.42	0.03	-2.01
135 Wholesale Trade Industries	3.63	7.96	4.33	1.37	1.95	0.66	0.11	0.23
142 Other Business Services Industries	0.45	4.60	4.15	2.15	1.68	1.85	0.91	-2.45
078 Motor Vehicle Parts and Accessories	0.37	3.72	3.35	3.47	-0.31	-0.03	-1.06	1.27
143 Professional Business Services	0.94	4.03	3.10	1.98	0.94	1.15	0.18	-1.15
154 Misc. Service Industries	0.62	3.02	2.39	-0.02	1.77	1.03	0.07	-0.46
076 Motor Vehicle Industry	0.11	2.32	2.21	2.26	-1.56	-0.28	0.18	1.59
085 Electronic Equipment Industries	0.40	1.82	1.42	1.58	-1.62	0.09	-0.39	1.75
136 Retail Trade Industries	2.34	3.74	1.40	-0.03	1.22	-0.79	0.03	0.96
137 Banks. Credit Union and Oth. Dep. Inst.	0.46	1.55	1.09	0.15	-0.01	0.80	-0.00	0.16
138 Trust. Other Finance and Real Estate	0.51	1.59	1.09	0.22	0.62	0.25	0.02	-0.03
074 Other Machinery and Equip. Industries	0.65	1.70	1.05	1.05	0.11	-0.12	-0.05	0.05
125 Other Transport and Services to Transport	0.07	1.10	1.03	0.13	0.56	0.66	0.03	-0.35
031 Plastic Products Industries	0.13	0.98	0.84	0.59	0.06	0.21	-0.04	0.03
150 Other Amusement and Recreational Serv.	0.03	0.59	0.56	0.56	0.16	-0.06	0.04	-0.14
070 Machine Shops Industry	0.15	0.69	0.55	0.49	0.16	0.05	-0.16	-0.00
108 Other Manufacturing Industry n.e.c.	0.54	1.04	0.50	0.52	0.12	-0.10	-0.09	0.06
011 Crude Petroleum and Natural Gas	0.60	1.09	0.50	0.47	-0.25	-0.01	0.14	0.14
030 Rubber Products Industries	0.29	0.77	0.48	0.55	0.13	-0.13	-0.15	0.08
118 Air Transport and Incidental Services	0.16	0.62	0.46	0.41	-0.04	0.03	-0.04	0.11
086 Office. Store and Business Machines	0.26	0.71	0.45	0.55	-0.16	-0.07	-0.16	0.29
075 Aircraft and Aircraft Parts Industries	1.17	1.62	0.44	0.56	-0.10	-0.14	0.04	0.09
041 Clothing Industry excl. Hosiery	0.25	0.66	0.41	0.45	0.05	-0.07	-0.01	-0.01
089 Other Elect. and Electronic Products	0.38	0.79	0.40	0.40	0.07	-0.06	-0.16	0.16
013 Services Related to Mineral Extraction	0.16	0.51	0.35	0.04	0.24	0.22	0.06	-0.21
066 Stamped. Pressed and Coated Metals	0.29	0.59	0.31	0.30	0.09	-0.09	-0.07	0.06
055 Printing and Publishing Industries	0.65	0.93	0.29	0.33	-0.01	-0.23	-0.04	0.23
048 Household Furniture Industries	0.04	0.33	0.29	0.30	0.03	-0.03	0.01	-0.02
131 Postal Service Industry	0.26	0.52	0.26	0.17	0.01	0.03	0.01	0.05

Table A.4B (cont'd)

Sorted by Size of Change	1961 Export Employ't as a % of Total Export Employ't	1992 Export Employ't as a % of Total Export Employ't	Change 1961–92 Export Employ't as a % of Total Export Employ't	Due to:				
				Change in Export Shares	Change in Employ't /Output Ratio	Change in Input/ Output Coeff's	Change in Import Coeff's	Residual /Interaction
124 Taxicab Industry	0.15	0.41	0.26	0.17	0.08	0.04	-0.04	0.01
144 Advertising Services	0.18	0.41	0.23	0.01	0.07	0.17	0.01	-0.02
132 Electric Power Systems Industry	0.77	1.00	0.23	-0.33	-0.21	0.39	0.00	0.38
121 Truck Transport Industries	2.92	3.13	0.21	-0.95	-0.56	0.99	0.10	0.64
130 Telecommunication Carriers and Other	0.53	0.74	0.21	0.20	-0.21	0.04	-0.01	0.19
068 Hardware Tool and Cutlery Industries	0.19	0.39	0.20	0.17	0.10	-0.04	-0.02	-0.00
134 Other Utility Industries n.e.c.	0.05	0.25	0.20	-0.00	0.01	0.19	-0.00	0.01
149 Motion Picture and Video Industries	0.05	0.20	0.15	0.10	0.01	0.02	0.01	0.01
002 Fishing and Trapping	1.24	1.38	0.14	-0.64	0.46	-0.14	0.22	0.24
057 Primary Steel Industries	1.10	1.24	0.14	0.30	-0.03	-0.15	-0.19	0.21
049 Office Furniture Industry	0.00	0.14	0.13	0.13	0.00	-0.01	0.01	0.00
145 Educational Services Industries	0.08	0.21	0.13	0.11	0.03	-0.02	0.02	-0.01
077 Truck. Bus Body and Trailer Industries	0.04	0.16	0.12	0.12	0.02	0.01	-0.00	-0.02
071 Other Metal Fabricating Industries	0.28	0.39	0.11	0.15	0.03	-0.08	-0.06	0.07
094 Glass and Glass Products Industries	0.10	0.21	0.11	0.13	-0.02	-0.11	-0.01	0.12
054 Other Converted Paper Prod. Industries	0.15	0.26	0.11	0.11	0.03	-0.08	-0.01	0.05
098 Plastic and Synthetic Resin Industries	0.16	0.26	0.10	0.13	-0.08	0.01	-0.03	0.07
050 Other Furniture and Fixture Industries	0.03	0.13	0.10	0.09	0.03	0.01	0.00	-0.01
073 Commercial Refrigeration Equipment	0.02	0.11	0.09	0.09	0.02	0.03	-0.04	-0.00
103 Chemicals and Chemical Products	0.43	0.52	0.09	0.08	-0.07	0.03	-0.07	0.12
065 Ornamental and Arch. Metal Products	0.06	0.15	0.09	0.08	0.01	0.03	0.00	-0.01
014 Meat and Meat Prod (excl. Poultry)	0.28	0.37	0.09	0.02	0.09	0.00	0.01	0.03
079 Railroad Rolling Stock Industry	0.11	0.20	0.09	0.14	-0.06	-0.02	-0.01	0.03
122 Urban Transit System Industry	0.01	0.10	0.08	0.07	0.05	-0.01	0.00	-0.03
105 Sporting Goods and Toys Industries	0.06	0.15	0.08	0.09	-0.01	-0.02	0.00	0.01
058 Steel Pipe and Tube Industry	0.03	0.11	0.08	0.05	0.04	-0.01	-0.00	0.00
059 Iron Foundries	0.16	0.23	0.08	0.08	-0.05	-0.00	-0.02	0.08
017 Fruit and Vegetable Processing	0.08	0.15	0.07	0.08	-0.01	-0.01	0.01	0.02
081 Misc. Transport. Equip. Industries	0.03	0.11	0.07	0.08	-0.06	-0.00	0.01	0.05

Table A.4B (cont'd)

Sorted by Size of Change	1961 Export Employ't as a % of Total Export Employ't	1992 Export Employ't as a % of Total Export Employ't	Change 1961-92 Export Employ't as a % of Total Export Employ't	Change in Export Shares	Change in Employ't /Output Ratio	Due to: Change in Input/Output Coeff's	Change in Import Coeff's	Residual /Interaction
127 Pipeline Transport Industries	0.11	0.18	0.07	0.01	0.04	-0.01	0.01	0.01
045 Sash. Door and Other Millwork Industries	0.23	0.30	0.07	0.06	0.04	-0.05	0.02	-0.00
056 Plate making. Typesetting and Bindery	0.08	0.15	0.07	0.06	0.02	-0.04	-0.00	0.02
022 Bread and Other Bakery Prod. Industries	0.04	0.11	0.06	0.07	0.00	-0.01	0.00	0.01
025 Soft Drink Industry	0.01	0.07	0.06	0.05	-0.05	0.01	0.00	0.05
102 Toilet Preparations Industry	0.01	0.06	0.06	0.05	0.01	-0.00	-0.00	-0.01
099 Pharmaceutical and Medicine Industry	0.09	0.14	0.05	0.06	-0.04	0.01	0.00	0.03
064 Power Boiler and Struct. Metal Industries	0.19	0.24	0.05	0.07	0.04	-0.10	0.01	0.04
063 Other Metal Rolling. Casting. etc.	0.15	0.20	0.05	-0.02	0.07	-0.05	-0.02	0.07
084 Record Players. Radio and TV Receivers	0.05	0.09	0.05	0.07	-0.03	-0.01	-0.05	0.07
151 Laundries and Cleaners	0.04	0.09	0.04	0.02	0.02	-0.01	-0.00	0.02
123 Interurban and Rural Transit Systems	0.01	0.06	0.04	0.05	-0.01	-0.01	-0.00	0.02
040 Carpet. Mat and Rug Industry	0.00	0.04	0.04	0.04	-0.01	-0.00	-0.00	0.01
038 Misc. Textile Products Industries	0.25	0.29	0.04	0.06	0.05	-0.05	-0.02	0.00
106 Sign and Display Industry	0.05	0.09	0.04	0.03	0.03	-0.03	-0.00	0.01
039 Contract Textile Dyeing and Finishing	0.02	0.06	0.04	0.04	0.01	0.01	-0.01	-0.02
146 Hospitals	0.02	0.05	0.03	0.04	-0.01	-0.01	0.00	0.01
101 Soap and Cleaning Compounds Industry	0.07	0.10	0.03	0.02	0.03	-0.02	-0.01	0.01
047 Other Wood Industries	0.22	0.25	0.03	0.12	-0.15	-0.03	0.02	0.07
107 Floor Tile. Linoleum. Coated Fabrics	0.03	0.06	0.03	0.04	0.00	-0.01	-0.01	0.01
100 Paint and Varnish Industry	0.11	0.13	0.03	0.05	-0.01	-0.00	-0.03	0.02
139 Insurance Industries	0.67	0.70	0.03	0.17	-0.10	-0.11	0.01	0.05
053 Paper Box and Bag Industries	0.27	0.30	0.03	0.06	0.03	-0.11	-0.02	0.06
082 Small Electrical Appliance Industry	0.02	0.05	0.03	0.03	0.01	-0.01	-0.00	0.00
087 Communic.. Energy Wire and Cable	0.13	0.15	0.02	0.03	0.01	-0.03	-0.02	0.03
153 Photographers	0.01	0.03	0.02	0.01	0.02	0.01	0.00	-0.00
015 Poultry Products	0.01	0.04	0.02	0.01	0.01	-0.00	0.00	-0.00
027 Brewery Products Industry	0.04	0.06	0.02	0.02	-0.00	-0.01	0.00	0.00
069 Heating Equipment Industry	0.03	0.05	0.02	0.02	0.01	-0.01	-0.00	0.00
033 Footwear Industry	0.07	0.09	0.02	0.02	0.01	-0.01	-0.01	0.01

Table A.4B (cont'd)

Sorted by Size of Change	1961 Export Employ't as a % of Total Export Employ't	1992 Export Employ't as a % of Total Export Employ't	Change 1961–92 Export Employ't as a % of Total Export Employ't	Due to:				
				Change in Export Shares	Change in Employ't /Output Ratio	Change in Input/ Output Coeff's	Change in Import Coeff's	Residual /Interaction
021 Biscuit Industry	0.02	0.04	0.02	0.02	-0.01	0.00	0.00	0.00
037 Broad Knitted Fabric Industry	0.01	0.03	0.02	0.02	-0.00	0.01	-0.00	-0.00
147 Other Health Services	0.00	0.01	0.01	0.00	0.00	0.01	0.00	-0.01
083 Major Appliances (Elec. and Non-Elec.)	0.08	0.09	0.01	0.02	-0.00	-0.01	-0.01	0.00
152 Other Personal Services	0.00	0.01	0.01	0.00	0.00	-0.00	0.00	0.00
104 Jewelry and Precious Metals Industry	0.14	0.15	0.01	0.01	0.02	-0.02	-0.00	0.00
093 Ready-Mix Concrete Industry	0.01	0.02	0.01	-0.00	0.01	0.00	0.00	0.00
028 Wine Industry	0.00	0.01	0.01	0.01	0.00	-0.00	-0.00	-0.00
052 Asphalt Roofing Industry	0.02	0.02	0.01	0.01	-0.01	-0.01	0.00	0.01
088 Battery Industry	0.03	0.04	0.01	0.01	0.01	-0.01	-0.01	0.01
092 Concrete Products Industry	0.02	0.03	0.00	0.01	0.00	-0.01	0.00	0.00
091 Cement Industry	0.03	0.03	0.00	0.01	0.00	-0.01	0.00	-0.00
117 Construction. Other Activities	0.01	0.02	0.00	0.00	0.01	-0.01	-0.00	0.01
034 Misc. Leather and Allied Prod. Ind	0.04	0.04	0.00	0.01	0.01	-0.00	-0.01	0.00
113 Gas and Oil Facility Construction	0.00	0.00	0.00	0.00	0.00	0.00	0.00	0.00
111 Non-Residential Bldg Construction	0.00	0.00	0.00	0.00	0.00	0.00	0.00	0.00
112 Road. Highway and Airstrip Constr.	0.00	0.00	0.00	0.00	0.00	0.00	0.00	0.00
114 Dams and Irrigation Projects	0.00	0.00	0.00	0.00	0.00	0.00	0.00	0.00
141 Owner Occupied Dwellings	0.00	0.00	0.00	0.00	0.00	0.00	0.00	0.00
116 Other Engineering Construction	0.00	0.00	0.00	0.00	0.00	0.00	0.00	0.00
115 Railway and Telephone Teleg. Constr.	0.00	0.00	0.00	0.00	0.00	0.00	0.00	0.00
110 Residential Construction	0.00	0.00	0.00	0.00	0.00	0.00	0.00	0.00
140 Govt. Royalties on Nat. Resources	0.00	0.00	0.00	0.00	0.00	0.00	0.00	0.00
096 Refined Petroleum and Coal Products	0.21	0.21	-0.00	0.05	-0.10	-0.00	-0.00	0.05
067 Wire and Wire Products Industries	0.31	0.30	-0.00	0.16	0.04	-0.23	-0.07	0.09
023 Cane and Beer Sugar Industry	0.02	0.01	-0.00	0.00	0.00	-0.01	0.00	0.00
126 Highway and Bridge Maintenance Ind.	0.01	0.01	-0.01	-0.00	-0.00	-0.00	0.00	0.00
020 Vegetable Oil Mills (excluding Corn)	0.03	0.02	-0.01	-0.01	-0.00	-0.00	0.00	0.00
042 Hosiery Industry	0.02	0.01	-0.01	-0.01	0.00	-0.00	0.00	0.00
133 Gas Distribution Systems Industry	0.12	0.10	-0.02	-0.00	-0.05	0.01	0.00	0.02

Table A.4B (cont'd)

Sorted by Size of Change	1961 Export Employ't as a % of Total Export Employ't	1992 Export Employ't as a % of Total Export Employ't	Change 1961–92 Export Employ't as a % of Total Export Employ't	Due to:				
				Change in Export Shares	Change in Employ't/Output Ratio	Change in Input/Output Coeff's	Change in Import Coeff's	Residual/Interaction
009 Salt Mines	0.04	0.02	-0.02	-0.01	-0.00	-0.01	0.00	-0.00
008 Non-Metal excl. Coal and Asbestos	0.28	0.25	-0.03	0.01	-0.26	-0.00	0.05	0.17
012 Quarries and Sand Pits	0.13	0.09	-0.04	-0.06	0.00	-0.01	0.00	0.03
061 Alum. Rolling, Casting and Extruding	0.24	0.20	-0.04	0.04	-0.13	0.03	-0.08	0.10
046 Wooden Box and Coffin Industries	0.10	0.06	-0.04	-0.01	-0.01	-0.01	-0.01	-0.00
062 Copper Rolling, Casting and Extruding	0.11	0.07	-0.04	-0.07	0.03	-0.06	-0.04	0.10
090 Clay Products Industries	0.06	0.01	-0.05	-0.02	-0.00	-0.01	-0.00	-0.01
036 Wool Yarn and Woven Cloth Industry	0.14	0.07	-0.07	-0.03	0.00	-0.04	-0.02	0.02
032 Leather Tanneries	0.09	0.02	-0.07	-0.07	0.00	0.00	-0.02	0.02
029 Tobacco Products Industries	0.13	0.06	-0.07	-0.02	-0.03	-0.01	0.00	-0.02
018 Dairy Products	0.17	0.09	-0.08	-0.05	-0.02	-0.01	0.00	-0.00
095 Non-Metallic Mineral Products n.e.c.	0.38	0.27	-0.11	-0.08	0.00	-0.06	-0.03	0.06
080 Shipbuilding and Repair Industry	0.25	0.11	-0.14	-0.14	-0.02	-0.00	0.01	0.01
035 Man-Made Fibre Yarn and Woven Cloth	0.51	0.34	-0.17	0.05	-0.05	-0.14	-0.06	0.03
019 Feed Industry	0.34	0.16	-0.18	-0.16	-0.00	-0.01	-0.01	0.00
024 Miscellaneous Food Industries	0.53	0.34	-0.19	-0.20	0.04	-0.06	-0.01	0.01
044 Veneer and Plywood Industries	0.36	0.16	-0.20	-0.17	-0.02	-0.03	0.01	0.01
129 Telecomm. Broadcasting Industry	0.42	0.21	-0.20	-0.08	-0.19	0.05	-0.00	0.01
026 Distillery Products Industry	0.31	0.09	-0.22	-0.25	0.01	-0.01	0.01	0.02
016 Fish Products Industry	1.11	0.87	-0.25	-0.31	0.07	-0.08	0.05	0.04
010 Coal Mines	0.52	0.25	-0.27	0.18	-0.89	-0.05	0.01	0.47
128 Storage and Warehousing Industries	0.78	0.49	-0.29	-0.56	0.17	-0.19	0.03	0.26
097 Industrial Chemicals Industries n.e.c.	1.05	0.63	-0.42	-0.09	-0.37	0.03	-0.05	0.05
072 Agricultural Implement Industry	0.72	0.21	-0.51	-0.57	0.02	-0.04	0.02	0.06
006 Iron Mines	0.79	0.22	-0.58	-0.48	-0.04	-0.03	0.03	-0.06
007 Asbestos Mines	0.72	0.10	-0.62	-1.06	0.04	-0.02	0.01	0.41
109 Repair Construction	2.11	1.28	-0.83	-0.41	-0.19	-0.43	0.02	0.19
004 Gold Mines	1.81	0.35	-1.46	-0.31	-0.64	-0.02	0.02	-0.50
120 Water Transport and Related Services	2.10	0.62	-1.48	-0.79	-0.18	-0.23	0.03	-0.30
043 Sawmills, Planing and Shingle Mills	3.85	1.99	-1.86	-0.98	-0.98	-0.08	0.17	0.02

Table A.4B (cont'd)

Sorted by Size of Change	1961	1992	Change 1961–92		Due to:			
	Export Employ't as a % of Total Export Employ't	Export Employ't as a % of Total Export Employ't	Export Employ't as a % of Total Export Employ't	Change in Export Shares	Change in Employ't /Output Ratio	Change in Input/ Output Coeff's	Change in Import Coeff's	Residual /Interaction
060 Non-Ferrous Smelting and Refining	3.18	1.20	-1.98	-1.79	-0.04	-0.10	-0.02	-0.03
005 Other Metal Mines	3.35	0.87	-2.48	-1.31	-0.14	-0.26	-0.05	-0.72
051 Pulp and Paper Industries	5.92	2.64	-3.27	-3.27	0.02	-0.33	0.14	0.17
119 Railway and Transport and Rel. Services	5.07	1.30	-3.77	-0.66	-0.37	-1.80	0.01	-0.94
003 Logging and Forestry	5.55	1.77	-3.78	-1.36	-1.17	-0.21	0.11	-1.15
001 Agriculture and Related	26.93	8.69	-18.24	-13.16	-3.23	-0.30	0.55	-2.09

APPENDIX 5
THE CHANGING INDUSTRIAL MIX OF IMPORTS
161-INDUSTRY AGGREGATION

Tables A.5A and A.5B show the detailed results behind the aggregates in Tables 13A and 13B in Section 5.3, using the full 161-industry calculations. In these tables the years 1961 and 1992 are shown, representing the span of our complete I/O data. In Table A5.A industries are listed in standard or numerical order from primary production through manufacturing and services. In Table A.5B the sectors are sorted from largest increase in export employment shares to largest decrease.

Those industries showing the largest increase in share of import employment are predominantly services of different types, including Accommodation and food services, Business and professional services, Wholesale trade, and Banking and other finance. Much the same sectors are also near the top of the list for exports (see Table A.3B). Motor vehicle parts and accessories is also near the top of the list, as imports of this sector have increased massively since 1961 under integration of the North American auto industry, with Canada primarily importing parts and exporting finished vehicles. Clothing, plastic products, Business machines and Electronic equipment also have increased significantly their share of employment "replaced" by imports.

At the bottom of the table are the sectors which have seen the largest declines in share of import employment. As can be seen, these include primary production sectors like Agriculture, and Coal mines, some manufactures like Agricultural implements, and Aircraft and parts, and particular services like Rail and water transport.

Finally, this appendix also presents the 161-industry decompositions of changes in employment shares attributable to imports from 1961 to 1992 in Tables A.6A and A.6B. Table A.6A presents the decomposition from 1961 through 1992 in numerical order while Table A.6B presents the same data sorted from largest positive to largest negative change.

Table A.5A Employment Shares: 1961 to 1992 – 161 Industries

	1961		1992		Change 1961–92	
	Import Employment as a % of Total Import Employment	Employment as a % of Total Employment	Import Employment as a % of Total Import Employment	Employment as a % of Total Employment	Import Employment as a % of Total Import Employment	Employment as a % of Total Employment
001 Agriculture and Related	12.42	2.04	4.77	1.24	-7.64	-0.80
002 Fishing and Trapping	0.44	0.07	0.36	0.09	-0.08	0.02
003 Logging and Forestry	1.06	0.17	0.38	0.10	-0.69	-0.08
004 Gold Mines	0.13	0.02	0.13	0.03	-0.00	0.01
005 Other Metal Mines	0.58	0.10	0.28	0.07	-0.30	-0.02
006 Iron Mines	0.39	0.06	0.10	0.03	-0.29	-0.04
007 Asbestos Mines	0.03	0.00	0.00	0.00	-0.03	-0.00
008 Non-Metal excl. Coal and Asbestos	0.41	0.07	0.10	0.03	-0.30	-0.04
009 Salt Mines	0.02	0.00	0.02	0.00	-0.01	0.00
010 Coal Mines	3.23	0.53	0.19	0.05	-3.04	-0.48
011 Crude Petroleum and Natural Gas	1.12	0.18	0.57	0.15	-0.56	-0.04
012 Quarries and Sand Pits	0.23	0.04	0.09	0.02	-0.14	-0.01
013 Services Related to Mineral Extraction	0.15	0.03	0.27	0.07	0.12	0.04
014 Meat and Meat Prod (excl. Poultry)	0.31	0.05	0.31	0.08	0.00	0.03
015 Poultry Products	0.04	0.01	0.08	0.02	0.04	0.01
016 Fish Products Industry	0.22	0.04	0.34	0.09	0.12	0.05
017 Fruit and Vegetable Processing	0.70	0.11	0.30	0.08	-0.40	-0.04
018 Dairy Products	0.12	0.02	0.12	0.03	-0.00	0.01
019 Feed Industry	0.16	0.03	0.13	0.03	-0.03	0.01
020 Vegetable Oil Mills (excluding Corn)	0.06	0.01	0.02	0.00	-0.04	-0.00
021 Biscuit Industry	0.10	0.02	0.05	0.01	-0.04	-0.00
022 Bread and Other Bakery Prod. Industries	0.04	0.01	0.11	0.03	0.07	0.02
023 Cane and Beer Sugar Industry	0.05	0.01	0.02	0.01	-0.03	-0.00
024 Miscellaneous Food Industries	0.70	0.12	0.50	0.13	-0.21	0.01
025 Soft Drink Industry	0.04	0.01	0.04	0.01	0.01	0.01
026 Distillery Products Industry	0.18	0.03	0.07	0.02	-0.11	-0.01
027 Brewery Products Industry	0.02	0.00	0.04	0.01	0.03	0.01
028 Wine Industry	0.05	0.01	0.09	0.02	0.04	0.02
029 Tobacco Products Industries	0.05	0.01	0.11	0.03	0.06	0.02
030 Rubber Products Industries	0.77	0.13	0.81	0.21	0.04	0.08
031 Plastic Products Industries	0.67	0.11	1.51	0.39	0.84	0.28

Table A.5A (cont'd)

	1961		1992		Change 1961–92	
	Import as a % of Total Import Employment	Employment as a % of Total Employment	Import as a % of Total Import Employment	Employment as a % of Total Employment	Import as a % of Total Import Employment	Employment as a % of Total Employment
032 Leather Tanneries	0.14	0.02	0.11	0.03	-0.03	0.00
033 Footwear Industry	0.45	0.07	0.79	0.21	0.34	0.13
034 Misc. Leather and Allied Prod. Ind	0.28	0.05	0.25	0.07	-0.03	0.02
035 Man-Made Fibre Yarn and Woven Cloth	3.14	0.52	0.76	0.20	-2.38	-0.32
036 Wool Yarn and Woven Cloth Industry	0.59	0.10	0.16	0.04	-0.43	-0.06
037 Broad Knitted Fabric Industry	0.24	0.04	0.11	0.03	-0.13	-0.01
038 Misc. Textile Products Industries	1.26	0.21	0.69	0.18	-0.57	-0.03
039 Contract Textile Dyeing and Finishing	0.11	0.02	0.15	0.04	0.04	0.02
040 Carpet. Mat and Rug Industry	0.09	0.01	0.11	0.03	0.02	0.01
041 Clothing Industry excl. Hosiery	1.53	0.25	2.71	0.70	1.18	0.45
042 Hosiery Industry	0.06	0.01	0.05	0.01	-0.00	0.00
043 Sawmills. Planing and Shingle Mills	0.65	0.11	0.24	0.06	-0.41	-0.04
044 Veneer and Plywood Industries	0.21	0.04	0.07	0.02	-0.14	-0.02
045 Sash. Door and Other Millwork Industries	0.10	0.02	0.21	0.06	0.11	0.04
046 Wooden Box and Coffin Industries	0.11	0.02	0.07	0.02	-0.04	-0.00
047 Other Wood Industries	0.15	0.03	0.06	0.02	-0.09	-0.01
048 Household Furniture Industries	0.33	0.06	0.58	0.15	0.24	0.10
049 Office Furniture Industry	0.06	0.01	0.07	0.02	0.02	0.01
050 Other Furniture and Fixture Industries	0.16	0.03	0.25	0.07	0.09	0.04
051 Pulp and Paper Industries	0.86	0.14	0.58	0.15	-0.28	0.01
052 Asphalt Roofing Industry	0.04	0.01	0.01	0.00	-0.02	-0.00
053 Paper Box and Bag Industries	0.51	0.08	0.36	0.09	-0.15	0.01
054 Other Converted Paper Prod. Industries	0.34	0.06	0.33	0.09	-0.01	0.03
055 Printing and Publishing Industries	2.35	0.39	1.94	0.51	-0.41	0.12
056 Plate making. Typesetting and Bindery	0.35	0.06	0.33	0.09	-0.02	0.03
057 Primary Steel Industries	2.44	0.40	1.48	0.39	-0.95	-0.01
058 Steel Pipe and Tube Industry	0.18	0.03	0.14	0.04	-0.04	0.01
059 Iron Foundries	0.58	0.10	0.36	0.09	-0.23	-0.00
060 Non-Ferrous Smelting and Refining	0.67	0.11	0.42	0.11	-0.25	-0.00
061 Alum. Rolling. Casting and Extruding	0.30	0.05	0.23	0.06	-0.07	0.01
062 Copper Rolling. Casting and Extruding	0.16	0.03	0.11	0.03	-0.05	0.00

Table A.5A (cont'd)

	1961		1992		Change 1961–92	
	Import Employment as a % of Total Import Employment	Import % of Total Employment	Import Employment as a % of Total Import Employment	Import % of Total Employment	Import % of Total Import Employment	Import % of Total Employment
063 Other Metal Rolling, Casting, etc.	0.21	0.03	0.18	0.05	-0.03	0.01
064 Power Boiler and Struct. Metal Industries	0.69	0.11	0.26	0.07	-0.43	-0.05
065 Ornamental and Arch. Metal Products	0.19	0.03	0.17	0.04	-0.02	0.01
066 Stamped. Pressed and Coated Metals	1.19	0.20	0.83	0.22	-0.36	0.02
067 Wire and Wire Products Industries	0.75	0.12	0.44	0.11	-0.30	-0.01
068 Hardware Tool and Cutlery Industries	0.95	0.16	0.94	0.25	-0.01	0.09
069 Heating Equipment Industry	0.19	0.03	0.12	0.03	-0.07	0.00
070 Machine Shops Industry	0.72	0.12	1.01	0.26	0.29	0.14
071 Other Metal Fabricating Industries	1.28	0.21	0.71	0.18	-0.57	-0.03
072 Agricultural Implement Industry	2.01	0.33	0.42	0.11	-1.58	-0.22
073 Commercial Refrigeration Equipment	0.18	0.03	0.30	0.08	0.11	0.05
074 Other Machinery and Equip. Industries	4.12	0.68	3.36	0.87	-0.76	0.20
075 Aircraft and Aircraft Parts Industries	2.34	0.38	0.96	0.25	-1.38	-0.14
076 Motor Vehicle Industry	0.91	0.15	1.14	0.30	0.23	0.15
077 Truck. Bus Body and Trailer Industries	0.21	0.03	0.33	0.09	0.12	0.05
078 Motor Vehicle Parts and Accessories	3.55	0.58	5.34	1.39	1.80	0.81
079 Railroad Rolling Stock Industry	0.18	0.03	0.17	0.04	-0.01	0.02
080 Shipbuilding and Repair Industry	0.46	0.08	0.11	0.03	-0.35	-0.05
081 Misc. Transport. Equip. Industries	0.17	0.03	0.15	0.04	-0.02	0.01
082 Small Electrical Appliance Industry	0.26	0.04	0.29	0.08	0.03	0.03
083 Major Appliances (Elec. and Non-Elec.)	0.73	0.12	0.33	0.09	-0.40	-0.03
084 Record Players. Radio and TV Receivers	0.34	0.06	0.39	0.10	0.04	0.04
085 Electronic Equipment Industries	1.89	0.31	2.51	0.65	0.63	0.34
086 Office. Store and Business Machines	0.74	0.12	1.64	0.43	0.90	0.30
087 Communic.. Energy Wire and Cable	0.19	0.03	0.18	0.05	-0.01	0.02
088 Battery Industry	0.07	0.01	0.08	0.02	0.01	0.01
089 Other Elect. and Electronic Products	1.80	0.30	1.69	0.44	-0.11	0.14
090 Clay Products Industries	0.53	0.09	0.19	0.05	-0.34	-0.04
091 Cement Industry	0.02	0.00	0.02	0.00	-0.01	0.00
092 Concrete Products Industry	0.04	0.01	0.02	0.01	-0.02	-0.00
093 Ready-Mix Concrete Industry	0.01	0.00	0.01	0.00	0.00	0.00

Table A.5A (cont'd)

	1961		1992		Change 1961–92	
	Import Employment as a % of Total Import Employment	Import as a % of Total Employment	Import Employment as a % of Total Import Employment	Import as a % of Total Employment	Import Employment as a % of Total Import Employment	Import as a % of Total Employment
094 Glass and Glass Products Industries	0.92	0.15	0.40	0.11	-0.52	-0.05
095 Non-Metallic Mineral Products n.e.c.	0.57	0.09	0.32	0.08	-0.25	-0.01
096 Refined Petroleum and Coal Products	0.29	0.05	0.16	0.04	-0.13	-0.01
097 Industrial Chemicals Industries n.e.c.	1.22	0.20	0.62	0.16	-0.61	-0.04
098 Plastic and Synthetic Resin Industries	0.39	0.06	0.33	0.09	-0.05	0.02
099 Pharmaceutical and Medicine Industry	0.29	0.05	0.39	0.10	0.10	0.05
100 Paint and Varnish Industry	0.21	0.03	0.20	0.05	-0.01	0.02
101 Soap and Cleaning Compounds Industry	0.16	0.03	0.18	0.05	0.03	0.02
102 Toilet Preparations Industry	0.03	0.01	0.18	0.05	0.15	0.04
103 Chemicals and Chemical Products	0.92	0.15	0.67	0.17	-0.24	0.02
104 Jewelry and Precious Metals Industry	0.38	0.06	0.31	0.08	-0.06	0.02
105 Sporting Goods and Toys Industries	0.50	0.08	0.67	0.17	0.17	0.09
106 Sign and Display Industry	0.10	0.02	0.14	0.04	0.03	0.02
107 Floor Tile. Linoleum. Coated Fabrics	0.22	0.04	0.11	0.03	-0.11	-0.01
108 Other Manufacturing Industry n.e.c.	2.74	0.45	2.58	0.67	-0.16	0.22
109 Repair Construction	1.46	0.24	0.89	0.23	-0.57	-0.01
110 Residential Construction	0.00	0.00	0.00	0.00	0.00	0.00
111 Non-Residential Bldg Construction	0.00	0.00	0.00	0.00	0.00	0.00
112 Road. Highway and Airstrip Constr.	0.00	0.00	0.00	0.00	0.00	0.00
113 Gas and Oil Facility Construction	0.00	0.00	0.00	0.00	0.00	0.00
114 Dams and Irrigation Projects	0.00	0.00	0.00	0.00	0.00	0.00
115 Railway and Telephone Teleg. Constr.	0.00	0.00	0.00	0.00	0.00	0.00
116 Other Engineering Construction	0.00	0.00	0.00	0.00	0.00	0.00
117 Construction. Other Activities	0.01	0.00	0.02	0.00	0.01	0.00
118 Air Transport and Incidental Services	0.23	0.04	0.80	0.21	0.57	0.17
119 Railway and Transport and Rel. Services	1.63	0.27	0.48	0.13	-1.14	-0.14
120 Water Transport and Related Services	1.00	0.17	0.30	0.08	-0.70	-0.09
121 Truck Transport Industries	1.22	0.20	1.10	0.29	-0.12	0.09
122 Urban Transit System Industry	0.02	0.00	0.18	0.05	0.16	0.04
123 Interurban and Rural Transit Systems	0.02	0.00	0.09	0.02	0.07	0.02
124 Taxicab Industry	0.26	0.04	0.61	0.16	0.35	0.12

Table A.5A (cont'd)	1961		1992		Change 1961–92	
	Import Employment as a % of Total Import Employment	Import % of Total Employment	Import Employment as a % of Total Import Employment	Import % of Total Employment	Import Employment as a % of Total Import Employment	Import % of Total Employment
125 Other Transport and Services to Transport	0.04	0.01	0.51	0.13	0.47	0.13
126 Highway and Bridge Maintenance Ind.	0.01	0.00	0.00	0.00	-0.00	-0.00
127 Pipeline Transport Industries	0.08	0.01	0.07	0.02	-0.01	0.01
128 Storage and Warehousing Industries	0.17	0.03	0.11	0.03	-0.06	0.00
129 Telecomm. Broadcasting Industry	0.27	0.04	0.27	0.07	-0.00	0.02
130 Telecommunication Carriers and Other	0.72	0.12	0.77	0.20	0.06	0.08
131 Postal Service Industry	0.38	0.06	0.45	0.12	0.07	0.05
132 Electric Power Systems Industry	0.52	0.08	0.64	0.17	0.13	0.08
133 Gas Distribution Systems Industry	0.13	0.02	0.08	0.02	-0.06	-0.00
134 Other Utility Industries n.e.c.	0.05	0.01	0.23	0.06	0.18	0.05
135 Wholesale Trade Industries	3.26	0.54	5.08	1.32	1.83	0.79
136 Retail Trade Industries	2.59	0.43	3.14	0.82	0.55	0.39
137 Banks. Credit Union and Oth. Dep. Inst.	0.73	0.12	1.83	0.48	1.11	0.36
138 Trust. Other Finance and Real Estate	0.79	0.13	1.83	0.47	1.04	0.34
139 Insurance Industries	0.51	0.08	0.62	0.16	0.11	0.08
140 Govt. Royalties on Nat. Resources	0.00	0.00	0.00	0.00	0.00	0.00
141 Owner Occupied Dwellings	0.00	0.00	0.00	0.00	0.00	0.00
142 Other Business Services Industries	1.19	0.20	5.23	1.36	4.04	1.16
143 Professional Business Services	1.70	0.28	3.65	0.95	1.95	0.67
144 Advertising Services	0.24	0.04	0.56	0.15	0.32	0.11
145 Educational Services Industries	0.04	0.01	0.12	0.03	0.08	0.02
146 Hospitals	0.03	0.01	0.08	0.02	0.04	0.01
147 Other Health Services	0.00	0.00	0.04	0.01	0.04	0.01
148 Accomm. and Food Services Industry	0.75	0.12	8.89	2.31	8.14	2.19
149 Motion Picture and Video Industries	0.25	0.04	0.24	0.06	-0.01	0.02
150 Other Amusement and Recreational Serv.	0.03	0.00	0.89	0.23	0.87	0.23
151 Laundries and Cleaners	0.06	0.01	0.10	0.03	0.04	0.02
152 Other Personal Services	0.00	0.00	0.01	0.00	0.01	0.00
153 Photographers	0.01	0.00	0.04	0.01	0.02	0.01
154 Misc. Service Industries	0.80	0.13	2.80	0.73	2.00	0.60
TOTAL	100.00	16.44	100.00	25.99	0.00	9.55

Table A.5B Employment Shares: 1961 to 1992 – 161 Industries – Sorted by Size of Change

	1961		1992		Change 1961–92	
	Import Employment as a % of Total Import Employment	Import Employment as a % of Total Employment	Import Employment as a % of Total Import Employment	Import Employment as a % of Total Employment	Import Employment as a % of Total Import Employment	Import Employment as a % of Total Employment
148 Accomm. and Food Services Industry	0.75	0.12	8.89	2.31	8.14	2.19
142 Other Business Services Industries	1.19	0.20	5.23	1.36	4.04	1.16
154 Misc. Service Industries	0.80	0.13	2.80	0.73	2.00	0.60
143 Professional Business Services	1.70	0.28	3.65	0.95	1.95	0.67
135 Wholesale Trade Industries	3.26	0.54	5.08	1.32	1.83	0.79
078 Motor Vehicle Parts and Accessories	3.55	0.58	5.34	1.39	1.80	0.81
041 Clothing Industry excl. Hosiery	1.53	0.25	2.71	0.70	1.18	0.45
137 Banks. Credit Union and Oth. Dep. Inst.	0.73	0.12	1.83	0.48	1.11	0.36
138 Trust. Other Finance and Real Estate	0.79	0.13	1.83	0.47	1.04	0.34
086 Office. Store and Business Machines	0.74	0.12	1.64	0.43	0.90	0.30
150 Other Amusement and Recreational Serv.	0.03	0.00	0.89	0.23	0.87	0.23
031 Plastic Products Industries	0.67	0.11	1.51	0.39	0.84	0.28
085 Electronic Equipment Industries	1.89	0.31	2.51	0.65	0.63	0.34
118 Air Transport and Incidental Services	0.23	0.04	0.80	0.21	0.57	0.17
136 Retail Trade Industries	2.59	0.43	3.14	0.82	0.55	0.39
125 Other Transport and Services to Transport	0.04	0.01	0.51	0.13	0.47	0.13
124 Taxicab Industry	0.26	0.04	0.61	0.16	0.35	0.12
033 Footwear Industry	0.45	0.07	0.79	0.21	0.34	0.13
144 Advertising Services	0.24	0.04	0.56	0.15	0.32	0.11
070 Machine Shops Industry	0.72	0.12	1.01	0.26	0.29	0.14
048 Household Furniture Industries	0.33	0.06	0.58	0.15	0.24	0.10
076 Motor Vehicle Industry	0.91	0.15	1.14	0.30	0.23	0.15
134 Other Utility Industries n.e.c.	0.05	0.01	0.23	0.06	0.18	0.05
105 Sporting Goods and Toys Industries	0.50	0.08	0.67	0.17	0.17	0.09
122 Urban Transit System Industry	0.02	0.00	0.18	0.05	0.16	0.04
102 Toilet Preparations Industry	0.03	0.01	0.18	0.05	0.15	0.04
132 Electric Power Systems Industry	0.52	0.08	0.64	0.17	0.13	0.04
077 Truck. Bus Body and Trailer Industries	0.21	0.03	0.33	0.09	0.12	0.08
016 Fish Products Industry	0.22	0.04	0.34	0.09	0.12	0.05
013 Services Related to Mineral Extraction	0.15	0.03	0.27	0.07	0.12	0.05
045 Sash. Door and Other Millwork Industries	0.10	0.02	0.21	0.06	0.11	0.04

Table A.5B (cont'd)

	1961		1992		Change 1961–92	
	Import Employment as a % of Total Import Employment	Import Employment as a % of Total Employment	Import Employment as a % of Total Import Employment	Import Employment as a % of Total Employment	Import Employment as a % of Total Import Employment	Import Employment as a % of Total Employment
073 Commercial Refrigeration Equipment	0.18	0.03	0.30	0.08	0.11	0.05
139 Insurance Industries	0.51	0.08	0.62	0.16	0.11	0.08
099 Pharmaceutical and Medicine Industry	0.29	0.05	0.39	0.10	0.10	0.05
050 Other Furniture and Fixture Industries	0.16	0.03	0.25	0.07	0.09	0.04
145 Educational Services Industries	0.04	0.01	0.12	0.03	0.08	0.02
131 Postal Service Industry	0.38	0.06	0.45	0.12	0.07	0.05
022 Bread and Other Bakery Prod. Industries	0.04	0.01	0.11	0.03	0.07	0.02
123 Interurban and Rural Transit Systems	0.02	0.00	0.09	0.02	0.07	0.02
130 Telecommunication Carriers and Other	0.72	0.12	0.77	0.20	0.06	0.08
029 Tobacco Products Industries	0.05	0.01	0.11	0.03	0.06	0.02
084 Record Players. Radio and TV Receivers	0.34	0.06	0.39	0.10	0.04	0.04
151 Laundries and Cleaners	0.06	0.01	0.10	0.03	0.04	0.02
039 Contract Textile Dyeing and Finishing	0.11	0.02	0.15	0.04	0.04	0.02
146 Hospitals	0.03	0.01	0.08	0.02	0.04	0.01
028 Wine Industry	0.05	0.01	0.09	0.02	0.04	0.02
147 Other Health Services	0.00	0.00	0.04	0.01	0.04	0.01
030 Rubber Products Industries	0.77	0.13	0.81	0.21	0.04	0.08
015 Poultry Products	0.04	0.01	0.08	0.02	0.04	0.01
106 Sign and Display Industry	0.10	0.02	0.14	0.04	0.03	0.02
082 Small Electrical Appliance Industry	0.26	0.04	0.29	0.08	0.03	0.03
101 Soap and Cleaning Compounds Industry	0.16	0.03	0.18	0.05	0.03	0.02
027 Brewery Products Industry	0.02	0.00	0.04	0.01	0.03	0.01
153 Photographers	0.01	0.00	0.04	0.01	0.02	0.01
040 Carpet. Mat and Rug Industry	0.09	0.01	0.11	0.03	0.02	0.01
049 Office Furniture Industry	0.06	0.01	0.07	0.02	0.02	0.01
088 Battery Industry	0.07	0.01	0.08	0.02	0.01	0.01
152 Other Personal Services	0.00	0.00	0.01	0.00	0.01	0.00
025 Soft Drink Industry	0.04	0.01	0.04	0.01	0.01	0.01
117 Construction. Other Activities	0.01	0.00	0.02	0.00	0.01	0.00
093 Ready-Mix Concrete Industry	0.01	0.00	0.01	0.00	0.00	0.00
014 Meat and Meat Prod (excl. Poultry)	0.31	0.05	0.31	0.08	0.00	0.03

Table A.5B (cont'd)

	1961		1992		Change 1961–92	
	Import Employment as a % of Total Import Employment	Import Employment as a % of Total Employment	Import Employment as a % of Total Import Employment	Import Employment as a % of Total Employment	Import Employment as a % of Total Import Employment	Import Employment as a % of Total Employment
111 Non-Residential Bldg Construction	0.00	0.00	0.00	0.00	0.00	0.00
110 Residential Construction	0.00	0.00	0.00	0.00	0.00	0.00
140 Govt. Royalties on Nat. Resources	0.00	0.00	0.00	0.00	0.00	0.00
116 Other Engineering Construction	0.00	0.00	0.00	0.00	0.00	0.00
141 Owner Occupied Dwellings	0.00	0.00	0.00	0.00	0.00	0.00
115 Railway and Telephone Teleg. Constr.	0.00	0.00	0.00	0.00	0.00	0.00
112 Road, Highway and Airstrip Constr.	0.00	0.00	0.00	0.00	0.00	0.00
113 Gas and Oil Facility Construction	0.00	0.00	0.00	0.00	0.00	0.00
114 Dams and Irrigation Projects	0.00	0.00	0.00	0.00	0.00	0.00
018 Dairy Products	0.12	0.02	0.12	0.03	-0.00	0.01
042 Hosiery Industry	0.06	0.01	0.05	0.01	-0.00	0.00
126 Highway and Bridge Maintenance Industries	0.01	0.00	0.00	0.00	-0.00	-0.00
129 Telecomm. Broadcasting Industry	0.27	0.04	0.27	0.07	-0.00	0.02
004 Gold Mines	0.13	0.02	0.13	0.03	-0.00	0.01
068 Hardware Tool and Cutlery Industries	0.95	0.16	0.94	0.25	-0.00	0.09
091 Cement Industry	0.02	0.00	0.02	0.00	-0.01	0.00
079 Railroad Rolling Stock Industry	0.18	0.03	0.17	0.04	-0.01	0.02
149 Motion Picture and Video Industries	0.25	0.04	0.24	0.06	-0.01	0.02
087 Communic.. Energy Wire and Cable	0.19	0.03	0.18	0.05	-0.01	0.02
127 Pipeline Transport Industries	0.08	0.01	0.07	0.02	-0.01	0.01
009 Salt Mines	0.02	0.00	0.02	0.00	-0.01	0.00
054 Other Converted Paper Prod. Industries	0.34	0.06	0.33	0.09	-0.01	0.03
100 Paint and Varnish Industry	0.21	0.03	0.20	0.05	-0.01	0.02
065 Ornamental and Arch. Metal Products	0.19	0.03	0.17	0.04	-0.02	0.01
092 Concrete Products Industry	0.04	0.01	0.02	0.01	-0.02	-0.00
056 Plate making, Typesetting and Bindery	0.35	0.06	0.33	0.09	-0.02	0.03
081 Misc. Transport. Equip. Industries	0.17	0.03	0.15	0.04	-0.02	0.01
052 Asphalt Roofing Industry	0.04	0.01	0.01	0.00	-0.02	-0.00
023 Cane and Beer Sugar Industry	0.05	0.01	0.02	0.01	-0.03	-0.00
007 Asbestos Mines	0.03	0.00	0.00	0.00	-0.03	-0.00
034 Misc. Leather and Allied Prod. Ind.	0.28	0.05	0.25	0.07	-0.03	0.02

Table A.5B (cont'd)

	1961		1992		Change 1961–92	
	Import Employment as a % of Total Import Employment	Import Employment as a % of Total Employment	Import Employment as a % of Total Import Employment	Import Employment as a % of Total Employment	Import Employment as a % of Total Import Employment	Import Employment as a % of Total Employment
019 Feed Industry	0.16	0.03	0.13	0.03	-0.03	0.01
032 Leather Tanneries	0.14	0.02	0.11	0.03	-0.03	0.00
063 Other Metal Rolling, Casting, etc.	0.21	0.03	0.18	0.05	-0.03	0.01
020 Vegetable Oil Mills (excluding Corn)	0.06	0.01	0.02	0.00	-0.04	-0.00
058 Steel Pipe and Tube Industry	0.18	0.03	0.14	0.04	-0.04	0.01
046 Wooden Box and Coffin Industries	0.11	0.02	0.07	0.02	-0.04	-0.00
021 Biscuit Industry	0.10	0.02	0.05	0.01	-0.04	-0.00
062 Copper Rolling, Casting and Extruding	0.16	0.03	0.11	0.03	-0.05	0.00
098 Plastic and Synthetic Resin Industries	0.39	0.06	0.33	0.09	-0.05	0.02
133 Gas Distribution Systems Industry	0.13	0.02	0.08	0.02	-0.06	-0.00
128 Storage and Warehousing Industries	0.17	0.03	0.11	0.03	-0.06	0.00
104 Jewelry and Precious Metals Industry	0.38	0.06	0.31	0.08	-0.06	0.02
069 Heating Equipment Industry	0.19	0.03	0.12	0.03	-0.07	0.00
061 Alum. Rolling, Casting and Extruding	0.30	0.05	0.23	0.06	-0.07	0.01
002 Fishing and Trapping	0.44	0.07	0.36	0.09	-0.08	0.02
047 Other Wood Industries	0.15	0.03	0.06	0.02	-0.09	-0.01
089 Other Elect. and Electronic Products	1.80	0.30	1.69	0.44	-0.11	0.14
107 Floor Tile, Linoleum, Coated Fabrics	0.22	0.04	0.11	0.03	-0.11	-0.01
026 Distillery Products Industry	0.18	0.03	0.07	0.02	-0.11	-0.01
121 Truck Transport Industries	1.22	0.20	1.10	0.29	-0.12	0.09
037 Broad Knitted Fabric Industry	0.24	0.04	0.11	0.03	-0.13	-0.01
096 Refined Petroleum and Coal Products	0.29	0.05	0.16	0.04	-0.13	-0.01
012 Quarries and Sand Pits	0.23	0.04	0.09	0.02	-0.14	-0.01
044 Veneer and Plywood Industries	0.21	0.04	0.07	0.02	-0.14	-0.02
053 Paper Box and Bag Industries	0.51	0.08	0.36	0.09	-0.15	0.01
108 Other Manufacturing Industry n.e.c.	2.74	0.45	2.58	0.67	-0.16	0.22
024 Miscellaneous Food Industries	0.70	0.12	0.50	0.13	-0.21	0.01
059 Iron Foundries	0.58	0.10	0.36	0.09	-0.23	-0.00
103 Chemicals and Chemical Products	0.92	0.15	0.67	0.17	-0.24	0.02
095 Non-Metallic Mineral Products n.e.c.	0.57	0.09	0.32	0.08	-0.25	-0.01
060 Non-Ferrous Smelting and Refining	0.67	0.11	0.42	0.11	-0.25	-0.00

Table A.5B (cont'd)

	1961		1992		Change 1961–92	
	Import Employment as a % of Total Import Employment	Import Employment as a % of Total Employment	Import Employment as a % of Total Import Employment	Import Employment as a % of Total Employment	Import Employment as a % of Total Import Employment	Import Employment as a % of Total Employment
051 Pulp and Paper Industries	0.86	0.14	0.58	0.15	-0.28	0.01
006 Iron Mines	0.39	0.06	0.10	0.03	-0.29	-0.04
005 Other Metal Mines	0.58	0.10	0.28	0.07	-0.30	-0.02
008 Non-Metal excl. Coal and Asbestos	0.41	0.07	0.10	0.03	-0.30	-0.04
067 Wire and Wire Products Industries	0.75	0.12	0.44	0.11	-0.30	-0.01
090 Clay Products Industries	0.53	0.09	0.19	0.05	-0.34	-0.04
080 Shipbuilding and Repair Industry	0.46	0.08	0.11	0.03	-0.35	-0.05
066 Stamped. Pressed and Coated Metals	1.19	0.20	0.83	0.22	-0.36	0.02
083 Major Appliances (Elec. and Non-Elec.)	0.73	0.12	0.33	0.09	-0.40	-0.03
017 Fruit and Vegetable Processing	0.70	0.11	0.30	0.08	-0.40	-0.04
043 Sawmills. Planing and Shingle Mills	0.65	0.11	0.24	0.06	-0.41	-0.04
055 Printing and Publishing Industries	2.35	0.39	1.94	0.51	-0.41	0.12
064 Power Boiler and Struct. Metal Industries	0.69	0.11	0.26	0.07	-0.43	-0.05
036 Wool Yarn and Woven Cloth Industry	0.59	0.10	0.16	0.04	-0.43	-0.06
094 Glass and Glass Products Industries	0.92	0.15	0.40	0.11	-0.52	-0.05
011 Crude Petroleum and Natural Gas	1.12	0.18	0.57	0.15	-0.56	-0.04
109 Repair Construction	1.46	0.24	0.89	0.23	-0.57	-0.01
071 Other Metal Fabricating Industries	1.28	0.21	0.71	0.18	-0.57	-0.03
038 Misc. Textile Products Industries	1.26	0.21	0.69	0.18	-0.57	-0.03
097 Industrial Chemicals Industries n.e.c.	1.22	0.20	0.62	0.16	-0.61	-0.04
003 Logging and Forestry	1.06	0.17	0.38	0.10	-0.69	-0.08
120 Water Transport and Related Services	1.00	0.17	0.30	0.08	-0.70	-0.09
074 Other Machinery and Equip. Industries	4.12	0.68	3.36	0.87	-0.76	0.20
057 Primary Steel Industries	2.44	0.40	1.48	0.39	-0.95	-0.01
119 Railway and Transport and Rel. Services	1.63	0.27	0.48	0.13	-1.14	-0.14
075 Aircraft and Aircraft Parts Industries	2.34	0.38	0.96	0.25	-1.38	-0.14
072 Agricultural Implement Industry	2.01	0.33	0.42	0.11	-1.58	-0.22
035 Man-Made Fibre Yarn and Woven Cloth	3.14	0.52	0.76	0.20	-2.38	-0.32
010 Coal Mines	3.23	0.53	0.19	0.05	-3.04	-0.48
001 Agriculture and Related	12.42	2.04	4.77	1.24	-7.64	-0.80
TOTAL	100.00	17.20	100.00	23.07	0.00	5.87

Table A.6A Decomposition of Changes in Employment Shares: 1961 to 1992 – 161 Industries

	1961	1992	Change 1961–92	Change in Import Shares	Due to:			Residual /Interaction
	Import Employ't as a % of Total Import Employ't	Import Employ't as a % of Total Import Employ't	Import Employ't as a % of Total Import Employ't		Change in Employ't /Output Ratio	Change in Input/ Output Coeff's	Change in Import Coeff's	
001 Agriculture and Related	12.42	4.77	-7.64	-4.68	-2.19	-0.58	0.23	-0.42
002 Fishing and Trapping	0.44	0.36	-0.08	-0.32	0.10	-0.07	0.06	0.14
003 Logging and Forestry	1.06	0.38	-0.69	-0.18	-0.29	-0.10	0.00	-0.12
004 Gold Mines	0.13	0.13	-0.00	0.06	-0.25	0.01	-0.00	0.18
005 Other Metal Mines	0.58	0.28	-0.30	-0.04	-0.07	-0.07	-0.06	-0.06
006 Iron Mines	0.39	0.10	-0.29	-0.24	-0.03	-0.02	0.02	-0.06
007 Asbestos Mines	0.03	0.00	-0.03	-0.03	0.00	-0.01	0.02	-0.01
008 Non-Metal excl. Coal and Asbestos	0.41	0.10	-0.30	-0.15	-0.12	-0.00	0.03	-0.06
009 Salt Mines	0.02	0.02	-0.01	-0.00	-0.00	-0.00	-0.00	0.00
010 Coal Mines	3.23	0.19	-3.04	-0.49	-0.73	-0.03	0.01	-1.79
011 Crude Petroleum and Natural Gas	1.12	0.57	-0.56	-0.51	-0.17	0.05	0.08	-0.00
012 Quarries and Sand Pits	0.23	0.09	-0.14	-0.15	-0.00	-0.01	0.00	0.02
013 Services Related to Mineral Extraction	0.15	0.27	0.12	-0.26	0.12	0.12	0.03	0.11
014 Meat and Meat Prod (excl. Poultry)	0.31	0.31	0.00	-0.08	0.06	-0.06	-0.00	0.08
015 Poultry Products	0.04	0.08	0.04	0.02	0.02	-0.00	0.00	-0.01
016 Fish Products Industry	0.22	0.34	0.12	0.10	0.01	-0.01	0.01	0.01
017 Fruit and Vegetable Processing	0.70	0.30	-0.40	-0.38	-0.05	-0.01	0.02	0.02
018 Dairy Products	0.12	0.12	-0.00	0.02	-0.04	-0.01	0.00	0.02
019 Feed Industry	0.16	0.13	-0.03	-0.02	-0.01	-0.01	-0.00	0.01
020 Vegetable Oil Mills (excluding Corn)	0.06	0.02	-0.04	-0.04	-0.00	-0.00	0.00	0.00
021 Biscuit Industry	0.10	0.05	-0.04	-0.04	-0.01	0.00	0.00	0.00
022 Bread and Other Bakery Prod. Industries	0.04	0.11	0.07	0.07	-0.01	-0.01	0.00	0.01
023 Cane and Beer Sugar Industry	0.05	0.02	-0.03	-0.02	0.00	-0.01	0.00	0.00
024 Miscellaneous Food Industries	0.70	0.50	-0.21	-0.29	0.03	-0.04	0.03	0.07
025 Soft Drink Industry	0.04	0.04	0.01	0.00	-0.04	0.02	0.00	0.02
026 Distillery Products Industry	0.18	0.07	-0.11	-0.13	0.01	-0.01	0.00	0.02
027 Brewery Products Industry	0.02	0.04	0.03	0.03	-0.00	-0.01	0.00	0.02
028 Wine Industry	0.05	0.09	0.04	0.03	0.01	-0.00	0.00	0.00
029 Tobacco Products Industries	0.05	0.11	0.06	0.08	-0.05	-0.01	0.00	0.04
030 Rubber Products Industries	0.77	0.81	0.04	0.13	0.10	-0.11	-0.10	0.02

| | 1961 | 1992 | Change 1961–92 | | Due to: | | | |
	Import Employ't as a % of Total Import Employ't	Import Employ't as a % of Total Import Employ't	Import Employ't as a % of Total Import Employ't	Change in Import Shares	Change in Employ't /Output Ratio	Change in Input/ Output Coeff's	Change in Import Coeff's	Residual /Interaction
031 Plastic Products Industries	0.67	1.51	0.84	0.45	-0.00	0.27	0.00	0.12
032 Leather Tanneries	0.14	0.11	-0.03	-0.01	0.00	0.00	-0.06	0.03
033 Footwear Industry	0.45	0.79	0.34	0.30	0.02	-0.04	0.05	0.02
034 Misc. Leather and Allied Prod. Ind.	0.28	0.25	-0.03	-0.06	0.02	-0.02	-0.01	0.03
035 Man-Made Fibre Yarn and Woven Cloth	3.14	0.76	-2.38	-1.46	-0.16	-0.20	-0.11	-0.45
036 Wool Yarn and Woven Cloth Industry	0.59	0.16	-0.43	-0.33	-0.00	-0.10	-0.01	0.01
037 Broad Knitted Fabric Industry	0.24	0.11	-0.13	-0.12	-0.02	0.02	0.00	-0.01
038 Misc. Textile Products Industries	1.26	0.69	-0.57	-0.65	0.09	-0.12	0.01	0.09
039 Contract Textile Dyeing and Finishing	0.11	0.15	0.04	0.02	0.02	0.07	-0.01	-0.06
040 Carpet. Mat and Rug Industry	0.09	0.11	0.02	0.03	-0.03	0.00	0.01	0.02
041 Clothing Industry excl. Hosiery	1.53	2.71	1.18	1.12	0.04	-0.13	0.13	0.02
042 Hosiery Industry	0.06	0.05	-0.00	-0.01	0.01	-0.01	0.00	0.00
043 Sawmills. Planing and Shingle Mills	0.65	0.24	-0.41	-0.17	-0.14	-0.05	0.01	-0.06
044 Veneer and Plywood Industries	0.21	0.07	-0.14	-0.11	-0.01	-0.03	0.00	0.00
045 Sash. Door and Other Millwork Ind.	0.10	0.21	0.11	0.10	0.02	-0.01	0.01	-0.01
046 Wooden Box and Coffin Industries	0.11	0.07	-0.04	-0.01	-0.02	-0.01	-0.01	0.00
047 Other Wood Industries	0.15	0.06	-0.09	-0.03	-0.04	-0.01	0.00	-0.02
048 Household Furniture Industries	0.33	0.58	0.24	0.22	0.02	-0.03	0.03	0.01
049 Office Furniture Industry	0.06	0.07	0.02	0.02	-0.00	-0.00	0.01	0.00
050 Other Furniture and Fixture Industries	0.16	0.25	0.09	0.06	0.04	-0.02	0.02	-0.01
051 Pulp and Paper Industries	0.86	0.58	-0.28	-0.06	-0.03	-0.16	-0.03	-0.01
052 Asphalt Roofing Industry	0.04	0.01	-0.02	-0.01	-0.01	-0.01	-0.00	0.01
053 Paper Box and Bag Industries	0.51	0.36	-0.15	-0.03	0.02	-0.13	-0.02	-0.00
054 Other Converted Paper Prod. Industries	0.34	0.33	-0.01	0.02	0.01	-0.07	-0.00	0.01
055 Printing and Publishing Industries	2.35	1.94	-0.41	-0.17	-0.15	-0.31	-0.00	0.03
056 Plate making. Typesetting and Bindery	0.35	0.33	-0.02	-0.07	0.03	-0.05	0.05	0.16
057 Primary Steel Industries	2.44	1.48	-0.95	-0.60	-0.13	-0.09	-0.17	0.05

Table A.6A (cont'd)

| | 1961 | 1992 | Change 1961–92 | Change in Import Shares | Change in Employ't /Output Ratio | Due to: | | Residual /Interaction |
	Import Employ't as a % of Total Import Employ't	Import Employ't as a % of Total Import Employ't	Import Employ't as a % of Total Import Employ't			Change in Input/ Output Coeff's	Change in Import Coeff's	
058 Steel Pipe and Tube Industry	0.18	0.14	-0.04	-0.20	0.05	0.00	0.00	0.11
059 Iron Foundries	0.58	0.36	-0.23	-0.18	-0.11	0.03	0.01	0.02
060 Non-Ferrous Smelting and Refining	0.67	0.42	-0.25	-0.15	-0.04	-0.01	-0.09	0.03
061 Alum. Rolling, Casting and Extruding	0.30	0.23	-0.07	0.05	-0.17	0.04	-0.09	0.11
062 Copper Rolling, Casting and Extruding	0.16	0.11	-0.05	0.01	0.05	-0.08	-0.05	0.03
063 Other Metal Rolling, Casting, etc.	0.21	0.18	-0.03	-0.10	0.06	-0.04	-0.03	0.07
064 Power Boiler and Struct. Metal Ind.	0.69	0.26	-0.43	-0.38	0.03	-0.14	0.01	0.06
065 Ornamental and Arch. Metal Products	0.19	0.17	-0.02	-0.02	0.01	-0.00	0.00	-0.00
066 Stamped, Pressed and Coated Metals	1.19	0.83	-0.36	-0.34	0.09	-0.14	-0.05	0.08
067 Wire and Wire Products Industries	0.75	0.44	-0.30	-0.16	0.04	-0.17	-0.05	0.04
068 Hardware Tool and Cutlery Industries	0.95	0.94	-0.01	-0.30	0.19	-0.06	0.03	0.13
069 Heating Equipment Industry	0.19	0.12	-0.07	-0.10	0.02	-0.02	0.00	0.03
070 Machine Shops Industry	0.72	1.01	0.29	0.12	0.19	-0.01	-0.09	0.08
071 Other Metal Fabricating Industries	1.28	0.71	-0.57	-0.51	0.01	-0.09	-0.04	0.05
072 Agricultural Implement Industry	2.01	0.42	-1.58	-1.86	0.02	-0.04	0.04	0.25
073 Commercial Refrigeration Equipment	0.18	0.30	0.11	0.07	0.04	0.01	-0.01	0.01
074 Other Machinery and Equip. Industries	4.12	3.36	-0.76	-1.08	0.02	-0.13	0.10	0.33
075 Aircraft and Aircraft Parts Industries	2.34	0.96	-1.38	-1.21	-0.13	-0.02	0.01	-0.02
076 Motor Vehicle Industry	0.91	1.14	0.23	0.61	-0.88	-0.08	0.09	0.49
077 Truck, Bus Body and Trailer Industries	0.21	0.33	0.12	0.08	0.02	-0.01	0.02	0.00
078 Motor Vehicle Parts and Accessories	3.55	5.34	1.80	2.28	-0.81	-0.11	-0.37	0.80
079 Railroad Rolling Stock Industry	0.18	0.17	-0.01	0.05	-0.07	-0.01	-0.00	0.02
080 Shipbuilding and Repair Industry	0.46	0.11	-0.35	-0.28	-0.03	-0.01	0.01	-0.04
081 Misc. Transport. Equip. Industries	0.17	0.15	-0.02	0.03	-0.10	-0.00	0.01	0.04
082 Small Electrical Appliance Industry	0.26	0.29	0.03	-0.01	0.06	-0.03	0.01	0.00
083 Major Appliances (Elec. and Non-Elec.)	0.73	0.33	-0.40	-0.39	-0.02	-0.02	0.01	0.02
084 Record Players, Radio and TV Receivers	0.34	0.39	0.04	0.16	-0.17	-0.02	-0.04	0.11
085 Electronic Equipment Industries	1.89	2.51	0.63	1.48	-2.55	0.25	-0.60	2.04
086 Office, Store and Business Machines	0.74	1.64	0.90	1.12	-0.50	-0.08	-0.30	0.65
087 Communic. Energy Wire and Cable	0.19	0.18	-0.01	0.04	0.00	-0.04	-0.02	0.02

Table A.6A (cont'd)

	1961 Import Employ't as a % of Total Import Employ't	1992 Import Employ't as a % of Total Import Employ't	Change 1961-92 Import Employ't as a % of Total Import Employ't	Change in Import Shares	Due to: Change in Employ't /Output Ratio	Change in Input/Output Coeff's	Change in Import Coeff's	Residual /Interaction
088 Battery Industry	0.07	0.08	0.01	0.01	0.01	-0.01	-0.00	0.00
089 Other Elect. and Electronic Products	1.80	1.69	-0.11	-0.06	0.05	-0.12	-0.12	0.14
090 Clay Products Industries	0.53	0.19	-0.34	-0.26	-0.03	-0.03	0.01	-0.03
091 Cement Industry	0.02	0.02	-0.01	-0.00	0.00	-0.00	0.00	0.00
092 Concrete Products Industry	0.04	0.02	-0.02	-0.02	0.00	-0.01	0.00	0.00
093 Ready-Mix Concrete Industry	0.01	0.01	0.00	-0.00	0.01	0.00	0.00	0.00
094 Glass and Glass Products Industries	0.92	0.40	-0.52	-0.37	-0.07	-0.10	0.00	0.01
095 Non-Metallic Mineral Products n.e.c.	0.57	0.32	-0.25	-0.17	-0.02	-0.09	-0.02	0.04
096 Refined Petroleum and Coal Products	0.29	0.16	-0.13	-0.04	-0.09	-0.00	-0.00	0.00
097 Industrial Chemicals Industries n.e.c.	1.22	0.62	-0.61	-0.18	-0.42	0.05	-0.05	0.00
098 Plastic and Synthetic Resin Industries	0.39	0.33	-0.05	0.01	-0.14	0.03	-0.03	0.07
099 Pharmaceutical and Medicine Industry	0.29	0.39	0.10	0.14	-0.15	0.02	0.02	0.07
100 Paint and Varnish Industry	0.21	0.20	-0.01	0.03	-0.04	-0.01	-0.02	0.01
101 Soap and Cleaning Compounds Industry	0.16	0.18	0.03	-0.00	0.04	-0.02	-0.00	0.01
102 Toilet Preparations Industry	0.03	0.18	0.15	0.13	0.03	-0.00	0.01	-0.02
103 Chemicals and Chemical Products	0.92	0.67	-0.24	-0.15	-0.14	0.02	-0.05	0.07
104 Jewelry and Precious Metals Industry	0.38	0.31	-0.06	-0.08	0.02	-0.02	0.00	0.02
105 Sporting Goods and Toys Industries	0.50	0.67	0.17	0.18	-0.07	-0.03	0.04	0.06
106 Sign and Display Industry	0.10	0.14	0.03	0.02	0.04	-0.03	-0.00	0.01
107 Floor Tile. Linoleum. Coated Fabrics	0.22	0.11	-0.11	-0.09	0.00	-0.02	-0.01	0.01
108 Other Manufacturing Industry n.e.c.	2.74	2.58	-0.16	-0.43	0.14	-0.10	-0.02	0.24
109 Repair Construction	1.46	0.89	-0.57	-0.15	-0.20	-0.28	-0.01	0.06
110 Residential Construction	0.00	0.00	0.00	0.00	0.00	0.00	0.00	0.00
111 Non-Residential Bldg Construction	0.00	0.00	0.00	0.00	0.00	0.00	0.00	0.00
112 Road. Highway and Airstrip Constr.	0.00	0.00	0.00	0.00	0.00	0.00	0.00	0.00
113 Gas and Oil Facility Construction	0.00	0.00	0.00	0.00	0.00	0.00	0.00	0.00
114 Dams and Irrigation Projects	0.00	0.00	0.00	0.00	0.00	0.00	0.00	0.00
115 Railway and Telephone Teleg. Constr.	0.00	0.00	0.00	0.00	0.00	0.00	0.00	0.00
116 Other Engineering Construction	0.00	0.00	0.00	0.00	0.00	0.00	0.00	0.00
117 Construction. Other Activities	0.01	0.02	0.01	0.00	0.01	-0.01	-0.00	0.00

	1961 Import Employ't as a % of Total Import Employ't	1992 Import Employ't as a % of Total Import Employ't	Change 1961-92 Import Employ't as a % of Total Import Employ't	Change in Import Shares	Change in Employ't/Output Ratio	Due to: Change in Input/Output Coeff's	Change in Import Coeff's	Residual/Interaction
118 Air Transport and Incidental Services	0.23	0.80	0.57	0.59	-0.11	-0.00	-0.01	0.11
119 Railway and Transport and Rel. Services	1.63	0.48	-1.14	0.04	-0.18	-0.69	-0.02	-0.29
120 Water Transport and Related Services	1.00	0.30	-0.70	-0.35	-0.12	-0.12	0.01	-0.12
121 Truck Transport Industries	1.22	1.10	-0.12	-0.10	-0.28	0.11	-0.03	0.18
122 Urban Transit System Industry	0.02	0.18	0.16	0.15	0.08	-0.01	0.01	-0.07
123 Interurban and Rural Transit Systems	0.02	0.09	0.07	0.08	-0.03	-0.01	0.00	0.02
124 Taxicab Industry	0.26	0.61	0.35	0.31	0.09	-0.00	-0.03	-0.02
125 Other Transport and Services to Transp.	0.04	0.51	0.47	0.18	0.25	0.27	-0.01	-0.22
126 Highway and Bridge Maintenance Ind.	0.01	0.00	-0.00	0.00	-0.00	-0.00	-0.00	0.00
127 Pipeline Transport Industries	0.08	0.07	-0.01	-0.05	0.01	0.01	0.00	0.02
128 Storage and Warehousing Industries	0.17	0.11	-0.06	-0.03	0.03	-0.11	0.00	0.05
129 Telecomm. Broadcasting Industry	0.27	0.27	-0.00	0.05	-0.27	0.07	0.00	0.14
130 Telecommunication Carriers and Other	0.72	0.77	0.06	0.17	-0.29	0.02	-0.01	0.16
131 Postal Service Industry	0.38	0.45	0.07	0.00	-0.02	0.05	-0.00	0.04
132 Electric Power Systems Industry	0.52	0.64	0.13	-0.14	-0.19	0.29	-0.02	0.18
133 Gas Distribution Systems Industry	0.13	0.08	-0.06	-0.04	-0.04	0.01	-0.00	0.01
134 Other Utility Industries n.e.c.	0.05	0.23	0.18	-0.02	-0.00	0.17	-0.00	0.03
135 Wholesale Trade Industries	3.26	5.08	1.83	-0.24	1.00	0.82	-0.15	0.40
136 Retail Trade Industries	2.59	3.14	0.55	-0.21	0.90	-0.79	-0.00	0.66
137 Banks. Credit Union and Oth. Dep. Inst.	0.73	1.83	1.11	0.25	-0.13	0.71	0.03	0.26
138 Trust. Other Finance and Real Estate	0.79	1.83	1.04	0.26	0.64	0.19	0.04	-0.10
139 Insurance Industries	0.51	0.62	0.11	0.23	-0.13	-0.04	0.01	0.04
140 Govt. Royalties on Nat. Resources	0.00	0.00	0.00	0.00	0.00	0.00	0.00	0.00
141 Owner Occupied Dwellings	0.00	0.00	0.00	0.00	0.00	0.00	0.00	0.00
142 Other Business Services Industries	1.19	5.23	4.04	1.50	1.70	1.64	0.92	-1.73
143 Professional Business Services	1.70	3.65	1.95	0.48	0.67	1.00	0.15	-0.35
144 Advertising Services	0.24	0.56	0.32	0.05	0.06	0.20	0.02	-0.02
145 Educational Services Industries	0.04	0.12	0.08	0.07	0.01	-0.01	0.01	-0.01

Table A.6A (cont'd)

	1961 Import Employ't as a % of Total Import Employ't	1992 Import Employ't as a % of Total Import Employ't	Change 1961–92 Import Employ't as a % of Total Import Employ't	Change in Import Shares	Change in Employ't /Output Ratio	Due to: Change in Input/ Output Coeff's	Change in Import Coeff's	Residual /Interaction
146 Hospitals	0.03	0.08	0.04	0.05	-0.01	-0.00	0.01	0.01
147 Other Health Services	0.00	0.04	0.04	0.03	0.02	0.01	0.00	-0.02
148 Accomm. and Food Services Industry	0.75	8.89	8.14	7.66	4.29	-0.51	0.32	-3.63
149 Motion Picture and Video Industries	0.25	0.24	-0.01	-0.08	-0.00	0.03	0.01	0.03
150 Other Amusement and Recreat. Serv.	0.03	0.89	0.87	0.86	0.20	-0.05	0.06	-0.20
151 Laundries and Cleaners	0.06	0.10	0.04	0.02	0.02	-0.02	0.00	0.02
152 Other Personal Services	0.00	0.01	0.01	0.01	0.00	-0.00	0.00	-0.00
153 Photographers	0.01	0.04	0.02	0.00	0.02	0.01	0.00	-0.00
154 Misc. Service Industries	0.80	2.80	2.00	-0.10	1.57	0.80	0.06	-0.33

Table A.6B Decomposition of Changes in Employment Shares: 1961 to 1992 – 161 Industries

Sorted by Size of Change	1961 Import Employ't as a % of Total Import Employ't	1992 Import Employ't as a % of Total Import Employ't	Change 1961–92 Import Employ't as a % of Total Import Employ't	Change in Import Shares	Due to: Change in Employ't /Output Ratio	Change in Input/ Output Coeff's	Change in Import Coeff's	Residual /Interaction
148 Accomm. and Food Services Industry	0.75	8.89	8.14	7.66	4.29	-0.51	0.32	-3.63
142 Other Business Services Industries	1.19	5.23	4.04	1.50	1.70	1.64	0.92	-1.73
154 Misc. Service Industries	0.80	2.80	2.00	-0.10	1.57	0.80	0.06	-0.33
143 Professional Business Services	1.70	3.65	1.95	0.48	0.67	1.00	0.15	-0.35
135 Wholesale Trade Industries	3.26	5.08	1.83	-0.24	1.00	0.82	-0.15	0.40
078 Motor Vehicle Parts and Accessories	3.55	5.34	1.80	2.28	-0.81	-0.11	-0.37	0.80
041 Clothing Industry excl. Hosiery	1.53	2.71	1.18	1.12	0.04	-0.13	0.13	0.02
137 Banks. Credit Union and Oth. Dep. Inst.	0.73	1.83	1.11	0.25	-0.13	0.71	0.03	0.26
138 Trust. Other Finance and Real Estate	0.79	1.83	1.04	0.26	0.64	0.19	0.04	-0.10
086 Office. Store and Business Machines	0.74	1.64	0.90	1.12	-0.50	-0.08	-0.30	0.65
150 Other Amusement and Recreat. Serv.	0.03	0.89	0.87	0.86	0.20	-0.05	0.06	-0.20
031 Plastic Products Industries	0.67	1.51	0.84	0.45	-0.00	0.27	0.00	0.12
085 Electronic Equipment Industries	1.89	2.51	0.63	1.48	-2.55	0.25	-0.60	2.04
118 Air Transport and Incidental Services	0.23	0.80	0.57	0.59	-0.11	-0.00	-0.01	0.11
136 Retail Trade Industries	2.59	3.14	0.55	-0.21	0.90	-0.79	-0.00	0.66
125 Other Transport and Services to Transp.	0.04	0.51	0.47	0.18	0.25	0.27	-0.01	-0.22
124 Taxicab Industry	0.26	0.61	0.35	0.31	0.09	-0.00	-0.03	-0.02
033 Footwear Industry	0.45	0.79	0.34	0.30	0.02	-0.04	0.05	0.02
144 Advertising Services	0.24	0.56	0.32	0.05	0.06	0.20	0.02	-0.02
070 Machine Shops Industry	0.72	1.01	0.29	0.12	0.19	-0.01	-0.09	0.08
048 Household Furniture Industries	0.33	0.58	0.24	0.22	0.02	-0.03	0.03	0.01
076 Motor Vehicle Industry	0.91	1.14	0.23	0.61	-0.88	-0.08	0.09	0.49
134 Other Utility Industries n.e.c.	0.05	0.23	0.18	-0.02	-0.00	0.17	-0.00	0.03
105 Sporting Goods and Toys Industries	0.50	0.67	0.17	0.18	-0.07	-0.03	0.04	0.06
122 Urban Transit System Industry	0.02	0.18	0.16	0.15	0.08	-0.01	0.01	-0.07
102 Toilet Preparations Industry	0.03	0.18	0.15	0.13	0.03	-0.00	0.01	-0.02
132 Electric Power Systems Industry	0.52	0.64	0.13	-0.14	-0.19	0.29	0.01	0.18
077 Truck. Bus Body and Trailer Industries	0.21	0.33	0.12	0.08	0.02	-0.01	-0.02	0.00
016 Fish Products Industry	0.22	0.34	0.12	0.10	0.01	-0.01	0.01	0.01

Table A.6B (cont'd)

Sorted by Size of Change	1961 Import Employ't as a % of Total Import Employ't	1992 Import Employ't as a % of Total Import Employ't	Change 1961-92 Import Employ't as a % of Total Import Employ't	Change in Import Shares	Due to: Change in Employ't /Output Ratio	Change in Input/ Output Coeff's	Change in Import Coeff's	Residual /Interaction
013 Services Related to Mineral Extraction	0.15	0.27	0.12	-0.26	0.12	0.12	0.03	0.11
045 Sash, Door and Other Millwork Ind.	0.10	0.21	0.11	0.10	0.02	-0.01	0.01	-0.01
073 Commercial Refrigeration Equipment	0.18	0.30	0.11	0.07	0.04	0.01	-0.01	0.01
139 Insurance Industries	0.51	0.62	0.11	0.23	-0.13	-0.04	0.01	0.04
099 Pharmaceutical and Medicine Industry	0.29	0.39	0.10	0.14	-0.15	0.02	0.02	0.07
050 Other Furniture and Fixture Industries	0.16	0.25	0.09	0.06	0.04	-0.02	0.02	-0.01
145 Educational Services Industries	0.04	0.12	0.08	0.07	0.01	-0.01	0.01	-0.01
131 Postal Service Industry	0.38	0.45	0.07	0.00	-0.02	0.05	-0.00	0.04
022 Bread and Other Bakery Prod. Industries	0.04	0.11	0.07	0.07	-0.01	-0.01	0.00	0.01
123 Interurban and Rural Transit Systems	0.02	0.09	0.07	0.08	-0.03	-0.01	0.00	0.02
130 Telecommunication Carriers and Other	0.72	0.77	0.06	0.17	-0.29	0.02	-0.01	0.16
029 Tobacco Products Industries	0.05	0.11	0.06	0.08	-0.05	-0.01	0.00	0.04
084 Record Players, Radio and TV Receivers	0.34	0.39	0.04	0.16	-0.17	-0.02	-0.04	0.11
151 Laundries and Cleaners	0.06	0.10	0.04	0.02	0.02	-0.02	0.00	0.02
039 Contract Textile Dyeing and Finishing	0.11	0.15	0.04	0.02	0.02	0.07	-0.01	-0.06
146 Hospitals	0.03	0.08	0.04	0.05	-0.01	-0.00	0.01	0.01
028 Wine Industry	0.05	0.09	0.04	0.03	0.01	-0.00	0.00	0.00
147 Other Health Services	0.00	0.04	0.04	0.03	0.02	0.01	0.00	-0.02
030 Rubber Products Industries	0.77	0.81	0.04	0.13	0.10	-0.11	-0.10	0.02
015 Poultry Products	0.04	0.08	0.04	0.02	0.02	-0.00	0.00	-0.01
106 Sign and Display Industry	0.10	0.14	0.03	0.02	0.04	-0.03	-0.00	0.01
082 Small Electrical Appliance Industry	0.26	0.29	0.03	-0.01	0.06	-0.03	0.01	0.00
101 Soap and Cleaning Compounds Industry	0.16	0.18	0.03	-0.00	0.04	-0.02	-0.00	0.01
027 Brewery Products Industry	0.02	0.04	0.03	0.03	-0.00	-0.01	0.00	0.00
153 Photographers	0.01	0.04	0.02	0.00	0.02	0.01	0.00	-0.00
040 Carpet, Mat and Rug Industry	0.09	0.11	0.02	0.03	-0.03	0.00	0.01	0.02
049 Office Furniture Industry	0.06	0.07	0.02	0.02	-0.00	-0.00	0.01	0.00
088 Battery Industry	0.07	0.08	0.01	0.01	0.01	-0.01	-0.00	0.00
152 Other Personal Services	0.00	0.01	0.01	0.01	0.00	-0.00	0.00	-0.00

Table A.6B (cont'd)

Sorted by Size of Change	1961 Import Employ't as a % of Total Import Employ't	1992 Import Employ't as a % of Total Import Employ't	Change 1961–92 Import Employ't as a % of Total Import Employ't	Change in Import Shares	Due to: Change in Employ't /Output Ratio	Due to: Change in Input/ Output Coeff's	Due to: Change in Import Coeff's	Residual /Interaction
025 Soft Drink Industry	0.04	0.04	0.01	0.00	-0.04	0.02	0.00	0.02
117 Construction. Other Activities	0.01	0.02	0.01	0.00	0.01	-0.01	-0.00	0.00
093 Ready-Mix Concrete Industry	0.01	0.01	0.00	-0.00	0.01	0.00	0.00	0.00
014 Meat and Meat Prod (excl. Poultry)	0.31	0.31	0.00	-0.08	0.06	-0.06	-0.00	0.08
111 Non-Residential Bldg Construction	0.00	0.00	0.00	0.00	0.00	0.00	0.00	0.00
110 Residential Construction	0.00	0.00	0.00	0.00	0.00	0.00	0.00	0.00
140 Govt. Royalties on Nat. Resources	0.00	0.00	0.00	0.00	0.00	0.00	0.00	0.00
116 Other Engineering Construction	0.00	0.00	0.00	0.00	0.00	0.00	0.00	0.00
141 Owner Occupied Dwellings	0.00	0.00	0.00	0.00	0.00	0.00	0.00	0.00
115 Railway and Telephone Teleg. Constr.	0.00	0.00	0.00	0.00	0.00	0.00	0.00	0.00
112 Road. Highway and Airstrip Constr.	0.00	0.00	0.00	0.00	0.00	0.00	0.00	0.00
113 Gas and Oil Facility Construction	0.00	0.00	0.00	0.00	0.00	0.00	0.00	0.00
114 Dams and Irrigation Projects	0.00	0.00	0.00	0.00	0.00	0.00	0.00	0.00
018 Dairy Products	0.12	0.12	-0.00	0.02	-0.04	-0.01	0.00	0.02
042 Hosiery Industry	0.06	0.05	-0.00	-0.01	0.01	-0.01	0.00	0.00
126 Highway and Bridge Maintenance Ind.	0.01	0.00	-0.00	0.00	-0.00	-0.00	-0.00	0.00
129 Telecomm. Broadcasting Industry	0.27	0.27	-0.00	0.05	-0.27	0.07	0.00	0.14
004 Gold Mines	0.13	0.13	-0.00	0.06	-0.25	0.01	-0.00	0.18
068 Hardware Tool and Cutlery Industries	0.95	0.94	-0.01	-0.30	0.19	-0.06	0.03	0.13
091 Cement Industry	0.02	0.02	-0.01	-0.00	0.00	-0.00	0.00	0.00
079 Railroad Rolling Stock Industry	0.18	0.17	-0.01	0.05	-0.07	-0.01	-0.00	0.02
149 Motion Picture and Video Industries	0.25	0.24	-0.01	-0.08	-0.00	0.03	0.01	0.03
087 Communic.. Energy Wire and Cable	0.19	0.18	-0.01	0.04	0.00	-0.04	-0.02	0.02
127 Pipeline Transport Industries	0.08	0.07	-0.01	-0.05	0.01	0.01	0.00	0.02
009 Salt Mines	0.02	0.02	-0.01	-0.00	-0.00	-0.00	-0.00	0.00
054 Other Converted Paper Prod. Industries	0.34	0.33	-0.01	0.02	0.01	-0.07	-0.00	0.03
100 Paint and Varnish Industry	0.21	0.20	-0.01	0.03	-0.04	-0.01	-0.02	0.01
065 Ornamental and Arch. Metal Products	0.19	0.17	-0.02	-0.02	0.01	-0.00	0.00	-0.00
092 Concrete Products Industry	0.04	0.02	-0.02	-0.02	0.00	-0.01	0.00	0.00

Table A.6B (cont'd)

Sorted by Size of Change	1961 Import Employ't as a % of Total Import Employ't	1992 Import Employ't as a % of Total Import Employ't	Change 1961-92 Import Employ't as a % of Total Import Employ't	Due to: Change in Import Shares	Change in Employ't /Output Ratio	Change in Input/ Output Coeff's	Change in Import Coeff's	Residual /Interaction
056 Plate making, Typesetting and Bindery	0.35	0.33	-0.02	-0.07	0.03	-0.05	0.01	0.05
081 Misc. Transport. Equip. Industries	0.17	0.15	-0.02	0.03	-0.10	-0.00	0.01	0.04
052 Asphalt Roofing Industry	0.04	0.01	-0.02	-0.01	-0.01	-0.01	-0.00	-0.00
023 Cane and Beer Sugar Industry	0.05	0.02	-0.03	-0.02	0.00	-0.01	0.00	0.00
007 Asbestos Mines	0.03	0.00	-0.03	-0.03	0.00	-0.01	-0.00	0.01
034 Misc. Leather and Allied Prod. Ind.	0.28	0.25	-0.03	-0.06	0.02	-0.02	-0.01	0.03
019 Feed Industry	0.16	0.13	-0.03	-0.02	-0.01	-0.01	-0.00	0.01
032 Leather Tanneries	0.14	0.11	-0.03	-0.01	0.00	0.00	-0.06	0.03
063 Other Metal Rolling, Casting, etc.	0.21	0.18	-0.03	-0.10	0.06	-0.04	-0.03	0.07
020 Vegetable Oil Mills (excluding Corn)	0.06	0.02	-0.04	-0.04	-0.00	-0.00	0.00	0.00
058 Steel Pipe and Tube Industry	0.18	0.14	-0.04	-0.20	0.05	0.00	0.00	0.11
046 Wooden Box and Coffin Industries	0.11	0.07	-0.04	-0.01	-0.02	-0.01	-0.01	0.00
021 Biscuit Industry	0.10	0.05	-0.04	-0.04	-0.01	0.00	0.00	0.00
062 Copper Rolling, Casting and Extruding	0.16	0.11	-0.05	0.01	0.05	-0.08	-0.05	0.03
098 Plastic and Synthetic Resin Industries	0.39	0.33	-0.05	0.01	-0.14	0.03	-0.03	0.07
133 Gas Distribution Systems Industry	0.13	0.08	-0.06	-0.04	-0.04	0.01	-0.00	0.01
128 Storage and Warehousing Industries	0.17	0.11	-0.06	-0.03	0.03	-0.11	0.00	0.05
104 Jewelry and Precious Metals Industry	0.38	0.31	-0.06	-0.08	0.02	-0.02	0.00	0.02
069 Heating Equipment Industry	0.19	0.12	-0.07	-0.10	0.02	-0.02	0.00	0.03
061 Alum. Rolling, Casting and Extruding	0.30	0.23	-0.07	0.05	-0.17	0.04	-0.09	0.11
002 Fishing and Trapping	0.44	0.36	-0.08	-0.32	0.10	-0.07	0.06	0.14
047 Other Wood Industries	0.15	0.06	-0.09	-0.03	-0.04	-0.01	0.00	-0.02
089 Other Elect. and Electronic Products	1.80	1.69	-0.11	-0.06	0.05	-0.12	-0.12	0.14
107 Floor Tile. Linoleum. Coated Fabrics	0.22	0.11	-0.11	-0.09	0.00	-0.02	-0.01	0.01
026 Distillery Products Industry	0.18	0.07	-0.11	-0.13	0.01	-0.01	0.00	0.02
121 Truck Transport Industries	1.22	1.10	-0.12	-0.10	-0.28	0.11	-0.03	0.18
037 Broad Knitted Fabric Industry	0.24	0.11	-0.13	-0.12	-0.02	0.02	0.00	-0.01
096 Refined Petroleum and Coal Products	0.29	0.16	-0.13	-0.04	-0.09	-0.00	-0.00	0.00
012 Quarries and Sand Pits	0.23	0.09	-0.14	-0.15	-0.00	-0.01	0.00	0.02

Table A.6B (cont'd)

Sorted by Size of Change	1961 Import Employ't as a % of Total Import Employ't	1992 Import Employ't as a % of Total Import Employ't	Change 1961–92 Import Employ't as a % of Total Import Employ't	Change in Import Shares	Due to: Change in Employ't /Output Ratio	Change in Input/ Output Coeff's	Change in Import Coeff's	Residual /Interaction
044 Veneer and Plywood Industries	0.21	0.07	-0.14	-0.11	-0.01	-0.03	0.00	0.00
053 Paper Box and Bag Industries	0.51	0.36	-0.15	-0.03	0.02	-0.13	-0.02	0.01
108 Other Manufacturing Industry n.e.c.	2.74	2.58	-0.16	-0.43	0.14	-0.10	-0.02	0.24
024 Miscellaneous Food Industries	0.70	0.50	-0.21	-0.29	0.03	-0.04	0.03	0.07
059 Iron Foundries	0.58	0.36	-0.23	-0.18	-0.11	0.03	0.01	0.02
103 Chemicals and Chemical Products	0.92	0.67	-0.24	-0.15	-0.14	0.02	-0.05	0.07
095 Non-Metallic Mineral Products n.e.c.	0.57	0.32	-0.25	-0.17	-0.02	-0.09	-0.02	0.04
060 Non-Ferrous Smelting and Refining	0.67	0.42	-0.25	-0.15	-0.04	-0.01	-0.09	0.03
051 Pulp and Paper Industries	0.86	0.58	-0.28	-0.06	-0.03	-0.16	-0.03	0.01
006 Iron Mines	0.39	0.10	-0.29	-0.24	-0.03	-0.02	0.02	-0.01
005 Other Metal Mines	0.58	0.28	-0.30	-0.04	-0.07	-0.07	-0.06	-0.06
008 Non-Metal excl. Coal and Asbestos	0.41	0.10	-0.30	-0.15	-0.12	-0.00	0.03	-0.06
067 Wire and Wire Products Industries	0.75	0.44	-0.30	-0.16	0.04	-0.17	-0.05	0.04
090 Clay Products Industries	0.53	0.19	-0.34	-0.26	-0.03	-0.03	0.01	-0.03
080 Shipbuilding and Repair Industry	0.46	0.11	-0.35	-0.28	-0.03	-0.01	0.01	-0.04
066 Stamped. Pressed and Coated Metals	1.19	0.83	-0.36	-0.34	0.09	-0.14	-0.05	0.08
083 Major Appliances (Elec. and Non-Elec.)	0.73	0.33	-0.40	-0.39	-0.02	-0.02	0.01	0.02
017 Fruit and Vegetable Processing	0.70	0.30	-0.40	-0.38	-0.05	-0.01	0.02	0.02
043 Sawmills. Planing and Shingle Mills	0.65	0.24	-0.41	-0.17	-0.14	-0.05	0.01	-0.06
055 Printing and Publishing Industries	2.35	1.94	-0.41	-0.17	-0.15	-0.31	0.05	0.16
064 Power Boiler and Struct. Metal Ind.	0.69	0.26	-0.43	-0.38	0.03	-0.14	0.01	0.06
036 Wool Yarn and Woven Cloth Industry	0.59	0.16	-0.43	-0.33	-0.00	-0.10	-0.01	0.01
094 Glass and Glass Products Industries	0.92	0.40	-0.52	-0.37	-0.07	-0.10	0.00	0.01
011 Crude Petroleum and Natural Gas	1.12	0.57	-0.56	-0.51	-0.17	0.05	0.08	-0.00
109 Repair Construction	1.46	0.89	-0.57	-0.15	-0.20	-0.28	-0.01	0.06
071 Other Metal Fabricating Industries	1.28	0.71	-0.57	-0.51	0.01	-0.09	-0.04	0.05
038 Misc. Textile Products Industries	1.26	0.69	-0.57	-0.65	0.09	-0.12	0.01	0.09
097 Industrial Chemicals Industries n.e.c.	1.22	0.62	-0.61	-0.18	-0.42	0.05	-0.05	0.00
003 Logging and Forestry	1.06	0.38	-0.69	-0.18	-0.29	-0.10	0.00	-0.12

Table A.6B (cont'd)

Sorted by Size of Change	1961 Import Employ't as a % of Total Import Employ't	1992 Import Employ't as a % of Total Import Employ't	Change 1961-92 Import Employ't as a % of Total Import Employ't	Change in Import Shares	Due to: Change in Employ't /Output Ratio	Due to: Change in Input/ Output Coeff's	Due to: Change in Import Coeff's	Residual /Interaction
120 Water Transport and Related Services	1.00	0.30	-0.70	-0.35	-0.12	-0.12	0.01	-0.12
074 Other Machinery and Equip. Industries	4.12	3.36	-0.76	-1.08	0.02	-0.13	0.10	0.33
057 Primary Steel Industries	2.44	1.48	-0.95	-0.60	-0.13	-0.09	-0.17	0.04
119 Railway and Transport and Rel. Services	1.63	0.48	-1.14	0.04	-0.18	-0.69	-0.02	-0.29
075 Aircraft and Aircraft Parts Industries	2.34	0.96	-1.38	-1.21	-0.13	-0.02	0.01	-0.02
072 Agricultural Implement Industry	2.01	0.42	-1.58	-1.86	0.02	-0.04	0.04	0.25
010 Coal Mines	3.23	0.19	-3.04	-0.49	-0.73	-0.03	0.01	-1.79
001 Agriculture and Related	12.42	4.77	-7.64	-4.68	-2.19	-0.58	0.23	-0.42

INDUSTRY CANADA RESEARCH PUBLICATIONS

INDUSTRY CANADA WORKING PAPER SERIES

No. 1 **Economic Integration in North America: Trends in Foreign Direct Investment and the Top 1,000 Firms,** Industry Canada, Micro-Economic Policy Analysis Staff including John Knubley, Marc Legault and P. Someshwar Rao, 1994.

No. 2 **Canadian-Based Multinationals: An Analysis of Activities and Performance,** Industry Canada, Micro-Economic Policy Analysis Staff including P. Someshwar Rao, Marc Legault and Ashfaq Ahmad, 1994.

No. 3 **International R&D Spillovers Between Industries in Canada and the United States,** Jeffrey I. Bernstein, Carleton University and National Bureau of Economic Research, under contract with Industry Canada, 1994.

No. 4 **The Economic Impact of Mergers and Acquisitions on Corporations,** Gilles Mcdougall, Micro-Economic Policy Analysis, Industry Canada, 1995.

No. 5 **Steppin' Out: An Analysis of Recent Graduates Into the Labour Market,** Ross Finnie, School of Public Administration, Carleton University and Statistics Canada, 1995.

No. 6 **Measuring the Compliance Cost of Tax Expenditures: The Case of Research and Development Incentives,** Sally Gunz, University of Waterloo, Alan Macnaughton, University of Waterloo, and Karen Wensley, Ernst & Young, Toronto, under contract with Industry Canada, 1996.

No. 7 **Governance Structure, Corporate Decision-Making and Firm Performance in North America,** P. Someshwar Rao and Clifton R. Lee-Sing, Micro-Economic Policy Analysis, Industry Canada, 1996.

No. 8 **Foreign Direct Investment and APEC Economic Integration,** Ashfaq Ahmad, P. Someshwar Rao and Colleen Barnes, Micro-Economic Policy Analysis, Industry Canada, 1996.

No. 9 **World Mandate Strategies for Canadian Subsidiaries,** Julian Birkinshaw, Institute of International Business, Stockholm School of Economics, under contract with Industry Canada, 1996.

No. 10 **R&D Productivity Growth in Canadian Communications Equipment and Manufacturing,** Jeffrey I. Bernstein, Carleton University and National Bureau of Economic Research, under contract with Industry Canada, 1996.

No. 11 **Long-run Perspective on Canadian Regional Convergence,** Serge Coulombe, Department of Economics, University of Ottawa, and Frank C. Lee, Industry Canada, 1996.

No. 12 **Implications of Technology and Imports on Employment and Wages in Canada,** Frank C. Lee, Industry Canada, 1996.

No. 13 **The Development of Strategic Alliances in Canadian Industries: A Micro Analysis,** Sunder Magun, Applied International Economics, 1996.

No. 14 **Employment Performance in the Knowledge-Based Economy,** Surendra Gera, Industry Canada, and Philippe Massé, Human Resources Development Canada, 1996.

No. 15 **The Knowledge-Based Economy: Shifts in Industrial Output,** Surendra Gera, Industry Canada, and Kurt Mang, Department of Finance, 1997.

INDUSTRY CANADA DISCUSSION PAPER SERIES

No. 1   **Multinationals as Agents of Change: Setting a New Canadian Policy on Foreign Direct Investment**, Lorraine Eden, Carleton University, 1994.

No. 2   **Technological Change and International Economic Institutions**, Sylvia Ostry, Centre for International Studies, University of Toronto, under contract with Industry Canada, 1995.

No. 3   **Canadian Corporate Governance: Policy Options**, Ronald. J. Daniels, Faculty of Law, University of Toronto, and Randall Morck, Faculty of Business, University of Alberta, 1996.

No. 4   **Foreign Direct Investment and Market Framework Policies: Reducing Frictions in APEC Policies on Competition and Intellectual Property**, Ronald Hirshhorn, 1996.

No. 5   **Industry Canada's Foreign Investment Research: Messages and Policy Implications**, Ronald Hirshhorn, 1997.

No. 6   **International Market Contestability and the New Issues at the World Trade Organization**, Edward M. Graham, Institute for International Economics, Washington (DC), under contract with Industry Canada, 1998.

No. 7   **Implications of Foreign Ownership Restrictions for the Canadian Economy – A Sectoral Analysis**, Steven Globerman, Western Washington University, under contract with Industry Canada, 1999.

INDUSTRY CANADA OCCASIONAL PAPER SERIES

No. 1   **Formal and Informal Investment Barriers in the G-7 Countries: The Country Chapters**, Industry Canada, Micro-Economic Policy Analysis Staff including Ashfaq Ahmad, Colleen Barnes, John Knubley, Rosemary D. MacDonald and Christopher Wilkie, 1994.

       Formal and Informal Investment Barriers in the G-7 Countries: Summary and Conclusions, Industry Canada, Micro-Economic Policy Analysis Staff including Ashfaq Ahmad, Colleen Barnes and John Knubley, 1994.

No. 2   **Business Development Initiatives of Multinational Subsidiaries in Canada**, Julian Birkinshaw, University of Western Ontario, under contract with Industry Canada, 1995.

No. 3   **The Role of R&D Consortia in Technology Development**, Vinod Kumar, Research Centre for Technology Management, Carleton University, and Sunder Magun, Centre for Trade Policy and Law, University of Ottawa and Carleton University, under contract with Industry Canada, 1995.

No. 4   **Gender Tracking in University Programs**, Sid Gilbert, University of Guelph, and Alan Pomfret, King's College, University of Western Ontario, 1995.

No. 5   **Competitiveness: Concepts and Measures**, Donald G. McFetridge, Department of Economics, Carleton University, 1995.

No. 6   **Institutional Aspects of R&D Tax Incentives: The SR&ED Tax Credit**, G. Bruce Doern, School of Public Administration, Carleton University, 1995.

No. 7   **Competition Policy as a Dimension of Economic Policy: A Comparative Perspective**, Robert D. Anderson and S. Dev Khosla, Economics and International Affairs Branch, Bureau of Competition Policy, Industry Canada, 1995.

No. 8   **Mechanisms and Practices for the Assessment of The Social and Cultural Implications of Science and Technology**, Liora Salter, Osgoode Hall Law School, University of Toronto, under contract with Industry Canada, 1995.

No. 9   **Science and Technology: Perspectives for Public Policy**, Donald G. McFetridge, Department of Economics, Carleton University, under contract with Industry Canada, 1995.

No. 10   **Endogenous Innovation and Growth: Implications for Canada**, Pierre Fortin, Université du Québec à Montréal and the Canadian Institute for Advanced Research, and Elhanan Helpman, Tel Aviv University and the Canadian Institute for Advanced Research, under contract with Industry Canada, 1995.

No. 11   **The University-Industry Relationship in Science and Technology**, Jérôme Doutriaux, University of Ottawa, and Margaret Barker, Meg Barker Consulting, under contract with Industry Canada, 1995.

No. 12   **Technology and the Economy: A Review of Some Critical Relationships**, Michael Gibbons, University of Sussex, under contract with Industry Canada, 1995.

No. 13   **Management Skills Development in Canada**, Keith Newton, Industry Canada, 1995.

No. 14   **The Human Factor in Firm's Performance: Management Strategies for Productivity and Competitiveness in the Knowledge-Based Economy**, Keith Newton, Industry Canada, 1996.

No. 15   **Payroll Taxation and Employment: A Literature Survey**, Joni Baran, Industry Canada, 1996.

No. 16   **Sustainable Development: Concepts, Measures, Market and Policy Failures at the Open Economy, Industry and Firm Levels**, Philippe Crabbé, Institute for Research on the Environment and Economy, University of Ottawa, 1997.

No. 17   **Measuring Sustainable Development: A Review of Current Practice,** Peter Hardi and Stephan Barg, with Tony Hodge and Laszlo Pinter, International Institute for Sustainable Development, 1997.

No. 18   **Reducing Regulatory Barriers to Trade: Lessons for Canada from the European Experience**, Ramesh Chaitoo and Michael Hart, Center for Trade Policy and Law, Carleton University, 1997.

No. 19   **Analysis of International Trade Dispute Settlement Mechanisms and Implications for Canada's Agreement on Internal Trade**, E. Wayne Clendenning and Robert J. Clendenning, E. Wayne Clendenning & Associates Inc., under contract with Industry Canada, 1997.

No. 20   **Aboriginal Businesses: Characteristics and Strategies for Growth**, David Caldwell and Pamela Hunt, Management Consulting Centre, under contract with Aboriginal Business Canada, Industry Canada, 1998.

CANADA IN THE 21ST CENTURY SERIES

No. 1   **Global Trends: 1980-2015 and Beyond**, J. Bradford De Long, University of California, Berkeley, under contract with Industry Canada, 1998.

No. 2   **Broad Liberalization Based on Fundamentals: A Framework for Canadian Commercial Policy**, Randy Wigle, Wilfrid Laurier University, under contract with Industry Canada, 1998.

No. 3   **North American Economic Integration: 25 Years Backward and Forward**, Gary C. Hufbauer and Jeffrey J. Schott, Institute for International Economics, Washington (DC), under contract with Industry Canada, 1998.

No. 4   **Demographic Trends in Canada, 1996-2006 : Implications for the Public and Private Sectors,** David K. Foot, Richard A. Loreto and Thomas W. McCormack, Madison Avenue Demographics Group, under contract with Industry Canada, 1998.

No. 5   **Capital Investment Challenges in Canada,** Ronald P. M. Giammarino, University of British Columbia, under contract with Industry Canada, 1998.

No. 6   **Looking to the 21st Century – Infrastructure Investments for Economic Growth and for the Welfare and Well-Being of Canadians,** Christian DeBresson, Université du Québec à Montréal, and Stéphanie Barker, Université de Montréal, under contract with Industry Canada, 1998.

No. 7   **The Implications of Technological Change for Human Resource Policy,** Julian R. Betts, University of California, San Diego, under contract with Industry Canada, 1998.

No. 8   **Economics and the Environment: The Recent Canadian Experience and Prospects for the Future,** Brian R. Copeland, University of British Columbia, under contract with Industry Canada, 1998.

No. 9   **Individual Responses to Changes in the Canadian Labour Market,** Paul Beaudry and David A. Green, University of British Columbia, under contract with Industry Canada, 1998.

No. 10 **The Corporate Response – Innovation in the Information Age,** Randall Morck, University of Alberta, and Bernard Yeung, University of Michigan, under contract with Industry Canada, 1998.

No. 11 **Institutions and Growth: Framework Policy as a Tool of Competitive Advantage for Canada,** Ronald J. Daniels, University of Toronto, under contract with Industry Canada, 1998.

PERSPECTIVES ON NORTH AMERICAN FREE TRADE SERIES

No. 1   **Can Small-Country Manufacturing Survive Trade Liberalization? Evidence from the Canada–U.S. Free Trade Agreement,** Keith Head and John Ries, University of British Columbia, under contract with Industry Canada, 1999.

No. 2   **Modelling Links Between Canadian Trade and Foreign Direct Investment,** W. Hejazi and A.E. Safarian, University of Toronto, under contract with Industry Canada, 1999.

No. 3   **Trade Liberalisation and the Migration of Skilled Workers,** Steven Globerman, Western Washington University and Simon Fraser University, under contract with Industry Canada, 1999.

No. 4   **The Changing Industry and Skill Mix of Canada's International Trade,** Peter Dungan and Steve Murphy, Institute for Policy Analysis, University of Toronto, under contract with Industry Canada, 1999.

JOINT PUBLICATIONS

Capital Budgeting in the Public Sector, in collaboration with the John Deutsch Institute, Jack Mintz and Ross S. Preston eds., 1994.

Infrastructure and Competitiveness, in collaboration with the John Deutsch Institute, Jack Mintz and Ross S. Preston eds., 1994.

Getting the Green Light: Environmental Regulation and Investment in Canada, in collaboration with the C.D. Howe Institute, Jamie Benidickson, G. Bruce Doern and Nancy Olewiler, 1994.

To obtain copies of documents published under the Research Publications Program, please contact:

Publications Officer
Micro-Economic Policy Analysis
Industry Canada
5th Floor, West Tower
235 Queen Street
Ottawa, Ontario, K1A 0H5

Tel.: (613) 952-5704
Fax: (613) 991-1261
E-mail: mepa.apme@ic.gc.ca

Programme des publications
de recherche d'Industrie Canada

PERSPECTIVES SUR LE LIBRE-ÉCHANGE NORD-AMÉRICAIN

ÉVOLUTION DU PROFIL SECTORIEL ET PROFESSIONNEL DU COMMERCE INTERNATIONAL DU CANADA

Par Peter Dungan et Steve Murphy,
Université de Toronto

Also available in English

Données de catalogage avant publication (Canada)

Dungan, D. Peter

Évolution du profil sectoriel et professionnel du commerce international du Canada

(Perspectives sur le libre-échange nord-américain)
Texte en français et en anglais disposé tête-bêche.
Titre de la p. de t. addit.: The changing industry and skill mix of Canada's international trade.
Comprend des références bibliographiques.
ISBN 0-662-64211-2
No de cat. C21-28/4-1999

1. Commerce extérieur et emploi – Canada.
2. Travail, Marché du – Canada.
3. Commerce international.
I. Murphy, Steven.
II. Canada. Industrie Canada.
III. Titre.
IV. Coll.

HD5710.75C3D86 1999   382.0971   C99-980165-1F

Vous trouverez, à la fin du présent ouvrage, des renseignements sur les documents publiés dans le cadre du Programme des publications de recherche et sur la façon d'en obtenir des exemplaires. Des sommaires des documents et cahiers de recherche publiés dans les diverses collections d'Industrie Canada, ainsi que le texte intégral de notre bulletin trimestriel, *MICRO*, peuvent être consultés sur *STRATEGIS*, le service d'information commerciale en direct du Ministère, à l'adresse http://strategis.ic.gc.ca.

Prière d'adresser tout commentaire à :

Someshwar Rao
Directeur
Analyse des investissements stratégiques
Analyse de la politique micro-économique
Industrie Canada
5e étage, tour ouest
235, rue Queen
Ottawa (Ontario) K1A 0H5

Tél. : (613) 941-8187
Fax : (613) 991-1261
Courriel : rao.someshwar@ic.gc.ca

Remerciements

Nous tenons à remercier Frank Lee, Surendra Gera et les participants à un atelier d'Industrie Canada qui ont fait des suggestions très utiles sur une version antérieure de la présente étude. Nous voudrions aussi remercier deux lecteurs-arbitres anonymes pour les commentaires pertinents qu'ils ont formulés. Bien entendu, nous demeurons seuls responsables de toute erreur qui pourrait subsister.

TABLE DES MATIÈRES

PRÉFACE

Vers le milieu des années 80, alors que la production et les marchés prenaient une orientation et une envergure de plus en plus internationales, le Canada risquait d'être relégué à la périphérie de l'économie mondiale. Notre pays ne possédait pas les éléments requis pour étendre sa participation aux marchés étrangers et nous risquions de perdre nos propres marchés. En outre, avec plus des deux tiers de nos exportations prenant la destination des États-Unis, et cette part allant en s'accroissant, nous étions fortement exposés aux sentiments protectionnistes montants dans ce pays. Essentiellement, notre prospérité passée nous avait rendus insouciants devant la situation précaire dans laquelle nous nous trouvions en tant que nation commerçante.

C'est dans un tel contexte que le gouvernement a pris les mesures nécessaires pour relancer et renforcer l'économie canadienne plutôt que de résister aux forces du changement qui se manifestaient dans le monde. L'approche du gouvernement a consisté à faire du secteur privé l'élément moteur de ce renouveau économique. Des politiques ont été mises en place pour encourager et récompenser l'esprit d'entreprise et faciliter l'adaptation au nouvel ordre économique.

Comme nation commerçante, un objectif évident était de mettre de l'ordre dans nos relations commerciales avec les États-Unis. Il fut convenu qu'un accord de libre-échange était nécessaire pour faire échec aux tendances protectionnistes qui se manifestaient aux États-Unis et accroître la sécurité d'accès du Canada au marché américain tout en améliorant la prévisibilité de nos relations commerciales avec notre voisin du Sud.

L'Accord de libre-échange Canada-États-Unis (ALE) est ainsi entré en vigueur en 1989. Cinq ans plus tard, soit en 1994, l'Accord de libre-échange nord-américain (ALENA) était conclu; essentiellement, il étendait les dispositions de l'ALE au marché en croissance rapide du Mexique.

Ces accords de libre-échange devaient accroître la prospérité du Canada en améliorant l'efficience et la productivité des entreprises canadiennes. On estime que de telles ententes sont mutuellement bénéfiques aux économies des parties en cause et qu'elles sont particulièrement profitables aux économies de taille relativement modeste comme celle du Canada. Dans un premier temps, ils exposent à la concurrence internationale les entreprises nationales jusque-là protégées. Puis, ils récompensent les sociétés innovatrices et productives en leur permettant d'avoir accès à des marchés de plus grande taille. En retour, ces effets accroissent les flux commerciaux entre les pays participants et améliorent l'efficience générale des économies signataires. L'ALE et l'ALENA ne font pas exception à cette règle et ces deux accords ont été signés dans l'espoir de concrétiser ces avantages pour l'économie canadienne après une période d'ajustement initiale. Néanmoins, des préoccupations légitimes se sont manifestées au sujet des fermetures possibles d'entreprises et des pertes d'emplois au Canada.

Plus de dix années se sont écoulées depuis l'entrée en vigueur de l'ALE — un délai suffisant pour nous permettre d'évaluer avec une certitude raisonnable les conséquences de l'Accord pour l'économie canadienne. Dans ce contexte, la Direction de l'analyse de la politique micro-économique a invité un groupe de spécialistes à faire un examen de l'économie canadienne à la lumière de l'ALE. Les six études qui découlent de cet exercice sont en voie de publication sous le thème général *Perspectives sur le libre-échange nord-américain*. Les auteurs de ces études abordent une vaste gamme de questions allant de l'impact de l'ALE sur les flux commerciaux interprovinciaux à ses conséquences sur la

performance de l'économie canadienne au chapitre de la productivité. En outre, la viabilité du secteur manufacturier canadien y est évaluée, de même que la relation entre les sorties d'investissement étranger direct et les flux commerciaux. Ces études traitent également des conséquences du commerce pour l'évolution de la structure industrielle du Canada et la composition des compétences, parallèlement à une évaluation des profils de migration entre le Canada et les États-Unis.

Peter Dungan et Steve Murphy entreprennent un examen de l'évolution de la composition industrielle et professionnelle des exportations et des importations canadiennes au cours des trois dernières décennies. La principale technique qu'ils utilisent est l'analyse entrées-sorties (E/S). Cette analyse est complétée par des données détaillées sur le secteur de l'éducation (représentant les compétences) tirées du Système de projections des professions au Canada (SPPC).

Ces données permettent aux auteurs de faire des estimations de la mesure dans laquelle l'emploi au Canada est associé aux exportations et aux importations et de vérifier si, avec le temps, les changements observés dans la composition industrielle de nos échanges ont eu un impact sur la composition de l'emploi et des compétences de la main-d'oeuvre. Une constatation clé qui ressort de l'étude de Dungan et Murphy est qu'en dépit de l'importance croissante des exportations dans l'activité économique totale, la croissance de la part de l'emploi attribuable aux exportations a été beaucoup moins prononcée. La principale raison avancée par les auteurs pour expliquer ce phénomène est que les exportations ont, de nos jours, un contenu en importations beaucoup plus élevé au niveau des intrants intermédiaires que par le passé. De même, si les biens que nous importons devaient être produits au Canada, notre technologie aurait tendance à les produire avec une proportion beaucoup plus grande d'intrants intermédiaires importés que par le passé.

Les auteurs constatent également que les changements observés dans la composition de l'emploi sont directement liés à la composition des exportations, ainsi qu'au degré de pénétration des importations au niveau des intrants intermédiaires. La productivité relative de la main-d'oeuvre et le changement technique sont considérés comme moins importants.

SOMMAIRE

Cette étude vise à examiner en détail la composition industrielle et professionnelle des exportations et des importations canadiennes en 1997 et à voir comment elle a évolué depuis 1961. Certaines questions importantes sous-tendent l'étude : Quelle proportion de l'emploi au Canada est associée aux exportations et comment la situation a-t-elle évolué au cours des trois dernières décennies? Dans quelle mesure les exportations canadiennes et l'emploi lié aux exportations dépendent-ils des matières premières et dans quelle mesure nos exportations ont-elles évolué vers la fabrication tertiaire et les services? Même si l'on observe une telle tendance, ses répercussions sur la composition professionnelle ne ressortent pas clairement : certains emplois du secteur primaire nécessitent des compétences considérables et sont très bien rémunérés, tandis que certains emplois du secteur manufacturier et des services ne demandent que peu de compétences et sont mal rémunérés. Dans quelle mesure la composition de l'emploi lié aux exportations canadiennes, sous l'angle de la scolarité et des compétences, a-t-elle évolué avec le temps et par rapport à l'emploi dans l'ensemble de l'économie? Du côté des importations, nous retrouvons la notion largement répandue selon laquelle une économie plus ouverte et une plus grande dépendance à l'égard des importations ont eu pour effet de réduire le nombre d'emplois peu spécialisés au Canada et ont abaissé les revenus des travailleurs les moins qualifiés. Dans quelle mesure pouvons-nous retracer une telle tendance dans les données de la période 1961-1997?

Les auteurs ont fait appel aux techniques d'analyse entrées-sorties pour répondre à ces questions et l'étude est enrichie de données sectorielles détaillées sur la scolarité provenant du Système de projections des professions au Canada (SPPC). Ils sont partis des études antérieures réalisées à Industrie Canada et ailleurs en utilisant des tableaux entrées-sorties annuels pour 1961 à 1992 et des données détaillées supplémentaires pour prolonger l'analyse jusqu'à 1997, en s'appuyant sur une désagrégation industrielle un peu plus étendue. Les résultats sont présentés sous forme tant agrégée que désagrégée, accompagnés de divers tests de sensibilité et d'une décompositions des sources des changements observés dans l'emploi lié aux exportations et au « remplacement des importations » au cours de la période 1961-1997.

Principales constatations

- Si la part des exportations et des importations dans l'économie canadienne a enregistré une forte croissance depuis 1961 — et plus particulièrement au cours des années 90 — la progression de la part de l'emploi attribuable aux exportations (ou « déplacée » par les importations) a été *beaucoup moins rapide*. La principale explication réside du côté de la pénétration des importations : aujourd'hui, les exportations ont un contenu en importations beaucoup plus élevé sous forme d'intrants intermédiaires que par le passé. Dans le cas des importations, si celles-ci devaient également être produites au Canada, la technologie actuelle nécessiterait un apport beaucoup plus important en intrants intermédiaires importés que dans les années 60.

- Lorsque les résultats sectoriels détaillés sont agrégés, les exportations canadiennes se retrouvent toujours *au-dessus de la moyenne* de la production totale du secteur des entreprises pour ce qui est de la productivité de la main-d'oeuvre — en particulier lorsque l'effet de l'agriculture dans les années 60 est neutralisé. Cependant, cette productivité relativement élevée de la main-d'oeuvre dans le secteur des exportations ne révèle pratiquement *aucune tendance à la hausse*. Parallèlement à une productivité plus élevée de la

main-d'oeuvre, on retrouve un rendement plus élevé du facteur travail dans le secteur d'exportation; mais encore une fois, cette performance relative des exportations ne révèle pratiquement aucune tendance temporelle. Étant donné que la part de l'emploi attribuable aux exportations a augmenté progressivement, nous pouvons en conclure que les exportations contribuent à relever à la fois le *niveau global* de la productivité de la main-d'oeuvre au Canada et le rendement du facteur travail.

- Les sources de changement de la composition de l'emploi lié aux exportations canadiennes sont principalement la composition des exportations finales et le degré de pénétration des importations au niveau des intrants intermédiaires. De façon générale, les variations intersectorielles au niveau de la productivité relative de la main-d'oeuvre, c'est-à-dire le « changement technique » intégré aux changements observés dans les coefficients entrées-sorties, ont une importance moindre. La même remarque peut être faite essentiellement pour ce qui est des changements dans la composition de l'emploi lié aux importations canadiennes.

- Les parts de l'emploi lié aux exportations ont changé dans une gamme plus étendue d'industries que ce que l'on aurait pu prévoir. Des dix groupes industriels dont la part de l'emploi lié aux exportations a augmenté de plus d'un point de pourcentage entre 1961 et 1997, quatre sont des industries de services (services personnels et autres, services aux entreprises, commerce et finance), mais les six autres sont des industries manufacturières diverses, dont certaines étaient prévisibles compte tenu du Pacte de l'automobile et de l'évolution de la technologie — par exemple les véhicules à moteur, les produits électriques et électroniques, et les produits en caoutchouc et en plastique — et certaines l'étaient beaucoup moins — comme le cuir, les textiles et le vêtement. Des quatre industries dont la part de l'emploi lié aux exportations affiche un recul de plus d'un point de pourcentage, les deux plus importantes diminutions touchent la production primaire (l'exploitation minière à l'exclusion du pétrole et du gaz et le secteur de l'agriculture, de l'exploitation forestière et de la pêche), l'une est une industrie de transformation de matières premières et de fabrication (papier et produits connexes et impression), tandis que la quatrième est l'industrie des transports.

- En combinant les résultats tirés de l'analyse entrées-sorties et les données sur la composition de la scolarité par industrie, on arrive à la conclusion que depuis 1961, la composition de l'emploi lié aux exportations canadiennes (directes et indirectes) a constamment évolué en faveur des industries où l'on retrouve des travailleurs plus scolarisés. Mais cela est également vrai de l'emploi *dans l'ensemble* du secteur des entreprises. Si nous comparons le secteur des exportations à l'ensemble du secteur des entreprises pour ce qui est de l'incidence des divers profils de scolarité, la conclusion qui s'en dégage est que l'emploi lié aux exportations est distribué de façon « bi-polaire ». Les exportations *dépassent* la moyenne de l'ensemble de l'économie pour ce qui est de l'emploi de travailleurs faiblement scolarisés et de l'emploi de travailleurs possédant une scolarité relativement avancée. Les ratios relatifs n'ont changé que très peu au cours des trois dernières décennies.

- La productivité de la main-d'oeuvre occupant des emplois « déplacés » par les importations (si ces dernières étaient produites avec la technologie canadienne) est invariablement *inférieure* à celle des emplois liés aux importations — même si elle est *supérieure* à la moyenne du secteur des entreprises au cours de la plupart des années. Le ratio a chuté aux environs de la moyenne de l'économie ces dernières années, ce qui indique qu'il y a eu

remplacement de certains des emplois les moins productifs. Néanmoins, les données montrent que les importations, dans l'ensemble, ne remplacent pas de façon particulièrement notable les emplois les moins productifs (qui sont probablement concentrés dans les services non commercialisables). Cependant, les importations déplacent « relativement » plus d'emplois que les exportations n'en ajoutent. Si les politiques macro-économiques peuvent contribuer à maintenir l'économie près du plein emploi et que le rythme du changement n'est pas trop rapide, cela veut dire que le Canada remplace des emplois peu productifs par des emplois hautement productifs grâce à l'expansion des échanges internationaux et s'en trouve ainsi avantagé.

• Si nous comparons les changements dans les parts de l'emploi des exportations et des importations, il est remarquable de constater que les hausses et les baisses les plus importantes sont survenues, dans bien des cas, dans les *mêmes* secteurs. Les services personnels, les services aux entreprises et le commerce font voir les augmentations les plus importantes pour ce qui est des parts de l'emploi tant des exportations que des importations, tandis que l'exploitation minière, l'agriculture et l'exploitation forestière montrent les diminutions les plus importantes des parts de l'emploi, tant pour les exportations que les importations. Le coefficient d'emploi dans les services liés aux exportations et aux importations canadiennes a augmenté, tandis que le coefficient d'emploi lié à la production de matières premières a diminué tant pour les exportations que pour les importations.

• L'analyse du profil de scolarité révèle que, du moins sous l'angle de la technologie canadienne et de la part de la scolarité par secteur, le contenu éducatif des importations canadiennes est supérieur à la moyenne du secteur des entreprises. Depuis quelques années, toutefois, cet écart a diminué, ce qui indique une certaine intensification de la concurrence provenant des importations dans les secteurs où l'on retrouve les travailleurs les moins qualifiés. Néanmoins, le contenu éducatif des importations canadiennes demeure au-dessus de la moyenne du secteur des entreprises. Ce résultat peut sembler en contradiction avec la conclusion précédente au sujet de la productivité de la main-d'oeuvre et du rendement du facteur travail. Cependant, il faut se rappeler que nous avons aussi constaté que la productivité et le rendement du facteur travail dans le secteur des importations étaient *supérieurs* à la moyenne du secteur des entreprises, même s'ils étaient inférieurs aux valeurs correspondantes pour les exportations. Un profil de scolarité supérieur à la moyenne du secteur des entreprises n'est pas incompatible avec cette dernière observation. L'anomalie réside peut-être dans le fait que la productivité et le rendement de la main-d'oeuvre liée aux *exportations* sont si élevés alors qu'au moins une partie du contenu éducatif est faible. Cependant, il est plus facile de comprendre cette anomalie si l'on se rappelle que la scolarité, interprétée au sens large, n'est pas le seul déterminant de la productivité et du rendement de la main-d'oeuvre; un coefficient élevé de capital et une forte dotation en ressources naturelles sont également des facteurs importants.

1. INTRODUCTION

Cette étude vise à examiner en détail la composition industrielle et professionnelle des exportations et des importations canadiennes en 1997 et à voir comment elle a évolué au cours des trois dernières décennies. Manifestement, certaines questions importantes sous-tendent cette étude. Le Canada, du moins à une époque, avait la réputation d'être un pays de « porteurs d'eau et de scieurs de bois » — autrement dit, d'être principalement un exportateur de matières premières et un importateur de biens finis. Dans quelle mesure cela est-il encore vrai? Dans quelle mesure nos exportations ont-elles évolué vers les produits manufacturiers tertiaires et les services? Même s'il y a eu un tel mouvement, les répercussions sur la composition professionnelle ne ressortent pas tout à fait clairement : au moins certains emplois du secteur primaire exigent des compétences considérables et sont très bien rémunérés, tandis que de nombreux emplois du secteur manufacturier et des services n'exigent que peu de compétences et sont mal rémunérés. Du côté des importations, il y a la perception largement répandue selon laquelle une économie plus ouverte et une plus grande dépendance à l'égard des importations ont contribué à réduire le nombre d'emplois peu qualifiés au Canada et ont provoqué une diminution des revenus des travailleurs les moins qualifiés.

La principale méthode utilisée est l'analyse entrées-sorties; cette méthode a été employée dans un certain nombre d'études récentes menées à Industrie Canada et par d'autres chercheurs canadiens. Cependant, nous avons pu étendre la période examinée dans les études antérieures en utilisant une série temporelle complète de tableaux entrées-sorties pour 1961 à 1992 et en y ajoutant des données détaillées supplémentaires par industrie pour prolonger l'analyse jusqu'à 1997. L'analyse entrées-sorties a été effectuée à un niveau passablement désagrégé, les calculs permettant d'examiner plus de 150 industries. Enfin, nous avons pu compléter l'analyse entrées-sorties à l'aide des données détaillées au niveau de l'industrie sur la composition des compétences, qui ont été tirées du Système de projections des professions au Canada (SPPC) pour les années 1986 et 1991. Ces données ont servi à faire des estimations de l'évolution de la composition de la scolarité ou des compétences liées aux exportations et aux importations, dans la mesure où les changements dans la composition des compétences sont attribuables aux changements dans la composition industrielle.

Trois réserves doivent être faites au sujet des méthodes et des résultats. Premièrement, il est important de noter que si la composition industrielle et professionnelle des exportations est une notion relativement claire, la notion de composition industrielle et professionnelle des importations signifie, dans le contexte de notre étude, la composition industrielle et professionnelle de la production équivalente ou concurrentielle au Canada et non la composition industrielle et professionnelle dans les pays étrangers d'où proviennent les importations. Deuxièmement, l'analyse entrées-sorties et les calculs connexes sur les compétences faits dans le cadre de l'étude peuvent permettre des descriptions et des associations importantes mais non nécessairement une « causalité ». À titre d'exemple, s'il est possible d'observer que les exportations sont associées à un nombre donné d'emplois à un moment précis, cela ne veut pas nécessairement dire que les exportations ont créé ou « causé » ces emplois, ni que les travailleurs ainsi employés demeureraient sans emploi en l'absence de ces exportations. La troisième réserve a trait au fait que la description et l'analyse sont fondées sur des rapports entrées-sorties survenus, du moins en partie, parce que les prix et les raretés relatifs étaient ce qu'ils étaient au cours d'une année donnée, bien que nous supposions qu'ils soient « fixes » (« technologie de Leontief »). Si les prix relatifs avaient été différents — par exemple en raison d'une politique monétaire ou d'une politique de change différente — alors des technologies différentes auraient pu être adoptées et des coefficients entrées-sorties différents auraient été observés. La présente étude vise surtout à offrir une première

description de ce qui s'est produit, en vue d'une analyse plus approfondie de la causalité et, éventuellement, de la formulation de recommandations axées sur les politiques.

L'étude se présente comme suit : le chapitre 2 renferme une description plus détaillée des données et des méthodes de calcul utilisées. Le chapitre 3 passe en revue certains des écrits antérieurs en faisant ressortir les différences et les progrès accomplis dans la présente étude par rapport aux travaux canadiens qui l'ont précédée. Le chapitre 4 renferme un examen de l'évolution du rôle joué par les exportations dans l'économie canadienne depuis 1961 et de la façon dont la production industrielle et la composition de l'emploi lié aux exportations a évolué avec le temps. Les changements dans la composition de l'emploi sont ventilés en quatre grandes composantes. Puis, en ajoutant des données sur la composition professionnelle par industrie, nous examinons la composition selon la scolarité/compétences des exportations canadiennes au cours des années récentes et, dans la mesure du possible, nous tentons de déterminer comment la composition globale a évolué avec le temps. Le chapitre 5 reprend l'analyse du chapitre 4 pour le secteur des importations. Enfin, le chapitre 6 renferme nos conclusions et un résumé des principales constatations. Des détails supplémentaires sur les calculs, les tests de sensibilité et les résultats industriels à un niveau plus détaillé sont présentés en appendice.

2. DONNÉES ET MÉTHODES

Aux fins d'étudier la composition des exportations et des importations canadiennes selon l'emploi et les compétences de 1961 à 1997, deux grandes sources de données ont été exploitées. La première est la série temporelle des tableaux entrées-sorties détaillés produite par Statistique Canada. L'Institute for Policy Analysis a recueilli cette série de données au fil des années et préparé diverses applications informatiques pour l'exploiter. Nos calculs entrées-sorties ont été faits à ce que Statistique Canada appelle le niveau de désagrégation « L » (« étendu »), qui nous permet d'examiner plus de 160 industries. Cet ensemble de données couvre la période 1961 à 1992 par tranche annuelle.

Malheureusement, au moment où l'étude a été réalisée, les tableaux entrées-sorties pour les années postérieures à 1992 n'étaient pas disponibles. Dans le but de pousser l'analyse jusqu'en 1997, nous avons recueilli des données sur le produit intérieur agrégé, les exportations, les importations et l'emploi et nous les avons jumelées aussi fidèlement que possible aux catégories de la désagrégation « L ». Nous avons combiné ces données aux tableaux entrées-sorties de 1992 pour prolonger notre analyse des exportations et des importations jusqu'en 1997. Cependant, les résultats pour la période 1993-1997 doivent être interprétés avec prudence, tant parce que nous avons utilisé uniquement les tableaux de 1992 que parce que notre jumelage des données publiées sur la production, l'emploi, etc. avec les catégories d'entrées-sorties demeure, au mieux, une approximation.

Pourquoi utiliser des données entrées-sorties? Pourquoi ne pas examiner simplement les industries « d'exportation » ou les industries qui « concurrencent les importations » et y dénombrer les emplois? La réponse aux deux questions réside dans la structure multi-sectorielle de la production ou, comme on le dit parfois, dans la « production de biens à l'aide de biens ». Si le Canada exporte des automobiles pour une certaine valeur et que l'industrie de l'automobile emploie un nombre donné de travailleurs, cela est une information valable qui, cependant, est loin de tout révéler. Les voitures exportées peuvent renfermer de l'acier produit au Canada et cet acier peut lui-même avoir été produit à partir de minerai de fer canadien. Une partie des employés des industries de l'acier et des mines ont donc été impliqués *indirectement* dans l'exportation de ces voitures et il est important de comptabiliser de façon appropriée l'emploi engendré par les exportations en tenant compte de ces intrants indirects. En outre, une bonne partie des voitures exportées peuvent avoir été produites à l'aide de pièces *importées* — ce qui n'aurait aucun effet sur l'emploi au Canada — tandis que les exportations d'un autre produit ou service, en apparence de moindre valeur, pourraient avoir un contenu canadien beaucoup plus important et, ainsi, un impact global plus grand sur l'emploi au Canada. Par conséquent, il est aussi important de tenir compte du contenu relatif en *importations* dans la production des intrants indirects.

Heureusement, le système de données entrées-sorties fournit, pour chaque année, un tableau de toutes ces interactions sectorielles et, par des manipulations appropriées, on peut déduire l'ensemble de la chaîne des facteurs de production entrant dans les exportations (ou qui auraient remplacé des importations). De là l'importance de la base de données entrées-sorties pour la présente étude. Les estimations de l'emploi engendré par les exportations (ou, de façon générale, des biens remplacés par les importations) qui sont tirées de ces données ne sont pas la somme des emplois dans ce que l'on considère comme les industries « axées sur les exportations », mais plutôt la somme des employés correspondant à la contribution des industries qui produisent pour l'exportation soit directement soit indirectement à toutes les étapes du processus de production.

Pour chacune des années de 1961 à 1997, nous avons procédé comme suit dans nos calculs initiaux sur la composition industrielle[1]. Nous débutons avec la matrice des demandes finales par

catégorie de demande finale et par industrie. Les colonnes de cette matrice correspondant aux exportations ou aux importations nous révèlent la ventilation industrielle des exportations et des importations pour l'année visée. (Dorénavant, nous mentionnerons uniquement les effets des exportations, mais la détermination de l'incidence des importations suit un cheminement très semblable)[2]. La colonne est ensuite multipliée par l'« inverse de Leontief » de la matrice des coefficients entrées-sorties pour estimer la production brute de chacune des 161 industries entrant dans les exportations pour cette année *avec* tous les intrants intermédiaires en remontant la chaîne de production. Pour ceux qui ne sont pas familiers avec la terminologie de l'analyse entrées-sorties, l'« inverse de Leontief » est simplement le résultat final des manipulations des données entrées-sorties requises pour dégager les effets de dépenses particulières (comme les exportations) sur la production industrielle en tenant compte de toutes les étapes de traitement intermédiaire. À noter également que les calculs que nous utilisons englobent aussi automatiquement la « perte » moyenne des importations pour les demandes de chaque industrie, tel qu'il ressort des données de l'année en cause. Les coefficients tirés des données entrées-sorties sont ensuite appliqués aux effets ainsi calculés de la production brute pour en arriver aux effets sur la production intérieure au coût des facteurs (ci-après le « produit intérieur »), l'emploi et les traitements et salaires gagnés — et, par conséquent, la rémunération moyenne dans les secteurs d'exportation. Ces résultats sont présentés et examinés tant en termes absolus qu'en tant que parts relatives du produit intérieur et de l'emploi total pour l'année visée.

En comparant nos calculs sur une base annuelle et pour différents intervalles de temps, nous pouvons voir comment a évolué la composition de la production et de l'emploi associés aux exportations canadiennes. Nous présentons des données détaillées pour l'ensemble des 161 industries mais, également, pour une agrégation plus restreinte au niveau de 24 industries afin de faire ressortir les grandes tendances de la production axée sur l'exportation.

La base de données entrées-sorties canadienne est disponible tant en dollars courants (nominaux) qu'en dollars constants (réels). Les données exprimées en dollars constants produites par Statistique Canada comportent des années de base différentes pour différents intervalles de temps et il est nécessaire de les intégrer si l'on veut obtenir une série temporelle complète de 1961 à 1992. Nous avons effectué nos calculs en utilisant principalement les tableaux renfermant des données nominales et cela, pour plusieurs raisons. Premièrement, puisque nous nous intéressons principalement à l'évolution des *parts* de la production et de l'emploi, il n'y a pas de distorsion attribuable à l'inflation dans nos calculs fondés sur les données nominales. Nous examinons simplement les changements dans les gains relatifs en dollars ou dans l'emploi relatif des différentes catégories d'exportation ou d'importation. Deuxièmement, il est très difficile de déflater la quantité considérable de données que renferment les tableaux entrées-sorties et la possibilité d'une erreur doit être prise en considération. Dans le cas présent, les données nominales sont des données brutes et elles risquent moins d'avoir été faussées par des jugements. Comme nous l'avons déjà indiqué, pour obtenir une série temporelle complète de données entrées-sorties réelles, plusieurs sous-périodes ayant des années de base différentes doivent être réunies, ce qui accroît encore le risque de distorsion. Enfin, on ne peut faire une projection sur la période 1992–1997 en termes *réels* pour les exportations et les importations au niveau et pour le genre de données détaillées requises par la désagrégation des tableaux entrées-sorties à 160 industries — du moins pas avec les ressources dont nous disposions. Pour avoir une série cohérente de 1961 à 1997, nous devions utiliser les données entrées-sorties nominales.

Afin de vérifier la sensibilité au choix des séries nominales et réelles, nous avons fait certains calculs, présentés ci-après, avec les *deux* ensembles de données pour la période 1961-1992 et nous avons comparé les résultats. Dans l'ensemble, les données nominales produisent des résultats généralement équivalents à ceux obtenus à l'aide des données réelles; là où elles diffèrent, les séries nominales sont

plus lisses d'une année à l'autre et intuitivement plus attrayantes. Étant donné que les changements sont observés pour l'ensemble de la période 1961-1997 ou pour des intervalles de dix ans à l'intérieur de cette période, il est important d'en connaître la source. Il y a deux sources possibles de changement dans la composition de la production liée aux exportations : premièrement, les changements dans la composition sectorielle des exportations canadiennes (qui ressortent de l'évolution des coefficients du vecteur des exportations dans la matrice de la demande finale) et, deuxièmement, les changements dans les procédés industriels utilisés pour produire les biens exportés (qui ressortent des changements observés dans les divers coefficients du système d'entrées-sorties). Nous avons décomposé ces deux éléments en appliquant la composition des exportations de 1961 aux coefficients entrées-sorties de 1971 et vice versa. Dans le système entrées-sorties, nous avons en outre différencié les changements observés dans les coefficients « techniques » d'entrées-sorties (ceux qui décrivent comment une industrie utilise les produits des autres industries comme intrants) et les changements observés dans les coefficients d'importation (qui traduisent l'évolution de la composition des importations et de la production intérieure servant à satisfaire la demande finale et intermédiaire de biens). Pour ce qui est de l'évolution de l'emploi lié aux exportations, une source supplémentaire de changement est l'évolution de la productivité relative de la main-d'oeuvre dans les différentes industries entre les années délimitant la comparaison. Encore une fois, cette source est identifiée séparément en examinant les changements des coefficients d'emploi/production entre les années comparées. Au total, quatre sources de changement dans l'emploi lié aux exportations ou aux importations sont examinées : 1) les changements dans la composition des exportations ou des importations, 2) les changements dans les coefficients « techniques » d'entrées-sorties, 3) les changements dans les besoins d'importation associés à la demande intermédiaire ou finale et 4) les changements dans la productivité relative de la main-d'oeuvre entre les divers secteurs[3].

La deuxième grande source de données utilisée dans la présente étude est la base de données sur l'emploi industriel par profession et par niveau de scolarité (compétences) maintenue par le groupe responsable du Système de projections des professions au Canada (SPPC) au sein de Développement des ressources humaines Canada. En coordonnant cette base de données avec la base de données entrées-sorties et en tenant compte de certains composants « non attribués » dans la base de données du SPPC, nous pouvons obtenir une désagrégation au niveau de 112 industries. Malheureusement, des données ne sont disponibles que pour deux années : 1991 et 1986[4]. Cela signifie que nous pouvons examiner les changements survenus dans le profil de scolarité uniquement *au sein des industries* entre ces deux dates. Nous avons examiné les changements dans le profil de scolarité entre 1986 et 1991, mais pour toutes les années antérieures à 1986, nous avons utilisé le profil de scolarité de 1986, tandis que pour les années 1992 à 1997, nous avons utilisé le profil de scolarité de 1991. Cependant, en utilisant les profils de scolarité de 1986 ou de 1991 avec les données entrées-sorties montrant comment la composition des exportations et des importations par industrie a changé de 1961 à 1986 et de 1991 à 1997, nous avons pu au moins tirer des enseignements précieux de l'évolution globale du profil des compétences qui découle des changements observés dans la composition *industrielle* au cours de ces périodes. En outre, les données entrées-sorties par industrie nous permettent non seulement de déterminer les changements dans la composition de l'emploi par industrie, mais également les changements dans la productivité de la main-d'oeuvre et le rendement global du facteur travail (de fait, l'impact des salaires).

L'application des données tirées du SPPC est relativement simple. Comme nous l'avons noté précédemment, les calculs d'entrées-sorties nous fournissent l'emploi par industrie associé aux exportations pour chacune des années examinées, au niveau de désagrégation de 161 industries. Premièrement, nous avons agrégé jusqu'au niveau de 112 industries permis par le SPPC. Puis, nous avons simplement réparti les estimations de l'emploi total à l'aide des parts tirées des données du SPPC en fonction de la ventilation souhaitée selon la scolarité (ou la profession, le cas échéant). Au terme de ces calculs, nous pouvons affirmer à peu près ce qui suit : en 1961, les exportations représentaient

x p. 100 de l'emploi total. Ces emplois étaient répartis parmi les niveaux de scolarité suivants : pas d'études secondaires, études secondaires, école technique, université et collège, diplôme d'études supérieures, etc. (mais ils faut se rappeler que nous avons utilisé les pondérations de scolarité de 1986 pour 1961!) Nous pouvons ensuite présenter les mêmes chiffres pour 1997 et certaines années intermédiaires puis les comparer aux données de 1961 pour faire ressortir les changements au niveau des proportions et des parts. Comme nous l'avons noté dans la présentation de l'analyse entrées-sorties, nous avons pu ventiler les effets au niveau de l'emploi entre les changements survenus dans la composition des exportations, les changements observés dans les coefficients techniques et d'importation (ou la structure de la production) et les changements observés dans la productivité relative de la main-d'oeuvre entre les divers secteurs. En outre, entre 1986 et 1991, nous avons pu mesurer la contribution découlant de l'évolution de la composition des compétences ou des professions *au sein* des diverses industries.

3. CONTEXTE ET ÉTUDES CONNEXES

Bien que l'objectif premier de la présente étude soit de produire de nouvelles données empiriques, nous avons examiné la documentation pertinente afin de voir si des études comparables avaient été réalisées pour le Canada ou pour d'autres nations industrialisées. Il existe, bien entendu, une vaste littérature sur l'incidence des changements observés dans les niveaux et les conditions du commerce extérieur sur l'emploi et les salaires, tant au niveau de l'économie qu'à celui d'industries particulières. La préoccupation politique sous-jacente est que l'intensification des échanges avec des pays en développement, où l'on verse de faibles salaires, aura un effet préjudiciable sur les industries où la main-d'oeuvre est peu spécialisée et faiblement rémunérée dans les pays industrialisés, ce qui entraînera un chômage plus élevé parmi les travailleurs peu spécialisés, et une diminution de leur pouvoir d'achat relatif (et, partant, un écart croissant entre les gains des travailleurs hautement spécialisés et peu spécialisés dans ces pays). Le principal fondement de cette analyse est le principe (la théorie) de Heckscher-Ohlin — dont l'énoncé central est que les pays qui exportent des biens utilisent de façon intensive les facteurs de production dont ils possèdent une abondance relative (Wood, 1995, p. 58). De nombreuses études ont été consacrées à ce sujet, notamment pour les États-Unis. Entre autres exemples, nous pouvons citer les textes de Freeman, Richardson et Wood parus dans un numéro spécial du *Journal of Economic Perspectives* en 1995, ainsi que les études de Sachs et Shatz et de Feenstra et Hanson, parues dans les *AEA Papers and Proceedings* de 1996. Un sommaire antérieur de la situation aux États-Unis est présenté dans Levy et Murnane (1992). En outre, on retrouve de nombreuses études consacrées à certains ou à l'ensemble des pays de l'OCDE, lesquelles englobent souvent des pays moins développés (PMD). Entre autres exemples, il y à l'étude de Lawrence (1996) et celle de Thygesen, Kosai et Lawrence (1996).

Cependant, s'il existe une abondante documentation sur la question fondamentale des échanges et des salaires pour les États-Unis et le Royaume-Uni, nous n'avons trouvé jusqu'à maintenant que peu de travaux empiriques consacrés au Canada. À titre d'exemple, le seul article pertinent publié ces dernières années est paru dans *Canadian Public Policy* (Gera et Mang, 1998), tandis que dans la *Revue canadienne d'économique*, la seule contribution importante parue ces dernières années est celle de Gaston et Trefler (1997) — qui porte essentiellement sur l'impact de l'Accord de libre-échange Canada-États-Unis. L'étude la plus récente qui se rapproche de la nôtre au niveau des objectifs et des méthodes est celle de Betts et McCurdy (1993). Ces auteurs ont utilisé des tableaux entrées-sorties pour 1961, 1971 et 1981 afin de préciser les sources de la variation totale de l'emploi au cours des deux sous-périodes à un niveau de désagrégation à 39 industries. Les sources de changement de l'emploi examinées sont notamment les changements observés dans les cinq grandes catégories de la demande finale, les coefficients techniques d'entrées-sorties, la productivité de la main-d'oeuvre et les heures travaillées par employé. En outre, les auteurs ont examiné les effets sur une ventilation professionnelle détaillée.

Si la documentation — à tout le moins pour les États-Unis et le Royaume-Uni — sur ce sujet général est vaste, relativement peu d'études parmi celles que nous avons consultées utilisent une approche empirique qui ressemble quelque peu à celle que nous avons employée ici. La presque totalité des études utilisent des données de panel sur les salaires ou pour un employeur ou un groupe d'employés particulier, ou se limitent à des secteurs économiques particuliers, définis de façon large ou étroite [par exemple le secteur de la fabrication (voir Betts, 1997)]. Notre méthode se fonde sur les techniques d'entrées-sorties et nous avons retrouvé uniquement deux références valables et immédiates à des études faisant appel à ces techniques d'analyse à l'extérieur du Canada : la première est celle de Gregory et Greenhalgh (1997), qui porte sur le Royaume-Uni, tandis que la seconde est une référence parue dans Tyson et Zysman (1988) à une étude d'entrées-sorties portant sur les États-Unis réalisée par l'Office of

Technology Assessment (1987), basée sur des données entrées-sorties beaucoup plus anciennes et qui est aujourd'hui passablement périmée.

Gregory et Greenhalgh (1997) ont utilisé des tableaux entrées-sorties exprimés en dollars courants pour les années 1979, 1985 et 1990 afin d'examiner les changements dans la demande de main-d'oeuvre au Royaume-Uni durant les années 80 et, en particulier, afin de déceler des preuves d'une « désindustrialisation » et de l'impact de l'évolution du commerce international sur le niveau et la répartition sectorielle de l'emploi ainsi que sur la rémunération globale. Les changements observés dans la production et l'emploi sectoriels sont décomposés en éléments axés sur la demande intérieure finale, les exportations, la pénétration des importations et les changements dans les achats intersectoriels (changement technique) et le changement technique en ce qu'il touche à la demande de main-d'oeuvre par unité de production. Si les résultats de l'étude — comme pour toutes les études de ce genre — se situent principalement au niveau du détail, quelques conclusions générales en ressortent : aucune source unique de « désindustrialisation » n'a pu être isolée. La pénétration des importations, la dissociation des services des secteurs de production de biens et le changement technique axé sur les économies de main-d'oeuvre sont tous des éléments qui contribuent à ce phénomène. La pénétration des importations est importante et assez généralisée mais ses effets sont atténués par la croissance des exportations. Le changement technique axé sur les économies de main-d'oeuvre a été plus important que les pertes de marché comme source de réduction de la demande de main-d'oeuvre — mais cet effet était apparent dans tous les secteurs au cours des années 80. L'étude révèle des indices d'un déplacement structurel provenant de la concurrence internationale qui oriente l'économie en direction des secteurs à valeur ajoutée ou de haute technologie, mais les données pour certains secteurs montrent qu'il n'en est pas toujours ainsi, en raison de l'augmentation des importations et de la faible valeur ajoutée associées à certains produits de haute technologie.

Dans le cas du Canada, les études qui se rapprochent le plus de l'approche que nous avons suivie ici, outre celle de Betts et McCurdy (1993) sont les études d'Industrie Canada réalisées par Gera et Mang (1997) [publiées subséquemment par Gera et Mang (1998)] et celle de Gera et Massé (1996). Chacune représente un progrès considérable par rapport aux travaux antérieurs de l'OCDE (1992) qui portaient uniquement sur la période 1981-1986 et un nombre limité d'industries agrégées. Gera et Mang (1998 et 1997) et Gera et Massé (1996) utilisent des tableaux entrées-sorties en dollars constants pour 1971, 1981, 1986 et 1991 au niveau de désagrégation le plus élevé possible (plus de 200 industries et plus de 600 biens). Dans le rapport final, les données sont présentées au niveau d'agrégation de 111 industries, ce qui demeure bien au delà des 33 secteurs identifiés dans l'étude de l'OCDE. Parce que les tableaux en dollars constants produits par Statistique Canada n'ont pas la même année de base, trois sous-périodes ont été examinées : 1971-1981, 1981-1986 et 1986-1991. Une décomposition très détaillée des sources de changement de la production et de l'emploi entre les années de référence a été effectuée. Enfin, à l'instar de Lee et Has (1991), les auteurs font une répartition des industries entre trois catégories de connaissance (élevée, moyenne et faible), pour examiner la performance relative des industries et de l'emploi selon l'intensité du savoir sur les périodes étudiées[5].

Ces études ont mené à une gamme étendue de conclusions que nous ne pouvons résumer complètement ici. Elles ont permis de déceler un changement structurel de grande envergure mais, ce qui est plus étonnant, le rythme de changement n'aurait pas accéléré entre 1971 et 1991 et les principaux secteurs de croissance sont demeurés les mêmes sur l'ensemble de la période. Bien entendu, il y a eu un déplacement relatif de l'emploi vers les services. L'intensité des compétences a augmenté dans le secteur manufacturier *et* dans celui des services — mais la plupart des emplois demeuraient concentrés dans les catégories de savoir faible et moyenne. Les auteurs ont constaté que les échanges internationaux jouaient un rôle de plus en plus important dans l'explication des taux de croissance relatifs des diverses

industries, y compris celles de ressources naturelles (où les effets intérieurs étaient souvent négatifs), tandis que les services devenaient plus exposés au commerce international. On a aussi constaté que l'expansion du commerce avait clairement une « orientation vers le savoir » [du moins pour les catégories définies par Lee et Has (1996)] : les industries de haut savoir du secteur des biens commercialisables semblent avoir profité le plus de l'essor des exportations; les industries de faible savoir ont vu leur déclin relatif accentué par la concurrence provenant des importations (Gera et Mang, 1998, p. 149).

À bien des égards, l'étude la plus récente qui se rapproche de la nôtre au niveau des objectifs et des méthodes est celle de Betts et McCurdy (1993). Les auteurs utilisent des tableaux entrées-sorties pour les années 1961, 1971 et 1981 afin de déterminer les sources de changement dans l'emploi total au cours des deux sous-périodes au niveau de désagrégation de 39 industries. Les sources de changement de l'emploi examinées sont notamment les changements observés dans les cinq grandes catégories de la demande finale et les changements dans les coefficients d'entrées-sorties techniques, la productivité de la main-d'oeuvre et les heures travaillées par employé. En outre, les auteurs examinent les effets sur une ventilation professionnelle détaillée. Entre autres résultats, ils ont établi que le taux plus élevé de la croissance de l'emploi dans le secteur privé au cours des années 70 par rapport aux années 60 était associé principalement à une croissance moins rapide de la productivité de la main-d'oeuvre étant donné que la croissance de la demande finale a fléchi au cours des années 70 par rapport aux années 60, notamment dans le secteur d'exportation. Les auteurs ont aussi constaté que la principale source de variation intersectorielle de la croissance de l'emploi durant les années 60 était les différences de taux de croissance de la productivité de la main-d'oeuvre, tandis que la principale source de variation intersectorielle de la croissance de l'emploi dans les années 70 était les différences de taux de croissance des secteurs de la demande finale.

Notre étude s'appuie sur ces travaux antérieurs. Ses principales caractéristiques sont notamment que les calculs ont été refaits jusqu'à un passé récent, qu'elle comporte une désagrégation industrielle plus poussée, qu'elle aborde toute une série d'aspects particuliers des exportations et des importations liées à la croissance de l'emploi et que nous utilisons des données désagrégées relativement récentes sur le profil de scolarité et de compétences des diverses industries.

Comme dans le cas des autres études fondées sur des données entrées-sorties que nous avons examinées brièvement ci-dessus, l'objectif premier est de *décrire* l'économie et les changements qu'elle subit progressivement afin d'approfondir notre compréhension et, éventuellement, de faire des recommandations utiles sur le plan des politiques. Comme l'ont fait remarquer Betts et McCurdy (1993, p. 289), l'analyse entrées-sorties demeure utile comme moyen d'évaluer l'importance relative des divers facteurs qui ont contribué aux changements dans les indicateurs économiques agrégés tels que l'emploi. Mais il importe de se rappeler que la description et l'association ne supposent pas nécessairement la causalité. À titre d'exemple, bien que les exportations puissent être associées à un certain nombre d'emplois, elles n'ont pas nécessairement créé ou « causé » ces emplois, pas plus que les travailleurs qui les occupent demeureraient sans emploi en l'absence des exportations (un marché du travail qui fonctionne bien les aurait éventuellement replacés dans un autre poste — mais sans nécessairement toucher des gains aussi importants)[6]. Une réserve connexe est que la description et l'analyse sont fondées sur les rapports entrées-sorties qui se sont produits, du moins en partie, uniquement en raison des prix et des raretés relatifs qui prévalaient au cours d'une année donnée, bien que nous supposions qu'ils soient « fixes » (« technologie de Leontief »). Si les prix relatifs avaient été différents — par exemple en raison d'une politique monétaire ou d'une politique de change différente — des technologies différentes auraient pu être adoptées et différents coefficients entrées-sorties auraient été observés. Encore une fois, l'objectif premier de l'analyse est de faire une description initiale de ce qui s'est produit, en vue de permettre une analyse plus approfondie de la causalité et, peut-être, la formulation de recommandations axées sur les politiques.

4. CHANGEMENTS DANS LA COMPOSITION INDUSTRIELLE ET PROFESSIONNELLE DES EXPORTATIONS CANADIENNES

Dans ce chapitre, nous examinons, à l'aide de données des Comptes nationaux et de calculs fondés sur une série temporelle de tableaux entrées-sorties, comment a évolué la place occupée par les exportations dans l'économie canadienne depuis 1961 et comment la composition de la production industrielle et de l'emploi lié aux exportations s'est modifiée avec le temps. Ensuite, en ajoutant des données sur le profil des compétences par industrie, nous analysons le profil de scolarité/compétences des exportations canadiennes au cours des années récentes et, dans la mesure du possible, nous tentons de déterminer comment ce profil a changé progressivement.

Les exportations dans l'économie canadienne, 1961-1997 : la perspective des Comptes nationaux

Nous débutons par un examen des données agrégées sur la place occupée par les exportations dans l'économie canadienne. Ces données proviennent des Comptes nationaux et seront les plus familières aux lecteurs. Une série de ratios ou d'indicateurs clés est présentée au tableau 1 pour la période 1961-1997.

Les colonnes 1 et 2 du tableau 1 (reproduites à la figure 1) montrent la croissance des exportations en proportion du PIB depuis 1961. Mesurées en dollars de 1992, les exportations sont passées de 12,5 p. 100 du PIB en 1961 à un peu plus de 37 p. 100 en 1997. Mesurées en dollars courants, elles sont passées de 17,7 p. 100 du PIB en 1961 à un peu plus de 40 p. 100 en 1997. Selon l'une et l'autre mesures, l'économie du Canada a, depuis 1961, évolué massivement vers les marchés mondiaux et le chapitre 5 montre une croissance correspondante des importations, alors que les marchés canadiens se sont ouverts au reste du monde. La croissance des exportations (et des importations) durant les années 90 est particulièrement impressionnante.

À noter que pour 1992, la dernière année pour laquelle nous possédons des données entrées-sorties, les parts des exportations dans le PIB sont identiques (27 p. 100) étant donné que l'année 1992 est l'année de base aux fins des Comptes nationaux. La différence dans la croissance des parts entre les mesures réelles et nominales peut s'expliquer par le mouvement du prix relatif des exportations au cours des 36 dernières années. (Par prix relatif, nous voulons dire le prix des exportations par rapport aux prix de l'ensemble des biens compris dans le PIB (qui comprend les exportations), tel que mesuré par le déflateur du PIB.) Comme on peut le voir à la colonne 3 du tableau 1, le prix relatif des exportations a diminué sensiblement entre 1961 et 1992, la plus grande partie du déclin étant survenue au cours des années 80 alors que les prix relatifs de l'énergie ont fléchi. Cependant, il a eu une modeste augmentation du prix relatif des exportations depuis 1992.

Ce redressement des prix relatifs signifie que la part des exportations exprimée en dollars constants (de 1992) a augmenté moins rapidement que la part exprimée en dollars courants depuis 1992 — bien que les deux variations soient énormes pour une période de cinq ans par rapport à la tendance historique. Étant donné que notre analyse entrées-sorties se concentre principalement sur les parts ou les ratios exprimés en dollars *courants*, il importe de garder à l'esprit cette distinction.

Il est intéressant de se demander si l'augmentation de la part des exportations (tant au cours des années récentes que depuis 1961) est davantage attribuable aux changements observés dans la part des exportations de biens ou celle des exportations de services. Les données des Comptes nationaux

(colonnes 4 et 5 du tableau 1 et figure 2) indiquent que si la part des exportations de biens et de services a augmenté par rapport au PIB, la plus grande partie de l'augmentation globale de la part des exportations est attribuable à la progression de la part des exportations de *biens*. Cela est vrai tant pour la période 1961-1992 pour laquelle nous disposons de données entrées-sorties, que pour la période subséquente de 1992-1997.

Enfin, le colonne 6 du tableau 1 montre les exportations en proportion non pas du PIB, mais du PIB du secteur privé au coût des facteurs. Cette dernière notion exclut la « production » gouvernementale (principalement les traitements et salaires des employés gouvernementaux et l'amortissement gouvernemental — qui n'ont aucun volet d'exportation important) et exclut les taxes indirectes (moins les subventions) qui sont incluses dans la notion de « prix du marché » du PIB agrégé. La plupart du travail d'analyse entrées-sorties présenté ci-après se concentre sur des comparaisons ou sur les changements observés dans les ratios d'exportation par rapport à cette notion de « production du secteur privé au coût des facteurs », qui est plus facilement accessible dans les tableaux et qui est la notion la plus significative à des fins de comparaison. La colonne 6 renferme les données équivalentes des Comptes nationaux et, comme on peut le constater, l'augmentation de la part des exportations va de 21,7 p. 100 en 1961 à 34 p. 100 en 1992 et, enfin, à près de 50 p. 100 en 1997. Le fait que la part des exportations dans le PIB total (en dollars courants) n'augmente pas autant (allant seulement de 17,7 p. 100 à 27,2 p. 100 entre 1961 et 1992) traduit la croissance du secteur gouvernemental durant cette période ainsi qu'une augmentation de la taxation indirecte moyenne.

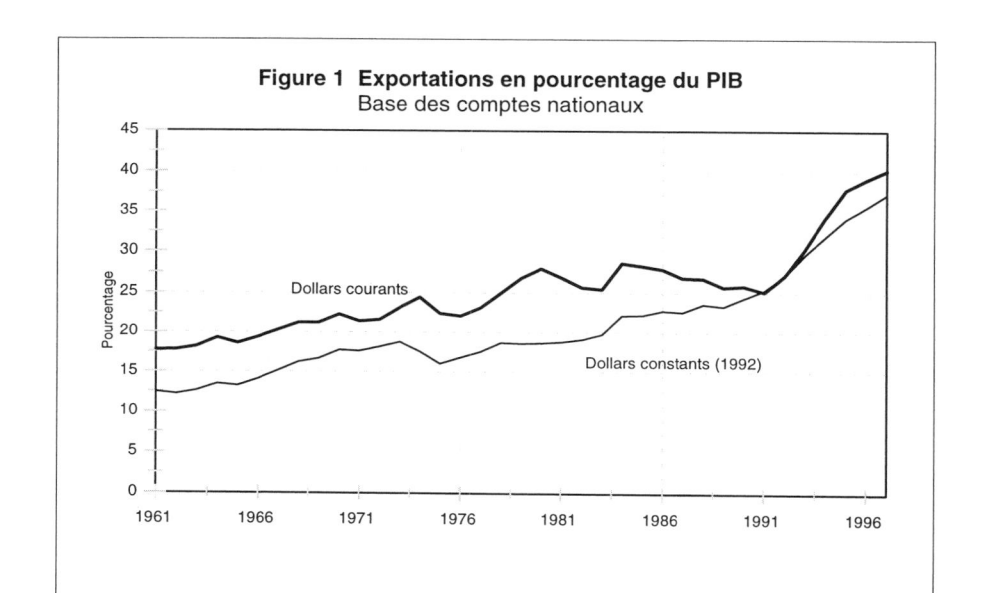

Figure 1   Exportations en pourcentage du PIB
Base des comptes nationaux

	Tableau 1 Les exportations agrégées dans les Comptes nationaux, 1961–1997					
	(1) **Exportations** **en % du PIB** **($ de 1992)**	**(2)** **Exportations** **en % du PIB** **($ courants)**	**(3)** **Ratio du** **déflateur des** **exportations** **au déflateur** **du PIB**	**(4)** **Exportations** **de biens en** **% du PIB** **($ courants)**	**(5)** **Exportations** **de services** **en % du PIB** **($ courants)**	**(6)** **Exportations** **en % du PIB** **du secteur** **privé au coût** **des facteurs**
1961	12,5	17,7	1,42	15,2	2,5	21,7
1962	12,2	17,8	1,46	15,2	2,6	21,8
1963	12,6	18,2	1,44	15,5	2,6	22,2
1964	13,5	19,3	1,43	16,6	2,6	23,6
1965	13,2	18,6	1,40	15,9	2,6	22,8
1966	14,1	19,4	1,37	16,6	2,7	23,8
1967	15,2	20,3	1,34	16,9	3,4	25,1
1968	16,2	21,2	1,31	18,5	2,6	26,2
1969	16,6	21,2	1,27	18,4	2,8	26,3
1970	17,7	22,3	1,26	19,3	2,9	27,5
1971	17,6	21,4	1,21	18,6	2,8	26,5
1972	18,2	21,6	1,19	19,0	2,6	26,8
1973	18,8	23,1	1,23	20,5	2,6	28,5
1974	17,5	24,5	1,40	21,7	2,7	30,0
1975	16,0	22,4	1,40	19,8	2,6	27,0
1976	16,8	22,1	1,31	19,5	2,6	26,8
1977	17,5	23,1	1,32	20,6	2,5	28,1
1978	18,7	25,0	1,34	22,3	2,7	30,2
1979	18,6	26,8	1,44	23,9	2,9	32,0
1980	18,7	28,0	1,50	25,1	2,9	33,2
1981	18,8	26,9	1,43	23,9	3,0	32,5
1982	19,1	25,7	1,34	22,8	2,9	31,3
1983	19,8	25,5	1,29	22,6	2,9	30,8
1984	22,2	28,7	1,29	25,7	2,9	34,5
1985	22,2	28,3	1,27	25,3	3,0	34,0
1986	22,8	27,9	1,22	24,5	3,4	33,9
1987	22,6	26,9	1,19	23,6	3,3	32,7
1988	23,6	26,8	1,13	23,5	3,3	32,7
1989	23,3	25,7	1,10	22,4	3,3	31,6
1990	24,4	25,9	1,06	22,4	3,5	32,0
1991	25,4	25,2	0,99	21,6	3,6	31,3
1992	27,2	27,2	1,00	23,4	3,8	34,0
1993	29,7	30,4	1,02	26,3	4,1	38,0
1994	31,9	34,3	1,07	29,9	4,4	42,7
1995	34,2	37,8	1,11	33,2	4,7	46,8
1996	35,7	39,1	1,10	34,2	4,9	48,3
1997	37,3	40,2	1,08	35,2	5,0	49,5

Les exportations dans l'économie canadienne : résultats agrégés de l'analyse entrées-sorties

Les calculs entrées-sorties visant à déterminer l'impact des exportations sur la production canadienne (la production intérieure) et l'emploi ont été effectués pour chaque année de la période 1961-1997[7]. L'incidence sur les diverses industries a été agrégée pour l'ensemble des industries afin d'obtenir l'impact au niveau de l'économie et les résultats sont résumés, par année, au tableau 2 et dans les figures 3 à 8. À noter encore une fois que ces résultats ne sont pas simplement la somme de la production ou de l'emploi dans les diverses industries considérées comme principalement « exportatrices »; plutôt, ce sont des estimations de l'ensemble de la production des emplois directs et *indirects* requis pour produire les exportations observées au cours de chacune des années.

La colonne 1 du tableau 2 fait pour ainsi dire le pont entre les données plus familières des Comptes nationaux et les calculs et notions d'entrées-sorties. Cette colonne montre les exportations (tirées de la base de données entrées-sorties) en proportion du produit intérieur du secteur des entreprises, c'est-à-dire la valeur ajoutée (provenant aussi de la base de données entrées-sorties). C'est l'équivalent le plus rapproché des données entrées-sorties apparaissant à la colonne 6 du tableau 1 et, comme on peut le voir, les deux parts estimatives et leurs variations entre 1961 et 1997 sont assez rapprochées. (Les différences sont attribuables à des modèles de classification différents et aux définitions différentes retenues pour le secteur gouvernemental.) À noter que les données entrées-sorties montrent une augmentation légèrement plus importante de la part des exportations entre 1961 et 1992 que les données des Comptes nationaux, même si les variations dans les parts sont presque identiques d'une mesure à l'autre lorsque nous projetons l'analyse jusqu'en 1997.

Passant à la colonne 4 du tableau 2 (et à la figure 3), nous arrivons au thème central de la présente étude — l'impact des exportations sur l'emploi[8]. Comme on peut le voir, la part de l'emploi lié aux exportations dans l'emploi total du secteur des entreprises a effectivement augmenté : de 17,1 p. 100 qu'il était en 1961, il avait atteint 23,1 p. 100 en 1992 et, enfin, 28,3 p. 100 en 1997 — mais l'augmentation de la part de l'emploi est beaucoup moins grande que l'augmentation de la part des exportations par rapport au produit du secteur des entreprises. C'est la première observation importante qui ressort des calculs entrées-sorties (à tout le moins pour les auteurs du présent rapport) : l'impact de la croissance des exportations sur l'emploi a été positif mais de beaucoup inférieur à ce que l'on aurait pu imaginer en examinant uniquement la part des exportations dans le PIB.

La recherche de la cause de l'augmentation moins élevée que prévu de la part de l'*emploi* lié aux exportations débute avec la productivité : une première hypothèse pourrait être que l'augmentation moins élevée que prévu est le résultat d'une hausse de la productivité relative de la main-d'oeuvre dans la production destinée à l'exportation. Le raisonnement fait ici est que le Canada a eu tendance à exporter davantage dans les secteurs où les gains de productivité de la main-d'oeuvre sont particulièrement importants. Cependant, les calculs entrées-sorties permettent de rejeter rapidement cette possibilité. La colonne 5 du tableau 2 (reproduite à la figure 6) montre que, si la productivité relative de la main-d'oeuvre dans la production (directe ou indirecte) destinée à l'exportation a toujours été supérieure à la moyenne du secteur des entreprises (le ratio est supérieur à 1,0), la croissance de la productivité *relative* de la main-d'oeuvre a été inégale et, de fait, elle a fléchi pour revenir presque à son niveau du milieu des années 60 en 1997. Le Canada exporte des biens et des services caractérisés par une productivité de la main-d'oeuvre relativement élevée; par conséquent, il n'y a pas eu de progression ininterrompue de la productivité relative de la main-d'oeuvre liée aux exportations entre les années 60 et les années 90 qui permettrait d'expliquer pourquoi la part de l'emploi attribuable aux exportations n'a pas augmenté au même rythme que la part des exportations dans le PIB.

Sur la question de la productivité relative des exportations, nous devons émettre une réserve : la diminution de la productivité relative de la main-d'oeuvre après 1988-1989 coïncide avec la récession de 1990-1992. Le phénomène de «l'accumulation de la main-d'oeuvre » a tendance à réduire la productivité de ce facteur dans tous les secteurs au cours d'une récession mais, étant donné que les exportations ont été touchées de façon particulièrement dure par la récession de 1990-1991 sous l'impact d'un dollar surévalué, il est possible que le phénomène d'accumulation de la main-d'oeuvre ait été proportionnellement plus important dans les secteurs d'exportation et que la productivité relative de la main-d'oeuvre dans ces secteurs en ait souffert. Puisque les coefficients d'entrées-sorties de 1992 ont été utilisés dans les calculs visant la période 1993-1997, alors tout effet persistant d'accumulation relative du facteur travail par secteur pour l'année 1992 contribuerait à maintenir à un bas niveau nos mesures de la productivité relative de la main-d'oeuvre liée aux exportations pour les années subséquentes.

Puisque la productivité relative de la main-d'oeuvre liée aux exportations n'a que peu augmenté depuis les années 60, il faudrait alors que l'augmentation de la part des exportations dans le produit intérieur du secteur des entreprises ait été assez comparable à l'augmentation de l'emploi — et les données de la colonne 2 du tableau 2 confirment ce point. Il est important de bien comprendre la différence entre les colonnes 1 et 2 : le dénominateur est le même dans chaque cas (le produit intérieur total du secteur des entreprises). Dans la colonne 1, le numérateur correspond aux ventes à l'exportation observées (tirées de la base de données entrées-sorties plus une projection pour les années postérieures à 1992), tandis que dans la colonne 2, le numérateur est l'*impact* (par le biais des calculs d'entrées-sorties de Leontief) de ces exportations sur le produit intérieur des diverses industries (qui sont ensuite agrégées). Si les *ventes* à l'exportation ont vu leur part du produit intérieur augmenter depuis 1961, l'effet de stimulation d'un dollar de vente à l'exportation sur le produit intérieur (directement ou indirectement) a *diminué*. En conséquence, le ratio des ventes à l'exportation au produit intérieur total des entreprises a augmenté plus rapidement que le ratio du produit intérieur *stimulé* par les exportations au produit intérieur total du secteur des entreprises (voir la figure 4).

La raison de cette baisse de l'impact des exportations est tout simplement la présence des importations : la colonne 3 du tableau 2 fait voir les importations requises pour produire les exportations en pourcentage du produit intérieur stimulé par les exportations. Comme on peut le voir, pour chaque dollar de produit intérieur attribuable aux exportations en 1961, un peu plus de 12 cents d'importations étaient requises. En 1992, ce chiffre avait atteint 40 cents et, en 1997, nos estimations imparfaites laissent penser qu'il se situait juste en-dessous de 50 cents. Comme le montre la figure 5, une partie de cette augmentation du contenu en importations des exportations est clairement imputable à la mise en place du Pacte de l'automobile entre le Canada et les États-Unis de 1966 au début des années 70. Cependant, l'impact des importations sur les exportations a augmenté constamment depuis, ce qui signifie que la part de la production (et de l'emploi) détenue par les exportations a augmenté beaucoup moins rapidement que la part globale des ventes à l'exportation dans le PIB.

Étant donné que la part d'importations que renferment les exportations a augmenté, nous pourrions nous attendre à ce que l'incidence *indirecte* des exportations sur la production et l'emploi ait augmenté relativement à l'incidence directe — traduisant une part plus importante d'exportations plus complexes ou manufacturées nécessitant une plus grande production intermédiaire. En partie, c'est ce qui s'est produit : de 1961 à la fin des années 80, on peut voir à l'examen des données de la colonne 7 du tableau 2 et de la figure 7 que le ratio de l'impact direct à l'impact total des exportations sur l'emploi a fléchi lentement, traduisant l'importance croissante des effets indirects. Pourtant, le taux de régression a été très graduel. De la fin des années 80 jusqu'à 1992, le ratio a cependant augmenté à nouveau, révélant une diminution des effets indirects relatifs. De 1993 à 1997, une augmentation importante de l'impact relatif de l'emploi induit directement et indirectement ressort des données, mais il faut se rappeler que nous avons utilisé les coefficients entrées-sorties techniques de 1992 pour l'ensemble de cette période.

Ce déplacement de la *composition* des exportations et des importations au cours des années 90 est tel qu'il aurait pu engendrer des effets directs plus importants que les effets indirects sur l'emploi lié à l'exportation, mais pour savoir si cette tendance a été compensée par l'évolution de la structure de la production, nous devrons attendre que des tableaux entrées-sorties soient disponibles pour les années postérieures à 1992.

Enfin, le système d'entrées-sorties nous permet de calculer les effets des exportations sur la rémunération totale du facteur travail. (Nous avons agrégé les traitements et salaires, le revenu supplémentaire du travail et le revenu tiré d'une entreprise non constituée en société dans cette catégorie.) Le rendement du facteur travail peut être exprimé sous forme de ratio par rapport à l'emploi engendré afin de déterminer le rendement relatif de la main-d'oeuvre liée à l'exportation. Comme le montrent les données de la colonne 8 du tableau 2 et la figure 8, ce ratio a augmenté constamment de 1961 au milieu des années 70 pour ensuite demeurer relativement constant jusqu'en 1992 — mais à une valeur supérieure à 1,0 (les calculs pour les années postérieures à 1992 ne sont pas disponibles). Une partie de l'augmentation du ratio observé de 1961 au début des années 70 est imputable au déclin relatif de l'agriculture dans les exportations et dans l'emploi lié aux exportations.

Avant de passer à des résultats plus désagrégés, deux tests de sensibilité effectués sur les calculs agrégés doivent être signalés : les calculs agrégés ont aussi été faits pour la période 1961-1992 à l'aide des tableaux entrées-sorties exprimés en dollars réels plutôt que nominaux et les calculs en valeurs nominales ont été répétés en excluant les exportations de produits agricoles parce que ce secteur a subi une profonde transformation structurelle, notamment au cours des années 60. Les détails de chaque test de sensibilité sont présentés à l'appendice 2. Brièvement, aucune de ces opérations n'entraîne un changement important dans les conclusions générales tirées de ce qui précède. Cependant, l'utilisation de données réelles dans les calculs engendre une diminution de la baisse de productivité relative de la main-d'oeuvre liée aux exportations pour la période 1990-1992, tandis que l'exclusion du secteur agricole produit des gains relatifs de la main-d'oeuvre liée aux exportations supérieurs à la moyenne de l'ensemble de l'économie pour *toutes* les décennies et non uniquement pour les années 60.

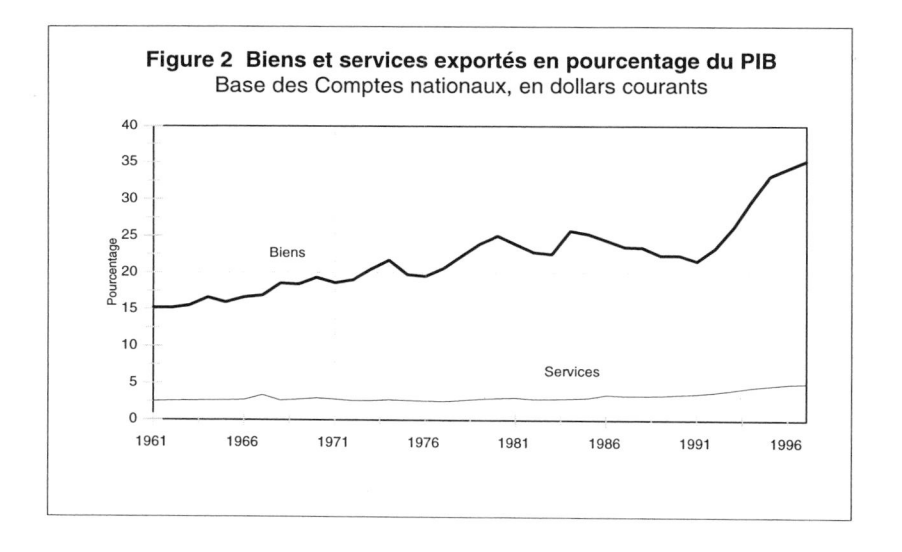

Figure 2 Biens et services exportés en pourcentage du PIB
Base des Comptes nationaux, en dollars courants

Tableau 2 Comparaisons des calculs entrées-sorties au niveau agrégé, exportations, 1961–1997

	(1) Exportations en % du produit intérieur du secteur des entreprises	(2) Produit intérieur intégré aux exportations en % du produit intérieur des entreprises	(3) Importations comprises dans les exportations en % du produit intérieur contenu dans les exportations	(4) Emploi lié aux exportations en % de l'emploi total des entreprises	(5) Productivité de la main-d'oeuvre liée aux exportations par rapport au secteur des entreprises	(6) Emploi direct lié aux exportations en % de l'emploi total	(7) Ratio emploi direct/total lié aux exportations	(8) Ratio du rendement de la main-d'oeuvre liée aux exportations à celui du secteur des entreprises
1961	20,82	17,83	12,29	17,20	1,04	9,46	0,55	0,92
1962	20,72	17,70	12,33	16,12	1,10	8,55	0,53	0,97
1963	21,32	18,19	12,52	16,74	1,09	8,94	0,53	0,97
1964	22,68	19,19	13,13	17,77	1,08	9,54	0,54	0,95
1965	21,76	18,35	13,40	16,61	1,10	8,74	0,53	0,98
1966	22,96	19,04	16,04	17,19	1,11	8,94	0,52	1,01
1967	23,90	19,32	18,82	17,47	1,11	8,83	0,51	1,01
1968	26,35	20,61	22,67	18,26	1,13	9,11	0,50	1,03
1969	26,47	20,50	23,86	17,66	1,16	8,69	0,49	1,06
1970	28,31	21,86	24,14	19,62	1,11	9,88	0,50	1,04
1971	27,46	21,06	24,81	19,38	1,09	9,78	0,50	1,03
1972	27,83	21,35	24,72	19,13	1,12	9,75	0,51	1,04
1973	29,33	22,80	23,60	19,27	1,18	9,81	0,51	1,06
1974	29,79	23,15	25,54	18,99	1,22	9,76	0,51	1,07
1975	27,28	21,01	27,47	17,83	1,18	9,13	0,51	1,07
1976	27,84	21,23	27,33	18,25	1,16	9,24	0,51	1,08
1977	29,70	22,26	29,28	19,17	1,16	9,59	0,50	1,08
1978	32,10	23,76	31,00	20,06	1,18	10,09	0,50	1,10
1979	33,66	25,57	28,20	20,58	1,24	10,45	0,50	1,10
1980	34,63	26,27	29,04	21,37	1,23	10,78	0,51	1,11
1981	33,63	24,76	30,95	20,91	1,18	10,52	0,50	1,09
1982	32,48	23,83	30,71	21,04	1,13	10,35	0,49	1,10
1983	32,16	23,97	29,78	20,98	1,14	10,42	0,50	1,08
1984	35,40	26,05	32,16	20,97	1,19	10,96	0,50	1,09
1985	35,16	25,43	34,55	20,99	1,21	10,28	0,49	1,11
1986	34,14	23,96	37,55	20,56	1,17	10,07	0,49	1,12

Tableau 2 (suite)

	(1) Exportations en % du produit intérieur du secteur des entreprises	(2) Produit intérieur intégré aux exportations en % du produit intérieur des entreprises	(3) Importations comprises dans les exportations en % du produit intérieur contenu dans les exportations	(4) Emploi lié aux exportations en % de l'emploi total des entreprises	(5) Productivité de la main-d'oeuvre liée aux exportations par rapport au secteur des entreprises	(6) Emploi direct lié aux exportations en % de l'emploi total	(7) Ratio emploi direct/total lié aux exportations	(8) Ratio du rendement de la main-d'oeuvre liée aux exportations à celui du secteur des entreprises
1987	32,85	23,75	33,60	20,24	1,17	9,86	0,49	1,10
1988	32,80	23,63	33,73	19,95	1,18	9,57	0,48	1,10
1989	31,82	22,76	34,45	19,55	1,16	9,32	0,48	1,10
1990	33,12	23,42	35,80	21,41	1,09	10,80	0,50	1,06
1991	32,28	22,82	36,69	21,75	1,05	10,99	0,51	1,06
1992	35,24	24,28	40,19	23,07	1,05	11,82	0,51	1,06
1993	38,39	25,75	44,00	23,60	1,09	13,13	0,56	n.d.
1994	42,34	28,07	45,74	25,40	1,11	15,48	0,61	n.d.
1995	45,63	30,28	45,58	26,90	1,13	17,44	0,65	n.d.
1996	46,44	30,80	45,75	27,86	1,11	18,55	0,67	n.d.
1997	47,66	31,17	47,97	28,31	1,10	19,28	0,68	n.d.

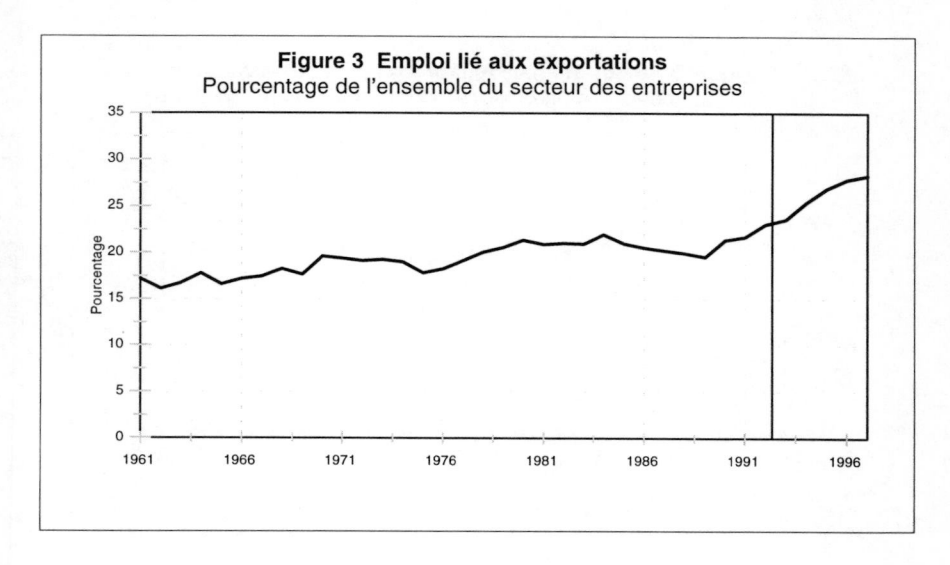

Figure 3 Emploi lié aux exportations
Pourcentage de l'ensemble du secteur des entreprises

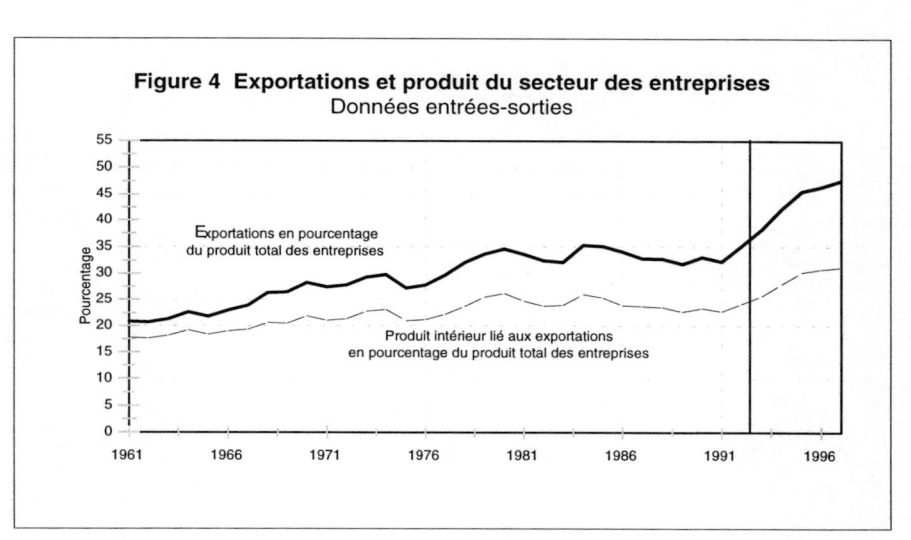

Figure 4 Exportations et produit du secteur des entreprises
Données entrées-sorties

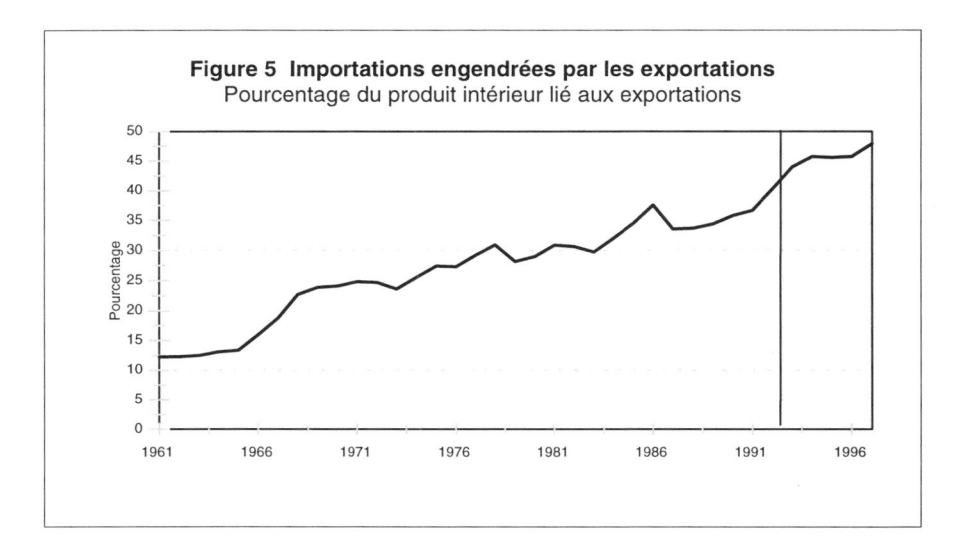

Figure 5 Importations engendrées par les exportations
Pourcentage du produit intérieur lié aux exportations

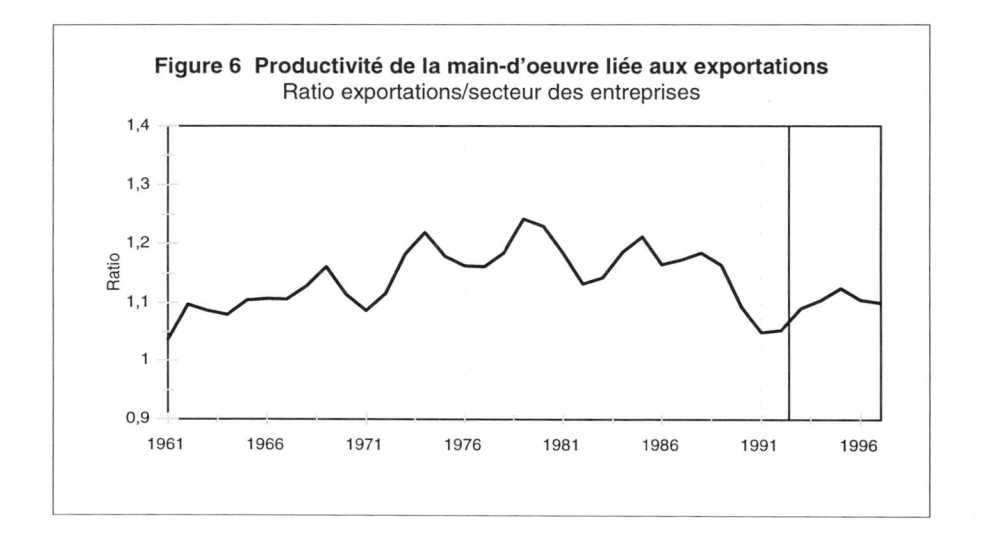

Figure 6 Productivité de la main-d'oeuvre liée aux exportations
Ratio exportations/secteur des entreprises

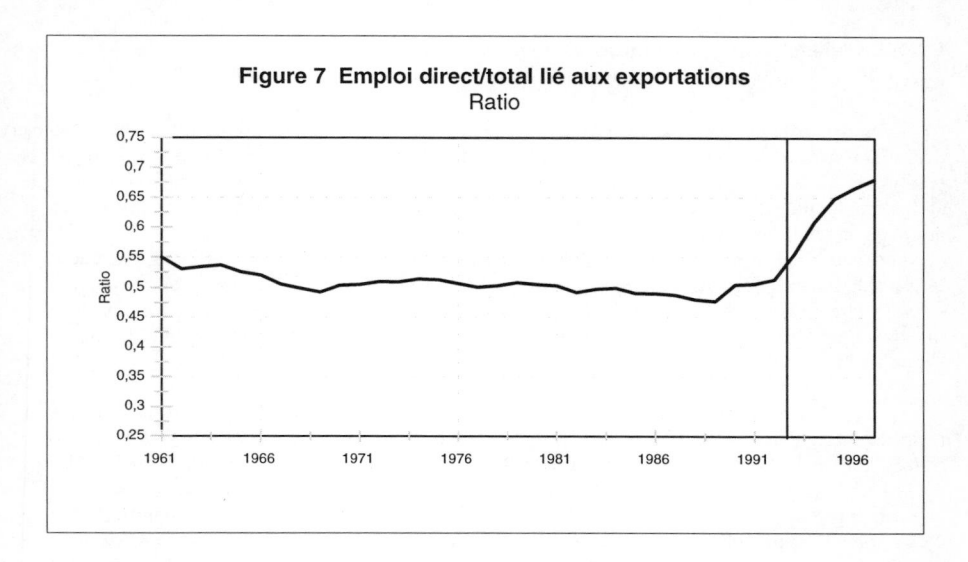

Figure 7 Emploi direct/total lié aux exportations
Ratio

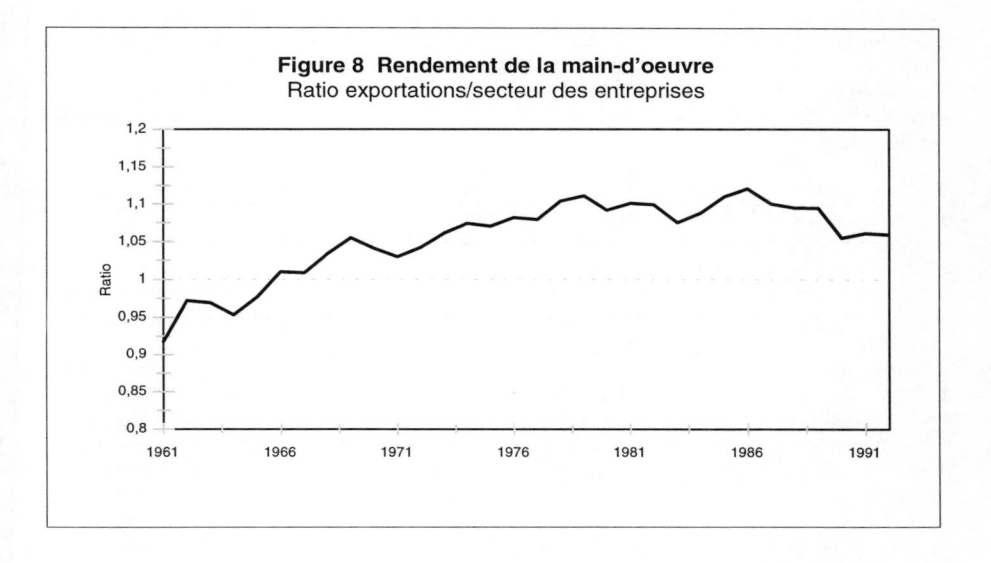

Figure 8 Rendement de la main-d'oeuvre
Ratio exportations/secteur des entreprises

Évolution de la composition industrielle des exportations : agrégation au niveau de 24 industries

Nous passons maintenant de l'examen des résultats agrégés à celui des résultats désagrégés. Les tableaux 3A et 3B font voir, pour une désagrégation spéciale au niveau (limité) de 24 industries produite pour la présente étude, l'emploi attribuable aux exportations en proportion de l'emploi total lié aux exportations et de l'emploi total, pour les années 1961 et 1997[10]. Le tableau montre également l'évolution de chacune des parts entre les deux années. Le tableau 3A fait voir ces parts classées par industrie — où le classement des industries suit l'ordre habituel, c'est-à-dire le secteur primaire, le secteur manufacturier, la construction et le secteur tertiaire (les services). Le tableau 3B fait voir les mêmes effets, mais classés selon l'ordre décroissant de l'augmentation de la part de l'emploi lié aux exportations. Le tableau 3C montre à nouveau les mêmes effets, mais cette fois classés selon l'importance de l'emploi lié aux exportations en 1997 en pourcentage de l'emploi total.

Les chiffres des tableaux 3A, 3B et 3C sont intéressants tant en raison de leur taille absolue au cours de chacune des années que pour les changements qu'ils révèlent entre 1961 et 1997. L'emploi (direct et indirect) lié aux exportations du secteur de l'agriculture, de l'exploitation forestière et de la pêche (AFP), par exemple, représentait 2,3 p. 100 de l'emploi total du secteur des entreprises en 1997 — une part appréciable de la proportion de 28,3 p. 100 de l'emploi total des entreprises représenté par *l'ensemble* de l'emploi lié aux exportations. De fait, parmi les 24 groupes d'industries représentés dans cette agrégation, seulement trois, tous des services, avaient une part de l'emploi total des entreprises plus élevée. Néanmoins, la pondération de l'agriculture, de l'exploitation forestière et de la pêche a changé sensiblement depuis 1961 : cette année-là, l'emploi lié aux exportations de cette industrie représentait 5,8 p. 100 de l'emploi total du secteur des entreprises — soit environ le tiers de la proportion de 17,2 p. 100 de l'emploi du secteur des entreprises représenté par *l'ensemble* des exportations. La diminution de 3,5 points de pourcentage est la plus importante, en valeur absolue, parmi les 24 industries de cette agrégation.

Un examen plus attentif des variations survenues entre 1961 et 1997 (tableau 3B) montre que sur dix groupes d'industries qui ont vu leur part de l'emploi lié aux exportations augmenter de plus d'un point de pourcentage, quatre sont des industries de services (services personnels et autres, services aux entreprises, commerce et finance). Les six autres sont des catégories manufacturières diverses, y compris certaines que l'on aurait pu prévoir en raison du Pacte de l'automobile et de l'évolution de la technologie depuis 1961 — par exemple les véhicules à moteur, les produits électriques et électroniques, les produits en caoutchouc et en plastique — et certains qui sont plus étonnants — comme le cuir, les textiles et le vêtement. Sur les quatre industries qui ont vu diminuer leur part de l'emploi lié aux exportations de plus d'un point de pourcentage, les deux baisses les plus importantes s'observent dans des industries de production primaire (l'exploitation minière à l'exclusion du pétrole et du gaz et l'agriculture, l'exploitation forestière et la pêche), une industrie appartient au groupe du traitement des matières premières et de la fabrication (papier et produits connexes et impression) et la quatrième est l'industrie des transports.

Des tableaux équivalents pour la désagrégation complète au niveau des 161 industries étudiées sont présentés à l'appendice 4, accompagnés d'une analyse des résultats.

Tableau 3A Parts de l'emploi, 1961 et 1997, groupe de 24 industries

Agrégation au niveau de 24 industries	1961		1997		Variation 1961-1997	
	Emploi lié à l'exportation en % de l'emploi total lié à l'exportation	Emploi lié à l'exportation en % de l'emploi total lié à l'exportation	Emploi lié à l'exportation en % de l'emploi total lié à l'exportation	Emploi lié à l'exportation en % de l'emploi total lié à l'exportation	Emploi lié à l'exportation en % de l'exportation lié à l'exportation	Emploi lié à l'exportation en % de l'emploi total
S1. Agriculture, forêt, pêche et piégeage	33,72	5,80	8,19	2,32	-25,53	-3,48
S2. Mines, sauf le pétrole et le gaz	7,80	1,34	2,11	0,60	-5,69	-0,74
S3. Pétrole brut et gaz naturel	0,60	0,10	0,87	0,24	0,27	0,14
S4. Aliments, boissons et tabac	3,14	0,54	2,45	0,69	-0,69	0,15
S5. Produits en caoutchouc et en plastique	0,42	0,07	2,42	0,68	1,99	0,61
S6. Cuir, textile et vêtement	1,40	0,24	2,84	0,80	1,44	0,56
S7. Produits en bois et mobilier	4,83	0,83	4,07	1,15	-0,76	0,32
S8. Papier, produits connexes et imprimerie	7,09	1,22	3,30	0,93	-3,79	-0,29
S9. Métaux primaires et fabrication métallique	6,46	1,11	5,64	1,60	-0,82	0,48
S10. Machinerie	1,39	0,24	2,45	0,69	1,06	0,45
S11. Véhicules à moteur et pièces	0,53	0,09	5,26	1,49	4,74	1,40
S12. Autre matériel de transport	1,57	0,27	1,98	0,56	0,41	0,29
S13. Produits électriques et électroniques	1,34	0,23	3,60	1,02	2,26	0,79
S14. Pétrole raffiné, prod. chimiques et non métall.	2,73	0,47	2,39	0,68	-0,35	0,21
S15. Autres produits fabriqués	0,82	0,14	1,84	0,52	1,02	0,38
S16. Construction	2,12	0,36	1,42	0,40	-0,70	0,04
S17. Transport et pipelines	10,61	1,82	7,53	2,13	-3,08	0,31
S18. Entreposage	0,78	0,13	0,64	0,18	-0,14	0,05
S19. Services publics	2,14	0,37	2,72	0,77	0,58	0,40
S20. Commerce	5,97	1,03	12,68	3,59	6,71	2,56
S21. Finances, assurance et immobilier	1,64	0,28	3,87	1,10	2,23	0,81
S22. Redev. gouv. et logements occupés par propr.	0,00	0,00	0,00	0,00	0,00	0,00
S23. Services commerciaux	1,57	0,27	10,65	3,02	9,08	2,74
S24. Services personnels et autres	1,32	0,23	11,11	3,15	9,79	2,92
TOTAL	100,00	17,20	100,00	28,31	0,00	11,11

Tableau 3B Parts de l'emploi, 1961 et 1997, groupe de 24 industries, classement selon la taille des variations

Agrégation au niveau de 24 industries	1961		1997		Variation 1961–1997	
	Emploi lié à l'exportation en % de l'emploi total lié à l'exportation	Emploi lié à l'exportation en % de l'emploi total	Emploi lié à l'exportation en % de l'emploi total lié à l'exportation	Emploi lié à l'exportation en % de l'emploi total	Emploi lié à l'exportation en % de l'emploi total lié à l'exportation	Emploi lié à l'exportation en % de l'emploi total
S24. Services personnels et autres	1,32	0,23	11,11	3,15	9,79	2,92
S23. Services aux entreprises	1,57	0,27	10,65	3,02	9,08	2,74
S20. Commerce	5,97	1,03	12,68	3,59	6,71	2,56
S11. Véhicules à moteur et pièces	0,53	0,09	5,26	1,49	4,74	1,40
S13. Produits électriques et électroniques	1,34	0,23	3,60	1,02	2,26	0,79
S21. Finances, assurance et immobilier	1,64	0,28	3,87	1,10	2,23	0,81
S5. Produits en caoutchouc et en plastique	0,42	0,07	2,42	0,68	1,99	0,61
S6. Cuir, textile et vêtement	1,40	0,24	2,84	0,80	1,44	0,56
S10. Machines	1,39	0,24	2,45	0,69	1,06	0,45
S15. Autres produits fabriqués	0,82	0,14	1,84	0,52	1,02	0,38
S19. Services publics	2,14	0,37	2,72	0,77	0,58	0,40
S12. Autre matériel de transport	1,57	0,27	1,98	0,56	0,41	0,29
S3. Pétrole brut et gaz naturel	0,60	0,10	0,87	0,24	0,27	0,14
S22. Redev. gouv. et logements occ. par propr.	0,00	0,00	0,00	0,00	0,00	0,00
S18. Entreposage	0,78	0,13	0,64	0,18	-0,14	0,05
S14. Pétrole raffiné, prod. chimiques et non métall.	2,73	0,47	2,39	0,68	-0,35	0,21
S4. Aliments, boissons et tabac	3,14	0,54	2,45	0,69	-0,69	0,15
S16. Construction	2,12	0,36	1,42	0,40	-0,70	0,04
S7. Produits en bois et mobilier	4,83	0,83	4,07	1,15	-0,76	0,32
S9. Métaux primaires et fabrication métallique	6,46	1,11	5,64	1,60	-0,82	0,48
S17. Transport et pipelines	10,61	1,82	7,53	2,13	-3,08	0,31
S8. Papier, produits connexes et imprimerie	7,09	1,22	3,30	0,93	-3,79	-0,29
S2. Mines, sauf le pétrole et le gaz	7,80	1,34	2,11	0,60	-5,69	-0,74
S1. Agriculture, forêt, pêche et piégeage	33,72	5,80	8,19	2,32	-25,53	-3,48
TOTAL	100,00	17,20	100,00	28,31	0,00	11,11

Tableau 3C Parts de l'emploi, 1961 et 1997, groupe de 24 industries, classement selon l'emploi lié à l'exportation en pourcentage de l'emploi total

Agrégation au niveau de 24 industries	1961		1997		Variation 1961–1997	
	Emploi lié à l'exportation en % de l'emploi total lié à l'exportation	Emploi lié à l'exportation en % de l'emploi total	Emploi lié à l'exportation en % de l'emploi total lié à l'exportation	Emploi lié à l'exportation en % de l'emploi total	Emploi lié à l'exportation en % de l'emploi total lié à l'exportation	Emploi lié à l'exportation en % de l'emploi total
S20. Commerce	5,97	1,03	12,68	3,59	6,71	2,56
S24. Services personnels et autres	1,32	0,23	11,11	3,15	9,79	2,92
S23. Services aux entreprises	1,57	0,27	10,65	3,02	9,08	2,74
S1. Agriculture, forêt, pêche et piégeage	33,72	5,8	8,19	2,32	-25,53	-3,48
S17. Transport et pipelines	10,61	1,82	7,53	2,13	-3,08	0,31
S9. Métaux primaires et fabrication métallique	6,46	1,11	5,64	1,60	-0,82	0,48
S11. Véhicules à moteur et pièces	0,53	0,09	5,26	1,49	4,74	1,40
S7. Produits en bois et mobilier	4,83	0,83	4,07	1,15	-0,76	0,32
S21. Finances, assurance et immobilier	1,64	0,28	3,87	1,10	2,23	0,81
S13. Produits électriques et électroniques	1,34	0,23	3,60	1,02	2,26	0,79
S8. Papier, produits connexes et imprimerie	7,09	1,22	3,30	0,93	-3,79	-0,29
S6. Cuir, textile et vêtement	1,4	0,24	2,84	0,80	1,44	0,56
S19. Services publics	2,14	0,37	2,72	0,77	0,58	0,40
S4. Aliments, boissons et tabac	3,14	0,54	2,45	0,69	-0,69	0,15
S10. Machines	1,39	0,24	2,45	0,69	1,06	0,45
S5. Produits en caoutchouc et en plastique	0,42	0,07	2,42	0,68	1,99	0,61
S14. Pétrole raffiné, prod. chimiques et non métall.	2,73	0,47	2,39	0,68	-0,35	0,21
S2. Mines, sauf le pétrole et le gaz	7,8	1,34	2,11	0,60	-5,69	-0,74
S12. Autre matériel de transport	1,57	0,27	1,98	0,56	0,41	0,29
S15. Autres produits fabriqués	0,82	0,14	1,84	0,52	1,02	0,38
S16. Construction	2,12	0,36	1,42	0,4	-0,7	0,04
S3. Pétrole brut et gaz naturel	0,60	0,10	0,87	0,24	0,27	0,14
S18. Entreposage	0,78	0,13	0,64	0,18	-0,14	0,05
S22. Redev. gouv. et logements occ. par propr.	0,00	0,00	0,00	0,00	0,00	0,00
TOTAL	100,00	17,20	100,00	28,31	0,00	11,11

Changements dans les effets sur l'emploi lié aux exportations pour certaines périodes choisies

Les tableaux sommaires présentés ci-dessus englobent une très longue période. Il est donc utile d'examiner les effets sur l'emploi pour diverses sous-périodes. Ces résultats sont présentés dans les tableaux 4A à 4D pour les période 1961-1971, 1971-1981, 1981-1991 et 1991-1997. Les tableaux portent uniquement sur l'agrégation au niveau de 24 industries et sont classés selon les changements observés dans l'emploi lié aux exportations en pourcentage de l'emploi total lié aux exportations. Enfin, un sommaire des changements d'une période à l'autre est présenté au tableau 5.

Si nous examinons le sommaire des changements observés d'une période à l'autre (tableau 5), un certain nombre d'observations ressortent : l'industrie de l'agriculture, de l'exploitation forestière et de la pêche, par exemple, a perdu du terrain pour ce qui est de l'emploi lié aux exportations dans toutes les sous-périodes mais, de loin, la diminution la plus importante s'est produite dans les années 60. Par la suite, le rythme du déclin qu'a connu ce secteur a été plus limité et constant. L'exploitation minière, par contre, a vu sa part de l'emploi des exportations diminuer au cours de chacune des sous-périodes, tandis que le secteur des aliments, boissons et tabac a connu des périodes de déclin et de hausse, les premières ayant prédominé.

Le secteur du cuir, des textiles et du vêtement et celui du bois et des meubles méritent une mention spéciale. Si les données ne sont pas trop sérieusement faussées par l'utilisation des tableaux entrées-sorties de 1992 pour faire des projections sur la période 1993-1997, les données présentées au tableau 11 indiquent un revirement intéressant de la part de l'emploi lié aux exportations entre 1991 et 1997, alors que les baisses précédentes (bois) ou une performance constante (cuir, etc.) ont cédé la place à des hausses importantes de la part de l'emploi lié aux exportations. Si le cadre de la présente étude ne nous permet pas de nous prononcer avec certitude, la coïncidence de ce renversement avec l'entrée en vigueur de l'Accord de libre-échange Canada-États-Unis (ALE) est évocateur. (Gaston et Trefler, 1997, ont aussi constaté un effet positif sur l'emploi découlant de l'ALE dans les industries du vêtement et du bois.)

Comme l'industrie des mines, celle du papier et des produits connexes a vu sa part de l'emploi lié aux exportations diminuer au cours de toutes les sous-périodes, tandis que celle des métaux primaires et de la fabrication métallique a vu sa part augmenter durant toutes les sous-périodes après les années 60. Cependant, l'industrie des machines a gagné du terrain au cours de toutes les sous-périodes sauf durant les années 80.

Pour l'industrie des véhicules à moteur et pièces, tous les gains enregistrés dans la part de l'emploi lié aux exportations ont eu lieu entre 1961 et 1971, au moment de la mise en oeuvre du Pacte de l'automobile. Par la suite, il y a eu une légère diminution nette de cette part. L'industrie des autres matériels de transport (rails, navires, avions et pièces) a également gagné du terrain au cours des premières sous-périodes, mais a enregistré une perte nette par la suite. Ce qui est peut-être étonnant, l'industrie des produits électriques a également enregistré son gain le plus important pour ce qui est de la part de l'emploi lié aux exportations durant la période 1961-1971. Cependant, cette industrie a aussi fait des gains considérables durant les années 80.

L'industrie du transport et des pipelines a vu sa part de l'emploi lié aux exportations diminuer au cours de toutes les sous-périodes, ce qui traduit peut-être un coefficient de transport progressivement moins élevé pour les exportations canadiennes avec le temps, ainsi que des gains de productivité plus élevés dans ces secteurs.

Pour ce qui est du commerce, des finances, des services aux entreprises et des services personnels, on observe des gains des parts de l'emploi lié aux exportations au cours de toutes les sous-périodes. Il est intéressant de noter que ce « déplacement vers les services » dans l'emploi lié aux exportations n'est pas un phénomène récent; en effet, les gains enregistrés dans la part de l'emploi pour les industries du commerce, des finances et des services aux entreprises étaient tout aussi importants dans les années 60 qu'au cours des périodes subséquentes. Seuls les services personnels et autres ont vu l'essentiel des gains dans la part de l'emploi lié aux exportations se produire après 1980.

Tableau 4A Parts de l'emploi, 1961 et 1971, groupe de 24 industries, classement selon la taille des variations

Agrégation au niveau de 24 industries	1961		1971		Variation 1961–1971	
	Emploi lié à l'exportation en % de l'exportation	Emploi lié à l'exportation en % de l'emploi total	Emploi lié à l'exportation en % de l'exportation	Emploi lié à l'exportation en % de l'emploi total	Emploi lié à l'exportation en % de l'exportation	Emploi lié à l'exportation en % de l'emploi total
S11. Véhicules à moteur et pièces	0,53	0,09	6,54	1,27	6,01	1,18
S20. Commerce	5,97	1,03	8,67	1,68	2,70	0,65
S23. Services aux entreprises	1,57	0,27	3,78	0,73	2,21	0,46
S9. Métaux primaires et fabrication métallique	6,46	1,11	8,44	1,63	1,97	0,52
S13. Produits électriques et électroniques	1,34	0,23	3,17	0,61	1,83	0,38
S24. Services personnels et autres	1,32	0,23	2,25	0,44	0,93	0,21
S12. Autre matériel de transport	1,57	0,27	2,39	0,46	0,83	0,19
S10. Machines	1,39	0,24	2,12	0,41	0,73	0,17
S5. Produits en caoutchouc et en plastique	0,42	0,07	1,04	0,20	0,62	0,13
S21. Finances, assurance et immobilier	1,64	0,28	2,26	0,44	0,61	0,15
S15. Autres produits fabriqués	0,82	0,14	1,20	0,23	0,38	0,09
S14. Pétrole raffiné, prod. chimiques et non métall.	2,73	0,47	3,08	0,60	0,35	0,13
S19. Services publics	2,14	0,37	2,49	0,48	0,35	0,11
S6. Cuir, textile et vêtement	1,40	0,24	1,70	0,33	0,30	0,09
S3. Pétrole brut et gaz naturel	0,60	0,10	0,87	0,17	0,28	0,07
S22. Redev. gouv. et logements occ. par propr.	0,00	0,00	0,00	0,00	0,00	0,00
S18. Entreposage	0,78	0,13	0,58	0,11	-0,21	-0,02
S4. Aliments, boissons et tabac	3,14	0,54	2,80	0,54	-0,34	0,00
S16. Construction	2,12	0,36	1,61	0,31	-0,51	-0,05
S7. Produits en bois et mobilier	4,83	0,83	4,23	0,82	-0,60	-0,01
S8. Papier, produits connexes et imprimerie	7,09	1,22	6,38	1,24	-0,70	0,02
S2. Mines, sauf le pétrole et le gaz	7,80	1,34	6,95	1,35	-0,84	0,01
S17. Transport et pipelines	10,61	1,82	9,37	1,82	-1,24	-0,01
S1. Agriculture, forêt, pêche et piégeage	33,72	5,80	18,07	3,50	-15,65	-2,30
TOTAL	100,00	17,20	100,00	19,38	0,00	2,18

Tableau 4B Parts de l'emploi, 1971 et 1981, groupe de 24 industries, classement selon la taille des variations

Agrégation au niveau de 24 industries	1971		1981		Variation 1971–1981	
	Emploi lié à l'exportation en % de l'emploi total	Emploi lié à l'exportation en % de l'emploi lié à l'exportation	Emploi lié à l'exportation en % de l'emploi total	Emploi lié à l'exportation en % de l'emploi lié à l'exportation	Emploi lié à l'exportation en % de l'emploi total	Emploi lié à l'exportation en % de l'emploi lié à l'exportation
S23. Services aux entreprises	3,78	0,73	6,76	1,41	2,98	0,68
S20. Commerce	8,67	1,68	10,31	2,16	1,64	0,48
S24. Services personnels et autres	2,25	0,44	3,32	0,69	1,06	0,26
S21. Finances, assurance et immobilier	2,26	0,44	3,24	0,68	0,98	0,24
S19. Services publics	2,49	0,48	3,21	0,67	0,72	0,19
S10. Machines	2,12	0,41	2,76	0,58	0,64	0,17
S5. Produits en caoutchouc et en plastique	1,04	0,20	1,31	0,27	0,27	0,07
S3. Pétrole brut et gaz naturel	0,87	0,17	1,05	0,22	0,18	0,05
S4. Aliments, boissons et tabac	2,80	0,54	2,89	0,60	0,09	0,06
S15. Autres produits fabriqués	1,20	0,23	1,29	0,27	0,08	0,04
S13. Produits électriques et électroniques	3,17	0,61	3,20	0,67	0,03	0,06
S22. Redev. gouv. et logements occ. par propr.	0,00	0,00	0,00	0,00	0,00	0,00
S18. Entreposage	0,58	0,11	0,52	0,11	-0,06	-0,00
S16. Construction	1,61	0,31	1,55	0,32	-0,06	0,01
S7. Produits en bois et mobilier	4,23	0,82	4,09	0,86	-0,14	0,04
S12. Autre matériel de transport	2,39	0,46	2,21	0,46	-0,18	-0,00
S14. Pétrole raffiné, prod. chimiques et non métall.	3,08	0,60	2,88	0,60	-0,20	-0,00
S6. Cuir, textile et vêtement	1,70	0,33	1,40	0,29	-0,30	-0,04
S17. Transport et pipelines	9,37	1,82	8,96	1,87	-0,41	0,06
S9. Métaux primaires et fabrication métallique	8,44	1,63	7,69	1,61	-0,75	-0,03
S8. Papier, produits connexes et imprimerie	6,38	1,24	5,47	1,14	-0,91	-0,09
S11. Véhicules à moteur et pièces	6,54	1,27	5,41	1,13	-1,13	-0,14
S2. Mines, sauf le pétrole et le gaz	6,95	1,35	4,95	1,03	-2,01	-0,31
S1. Agriculture, forêt, pêche et piégeage	18,07	3,50	15,52	3,25	-2,55	-0,26
TOTAL	100,00	19,38	100,00	20,91	0,00	1,53

Tableau 4C Parts de l'emploi, 1981 et 1991, groupe de 24 industries, classement selon la taille des variations

Agrégation au niveau de 24 industries	1981		1991		Variation 1981–1991	
	Emploi lié à l'exportation en % de l'emploi total lié à l'exportation	Emploi lié à l'exportation en % de l'emploi total	Emploi lié à l'exportation en % de l'emploi total lié à l'exportation	Emploi lié à l'exportation en % de l'emploi total	Emploi lié à l'exportation en % de l'emploi total lié à l'exportation	Emploi lié à l'exportation en % de l'emploi total
S24. Services personnels et autres	3.32	0.69	10.03	2.18	6.72	1.49
S23. Services aux entreprises	6.76	1.41	8.91	1.94	2.15	0.52
S20. Commerce	10.31	2.16	11.61	2.52	1.30	0.37
S11. Véhicules à moteur et pièces	5.41	1.13	6.11	1.33	0.70	0.20
S21. Finances, assurance et immobilier	3.24	0.68	3.83	0.83	0.59	0.16
S13. Produits électriques et électroniques	3.20	0.67	3.72	0.81	0.52	0.14
S5. Produits en caoutchouc et en plastique	1.31	0.27	1.72	0.37	0.41	0.10
S6. Cuir, textile et vêtement	1.40	0.29	1.64	0.36	0.24	0.06
S15. Autres produits fabriqués	1.29	0.27	1.46	0.32	0.18	0.05
S3. Pétrole brut et gaz naturel	1.05	0.22	1.15	0.25	0.09	0.03
S18. Entreposage	0.52	0.11	0.54	0.12	0.02	0.01
S22. Redev. gouv. et logements occ. par propr.	0.00	0.00	0.00	0.00	0.00	0.00
S12. Autre matériel de transport	2.21	0.46	2.11	0.46	-0.10	-0.00
S16. Construction	1.55	0.32	1.30	0.28	-0.25	-0.04
S14. Pétrole raffiné, prod. chimiques et non métall.	2.88	0.60	2.62	0.57	-0.26	-0.03
S19. Services publics	3.21	0.67	2.79	0.61	-0.43	-0.07
S4. Aliments, boissons et tabac	2.89	0.60	2.38	0.52	-0.51	-0.09
S10. Machines	2.76	0.58	1.99	0.43	-0.78	-0.15
S8. Papier, produits connexes et imprimerie	5.47	1.14	4.60	1.00	-0.88	-0.14
S7. Produits en bois et mobilier	4.09	0.86	3.12	0.68	-0.97	-0.18
S17. Transport et pipelines	8.96	1.87	7.74	1.68	-1.21	-0.19
S9. Métaux primaires et fabrication métallique	7.69	1.61	6.47	1.41	-1.22	-0.20
S2. Mines, sauf le pétrole et le gaz	4.95	1.03	3.00	0.65	-1.95	-0.38
S1. Agriculture, forêt, pêche et piégeage	15.52	3.25	11.16	2.43	-4.36	-0.82
TOTAL	100.00	20.91	100.00	21.75	-0.00	0.84

Tableau 4D Parts de l'emploi, 1991 et 1997, groupe de 24 industries, classement selon la taille des variations

Agrégation au niveau de 24 industries	1991		1997		Variation 1991-1997	
	Emploi lié à l'exportation en % de l'exportation	Emploi lié à l'exportation en % de l'emploi total	Emploi lié à l'exportation en % de l'exportation	Emploi lié à l'exportation en % de l'emploi total	Emploi lié à l'exportation en % de l'exportation	Emploi lié à l'exportation en % de l'emploi total
S23. Services aux entreprises	8,91	1,94	10,65	3,02	1,74	1,08
S6. Cuir, textile et vêtement	1,64	0,36	2,84	0,80	1,20	0,45
S24. Services personnels et autres	10,03	2,18	11,11	3,15	1,08	0,96
S20. Commerce	11,61	2,52	12,68	3,59	1,07	1,06
S7. Produits en bois et mobilier	3,12	0,68	4,07	1,15	0,94	0,47
S5. Produits en caoutchouc et en plastique	1,72	0,37	2,42	0,68	0,70	0,31
S10. Machines	1,99	0,43	2,45	0,69	0,46	0,26
S15. Autres produits fabriqués	1,46	0,32	1,84	0,52	0,38	0,20
S16. Construction	1,30	0,28	1,42	0,40	0,12	0,12
S18. Entreposage	0,54	0,12	0,64	0,18	0,10	0,06
S4. Aliments, boissons et tabac	2,38	0,52	2,45	0,69	0,07	0,18
S21. Finances, assurance et immobilier	3,83	0,83	3,87	1,10	0,04	0,26
S22. Redev. gouv. et logements occ. par propr.	0,00	0,00	0,00	0,00	0,00	0,00
S19. Services publics	2,79	0,61	2,72	0,77	-0,07	0,16
S13. Produits électriques et électroniques	3,72	0,81	3,60	1,02	-0,12	0,21
S12. Autre matériel de transport	2,11	0,46	1,98	0,56	-0,13	0,10
S17. Transport et pipelines	7,74	1,68	7,53	2,13	-0,22	0,45
S14. Pétrole raffiné, prod. chimiques et non métall.	2,62	0,57	2,39	0,68	-0,23	0,11
S3. Pétrole brut et gaz naturel	1,15	0,25	0,87	0,24	-0,28	0,00
S9. Métaux primaires et fabrication métallique	6,47	1,41	5,64	1,60	-0,83	0,19
S11. Véhicules à moteur et pièces	6,11	1,33	5,26	1,49	-0,85	0,16
S2. Mines, sauf le pétrole et le gaz	3,00	0,65	2,11	0,60	-0,89	-0,06
S8. Papier, produits connexes et imprimerie	4,60	1,00	3,30	0,93	-1,30	-0,07
S1. Agriculture, forêt, pêche et piégeage	11,16	2,43	8,19	2,32	-2,97	-0,11
TOTAL	100,00	21,75	100,00	28,31	0,00	6,57

Tableau 5 Parts de l'emploi, variations de 1961 à 1997, groupe de 24 industries					
Emploi lié à l'exportation en % de l'emploi total lié à l'exportation					
Agrégation au niveau de 24 industries	**1961–1997**	**1961–1971**	**1971–1981**	**1981–1991**	**1991–1997**
S1. Agriculture, forêt, pêche et piégeage	-25,5	-15,7	-2,5	-4,4	-3,0
S2. Mines, sauf le pétrole et le gaz	-5,7	-0,8	-2,0	-1,9	-0,9
S3. Pétrole brut et gaz naturel	0,3	0,3	0,2	0,1	-0,3
S4. Aliments, boissons et tabac	-0,7	-0,3	0,1	-0,5	0,1
S5. Produits en caoutchouc et en plastique	2,0	0,6	0,3	0,4	0,7
S6. Cuir, textile et vêtement	1,4	0,3	-0,3	0,2	1,2
S7. Produits en bois et mobilier	-0,8	-0,6	-0,1	-1,0	0,9
S8. Papier, produits connexes et imprimerie	-3,8	-0,7	-0,9	-0,9	-1,3
S9. Métaux primaires et fabrication métallique	-0,8	2,0	-0,7	-1,2	-0,8
S10. Machines	1,1	0,7	0,6	-0,8	0,5
S11. Véhicules à moteur et pièces	4,7	6,0	-1,1	0,7	-0,8
S12. Autre matériel de transport	0,4	0,8	-0,2	-0,1	-0,1
S13. Produits électriques et électroniques	2,3	1,8	0,0	0,5	-0,1
S14. Pétrole raffiné, prod. chimiques et non métall.	-0,3	0,4	-0,2	-0,3	-0,2
S15. Autres produits fabriqués	1,0	0,4	0,1	0,2	0,4
S16. Construction	-0,7	-0,5	-0,1	-0,3	0,1
S17. Transport et pipelines	-3,1	-1,2	-0,4	-1,2	-0,2
S18. Entreposage	-0,1	-0,2	-0,1	0,0	0,1
S19. Services publics	0,6	0,4	0,7	-0,4	-0,1
S20. Commerce	6,7	2,7	1,6	1,3	1,1
S21. Finances, assurance et immobilier	2,2	0,6	1,0	0,6	0,0
S22. Redev. gouv. et logements occ. par propr.	0,0	0,0	0,0	0,0	0,0
S23. Services aux entreprises	9,1	2,2	3,0	2,2	1,7
S24. Services personnels et autres	9,8	0,9	1,1	6,7	1,1

Décomposition des changements dans la structure d'emploi des exportations, 1961-1997

Comme nous l'avons noté précédemment au chapitre 2 en traitant des méthodes, il est possible de décomposer en divers éléments les changements observés dans les parts de l'emploi lié à l'exportation entre deux années. Même si la décomposition est exhaustive (autrement dit, si tous les composants considérés changent simultanément entre l'année de base et l'année de comparaison), ils expliquent exactement la totalité du changement observé entre ces années), les composants sont en interaction les uns avec les autres de sorte que la somme des effets individuels ne correspond pas au total, laissant un terme d'interaction résiduel.

En gardant cela à l'esprit, nous avons tenu compte des composants suivants dans l'examen des changements des parts de l'emploi lié aux exportations entre deux années : 1) les changements dans les parts des exportations : ce sont les pondérations des 161 industries entrant dans les calculs d'entrées-sorties pour les exportations à mesure qu'elles changent entre l'année de base et l'année de comparaison; 2) les changements dans le ratio emploi/production : il s'agit du ratio de l'emploi (nombre de personnes) à la production (ventes totales) pour chacune des 161 industries entrant dans nos calculs d'entrées-sorties; 3) les changements dans les coefficients entrées-sorties : les « coefficients techniques » qui décrivent les parts des 161 intrants industriels possibles pour chacune des 161 industries productrices; enfin, 4) les changements dans les coefficients d'importation : ce sont les parts de toute nouvelle demande (autre que les exportations) d'une industrie qui va aux importations plutôt que d'être satisfaite par la production intérieure.

Les décompositions ont été effectuées pour différentes périodes aux niveaux d'agrégation à 24 et à 161 industries. Le tableau 6A montre la décomposition des changements entre 1961 et 1997 pour l'agrégation à 24 industries, par ordre numérique, tandis que le tableau 6B renferme les mêmes données, mais classées selon l'ordre décroissant des variations. Les tableaux A.4A et A.4B de l'appendice 4 font voir les décompositions des changements entre 1961 et 1992 pour la désagrégation à 161 industries. Enfin, les tableaux 7A à 7D montrent les décompositions au niveau d'agrégation à 24 industries pour les sous-périodes 1961-1971, 1971-1981, 1981-1991 et 1991-1997, respectivement.

Nous discuterons principalement des résultats présentés au tableau 6B, pour la période 1961-1997 au niveau d'agrégation à 24 industries. L'industrie des services personnels et autres est celle qui affiche le changement positif le plus important pour ce qui est de la part de l'emploi lié aux exportations durant la période 1961-1997. Comme nous pouvons le voir, l'augmentation est principalement attribuable à deux facteurs : une augmentation de la part relative des exportations de cette industrie ou des industries qui utilisent intensivement la production de cette dernière, ainsi qu'une diminution du contenu *relatif* en importations — ce qui a un effet positif sur la part de l'emploi du secteur et qui explique par conséquent le signe positif. Pour les services aux entreprises, qui est la deuxième industrie ayant enregistré le gain le plus important pour la part de l'emploi, ces deux facteurs sont également présents mais ils s'accompagnent d'une *perte* relative de la productivité de la main-d'oeuvre (qui vient ajouter à la part de l'emploi et, par conséquent, a un signe positif) ainsi que par une utilisation accrue de ces services dans les autres secteurs d'exportation (comme l'indique la valeur 1,17 dans la colonne Variation des coefficients entrées-sorties. Pour le commerce, qui a enregistré le troisième gain le plus important au niveau de la part de l'emploi, la principale source de changement est, de loin, une diminution relative du contenu en importations. On observe également une certaine contribution positive des changements observés dans la composition des exportations, mais ce secteur a connu une amélioration de la productivité relative de la main-d'oeuvre, ce qui a eu une influence négative sur le ratio emploi/production.

L'industrie des véhicules à moteur et pièces et celle des produits électriques et électroniques se ressemblent dans la mesure où les deux ont vu leur part de l'emploi lié à l'exportation augmenter, principalement en raison des changements survenus dans la composition des exportations du Canada — largement compensée toutefois par l'effet du contenu en importations. L'industrie des produits en caoutchouc et en plastique (principalement ces derniers) et celle du cuir, des textiles et du vêtement ont cependant vu leur part de l'emploi lié à l'exportation augmenter principalement en raison des gains enregistrés dans la composition des exportations *et* d'une diminution du contenu relatif en importations.

Tournant notre attention vers les secteurs qui ont enregistré les pertes les plus importantes dans la part de l'emploi lié à l'exportation, de nombreux profils différents ressortent encore une fois. L'industrie des transports et des pipelines a vu sa part de l'emploi diminuer principalement en raison de la composition des exportations : en 1997, le Canada exportait relativement plus de biens et de services ayant un coefficient de transport moins élevé qu'en 1961. Même si la composition des divers types de transport a changé, cette diminution n'est attribuable ni au fait que certains biens d'exportation nécessitent moins de transport qu'auparavant (ce qui serait ressorti comme une valeur négative dans la colonne Variation des coefficients entrées-sorties), ni à une amélioration de la productivité relative de la main-d'oeuvre dans le secteur des transports (qui serait ressortie des valeurs figurant dans la colonnes Variation du ratio emploi/production).

L'industrie des papiers, des produits connexes et de l'impression fait voir un tableau un peu plus diversifié pour ce qui est des causes de la baisse de la part de l'emploi lié aux exportations : les changements dans la composition des exportations demeurent la principale cause, mais l'amélioration de la productivité relative de la main-d'oeuvre (coefficient de -0,74 dans la colonne Variation du ratio emploi/production) et une pénétration relativement plus importante des importations comme source d'intrants intermédiaires pour les exportations (-0,42) ont également joué. Le secteur des mines et celui de l'agriculture et de la forêt ont également vu leurs parts de l'emploi lié aux exportations diminuer tant en raison des changements survenus dans la composition des exportations que de la pénétration accrue des importations au niveau des intrants intermédiaires. Dans le secteur de l'agriculture et de la forêt, on note également une faible contribution négative provenant d'une amélioration de la productivité de la main-d'oeuvre ainsi qu'un effet positif compensateur découlant d'une plus grande utilisation des intrants intermédiaires du secteur de l'agriculture et de la forêt dans les autres exportations (coefficient de 0,82 dans la colonne Variation des coefficients entrées-sorties).

Si nous examinons l'ensemble des décompositions sectorielles présentées aux tableaux 6A et 6B, on peut voir que les principales causes des changements observés dans les parts de l'emploi lié à l'exportation sont la composition des exportations elle-même, suivie dans bien des cas des changements observés dans la pénétration relative des importations au niveau des intrants intermédiaires. Les variations de la productivité relative de la main-d'oeuvre sont, à une ou deux exceptions près, beaucoup moins importantes, tandis que les changements dans les coefficients d'entrées-sorties techniques sont le facteur le moins important. Cependant, cette dernière remarque doit être tempérée par le fait que pour l'intervalle 1993-1997, qui s'inscrit dans la période plus longue de 1961 à 1997 étudiée, les coefficients d'entrées-sorties techniques étaient fixes parce que nous avons utilisé les coefficients de 1992 pour les années subséquentes.

Tableau 6A Décomposition des variations des parts de l'emploi, 1961–1997, groupe de 24 industries

	1961 — Emploi lié à l'exportation en % de l'emploi total lié à l'exportation	1997 — Emploi lié à l'exportation en % de l'emploi total lié à l'exportation	Variation 1961–1997 — Emploi lié à l'exportation en % de l'emploi total lié à l'exportation	Attribuable à : Variation de la part des exportations	Attribuable à : Variation du ratio emploi/production	Attribuable à : Variation des coefficients entrées-sorties	Attribuable à : Variation des coefficients d'importation	Attribuable à : Interaction résiduelle
S1. Agriculture, forêt, pêche et piégeage	33,72	8,19	-25,53	-14,83	-0,64	0,82	-5,56	-5,33
S2. Mines, sauf le pétrole et le gaz	7,80	2,11	-5,69	-4,69	-0,23	-0,01	-1,38	0,61
S3. Pétrole brut et gaz naturel	0,60	0,87	0,27	0,36	-0,03	0,07	-0,39	0,26
S4. Aliments, boissons et tabac	3,14	2,45	-0,69	-1,10	-0,27	0,15	0,15	0,39
S5. Produits en caoutchouc et en plastique	0,42	2,42	1,99	1,86	-0,02	0,52	0,52	0,04
S6. Cuir, textile et vêtement	1,40	2,84	1,44	1,76	-0,39	-0,40	0,47	-0,21
S7. Produits en bois et mobilier	4,83	4,07	-0,76	0,06	-0,45	-0,20	-1,46	0,72
S8. Papier, produits connexes et imprimerie	7,09	3,30	-3,79	-2,71	-0,74	0,36	-0,42	0,06
S9. Métaux primaires et fabrication métallique	6,46	5,64	-0,82	0,46	-0,78	0,02	-0,23	0,64
S10. Machines	1,39	2,45	1,06	1,17	-0,23	0,36	-0,01	0,21
S11. Véhicules à moteur et pièces	0,53	5,26	4,74	4,93	-0,23	-0,09	-3,29	3,92
S12. Autre matériel de transport	1,57	1,98	0,41	0,71	-0,21	-0,60	-0,32	0,37
S13. Produits électriques et électroniques	1,34	3,60	2,26	2,80	0,16	-0,09	-2,11	1,87
S14. Pétrole raffiné, prod. chimiques et non métall.	2,73	2,39	-0,35	0,58	-0,23	-0,47	-1,06	0,66
S15. Autres produits fabriqués	0,82	1,84	1,02	1,02	-0,11	-0,13	0,33	-0,13
S16. Construction	2,12	1,42	-0,70	-0,67	-0,56	-0,29	0,01	0,51
S17. Transport et pipelines	10,61	7,53	-3,08	-2,43	0,20	-0,09	0,01	-0,96
S18. Entreposage	0,78	0,64	-0,14	-0,83	-0,26	0,06	0,31	0,57
S19. Services publics	2,14	2,72	0,58	-0,20	0,65	-0,02	-0,72	0,86
S20. Commerce	5,97	12,68	6,71	0,91	-0,48	0,19	4,05	2,03
S21. Finances, assurance et immobilier	1,64	3,87	2,23	0,38	0,83	-0,03	0,58	0,47
S22. Redev. gouv. et logements occ. par propr.	0,00	0,00	0,00	0,00	0,00	0,00	0,00	0,00
S23. Services aux entreprises	1,57	10,65	9,08	4,71	3,54	1,17	4,21	-4,56
S24. Services personnels et autres	1,32	11,11	9,79	5,72	0,48	0,29	6,30	-3,00
TOTAL	100,00	100,00	0,00	0,00	0,00	0,00	0,00	0,00

Tableau 6B Décomposition des variations des parts de l'emploi, 1961–1997, groupe de 24 industries

Classement selon la taille des variations	1961 — Emploi lié à l'exportation en % de l'emploi total lié à l'exportation	1997 — Emploi lié à l'exportation en % de l'emploi total lié à l'exportation	Variation 1961–1997 — Emploi lié à l'exportation en % de l'emploi total lié à l'exportation	Variation 1961–1997 Emploi lié à l'exportation — Variation de la part des exportations	Attribuable à : Variation du ratio emploi/ production	Variation des coefficients entrées-sorties	Variation des coefficients d'importation	Interaction résiduelle
S24. Services personnels et autres	1,32	11,11	9,79	5,72	0,48	0,29	6,30	-3,00
S23. Services aux entreprises	1,57	10,65	9,08	4,71	3,54	1,17	4,21	-4,56
S20. Commerce	5,97	12,68	6,71	0,91	-0,48	0,19	4,05	2,03
S11. Véhicules à moteur et pièces	0,53	5,26	4,74	4,93	-0,23	-0,60	-3,29	3,92
S13. Produits électriques et électroniques	1,34	3,60	2,26	2,80	0,16	-0,47	-2,11	1,87
S21. Finances, assurance et immobilier	1,64	3,87	2,23	0,38	0,83	-0,03	0,58	0,47
S5. Produits en caoutchouc et en plastique	0,42	2,42	1,99	1,86	-0,02	-0,40	0,52	0,04
S6. Cuir, textile et vêtement	1,40	2,84	1,44	1,76	-0,39	-0,20	0,47	-0,21
S10. Machines	1,39	2,45	1,06	1,17	-0,23	-0,09	-0,01	0,21
S15. Autres produits fabriqués	0,82	1,84	1,02	1,02	-0,11	-0,09	0,33	-0,13
S19. Services publics	2,14	2,72	0,58	-0,20	0,65	-0,02	-0,72	0,86
S12. Autre matériel de transport	1,57	1,98	0,41	0,71	-0,21	-0,13	-0,32	0,37
S3. Pétrole brut et gaz naturel	0,60	0,87	0,27	0,36	-0,03	0,07	-0,39	0,26
S22. Redev. gouv. et logements occ. par propr.	0,00	0,00	0,00	0,00	0,00	0,00	0,00	0,00
S18. Entreposage	0,78	0,64	-0,14	-0,83	-0,26	0,06	0,31	0,57
S14. Pétrole raffiné, prod. chimiques et non métall.	2,73	2,39	-0,35	0,58	-0,23	-0,29	-1,06	0,66
S4. Aliments, boissons et tabac	3,14	2,45	-0,69	-1,10	-0,27	0,15	0,15	0,39
S16. Construction	2,12	1,42	-0,70	-0,67	-0,56	0,00	0,15	0,51
S7. Produits en bois et mobilier	4,83	4,07	-0,76	0,06	-0,45	0,36	-1,46	0,72
S9. Métaux primaires et fabrication métallique	6,46	5,64	-0,82	0,46	-0,78	-0,92	-0,23	0,64
S17. Transport et pipelines	10,61	7,53	-3,08	-2,43	0,20	0,09	0,01	-0,96
S8. Papier, produits connexes et imprimerie	7,09	3,30	-3,79	-2,71	-0,74	0,02	-0,42	0,06
S2. Mines, sauf le pétrole et le gaz	7,80	2,11	-5,69	-4,69	-0,23	-0,01	-1,38	0,61
S1. Agriculture, forêt, pêche et piégeage	33,72	8,19	-25,53	-14,83	-0,64	0,82	-5,56	-5,33
TOTAL	100,00	100,00	0,00	0,00	0,00	0,00	0,00	0,00

Tableau 7A Décomposition des variations des parts de l'emploi, 1961–1971, groupe de 24 industries

Classement selon la taille des variations	1961 — Emploi lié à l'exportation en % de l'emploi total lié à l'exportation	1971 — Emploi lié à l'exportation en % de l'emploi total lié à l'exportation	Variation 1961-1971 — Emploi lié à l'exportation en % de l'emploi total lié à l'exportation	Attribuable à : Variation de la part des exportations	Variation du ratio emploi/ production	Variation des coefficients entrées-sorties	Variation des coefficients d'importation	Interaction résiduelle
S11. Véhicules à moteur et pièces	0,53	6,54	6,01	6,12	-0,01	-0,84	-1,52	2,25
S20. Commerce	5,97	8,67	2,70	0,99	0,23	-0,01	1,22	0,27
S23. Services aux entreprises	1,57	3,78	2,21	1,28	0,21	0,21	0,72	-1,13
S9. Métaux primaires et fabrication métallique	6,46	8,44	1,97	1,37	1,12	-0,11	0,74	0,21
S13. Produits électriques et électroniques	1,34	3,17	1,83	1,72	-0,00	-0,12	0,32	-0,09
S24. Services personnels et autres	1,32	2,25	0,93	0,39	0,09	-0,00	0,56	-0,11
S12. Autre matériel de transport	1,57	2,39	0,83	0,82	-0,05	-0,02	-0,13	0,21
S10. Machines	1,39	2,12	0,73	0,77	0,06	0,00	-0,08	-0,02
S5. Produits en caoutchouc et en plastique	0,42	1,04	0,62	0,53	0,14	-0,05	0,05	-0,05
S21. Finances, assurance et immobilier	1,64	2,26	0,61	0,77	0,19	-0,00	0,29	0,00
S15. Autres produits fabriqués	0,82	1,20	0,38	0,38	0,13	-0,03	0,05	-0,04
S14. Pétrole raffiné, prod. chimiques et non métall.	2,73	3,08	0,35	-0,04	0,02	0,02	0,09	0,09
S19. Services publics	2,14	2,49	0,35	0,05	0,15	0,00	0,32	0,04
S6. Cuir, textile et vêtement	1,40	1,70	0,30	0,34	-0,11	0,01	0,10	-0,01
S3. Pétrole brut et gaz naturel	0,60	0,87	0,28	0,34	-0,11	0,03	-0,15	0,06
S22. Redev. gouv. et logements occ. par propr.	0,00	0,00	0,00	0,00	0,00	0,00	0,00	0,00
S18. Entreposage	0,78	0,58	-0,21	-0,19	-0,07	0,01	0,04	0,00
S4. Aliments, boissons et tabac	3,14	2,80	-0,34	-0,44	-0,11	0,07	0,16	-0,02
S16. Construction	2,12	1,61	-0,51	-0,01	-0,24	0,02	-0,23	-0,05
S7. Produits en bois et mobilier	4,83	4,23	-0,60	-0,35	0,03	0,13	-0,36	-0,05
S8. Papier, produits connexes et imprimerie	7,09	6,38	-0,70	-2,07	-0,41	0,12	1,14	0,51
S2. Mines, sauf le pétrole et le gaz	7,80	6,95	-0,84	-2,34	0,22	0,02	0,60	0,66
S17. Transport et pipelines	10,61	9,37	-1,24	-0,38	-0,07	0,18	-0,86	-0,11
S1. Agriculture, forêt, pêche et piégeage	33,72	18,07	-15,65	-9,44	-0,96	0,52	-3,14	-2,63

Tableau 7B Décomposition des variations des parts de l'emploi, 1971–1981, groupe de 24 industries

Classement selon la taille des variations	1971	1981	Variation 1971-1981	Attribuable à :				
	Emploi lié à l'exportation en % de l'emploi total lié à l'exportation	Emploi lié à l'exportation en % de l'emploi total lié à l'exportation	Emploi lié à l'exportation en % de l'emploi total lié à l'exportation	Variation de la part des exportations	Variation du ratio emploi/ production	Variation des coefficients entrées-sorties	Variation des coefficients d'importation	Interaction résiduelle
S23. Services aux entreprises	3,78	6,76	2,98	0,75	0,58	0,03	1,87	-0,24
S20. Commerce	8,67	10,31	1,64	0,42	-0,62	0,02	1,93	-0,12
S24. Services personnels et autres	2,25	3,32	1,06	-0,24	0,21	0,04	1,07	-0,02
S21. Finances, assurance et immobilier	2,26	3,24	0,98	0,16	0,11	-0,01	0,81	-0,09
S19. Services publics	2,49	3,21	0,72	0,50	0,06	0,03	0,08	0,04
S10. Machines	2,12	2,76	0,64	0,64	0,06	-0,01	0,04	-0,08
S5. Produits en caoutchouc et en plastique	1,04	1,31	0,27	0,24	0,01	-0,02	0,11	-0,07
S3. Pétrole brut et gaz naturel	0,87	1,05	0,18	0,38	0,16	0,03	-0,66	0,27
S4. Aliments, boissons et tabac	2,80	2,89	0,09	0,01	0,07	0,05	0,01	-0,06
S15. Autres produits fabriqués	1,20	1,29	0,08	0,20	-0,04	-0,02	-0,09	0,03
S13. Produits électriques et électroniques	3,17	3,20	0,03	0,33	0,03	-0,12	-0,21	0,00
S22. Redev. gouv. et logements occ. par propr.	0,00	0,00	0,00	0,00	0,00	0,00	0,00	0,00
S18. Entreposage	0,58	0,52	-0,06	-0,19	-0,06	0,01	0,13	0,05
S16. Construction	1,61	1,55	-0,06	0,06	-0,12	0,02	-0,13	0,12
S7. Produits en bois et mobilier	4,23	4,09	-0,14	-0,34	0,13	0,06	0,11	-0,10
S12. Autre matériel de transport	2,39	2,21	-0,18	-0,15	0,02	0,03	-0,20	0,13
S14. Pétrole raffiné, prod. chimiques et non métall.	3,08	2,88	-0,20	0,28	0,27	0,08	-1,35	0,52
S6. Cuir, textile et vêtement	1,70	1,40	-0,30	-0,13	-0,11	-0,03	0,01	-0,05
S17. Transport et pipelines	9,37	8,96	-0,41	-0,91	-0,16	0,13	0,79	-0,26
S9. Métaux primaires et fabrication métallique	8,44	7,69	-0,75	-0,19	-0,02	-0,38	-0,07	-0,09
S8. Papier, produits connexes et imprimerie	6,38	5,47	-0,91	0,05	-0,06	0,09	-0,81	-0,18
S11. Véhicules à moteur et pièces	6,54	5,41	-1,13	-1,99	0,01	-0,21	0,92	0,15
S2. Mines, sauf le pétrole et le gaz	6,95	4,95	-2,01	-0,22	-0,37	-0,14	-1,77	0,50
S1. Agriculture, forêt, pêche et piégeage	18,07	15,52	-2,55	0,33	-0,16	0,30	-2,58	-0,44

Tableau 7C Décomposition des variations des parts de l'emploi, 1981 à 1991, groupe de 24 industries

Classement selon la taille des variations	1981 — Emploi lié à l'exportation en % de l'emploi total lié à l'exportation	1991 — Emploi lié à l'exportation en % de l'emploi total lié à l'exportation	Variation 1981-1991 — Emploi lié à l'exportation en % de l'emploi total lié à l'exportation	Attribuable à : Variation de la part des exportations	Variation du ratio emploi/production	Variation des coefficients entrées-sorties	Variation des coefficients d'importation	Interaction résiduelle
S24. Services personnels et autres	3,32	10,03	6,72	5,68	0,29	-0,26	1,05	-0,03
S23. Services aux entreprises	6,76	8,91	2,15	1,69	0,66	0,25	-0,71	0,27
S20. Commerce	10,31	11,61	1,30	0,17	0,88	0,08	0,35	-0,19
S11. Véhicules à moteur et pièces	5,41	6,11	0,70	1,31	-0,34	0,56	-0,61	-0,22
S21. Finances, assurance et immobilier	3,24	3,83	0,59	0,31	0,83	-0,02	-0,90	0,37
S13. Produits électriques et électroniques	3,20	3,72	0,52	1,49	-0,01	-0,30	-1,28	0,62
S5. Produits en caoutchouc et en plastique	1,31	1,72	0,41	0,37	-0,02	-0,15	0,27	-0,07
S6. Cuir, textile et vêtement	1,40	1,64	0,24	0,34	-0,10	-0,11	0,14	-0,03
S15. Autres produits fabriqués	1,29	1,46	0,18	0,06	-0,09	-0,05	0,18	0,08
S3. Pétrole brut et gaz naturel	1,05	1,15	0,09	-0,44	-0,28	0,05	0,52	0,24
S18. Entreposage	0,52	0,54	0,02	0,01	-0,04	0,00	0,07	-0,02
S22. Redev. gouv. et logement occ. par propr.	0,00	0,00	0,00	0,00	0,00	0,00	0,00	0,00
S12. Autre matériel de transport	2,21	2,11	-0,10	0,19	-0,08	0,05	-0,09	-0,17
S16. Construction	1,55	1,30	-0,25	-0,22	-0,20	-0,01	0,20	-0,02
S14. Pétrole raffiné, prod. chimiques et non métall.	2,88	2,62	-0,26	0,05	-0,24	-0,02	0,21	-0,06
S19. Services publics	3,21	2,79	-0,43	-0,21	0,49	-0,03	-0,78	0,10
S4. Aliments, boissons et tabac	2,89	2,38	-0,51	-0,27	-0,20	-0,02	0,08	-0,09
S10. Machines	2,76	1,99	-0,78	-0,97	-0,19	-0,02	0,33	0,08
S8. Papier, produits connexes et imprimerie	5,47	4,60	-0,88	-0,57	-0,26	-0,08	0,23	-0,20
S7. Produits en bois et mobilier	4,09	3,12	-0,97	-0,24	-0,20	0,02	-0,23	-0,32
S17. Transport et pipelines	8,96	7,74	-1,21	0,15	-0,22	-0,17	-0,63	-0,34
S9. Métaux primaires et fabrication métallique	7,69	6,47	-1,22	-0,88	-0,67	-0,03	0,64	-0,28
S2. Mines, sauf le pétrole et le gaz	4,95	3,00	-1,95	-1,55	-0,25	0,17	-0,07	-0,25
S1. Agriculture, forêt, pêche et piégeage	15,52	11,16	-4,36	-6,46	0,25	0,27	1,03	0,55

Tableau 7D Décomposition des variations des parts de l'emploi, 1991-1997, groupe de 24 industries

Classement selon la taille des variations	1991	1997	Variation 1991-1997	Attribuable à :				
	Emploi lié à l'exportation en % de l'emploi total lié à l'exportation	Emploi lié à l'exportation en % de l'emploi total lié à l'exportation	Emploi lié à l'exportation en % de l'emploi total lié à l'exportation	Variation de la part des exportations	Variation du ratio emploi/ production	Variation des coefficients entrées-sorties	Variation des coefficients d'importation	Interaction résiduelle
S23. Services aux entreprises	8.91	10.65	1.74	0.00	0.19	0.01	1.46	0.08
S6. Cuir, textile et vêtement	1.64	2.84	1.20	1.19	-0.02	-0.12	0.30	-0.15
S24. Services personnels et autres	10.03	11.11	1.08	-1.36	0.03	0.24	1.84	0.33
S20. Commerce	11.61	12.68	1.07	-0.18	-0.28	0.11	1.23	0.18
S7. Produits en bois et mobilier	3.12	4.07	0.94	1.16	-0.03	0.13	-0.50	0.20
S5. Produits en caoutchouc et en plastique	1.72	2.42	0.70	0.79	-0.00	-0.22	0.16	-0.03
S10. Machines	1.99	2.45	0.46	0.66	-0.00	-0.08	-0.19	0.07
S15. Autres produits fabriqués	1.46	1.84	0.38	0.38	0.09	0.01	0.18	-0.28
S16. Construction	1.30	1.42	0.12	-0.13	-0.01	-0.01	0.22	0.04
S18. Entreposage	0.54	0.64	0.10	-0.11	0.00	0.02	0.15	0.03
S4. Aliments, boissons et tabac	2.38	2.45	0.07	-0.15	0.02	0.06	0.15	-0.01
S21. Finances, assurance et immobilier	3.83	3.87	0.04	-0.01	-0.20	-0.02	0.22	0.06
S22. Redev. gouv. et logements occ. par propr.	0.00	0.00	0.00	0.00	0.00	0.00	0.00	0.00
S19. Services publics	2.79	2.72	-0.07	-0.07	0.05	-0.01	-0.07	0.03
S13. Produits électriques et électroniques	3.72	3.60	-0.12	0.64	0.35	0.20	-0.28	-1.04
S12. Autre matériel de transport	2.11	1.98	-0.13	-0.08	-0.01	-0.14	-0.28	0.04
S17. Transport et pipelines	7.74	7.53	-0.22	-1.00	-0.03	0.06	0.05	0.21
S14. Pétrole raffiné, prod. chimiques et non métall.	2.62	2.39	-0.23	0.31	0.01	-0.18	-0.40	0.02
S3. Pétrole brut et gaz naturel	1.15	0.87	-0.28	-0.02	0.01	-0.03	-0.23	-0.00
S9. Métaux primaires et fabrication métallique	6.47	5.64	-0.83	0.45	-0.08	-0.32	-0.90	0.02
S11. Véhicules à moteur et pièces	6.11	5.26	-0.85	0.35	0.02	0.09	-1.51	0.20
S2. Mines, sauf le pétrole et le gaz	3.00	2.11	-0.89	-0.95	-0.01	-0.09	0.02	0.15
S8. Papier, produits connexes et imprimerie	4.60	3.30	-1.30	-0.66	-0.05	0.01	-0.46	-0.15
S1. Agriculture, forêt, pêche et piégeage	11.16	8.19	-2.97	-1.21	-0.07	0.29	-1.98	0.01

Évolution de la composition professionnelle des exportations canadiennes

L'utilisation des données du SPPC pour 1986 et 1991 nous permet d'identifier le profil des « compétences » ou de la « scolarité » de l'emploi dans 112 industries — toutes tirées des données entrées-sorties de la désagrégation à 161 industries ou représentant une combinaison de certaines de ces industries.

Les six catégories de scolarité permettent de répartir les personnes employées selon le diplôme ou le certificat le plus élevé obtenu. Ce sont : 1) secondaire non terminé, 2) études secondaires, 3) certificat ou diplôme de métier, 4) certificat ou diplôme d'études postsecondaires non universitaires, 5) certificat ou diplôme d'études universitaires allant jusqu'au baccalauréat et 6) diplôme d'études supérieures. Le tableau 8A montre les parts de l'emploi selon la désagrégation à 112 industries pour 1991, tandis que le tableau 8B montre les parts de l'emploi pour l'année 1986. Le tableau 8C fait voir la différence entre la part de 1991 et la part de 1986; ces données indiquent donc la mesure dans laquelle les parts ont changé tant au niveau agrégé que par industrie entre 1986 et 1991. Ces tableaux montrent également la concordance entre les 112 industries de la base de données du SPPC et la désagrégation plus poussée des données entrées-sorties à 161 industries. Par souci de commodité, nous avons aussi agrégé les 112 industries au niveau de notre ensemble plus restreint de 24 industries en utilisant les pondérations de l'emploi lié à l'exportation. Les parts pour les années 1991 et 1986 sont présentées, respectivement, dans les tableaux 9A et 9B, tandis que les différences entre ces deux années apparaissent dans le tableau 9C.

Les totaux du tableau 9A indiquent qu'en 1991, 34 p. 100 des employés non gouvernementaux n'avaient pas complété leurs études secondaires tandis qu'une autre tranche de 26 p. 100 avaient complété seulement leurs études secondaires. Un autre groupe de 27 p. 100 possédaient soit un certificat, soit un diplôme de métier, soit un diplôme d'études postsecondaires non universitaires. Enfin, 13 p. 100 de ces personnes détenaient soit un baccalauréat, soit un diplôme d'études supérieures. Parmi les diverses industries, la variation autour de ces parts globales est considérable : dans le secteur de l'agriculture, de la forêt et de la pêche, 53 p. 100 de la main-d'oeuvre ne possédaient pas de diplôme d'études secondaires; dans le secteur du cuir, des textiles et du vêtement et dans celui des aliments, boissons et tabac, la proportion était, respectivement de 52 et 50 p. 100. Les autres secteurs manufacturiers affichaient aussi des proportions relativement élevées de travailleurs peu scolarisés, notamment le papier et le meuble (48 p. 100), les produits en caoutchouc et en plastique (41 p. 100) et l'industrie des véhicules à moteur et des pièces (41 p. 100). Parmi les secteurs où la part des travailleurs ne possédant pas un diplôme d'études secondaires était la plus basse, mentionnons les services aux entreprises (12 p. 100), le pétrole brut (14 p. 100), les finances, l'assurance et l'immobilier (16 p. 100) et, enfin, les services publics (19 p. 100).

On retrouve plus particulièrement les personnes détenant des certificats de métier dans l'exploitation minière, le papier et l'impression, les métaux primaires, les machines et les autres matériels de transport, ainsi que dans la fabrication et la construction. Les diplômes postsecondaires non universitaires recueillent une part plus élevée dans les industries suivantes : autre matériel de transport, produits électriques et électroniques, services publics, finances, assurance et immobilier et services aux entreprises.

Les diplômes universitaires, au niveau du baccalauréat ou des études supérieures, se retrouvent principalement dans les secteurs du pétrole brut et des services aux entreprises, suivis des autres matériels de transport, des produits électriques et électroniques, des produits du pétrole raffiné et des produits chimiques, des services publics et, enfin, des finances, de l'assurance et de l'immobilier.

Le tableau 9C permet de voir qu'il y a eu augmentation générale du niveaux de scolarité au sein de la population active même au cours de la période de cinq ans allant de 1986 à 1991[10]. La part des personnes employées qui ne possèdent pas un diplôme d'études secondaires a reculé de 4 p. 100 et chacune des catégories au delà des études secondaires a enregistré des gains variant entre un et deux points de pourcentage. L'amélioration s'est manifestée dans tous les secteurs, sauf celui des services personnels et autres, où la part de la main-d'oeuvre qui ne possède pas un diplôme d'études secondaires a augmenté de quatre points de pourcentage. Cependant, il faut se rappeler que ce chiffre représente la moyenne pondérée d'un certain nombre d'éléments, le facteur de pondération étant l'emploi lié aux exportations au cours de l'année visée. Un examen rapide du tableau 8C permet de constater que la plupart des éléments de ce secteur montrent à tout le moins une certaine réduction de la part des travailleurs qui ne possèdent pas une formation secondaire. La hausse dans cette catégorie traduit par conséquent un déplacement des exportations vers les secteurs affichant une part plus élevée de travailleurs ne possédant pas de diplôme d'études secondaires.

En appliquant ces parts de la scolarité aux résultats de l'emploi examinés précédemment, nous pouvons obtenir les parts de la scolarité correspondant à l'emploi non gouvernemental et à l'emploi lié aux exportations pour chacune des années de 1961 à 1997. Comme nous l'avons noté précédemment, le profil de scolarité de 1986 doit être utilisé pour l'ensemble de la période 1961-1986, tandis que le profil de 1991 a été utilisé pour les années 1992 à 1997. Les années entre 1986 et 1991 ont été calculées à l'aide de moyennes pondérées simples des deux années de base. Nous tenons à faire une mise en garde : les résultats présentés pour les périodes 1961-1985 et 1992-1997 n'ont qu'une valeur indicative : ils montrent comment les profils de compétences *agrégés* auraient changé au cours de ces périodes en raison des changements observés dans l'emploi du secteur des entreprises ou l'emploi lié aux exportations *si les niveaux de scolarité dans les diverses industries étaient, individuellement, demeurés les mêmes*[11].

Le tableau 10A présente les calculs des parts de la scolarité liée aux exportations, tandis que le tableau 10B fait voir les parts de la scolarité correspondantes pour l'ensemble du secteur des entreprises. Les séries contenues dans chacun de ces tableaux sont reproduites aux figures 9 et 10. Les ratios des parts de la scolarité liée à l'exportation à celles de l'ensemble du secteur des entreprises sont présentés au tableau 10C et cette série est reproduite aux figures 11 et 12.

Au tableau 10A, nous pouvons observer que la composition industrielle des exportations au Canada a changé depuis 1961 de manière à accroître la part de l'emploi détenue par des personnes possédant une scolarité postsecondaire (et secondaire) et à réduire la part de l'emploi des personnes qui ne possèdent pas une formation secondaire. Il faut se rappeler que jusqu'en 1986, ce déplacement traduisait *uniquement* l'évolution de la composition industrielle parce que le profil de scolarité de chaque industrie est (nécessairement) maintenu au niveau de 1986. En outre, la composition industrielle des exportations a continué de changer après 1991 en privilégiant les secteurs où l'on retrouve les besoins de scolarité les plus élevés. Encore une fois, après 1991, l'évolution des parts de la scolarité qui ressort des données du tableau 10A ne traduit que les changements survenus dans la composition industrielle des exportations étant donné que le profil de scolarité de chaque industrie est maintenu à son niveau de 1991. Ce n'est qu'entre 1986 et 1991 que les changements observés dans le profil de scolarité des exportations englobent les améliorations survenues dans les profils de scolarité des diverses industries prises individuellement. Un examen attentif du tableau 10A et, en particulier, de la figure 9 (où les résultats pour la période 1986-1991 sont séparés par des barres verticales), révèle que l'amélioration du profil de scolarité, selon nos calculs, aurait été plus rapide entre 1986 et 1991.

Bref, les calculs montrent que depuis 1961, la composition des exportations canadiennes (en tenant compte à la fois de l'emploi direct et indirect) a constamment évolué en faveur des industries où

l'on retrouve les travailleurs les plus scolarisés. Si l'amélioration du niveau de scolarité dans l'industrie entre 1986 et 1991 est, comme il est vraisemblable, indicatif d'une tendance à plus long terme vers le relèvement du niveau de scolarité dans les diverses industries, alors le coefficient de scolarité de l'emploi lié aux exportations pourrait avoir augmenté encore plus, entre 1961 et 1997, que les résultats du tableau 10A et de la figure 9 ne le laissent entendre.

Cependant, même si le tableau 10A indique effectivement que les exportations canadiennes ont vu leur coefficient de « scolarité » augmenter depuis 1961, un examen des données du tableau 10B et de la figure 10 montre que l'on peut dire essentiellement la même chose de *l'ensemble* du secteur des entreprises. Cela soulève la question de savoir si le coefficient de scolarité associé aux exportations a augmenté relativement plus, ou moins, que celui de la production totale des entreprises au cours de la période 1961-1997.

Cette question est examinée dans le tableau 10C et les figures 11 et 12 qui montent les *ratios* des parts de la scolarité liée aux exportations à celles de l'ensemble du secteur des entreprises — autrement dit, les chiffres du tableau 10A ont été divisés par ceux du tableau 10B, pour chaque année et niveau de scolarité. La valeur 1,074 apparaissant à la première ligne de la colonne 1 du tableau 10C signifie donc qu'en 1961, la part de l'emploi lié aux exportations détenue par des personnes qui n'avaient pas terminé leurs études secondaires correspondait à 1,074 fois la part des personnes qui n'avaient pas terminé leurs études secondaires dans l'ensemble de la main-d'oeuvre du secteur des entreprises. De même, en 1961, la part détenue par les personnes détenant des emplois liés aux exportations qui possédaient un diplôme d'études supérieures représentait 0,99 de la part des personnes possédant un tel diplôme parmi l'ensemble des employés du secteur des entreprises.

Le tableau 10C et les figures 11 et 12 révèlent que la scolarité des personnes dont l'emploi est lié aux exportations est distribuée de façon « bi-polaire » et l'a généralement toujours été. L'emploi lié aux exportations est plus concentré parmi le groupe des travailleurs qui ne possèdent pas une formation secondaire, comparativement à l'ensemble de la population active et, ce qui étonne moins, parmi le groupe des personnes qui détiennent un certificat ou un diplôme de métier. Par rapport à l'ensemble de l'économie, le secteur d'exportation utilise moins de personnes ayant un diplôme d'études secondaires mais plus de personnes possédant un diplôme d'études supérieures et, ces dernières années, plus de personnes détenant un baccalauréat. La proportion des employés possédant une formation postsecondaire non universitaire est pratiquement la même que dans l'ensemble de l'économie.

Comme le montrent les tableaux et figures, ces ratios ont changé relativement peu au cours des trois décennies étudiées. La proportion des personnes employées qui n'ont qu'une formation secondaire a augmenté progressivement depuis 1980 pour rejoindre le niveau de l'ensemble du secteur des entreprises, tandis que la proportion des personnes ayant fait des études supérieures a commencé à diminuer vers la fin des années 80, bien qu'elle demeure supérieure à la moyenne du secteur des entreprises. Tel que noté, il y a eu une hausse progressive du ratio des détenteurs de baccalauréat, partant d'un niveau inférieur ou égal à celui du secteur des entreprises au cours des années 60 et des années 70 pour dépasser légèrement ce niveau durant les années 90. Au risque de faire une généralisation excessive, et en gardant à l'esprit les limitations affectant nos données, il semblerait que le Canada ait pratiquement deux secteurs d'exportation distincts : un qui utilise davantage de travailleurs peu spécialisés, orientés vers les métiers, que la proportion observée dans l'ensemble de l'économie (dans des industries aussi diversifiés que l'agriculture et la forêt, les véhicules à moteur et l'alimentation et l'hébergement), et un autre qui utilise les services de travailleurs plus scolarisés que la moyenne de l'ensemble de l'économie (encore une fois dans des industries aussi diversifiées que le pétrole brut, les autres matériels de transport (en particulier les aéronefs), les produits électriques et électroniques, le raffinage du pétrole et les produits chimiques,

les finances ainsi que les services aux entreprises). En termes simples, ce clivage pourrait traduire le caractère bi-polaire de la clientèle visée par les exportations canadiennes : selon la théorie, les exportations devraient intégrer des facteurs de production dont le pays exportateur possède une abondance relative. Comparativement aux États-Unis, le Canada a une « abondance relative » de travailleurs relativement moins scolarisés (souvent conjuguée à une abondance relative de matières premières). Mais, comparativement à de nombreux partenaires commerciaux autres que les États-Unis, le Canada possède une abondance relative de travailleurs hautement scolarisés et ses exportations traduisent cet état de fait.

Tableau 8A   Parts selon le niveau de scolarité/compétence, 1991, 112 industries (données sur SPPC)

	Secondaire non terminé	Études secondaires	Certificat ou diplôme professionnel	Diplôme d'études post-secondaires non universitaires	Diplôme universitaires jusqu'au baccalauréat	Études universitaires diplômes d'études supérieures	Tous les diplômes	Numéros équivalents de la classification à 161 industries
001 Agriculture et industries connexes	0,54	0,21	0,10	0,08	0,05	0,02	0,02	1
002 Pêche et piégeage	0,60	0,16	0,13	0,06	0,04	0,01	0,01	2
003 Abattage et foresterie	0,43	0,24	0,14	0,11	0,07	0,01	0,01	3
004 Mines métalliques	0,36	0,19	0,24	0,12	0,07	0,02	0,02	4-6
005 Mines non métalliques	0,37	0,20	0,25	0,10	0,07	0,02	0,01	7-9
006 Mines de charbon	0,35	0,19	0,30	0,10	0,06	0,02	0,02	10
007 Pétrole brut et gaz naturel	0,14	0,21	0,17	0,18	0,23	0,07	0,07	11
008 Carrières et sablières	0,54	0,22	0,13	0,06	0,04	0,00	0,01	12
009 Services connexes à l'extraction minière	0,39	0,22	0,18	0,12	0,07	0,02	0,02	13
010 Viande et volaille	0,51	0,25	0,11	0,07	0,04	0,01	0,01	14-15
011 Produits du poisson	0,63	0,17	0,11	0,05	0,03	0,01	0,01	16
012 Transformation des fruits et légumes	0,46	0,25	0,12	0,09	0,07	0,01	0,01	17
013 Produits laitiers	0,38	0,29	0,13	0,12	0,06	0,01	0,01	18
014 Moulins d'huile végétale (sauf le maïs)	0,30	0,17	0,19	0,17	0,13	0,04	0,04	20
015 Pain, biscuits et autres produits de boulangerie	0,47	0,27	0,12	0,08	0,05	0,01	0,01	21-22
016 Sucre de canne et de betterave	0,43	0,28	0,10	0,10	0,08	0,01	0,01	23
017 Industries alimentaires diverses	0,39	0,27	0,11	0,11	0,10	0,02	0,02	19+24
018 Boissons gazeuses	0,38	0,31	0,13	0,08	0,08	0,02	0,02	25
019 Produits de distillerie	0,28	0,30	0,14	0,13	0,11	0,04	0,04	26
020 Produits brassicoles	0,28	0,33	0,14	0,12	0,10	0,03	0,03	27
021 Vin	0,24	0,34	0,11	0,11	0,16	0,04	0,04	28
022 Produits du tabac	0,31	0,28	0,12	0,17	0,10	0,02	0,02	29
023 Produits en caoutchouc	0,40	0,25	0,16	0,12	0,06	0,01	0,01	30
024 Industries des produits en plastique	0,42	0,28	0,12	0,10	0,06	0,02	0,02	31
025 Cuir et chaussure	0,58	0,24	0,08	0,06	0,03	0,01	0,01	32-34
026 Textiles primaires	0,45	0,26	0,13	0,09	0,05	0,02	0,01	35-37
027 Produits textiles (sauf les tapis)	0,49	0,25	0,09	0,09	0,06	0,02	0,02	38-40
028 Vêtement et bonneterie	0,56	0,24	0,08	0,06	0,05	0,01	0,01	41-42
029 Scieries, atel. de rabotage et usines de bardeaux	0,50	0,21	0,18	0,07	0,03	0,01	0,01	43
030 Plaqués et contreplaqués	0,50	0,26	0,13	0,08	0,03	0,01	0,01	44
031 Châssis, portes et autres ouvrages de menuiserie	0,41	0,29	0,16	0,10	0,04	0,01	0,01	45

Tableau 8A (suite)

	Secondaire non terminé	Études secondaires	Certificat ou diplôme professionnel non universitaires	Diplôme d'études post-secondaires baccalauréat	Études universitaires jusqu'au baccalauréat	Tous les diplômes d'études supérieures équivalents	Numéros de la classification à 161 industries
032 Boîtes en bois et cercueils	0,46	0,32	0,08	0,09	0,05	0,01	46
033 Autres industries du bois	0,45	0,25	0,15	0,10	0,04	0,01	47
034 Meubles et appareils d'éclairage	0,45	0,25	0,15	0,09	0,05	0,01	48-50
035 Pâtes et papiers	0,27	0,27	0,24	0,13	0,08	0,02	51
036 Autres produits du papier	0,40	0,29	0,11	0,11	0,07	0,02	52-54
037 Imprimerie et édition	0,27	0,30	0,13	0,11	0,12	0,03	55
038 Clichage, composition et reliure	0,31	0,32	0,14	0,15	0,08	0,01	56
039 Industries de l'acier primaire	0,36	0,24	0,14	0,14	0,08	0,01	57
040 Canalisations et tuyaux d'acier	0,39	0,22	0,21	0,11	0,06	0,01	58
041 Fonderies de fer	0,47	0,20	0,20	0,09	0,04	0,01	59
042 Fonte et affinage des métaux non ferreux	0,27	0,21	0,26	0,15	0,09	0,02	60
043 Laminage, moulage et extrusion de l'aluminium	0,30	0,26	0,18	0,14	0,09	0,03	61
044 Laminage, moulage et extrusion du cuivre	0,34	0,32	0,14	0,13	0,05	0,01	62
045 Laminage, moulage, etc. d'autres métaux	0,40	0,21	0,17	0,11	0,07	0,01	63
046 Chaudières et métaux de charpente	0,31	0,19	0,29	0,11	0,07	0,03	64
047 Prod. métall. décoratifs et architecturaux	0,40	0,27	0,17	0,13	0,06	0,02	65
048 Métal embouti, pressé et enrobé	0,37	0,25	0,18	0,11	0,07	0,01	66
049 Tréfilage et produits tréfilés	0,40	0,26	0,16	0,10	0,06	0,02	67
050 Art. de quincaillerie, outils et couteaux	0,31	0,24	0,26	0,13	0,05	0,01	68
051 Matériel de chauffage	0,34	0,23	0,21	0,14	0,07	0,01	69
052 Ateliers d'usinage	0,25	0,20	0,38	0,13	0,03	0,01	70
053 Autres métaux ouvrés	0,36	0,25	0,19	0,13	0,06	0,02	71
054 Instruments agricoles	0,40	0,24	0,17	0,12	0,06	0,01	72
055 Équipement de réfrigération commercial	0,30	0,26	0,23	0,12	0,07	0,02	73
056 Autres machines et matériel	0,27	0,22	0,23	0,17	0,09	0,02	74
057 Aéronautique et pièces d'avion	0,19	0,21	0,22	0,21	0,13	0,04	75
058 Véhicules à moteur	0,36	0,28	0,17	0,10	0,07	0,02	76
059 Camions, carross. d'autobus et remorques	0,42	0,25	0,19	0,09	0,05	0,01	77
060 Pièces et accessoires de véh. à moteur	0,43	0,26	0,14	0,10	0,05	0,01	78
061 Matériel ferroviaire roulant	0,30	0,24	0,23	0,15	0,06	0,01	79
062 Construction et réparation de navires	0,26	0,13	0,37	0,17	0,05	0,01	80

Tableau 8A (suite)

	Secondaire non terminé	Études secondaires	Certificat ou diplôme professionnel	Diplôme d'études post-secondaires non universitaires	Études universitaires jusqu'au baccalauréat	Tous les diplômes d'études supérieures équivalents	Numéros de la classification à 161 industries
063 Matériel de transport divers	0,39	0,23	0,19	0,10	0,07	0,02	81
064 Petits appareils électriques	0,41	0,27	0,12	0,13	0,06	0,00	82
065 Gros appareils (électriques et non électriques)	0,42	0,27	0,15	0,11	0,05	0,01	83
066 Tourne-disques, radios et téléviseurs	0,30	0,28	0,09	0,16	0,14	0,02	84
067 Matériel électronique	0,19	0,23	0,11	0,23	0,18	0,06	85
068 Machines de bureau et de magasin	0,14	0,24	0,11	0,22	0,21	0,08	86
069 Autres produits élect. et électroniques	0,33	0,24	0,14	0,16	0,11	0,03	87-89
070 Matériaux en céramique	0,38	0,26	0,13	0,11	0,08	0,03	90
071 Ciment	0,4	0,23	0,17	0,10	0,09	0,01	91
072 Produits en béton	0,47	0,24	0,14	0,09	0,06	0,01	92
073 Béton prémélangé	0,51	0,21	0,14	0,09	0,04	0,01	93
074 Verre et produits en verre	0,44	0,26	0,14	0,09	0,05	0,01	94
075 Produits minéraux non métalliques n.c.a.	0,40	0,24	0,15	0,11	0,08	0,02	95
076 Produits du pétrole et du charbon raffinés	0,19	0,27	0,21	0,18	0,11	0,04	96
077 Produits chimiques industriels n.c.a.	0,18	0,25	0,19	0,19	0,15	0,05	97
078 Plastiques et résines synthétiques	0,24	0,30	0,16	0,14	0,13	0,04	98
079 Prod. pharmaceutiques et médicaments	0,15	0,24	0,08	0,17	0,25	0,10	99
080 Peintures et vernis	0,30	0,33	0,11	0,13	0,11	0,02	100
081 Savons et prod. de nettoyage	0,24	0,32	0,09	0,13	0,17	0,04	101
082 Produits de toilette	0,29	0,28	0,10	0,16	0,13	0,04	102
083 Produits chimiques	0,27	0,27	0,13	0,15	0,14	0,04	103
084 Bijouterie et métaux précieux	0,39	0,28	0,13	0,12	0,07	0,01	104
085 Articles de sport et jouets	0,42	0,28	0,13	0,10	0,08	0,01	105
086 Enseignes et étalages	0,29	0,31	0,15	0,16	0,07	0,02	106
087 Autres industries manufacturières	0,31	0,27	0,13	0,17	0,10	0,03	107-108
088 Construction	0,37	0,23	0,25	0,10	0,05	0,01	109-117
089 Transport aérien et services connexes	0,14	0,31	0,19	0,23	0,11	0,02	118
090 Transport ferroviaire et services connexes	0,35	0,27	0,21	0,10	0,06	0,01	119
091 Transport par eau et services connexes	0,31	0,22	0,21	0,17	0,07	0,02	120
092 Camionnage	0,51	0,25	0,14	0,07	0,03	0,00	121
093 Transport en commun	0,40	0,29	0,15	0,10	0,04	0,01	122-123

Tableau 8A (suite)

	Secondaire non terminé	Études secondaires	non universitaires		universitaires		Numéros de la classification à 161 industries
			Certificat ou diplôme professionnel	Diplôme d'études post-secondaires	Études universitaires jusqu'au baccalauréat	Études universitaires diplômes d'études supérieures / Tous les diplômes équivalents	
094 Autres transports et services connexes	0,47	0,25	0,13	0,08	0,05	0,02	124-126
095 Transport par pipelines	0,15	0,24	0,18	0,22	0,16	0,05	127
096 Stockage et entreposage	0,38	0,33	0,12	0,09	0,05	0,02	128
097 Télécommunications et radiodiffusion	0,12	0,25	0,11	0,29	0,18	0,05	129
098 Transporteurs de télécomm. et autres	0,15	0,36	0,13	0,20	0,13	0,03	130
099 Services postaux	0,32	0,38	0,10	0,11	0,07	0,01	131
100 Systèmes d'énergie électrique	0,12	0,22	0,24	0,23	0,14	0,05	132
101 Systèmes de distribution du gaz	0,18	0,29	0,18	0,17	0,14	0,03	133
102 Autres services publics n.c.a.	0,39	0,23	0,16	0,12	0,07	0,02	134
103 Commerce de gros	0,30	0,31	0,14	0,14	0,10	0,02	135
104 Commerce de détail	0,36	0,34	0,13	0,10	0,06	0,01	136
105 Finances, assurance et immobilier	0,16	0,34	0,10	0,19	0,17	0,04	137-139
106 Autres services commerciaux	0,12	0,22	0,09	0,20	0,26	0,11	142-144
107 Services éducatifs	0,10	0,13	0,06	0,11	0,35	0,25	145
108 Services hospitaliers et de santé	0,17	0,16	0,12	0,31	0,15	0,10	146-147
109 Hébergement et restauration	0,46	0,32	0,08	0,09	0,05	0,01	148
110 Cinéma, divertissements et loisirs	0,30	0,32	0,08	0,13	0,13	0,03	149-150
111 Services personnels et domestiques	0,34	0,23	0,26	0,11	0,05	0,01	151-152
112 Autres services et organisations	0,30	0,25	0,13	0,14	0,12	0,07	153-154
TOTAL, SECTEUR NON GOUVERNEMENTAL	0,30	0,26	0,13	0,14	0,12	0,05	1-154

Tableau 8B Parts selon le niveau de scolarité/compétence, 1986, 112 industries (données du SPPC)

	Secondaire non terminé	Études secondaires	Certificat ou diplôme professionnel non universitaires	Diplôme d'études post-secondaires baccalauréat	Études universitaires jusqu'au baccalauréat	Études universitaires diplômes d'études supérieures	Tous les équivalents de la classification à 161 industries	Numéros industries
001 Agriculture et industries connexes	0.58	0.21	0.08	0.07	0.06	0.01		1
002 Pêche et piégeage	0.65	0.15	0.11	0.05	0.03	0.01		2
003 Abattage et foresterie	0.49	0.22	0.12	0.1	0.06	0.01		3
004 Mines métalliques	0.41	0.20	0.23	0.09	0.06	0.01		4-6
005 Mines non métalliques	0.39	0.20	0.23	0.11	0.06	0.01		7-9
006 Mines de charbon	0.36	0.18	0.28	0.10	0.06	0.01		10
007 Pétrole brut et gaz naturel	0.16	0.23	0.14	0.17	0.24	0.06		11
008 Carrières et sablières	0.57	0.22	0.13	0.05	0.02	0.00		12
009 Services connexes à l'extraction minière	0.42	0.23	0.15	0.09	0.08	0.02		13
010 Viande et volaille	0.54	0.25	0.10	0.06	0.04	0.01		14-15
011 Produits du poisson	0.68	0.15	0.11	0.04	0.02	0.00		16
012 Transformation des fruits et légumes	0.51	0.22	0.10	0.09	0.07	0.01		17
013 Produits laitiers	0.43	0.28	0.12	0.10	0.05	0.01		18
014 Moulins d'huile végétale (sauf le maïs)	0.34	0.17	0.18	0.10	0.10	0.03		20
015 Pain, biscuits et autres produits de boulangerie	0.52	0.27	0.10	0.07	0.04	0.01		21-22
016 Sucre de canne et betterave	0.52	0.23	0.10	0.08	0.06	0.01		23
017 Industries alimentaires diverses	0.41	0.28	0.09	0.10	0.09	0.02		19+24
018 Boissons gazeuses	0.41	0.33	0.10	0.08	0.06	0.01		25
019 Produits de distillerie	0.31	0.30	0.13	0.08	0.13	0.04		26
020 Produits brassicoles	0.32	0.33	0.14	0.10	0.10	0.02		27
021 Vin	0.32	0.30	0.11	0.12	0.12	0.02		28
022 Produits du tabac	0.40	0.26	0.11	0.14	0.08	0.02		29
023 Produits en caoutchouc	0.42	0.27	0.15	0.09	0.05	0.01		30
024 Produits en plastique	0.45	0.28	0.11	0.09	0.06	0.01		31
025 Cuir et chaussure	0.63	0.22	0.06	0.05	0.03	0.01		32-34
026 Textiles primaires	0.50	0.26	0.11	0.05	0.04	0.01		35-37
027 Produits textiles (sauf les tapis)	0.50	0.27	0.09	0.08	0.05	0.01		38-40
028 Vêtement et bonneterie	0.62	0.22	0.07	0.05	0.03	0.01		41-42
029 Scieries, atel. de rabotage et usines de bardeaux	0.53	0.21	0.17	0.06	0.03	0.00		43
030 Plaqués et contreplaqués	0.55	0.23	0.14	0.06	0.03	0.01		44
031 Châssis, portes et autres ouvrages de menuiserie	0.47	0.28	0.14	0.08	0.03	0.00		45
032 Boîtes en bois et cercueils	0.56	0.27	0.10	0.05	0.02	0.01		46

Tableau 8B (suite)

	Secondaire non terminé	Études secondaires	Certificat ou diplôme professionnel	Diplôme d'études post-secondaires non universitaires	Études universitaires diplômes d'études jusqu'au baccalauréat	Tous les diplômes équivalents d'études supérieures	Numéros de la classification à 161 industries
033 Autres industries du bois	0,49	0,23	0,16	0,07	0,04	0,01	47
034 Meubles et appareils d'éclairage	0,48	0,26	0,13	0,08	0,04	0,01	48-50
035 Pâtes et papiers	0,33	0,28	0,21	0,11	0,06	0,01	51
036 Autres produits en papier	0,46	0,28	0,1	0,09	0,05	0,01	52-54
037 Imprimerie et édition	0,29	0,33	0,13	0,13	0,05	0,02	55
038 Clichage, composition et reliure	0,30	0,33	0,14	0,10	0,07	0,01	56
039 Acier primaire	0,39	0,25	0,19	0,14	0,07	0,01	57
040 Canalisations et tuyaux d'acier	0,44	0,25	0,17	0,10	0,05	0,01	58
041 Fonderies de fer	0,51	0,21	0,09	0,08	0,05	0,01	59
042 Fonte et affinage des métaux non ferreux	0,34	0,23	0,22	0,12	0,07	0,02	60
043 Laminage, moulage et extrusion de l'aluminium	0,33	0,31	0,15	0,11	0,07	0,02	61
044 Laminage, moulage et extrusion du cuivre	0,44	0,27	0,14	0,11	0,03	0,01	62
045 Laminage, moulage, etc. d'autres métaux	0,43	0,22	0,16	0,12	0,06	0,01	63
046 Chaudières et métaux de charpente	0,32	0,21	0,28	0,12	0,06	0,02	64
047 Prod. métall. décoratifs et architecturaux	0,43	0,27	0,15	0,10	0,05	0,01	65
048 Métal embouti, pressé et enrobé	0,41	0,26	0,16	0,09	0,06	0,01	66
049 Tréfilage et produits tréfilés	0,45	0,26	0,14	0,10	0,05	0,01	67
050 Art. de quincaillerie, outils et couteaux	0,35	0,26	0,23	0,12	0,04	0,01	68
051 Matériel de chauffage	0,37	0,25	0,16	0,13	0,07	0,02	69
052 Ateliers d'usinage	0,27	0,23	0,35	0,11	0,03	0,00	70
053 Autres industries métallurgiques	0,41	0,25	0,18	0,10	0,05	0,01	71
054 Instruments agricoles	0,38	0,24	0,19	0,12	0,06	0,02	72
055 Équipement de réfrigération commercial	0,33	0,27	0,19	0,12	0,07	0,01	73
056 Autres machines et matériel	0,28	0,25	0,23	0,15	0,07	0,02	74
057 Aéronautique et pièces d'avion	0,23	0,26	0,19	0,17	0,11	0,03	75
058 Véhicules à moteur	0,44	0,27	0,15	0,08	0,05	0,01	76
059 Camions, carross. d'autobus et remorques	0,43	0,25	0,2	0,09	0,03	0,00	77
060 Pièces et accessoires de véh. à moteur	0,46	0,26	0,13	0,09	0,04	0,01	78
061 Matériel ferroviaire roulant	0,33	0,20	0,25	0,14	0,06	0,02	79
062 Construction et réparation de navires	0,32	0,17	0,33	0,13	0,05	0,01	80
063 Matériel de transport divers	0,40	0,24	0,21	0,10	0,04	0,01	81

Tableau 8B (suite)

	Secondaire non terminé	Études secondaires	Certificat ou diplôme professionnel	Diplôme d'études post-secondaires	Études universitaires jusqu'au baccalauréat	Tous les diplômes d'études supérieures	Numéros équivalents de la classification à 161 industries
			non universitaires				
064 Petits appareils électriques	0,43	0,28	0,13	0,10	0,05	0,01	82
065 Gros appareils (électriques et non électr.)	0,45	0,28	0,12	0,10	0,04	0,01	83
066 Tourne-disques, radios et téléviseurs	0,39	0,25	0,12	0,14	0,01	0,02	84
067 Matériel électronique	0,25	0,24	0,11	0,21	0,15	0,05	85
068 Machines de bureau et de magasin	0,13	0,28	0,09	0,24	0,21	0,05	86
069 Autres produits élect. et électroniques	0,38	0,26	0,13	0,12	0,08	0,02	87-89
070 Matériaux en céramique	0,48	0,25	0,09	0,09	0,07	0,02	90
071 Ciment	0,36	0,25	0,20	0,10	0,08	0,02	91
072 Produits en béton	0,50	0,24	0,12	0,10	0,05	0,01	92
073 Béton prémélangé	0,53	0,22	0,14	0,09	0,03	0,01	93
074 Verre et produits en verre	0,48	0,26	0,12	0,08	0,05	0,01	94
075 Produits minéraux non métalliques n.c.a.	0,43	0,25	0,12	0,10	0,08	0,02	95
076 Produits du pétrole et du charbon raffinés	0,17	0,29	0,17	0,16	0,16	0,05	96
077 Produits chimiques industriels n.c.a.	0,20	0,26	0,18	0,15	0,16	0,05	97
078 Plastiques et résines synthétiques	0,24	0,31	0,14	0,15	0,12	0,04	98
079 Prod. pharmaceutiques et médicaments	0,22	0,27	0,07	0,14	0,24	0,06	99
080 Peintures et vernis	0,33	0,32	0,10	0,12	0,12	0,02	100
081 Savons et prod. de nettoyage	0,30	0,28	0,09	0,14	0,15	0,04	101
082 Produits de toilette	0,32	0,31	0,09	0,14	0,12	0,03	102
083 Produits chimiques	0,30	0,27	0,13	0,14	0,13	0,03	103
084 Bijouterie et métaux précieux	0,43	0,29	0,10	0,10	0,07	0,02	104
085 Articles de sport et jouets	0,46	0,29	0,10	0,09	0,05	0,01	105
086 Enseignes et étalages	0,36	0,30	0,16	0,12	0,06	0,01	106
087 Autres industries manufacturières	0,35	0,28	0,12	0,14	0,08	0,02	107-108
088 Construction	0,41	0,23	0,24	0,08	0,04	0,01	109-117
089 Transport aérien et services connexes	0,17	0,34	0,17	0,20	0,10	0,02	118
090 Transport ferroviaire et services connexes	0,40	0,28	0,18	0,08	0,05	0,01	119
091 Transport par eau et services connexes	0,36	0,22	0,20	0,15	0,06	0,01	120
092 Camionnage	0,56	0,24	0,12	0,05	0,02	0,00	121
093 Transport en commun	0,44	0,29	0,14	0,08	0,04	0,01	122-123
094 Autres transports et services connexes	0,51	0,25	0,12	0,07	0,04	0,01	124-126
095 Transport par pipelines	0,17	0,28	0,16	0,19	0,16	0,04	127

Tableau 8B (suite)

	Secondaire non terminé	Études secondaires	Certificat ou diplôme professionnel	Diplôme d'études post-secondaires	Études universitaires jusqu'au baccalauréat	Tous les diplômes d'études supérieures	Numéros équivalents de la classification à 161 industries
			secondaires non universitaires		universitaires		
096 Stockage et entreposage	0,46	0,31	0,11	0,08	0,04	0,01	128
097 Télécommunications et radiodiffusion	0,13	0,30	0,10	0,26	0,17	0,04	129
098 Transporteurs de télécomm. et autres	0,19	0,40	0,12	0,17	0,10	0,02	130
099 Services postaux	0,38	0,38	0,08	0,09	0,05	0,01	131
100 Systèmes d'énergie électrique	0,15	0,25	0,23	0,19	0,12	0,05	132
101 Systèmes de distribution du gaz	0,22	0,29	0,19	0,15	0,12	0,02	133
102 Autres services publics n.c.a.	0,49	0,23	0,14	0,09	0,04	0,01	134
103 Commerce de gros	0,33	0,32	0,13	0,13	0,08	0,01	135
104 Commerce de détail	0,38	0,34	0,13	0,09	0,06	0,01	136
105 Finances, assurance et immobilier	0,19	0,37	0,10	0,16	0,14	0,03	137-139
106 Autres services commerciaux	0,13	0,24	0,08	0,20	0,25	0,10	142-144
107 Services éducatifs	0,11	0,13	0,05	0,11	0,37	0,23	145
108 Services hospitaliers et de santé	0,18	0,17	0,11	0,31	0,19	0,04	146-147
109 Hébergement et restauration	0,49	0,31	0,08	0,07	0,04	0,01	148
110 Cinéma, divertissements et loisirs	0,32	0,34	0,08	0,12	0,12	0,03	149-150
111 Services personnels et domestiques	0,37	0,23	0,27	0,09	0,03	0,00	151-152
112 Autres services et organisations	0,30	0,26	0,12	0,13	0,12	0,06	153-154
TOTAL, SECTEUR NON GOUVERNEMENTAL	0,33	0,26	0,13	0,13	0,11	0,04	1-154

Tableau 8C Parts selon le niveau de scolarité/compétence, variations, 1986–1991 (données du SPPC)

	Secondaire non terminé	Études secondaires	Certificat ou diplôme professionnel	Diplôme d'études post-secondaires non universitaires	Études universitaires jusqu'au baccalauréat	Tous les diplômes d'études supérieures	Numéros équivalents de la classification à 161 industries
001 Agriculture et industries connexes	-0.04	0.01	0.02	0.01	0.00	0.01	1
002 Pêche et piégeage	-0.05	0.01	0.02	0.01	0.00	0.00	2
003 Abattage et foresterie	-0.05	0.03	0.01	0.01	0.00	0.00	3
004 Mines métalliques	-0.05	-0.00	0.01	0.02	0.01	0.01	4-6
005 Mines non métalliques	-0.02	-0.00	0.01	-0.01	0.01	0.00	7-9
006 Mines de charbon	-0.02	0.01	0.01	0.01	0.00	0.00	10
007 Pétrole brut et gaz naturel	-0.01	-0.01	0.03	0.01	-0.02	0.00	11
008 Carrières et sablières	-0.03	-0.00	0.03	0.01	0.02	-0.00	12
009 Services connexes à l'extraction minière	-0.03	-0.02	0.03	0.02	-0.01	-0.00	13
010 Viande et volaille	-0.03	0.00	0.01	0.01	-0.01	0.00	14-15
011 Produits du poisson	-0.05	0.02	0.01	0.01	0.01	0.00	16
012 Transformation des fruits et légumes	-0.05	0.02	0.02	0.01	-0.00	0.00	17
013 Produits laitiers	-0.05	0.01	0.01	0.01	0.01	-0.00	18
014 Moulins d'huile végétale (sauf le maïs)	-0.04	-0.00	0.01	-0.00	0.03	-0.00	19+24
015 Pain, biscuits et autres produits de boulangerie	-0.05	0.00	0.02	0.02	0.01	0.00	20
016 Sucre de canne et betterave	-0.09	0.05	0.00	0.02	0.02	-0.00	21-22
017 Industries alimentaires diverses	-0.03	-0.01	0.01	0.01	0.01	0.01	23
018 Boissons gazeuses	-0.03	-0.02	0.03	-0.01	0.03	0.01	25
019 Produits de distillerie	-0.04	0.00	0.01	0.03	-0.01	0.01	26
020 Produits brassicoles	-0.03	-0.00	0.00	0.02	0.01	0.00	27
021 Vin	-0.08	0.04	-0.00	-0.01	0.03	0.02	28
022 Produits du tabac	-0.09	0.02	0.02	0.03	0.02	0.00	29
023 Produits en caoutchouc	-0.02	-0.01	0.01	0.02	0.01	0.00	30
024 Produits en plastique	-0.04	-0.01	0.02	0.02	0.01	0.01	31
025 Cuir et chaussure	-0.05	0.02	0.02	0.01	0.00	0.00	32-34
026 Textiles primaires	-0.05	0.00	0.01	0.01	0.01	0.01	35-37
027 Produits textiles (sauf les tapis)	-0.01	-0.02	0.01	0.01	0.01	0.01	38-40
028 Vêtement et bonneterie	-0.05	0.02	0.00	0.01	0.01	0.00	41-42
029 Scieries, atel. de rabotage et usines de bardeaux	-0.04	0.00	0.00	0.02	0.00	-0.00	43
030 Plaqués et contreplaqués	-0.05	0.03	0.02	0.01	0.00	-0.00	44
031 Châssis, portes et autres ouvrages de menuiserie	-0.06	0.01	0.01	0.02	0.01	0.00	45
032 Boîtes en bois et cercueils	-0.10	0.05	-0.02	0.03	0.03	-0.00	46

Tableau 8C (suite)

	Secondaire non terminé	Études secondaires	Certificat ou diplôme professionnel	Diplôme d'études post-secondaires non universitaires	Études universitaires jusqu'au baccalauréat	Tous les diplômes d'études supérieures	Numéros équivalents de la classification à 161 industries
033 Autres industries du bois	-0,04	0,02	-0,01	0,03	0,00	-0,00	47
034 Meubles et appareils d'éclairage	-0,03	-0,00	0,02	0,01	0,00	0,00	48-50
035 Pâtes et papiers	-0,06	-0,01	0,03	0,02	0,02	0,01	51
036 Autres produits en papier	-0,07	0,01	0,01	0,03	0,02	0,01	52-54
037 Imprimerie et édition	-0,02	-0,03	-0,00	0,02	0,02	0,01	55
038 Clichage, composition et reliure	0,01	-0,01	-0,00	0,00	0,00	0,00	56
039 Acier primaire	-0,03	-0,01	0,02	0,01	0,01	0,00	57
040 Canalisations et tuyaux d'acier	-0,03	-0,01	0,02	0,01	0,01	-0,00	58
041 Fonderies de fer	-0,04	-0,02	0,04	0,02	0,02	-0,00	59
042 Fonte et affinage des métaux non ferreux	-0,07	-0,01	0,06	0,01	-0,01	-0,00	60
043 Laminage, moulage et extrusion de l'aluminium	-0,03	-0,01	0,04	0,02	0,01	0,00	61
044 Laminage, moulage et extrusion du cuivre	-0,02	-0,05	0,02	0,03	0,02	0,01	62
045 Laminage, moulage, etc. d'autres métaux	-0,10	0,06	0,00	0,02	0,02	0,00	63
046 Chaudières et métaux de charpente	-0,02	-0,01	0,01	-0,00	0,01	0,02	64
047 Prod. métall. décoratifs et architecturaux	-0,02	-0,02	0,02	0,02	0,00	0,00	65
048 Métal embouti, pressé et enrobé	-0,05	-0,00	0,02	-0,00	-0,00	0,00	66
049 Tréfilage et produits tréfilés	-0,04	-0,01	0,02	0,02	0,01	0,01	67
050 Art. de quincaillerie, outils et couteaux	-0,04	0,01	0,03	-0,00	0,01	0,01	68
051 Matériel de chauffage	-0,03	-0,02	0,05	0,01	0,01	-0,01	69
052 Ateliers d'usinage	-0,02	-0,03	0,05	0,01	0,00	-0,01	70
053 Autres métaux ouvrés	-0,05	-0,03	0,03	0,01	0,00	0,01	71
054 Instruments agricoles	0,02	0,00	0,01	0,02	0,01	0,01	72
055 Équipement de réfrigération commercial	-0,03	-0,01	0,04	0,00	0,00	0,01	73
056 Autres machines et matériel	-0,01	-0,03	0,00	0,01	0,02	0,00	74
057 Aéronautique et pièces d'avion	-0,05	-0,05	0,03	0,02	0,01	0,01	75
058 Véhicules à moteur	-0,07	0,01	0,02	0,00	0,01	0,01	76
059 Camions, carross. d'autobus et remorques	-0,03	-0,01	-0,01	0,01	0,02	0,00	77
060 Pièces et accessoires de véh. à moteur	-0,03	0,00	0,00	0,01	0,01	0,00	78
061 Matériel ferroviaire roulant	-0,02	0,04	-0,02	0,01	-0,00	-0,00	79
062 Construction et réparation de navires	-0,06	-0,04	0,05	0,04	0,01	0,00	80
063 Matériel de transport divers	-0,01	-0,01	-0,02	-0,00	0,02	0,01	81
064 Petits appareils électriques	-0,03	-0,01	-0,00	0,03	0,02	-0,01	82

Tableau 8C (suite)

	Secondaire non terminé	Études secondaires	Certificat ou diplôme professionnel	Diplôme d'études post-secondaires non universitaires	Études universitaires jusqu'au baccalauréat	Tous les diplômes d'études supérieures	Numéros équivalents de la classification à 161 industries
065 Gros appareils (électriques et non électr.)	-0.03	-0.02	0.03	0.01	0.02	-0.00	83
066 Tourne-disques, radios et téléviseurs	-0.08	0.04	-0.02	0.02	0.04	-0.00	84
067 Matériel électronique	-0.05	-0.01	0.00	0.02	0.03	0.01	85
068 Machines de bureau et de magasin	0.01	-0.04	0.02	-0.02	-0.00	0.03	86
069 Autres produits élect. et électroniques	-0.05	-0.02	0.01	0.03	0.02	0.01	87-89
070 Matériaux en céramique	-0.10	0.02	0.05	0.02	0.01	0.01	90
071 Ciment	0.03	-0.02	-0.03	0.02	-0.01	-0.01	91
072 Produits en béton	-0.03	-0.00	0.01	0.01	0.01	0.00	92
073 Béton prémélangé	-0.02	-0.01	0.00	0.02	0.01	-0.00	93
074 Verre et produits en verre	-0.04	0.00	0.02	0.01	0.01	-0.00	94
075 Produits minéraux non métalliques n.c.a.	-0.04	-0.01	0.02	0.01	0.00	0.00	95
076 Produits du pétrole et du charbon raffinés	0.02	-0.02	0.04	0.02	0.00	-0.00	96
077 Produits chimiques industriels n.c.a.	-0.03	-0.01	0.01	0.02	-0.01	-0.00	97
078 Plastiques et résines synthétiques	-0.01	-0.00	0.02	0.04	-0.01	-0.00	98
079 Prod. pharmaceutiques et médicaments	-0.06	-0.02	0.02	-0.01	0.00	-0.00	99
080 Peintures et vernis	-0.03	0.01	0.01	0.03	0.01	0.04	100
081 Savons et prod. de nettoyage	-0.06	0.04	0.00	0.01	-0.01	0.00	101
082 Produits de toilette	-0.03	-0.03	0.01	0.03	0.02	0.00	102
083 Produits chimiques	-0.03	-0.01	0.00	0.01	0.01	0.01	103
084 Bijouterie et métaux précieux	-0.05	-0.01	0.03	0.02	0.00	-0.00	104
085 Articles de sport et jouets	-0.04	-0.01	0.03	0.01	0.00	0.00	105
086 Enseignes et étalages	-0.06	0.01	-0.01	0.04	0.03	0.01	106
087 Autres industries manufacturières	-0.04	-0.02	0.01	0.02	0.02	0.01	107-108
088 Construction	-0.04	0.00	0.01	0.02	0.01	0.00	109-117
089 Transport aérien et services connexes	-0.03	-0.04	0.02	0.03	0.01	0.00	118
090 Transport ferroviaire et services connexes	-0.06	-0.00	0.04	0.01	0.01	0.00	119
091 Transport par eau et services connexes	-0.05	0.00	0.01	0.02	0.01	0.00	120
092 Camionnage	-0.05	0.01	0.02	0.02	0.00	0.00	121
093 Transport en commun	-0.04	0.00	0.01	0.02	0.00	0.00	122-123
094 Autres transports et services connexes	-0.04	-0.00	0.02	0.01	0.01	0.01	124-126
095 Transport par pipelines	-0.02	-0.04	0.01	0.03	-0.00	0.02	127
096 Stockage et entreposage	-0.07	0.02	0.01	0.02	0.01	0.01	128

Tableau 8C (suite)

	Secondaire non terminé	Études secondaires	Certificat ou diplôme professionnel	Diplôme d'études post-secondaires non universitaires	Études universitaires jusqu'au baccalauréat	Tous les diplômes d'études supérieures	Numéros équivalents de la classification à 161 industries
097 Télécommunications et radiodiffusion	-0.01	-0.05	0.01	0.03	0.01	0.01	129
098 Transporteurs de télécomm. et autres	-0.04	-0.04	0.01	0.04	0.03	0.01	130
099 Services postaux	-0.05	-0.01	0.02	0.02	0.02	0.01	131
100 Systèmes d'énergie électrique	-0.04	-0.03	0.01	0.03	0.02	0.01	132
101 Systèmes de distribution du gaz	-0.04	0.00	-0.01	0.02	0.02	0.01	133
102 Autres services publics n.c.a.	-0.09	0.00	0.02	0.03	0.03	0.01	134
103 Commerce de gros	-0.03	-0.02	0.01	0.02	0.01	0.01	135
104 Commerce de détail	-0.03	0.01	0.00	0.01	0.01	0.00	136
105 Finances, assurance et immobilier	-0.03	-0.03	0.00	0.02	0.02	0.01	137-139
106 Autres services commerciaux	-0.01	-0.02	0.00	0.01	0.01	0.01	142-144
107 Services éducatifs	-0.01	0.00	0.00	-0.00	-0.02	0.02	145
108 Services hospitaliers et de santé	-0.01	-0.00	0.00	-0.00	-0.04	0.06	146-147
109 Hébergement et restauration	-0.03	0.00	0.00	0.01	0.01	0.00	148
110 Cinéma, divertissements et loisirs	-0.01	-0.02	0.01	0.01	0.01	0.00	149-150
111 Services personnels et domestiques	-0.03	0.00	-0.01	0.02	0.02	0.00	151-152
112 Autres services et organisations	-0.00	-0.01	0.01	0.01	-0.00	0.00	153-154
TOTAL, SECTEUR NON GOUVERNEMENTAL	-0.04	-0.01	0.01	0.02	0.01	0.01	1-154

Tableau 9A Parts des exportations selon le niveau de scolarité/compétence, 1991, groupe de 24 industries (pondération de l'emploi lié aux exportations)

Agrégation au niveau de 24 industries	Secondaire non terminé	Études secondaires	Certificat ou diplôme professionnel	Diplôme d'études post-secondaires non universitaires	Études universitaires jusqu'au baccalauréat	Tous les diplômes d'études supérieures
S1. Agriculture, forêt, pêche et piégeage	0,53	0,21	0,11	0,08	0,05	0,02
S2. Mines, sauf le pétrole et le gaz	0,37	0,20	0,24	0,11	0,06	0,02
S3. Pétrole brut et gaz naturel	0,14	0,21	0,17	0,18	0,23	0,07
S4. Aliments, boissons et tabac	0,50	0,23	0,12	0,08	0,06	0,01
S5. Produits en caoutchouc et en plastique	0,41	0,27	0,14	0,11	0,06	0,02
S6. Cuir, textile et vêtement	0,52	0,25	0,10	0,08	0,05	0,01
S7. Produits en bois et mobilier	0,48	0,23	0,17	0,08	0,04	0,01
S8. Papier, produits connexes et imprimerie	0,28	0,28	0,20	0,13	0,09	0,02
S9. Métaux primaires et fabrication métallique	0,33	0,23	0,24	0,12	0,06	0,02
S10. Machines	0,29	0,22	0,22	0,16	0,08	0,02
S11. Véhicules à moteur et pièces	0,41	0,27	0,15	0,10	0,06	0,01
S12. Autre matériel de transport	0,21	0,21	0,23	0,20	0,12	0,04
S13. Produits électriques et électroniques	0,23	0,24	0,12	0,20	0,16	0,05
S14. Pétrole raffiné, prod. chimiques et non métall.	0,27	0,27	0,15	0,15	0,13	0,04
S15. Autres produits fabriqués	0,33	0,27	0,13	0,16	0,09	0,02
S16. Construction	0,37	0,23	0,25	0,10	0,05	0,01
S17. Transport et pipelines	0,42	0,26	0,16	0,10	0,05	0,01
S18. Entreposage	0,38	0,33	0,12	0,09	0,05	0,02
S19. Services publics	0,19	0,29	0,17	0,19	0,12	0,03
S20. Commerce	0,32	0,32	0,14	0,13	0,08	0,02
S21. Finances, assurance et immobilier	0,16	0,34	0,10	0,19	0,17	0,04
S22. Redev. gouv. et logements occ. par propr.	0,00	0,00	0,00	0,00	0,00	0,00
S23. Services aux entreprises	0,12	0,22	0,09	0,20	0,26	0,11
S24. Services personnels et autres	0,39	0,29	0,10	0,11	0,08	0,03
TOTAL	0,34	0,26	0,14	0,13	0,10	0,03

Tableau 9B Parts des exportations selon le niveau de scolarité/compétence, 1986,
groupe de 24 industries (pondération de l'emploi lié aux exportations)

Agrégation au niveau de 24 industries	Secondaire non terminé	Études secondaires	Certificat ou diplôme professionnel	Diplôme d'études post-secondaires non universitaires	Études universitaires jusqu'au baccalauréat	Tous les diplômes d'études supérieures
S1. Agriculture, forêt, pêche et piégeage	0,57	0,20	0,09	0,08	0,05	0,01
S2. Mines, sauf le pétrole et le gaz	0,41	0,20	0,22	0,09	0,06	0,01
S3. Pétrole brut et gaz naturel	0,16	0,23	0,14	0,17	0,24	0,06
S4. Aliments, boissons et tabac	0,56	0,21	0,11	0,06	0,05	0,01
S5. Produits en caoutchouc et en plastique	0,44	0,28	0,13	0,06	0,06	0,01
S6. Cuir, textile et vêtement	0,56	0,24	0,08	0,09	0,06	0,01
S7. Produits en bois et mobilier	0,52	0,22	0,16	0,06	0,04	0,01
S8. Papier, produits connexes et imprimerie	0,33	0,29	0,18	0,06	0,03	0,01
S9. Métaux primaires et fabrication métallique	0,38	0,24	0,20	0,11	0,07	0,01
S10. Machines	0,30	0,25	0,22	0,11	0,06	0,01
S11. Véhicules à moteur et pièces	0,45	0,26	0,14	0,09	0,07	0,02
S12. Autre matériel de transport	0,26	0,25	0,21	0,16	0,05	0,01
S13. Produits électriques et électroniques	0,27	0,26	0,11	0,19	0,09	0,03
S14. Pétrole raffiné, prod. chimiques et non métall.	0,30	0,27	0,14	0,13	0,14	0,04
S15. Autres produits fabriqués	0,37	0,28	0,12	0,13	0,12	0,03
S16. Construction	0,41	0,23	0,24	0,08	0,07	0,02
S17. Transport et pipelines	0,48	0,25	0,14	0,08	0,04	0,01
S18. Entreposage	0,46	0,31	0,11	0,08	0,04	0,01
S19. Services publics	0,23	0,32	0,16	0,17	0,10	0,03
S20. Commerce	0,34	0,33	0,13	0,12	0,07	0,01
S21. Finances, assurance et immobilier	0,19	0,37	0,10	0,16	0,14	0,03
S22. Redev. gouv. et logements occ. par propr.	0,00	0,00	0,00	0,00	0,00	0,00
S23. Services aux entreprises	0,13	0,24	0,08	0,20	0,25	0,10
S24. Services personnels et autres	0,35	0,27	0,11	0,12	0,11	0,05
TOTAL	0,38	0,26	0,14	0,11	0,09	0,02

Tableau 9C Parts des exportations selon le niveau de scolarité/compétence, variations 1986–1991, groupe de 24 industries

Agrégation au niveau de 24 industries	Secondaire non terminé	Études secondaires	Certificat ou diplôme professionnel	Diplôme d'études post-secondaires non universitaires	Études universitaires jusqu'au baccalauréat	Tous les diplômes d'études supérieures
S1. Agriculture, forêt, pêche et piégeage	-0.04	0.01	0.02	0.01	-0.00	0.01
S2. Mines, sauf le pétrole et le gaz	-0.04	-0.00	0.01	0.02	0.00	0.01
S3. Pétrole brut et gaz naturel	-0.01	-0.01	0.03	0.01	-0.01	0.00
S4. Aliments, boissons et tabac	-0.06	0.02	0.01	0.01	0.01	0.00
S5. Produits en caoutchouc et en plastique	-0.03	-0.01	0.01	0.02	0.01	0.00
S6. Cuir, textile et vêtement	-0.04	0.01	0.01	0.02	0.01	0.00
S7. Produits en bois et mobilier	-0.04	0.01	0.01	0.01	0.01	0.00
S8. Papier, produits connexes et imprimerie	-0.05	-0.01	0.02	0.02	0.02	0.01
S9. Métaux primaires et fabrication métallique	-0.04	-0.01	0.01	0.02	0.01	0.00
S10. Machines	-0.01	-0.02	0.03	0.01	0.01	0.00
S11. Véhicules à moteur et pièces	-0.05	0.00	0.00	0.01	0.01	0.00
S12. Autre matériel de transport	-0.05	-0.04	0.01	0.02	0.02	0.01
S13. Produits électriques et électroniques	-0.04	-0.02	0.00	0.04	0.02	0.01
S14. Pétrole raffiné, prod. chimiques et non métall.	-0.03	-0.01	0.01	0.02	0.02	0.01
S15. Autres produits fabriqués	-0.05	-0.01	0.01	0.03	0.02	0.01
S16. Construction	-0.04	0.00	0.01	0.02	0.01	0.00
S17. Transport et pipelines	-0.06	0.00	0.02	0.02	0.01	0.00
S18. Entreposage	-0.07	0.02	0.01	0.02	0.01	0.00
S19. Services publics	-0.04	-0.02	0.01	0.02	0.02	0.00
S20. Commerce	-0.03	-0.01	0.01	0.03	0.02	0.01
S21. Finances, assurance et immobilier	-0.03	-0.03	0.00	0.01	0.01	0.01
S22. Redev. gouv. et logements occ. par propr.	0.00	0.00	0.00	0.02	0.02	0.00
S23. Services aux entreprises	-0.01	-0.02	0.00	0.00	0.01	0.01
S24. Services personnels et autres	0.04	0.02	-0.01	-0.01	-0.02	-0.02
TOTAL	-0.04	-0.00	0.01	0.02	0.01	0.01

	Secondaire non terminé	Études secondaires	Certificat ou diplôme professionnel	Diplôme d'études post-secondaires non universitaires	Études universitaires jusqu'au baccalauréat	Tous les diplômes d'études supérieures
Tableau 10A Parts des exportations selon le niveau de scolarité/compétence, 1961–1997						
1961	0,441	0,240	0,140	0,098	0,066	0,014
1962	0,430	0,242	0,144	0,100	0,068	0,015
1963	0,431	0,242	0,143	0,100	0,068	0,015
1964	0,434	0,242	0,140	0,100	0,068	0,015
1965	0,428	0,244	0,142	0,101	0,069	0,016
1966	0,420	0,247	0,144	0,103	0,070	0,016
1967	0,411	0,249	0,146	0,105	0,072	0,017
1968	0,406	0,251	0,147	0,106	0,072	0,018
1969	0,397	0,254	0,148	0,108	0,074	0,019
1970	0,401	0,253	0,147	0,107	0,074	0,018
1971	0,405	0,252	0,145	0,106	0,074	0,018
1972	0,403	0,252	0,145	0,107	0,074	0,018
1973	0,403	0,253	0,144	0,107	0,074	0,018
1974	0,402	0,253	0,144	0,107	0,075	0,019
1975	0,399	0,254	0,144	0,108	0,076	0,019
1976	0,395	0,255	0,145	0,109	0,077	0,019
1977	0,396	0,255	0,144	0,108	0,077	0,020
1978	0,393	0,256	0,143	0,109	0,078	0,020
1979	0,390	0,256	0,143	0,110	0,080	0,021
1980	0,391	0,255	0,141	0,111	0,081	0,021
1981	0,388	0,256	0,141	0,112	0,082	0,022
1982	0,386	0,257	0,140	0,112	0,083	0,022
1983	0,389	0,257	0,137	0,112	0,083	0,022
1984	0,386	0,258	0,136	0,113	0,084	0,022
1985	0,379	0,260	0,136	0,114	0,086	0,023
1986	0,378	0,260	0,138	0,114	0,086	0,023
1987	0,373	0,259	0,139	0,117	0,088	0,024
1988	0,364	0,258	0,141	0,121	0,090	0,026
1989	0,352	0,257	0,145	0,125	0,093	0,028
1990	0,350	0,259	0,143	0,126	0,093	0,028
1991	0,341	0,258	0,144	0,130	0,097	0,030
1992	0,343	0,258	0,143	0,130	0,097	0,030
1993	0,339	0,260	0,142	0,130	0,098	0,030
1994	0,337	0,260	0,142	0,131	0,099	0,031
1995	0,336	0,261	0,142	0,131	0,099	0,031
1996	0,335	0,261	0,141	0,132	0,100	0,031
1997	0,338	0,260	0,140	0,131	0,100	0,031

	Secondaire non terminé	Études secondaires	Certificat ou diplôme professionnel	Diplôme d'études post-secondaires non universitaires	Études universitaires jusqu'au baccalauréat	Tous les diplômes d'études supérieures
			Tableau 10B Parts de l'emploi du secteur des entreprises selon le niveau de scolarité/compétence, 1961–1997			
1961	0,411	0,269	0,136	0,102	0,068	0,015
1962	0,408	0,270	0,136	0,102	0,069	0,015
1963	0,406	0,270	0,136	0,103	0,069	0,015
1964	0,404	0,271	0,137	0,103	0,070	0,015
1965	0,402	0,271	0,138	0,104	0,070	0,016
1966	0,398	0,272	0,139	0,105	0,071	0,016
1967	0,396	0,273	0,138	0,105	0,071	0,016
1968	0,395	0,273	0,138	0,106	0,072	0,016
1969	0,393	0,274	0,137	0,106	0,073	0,017
1970	0,390	0,275	0,137	0,107	0,073	0,017
1971	0,389	0,275	0,137	0,107	0,074	0,017
1972	0,387	0,277	0,137	0,108	0,075	0,017
1973	0,385	0,277	0,137	0,108	0,075	0,018
1974	0,383	0,278	0,137	0,109	0,076	0,018
1975	0,381	0,279	0,136	0,109	0,077	0,018
1976	0,381	0,279	0,136	0,109	0,077	0,018
1977	0,378	0,279	0,136	0,110	0,078	0,019
1978	0,378	0,280	0,135	0,110	0,079	0,019
1979	0,377	0,280	0,135	0,111	0,079	0,019
1980	0,375	0,280	0,134	0,111	0,080	0,020
1981	0,374	0,280	0,134	0,112	0,081	0,020
1982	0,370	0,281	0,133	0,113	0,082	0,021
1983	0,370	0,281	0,131	0,113	0,083	0,021
1984	0,370	0,282	0,131	0,113	0,084	0,021
1985	0,368	0,282	0,131	0,114	0,084	0,021
1986	0,368	0,282	0,131	0,114	0,084	0,021
1987	0,361	0,281	0,133	0,117	0,086	0,022
1988	0,353	0,280	0,135	0,120	0,088	0,024
1989	0,346	0,278	0,137	0,123	0,090	0,025
1990	0,338	0,277	0,138	0,127	0,093	0,027
1991	0,330	0,276	0,140	0,131	0,096	0,029
1992	0,329	0,276	0,139	0,131	0,096	0,029
1993	0,330	0,276	0,138	0,131	0,096	0,029
1994	0,330	0,276	0,138	0,131	0,096	0,029
1995	0,328	0,276	0,138	0,131	0,097	0,030
1996	0,328	0,275	0,138	0,131	0,098	0,030
1997	0,326	0,275	0,137	0,132	0,099	0,030

	Tableau 10C Ratio des parts de l'emploi, exportations/secteur des entreprises, 1961–1997					
	Secondaire non terminé	Études secondaires	Certificat ou diplôme professionnel	Diplôme d'études post-secondaires non universitaires	Études universitaires jusqu'au baccalauréat	Tous les diplômes d'études supérieures
1961	1,074	0,892	1,029	0,966	0,976	0,990
1962	1,054	0,898	1,057	0,981	0,990	1,031
1963	1,061	0,897	1,046	0,976	0,983	1,020
1964	1,073	0,896	1,025	0,969	0,978	1,004
1965	1,064	0,901	1,029	0,975	0,988	1,027
1966	1,056	0,907	1,036	0,981	0,991	1,037
1967	1,038	0,913	1,056	0,998	1,003	1,071
1968	1,027	0,918	1,069	1,004	1,006	1,088
1969	1,012	0,925	1,076	1,015	1,025	1,127
1970	1,028	0,918	1,067	1,003	1,009	1,087
1971	1,040	0,913	1,058	0,994	1,000	1,066
1972	1,042	0,913	1,060	0,991	0,995	1,058
1973	1,046	0,914	1,056	0,987	0,989	1,045
1974	1,049	0,912	1,051	0,986	0,992	1,044
1975	1,045	0,911	1,062	0,988	0,993	1,046
1976	1,038	0,914	1,068	0,992	0,999	1,063
1977	1,046	0,913	1,062	0,987	0,991	1,051
1978	1,040	0,915	1,064	0,991	0,997	1,066
1979	1,036	0,916	1,058	0,999	1,009	1,079
1980	1,043	0,912	1,052	0,995	1,008	1,074
1981	1,038	0,912	1,054	1,001	1,016	1,087
1982	1,042	0,913	1,053	0,996	1,011	1,076
1983	1,050	0,913	1,043	0,989	1,002	1,059
1984	1,043	0,917	1,041	0,995	1,011	1,075
1985	1,031	0,923	1,042	1,006	1,027	1,098
1986	1,026	0,923	1,052	1,007	1,026	1,106
1987	1,033	0,923	1,044	1,002	1,021	1,088
1988	1,029	0,922	1,046	1,005	1,027	1,089
1989	1,019	0,924	1,058	1,012	1,034	1,087
1990	1,038	0,937	1,031	0,994	1,004	1,027
1991	1,035	0,935	1,035	0,995	1,013	1,033
1992	1,042	0,934	1,027	0,991	1,011	1,030
1993	1,027	0,941	1,030	1,000	1,023	1,041
1994	1,023	0,943	1,024	1,003	1,031	1,052
1995	1,023	0,947	1,027	1,001	1,023	1,038
1996	1,022	0,949	1,026	1,002	1,022	1,032
1997	1,035	0,946	1,016	0,994	1,012	1,023

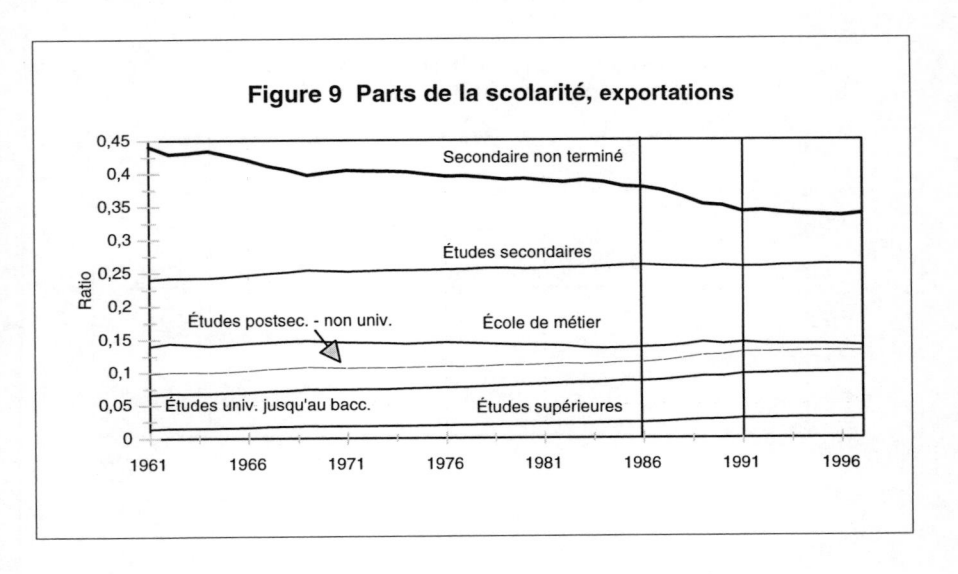

Figure 9 Parts de la scolarité, exportations

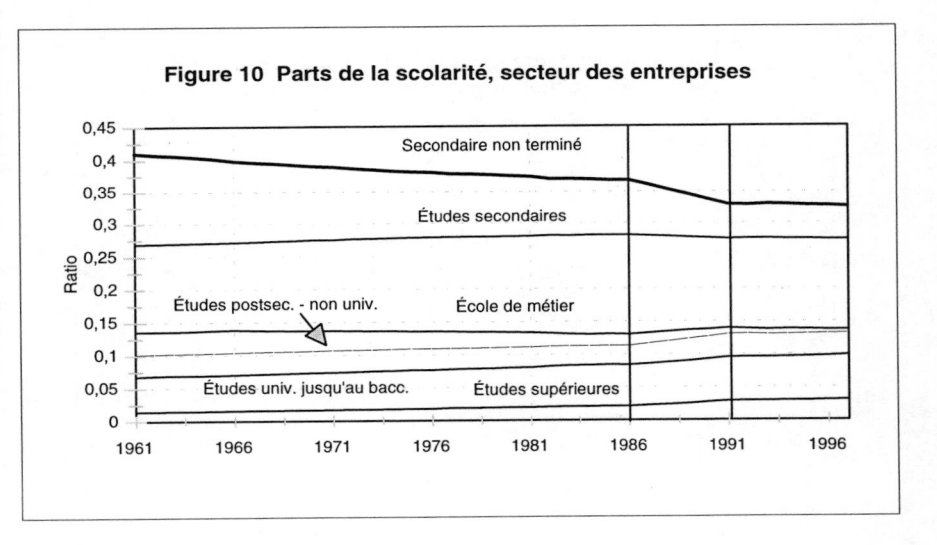

Figure 10 Parts de la scolarité, secteur des entreprises

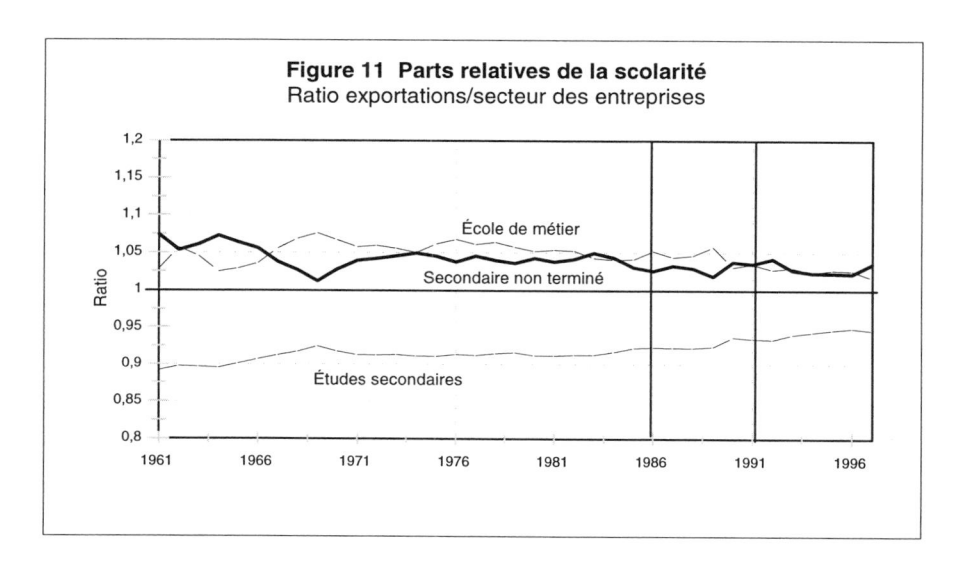

Figure 11 Parts relatives de la scolarité
Ratio exportations/secteur des entreprises

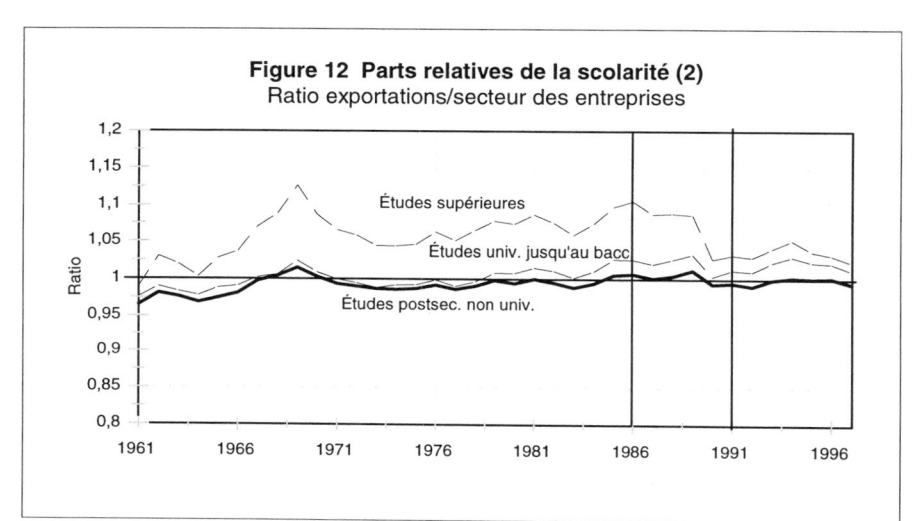

Figure 12 Parts relatives de la scolarité (2)
Ratio exportations/secteur des entreprises

5. CHANGEMENTS DANS LA COMPOSITION INDUSTRIELLE ET PROFESSIONNELLE DES IMPORTATIONS CANADIENNES

Dans le chapitre précédent, nous avons examiné la place occupée par les exportations dans l'économie canadienne et la façon dont la composition des exportations avait progressivement changé du point de vue de la production industrielle et de l'emploi. Dans le présent chapitre, nous reprenons ces calculs et analyses pour les importations. Nécessairement, les résultats présentés ici sont un peu plus spéculatifs que ceux du chapitre précédent. Dans le chapitre précédent, nous examinions, sous réserve des limitations qui affectent nos données, quelles combinaisons de compétences et d'intrants industriels ont été *réellement utilisées* pour produire les exportations canadiennes. Dans le présent chapitre, nous cherchons à déterminer quelles combinaisons d'intrants industriels et de compétences *auraient été utilisées* pour produire les importations canadiennes au Canada plutôt qu'à l'étranger avec la technologie et la main-d'oeuvre canadiennes actuelles. Puisque ces biens ont été effectivement importés, il est probable que différentes technologies et différents profils de compétences ont servi à les produire à l'étranger. Néanmoins, cet exercice est utile parce qu'il permet de montrer, au moment où les importations dans l'économie canadienne augmentent, quels auraient été la composition industrielle et le profil des compétences au Canada et où les pressions exercées par les importations se font le plus durement sentir.

Comme nous l'avons indiqué au chapitre 2, on peut se demander où cette substitution hypothétique de la production intérieure aux importations devrait prendre fin. Selon la technologie qui ressort des tableaux entrées-sorties canadiens, pour produire au pays une partie ou la totalité des biens que nous avons historiquement importés, il aurait fallu importer d'autres biens qui servent d'intrants intermédiaires. Plutôt que de tenter de remplacer toutes les importations entrant dans la chaîne de production, ce qui nous aurait amenés de plus en plus loin de la réalité et de la structure de production canadienne, nous avons choisi de modéliser la production intérieure uniquement pour les importations observées. Toutes les autres importations requises pour « produire » ces importations au pays sont laissées sans contrainte et nous n'avons pas cherché à les remplacer par une production intérieure. Pour cette raison et les autres, énoncées ci-dessus, lorsque nous parlons de production ou d'emploi « remplacé par les importations » en décrivant les résultats qui ressortent de nos calculs, il faut interpréter avec beaucoup de prudence tant les termes observés que les résultats.

Les importations dans l'économie canadienne, 1961-1997 : perspective des Comptes nationaux

Comme dans le cas des exportations, nous commençons par un examen de données agrégées des Comptes nationaux pour préciser la place qu'occupent les importations dans l'économie canadienne. Une série de ratios ou d'indicateurs clés est présentée pour la période 1961-1997 au tableau 11 et reproduite dans les figures 13 et 14.

Les données des colonnes 1 et 2 du tableau 11 (reproduites à la figure 13) montrent la croissance des importations en proportion du PIB depuis 1961. Mesurées en dollars de 1992, les importations sont passées de 10,8 p. 100 du PIB en 1961 à un peu plus de 36 p. 100 en 1997. Mesurées en dollars courants, elles sont passées de 18,2 p. 100 du PIB en 1961 à 38,5 p. 100 en 1997. À noter que, pour 1992, soit la dernière année pour laquelle nous disposions de données pour l'analyse entrées-sorties, les parts des importations dans le PIB sont identiques à 27,5 p. 100 puisqu'il s'agit de l'année de base utilisée aux fins des Comptes nationaux.

La différence observée dans les parts de croissance peut s'expliquer par le mouvement des prix relatifs des importations au cours des 36 dernières années. (Par prix relatif, nous voulons dire le prix des importations par rapport aux prix de l'ensemble des biens compris dans le PIB tel que mesuré par le déflateur du PIB.) Comme il ressort des données de la colonne 3 du tableau 11, le prix relatif des importations a diminué de façon significative entre 1961 et 1992, surtout durant les années 80 au moment où les prix relatifs de l'énergie et des autres produits de base ont fléchi. Cependant, on constate une modeste augmentation du prix relatif des importations depuis 1992.

Cette hausse du prix relatif des importations a fait en sorte que la part des importations exprimée en dollars constants (de 1992) a augmenté moins que la part exprimée en dollars courants depuis 1992 — même si les deux hausses, comme dans le cas des exportations, sont très importantes pour une période de cinq ans par rapport à l'expérience historique.

Comme nous l'avons fait pour les exportations, il est intéressant de se demander si cette hausse (au cours des dernières années et depuis 1961) est davantage attribuable aux changements survenus dans la part des importations de biens ou la part des importations de services. Même si les données des Comptes nationaux (colonnes 4 et 5 du tableau 11 et figure 14) indiquent que tant la part des importations de biens que celle des importations de services a augmenté dans le PIB, la principale source de l'augmentation globale de la part des importations est la hausse de la part des importations de *biens*. Cela est vrai pour la période 1961-1992, à l'égard de laquelle nous possédons des données entrées-sorties et pour la période subséquente de 1992 à 1997.

Enfin, la colonne 6 du tableau 11 montre les importations exprimées en proportion non pas du PIB mais du PIB du secteur privé au coût des facteurs. Cette dernière notion exclut la « production » gouvernementale et les taxes indirectes (moins les subventions) comprises dans la notion de « prix du marché » du PIB agrégé. La plus grande partie de l'analyse entrées-sorties que nous présentons ci-après porte sur les comparaisons ou les changements des ratios des importations à cette notion de « production du secteur privé au coût des facteurs ». La colonne 6 renferme les données équivalentes tirées des Comptes nationaux et, comme on peut le voir, la part des importations est passée de 22,3 p. 100 en 1961 à 34,5 p. 100 en 1992 et, enfin, à un peu plus de 47 p. 100 en 1997. Comme pour les exportations, le fait que la part des importations dans le PIB total (en dollars courants) n'ait pas augmenté aussi rapidement (de 18,2 à 27,5 p. 100 entre 1961 et 1992) s'explique par la croissance du secteur gouvernemental au cours de cette période et l'augmentation des impôts indirects moyens.

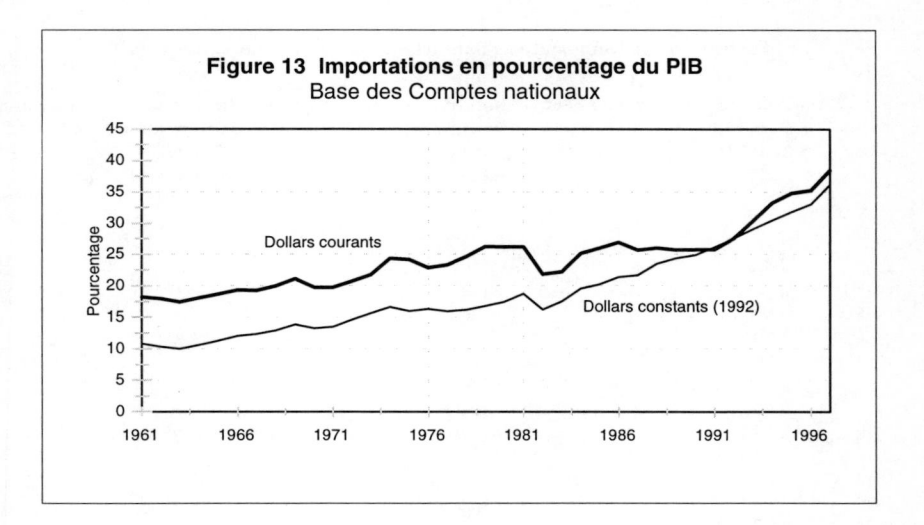

Figure 13 Importations en pourcentage du PIB
Base des Comptes nationaux

Tableau 11 Les importations dans les Comptes nationaux, 1961–1997					
(1) Importations en % du PIB ($ de 1992)	(2) Importations en % du PIB ($ courants)	(3) Ratio du déflateur des importations à celui du PIB	(4) Importations de biens en % du PIB ($ courants)	(5) Importations de services en % du PIB ($ courants)	(6) Importations en % du PIB du secteur privé au coût des facteurs
1961	10,8	18,2	1,68	14,5	3,7	22,3
1962	10,4	18,0	1,73	14,5	3,5	22,1
1963	10,0	17,5	1,74	14,2	3,3	21,4
1964	10,6	18,1	1,70	14,7	3,4	22,2
1965	11,3	18,7	1,65	15,4	3,3	23,0
1966	12,0	19,3	1,60	16,0	3,3	23,7
1967	12,3	19,3	1,56	15,9	3,4	23,8
1968	12,9	20,0	1,55	16,6	3,4	24,7
1969	13,9	21,1	1,52	17,3	3,8	26,1
1970	13,3	19,7	1,49	15,8	3,9	24,4
1971	13,5	19,8	1,47	16,0	3,8	24,5
1972	14,6	20,7	1,42	17,1	3,6	25,7
1973	15,6	21,7	1,39	18,1	3,7	26,7
1974	16,7	24,3	1,46	20,6	3,7	29,8
1975	16,0	24,1	1,51	20,1	4,0	29,1
1976	16,3	22,8	1,40	18,8	4,1	27,7
1977	15,9	23,3	1,46	19,2	4,1	28,3
1978	16,2	24,6	1,52	20,4	4,2	29,8
1979	16,8	26,3	1,56	22,3	3,9	31,4
1980	17,4	26,2	1,50	22,1	4,0	31,0
1981	18,7	26,2	1,40	22,1	4,1	31,6
1982	16,2	21,8	1,34	17,9	3,9	26,6
1983	17,5	22,2	1,27	18,3	3,9	26,9
1984	19,6	25,1	1,28	21,2	3,9	30,3
1985	20,2	26,0	1,29	22,0	4,0	31,2
1986	21,4	26,9	1,26	22,5	4,4	32,7
1987	21,7	25,7	1,18	21,4	4,3	31,3
1988	23,5	26,0	1,11	21,7	4,3	31,7
1989	24,4	25,7	1,05	21,2	4,5	31,6
1990	24,9	25,8	1,04	20,8	5,0	31,8
1991	26,2	25,8	0,99	20,6	5,2	32,1
1992	27,5	27,5	1,00	22,1	5,4	34,5
1993	29,1	30,4	1,05	24,5	5,9	38,0
1994	30,5	33,3	1,09	27,4	5,9	41,4
1995	31,9	34,8	1,09	28,9	5,9	43,1
1996	33,1	35,3	1,06	29,2	6,1	43,6
1997	36,2	38,5	1,06	32,5	6,0	47,4

Les importations dans l'économie canadienne : résultats agrégés de l'analyse entrées-sorties

Les calculs entrées-sorties visant à déterminer l'impact du remplacement des importations historiques (du moins au cours de la première « ronde ») sur la production intérieure et l'emploi au Canada ont été effectués pour chacune des années de 1961 à 1997[12]. Les effets au niveau de chaque industrie ont été agrégés pour l'ensemble des industries afin d'obtenir une estimation de l'impact sur l'ensemble de l'économie. Ces données sont présentées de façon sommaire, par année, au tableau 12 et dans les figures 15 à 20. Comme dans le cas des calculs faits pour les exportations, ces résultats agrégés présentent un tableau complet des répercussions finales sur la production et l'emploi — dans ce cas, du remplacement hypothétique des importations. Ces données ne sont pas simplement la somme des niveaux de production ou d'emploi des diverses industries qui sont considérées comme étant principalement « en concurrence avec les importations »; plutôt, il s'agit d'estimations de l'ensemble de la production et de l'emploi direct et indirect requis pour produire au pays la première ronde d'importations observées pour chacune des années étudiées.

La colonne 1 du tableau 12 fait le lien entre les données plus familières des Comptes nationaux et les calculs et notions d'entrées-sorties. Cette colonne montre les importations (tirées de la base de données entrées-sorties) en tant que part du produit intérieur du secteur des entreprises, c'est-à-dire la valeur ajoutée (tirée également de la base de données entrées-sorties). C'est l'équivalent le plus rapproché des données entrées-sorties de la colonne 6 du tableau 11. Les écarts sont plus importants que dans le cas des exportations mais, encore une fois, ils sont attribuables aux différences dans les systèmes de classification et la définition donnée au secteur gouvernemental. Ils traduisent également des écarts possibles par rapport à notre propre mise à jour des données entrées-sorties agrégées pour les importations après 1992.

Passant à la colonne 4 du tableau 12 (et à la figure 21), nous en arrivons au thème central de la présente étude: l'impact sur l'emploi. Comme on peut le voir, la part de l'emploi « remplacé par les importations » dans l'emploi total du secteur des entreprises a effectivement augmenté : elle est passée de 16,4 p. 100 en 1961 à 26,0 p. 100 en 1992 et, enfin, à 32,7 p. 100 en 1997; mais, comme pour les exportations, l'augmentation de la part de l'emploi est de beaucoup inférieure à l'augmentation de la part des importations dans le produit du secteur des entreprises. La raison est la même : la « pénétration » accrue des importations; on peut voir à la colonne 3 du tableau 12 qu'en 1961, si le Canada avait tenté de produire ce qu'il importait, il aurait eu besoin d'importations supplémentaires représentant environ 20 p. 100 du produit intérieur qui aurait été engendré en remplaçant la première ronde d'importations. En 1997, ce chiffre avait augmenté à plus de 50 p. 100. Ainsi, même s'il y a eu une croissance considérable de l'emploi et du produit intérieur (voir la colonne 2) « déplacés » par les importations, cette croissance n'a pas été aussi importante que celle de la part des importations dans le PIB lui-même (figure 16).

La comparaison des répercussions sur l'emploi des exportations et du « remplacement des importations » fait ressortir certaines observations intéressantes (colonne 4 des tableaux 2 et 12 et figures 3 et 15). L'emploi « déplacé » par les importations en 1961, soit 16,4 p. 100 de l'emploi total des entreprises, était largement inférieur à la part de 17,2 p. 100 de l'emploi attribuable aux exportations. (Les deux mesures, rappelons-le, englobent l'emploi lié à l'ensemble des intrants intermédiaires.) Cependant, en 1992, ce chiffre avait atteint 26 p. 100 pour les importations et 23,1 p. 100 pour les exportations; en 1997, il avait encore augmenté à 32,7 p. 100 pour les importations et à 28,3 p. 100 pour les exportations. Autrement dit, les importations semblent avoir remplacé plus d'emplois que les exportations n'en ont créés. Pourquoi en est-il ainsi? Et, comme il peut sembler à première vue, est-ce que cela est mauvais pour l'économie canadienne? Les réponses à ces deux questions sont étroitement liées.

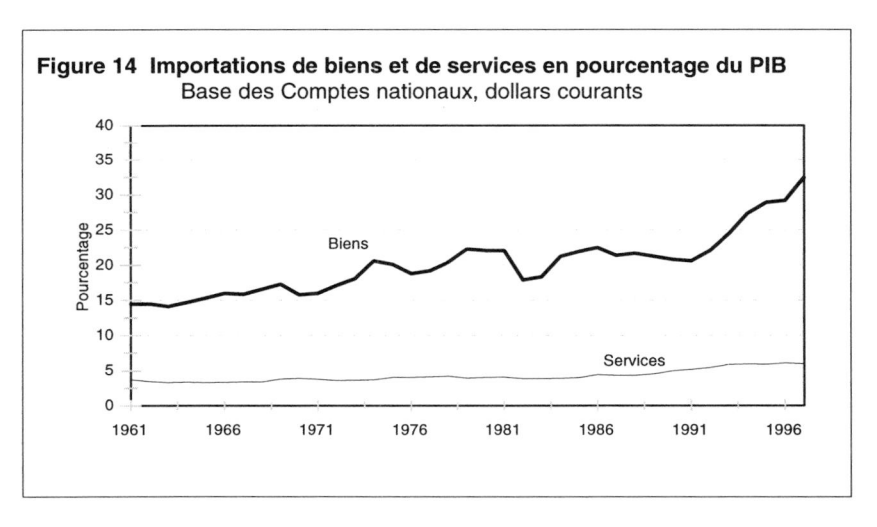

Figure 14 Importations de biens et de services en pourcentage du PIB
Base des Comptes nationaux, dollars courants

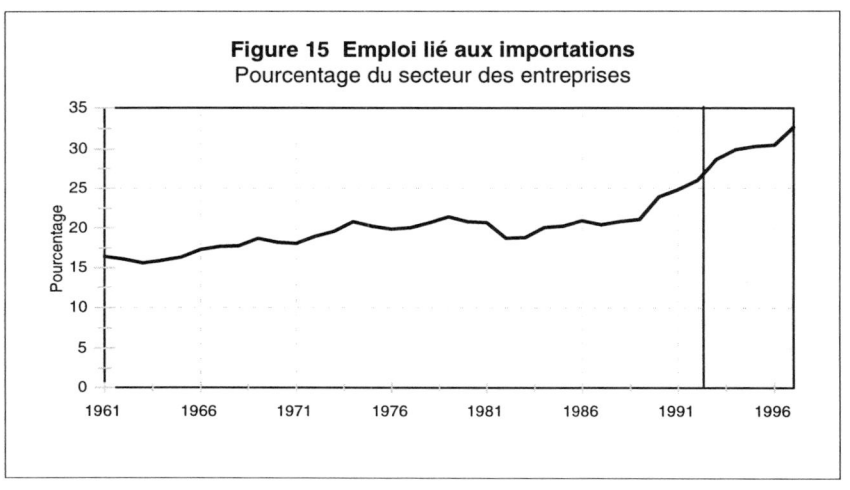

Figure 15 Emploi lié aux importations
Pourcentage du secteur des entreprises

Le principal indice ressort d'une comparaison de la productivité moyenne de la main-d'oeuvre calculée pour les exportations et les « importations remplacées » — voir la colonne 5 des tableaux 2 et 12 et les figures 6 et 18. Comme on peut le constater, la productivité de la main-d'oeuvre liée au « remplacement des importations » est invariablement inférieure à celle des exportations (elle est égale ou légèrement supérieure à la moyenne de l'ensemble de l'économie) et, de fait, elle a chuté en termes relatifs au cours des dernières années. Par conséquent, même si les importations ont en réalité augmenté légèrement moins vite que les exportations par rapport au PIB, parce qu'elles correspondent à une production ayant une productivité inférieure (du moins en fonction de la technologie canadienne), elles ont eu tendance à « déplacer » plus d'emplois. Cependant, si nous retenons le principe macro-économique classique voulant que les économies tendent vers le plein emploi à long terme, quelle que

soit la composition de leur production, alors la conséquence d'une augmentation des échanges internationaux n'a pas été une perte d'emplois permanente mais, plutôt, le remplacement d'une production à faible productivité (que nous importons), par une production à productivité plus élevée (que nous exportons) — laissant l'économie canadienne avec un gain net par rapport à ce qu'il en serait autrement. En outre, ce résultat est conforme à celui prédit par la théorie du commerce international. Ce n'est que dans la mesure où l'évolution des échanges s'est produite trop rapidement pour permettre un ajustement complet de la population active que l'accroissement du commerce international a « coûté des emplois » en haussant le chômage structurel (les travailleurs déplacés par les importations qui ne peuvent être employés ailleurs dans l'économie) et le taux de chômage de plein emploi.

Un autre élément qui requiert notre attention au tableau 12 est l'importance relative de l'emploi direct et indirect associé au « remplacement des importations » (colonnes 6 et 7 et figure 19). Comme on peut le voir, le ratio emploi direct/total lié au « remplacement des importations » a oscillé légèrement en deçà de 60 p. 100 jusqu'en 1992, puis il a augmenté rapidement par la suite. La hausse subséquente à 1992, que l'on observe aussi pour les exportations, doit être interprétée avec prudence parce que nous ne disposons pas de tableaux entrées-sorties pour ces années. Avant les années 90, la constance de ce ratio est remarquable, ce qui voudrait dire qu'il n'y a eu aucun « renforcement » de la technologie intersectorielle dans le phénomène du « remplacement des importations » tout au long de cette période. Il faut noter également le fait que le ratio de remplacement des importations est plus élevé que pour les exportations (en comparant les figures 7 et 19). Ainsi, la composition des importations canadiennes, si celles-ci devaient être produites avec la technologie canadienne, supposerait moins d'intrants intermédiaires (et plus d'intrants importés) que la composition des exportations canadiennes.

Enfin, comme pour les exportations, le système entrées-sorties nous permet de calculer les effets du « remplacement des importations » sur la rémunération totale de la main-d'oeuvre (en amalgamant les traitements et salaires, le revenu supplémentaire du travail et le revenu des entreprises non constituées en société dans cette catégorie). Le rendement de la main-d'oeuvre peut être exprimé sous forme de ratio à l'emploi engendré afin de déterminer le rendement relatif de ce facteur dans le remplacement des importations. Comme le montrent la colonne 8 du tableau 12 et la figure 20, ce ratio est demeuré relativement stable entre 1961 et 1976, puis il a augmenté pour se situer à un niveau légèrement supérieur à la fin des années 70 et, enfin, il a chuté après 1988. Mais en tout temps, il a été supérieur à 1,0, ce qui indique que le rendement de la main-d'oeuvre a été supérieur à la moyenne du secteur des entreprises. Toutefois, lorsque nous comparons ces chiffres au rendement de la main-d'oeuvre liée à l'exportation, (tableau 2 et figure 8), le rendement de la main-d'oeuvre liée au remplacement des importations a été systématiquement inférieur depuis le début des années 70 (lorsque l'effet de l'agriculture est atténué). Cela était prévisible, compte tenu du fait que la productivité de la main-d'oeuvre liée au « remplacement des importations » semble également inférieure à celle des exportations, selon nos calculs. Encore une fois, il s'ensuit que le commerce international aurait permis au Canada de substituer des emplois relativement mieux rémunérés à des emplois relativement moins bien rémunérés. Cependant, il faut garder à l'esprit que même le rendement de la main-d'oeuvre liée au remplacement des importations est supérieur à la moyenne du secteur des entreprises. Cela signifie, évidemment, qu'il demeure un important volet de l'économie où les travailleurs sont relativement mal payés et peu exposés à la concurrence internationale — certains services, la construction et certaines activités manufacturières localisées (comme la production du ciment). Si le Canada tire un avantage net du commerce international, dans l'ensemble, il n'importe pas de biens qui, du moins en fonction de sa propre technologie, seraient produits par des travailleurs faiblement rémunérés et dont la productivité est peu élevée.

Tableau 12 Comparaisons tirées des calculs entrées-sorties au niveau agrégé, importations, 1961–1997

	(1) Importations en % du produit intérieur du secteur des entreprises	(2) Produit intérieur lié aux importations en % du produit intérieur des entreprises	(3) « Importations » liées aux importations en % du produit intérieur lié aux importations	(4) Emploi lié aux importations en % de l'emploi total des entreprises	(5) Productivité de la main-d'oeuvre liée aux importations par rapport au secteur des entreprises	(6) Emploi direct lié aux importations en % de l'emploi total	(7) Ratio emploi direct/total lié aux importations	(8) Ratio du rendement de la main-d'oeuvre liée aux importations à celui du secteur des entreprises
1961	21,31	17,03	20,01	16,44	1,04	9,55	0,58	1,01
1962	21,37	17,15	19,66	16,10	1,06	9,33	0,58	1,01
1963	20,77	16,75	19,31	15,60	1,07	8,97	0,57	1,01
1964	21,45	17,15	20,18	15,94	1,08	9,21	0,58	1,02
1965	22,14	17,67	20,78	16,34	1,08	9,39	0,57	1,03
1966	23,29	18,42	22,34	17,30	1,06	9,92	0,57	1,02
1967	23,83	18,60	23,82	17,72	1,05	10,19	0,58	1,02
1968	24,93	18,99	23,86	17,78	1,07	10,21	0,57	1,03
1969	26,43	19,96	26,48	18,71	1,07	10,74	0,57	1,04
1970	24,91	18,76	27,32	18,24	1,03	10,52	0,58	1,04
1971	25,39	18,98	27,41	18,07	1,05	10,29	0,57	1,04
1972	27,02	20,05	28,37	18,98	1,05	10,83	0,57	1,03
1973	27,83	20,64	29,35	19,60	1,06	11,23	0,57	1,03
1974	31,29	23,14	29,69	20,81	1,11	11,86	0,57	1,03
1975	30,15	22,31	31,15	20,24	1,10	11,44	0,57	1,03
1976	28,94	21,38	31,85	19,89	1,08	11,34	0,57	1,03
1977	29,71	21,58	31,12	20,05	1,08	11,36	0,57	1,04
1978	31,47	22,54	33,17	20,70	1,09	11,79	0,57	1,06
1979	33,39	23,89	35,07	21,44	1,11	12,23	0,57	1,08
1980	32,55	23,53	35,80	20,82	1,13	11,92	0,57	1,08
1981	32,82	23,41	34,83	20,82	1,13	11,88	0,57	1,09
1982	27,65	20,15	35,32	20,69	1,08	10,68	0,57	1,09
1983	27,57	19,94	31,94	18,74	1,06	10,69	0,57	1,07
1984	30,86	22,02	33,62	18,83	1,10	11,42	0,57	1,07
1985	32,05	22,41	36,13	20,09	1,11	11,45	0,56	1,09
1986	33,08	22,57	39,12	20,27	1,08	11,88	0,57	1,08
1987	31,62	21,74	41,68	20,92	1,06	11,47	0,56	1,07
1988	32,09	22,20	40,58	20,43	1,06	11,77	0,56	1,07
1989	32,10	22,26	39,00	21,11	1,05	11,96	0,57	1,05

Tableau 12 (suite)

	(1) Importations en % du produit intérieur du secteur des entreprises	(2) Produit intérieur lié aux importations en % du produit intérieur des entreprises	(3) « Importations » liées aux importations en % du produit intérieur des entreprises	(4) Emploi lié aux importations en % de l'emploi total des entreprises	(5) Productivité de la main-d'oeuvre liée aux importations par rapport au secteur des entreprises	(6) Emploi direct lié aux importations en % de l'emploi total	(7) Ratio emploi direct/total lié aux importations	(8) Ratio du rendement de la main-d'oeuvre liée aux importations à celui du secteur des entreprises
1990	34,14	23,83	37,87	23,92	1,00	14,20	0,59	1,01
1991	34,54	23,99	39,38	24,84	0,97	14,75	0,59	1,01
1992	37,15	25,25	42,27	25,99	0,97	15,60	0,60	1,01
1993	42,59	28,45	44,89	28,64	0,99	18,51	0,65	n.d.
1994	46,32	30,46	47,25	29,91	1,02	21,06	0,70	n.d.
1995	47,72	31,24	47,94	30,30	1,03	22,40	0,74	n.d.
1996	47,54	30,93	48,87	30,47	1,01	22,78	0,75	n.d.
1997	52,37	33,51	51,50	32,69	1,03	24,90	0,76	n.d.

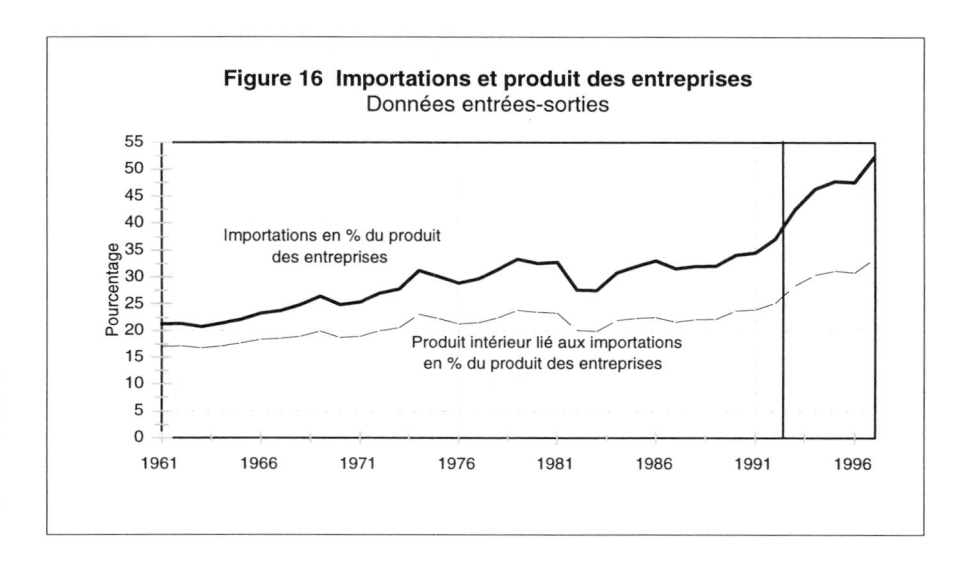

Figure 16 Importations et produit des entreprises
Données entrées-sorties

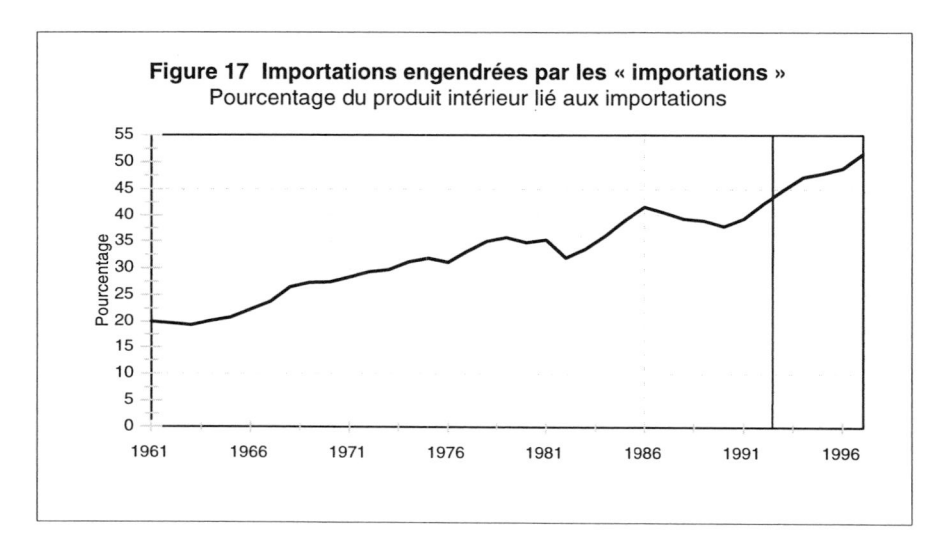

Figure 17 Importations engendrées par les « importations »
Pourcentage du produit intérieur lié aux importations

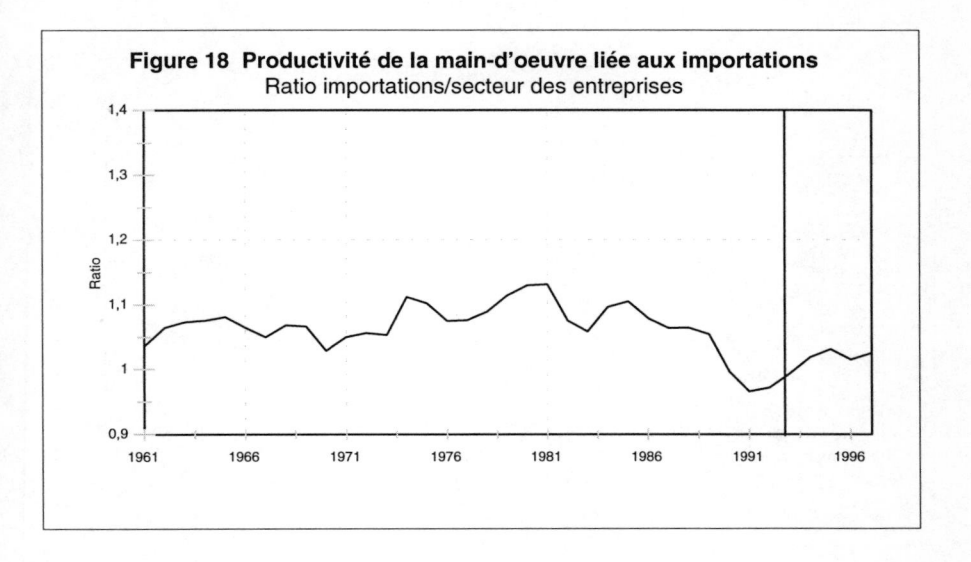

Figure 18 Productivité de la main-d'oeuvre liée aux importations
Ratio importations/secteur des entreprises

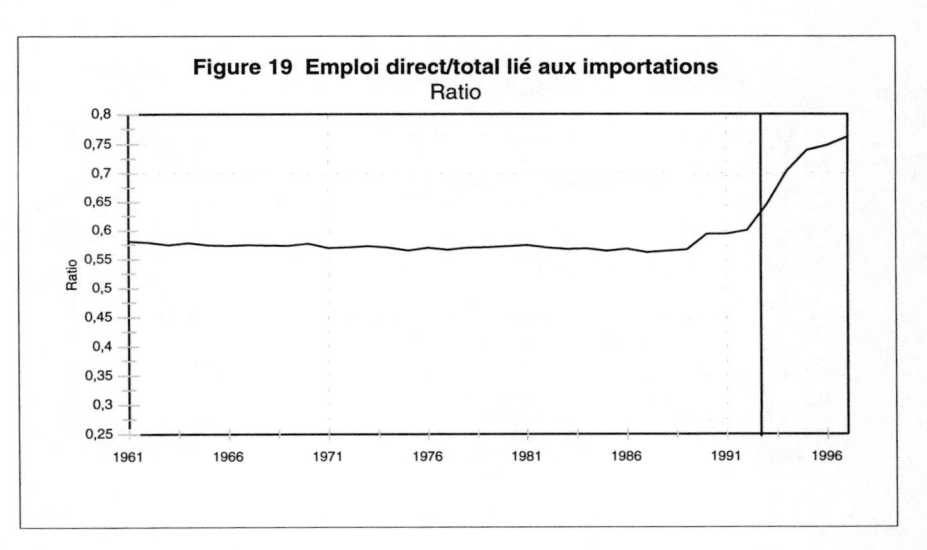

Figure 19 Emploi direct/total lié aux importations
Ratio

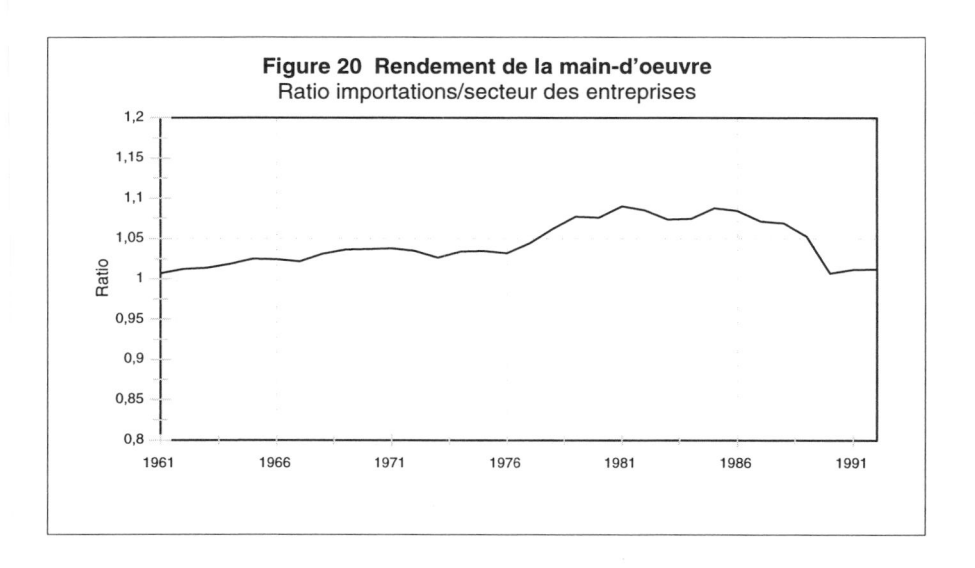

Figure 20 Rendement de la main-d'oeuvre
Ratio importations/secteur des entreprises

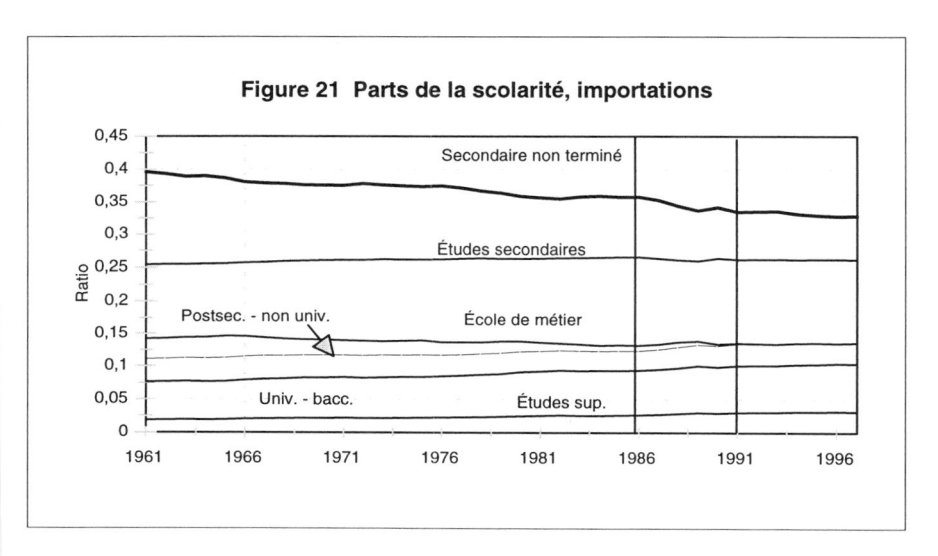

Figure 21 Parts de la scolarité, importations

Évolution de la composition industrielle des importations : agrégation au niveau de 24 industries

Comme dans le cas des exportations, nous passons maintenant de l'examen des résultats agrégés à celui des résultats désagrégés et aux changements qui sont survenus avec le temps. Les tableaux 13A et 13B montrent, pour l'agrégation à 24 industries, l'emploi attribuable aux importations dans chaque industrie

en proportion de l'emploi total lié aux importations et de l'emploi total, pour les années 1961 et 1997. Le tableau montre également le changement observé dans les parts entre ces deux années. Le tableau 13A fait voir ces parts classées par industrie, tandis que le tableau 13B fait voir les effets, classés par ordre décroissant de l'augmentation de la part de l'emploi lié à l'importation. Le tableau 13C fait voir les mêmes effets, mais classés par ordre décroissant de l'emploi lié à l'importation en 1997 en pourcentage de l'emploi total.

Les données des tableaux 13A, B et C sont intéressantes tant en termes absolus, pour chacune des années, que pour ce qui est des changements observés entre 1961 et 1997. En 1997, les trois premières industries quant à la part de l'emploi total représentée par l'emploi lié au « remplacement des importations » étaient toutes des industries de services : services personnels et autres, services aux entreprises et commerce. Étant donné que les importations de services ne sont pas un élément très important des importations totales, on peut voir que la plus grande partie, sinon la totalité, de l'impact de ces services provient des intrants indirects qui contribuent au « remplacement des importations ». Les autres industries dont l'impact au niveau du remplacement des importations se situe entre 2 et 3 p. 100 de l'emploi total du secteur des entreprises sont celles des métaux primaires et de la fabrication métallique (2,4 p. 100), des véhicules à moteur et pièces (2,0 p. 100) et des produits électriques et électroniques (2,6 p. 100). Chacune de ces industries et les trois industries de services mentionnées plus haut figurent aussi dans le peloton pour ce qui est de l'emploi lié aux exportations en 1997, ce qui indique une spécialisation des échanges dans ces industries, qui engendre un important commerce bilatéral.

Si l'on examine plus attentivement les changements survenus entre 1961 et 1997, nous pouvons constater au tableau 13B que, sur les sept industries qui ont vu leur part de l'emploi lié à l'importation augmenter de plus d'un point de pourcentage, quatre étaient des industries de services (services personnels et autres, services aux entreprises, commerce et finance). Les trois autres étaient des industries manufacturières diverses que l'on aurait pu prévoir compte tenu du Pacte de l'automobile et de l'évolution de la technologie : les véhicules à moteur, les produits électriques et électroniques et les produits en caoutchouc et en plastique. Huit industries ont vu leur part de l'emploi lié à l'importation diminuer de plus d'un point de pourcentage : les deux premières sont des industries de production primaire (exploitation minière à l'exclusion du pétrole et du gaz, et agriculture, forêt et pêche). Les autres sont toutes des industries manufacturières et, dans biens des cas, leur présence parmi ce groupe indique que l'économie canadienne a progressé sur la voie du traitement intérieur des matières premières au fil des années depuis 1961 — par exemple les métaux primaires, les produits tirés du pétrole brut et les produits chimiques et, enfin, le papier et les produits connexes. D'autres industries révèlent également une certaine maturation du secteur manufacturier canadien au cours de la période, entraînant (en termes relatifs) un certain remplacement des importations — comme l'industrie des machines et celle des autres matériels de transport.

Si l'on compare les tableaux équivalents pour les exportations et les importations (les tableaux 3B et 13B), il est peut être remarquable que les secteurs qui ont enregistré les hausses et les baisses les plus importantes de la part de l'emploi sont pratiquement les mêmes dans chaque cas : services personnels, services aux entreprises et commerce en tête de liste et exploitation minière et agriculture et forêt au bas de la liste. *Tant* les exportations que les importations canadiennes ont vu leur coefficient d'emploi lié aux services augmenter, tandis que le coefficient d'emploi lié à la production de matières premières a fléchi.

Une analyse de l'évolution de la composition industrielle des importations pour la désagrégation à 161 industries est présentée à l'appendice 5.

Tableau 13A Parts de l'emploi, 1961 et 1997, groupe de 24 industries

Agrégation au niveau de 24 industries	1961		1997		Variation 1961–1997	
	Emploi lié à l'importation en % de l'emploi total lié à l'importation	Emploi lié à l'importation en % de l'emploi total	Emploi lié à l'importation en % de l'emploi total lié à l'importation	Emploi lié à l'importation en % de l'emploi total	Emploi lié à l'importation en % de l'emploi total lié à l'importation	Emploi lié à l'importation en % de l'emploi total
S1. Agriculture, forêt, pêche et piégeage	13,92	2,29	3,69	1,21	-10,22	-1,08
S2. Mines, sauf le pétrole et le gaz	5,18	0,85	1,08	0,35	-4,10	-0,50
S3. Pétrole brut et gaz naturel	1,12	0,18	0,48	0,16	-0,64	-0,03
S4. Aliments, boissons et tabac	2,83	0,47	2,13	0,70	-0,70	0,23
S5. Produits en caoutchouc et en plastique	1,44	0,24	3,03	0,99	1,58	0,75
S6. Cuir, textile et vêtement	7,88	1,30	5,81	1,90	-2,07	0,60
S7. Produits en bois et mobilier	1,78	0,29	1,49	0,49	-0,29	0,19
S8. Papier, produits connexes et imprimerie	4,45	0,73	3,12	1,02	-1,32	0,29
S9. Métaux primaires et fabrication métallique	10,49	1,72	7,26	2,37	-3,23	0,65
S10. Machines	6,31	1,04	5,16	1,69	-1,14	0,65
S11. Véhicules à moteur et pièces	4,67	0,77	6,22	2,03	1,55	1,26
S12. Autre matériel de transport	3,15	0,52	1,75	0,57	-1,40	0,06
S13. Produits électriques et électroniques	6,02	0,99	8,05	2,63	2,03	1,64
S14. Pétrole raffiné, prod. chimiques et non métall.	5,61	0,92	3,36	1,10	-2,25	0,18
S15. Autres produits fabriqués	3,95	0,65	4,40	1,44	0,46	0,79
S16. Construction	1,47	0,24	1,02	0,33	-0,45	0,09
S17. Transport et pipelines	4,51	0,74	4,26	1,39	-0,25	0,65
S18. Entreposage	0,17	0,03	0,13	0,04	-0,03	0,02
S19. Services publics	2,07	0,34	2,35	0,77	0,28	0,43
S20. Commerce	5,85	0,96	8,85	2,89	2,99	1,93
S21. Finances, assurance et immobilier	2,03	0,33	4,13	1,35	2,11	1,02
S22. Redev. gouv. et logements occ. par propr.	0,00	0,00	0,00	0,00	0,00	0,00
S23. Services aux entreprises	3,13	0,51	10,33	3,38	7,2	2,86
S24. Services personnels et autres	1,97	0,32	11,88	3,88	9,9	3,56
TOTAL	100,00	16,44	100,00	32,69	-0,00	16,25

Tableau 13B Parts de l'emploi, 1961 à 1997, groupe de 24 industries, classement selon la taille des variations

Agrégation au niveau de 24 industries	1961		1997		Variation 1961–1997	
	Emploi lié à l'importation en % de l'importation	Emploi lié à l'importation en % de l'emploi total	Emploi lié à l'importation en % de l'importation	Emploi lié à l'importation en % de l'emploi total	Emploi lié à l'importation en % de l'importation	Emploi lié à l'importation en % de l'emploi total
S24. Services personnels et autres	1,97	0,32	11,88	3,88	9,90	3,56
S23. Services aux entreprises	3,13	0,51	10,33	3,38	7,20	2,86
S20. Commerce	5,85	0,96	8,85	2,89	2,99	1,93
S21. Finances, assurance et immobilier	2,03	0,33	4,13	1,35	2,11	1,02
S13. Produits électriques et électroniques	6,02	0,99	8,05	2,63	2,03	1,64
S5. Produits en caoutchouc et en plastique	1,44	0,24	3,03	0,99	1,58	0,75
S11. Véhicules à moteur et pièces	4,67	0,77	6,22	2,03	1,55	1,26
S15. Autres produits fabriqués	3,95	0,65	4,4	1,44	0,46	0,79
S19. Services publics	2,07	0,34	2,35	0,77	0,28	0,43
S22. Redev. gouv. et logements occ. par propr.	0,00	0,00	0,00	0,00	0,00	0,00
S18. Entreposage	0,17	0,03	0,13	0,04	-0,03	0,02
S17. Transport et pipelines	4,51	0,74	4,26	1,39	-0,25	0,65
S7. Produits en bois et mobilier	1,78	0,29	1,49	0,49	-0,29	0,19
S16. Construction	1,47	0,24	1,02	0,33	-0,45	0,09
S3. Pétrole brut et gaz naturel	1,12	0,18	0,48	0,16	-0,64	-0,03
S4. Aliments, boissons et tabac	2,83	0,47	2,13	0,70	-0,70	0,23
S10. Machines	6,31	1,04	5,16	1,69	-1,14	0,65
S8. Papier, produits connexes et imprimerie	4,45	0,73	3,12	1,02	-1,32	0,29
S12. Autre matériel de transport	3,15	0,52	1,75	0,57	-1,40	0,06
S6. Cuir, textile et vêtement	7,88	1,30	5,81	1,90	-2,07	0,60
S14. Pétrole raffiné, prod. chimiques et non métall.	5,61	0,92	3,36	1,10	-2,25	0,18
S9. Métaux primaires et fabrication métallique	10,49	1,72	7,26	2,37	-3,23	0,65
S2. Mines, sauf le pétrole et le gaz	5,18	0,85	1,08	0,35	-4,10	-0,50
S1. Agriculture, forêt, pêche et piégeage	13,92	2,29	3,69	1,21	-10,22	-1,08
TOTAL	100,00	16,44	100,00	32,69	0,00	16,25

Tableau 13C Parts de l'emploi, 1961 et 1997, groupes de 24 industries, classement selon l'emploi lié à l'importation en % de l'emploi total

Agrégation au niveau de 24 industries	1961		1997		Variation 1961–1997	
	Emploi lié à l'importation en % de l'emploi total lié à l'importation	Emploi lié à l'importation en % de l'emploi total	Emploi lié à l'importation en % de l'emploi total lié à l'importation	Emploi lié à l'importation en % de l'emploi total	Emploi lié à l'importation en % de l'emploi total lié à l'importation	Emploi lié à l'importation en % de l'emploi total
S24. Services personnels et autres	1,97	0,32	11,88	3,88	9,90	3,56
S23. Services aux entreprises	3,13	0,51	10,33	3,38	7,20	2,86
S20. Commerce	5,85	0,96	8,85	2,89	2,99	1,93
S13. Produits électriques et électroniques	6,02	0,99	8,05	2,63	2,03	1,64
S9. Métaux primaires et fabrication métallique	10,49	1,72	7,26	2,37	-3,23	0,65
S11. Véhicules à moteur et pièces	4,67	0,77	6,22	2,03	1,55	1,26
S6. Cuir, textile et vêtement	7,88	1,30	5,81	1,90	-2,07	0,60
S10. Machines	6,31	1,04	5,16	1,69	-1,14	0,65
S15. Autres produits fabriqués	3,95	0,65	4,40	1,44	0,46	0,79
S17. Transport et pipelines	4,51	0,74	4,26	1,39	-0,25	0,65
S21. Finances, assurance et immobilier	2,03	0,33	4,13	1,35	2,11	1,02
S1. Agriculture, forêt, pêche et piégeage	13,92	2,29	3,69	1,21	-10,22	-1,08
S14. Pétrole raffiné, prod. chimiques et non métall.	5,61	0,92	3,36	1,10	-2,25	0,18
S8. Papier, produits connexes et imprimerie	4,45	0,73	3,12	1,02	-1,32	0,29
S5. Produits en caoutchouc et en plastique	1,44	0,24	3,03	0,99	1,58	0,75
S19. Services publics	2,07	0,34	2,35	0,77	0,28	0,43
S4. Aliments, boissons et tabac	2,83	0,47	2,13	0,70	-0,70	0,23
S12. Autre matériel de transport	3,15	0,52	1,75	0,57	-1,40	0,06
S7. Produits en bois et mobilier	1,78	0,29	1,49	0,49	-0,29	0,19
S2. Mines, sauf le pétrole et le gaz	5,18	0,85	1,08	0,35	-4,10	-0,50
S16. Construction	1,47	0,24	1,02	0,33	-0,45	0,09
S3. Pétrole brut et gaz naturel	1,12	0,18	0,48	0,16	-0,64	-0,03
S18. Entreposage	0,17	0,03	0,13	0,04	-0,03	0,02
S22. Redev. gouv. et logements occ. par propr.	0,00	0,00	0,00	0,00	0,00	0,00
TOTAL	100,00	16,44	100,00	32,69	-0,00	16,25

Changements dans les effets sur l'emploi lié aux importations pour certaines périodes choisies

Les tableaux sommaires et détaillés présentés ci-dessus portent sur de très longues périodes, soit de 1961 à 1997 ou de 1961 à 1992. Il est également utile de sélectionner des années intermédiaires afin d'examiner l'impact sur l'emploi lié à l'importation au cours de ces années en notant comment il a pu changer au fil des diverses sous-périodes. Ces résultats sont présentés dans les tableaux 14A à D pour les périodes 1961-1971, 1971-1981, 1981-1991 et 1991-1997. Les tableaux renferment uniquement les données correspondant à l'agrégation au niveau de 24 industries, classées par ordre décroissant du changement observé dans l'emploi lié à l'importation en pourcentage de l'emploi total lié à l'importation. Enfin, un sommaire des changements d'une période à l'autre est présenté au tableau 15.

À l'examen du sommaire des changements survenus d'une période à l'autre (tableau 15), un certain nombre d'observations ressortent : le secteur de l'agriculture, de la forêt et de la pêche a, comme dans le cas des exportations, vu sa « part » de l'emploi lié au remplacement des importations diminuer durant toutes les sous-périodes mais, de loin, la diminution la plus importante s'est produite dans les années 60. Par la suite, le rythme du déclin dans ce secteur a été plus lent et stable, mais il semble qu'il ait à nouveau augmenté au cours des années 90. Par ailleurs, dans le secteur des mines, on constate une diminution de la part de l'emploi lié à l'importation principalement durant les années 60 et les années 90. La pénétration relative des importations dans le secteur des aliments, des boissons et du tabac s'est produite principalement durant les années 60, tandis que le déclin de la pénétration des importations dans le secteur du cuir, des textiles et du vêtement s'est produit au cours des années 60 et des années 70.

Dans l'industrie des métaux et des machines, on observe une forte période de déclin de la pénétration relative des importations durant les années 80. Au cours des années 90, les importations de machines ont rebondi, partiellement stimulées par la très forte demande d'investissement en machinerie. Dans l'industrie des véhicules à moteur et des pièces, on observe une importante hausse de la part de l'emploi lié à l'importation durant les années 60 sous l'effet du Pacte de l'automobile. Depuis, cette augmentation s'est progressivement effritée d'environ la moitié.

Il est intéressant de constater que la hausse de la part de l'emploi lié à l'importation dans l'industrie des produits électriques et électroniques n'est pas un phénomène récent. La moitié de l'augmentation de la part observée s'est produite durant les années 60; cette part a enregistré une baisse durant les années 80 avant d'augmenter à nouveau dans les années 90.

Enfin, comme nous l'avons noté précédemment, les hausses les plus importantes des parts de l'emploi lié à l'importation se situent du côté des grands services. Mais, cela n'est pas non plus un phénomène récent. Ainsi, la principale augmentation de la part de l'emploi lié à l'importation dans l'industrie des services aux entreprises a eu lieu durant les années 60 et les années 70 et, dans l'industrie des finances, durant les années 70. Pour le commerce (principalement le commerce de gros), encore une fois les gains les plus importants au niveau des parts ont été faits durant les années 60 et les années 70. Cependant, pour les services personnels, on observe une augmentation considérable de la part durant les années 80 et un déclin relatif durant les années 90.

Décomposition des changements dans la structure d'emploi des importations, 1961-1997

Comme dans le cas des exportations, il est possible de décomposer les changements dans les parts de l'emploi lié à l'importation entre deux années en diverses composantes : 1) les changements dans les parts des importations, 2) les changements dans le ratio emploi/production, 3) les changements dans les coefficients entrées-sorties et 4) les changements dans les coefficients d'importation.

Nous avons procédé à une décomposition pour différentes périodes, aux niveaux d'agrégation à 24 industries et à 161 industries. Le tableau 16A renferme les résultats de la décomposition des changements qui se sont produits entre 1961 et 1997 au niveau d'agrégation à 24 industries, classées par ordre numérique, tandis que le tableau 16B renferme les mêmes données classées selon l'ordre décroissant des changements observés, du changement positif le plus important au changement négatif le plus important. La décomposition au niveau d'agrégation à 161 industries est présentée à l'appendice 5. Enfin, les tableaux 17A à 17D font voir les décompositions pour l'agrégation à 24 industries et les sous-périodes 1961-1971, 1971-1981, 1981-1991 et 1991-1997, respectivement.

Nous examinerons principalement les résultats du tableau 16B pour la période 1961-1997 au niveau d'agrégation à 24 industries. Il n'est pas étonnant de constater de nombreuses similitudes entre les données de ce tableau et les données équivalentes pour les parts de l'emploi lié à l'exportation (tableau 6B). Cela s'explique partiellement par le fait que les changements survenus entre 1961 et 1997 dans les ratios emploi/production, les coefficients entrées-sorties et les coefficients d'importation sont les mêmes entre ces deux années, peu importe que nous analysions les exportations ou les importations. Seul le premier élément de la décomposition — la part des importations dans le cas présent — diffère. Bien entendu, les résultats présentés dans les autres colonnes ne sont pas identiques en raison de l'emploi de pondérations différentes aux fins de l'agrégation et des interactions différentes avec les parts des exportations et des importations.

Pour les secteurs qui font voir les changements de la part de l'emploi les plus importants, les principales sources sont, comme dans le cas des exportations, les parts des importations elles-mêmes et les coefficients d'importation. Les changements dans le ratio relatif emploi/production et dans les coefficients entrées-sorties jouent un rôle beaucoup moins important.

Il y a toutefois quelques exceptions : les changements dans le ratio emploi/production sont un élément important de l'évolution de la part de l'emploi lié à l'importation dans les industries des services aux entreprises, des produits électriques et électroniques, du papier et, enfin, des métaux primaires. Les changements dans les coefficients entrées-sorties sont importants, encore une fois, dans l'industrie des services aux entreprises et dans celle des métaux primaires.

Pour les autres industries, nous observons divers profils d'influence. Dans certains cas, les parts des importations et les coefficients d'importation se renforcent; dans d'autres cas ils se neutralisent.

Tableau 14A Parts de l'emploi, 1961 et 1971, groupe de 24 industries, classement selon la taille des variations

Agrégation au niveau de 24 industries	1961		1971		Variation 1961–1971	
	Emploi lié à l'importation en % de l'emploi total lié à l'importation	Emploi lié à l'importation en % de l'emploi total	Emploi lié à l'importation en % de l'emploi total lié à l'importation	Emploi lié à l'importation en % de l'emploi total	Emploi lié à l'importation en % de l'emploi total lié à l'importation	Emploi lié à l'importation en % de l'emploi total
S11. Véhicules à moteur et pièces	4,67	0,77	8,39	1,52	3,72	0,75
S23. Services aux entreprises	3,13	0,51	5,76	1,04	2,63	0,53
S20. Commerce	5,85	0,96	7,23	1,31	1,37	0,34
S13. Produits électriques et électroniques	6,02	0,99	7,27	1,31	1,25	0,32
S9. Métaux primaires et fabrication métallique	10,49	1,72	11,69	2,11	1,20	0,39
S21. Finances, assurance et immobilier	2,03	0,33	2,93	0,53	0,90	0,20
S24. Services personnels et autres	1,97	0,32	2,78	0,50	0,81	0,18
S5. Produits en caoutchouc et en plastique	1,44	0,24	2,07	0,37	0,63	0,14
S19. Services publics	2,07	0,34	2,39	0,43	0,32	0,09
S15. Autres produits fabriqués	3,95	0,65	4,19	0,76	0,24	0,11
S22. Redev. gouv. et logements occ. par propr.	0,00	0,00	0,00	0,00	0,00	0,00
S18. Entreposage	0,17	0,03	0,13	0,02	-0,04	-0,00
S10. Machines	6,31	1,04	6,15	1,11	-0,16	0,07
S16. Construction	1,47	0,24	1,15	0,21	-0,32	-0,03
S8. Papier, produits connexes et imprimerie	4,45	0,73	4,09	0,74	-0,36	0,01
S3. Pétrole brut et gaz naturel	1,12	0,18	0,74	0,13	-0,38	-0,05
S14. Pétrole raffiné, prod. chimiques et non métall.	5,61	0,92	5,21	0,94	-0,40	0,02
S7. Produits en bois et mobilier	1,78	0,29	1,37	0,25	-0,41	-0,05
S6. Cuir, textile et vêtement	7,88	1,30	7,38	1,33	-0,50	0,04
S17. Transport et pipelines	4,51	0,74	3,95	0,71	-0,55	-0,03
S4. Aliments, boissons et tabac	2,83	0,47	2,13	0,39	-0,70	-0,08
S12. Autre matériel de transport	3,15	0,52	2,12	0,38	-1,03	-0,13
S2. Mines, sauf le pétrole et le gaz	5,18	0,85	3,06	0,55	-2,12	-0,30
S1. Agriculture, forêt, pêche et piégeage	13,92	2,29	7,81	1,41	-6,11	-0,88
TOTAL	100,00	16,44	100,00	18,07	-0,00	1,63

Tableau 14B Parts de l'emploi, 1971 et 1981, groupe de 24 industries, classement selon la taille des variations

Agrégation au niveau de 24 industries	1971		1981		Variation 1971-1981	
	Emploi lié à l'importation en % de l'emploi total lié à l'importation	Emploi lié à l'importation en % de l'emploi total	Emploi lié à l'importation en % de l'emploi total lié à l'importation	Emploi lié à l'importation en % de l'emploi total	Emploi lié à l'importation en % de l'emploi total lié à l'importation	Emploi lié à l'importation en % de l'emploi total
S23. Services aux entreprises	5,76	1,04	9,24	1,91	3,48	0,87
S21. Finances, assurance et immobilier	2,93	0,53	4,21	0,87	1,28	0,34
S24. Services personnels et autres	2,78	0,50	4,06	0,84	1,28	0,34
S20. Commerce	7,23	1,31	8,23	1,70	1,00	0,40
S12. Autre matériel de transport	2,12	0,38	2,66	0,55	0,54	0,17
S3. Pétrole brut et gaz naturel	0,74	0,13	1,07	0,22	0,33	0,09
S10. Machines	6,15	1,11	6,44	1,33	0,29	0,22
S13. Produits électriques et électroniques	7,27	1,31	7,54	1,56	0,27	0,25
S19. Services publics	2,39	0,43	2,59	0,54	0,21	0,11
S7. Produits en bois et mobilier	1,37	0,25	1,46	0,30	0,10	0,06
S22. Redev. gouv. et logements occ. par propr.	0,00	0,00	0,00	0,00	0,00	0,00
S18. Entreposage	0,13	0,02	0,13	0,03	-0,00	0,00
S5. Produits en caoutchouc et en plastique	2,07	0,37	2,05	0,42	-0,02	0,05
S16. Construction	1,15	0,21	1,10	0,23	-0,05	0,02
S4. Aliments, boissons et tabac	2,13	0,39	2,00	0,41	-0,14	0,03
S17. Transport et pipelines	3,95	0,71	3,68	0,76	-0,28	0,05
S15. Autres produits fabriqués	4,19	0,76	3,85	0,80	-0,34	0,04
S11. Véhicules à moteur et pièces	8,39	1,52	7,77	1,61	-0,62	0,09
S2. Mines, sauf le pétrole et le gaz	3,06	0,55	2,37	0,49	-0,69	-0,06
S8. Papier, produits connexes et imprimerie	4,09	0,74	3,35	0,69	-0,74	-0,05
S14. Pétrole raffiné, prod. chimiques et non métall.	5,21	0,94	4,05	0,84	-1,16	-0,10
S9. Métaux primaires et fabrication métallique	11,69	2,11	10,29	2,13	-1,40	0,02
S6. Cuir, textile et vêtement	7,38	1,33	5,73	1,18	-1,66	-0,15
S1. Agriculture, forêt, pêche et piégeage	7,81	1,41	6,12	1,27	-1,69	-0,14
TOTAL	100,00	18,07	100,00	20,69	0,00	2,62

Tableau 14C Parts de l'emploi, 1981 et 1991, groupe de 24 industries, classement selon la taille des variations

Agrégation au niveau de 24 industries	1981		1991		Variation 1981-1991	
	Emploi lié à l'importation en % de l'emploi total lié à l'importation	Emploi lié à l'importation en % de l'emploi total	Emploi lié à l'importation en % de l'emploi total lié à l'importation	Emploi lié à l'importation en % de l'emploi total	Emploi lié à l'importation en % de l'emploi total lié à l'importation	Emploi lié à l'importation en % de l'emploi total
S24. Services personnels et autres	4,06	0,84	13,18	3,27	9,12	2,43
S17. Transport et pipelines	3,68	0,76	4,12	1,02	0,44	0,26
S5. Produits en caoutchouc et en plastique	2,05	0,42	2,40	0,60	0,35	0,17
S7. Produits en bois et mobilier	1,46	0,30	1,73	0,43	0,27	0,13
S21. Finances, assurance et immobilier	4,21	0,87	4,47	1,11	0,26	0,24
S8. Papier, produits connexes et imprimerie	3,35	0,69	3,54	0,88	0,19	0,19
S4. Aliments, boissons et tabac	2,00	0,41	2,17	0,54	0,18	0,13
S6. Cuir, textile et vêtement	5,73	1,18	5,86	1,46	0,13	0,27
S23. Services aux entreprises	9,24	1,91	9,25	2,30	0,01	0,39
S20. Commerce	8,23	1,70	8,24	2,05	0,01	0,34
S22. Redev. gouv. et logements occ. par propr.	0,00	0,00	0,00	0,00	0,00	0,00
S18. Entreposage	0,13	0,03	0,10	0,03	-0,02	-0,00
S15. Autres produits fabriqués	3,85	0,80	3,76	0,93	-0,09	0,14
S19. Services publics	2,59	0,54	2,40	0,60	-0,20	0,06
S16. Construction	1,10	0,23	0,90	0,22	-0,21	-0,01
S3. Pétrole brut et gaz naturel	1,07	0,22	0,64	0,16	-0,43	-0,06
S14. Pétrole raffiné, prod. chimiques et non métall.	4,05	0,84	3,60	0,90	-0,45	0,06
S1. Agriculture, forêt, pêche et piégeage	6,12	1,27	5,49	1,36	-0,63	0,10
S13. Produits électriques et électroniques	7,54	1,56	6,77	1,68	-0,76	0,12
S12. Autre matériel de transport	2,66	0,55	1,56	0,39	-1,10	-0,16
S11. Véhicules à moteur et pièces	7,77	1,61	6,67	1,66	-1,10	0,05
S2. Mines, sauf le pétrole et le gaz	2,37	0,49	1,15	0,29	-1,22	-0,21
S10. Machines	6,44	1,33	4,11	1,02	-2,33	-0,31
S9. Métaux primaires et fabrication métallique	10,29	2,13	7,87	1,95	-2,42	-0,17
TOTAL	100,00	20,69	100,00	24,84	0,00	4,15

Tableau 14D Parts de l'emploi, 1991 et 1997, groupe de 24 industries, classement selon la taille des variations

Agrégation au niveau de 24 industries	1991		1997		Variation 1991–1997	
	Emploi lié à l'importation en % de l'emploi total lié à l'importation	Emploi lié à l'importation en % de l'emploi total	Emploi lié à l'importation en % de l'emploi total lié à l'importation	Emploi lié à l'importation en % de l'emploi total	Emploi lié à l'importation en % de l'emploi total lié à l'importation	Emploi lié à l'importation en % de l'emploi total
S13. Produits électriques et électroniques	6,77	1,68	8,05	2,63	1,28	0,95
S23. Services aux entreprises	9,25	2,30	10,33	3,38	1,08	1,08
S10. Machines	4,11	1,02	5,16	1,69	1,05	0,67
S15. Autres produits fabriqués	3,76	0,93	4,40	1,44	0,65	0,51
S5. Produits en caoutchouc et en plastique	2,40	0,60	3,03	0,99	0,63	0,39
S20. Commerce	8,24	2,05	8,85	2,89	0,61	0,85
S12. Autre matériel de transport	1,56	0,39	1,75	0,57	0,19	0,18
S17. Transport et pipelines	4,12	1,02	4,26	1,39	0,14	0,37
S16. Construction	0,90	0,22	1,02	0,33	0,13	0,11
S18. Entreposage	0,10	0,03	0,13	0,04	0,03	0,02
S22. Redev. gouv. et logements occ. par propr.	0,00	0,00	0,00	0,00	0,00	0,00
S4. Aliments, boissons et tabac	2,17	0,54	2,13	0,70	-0,04	0,16
S6. Cuir, textile et vêtement	5,86	1,46	5,81	1,90	-0,04	0,45
S19. Services publics	2,40	0,60	2,35	0,77	-0,05	0,17
S2. Mines, sauf le pétrole et le gaz	1,15	0,29	1,08	0,35	-0,07	0,07
S3. Pétrole brut et gaz naturel	0,64	0,16	0,48	0,16	-0,17	-0,00
S7. Produits en bois et mobilier	1,73	0,43	1,49	0,49	-0,24	0,06
S14. Pétrole raffiné, prod. chimiques et non métall.	3,60	0,90	3,36	1,10	-0,25	0,20
S21. Finances, assurance et immobilier	4,47	1,11	4,13	1,35	-0,34	0,24
S8. Papier, produits connexes et imprimerie	3,54	0,88	3,12	1,02	-0,42	0,14
S11. Véhicules à moteur et pièces	6,67	1,66	6,22	2,03	-0,45	0,38
S9. Métaux primaires et fabrication métallique	7,87	1,95	7,26	2,37	-0,61	0,42
S24. Services personnels et autres	13,18	3,27	11,88	3,88	-1,30	0,61
S1. Agriculture, forêt, pêche et piégeage	5,49	1,36	3,69	1,21	-1,80	-0,16
TOTAL	100,00	24,84	100,00	32,69	-0,00	7,85

Tableau 15 Parts de l'emploi, variations de 1961 à 1997, groupe de 24 industries

Emploi lié à l'importation en pourcentage de l'emploi total lié à l'importation

Agrégation au niveau de 24 industries	1961–1997	1961–1971	1971–1981	1981–1991	1991–1997
S1. Agriculture, forêt, pêche et piégeage	-10,2	-6,1	-1,7	-0,6	-1,8
S2. Mines, sauf le pétrole et le gaz	-4,1	-2,1	-0,7	-1,2	-0,1
S3. Pétrole brut et gaz naturel	-0,6	-0,4	0,3	-0,4	-0,2
S4. Aliments, boissons et tabac	-0,7	-0,7	-0,1	0,2	-0,0
S5. Produits en caoutchouc et en plastique	1,6	0,6	-0,0	0,3	0,6
S6. Cuir, textile et vêtement	-2,1	-0,5	-1,7	0,1	-0,0
S7. Produits en bois et mobilier	-0,3	-0,4	0,1	0,3	-0,2
S8. Papier, produits connexes et imprimerie	-1,3	-0,4	-0,7	0,2	-0,4
S9. Métaux primaires et fabrication métallique	-3,2	1,2	-1,4	-2,4	-0,6
S10. Machines	-1,1	-0,2	0,3	-2,3	1,1
S11. Véhicules à moteur et pièces	1,5	3,7	-0,6	-1,1	-0,5
S12. Autre matériel de transport	-1,4	-1,0	0,5	-1,1	0,2
S13. Produits électriques et électroniques	2,0	1,3	0,3	-0,8	1,3
S14. Pétrole raffiné, prod. chimiques et non métall.	-2,2	-0,4	-1,2	-0,4	-0,2
S15. Autres produits fabriqués	0,5	0,2	-0,3	-0,1	0,6
S16. Construction	-0,4	-0,3	-0,0	-0,2	0,1
S17. Transport et pipelines	-0,3	-0,6	-0,3	0,4	0,1
S18. Entreposage	-0,0	-0,0	-0,0	-0,0	0,0
S19. Services publics	0,3	0,3	0,2	-0,2	-0,1
S20. Commerce	3,0	1,4	1,0	0,0	0,6
S21. Finances, assurance et immobilier	2,1	0,9	1,3	0,3	-0,3
S22. Redev. gouv. et logements occ. par propr.	0,0	0,0	0,0	0,0	0,0
S23. Services aux entreprises	7,2	2,6	3,5	0,0	1,1
S24. Services personnels et autres	9,9	0,8	1,3	9,1	-1,3

Tableau 16A Décomposition des variations des parts de l'emploi, 1961-1997, groupe de 24 industries

	1961	1997	Variation 1961-1997	Attribuable à :				
	Emploi lié à l'importation en % de l'emploi total lié à l'importation	Emploi lié à l'importation en % de l'emploi total lié à l'importation	Emploi lié à l'importation en % de l'emploi total lié à l'importation	Variation de la part des importations	Variation du ratio emploi/production	Variation des coefficients entrées-sorties	Variation des coefficients d'importation	Interaction résiduelle
S1. Agriculture, forêt, pêche et piégeage	13,92	3,69	-10,22	-5,10	-0,64	0,30	-3,08	-1,70
S2. Mines, sauf le pétrole et le gaz	5,18	1,08	-4,10	-1,22	-0,09	-0,10	-0,89	-1,80
S3. Pétrole brut et gaz naturel	1,12	0,48	-0,64	-0,42	0,01	0,03	-0,26	-0,00
S4. Aliments, boissons et tabac	2,83	2,13	-0,70	-1,19	-0,21	0,11	-0,01	0,60
S5. Produits en caoutchouc et en plastique	1,44	3,03	1,58	1,20	0,03	-0,29	0,46	0,18
S6. Cuir, textile et vêtement	7,88	5,81	-2,07	-1,72	-0,58	-0,02	0,64	-0,38
S7. Produits en bois et mobilier	1,78	1,49	-0,29	-0,05	-0,19	0,06	-0,18	0,06
S8. Papier, produits connexes et imprimerie	4,45	3,12	-1,32	-0,82	-0,79	-0,04	-0,20	0,53
S9. Métaux primaires et fabrication métallique	10,49	7,26	-3,23	-2,00	-0,88	-0,90	-0,56	1,11
S10. Machines	6,31	5,16	-1,14	-1,33	-0,39	0,19	-0,28	0,67
S11. Véhicules à moteur et pièces	4,67	6,22	1,55	2,71	-0,33	-0,02	-2,92	2,11
S12. Autre matériel de transport	3,15	1,75	-1,40	-0,83	-0,15	-0,15	-0,46	0,19
S13. Produits électriques et électroniques	6,02	8,05	2,03	3,73	1,18	0,37	-3,41	0,16
S14. Pétrole raffiné, prod. chimiques et non métall.	5,61	3,36	-2,25	-0,83	-0,26	-0,20	-1,46	0,50
S15. Autres produits fabriqués	3,95	4,40	0,46	-0,16	-0,17	0,09	0,48	0,22
S16. Construction	1,47	1,02	-0,45	-0,20	-0,40	-0,04	-0,05	0,25
S17. Transport et pipelines	4,51	4,26	-0,25	0,71	-0,31	-0,22	0,11	-0,54
S18. Entreposage	0,17	0,13	-0,03	-0,05	-0,15	-0,00	0,06	0,11
S19. Services publics	2,07	2,35	0,28	-0,06	0,60	-0,10	-0,88	0,71
S20. Commerce	5,85	8,85	2,99	-0,64	-0,19	-0,37	2,48	1,72
S21. Finances, assurance et immobilier	2,03	4,13	2,11	0,51	0,67	-0,01	0,41	0,54
S22. Redev. gouv. et logements occ. par propr.	0,00	0,00	0,00	0,00	0,00	0,00	0,00	0,00
S23. Services aux entreprises	3,13	10,33	7,20	1,47	3,04	1,02	3,61	-1,94
S24. Services personnels et autres	1,97	11,88	9,90	6,31	0,18	0,31	6,39	-3,29
TOTAL	100,00	100,00	-0,00	0,00	-0,00	-0,00	0,00	0,00

Tableau 16B Décomposition des variations des parts de l'emploi, 1961–1997, groupe de 24 industries

Classement selon la taille des variations	1961 Emploi lié à l'importation en % de l'emploi total lié à l'importation	1997 Emploi lié à l'importation en % de l'emploi total lié à l'importation	Variation 1961-1997 Emploi lié à l'importation en % de l'emploi total lié à l'importation	Attribuable à : Variation de la part des importations	Variation du ratio emploi/ production	Variation des coefficients entrées-sorties	Variation des coefficients d'importation	Interaction résiduelle
S24. Services personnels et autres	1,97	11,88	9,90	6,31	0,18	0,31	6,39	-3,29
S23. Services aux entreprises	3,13	10,33	7,20	1,47	3,04	1,02	3,61	-1,94
S20. Commerce	5,85	8,85	2,99	-0,64	-0,19	-0,37	2,48	1,72
S21. Finances, assurance et immobilier	2,03	4,13	2,11	0,51	0,67	-0,01	0,41	0,54
S13. Produits électriques et électroniques	6,02	8,05	2,03	3,73	1,18	0,37	-3,41	0,16
S5. Produits en caoutchouc et en plastique	1,44	3,03	1,58	1,20	0,03	-0,29	0,46	0,18
S11. Véhicules à moteur et pièces	4,67	6,22	1,55	2,71	-0,33	-0,02	-2,92	2,11
S15. Autres produits fabriqués	3,95	4,40	0,46	-0,16	-0,17	0,09	0,48	0,22
S19. Services publics	2,07	2,35	0,28	-0,06	0,60	-0,10	-0,88	0,71
S22. Redev. gouv. et logements occ. par propr.	0,00	0,00	0,00	0,00	0,00	0,00	0,00	0,00
S18. Entreposage	0,17	0,13	-0,03	-0,05	-0,15	-0,00	0,06	0,11
S17. Transport et pipelines	4,51	4,26	-0,25	0,71	-0,31	-0,22	0,11	-0,54
S7. Produits en bois et mobilier	1,78	1,49	-0,29	-0,05	-0,19	0,06	-0,18	0,06
S16. Construction	1,47	1,02	-0,45	-0,20	-0,40	0,06	-0,05	0,25
S3. Pétrole brut et gaz naturel	1,12	0,48	-0,64	-0,42	0,01	0,03	-0,26	-0,00
S4. Aliments, boissons et tabac	2,83	2,13	-0,70	-1,19	-0,21	0,11	-0,01	0,60
S10. Machines	6,31	5,16	-1,14	-1,33	-0,39	0,19	-0,28	0,67
S8. Papier, produits connexes et imprimerie	4,45	3,12	-1,32	-0,82	-0,79	-0,04	-0,20	0,53
S12. Autre matériel de transport	3,15	1,75	-1,40	-0,83	-0,15	-0,15	-0,46	0,19
S6. Cuir, textile et vêtement	7,88	5,81	-2,07	-1,72	-0,58	-0,15	0,64	-0,38
S14. Pétrole raffiné, prod. chimiques et non métall.	5,61	3,36	-2,25	-0,83	-0,26	-0,20	-1,46	0,50
S9. Métaux primaires et fabrication métallique	10,49	7,26	-3,23	-2,00	-0,88	-0,90	-0,56	1,11
S2. Mines, sauf le pétrole et le gaz	5,18	1,08	-4,10	-1,22	-0,09	-0,10	-0,89	-1,80
S1. Agriculture, forêt, pêche et piégeage	13,92	3,69	-10,22	-5,10	-0,64	0,30	-3,08	-1,70
TOTAL	100,00	100,00	-0,00	0,00	-0,00	-0,00	0,00	0,00

Tableau 17A Décomposition des variations des parts de l'emploi, 1961–1971, groupe de 24 industries

Classement selon la taille des variations	1961 — Emploi lié à l'importation en % de l'emploi total lié à l'importation	1971 — Emploi lié à l'importation en % de l'emploi total lié à l'importation	Variation 1961–1971 — Emploi lié à l'importation en % de l'emploi total lié à l'importation	Variation de la part des importations	Attribuable à : Variation du ratio emploi/ production	Variation des coefficients entrées-sorties	Variation des coefficients d'importation	Interaction résiduelle
S11. Véhicules à moteur et pièces	4.67	8.39	3.72	4.76	0.03	-0.63	-1.87	1.42
S23. Services aux entreprises	3.13	5.76	2.63	0.97	1.09	0.30	0.99	-0.72
S20. Commerce	5.85	7.23	1.37	0.43	-0.09	-0.05	0.90	0.19
S13. Produits électriques et électroniques	6.02	7.27	1.25	0.80	0.02	-0.18	0.59	0.02
S9. Métaux primaires et fabrication métallique	10.49	11.69	1.20	0.43	0.04	-0.19	0.74	0.18
S21. Finances, assurance et immobilier	2.03	2.93	0.90	0.37	0.22	0.01	0.36	-0.07
S24. Services personnels et autres	1.97	2.78	0.81	0.21	-0.01	0.02	0.65	-0.06
S5. Produits en caoutchouc et en plastique	1.44	2.07	0.63	0.51	0.12	-0.02	0.05	-0.04
S19. Services publics	2.07	2.39	0.32	0.06	0.11	0.01	0.07	0.06
S15. Autres produits fabriqués	3.95	4.19	0.24	0.18	0.02	0.04	0.05	-0.05
S22. Redev. gouv. et logements occ. par propr.	0.00	0.00	0.00	0.00	0.00	0.00	0.00	0.00
S18. Entreposage	0.17	0.13	-0.04	-0.02	-0.03	0.00	0.01	0.01
S10. Machines	6.31	6.15	-0.16	0.09	0.05	0.11	-0.37	-0.04
S16. Construction	1.47	1.15	-0.32	-0.11	-0.13	0.02	-0.19	0.09
S8. Papier, produits connexes et imprimerie	4.45	4.09	-0.36	-0.50	-0.13	0.06	0.39	0.14
S3. Pétrole brut et gaz naturel	1.12	0.74	-0.38	-0.24	-0.45	0.03	-0.15	-0.03
S14. Pétrole raffiné, prod. chimiques et non métall.	5.61	5.21	-0.40	-0.69	0.01	0.07	0.34	0.09
S7. Produits en bois et mobilier	1.78	1.37	-0.41	-0.35	-0.20	0.04	-0.06	-0.00
S6. Cuir, textile et vêtement	7.88	7.38	-0.50	-0.80	-0.03	0.09	-0.06	-0.00
S17. Transport et pipelines	4.51	3.95	-0.55	-0.06	-0.13	0.09	0.25	0.10
S4. Aliments, boissons et tabac	2.83	2.13	-0.70	-0.92	-0.16	0.02	-0.40	0.04
S12. Autre matériel de transport	3.15	2.12	-1.03	-1.00	-0.04	0.06	0.11	0.09
S2. Mines, sauf le pétrole et le gaz	5.18	3.06	-2.12	-0.87	0.12	0.00	-0.71	-0.66
S1. Agriculture, forêt, pêche et piégeage	13.92	7.81	-6.11	-3.27	-0.53	0.24	-1.68	-0.87

Tableau 17B Décomposition des variations des parts de l'emploi, 1971–1981, groupe de 24 industries

Classement selon la taille des variations	1971	1981	Variation 1971-1981	Attribuable à :				
	Emploi lié à l'importation en % de l'emploi total lié à l'importation	Emploi lié à l'importation en % de l'emploi total lié à l'importation	Emploi lié à l'importation en % de l'emploi total lié à l'importation	Variation de la part des importations	Variation du ratio emploi /production	Variation des coefficients entrées-sorties	Variation des coefficients d'importation	Interaction résiduelle
S23. Services aux entreprises	5,76	9,24	3,48	0,81	0,53	0,15	2,26	-0,27
S21. Finances, assurance et immobilier	2,93	4,21	1,28	0,33	0,10	0,03	0,94	-0,12
S24. Services personnels et autres	2,78	4,06	1,28	-0,09	0,21	0,06	1,19	-0,10
S20. Commerce	7,23	8,23	1,00	0,32	-0,52	-0,05	1,31	-0,07
S12. Autre matériel de transport	2,12	2,66	0,54	0,68	0,02	0,06	-0,36	0,14
S3. Pétrole brut et gaz naturel	0,74	1,07	0,33	0,51	0,12	0,04	-0,74	0,40
S10. Machines	6,15	6,44	0,29	0,37	0,11	0,11	-0,19	-0,10
S13. Produits électriques et électroniques	7,27	7,54	0,27	0,94	0,04	-0,13	-0,63	0,04
S19. Services publics	2,39	2,59	0,21	0,06	0,04	0,01	0,07	0,03
S7. Produits en bois et mobilier	1,37	1,46	0,10	0,16	-0,01	-0,02	-0,02	-0,04
S22. Redev. gouv. et logements occ. par propr.	0,00	0,00	0,00	0,00	0,00	0,01	0,00	0,00
S18. Entreposage	0,13	0,13	-0,00	-0,00	-0,04	0,00	0,03	0,01
S5. Produits en caoutchouc et en plastique	2,07	2,05	-0,02	-0,10	0,03	0,00	0,04	0,01
S16. Construction	1,15	1,10	-0,05	0,15	-0,17	0,00	-0,14	0,12
S4. Aliments, boissons et tabac	2,13	2,00	-0,14	-0,09	0,05	0,04	-0,10	-0,03
S17. Transport et pipelines	3,95	3,68	-0,28	-0,09	-0,31	-0,01	0,25	-0,12
S15. Autres produits fabriqués	4,19	3,85	-0,34	-0,45	0,05	0,03	-0,02	0,03
S11. Véhicules à moteur et pièces	8,39	7,77	-0,62	-1,96	0,01	-0,08	1,25	0,15
S2. Mines, sauf le pétrole et le gaz	3,06	2,37	-0,69	0,56	-0,19	-0,19	-1,40	0,54
S8. Papier, produits connexes et imprimerie	4,09	3,35	-0,74	-0,35	-0,09	0,03	-0,29	-0,03
S14. Pétrole raffiné, prod. chimiques et non métall.	5,21	4,05	-1,16	-0,34	0,31	0,13	-1,49	0,24
S9. Métaux primaires et fabrication métallique	11,69	10,29	-1,40	-0,05	-0,15	-0,43	-0,49	-0,28
S6. Cuir, textile et vêtement	7,38	5,73	-1,66	-1,09	-0,21	0,09	-0,14	-0,31
S1. Agriculture, forêt, pêche et piégeage	7,81	6,12	-1,69	-0,28	0,06	0,10	-1,32	-0,24

Tableau 17C Décomposition des variations des parts de l'emploi, 1981–1991, groupe de 24 industries

Classement selon la taille des variations	1981 Emploi lié à l'importation en % de l'emploi total lié à l'importation	1991 Emploi lié à l'importation en % de l'emploi total lié à l'importation	Variation 1981–1991 Emploi lié à l'importation en % de l'emploi total lié à l'importation	Attribuable à : Variation de la part des importations	Variation du ratio emploi/ production	Variation des coefficients entrées-sorties	Variation des coefficients d'importation	Interaction résiduelle
S24. Services personnels et autres	4,06	13,18	9,12	8,40	0,08	-0,12	1,19	-0,43
S17. Transport et pipelines	3,68	4,12	0,44	1,03	-0,15	-0,13	-0,30	-0,02
S5. Produits en caoutchouc et en plastique	2,05	2,40	0,35	0,19	0,02	-0,11	0,38	-0,12
S7. Produits en bois et mobilier	1,46	1,73	0,27	0,35	-0,08	-0,00	0,15	-0,15
S21. Finances, assurance et immobilier	4,21	4,47	0,26	0,30	0,71	0,01	-1,09	0,34
S8. Papier, produits connexes et imprimerie	3,35	3,54	0,20	0,54	-0,17	-0,10	0,05	-0,12
S4. Aliments, boissons et tabac	2,00	2,17	0,18	0,30	-0,15	-0,01	0,05	-0,01
S6. Cuir, textile et vêtement	5,73	5,86	0,13	0,35	-0,28	-0,14	0,44	-0,25
S23. Services aux entreprises	9,24	9,25	0,01	-0,25	0,83	0,28	-0,78	-0,06
S20. Commerce	8,23	8,24	0,01	-1,18	0,94	0,04	0,14	0,07
S22. Redev. gouv. et logements occ. par propr.	0,00	0,00	0,00	0,00	0,00	0,00	0,00	0,00
S18. Entreposage	0,13	0,10	-0,02	-0,01	-0,02	0,00	0,01	0,00
S15. Autres produits fabriqués	3,85	3,76	-0,09	-0,18	-0,18	-0,02	0,39	-0,10
S19. Services publics	2,59	2,40	-0,20	-0,03	0,40	-0,02	-0,70	0,16
S16. Construction	1,10	0,90	-0,21	-0,18	-0,11	-0,00	0,13	-0,05
S3. Pétrole brut et gaz naturel	1,07	0,64	-0,43	-1,08	-0,17	0,04	0,29	0,50
S1. Agriculture, forêt, pêche et piégeage	4,05	3,60	-0,45	-0,01	-0,27	-0,19	0,11	-0,09
S14. Pétrole raffiné, prod. chimiques et non métall.	6,12	5,49	-0,63	-1,38	-0,25	0,10	0,68	0,22
S13. Produits électriques et électroniques	7,54	6,77	-0,76	1,28	0,02	-0,34	-2,08	0,36
S12. Autre matériel de transport	2,66	1,56	-1,10	-0,82	-0,03	0,05	-0,08	-0,21
S11. Véhicules à moteur et pièces	7,77	6,67	-1,10	-0,34	-0,19	0,48	-0,67	-0,39
S2. Mines, sauf le pétrole et le gaz	2,37	1,15	-1,22	-1,32	-0,10	0,14	0,01	0,05
S10. Machines	6,44	4,11	-2,33	-3,22	-0,23	0,04	0,65	0,43
S9. Métaux primaires et fabrication métallique	10,29	7,87	-2,42	-2,74	-0,58	0,01	1,03	-0,14

Tableau 17D Décomposition des variations des parts de l'emploi, 1991–1997, groupe de 24 industries

Classement selon la taille des variations	1991 — Emploi lié à l'importation en % de l'emploi total lié à l'importation	1997 — Emploi lié à l'importation en % de l'emploi total lié à l'importation	Variation 1991-1997 — Emploi lié à l'importation en % de l'emploi total lié à l'importation	Variation de la part des importations	Variation du ratio emploi/ production	Attribuable à : Variation des coefficients entrées- sorties	Variation des coefficients d'importation	Interaction résiduelle
S13. Produits électriques et électroniques	6,77	8,05	1,28	2,44	1,39	1,30	0,18	4,03
S23. Services aux entreprises	9,25	10,33	1,08	-0,30	-0,00	-0,07	1,06	0,39
S10. Machines	4,11	5,16	1,05	1,34	-0,00	-0,02	-0,48	0,30
S15. Autres produits fabriqués	3,76	4,40	0,65	0,58	0,10	0,07	0,29	-0,39
S5. Produits en caoutchouc et en plastique	2,40	3,03	0,63	0,66	-0,04	0,07	0,17	0,06
S20. Commerce	8,24	8,85	0,61	0,00	-0,27	-0,23	0,67	0,37
S12. Autre matériel de transport	1,56	1,75	0,19	0,29	-0,03	-0,17	-0,02	0,10
S17. Transport et pipelines	4,12	4,26	0,14	-0,32	-0,06	-0,15	0,38	0,24
S16. Construction	0,90	1,02	0,14	-0,01	-0,01	-0,10	0,14	0,05
S18. Entreposage	0,10	0,13	0,03	-0,00	-0,01	-0,04	0,05	0,01
S22. Redev., gouv., et logements occ. par propr.	0,00	0,00	0,00	0,00	0,00	0,00	0,00	0,00
S4. Aliments, boissons et tabac	2,17	2,13	-0,04	-0,23	-0,01	0,03	0,08	0,09
S6. Cuir, textile et vêtement	5,86	5,81	-0,04	-0,52	-0,12	-0,11	0,43	0,26
S19. Services publics	2,40	2,35	-0,05	0,02	0,02	-0,06	-0,13	0,09
S2. Mines, sauf le pétrole et le gaz	1,15	1,08	-0,07	0,07	-0,02	-0,05	-0,05	0,05
S3. Pétrole brut et gaz naturel	0,64	0,48	-0,17	0,00	-0,00	-0,04	-0,14	0,02
S7. Produits en bois et mobilier	1,73	1,49	-0,24	-0,09	-0,04	0,01	-0,15	0,03
S14. Pétrole raffiné, prod. chimiques et non métall.	3,60	3,36	-0,25	0,26	-0,04	-0,17	-0,50	0,03
S21. Finances, assurance et immobilier	4,47	4,13	-0,34	-0,37	-0,26	-0,05	0,13	0,21
S8. Papier, produits connexes et imprimerie	3,54	3,12	-0,42	-0,33	-0,12	-0,04	-0,08	0,16
S11. Véhicules à moteur et pièces	6,67	6,22	-0,45	0,57	-0,09	0,14	-1,37	0,29
S9. Métaux primaires et fabrication métallique	7,87	7,26	-0,61	0,80	-0,14	-0,43	-1,28	0,45
S24. Services personnels et autres	13,18	11,88	-1,30	-4,20	-0,11	0,17	1,73	1,10
S1. Agriculture, forêt, pêche et piégeage	5,49	3,69	-1,80	-0,67	-0,07	0,08	-1,10	-0,03

Évolution de la composition professionnelle des importations canadiennes

Comme dans le cas des exportations, nous pouvons maintenant appliquer les parts de la scolarité par industrie aux effets sur l'emploi pour nous faire une idée du profil de scolarité (au Canada) de l'emploi « déplacé » par les importations. Les résultats pour les années autres que l'intervalle 1981-1991 doivent être vus comme étant simplement indicatifs parce qu'ils traduisent uniquement les changements dans la composition de l'emploi par secteur et non les changements dans le profil de scolarité des diverses industries.

Le lecteur est invité à consulter la rubrique Évolution de la composition professionnelle des exportations canadiennes ci-dessus, qui renferme une description plus détaillée des données de base du SPPC et une liste des parts de la scolarité pour les 112 industries disponibles au niveau de désagrégation le plus détaillé. Ces données ont été agrégées au niveau de 24 industries en utilisant les facteurs de pondération de l'emploi lié à l'importation des tableaux 18A et 18B, respectivement, pour les années 1991 et 1986.

Le tableau 19A renferme les résultats des calculs des parts de la scolarité pour les importations, tandis que le tableau 10B, présenté précédemment au chapitre 4, fait voir les parts correspondantes pour l'ensemble du secteur des entreprises. Les séries présentées au tableau 19A sont reproduites à la figure 21.

Comme pour les exportations, la principale préoccupation ne vise pas les parts absolues de la scolarité liée aux importations au cours de la période 1961-1997, mais plutôt la façon dont elles se comparent à l'ensemble de l'économie. Les ratios des parts de la scolarité liée aux importations à celles de l'ensemble du secteur des entreprises sont présentés au tableau 19B et les séries de ce tableau sont reproduites aux figures 22 et 23. Celles-ci sont examinées d'abord, puis comparées aux résultats obtenus pour les exportations présentés au tableaux 10C et aux figures 11 et 12.

Le tableau 19B et les figures 22 et 23 font ressortir assez clairement que, sur l'ensemble de la période, le contenu en scolarité des importations canadiennes a été — du moins selon la technologie canadienne et les parts de la scolarité par secteur — *supérieur* à la moyenne du secteur des entreprises. Cependant, au cours des dernières années, on observe des signes évidents d'une diminution de l'écart par rapport au niveau de scolarité moyen associé à la production canadienne. Cela indiquerait un déplacement relativement plus important des emplois occupés par des Canadiens peu qualifiés par des importations ces dernières années, mais la moyenne pour l'ensemble des importations demeure supérieure au niveau moyen des compétences au Canada.

Comme on peut le voir à la figure 22, la part des employés n'ayant qu'une formation secondaire dans l'emploi lié à l'importation n'a représenté qu'environ 0.95 p. 100 de la part correspondante du secteur des entreprises presque sans interruption depuis 1961. Durant la plus grande partie de la période écoulée depuis 1961, la part des employés liés aux « importations » qui ne possédaient pas de diplôme d'études secondaires a aussi été légèrement inférieure à celle de l'ensemble du secteur des entreprises; mais ce ratio s'est modifié vers 1990, de sorte que la part des employés n'ayant pas un diplôme d'études secondaires parmi le contingent lié aux « importations » était légèrement supérieure à la moyenne de l'ensemble du secteur des entreprises. La même année, il y a eu un déplacement de la proportion relative d'employés possédant un diplôme d'école de métier — l'emploi lié à l'importation passant d'un niveau légèrement supérieur à un niveau légèrement inférieur à la moyenne du secteur des entreprises. Comme il ressort de la figure 23, les parts correspondant à une scolarité postsecondaire parmi les personnes dont l'emploi est lié aux importations ont systématiquement dépassé la moyenne du secteur des entreprises. Cependant, toutes ces valeurs ont convergé vers la moyenne du secteur des entreprises à compter de la fin des années 80.

Tableau 18A Parts des importations selon le niveau de scolarité/compétence, 1991, groupe de 24 industries (pondération de l'emploi lié aux importations)

Agrégation au niveau de 24 industries	Secondaire non terminé	Études secondaires	Certificat ou diplôme professionnel	Diplôme d'études post-secondaires non universitaires	Études universitaires jusqu'au baccalauréat	Tous les diplômes d'études supérieures
S1. Agriculture, forêt, pêche et piégeage	0,53	0,21	0,10	0,08	0,05	0,02
S2. Mines, sauf le pétrole et le gaz	0,38	0,20	0,23	0,11	0,06	0,02
S3. Pétrole brut et gaz naturel	0,14	0,21	0,17	0,18	0,23	0,07
S4. Aliments, boissons et tabac	0,44	0,26	0,12	0,09	0,07	0,02
S5. Produits en caoutchouc et en plastique	0,41	0,27	0,14	0,11	0,06	0,02
S6. Cuir, textile et vêtement	0,53	0,25	0,09	0,07	0,05	0,01
S7. Produits en bois et mobilier	0,45	0,25	0,15	0,09	0,04	0,01
S8. Papier, produits connexes et imprimerie	0,30	0,30	0,15	0,14	0,10	0,02
S9. Métaux primaires et fabrication métallique	0,34	0,23	0,23	0,12	0,06	0,01
S10. Machines	0,29	0,23	0,22	0,16	0,08	0,02
S11. Véhicules à moteur et pièces	0,42	0,26	0,14	0,10	0,06	0,01
S12. Autre matériel de transport	0,22	0,21	0,23	0,19	0,11	0,03
S13. Produits électriques et électroniques	0,25	0,24	0,12	0,19	0,15	0,05
S14. Pétrole raffiné, prod. chimiques et non métall.	0,28	0,27	0,14	0,14	0,13	0,04
S15. Autres produits fabriqués	0,33	0,27	0,13	0,15	0,09	0,02
S16. Construction	0,37	0,23	0,25	0,10	0,05	0,01
S17. Transport et pipelines	0,38	0,26	0,16	0,12	0,06	0,01
S18. Entreposage	0,38	0,33	0,12	0,09	0,05	0,02
S19. Services publics	0,19	0,30	0,16	0,19	0,12	0,03
S20. Commerce	0,32	0,32	0,13	0,13	0,08	0,02
S21. Finances, assurance et immobilier	0,16	0,34	0,10	0,19	0,17	0,04
S22. Redev. gouv. et logements occ. par propr.	0,00	0,00	0,00	0,00	0,00	0,00
S23. Services aux entreprises	0,12	0,22	0,09	0,20	0,26	0,11
S24. Services personnels et autres	0,40	0,30	0,09	0,11	0,08	0,03
TOTAL	0,33	0,26	0,14	0,13	0,10	0,03

Tableau 18B Parts des importations selon le niveau de scolarité/compétence, 1986, groupe de 24 industries
(pondération de l'emploi lié aux importations)

Agrégation au niveau de 24 industries	Secondaire non terminé	Études secondaires	Certificat ou diplôme professionnel	Diplôme d'études post-secondaires non universitaires	Études universitaires jusqu'au baccalauréat	Tous les diplômes d'études supérieures
S1. Agriculture, forêt, pêche et piégeage	0.58	0.20	0.08	0.07	0.05	0.01
S2. Mines, sauf le pétrole et le gaz	0.41	0.20	0.22	0.09	0.06	0.01
S3. Pétrole brut et gaz naturel	0.16	0.23	0.14	0.17	0.24	0.06
S4. Aliments, boissons et tabac	0.49	0.24	0.10	0.08	0.07	0.01
S5. Produits en caoutchouc et en plastique	0.44	0.28	0.13	0.09	0.06	0.01
S6. Cuir, textile et vêtement	0.57	0.24	0.08	0.06	0.04	0.01
S7. Produits en bois et mobilier	0.51	0.24	0.14	0.07	0.03	0.01
S8. Papier, produits connexes et imprimerie	0.33	0.31	0.15	0.12	0.08	0.02
S9. Métaux primaires et fabrication métallique	0.38	0.25	0.20	0.11	0.05	0.01
S10. Machines	0.30	0.25	0.22	0.15	0.07	0.02
S11. Véhicules à moteur et pièces	0.45	0.26	0.14	0.09	0.05	0.01
S12. Autre matériel de transport	0.26	0.25	0.21	0.16	0.09	0.03
S13. Produits électriques et électroniques	0.28	0.26	0.11	0.18	0.13	0.04
S14. Pétrole raffiné, prod. chimiques et non métall.	0.31	0.27	0.13	0.13	0.13	0.03
S15. Autres produits fabriqués	0.37	0.28	0.12	0.13	0.08	0.02
S16. Construction	0.41	0.23	0.24	0.08	0.04	0.01
S17. Transport et pipelines	0.46	0.26	0.14	0.09	0.04	0.01
S18. Entreposage	0.46	0.31	0.11	0.08	0.05	0.01
S19. Services publics	0.23	0.31	0.14	0.16	0.10	0.03
S20. Commerce	0.35	0.33	0.13	0.16	0.07	0.01
S21. Finances, assurance et immobilier	0.19	0.37	0.10	0.11	0.07	0.03
S22. Redev. gouv. et logements occ. par propr.	0.00	0.00	0.00	0.00	0.00	0.00
S23. Services aux entreprises	0.13	0.24	0.08	0.20	0.25	0.10
S24. Services personnels et autres	0.36	0.28	0.10	0.12	0.10	0.04
TOTAL	0.36	0.27	0.13	0.12	0.09	0.03

Tableau 19A Parts de la scolarité/compétence dans les importations, 1961–1997					
	Secondaire non complété	Études secondaires	Certificat ou diplôme professionnel	Diplôme d'études post-secondaires non universitaires	Études universitaires jusqu'au baccalauréat	Tous les diplômes d'études supérieures
1961	0,396	0,255	0,142	0,111	0,076	0,019
1962	0,394	0,255	0,143	0,112	0,077	0,019
1963	0,390	0,256	0,145	0,113	0,078	0,019
1964	0,390	0,256	0,145	0,113	0,077	0,019
1965	0,387	0,257	0,146	0,113	0,077	0,019
1966	0,381	0,258	0,146	0,115	0,079	0,021
1967	0,379	0,259	0,144	0,116	0,081	0,021
1968	0,378	0,260	0,142	0,116	0,082	0,021
1969	0,377	0,261	0,141	0,117	0,083	0,022
1970	0,376	0,261	0,141	0,117	0,083	0,022
1971	0,376	0,262	0,140	0,117	0,083	0,022
1972	0,378	0,262	0,139	0,116	0,083	0,022
1973	0,377	0,263	0,138	0,117	0,083	0,022
1974	0,375	0,263	0,139	0,117	0,084	0,022
1975	0,374	0,263	0,140	0,117	0,084	0,022
1976	0,375	0,263	0,137	0,117	0,085	0,023
1977	0,371	0,264	0,137	0,118	0,086	0,023
1978	0,367	0,265	0,137	0,119	0,088	0,024
1979	0,364	0,264	0,138	0,120	0,089	0,024
1980	0,359	0,264	0,138	0,122	0,091	0,025
1981	0,357	0,265	0,137	0,123	0,093	0,026
1982	0,355	0,265	0,135	0,124	0,094	0,026
1983	0,358	0,266	0,134	0,123	0,093	0,026
1984	0,359	0,266	0,132	0,123	0,093	0,026
1985	0,358	0,266	0,133	0,123	0,094	0,026
1986	0,358	0,266	0,132	0,123	0,094	0,026
1987	0,353	0,264	0,134	0,126	0,096	0,027
1988	0,344	0,262	0,137	0,130	0,098	0,029
1989	0,337	0,261	0,138	0,133	0,101	0,030
1990	0,342	0,265	0,134	0,131	0,099	0,030
1991	0,335	0,263	0,136	0,134	0,101	0,031
1992	0,336	0,263	0,135	0,134	0,101	0,031
1993	0,336	0,263	0,134	0,134	0,101	0,031
1994	0,331	0,263	0,136	0,135	0,103	0,032
1995	0,330	0,263	0,136	0,136	0,103	0,032
1996	0,328	0,263	0,135	0,136	0,104	0,032
1997	0,329	0,263	0,136	0,137	0,104	0,032

	Tableau 19B Ratio des parts de la scolarité/compétence dans les importations à l'emploi du secteur des entreprises, 1961–1997					
	Secondaire non terminé	Études secondaires	Certificat ou diplôme professionnel	Diplôme d'études post-secondaires non universitaires	Études universitaires jusqu'au baccalauréat	Tous les diplômes d'études supérieures
1961	965	0,948	1,044	1,097	1,123	1,284
1962	965	0,948	1,050	1,094	1,115	1,271
1963	0,959	0,947	1,061	1,100	1,120	1,283
1964	0,965	0,947	1,057	1,092	1,107	1,257
1965	0,963	0,948	1,060	1,092	1,104	1,248
1966	0,957	0,949	1,051	1,100	1,126	1,294
1967	0,956	0,949	1,043	1,105	1,133	1,310
1968	0,958	0,950	1,034	1,100	1,134	1,319
1969	0,959	0,950	1,028	1,101	1,139	1,323
1970	0,964	0,949	1,025	1,097	1,128	1,295
1971	0,966	0,951	1,017	1,095	1,128	1,293
1972	0,978	0,947	1,015	1,081	1,108	1,257
1973	0,978	0,949	1,012	1,082	1,105	1,249
1974	0,979	0,945	1,016	1,077	1,106	1,250
1975	0,980	0,943	1,030	1,072	1,094	1,233
1976	0,985	0,944	1,008	1,072	1,104	1,247
1977	0,982	0,946	1,010	1,074	1,105	1,243
1978	0,972	0,947	1,020	1,083	1,114	1,257
1979	0,966	0,945	1,027	1,089	1,123	1,272
1980	0,957	0,944	1,030	1,098	1,140	1,293
1981	0,955	0,944	1,023	1,104	1,150	1,302
1982	0,958	0,943	1,021	1,100	1,141	1,277
1983	0,967	0,945	1,020	1,091	1,118	1,240
1984	0,972	0,944	1,009	1,087	1,118	1,243
1985	0,973	0,945	1,012	1,085	1,114	1,234
1986	0,971	0,944	1,009	1,085	1,122	1,250
1987	0,977	0,941	1,009	1,076	1,112	1,218
1988	0,973	0,938	1,019	1,080	1,110	1,201
1989	0,974	0,937	1,011	1,076	1,116	1,191
1990	1,012	0,956	0,970	1,033	1,060	1,088
1991	1,016	0,954	0,973	1,028	1,057	1,074
1992	1,020	0,953	0,970	1,023	1,056	1,070
1993	1,016	0,953	0,975	1,027	1,058	1,067
1994	1,005	0,953	0,980	1,035	1,071	1,085
1995	1,004	0,955	0,984	1,037	1,066	1,072
1996	1,000	0,958	0,984	1,038	1,068	1,071
1997	1,007	0,955	0,989	1,036	1,054	1,048

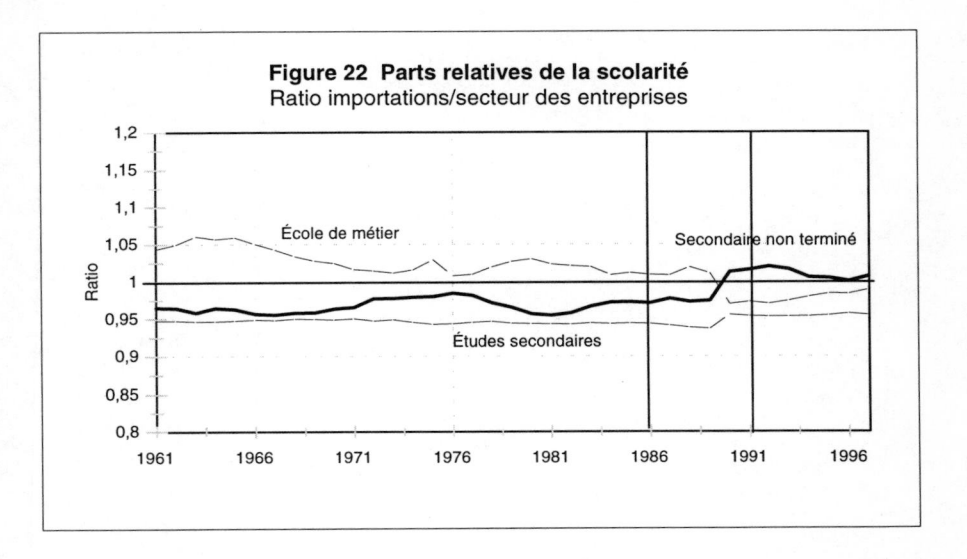

Figure 22 Parts relatives de la scolarité
Ratio importations/secteur des entreprises

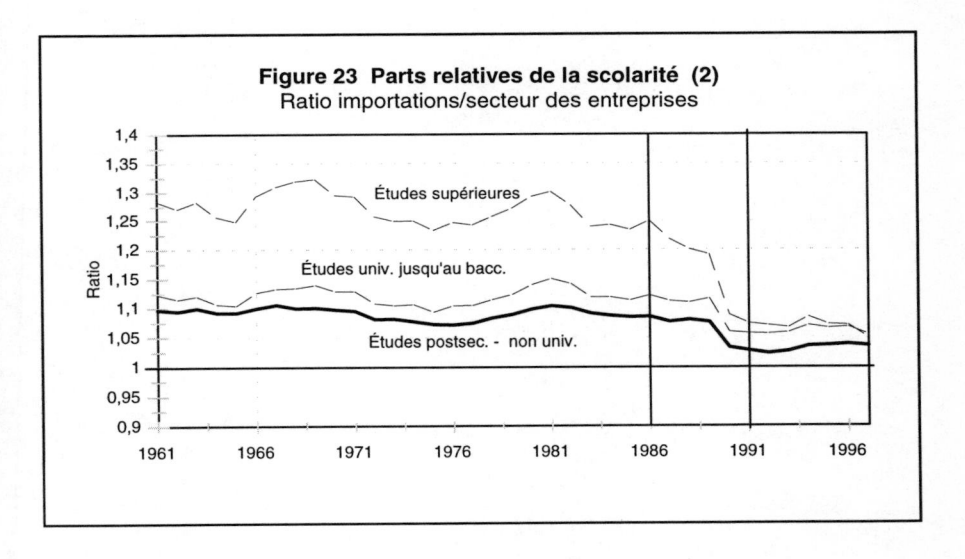

Figure 23 Parts relatives de la scolarité (2)
Ratio importations/secteur des entreprises

6. CONCLUSIONS

La valeur d'une étude telle que la nôtre réside en partie dans les résultats des calculs détaillés qui y sont présentés, dans la mesure où ils sont un peu plus à jour et complets que ceux des études antérieures. Avec de la chance, ces résultats peuvent permettre à d'autres chercheurs ainsi qu'aux lecteurs de trouver réponse à leurs questions sur divers aspects et, peut-être, de suggérer de nouvelles questions.

Quoi qu'il en soit, nous avons tenté de tirer quelques grandes conclusions de l'étude. Certaines ont déjà été évoquées dans les chapitres qui précèdent.

1) Si la part des exportations et des importations dans l'économie canadienne a progressé rapidement depuis 1961 — et en particulier après 1990 — la croissance de la part de l'emploi attribuable aux exportations (ou « déplacé » par les importations) a été *beaucoup moins rapide*. La principale raison de ce phénomène est la pénétration des importations : aujourd'hui, les exportations ont un contenu en intrants intermédiaires importés beaucoup plus élevé que par le passé. Quant aux importations, si elles devaient être produites au Canada, la technologie actuelle ferait en sorte qu'elles nécessiteraient beaucoup plus d'intrants intermédiaires importés que dans les années 60.

2) Lorsque nous agrégeons nos résultats sectoriels, la productivité de la main-d'oeuvre liée aux exportations canadiennes est toujours supérieure à la moyenne de la production totale du secteur des entreprises — notamment lorsque l'effet de l'agriculture dans les années 60 est exclu. Cependant, cette productivité relativement élevée de la main-d'oeuvre liée aux exportations n'affiche pratiquement *aucune tendance à la hausse*. Parallèlement à une productivité élevée, nous observons que la main-d'oeuvre liée aux exportations a un rendement élevé mais, encore une fois, cette performance relative des exportations ne montre pratiquement aucune tendance temporelle. Cependant, étant donné que la part de l'emploi attribuable aux exportations a augmenté constamment, on pourrait en conclure que les exportations contribuent à relever le *niveau global* de la productivité et le rendement de la main-d'oeuvre au Canada.

3) Les sources de changement dans la composition de l'emploi lié à l'exportation canadienne sont principalement la composition des exportations finales et le degré de pénétration des importations au niveau des intrants intermédiaires. Les changements entre les secteurs dans la productivité relative de la main-d'oeuvre, c'est-à-dire le « changement technique » incorporé à l'évolution des coefficients entrées-sorties, sont généralement moins importants, bien que pour certaines industries ils puissent demeurer primordiaux (par exemple le transport ferroviaire). La même observation s'applique essentiellement aux changements observés dans la composition de l'emploi lié à aux importations canadiennes.

4) Les changements dans les parts de l'emploi lié à l'exportation ont touché une gamme plus étendue d'industries que ce que l'on aurait pu prédire. Sur dix groupes industriels qui ont vu leur part de l'emploi lié à l'exportation augmenter par plus d'un point de pourcentage entre 1961 et 1997, quatre sont des industries de services (services personnels et autres, services aux entreprises, commerce et finance), tandis que les six autres sont des industries manufacturières diverses, dont certaines étaient prévisibles compte tenu de la signature du Pacte de l'automobile et de l'évolution de la technologie — par exemple les véhicules à moteur, les produits électriques et électroniques et les produits en caoutchouc et en plastique — et certains qui étonnent un peu — comme le cuir, les textiles et le vêtement. Parmi les quatre industries qui montrent une diminution de la part de l'emploi lié à l'exportation de plus d'un point de pourcentage, les deux

reculs les plus importants touchent la production primaire (l'exploitation minière à l'exclusion du pétrole et du gaz, et l'agriculture, la forêt et la pêche), l'une est une industrie de transformation de matières premières et de fabrication (papier, produits connexes et impression), tandis que la quatrième est l'industrie des transports. On pourrait aussi s'étonner de la période où ces changements se sont produits : à titre d'exemple, l'industrie des véhicules à moteur a enregistré presque tous ses gains de la part de l'emploi lié à l'exportation entre 1961 et 1971, tandis que l'augmentation de la part de l'emploi lié à l'exportation dans les secteurs du commerce, des finances et des services aux entreprises a été aussi importante dans les années 60 qu'au cours des autres périodes. Bref, il est important d'examiner les résultats détaillés pour chaque industrie.

5)   En combinant les résultats entrées-sorties avec les données sur le profil de scolarité par industrie nous pouvons constater que, depuis 1961, la composition des exportations canadiennes selon l'emploi (direct et indirect) a constamment évolué vers les industries qui embauchent des travailleurs plus scolarisés. Cependant, cela est aussi vrai de l'emploi dans l'ensemble du secteur des entreprises. Si nous comparons les exportations au secteur des entreprises pour ce qui est de l'utilisation relative des différents profils de scolarité, la conclusion qui s'en dégage est que l'emploi lié à l'exportation a une distribution « bi-polaire ». Le secteur d'exportation emploie proportionnellement plus de travailleurs peu scolarisés et de travailleurs très scolarisés que la moyenne de l'économie. Les ratios relatifs n'ont changé que très peu au cours des trois dernières décennies.

6)   La productivité de la main-d'oeuvre occupant les postes « déplacés » par les importations (si celles-ci devaient être produites avec la technologie canadienne) est systématiquement inférieure à celle des exportations — bien qu'elle soit tout de même supérieure à la moyenne du secteur des entreprises pour la plupart des années. Le ratio a chuté autour de la moyenne de l'ensemble de l'économie ces dernières années. Par conséquent, les données indiquent que, dans l'ensemble, les importations ne remplacent pas des emplois dont la productivité est exceptionnellement faible (lesquels sont probablement concentrés dans les services non commercialisables). Cependant, les importations déplacent « relativement » plus d'emplois que les exportations n'en ajoutent. Si les politiques macro-économiques peuvent maintenir l'économie près du seuil de plein emploi et si le rythme de changement n'est pas trop rapide, le Canada serait en mesure de remplacer des emplois à faible productivité par des emplois à productivité plus élevée grâce à une expansion du commerce international, ce qui serait à son avantage.

7)   En comparant les changements dans les parts de l'emploi lié à l'exportation et à l'importation, on remarque immédiatement que les hausses et les baisses les plus importantes se retrouvent, dans bien des cas, dans les *mêmes* secteurs. Les services personnels, les services aux entreprises et le commerce ont connu des augmentations de la part de l'emploi parmi les plus élevées, tant pour les exportations que pour les importations, tandis que l'exploitation minière, l'agriculture et la forêt accusent les baisses les plus fortes des parts de l'emploi, tant pour les exportations que pour les importations. Les exportations et les importations canadiennes ont vu leur coefficient d'emploi lié aux services augmenter, tandis que le coefficient d'emploi lié à la production de matières premières a fléchi.

8)   Les calculs portant sur le profil de scolarité montrent qu'à tout le moins pour la part de la technologie canadienne et de la scolarité par secteur, le contenu en éducation des importations canadiennes a dépassé celui de la moyenne du secteur des entreprises. Ces dernières années, toutefois, l'écart s'est rétréci, ce qui indiquerait une concurrence accrue en provenance des importations dans les secteurs qui emploient des travailleurs peu spécialisés. Néanmoins, les importations canadiennes continuent de dépasser la moyenne du secteur des entreprises pour ce

qui est du contenu en éducation. Ce résultat peut sembler contraire à la conclusion précédente sur la productivité et le rendement de la main-d'oeuvre. Mais, il faut se rappeler que nous avons constaté que la productivité et le rendement de la main-d'oeuvre liée à l'importation étaient *supérieurs* à la moyenne du secteur des entreprises, tout en étant *inférieurs* à la productivité et au rendement de la main-d'oeuvre liée à l'exportation. Ces deux observations ne sont pas incompatibles. L'anomalie, c'est peut-être que la productivité et le rendement liés aux exportations sont si élevés alors que le profil de scolarité est faible, du moins dans certains cas. Cette anomalie est plus facile à comprendre si l'on se rappelle que l'éducation, mesurée de façon étendue, n'est pas le seul facteur déterminant de la productivité ou du rendement du facteur travail. Une forte capitalisation ou une riche dotation en ressources naturelles peuvent permettre à une main-d'oeuvre relativement peu scolarisée d'être hautement productive et bien rémunérée, comme cela semble être le cas de certaines industries d'exportation canadiennes telles que celles des véhicules à moteur et des produits métalliques.

NOTES

1   Pour plus de détails, voir l'appendice 1.

2   À noter partout dans le texte : les importations signifient les importations nettes de toute réexportation.

3   Courakis, Maskus et Webster (1997) soulignent que le fait de « répartir le blâme » entre la mondialisation (intensification des échanges) et le changement technique dans l'analyse des pertes (variations) d'emplois pourrait être une fausse dichotomie qui ne cadre pas avec la théorie du commerce, parce que les deux effets seraient eux-mêmes le résultat de l'évolution sous-jacente de la technologie et des goûts. Cette observation peut être pertinente pour ce qui est d'évaluer la causalité ou de formuler des politiques, mais notre étude vise simplement à déterminer ce que les données révèlent sur la contribution relative des divers facteurs.

4   Les ensembles de données pour 1986 et 1991 ne sont pas parfaitement comparables et il a fallu faire intervenir une part de jugement pour les rapprocher.

5   Une autre méthode permettant d'examiner l'impact des importations et de la technologie sur l'emploi et les salaires sans recourir aux techniques d'analyse entrées-sorties est présentée dans Lee (1996).

6   Nous sommes reconnaissants envers un lecteur-arbitre anonyme qui a porté ce point à notre attention et présenté cet exemple particulier.

7   Il faut se rappeler que, pour la période 1993-1997, nous avons utilisé les coefficients entrées-sorties de 1992, tandis que les coefficients des exportations, des parts de l'emploi et des importations ont été estimés pour chacune de ces années.

8   À noter qu'ici et ailleurs dans l'étude, l'emploi est mesuré par le nombre de personnes employées et non par le nombre d'heures travaillées. L'emploi peut comprendre les postes à temps partiel comme cela se fait, par exemple, dans l'Enquête sur la population active. Les conclusions au sujet des parts de l'emploi et de la productivité de la main-d'oeuvre peuvent être faussées si on néglige de prendre en considération les changements survenus dans le nombre d'heures travaillées par employé.

9   Les détails de l'agrégation et des codes de la CTI de la désagrégation la plus poussée, c'est-à-dire à 161 industries, figurent à l'appendice 3.

10   Malheureusement, nous ne pouvons être sûrs qu'une scolarité plus élevée se traduise par de meilleures compétences ou habiletés au sein de la population active. Cela pourrait simplement refléter, pour reprendre l'expression d'un expert-arbitre anonyme, le phénomène de la « diplomatie rampante » : un emploi peut ne pas exiger plus de compétences qu'auparavant mais nécessiter maintenant un diplôme universitaire (peut-être parce qu'un plus grand nombre de diplômés sont aujourd'hui disponibles), alors qu'un diplôme d'études secondaires était autrefois suffisant.

11   À la lumière du problème de la « diplomatie rampante » (voir la note précédente), l'utilisation de critères de scolarité relativement fixes dans l'industrie pourrait comporter certains avantages en

permettant d'identifier comment l'évolution de la composition industrielle des exportations a influé sur la demande de compétences avec le temps.

12   Comme dans l'analyse des exportations, nous avons utilisé les coefficients entrées-sorties de 1992 pour les années 1993 à 1997, tandis que les niveaux d'importation, les parts de l'emploi et les coefficients d'importation ont été estimés pour chacune des années.

BIBLIOGRAPHIE

Betts, Julian R., « The Skill Bias of Technological Change in Canadian Manufacturing Industries », *Review of Economics and Statistics*, vol. LXXIX, n° 1, février 1997, p. 146-150.

_____ , « Two Exact, Non-Arbitrary and General Methods of Decomposing Temporal Change », *Economics Letters*, vol. 30, 1989, p. 151-156.

Betts, Julian R. et Thomas McCurdy, « Sources of Employment Growth by Occupation and Industry in Canada », *Relations industrielles*, vol. 48, n° 2, 1993, p. 285-304.

Courakis, Anthony, Keith E. Maskus et Allan Webster, « Occupational Employment and Wage Changes in the UK: Commerce and Technology Effects », paru dans *International Commerce and Labour Markets*, publié sous la direction de Jitendralal Borkakoti et Chris Milner, St. Martin's Press, New York, 1997.

Feenstra, Robert C. et Gordon H. Hanson, « Globalization, Outsourcing and Wage Inequality », *American Economic Review - Papers and Proceedings*, vol. 86, n° 2, mai 1996, p. 240-245.

Freeman, Richard B., « Are Your Wages Set in Beijing? », *Journal of Economic Perspectives*, vol. 9, n° 3, été 1995, p. 15-32.

Gaston, Noel et Daniel Trefler, « The Labour-Market Consequences of the Canada-U.S. Free Commerce Agreement », *Canadian Journal of Economics*, XXX, n° 1, février 1997, p. 18-41.

Gera, Surendra et Kurt Mang, « The Knowledge-Based Economy: Shifts in Industrial Output », *Canadian Public Policy/Analyse de Politiques*, vol. XXIV, n° 2, juin 1998, p. 149-184.

_____ , *L'économie du savoir et l'évolution de la production industrielle*, Industrie Canada, Document de travail n° 15, janvier 1997.

Gera, Surendra et Philippe Massé, *Performance de l'emploi dans l'économie du savoir*, Industre Canada, Document de travail n° 14, décembre 1996.

Gregory, Mary et Christine Greenhalgh, « International Commerce, Deindustrialization and Labour Demand: An Input-Output Study for the UK (1979–90) », paru dans *International Commerce and Labour Markets*, publié sous la direction de Jitendralal Borkakoti et Chris Milner, St. Martin's Press, New York, 1997.

Lawrence, Robert Z., *Single World, Divided Nations*, Brookings Institution Press, Washington (DC), et Centre de développement économique de l'OCDE, Paris, 1996.

Lee, Frank, *Les répercussions de la technologie et des importations sur l'emploi et les salaires au Canada,* Industrie Canada, Document de travail n° 12, juillet 1996.

Lee, Frank et H. Has, « Évolution quantitative des industries à forte concentration de savoir par rapport aux industries à faible concentration de savoir », paru dans *La croissance fondée sur le savoir et son incidence sur les politiques microéconomiques,* publié sous la direction de P. Howitt, Documents de recherche d'Industrie Canada, University of Calgary Press, Calgary, 1996.

Levy, Frank et Richard J. Murnane, « U.S. Earnings Levels and Earnings Inequality: A Review of Recent Trends and Proposed Explanations », *Journal of Economic Literature*, vol. XXX, n° 3, septembre 1992.

Organisation de coopération et de développement économiques, *Structural Change and Industrial Performance: A Seven-Country Growth Decomposition Study*, OCDE, Paris, 1992.

Richardson, J. David, « Income Inequality and Commerce: How to Think, What to Conclude », *Journal of Economic Perspectives*, vol. 9, n° 3, été 1995, p. 33-55.

Sachs, Jeffrey D. et Howard J. Shatz, « U.S. Commerce with Developing Countries and Wage Inequality », *American Economic Review - Papers and Proceedings*, vol. 86, n° 2, mai 1996, p. 234-239.

Thygesen, Niels, Yutaka Kosai et Robert Z. Lawrence, *Globalization and Trilateral Labor Markets, A Report to the Trilateral Commission,* n° 49, The Trilateral Commission, New York, 1996.

Tyson, Laura D'Andrea et John Zysman, « Commerce and Employment: An Overview of the Issues and Evidence », paru dans *The Dynamics of Commerce and Employment*, publié sous la direction de Laura D'Andrea Tyson, William T. Dickens et John Zysman, Ballinger, Cambridge, 1988.

Wood, Adrian, « How Commerce Hurt Unskilled Workers », *Journal of Economic Perspectives*, vol. 9, n° 3, été 1995, p. 57–80.

APPENDICE 1
DESCRIPTION DÉTAILLÉE DES CALCULS

Dans cet appendice, nous décrivons plus en détail et dans une forme un peu plus algébrique les calculs qui sous-tendent les résultats présentés dans le document. De façon très approximative, la notation suivante est tirée de Gera et Mang (1997, p. 69-70).

Pour débuter, envisageons les calculs pour une seule année (disons 1992) en se rappelant qu'il y a 161 industries dans l'agrégation « L » employée.

La relation entrées-sorties fondamentale pour cette année et toute autre se présente comme suit :

$$g = Bg + fo + fx + fm \tag{1}$$

où

- g : vecteur 1 x 161 de la production brute totale pour chaque industrie
- B : matrice des coefficients d'intrants directs b_{ij} — les besoins directs en intrants de l'industrie i pour la production d'une unité de bien de l'industrie j
- fo : vecteur 1 x 161 de toutes les demandes finales autres que les exportations et les importations moins les ré-exportations
- fx : vecteur 1 x 161 de toutes les exportations
- fm : vecteur 1 x 161 de toutes les importations moins les ré-exportations (définies comme valeurs négatives)

À noter que Bg représente toutes les demandes intermédiaires sur la production d'un secteur industriel, tandis que la somme de $fo + fx + fm$ représente l'ensemble de la demande finale nette sur la production d'un secteur. Ces deux éléments doivent être exactement égaux à la production totale d'un secteur (g) étant donné que les variations de stocks, intentionnelles ou non, font partie de fo.

Afin d'établir l'impact sur g de tout changement dans l'un des composants de la demande finale, f, certains jugements doivent être faits en ce qui a trait aux « pertes » de demande dans la chaîne de production antérieure. Dans le modèle entrées-sorties standard de Statistique Canada, ainsi que dans les travaux de Gera et Mang (1997), on suppose qu'il y a trois sources de pertes : les importations, la demande desservie à même les stocks et la demande desservie par la « production gouvernementale », c'est-à-dire la prestation de services gouvernementaux et d'infrastructure. Nous adoptons la solution plus simple de permettre uniquement les pertes liées à la consommation. À notre avis, la prestation de services gouvernementaux est largement fixe au cours d'une année et varierait très peu même si la demande accusait des changements relativement importants. Ce terme est, de toute façon, très restreint. On peut également s'interroger sur la mesure dans laquelle des changements importants au niveau de la demande pourraient être satisfaits à même les stocks, mais le point plus pertinent est que les « ratios » des stocks à partir desquels la perte devrait être calculée peuvent varier considérablement dans certains secteurs d'une année à l'autre, engendrant, selon nous, des écarts importants et inacceptables dans les résultats et les impacts. Par conséquent, nous nous sommes limités aux pertes liées aux importations où la perte moyenne dans tout secteur pour une année donnée est définie comme étant le ratio des importations à la production intérieure *moins les exportations* pour ce secteur au cours de l'année. Les exportations ne sont pas incluses dans le calcul de la perte moyenne liée aux importations étant donné que les ré-exportations ont déjà été soustraites et que les exportations ne proviendront que de la production intérieure.

Ainsi, nous supposons une équation des importations prenant la forme suivante :

$$fm = M \cdot (Bg + fo) = M \cdot (g - fx) \tag{2}$$

Où M est une matrice dont les diagonales ne comportent pas de zéro et où les éléments des diagonales pour la colonne et la ligne i sont définis comme suit :

$$M_{ii} = fm_i / (g_i - fx_i) \tag{3}$$

Par conséquent, l'équation (1) peut être réécrite ainsi :

$$g = Bg + fo + fx + M(g\text{-}fx) \tag{3}$$

En solutionnant pour g, nous procédons de la façon suivante :

$$g - Bg - Mg = fo + fx - Mfx$$

$$(I - B - M)\, g = fo + (I - M)\, fx$$

$$g = (I - B - M)^{-1} \cdot (fo + (I - M)\, fx). \tag{4}$$

En solutionnant pour les *changements* dans fx, nous obtenons :

$$\Delta g = (I - B - M)^{-1} \cdot (I - M) \cdot \Delta fx \tag{5}$$

L'équation 5 est donc l'équation utilisée pour obtenir le changement dans la production par secteur (le changement dans g) pour un changement donné de fx. Dans notre cas, le montant que nous entrons pour représenter le changement dans fx est le niveau réel de fx au cours de l'année examinée.

À l'aide des données entrées-sorties de chacune des années, des ratios supplémentaires pour la production intérieure (la valeur ajoutée) par unité de production totale, l'emploi par unité de production totale et le rendement du facteur travail par unité de production totale peuvent être calculés. Ces ratios sont ensuite appliqués à Δg, tel que nous l'avons calculé précédemment afin d'obtenir les effets des exportations au cours de cette année sur la production intérieure, l'emploi et le rendement du facteur travail pour chaque industrie :

$rdp_i = dp_i / g_i$, où rdp et dp sont les ratios et les niveaux de la production intérieure

$re_i = e_i / g_i$, où re et e sont les ratios et les niveaux de l'emploi exprimés en nombre de personnes

$rw_i = w_i / g_i$, où rw et w sont les ratios et les niveaux du rendement de la main-d'oeuvre.

Alors :

$$\Delta dp = rdp \cdot \Delta g$$

$$\Delta e = re \cdot \Delta g$$

$$\Delta w = rw \cdot \Delta g$$

Décomposition :

Pour toute paire d'années, disons 1961 et 1992, l'emploi attribuable aux exportations pour cette année peut être calculé ainsi :

$$\Delta e_{92} = re_{92} \cdot (I - B_{92} - M_{92})^{-1} \cdot (I - M_{92}) \cdot fx_{92}, \text{ et} \tag{6}$$

$$\Delta e_{61} = re_{61} \cdot (I - B_{61} - M_{61})^{-1} \cdot (I - M_{61}) \cdot fx_{61} \tag{7}$$

Afin de déterminer les contributions autonomes, le calcul de Δe_{92} est répété successivement à l'aide de re_{61}, B_{61}, M_{61} et fx_{61}. Étant donné que nous présentons des ratios du nombre d'employés dans les différentes industries à l'emploi total, nous utilisons les parts des industries dans fx_{61} plutôt que les niveaux, mais le calcul alternatif aboutit au même résultat.

Cette décomposition est moins élaborée que la décomposition de la croissance utilisée par Gera et Mang (1997, p. 71-74), mais elle a pour but premier de faire ressortir les principaux facteurs qui contribuent aux changements observés dans la part de l'emploi entre deux années. La décomposition est complète au sens où, si les quatre éléments de 1961 (fx_{61}, re_{61}, etc.) devaient être entrés ensemble dans l'équation (6), alors nous obtiendrons évidemment l'équation (7) et toute la différence entre les deux années sera expliquée. Cependant, en raison de l'interaction entre les termes, la somme des éléments individuels ne correspond pas au changement total et, par conséquent, un terme résiduel ou d'interaction est présenté dans les tableaux de décomposition. En autant que nous puissions dire, toute tentative visant à « répartir » le terme d'interaction sera arbitraire. Si le terme d'interaction devait être réparti de façon proportionnelle, il n'y aurait évidemment aucun changement dans les pondérations relatives des éléments contribuants. (Voir Betts, 1989, qui renferme un autre modèle de décomposition où le terme résiduel est supprimé).

APPENDICE 2
TEST DE SENSIBILITÉ DES CALCULS
AGRÉGÉS POUR LES EXPORTATIONS

Dans cet appendice, nous présentons les résultats détaillés de deux ensembles de calculs portant sur les exportations. Le premier utilise des données et des tableaux entrées-sorties exprimés en valeurs réelles (dollars constants); le second exclut l'agriculture des calculs.

Utilisation des données exprimées en dollars constants

Tel qu'indiqué au chapitre 2, nous avons fait la plupart des calculs présentés dans cette étude à l'aide de données nominales, tirées soit du système entrées-sorties soit d'autres sources. L'utilisation de données nominales nous permet de prolonger certains des calculs sur la période 1993-1997 et d'éviter les difficultés inhérentes aux calculs d'une nouvelle base entre des séries différentes de tableaux entrées-sorties exprimés en valeurs réelles. Néanmoins, nous avons pu effectuer certains des calculs décrits précédemment à l'aide de données exprimées en dollars constants (réels) et voir s'il en découlait des différences importantes au niveau des résultats et des répercussions.

Au tableau A.1, nous présentons des résultats agrégés conceptuellement identiques à ceux du tableau 2 du chapitre 4, sauf que notre série en chaîne de tableaux entrées-sorties exprimés en valeurs réelles a été utilisée. Les données ne peuvent être prolongées au delà de 1992 et le calcul du rendement de la main-d'oeuvre ne peut être fait. Les colonnes du tableau 2 et du tableau A.1 peuvent être comparées directement afin de voir les différences découlant de l'utilisation des valeurs réelles et nominales; plusieurs de ces comparaisons sont présentées dans les figures A.1 à A.3.

La figure A.1 compare l'emploi dans les exportations, en pourcentage de l'ensemble du secteur des entreprises, selon les deux calculs. Les deux séries font voir un profil d'augmentation graduelle après 1961, les hausses étant un peu plus fortes dans le cas des calculs effectués avec des données réelles durant les années 60. Dans chaque cas, il y a diminution de la part de l'emploi lié aux exportations après 1984, mais la diminution n'est pas plus rapide dans les calculs faits avec les valeurs réelles — et un peu plus difficile à comprendre. Après 1984, les résultats des deux séries sont presque identiques. Par conséquent, les deux séries montrent que la part de l'emploi au Canada attribuable aux exportations n'a augmenté que graduellement de 1961 à 1992. Les calculs effectués avec les données réelles font voir que cette part a une tendance plus prononcée et affiche une baisse étonnante après 1984, laquelle n'avait pas encore été rattrapée en 1992.

La figure A.2 compare le produit intérieur attribuable aux exportations en tant que part du produit total des entreprises, à l'aide des séries nominales et réelles. Le profil est à peu près le même que pour l'emploi, montrant une tendance graduelle à la hausse qui, dans les calculs faits avec les données réelles, est un peu plus volatile. À noter qu'à partir de la fin des années 80, les données réelles font voir une augmentation un peu plus rapide de la part des exportations dans le PIB que les données nominales.

Enfin, les deux calculs de la productivité de la main-d'oeuvre liée aux exportations sont comparés à la figure A.3. Les résultats indiquent qu'il n'y a pas eu de tendance prononcée de ce terme : il a toujours été plus élevé que la moyenne de l'ensemble de l'économie (il est toujours supérieur à 1,0), mais nous n'observons aucune tendance marquée. Les calculs effectués à l'aide des données réelles montrent une diminution significative de la productivité relative au milieu des années 70, dont la plus

grande partie a été progressivement récupérée. Contrairement aux données nominales, les données réelles montrent relativement peu de baisse après la fin des années 80, ce qui laisse penser que le fléchissement de la série nominale est attribuable à une appréciation relative des exportations plutôt qu'à une baisse de la productivité relative des facteurs matériels.

Exclusion des exportations de produits agricoles

Parce que l'agriculture est une importante source d'exportations et parce que ce secteur a subi une profonde transformation structurelle, notamment dans les années 60, nous avons calculé les mesures nominales agrégées du tableau 2 (chapitre 4) en *excluant* les exportations agricoles aux fins de comparaison. (À noter que ce sont les exportations de produits agricoles que nous avons exclues du calcul; il pourrait y avoir un certain impact indirect par l'intermédiaire du secteur agricole si celui-ci doit produire des intrants indirects pour d'autres exportations). Ce calcul fournit un exemple de la façon dont d'autres exclusions pourraient être effectuées dans les calculs, même si ces variations (qui peuvent être assez importantes) n'ont pas été incluses dans la présente étude.

Le tableau A.2 résume les calculs annuels agrégés en excluant les exportations agricoles; les résultats présentés ici devraient être comparés aux calculs équivalents faits avec des valeurs nominales agrégées où ces exportations étaient incluses (tableau 2 du chapitre 4). Les figures A.4 à A.6 comparent les deux calculs pour trois indicateurs clés.

La figure A.4 montre le ratio de l'emploi attribuable aux exportations à l'emploi total du secteur des entreprises, tant pour l'ensemble des exportations (tableau 2) qu'en excluant les exportations de produits agricoles. Comme on peut le voir, les exportations agricoles comptaient davantage dans les années 60, même si leur poids, exprimé en dollars, demeurait important dans les années 80. L'inclusion ou l'exclusion des exportations agricoles ne modifie pas le jugement que l'on peut porter au sujet des tendances.

La figure A.5 reproduit l'évolution de la productivité de la main-d'oeuvre liée aux exportations avec et sans les exportations agricoles. Comme on peut le constater, l'exclusion des exportations agricoles a pour effet d'aplanir encore davantage la tendance et rend la productivité de la main-d'oeuvre liée aux exportations clairement supérieure à la productivité moyenne de la main-d'oeuvre sur l'ensemble des trois décennies.

Enfin, la figure A.6 fait voir le rendement du facteur travail (y compris le revenu tiré des entreprises non constituées en société) lié aux exportations par rapport à l'ensemble du secteur des entreprises. Lorsque les exportations agricoles sont exclues, l'emploi lié aux exportations montre un rendement supérieur à la moyenne du secteur des entreprises pour toutes les décennies. Cependant, la tendance fondamentale demeure inchangée : à la hausse jusqu'au milieu des années 80, suivie d'un léger repli par la suite.

Tableau A.1 Comparaisons tirées des calculs entrées-sorties au niveau agrégé, exportations, valeurs réelles, 1961-1992

	(1) Exportations en % du produit intérieur du secteur intérieur des entreprises	(2) Produit intérieur lié aux exportations en % du produit intérieur des entreprises	(3) Importations liées aux exportations en % du produit intérieur lié aux exportations	(4) Emploi lié aux exportations en % de l'emploi total des entreprises	(5) Productivité de la main-d'oeuvre liée aux exportations par rapport au secteur des entreprises	(6) Emploi direct lié aux exportations en % de l'emploi total	(7) Ratio de l'emploi direct à l'emploi total lié aux exportations
1961	25,39	20,66	18,48	17,62	1,17	9,59	0,54
1962	25,38	20,79	17,64	16,90	1,23	8,92	0,53
1963	25,96	21,25	17,90	17,67	1,20	9,34	0,53
1964	27,51	22,52	17,76	18,68	1,21	9,77	0,52
1965	26,71	21,66	18,82	18,10	1,20	9,53	0,53
1966	28,81	22,50	23,48	19,08	1,18	10,08	0,53
1967	31,51	23,54	28,95	19,82	1,19	10,40	0,52
1968	35,73	26,08	32,29	21,39	1,22	11,13	0,52
1969	37,77	26,72	36,64	21,45	1,25	11,25	0,52
1970	40,57	28,39	38,33	23,30	1,22	12,66	0,52
1971	40,50	28,45	38,13	22,98	1,24	12,34	0,54
1972	41,96	29,45	38,33	22,87	1,29	12,53	0,54
1973	43,23	30,40	38,07	22,63	1,34	12,32	0,55
1974	40,08	28,02	38,74	21,41	1,31	11,45	0,54
1975	37,19	25,38	41,85	20,41	1,24	10,96	0,53
1976	37,93	25,27	45,56	21,28	1,19	11,52	0,53
1977	39,25	25,51	49,28	22,40	1,14	11,97	0,54
1978	41,78	25,21	60,93	22,80	1,11	12,85	0,54
1979	40,32	26,65	46,35	23,65	1,13	12,87	0,53
1980	39,59	25,95	47,15	24,05	1,08	12,92	0,56
1981	39,81	26,33	46,05	24,41	1,08	13,08	0,54
1982	40,99	26,21	51,02	24,66	1,06	13,15	0,54
1983	43,29	27,27	53,58	24,90	1,10	13,43	0,54
1984	49,22	30,46	56,48	26,75	1,14	14,51	0,54
1985	36,17	25,48	36,92	21,83	1,17	11,05	0,51
1986	34,14	23,96	37,55	20,85	1,15	10,21	0,49
1987	33,85	24,16	35,43	20,46	1,18	10,00	0,49
1988	34,79	24,28	38,56	20,20	1,20	9,71	0,48
1989	34,35	23,74	40,09	19,70	1,20	9,44	0,48
1990	37,02	25,29	41,91	21,85	1,16	11,09	0,51
1991	38,44	26,19	42,21	22,62	1,16	11,61	0,51
1992	41,37	27,64	45,01	23,63	1,17	12,27	0,52

Tableau A.2 Comparaisons tirées des calculs entrées-sorties au niveau agrégé, exportations, 1961–1997

Agriculture exclue

	(1) Exportations en % du produit intérieur du secteur des entreprises	(2) Produit intérieur lié aux exportations en % du produit intérieur lié aux exportations	(3) Importations liées aux exportations en % du produit intérieur lié aux exportations	(4) Emploi lié aux exportations en % de l'emploi total des entreprises	(5) Productivité de la main-d'oeuvre liée aux exportations par rapport au secteur des entreprises	(6) Emploi direct lié aux exportations en % de l'emploi total	(7) Ratio de l'emploi direct lié aux exportations	(8) Ratio du rendement de la main-d'oeuvre liée aux exportations à celui du secteur des entreprises
1961	19,34	17,01	13,15	14,61	1,16	6,68	0,46	1,01
1962	19,77	17,09	13,28	14,53	1,18	6,65	0,46	1,02
1963	20,12	17,43	13,67	14,95	1,17	6,82	0,46	1,02
1964	21,12	18,22	14,22	15,34	1,19	6,98	0,45	1,02
1965	20,56	17,56	14,45	14,76	1,19	6,75	0,46	1,03
1966	21,77	18,17	17,58	15,62	1,16	7,17	0,46	1,04
1967	23,32	18,96	19,82	16,49	1,15	7,63	0,46	1,04
1968	26,13	20,46	23,73	17,69	1,16	8,22	0,46	1,05
1969	26,69	20,60	24,68	17,58	1,16	8,30	0,47	1,06
1970	28,02	21,60	25,19	18,84	1,17	8,89	0,47	1,07
1971	26,88	20,66	26,07	18,32	1,15	8,54	0,47	1,06
1972	27,22	20,95	25,87	18,07	1,13	8,57	0,47	1,08
1973	28,72	22,26	25,08	18,23	1,16	8,66	0,47	1,08
1974	28,83	22,37	27,46	17,62	1,22	8,28	0,47	1,10
1975	26,51	20,38	29,53	16,66	1,27	7,80	0,47	1,10
1976	27,29	20,81	28,85	17,34	1,22	8,16	0,47	1,11
1977	29,10	21,84	30,69	18,15	1,20	8,46	0,47	1,12
1978	31,75	23,45	32,43	19,25	1,20	9,16	0,48	1,13
1979	33,27	25,22	29,49	19,65	1,22	9,46	0,48	1,14
1980	33,77	25,68	30,57	20,06	1,28	9,43	0,47	1,14
1981	32,87	24,18	32,65	19,75	1,28	9,30	0,47	1,13
1982	31,58	23,21	32,42	19,84	1,22	9,08	0,46	1,14
1983	31,12	23,40	31,16	19,55	1,17	8,93	0,46	1,13
1984	34,65	25,55	33,56	20,67	1,20	9,61	0,46	1,13
1985	34,78	25,15	35,68	20,10	1,24	9,33	0,46	1,15
1986	34,09	23,78	38,73	20,00	1,25	9,44	0,47	1,14
1987	32,56	23,50	34,44	19,48	1,19	9,28	0,48	1,13
1988	32,47	23,34	34,71	19,18	1,22	8,94	0,47	1,12

Tableau A.2 (suite)

Agriculture exclue

	(1) Exportations en % du produit intérieur du secteur des entreprises	(2) Produit intérieur lié aux exportations en % du produit intérieur des entreprises	(3) Importations liées aux exportations en % du produit intérieur lié aux exportations	(4) Emploi lié aux exportations en % de l'emploi total des entreprises	(5) Productivité de la main-d'oeuvre liée aux exportations par rapport au secteur des entreprises	(6) Emploi direct lié aux exportations en % de l'emploi total	(7) Ratio de l'emploi direct lié aux exportations total lié aux exportations	(8) Ratio du rendement de la main-d'oeuvre liée aux exportations à celui du secteur des entreprises
1989	31,63	22,60	35,20	19,04	1,19	8,87	0,47	1,12
1990	32,77	23,19	36,58	20,78	1,12	10,31	0,50	1,08
1991	31,93	22,59	37,47	21,12	1,07	10,52	0,50	1,09
1992	34,74	23,95	41,14	22,17	1,08	11,16	0,50	1,09
1993	38,36	25,64	44,79	23,22	1,10	12,88	0,55	n.d.
1994	42,47	28,06	46,61	25,24	1,11	15,18	0,60	n.d.
1995	45,91	30,35	46,48	26,86	1,13	17,11	0,64	n.d.
1996	47,01	31,04	46,84	28,04	1,1	18,13	0,65	n.d.
1997	47,74	31,08	49,04	28,03	1,1	18,71	0,67	n.d.

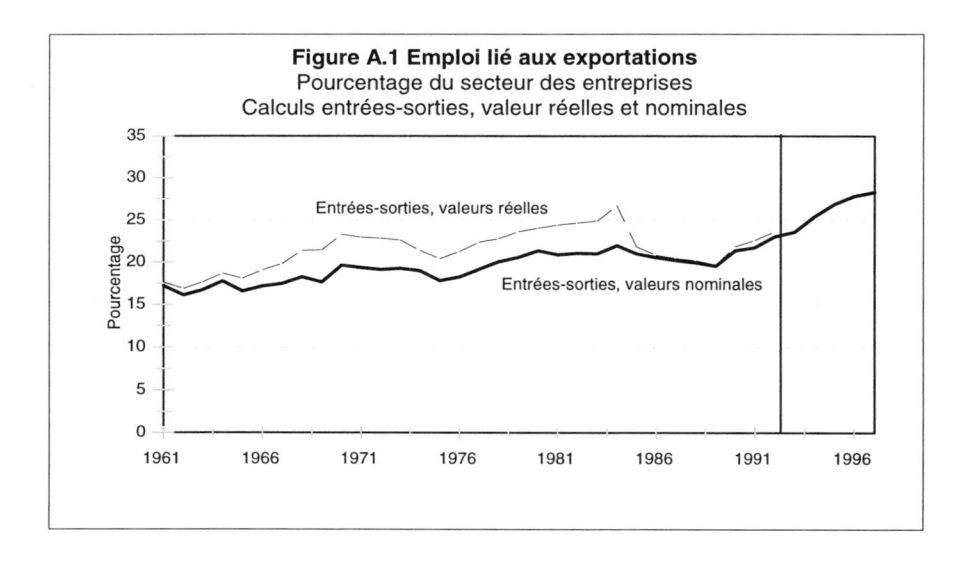

Figure A.1 Emploi lié aux exportations
Pourcentage du secteur des entreprises
Calculs entrées-sorties, valeur réelles et nominales

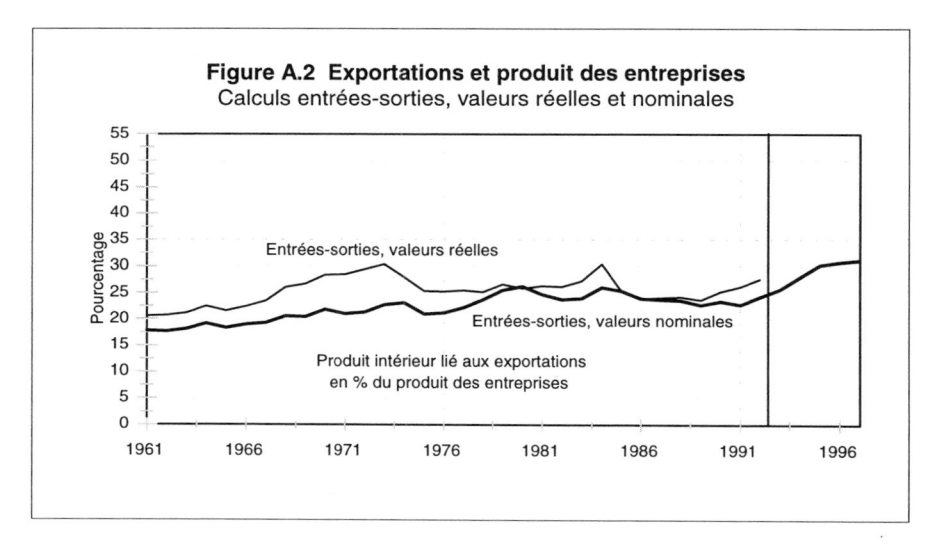

Figure A.2 Exportations et produit des entreprises
Calculs entrées-sorties, valeurs réelles et nominales

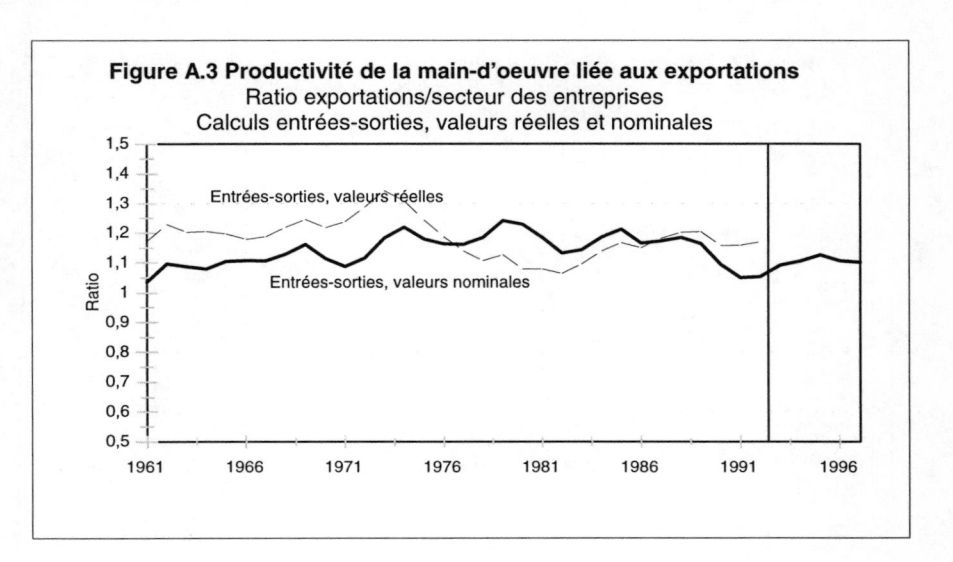

Figure A.3 Productivité de la main-d'oeuvre liée aux exportations
Ratio exportations/secteur des entreprises
Calculs entrées-sorties, valeurs réelles et nominales

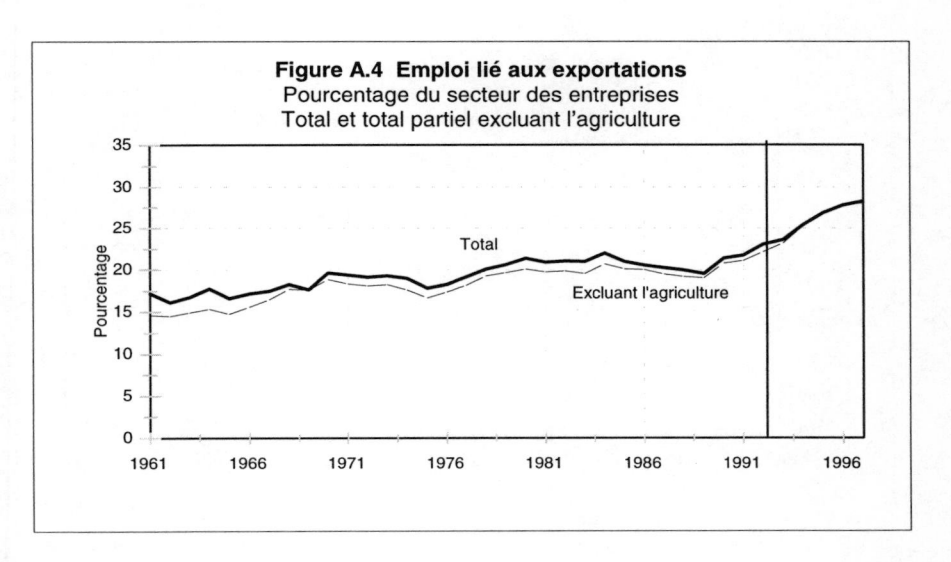

Figure A.4 Emploi lié aux exportations
Pourcentage du secteur des entreprises
Total et total partiel excluant l'agriculture

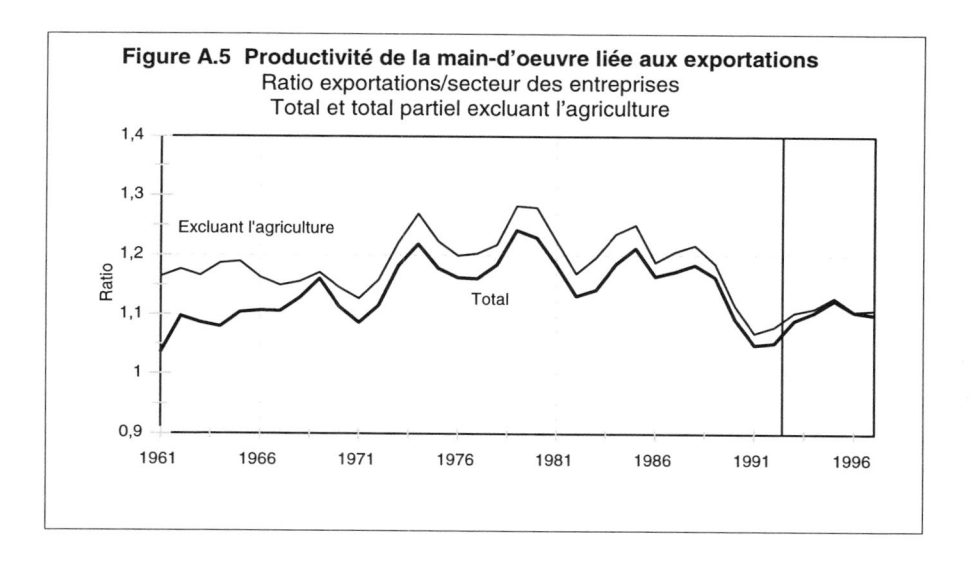

Figure A.5 Productivité de la main-d'oeuvre liée aux exportations
Ratio exportations/secteur des entreprises
Total et total partiel excluant l'agriculture

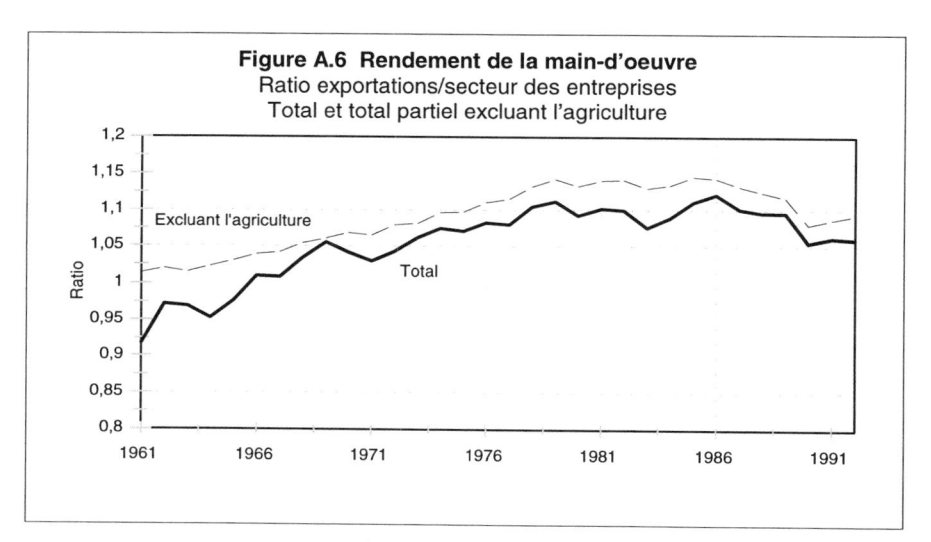

Figure A.6 Rendement de la main-d'oeuvre
Ratio exportations/secteur des entreprises
Total et total partiel excluant l'agriculture

APPENDICE 3
AGRÉGATION AU NIVEAU DE 24 INDUSTRIES
– PARAMÈTRES D'AGRÉGATION

Agrégation au niveau de 24 industries	Entrées-sorties composants de l'agrégation entre « L » à 161 industries	SPPC composants de l'agrégation à 112 industries	Groupes de la CTI
S1. Agriculture, forêt, pêche et piégeage	1-3	1-3	01-05
S2. Mines, sauf le pétrole et le gaz	4-10, 12-13	4-6, 8–9	06, 08, 09
S3. Pétrole brut et gaz naturel	11	7	07
S4. Aliments, boissons et tabac	14-29	10-22	10-12
S5. Produits en caoutchouc et en plastique	30,31	23,24	15, 16
S6. Cuir, textile et vêtement	32-42	25-28	17-19, 24
S7. Produits en bois et mobilier	43-50	29-34	25, 26
S8. Papier, produits connexes et imprimerie	51-56	35-38	27, 28
S9. Métaux primaires et fabrication métallique	57-71	39-53	29, 30
S10. Machines	72-74	54-56	31
S11. Véhicules à moteur et pièces	76-78	58-60	323-325
S12. Autre matériel de transport	75, 79-81	57, 61-63	321, 326-329
S13. Produits électriques et électroniques	82-89	64-69	33
S14. Pétrole raffiné, prod. chimiques et non métall.	90-103	70-83	35-37
S15. Autres produits fabriqués	104-108	84-87	39
S16. Construction	109-117	88	40-44
S17. Transport et pipelines	118-127	89-95	45, 46
S18. Entreposage	128	96	47
S19. Services publics	129-134	97-102	48, 49
S20. Commerce	135, 136	103, 104	50-69
S21. Finances, assurance et immobilier	137-139	105	70-74
S22. Redev. gouv. et logements occupés par propr.	140, 141	aucune	75,76
S23. Services aux entreprises	142-144	106	77
S24. Services personnels et autres	145-154	107-112	85-99

APPENDICE 4
ÉVOLUTION DE LA COMPOSITION INDUSTRIELLE DES EXPORTATIONS :
AGRÉGATION AU NIVEAU DE 161 INDUSTRIES

Les tableaux A.3A et A.3B montrent les résultats détaillés qui sous-tendent les données agrégées des tableaux 3A et 3B, au chapitre 4, obtenus dans les calculs faits avec la série complète de 161 industries. Ces tableaux font voir les années 1961 et 1992, qui bornent l'intervalle complet de nos données entrées-sorties. Au tableau A.3A, les industries sont classées selon l'ordre numérique habituel, allant de la production primaire aux industries manufacturières et aux services. Au tableau A.3B, les secteurs sont classés selon l'ordre décroissant de l'augmentation de la part de l'emploi lié aux exportations.

Les industries qui montrent les augmentations les plus importantes de la part de l'emploi lié aux exportations appartiennent principalement à trois groupes[1] : le premier et le plus nombreux est celui des industries de services de tous genres, allant de l'hébergement et des services alimentaires aux services aux entreprises et aux services professionnels et jusqu'au commerce et aux services bancaires. Dans la section qui suit, consacrée aux décompositions, nous analysons la mesure dans laquelle cette augmentation de l'emploi dans les services est attribuable à une expansion des exportations directes dans ces industries et au fait que d'autres industries utilisent davantage de services comme intrants (ou à l'évolution de la productivité relative de la main-d'oeuvre dans les divers secteurs). Pour l'instant, le fait que les exportations de services n'aient pas augmenté significativement par rapport aux exportations de biens entre 1961 et 1992 (comme nous pouvons le voir au tableau 1) laisse penser que c'est en grande partie les changements survenus au niveau des facteurs intermédiaires qui entrent dans les exportations ou l'évolution de la productivité sectorielle relative qui est responsable de ce déplacement.

Le second groupe d'industries qui a vu sa part de l'emploi lié aux exportations augmenter est celui des véhicules à moteur et des pièces et accessoires de véhicules à moteur. Ce résultat n'est pas surprenant compte tenu du Pacte de l'automobile et de l'expansion et de l'intégration continues de l'industrie de l'automobile en Amérique du Nord. On notera également avec un certain optimisme que le troisième élément important de l'expansion des parts de l'emploi lié aux exportations est le groupe des industries du matériel électronique, ce qui indique que le Canada a trouvé le moyen d'exploiter des occasions d'exportation importantes dans ce secteur en expansion à l'échelle mondiale.

Au bas du tableau, on retrouve les secteurs qui ont enregistré les diminutions les plus importantes de la part de l'emploi lié aux exportations. Comme on peut le voir, ce sont des industries de production primaire telles que l'agriculture, l'exploitation forestière et, en partie, les mines, ainsi que les secteurs connexes comme la fonte et l'affinage des métaux non ferreux, les pâtes et papiers et les scieries. Il faut également signaler la diminution de la part du transport ferroviaire depuis 1961; à mesure que les exportations ont augmenté, on a eu tendance à les expédier de moins en moins par chemin de fer.

Enfin, nous présentons aussi dans cet appendice les décompositions au niveau de 161 industries des changements observés dans les parts de l'emploi entre 1961 et 1992 (tableaux A.4A et A.4B).

---

[1] Le classement a aussi tendance à être le même pour l'emploi lié aux exportations en pourcentage de l'emploi *total*, mais il peut y avoir de légères différences en raison du fait que l'emploi lié aux exportations a lui-même changé par rapport à l'emploi total durant cette période.

Tableau A.3A Parts de l'emploi, 1961 et 1992, 161 industries

	1961		1992		Variation 1961-1992	
	Emploi lié à l'exportation en % de l'emploi total lié à l'exportation	Emploi lié à l'exportation en % de l'emploi total	Emploi lié à l'exportation en % de l'emploi total lié à l'exportation	Emploi lié à l'exportation en % de l'emploi total	Emploi lié à l'exportation en % de l'emploi total lié à l'exportation	Emploi lié à l'exportation en % de l'emploi total
001 Agriculture et ind. connexes	26,93	4,63	8,69	2,01	-18,24	-2,63
002 Pêche et piégeage	1,24	0,21	1,38	0,32	0,14	0,11
003 Abattage et foresterie	5,55	0,95	1,77	0,41	-3,78	-0,55
004 Mines d'or	1,81	0,31	0,35	0,08	-1,46	-0,23
005 Autres mines métalliques	3,35	0,58	0,87	0,20	-2,48	-0,38
006 Mines de fer	0,79	0,14	0,22	0,05	-0,58	-0,09
007 Mines d'amiante	0,72	0,12	0,10	0,02	-0,62	-0,10
008 Mines non mét. sauf charbon et amiante	0,28	0,05	0,25	0,06	-0,03	0,01
009 Mines de sel	0,04	0,01	0,02	0,00	-0,02	-0,00
010 Mines de charbon	0,52	0,09	0,25	0,06	-0,27	-0,03
011 Pétrole brut et gaz naturel	0,60	0,10	1,09	0,25	0,50	0,15
012 Carrières et sablières	0,13	0,02	0,09	0,02	-0,04	-0,00
013 Services connexes à l'extraction min.	0,16	0,03	0,51	0,12	0,35	0,09
014 Viande et prod. viande (sauf volaille)	0,28	0,05	0,37	0,09	0,09	0,04
015 Produits de la volaille	0,01	0,00	0,04	0,01	0,02	0,01
016 Produits du poisson	1,11	0,19	0,87	0,20	-0,25	0,01
017 Transformation des fruits et légumes	0,08	0,01	0,15	0,04	0,07	0,02
018 Produits laitiers	0,17	0,03	0,09	0,02	-0,08	-0,01
019 Nourriture pour animaux	0,34	0,06	0,16	0,04	-0,18	-0,02
020 Raffin. d'huile végétale (sauf maïs)	0,03	0,00	0,02	0,00	-0,01	-0,00
021 Biscuits	0,02	0,00	0,04	0,01	0,02	0,01
022 Pain et autres prod. de boulangerie	0,04	0,01	0,11	0,02	0,06	0,02
023 Sucre de canne et de betterave	0,02	0,00	0,01	0,00	-0,00	0,00
024 Industries alimentaires diverses	0,53	0,09	0,34	0,08	-0,19	-0,01
025 Boissons gazeuses	0,01	0,00	0,07	0,02	0,06	0,01
026 Produits de distillerie	0,31	0,05	0,09	0,02	-0,22	-0,03
027 Produits brassicoles	0,04	0,01	0,06	0,01	0,02	0,01
028 Vin	0,00	0,00	0,01	0,00	0,01	0,00
029 Produits du tabac	0,13	0,02	0,06	0,01	-0,07	-0,01
030 Produits en caoutchouc	0,29	0,05	0,77	0,18	0,48	0,13

Tableau A.3A (suite)

	1961		1992		Variation 1961–1992	
	Emploi lié à l'exportation en % de l'emploi total lié à l'exportation	Emploi lié à l'exportation en % de l'emploi total	Emploi lié à l'exportation en % de l'emploi total lié à l'exportation	Emploi lié à l'exportation en % de l'emploi total	Emploi lié à l'exportation en % de l'emploi total lié à l'exportation	Emploi lié à l'exportation en % de l'emploi total
031 Produits en plastique	0,13	0,02	0,98	0,23	0,84	0,20
032 Tanneries de cuir	0,09	0,02	0,02	0,01	-0,07	-0,01
033 Chaussure	0,07	0,01	0,09	0,02	0,02	0,01
034 Cuir et produits connexes	0,04	0,01	0,04	0,02	0,00	0,01
035 Fibres chimiques, fils et textiles tissés	0,51	0,09	0,34	0,08	-0,17	-0,01
036 Fils de laine et textiles tissés	0,14	0,02	0,07	0,02	-0,07	-0,01
037 Tricots	0,01	0,00	0,03	0,01	0,02	0,00
038 Autres produits textiles	0,25	0,04	0,29	0,07	0,04	0,02
039 Achèvement et teinture de tissus	0,02	0,00	0,06	0,01	0,04	0,01
040 Moquettes, paillassons et tapis	0,00	0,00	0,04	0,01	0,04	0,01
041 Vêtement, sauf bonneterie	0,25	0,04	0,66	0,15	0,41	0,11
042 Bonneterie	0,02	0,00	0,01	0,00	-0,01	-0,00
043 Scieries, atel. rabotage et usi. de bardeaux	3,85	0,66	1,99	0,46	-1,86	-0,20
044 Plaqués et contreplaqués	0,36	0,06	0,16	0,04	-0,20	-0,03
045 Châssis, portes et autres ouvr. de menuis.	0,23	0,04	0,30	0,07	0,07	0,03
046 Boîtes en bois et cercueils	0,10	0,02	0,06	0,01	-0,04	-0,00
047 Autres industries du bois	0,22	0,04	0,25	0,06	0,03	0,02
048 Ameublement de maison	0,04	0,01	0,33	0,08	0,29	0,07
049 Ameublement de bureau	0,00	0,00	0,14	0,03	0,13	0,03
050 Autres mobiliers et app. d'éclairage	0,03	0,01	0,13	0,03	0,10	0,02
051 Pâtes et papiers	5,92	1,02	2,64	0,61	-3,27	-0,41
052 Papier-toiture asphalté	0,02	0,00	0,02	0,01	0,01	0,00
053 Boîtes en carton et sacs en papier	0,27	0,05	0,30	0,07	0,03	0,02
054 Autres prod. de papier façonné	0,15	0,03	0,26	0,06	0,11	0,03
055 Imprimerie et édition	0,65	0,11	0,93	0,22	0,29	0,10
056 Clichage, composition et reliure	0,08	0,01	0,15	0,03	0,07	0,02
057 Acier primaire	1,10	0,19	1,24	0,29	0,14	0,10
058 Canalisations et tuyaux d'acier	0,03	0,00	0,11	0,02	0,08	0,02
059 Fonderies de fer	0,16	0,03	0,23	0,05	0,08	0,03
060 Fonte et affinage métaux non-ferreux	3,18	0,55	1,20	0,28	-1,98	-0,27

Tableau A.3A (suite)

	1961		1992		Variation 1961–1992	
	Emploi lié à l'exportation en % de l'emploi total lié à l'exportation	Emploi lié à l'exportation en % de l'emploi total	Emploi lié à l'exportation en % de l'emploi total lié à l'exportation	Emploi lié à l'exportation en % de l'emploi total	Emploi lié à l'exportation en % de l'emploi total lié à l'exportation	Emploi lié à l'exportation en % de l'emploi total
061 Laminage, moulage et extr. de l'alum.	0,24	0,04	0,20	0,05	-0,04	0,01
062 Laminage, moulage et extr. du cuivre	0,11	0,02	0,07	0,02	-0,04	-0,00
063 Laminage, moulage, etc. d'autres métaux	0,15	0,03	0,20	0,05	0,05	0,02
064 Chaudières et métaux de charpente	0,19	0,03	0,24	0,06	0,05	0,02
065 Prod. métall. décoratifs et architecturaux	0,06	0,01	0,15	0,04	0,09	0,02
066 Métal embouti, pressé et enrobé	0,29	0,05	0,59	0,14	0,31	0,09
067 Tréfilage et produits tréfilés	0,31	0,05	0,30	0,07	-0,00	0,02
068 Art. de quincaillerie, outils et couteaux	0,19	0,03	0,39	0,09	0,20	0,06
069 Matériel de chauffage	0,03	0,01	0,05	0,01	0,02	0,01
070 Ateliers d'usinage	0,15	0,03	0,69	0,16	0,55	0,13
071 Autres métaux ouvrés	0,28	0,05	0,39	0,09	0,11	0,04
072 Instruments agricoles	0,72	0,12	0,21	0,05	-0,51	-0,07
073 Équipement de réfrigération commercial	0,02	0,00	0,11	0,03	0,10	0,02
074 Autres machines et matériel	0,65	0,11	1,70	0,39	1,05	0,28
075 Aéronautique et pièces d'avion	1,17	0,20	1,62	0,37	0,44	0,17
076 Véhicules à moteur	0,11	0,02	2,32	0,54	2,21	0,52
077 Camions, carross. d'autobus et remorques	0,04	0,01	0,16	0,04	0,12	0,03
078 Pièces et accessoires de véh. à moteur	0,37	0,06	3,72	0,86	3,35	0,79
079 Matériel ferroviaire roulant	0,11	0,02	0,20	0,05	0,09	0,03
080 Construction et réparation de navires	0,25	0,04	0,11	0,03	-0,14	-0,02
081 Matériel de transport divers	0,03	0,01	0,11	0,02	0,07	0,02
082 Petits appareils électriques	0,02	0,01	0,05	0,01	0,03	0,01
083 Gros app. (élect. et non électr.)	0,08	0,01	0,09	0,02	0,01	0,01
084 Tourne-disques, radios et téléviseurs	0,05	0,01	0,09	0,02	0,05	0,01
085 Matériel électronique	0,40	0,07	1,82	0,42	1,42	0,35
086 Machines de bureau et de magasin	0,26	0,04	0,71	0,16	0,45	0,12
087 Fils et câbles de transm. et d'énergie	0,13	0,02	0,15	0,03	0,02	0,01
088 Batteries	0,03	0,01	0,04	0,01	0,01	0,00
089 Autres prod. élect. et électroniques	0,38	0,07	0,79	0,18	0,40	0,12
090 Matériaux en céramique	0,06	0,01	0,01	0,00	-0,05	-0,01

Tableau A.3A (suite)

	1961		1992		Variation 1961–1992	
	Emploi lié à l'exportation en % de l'emploi total lié à l'exportation	Emploi lié à l'exportation en % de l'emploi total	Emploi lié à l'exportation en % de l'emploi total lié à l'exportation	Emploi lié à l'exportation en % de l'emploi total	Emploi lié à l'exportation en % de l'emploi total lié à l'exportation	Emploi lié à l'exportation en % de l'emploi total
091 Ciment	0,03	0,00	0,03	0,01	0,00	0,00
092 Produits en béton	0,02	0,00	0,03	0,01	0,00	0,00
093 Béton prémélangé	0,01	0,00	0,02	0,00	0,01	0,00
094 Verre et produits en verre	0,10	0,02	0,21	0,05	0,11	0,03
095 Produits minéraux non métalliques n.c.a.	0,38	0,07	0,27	0,06	-0,11	-0,00
096 Produits du pétrole et du charbon raffinés	0,21	0,04	0,21	0,05	-0,00	0,01
097 Produits chimiques industriels n.c.a.	1,05	0,18	0,63	0,15	-0,42	-0,04
098 Plastiques et résines synthétiques	0,16	0,03	0,26	0,06	0,10	0,03
099 Prod. pharmaceutiques et médicaments	0,09	0,02	0,14	0,03	0,05	0,02
100 Peintures et vernis	0,11	0,02	0,13	0,03	0,03	0,01
101 Savons et prod. de nettoyage	0,07	0,01	0,10	0,02	0,03	0,01
102 Produits de toilette	0,01	0,00	0,06	0,01	0,06	0,01
103 Produits chimiques	0,43	0,07	0,52	0,12	0,09	0,05
104 Bijouterie et métaux précieux	0,14	0,02	0,15	0,03	0,01	0,01
105 Articles de sport et jouets	0,06	0,01	0,15	0,03	0,08	0,02
106 Enseignes et étalages	0,05	0,01	0,09	0,02	0,04	0,01
107 Carreaux, linoléum et tissus enduits	0,03	0,00	0,06	0,01	0,03	0,01
108 Autres industries manufacturières n.c.a.	0,54	0,09	1,04	0,24	0,50	0,15
109 Réparation, construction	2,11	0,36	1,28	0,30	-0,83	-0,07
110 Construction résidentielle	0,00	0,00	0,00	0,00	0,00	0,00
111 Construction d'immeubles non résid.	0,00	0,00	0,00	0,00	0,00	0,00
112 Const. de routes, autor. et pistes d'atterr.	0,00	0,00	0,00	0,00	0,00	0,00
113 Const. d'install. gazières et pétrolières	0,00	0,00	0,00	0,00	0,00	0,00
114 Projets de barrages et d'irrigation	0,00	0,00	0,00	0,00	0,00	0,00
115 Const. de ch. fer et lignes tél. et télég.	0,00	0,00	0,00	0,00	0,00	0,00
116 Autres travaux d'ingénierie	0,00	0,00	0,00	0,00	0,00	0,00
117 Autres activités de construction	0,01	0,00	0,02	0,00	0,00	0,00
118 Transport aérien et services connexes	0,16	0,03	0,62	0,14	0,46	0,11
119 Transport ferroviaire et services connexes	5,07	0,87	1,30	0,30	-3,77	-0,57
120 Transport par eau et services connexes	2,10	0,36	0,62	0,14	-1,48	-0,22

Tableau A.3A (suite)

	1961		1992		Variation 1961–1992	
	Emploi lié à l'exportation en % de l'emploi total lié à l'exportation	Emploi lié à l'exportation en % de l'emploi total	Emploi lié à l'exportation en % de l'emploi total lié à l'exportation	Emploi lié à l'exportation en % de l'emploi total	Emploi lié à l'exportation en % de l'emploi total lié à l'exportation	Emploi lié à l'exportation en % de l'emploi total
121 Camionnage	2,92	0,50	3,13	0,72	0,21	0,22
122 Systèmes de transport urbain	0,01	0,00	0,10	0,02	0,08	0,02
123 Systèmes de transport interurbain et rural	0,01	0,00	0,06	0,01	0,04	0,01
124 Industrie du taxi	0,15	0,03	0,41	0,10	0,26	0,07
125 Autres transports et services connexes	0,07	0,01	1,10	0,25	1,03	0,24
126 Entr. des ponts et des autoroutes	0,01	0,00	0,01	0,00	-0,01	-0,00
127 Transport par pipelines	0,11	0,02	0,18	0,04	0,07	0,02
128 Stockage et entreposage	0,78	0,13	0,49	0,11	-0,29	-0,02
129 Télécommunications et radiodiffusion	0,42	0,07	0,21	0,05	-0,20	-0,02
130 Entreprises de télécomm. et autres	0,53	0,09	0,74	0,17	0,21	0,08
131 Services postaux	0,26	0,04	0,52	0,12	0,26	0,08
132 Systèmes d'énergie électrique	0,77	0,13	1,00	0,23	0,23	0,10
133 Systèmes de distribution du gaz	0,12	0,02	0,10	0,02	-0,02	0,00
134 Autres services publics n.c.a.	0,05	0,01	0,25	0,06	0,20	0,05
135 Commerce de gros	3,63	0,63	7,96	1,84	4,33	1,21
136 Commerce de détail	2,34	0,40	3,74	0,86	1,40	0,46
137 Banq., coop. de crédit et autr. inst. dépôt	0,46	0,08	1,55	0,36	1,09	0,28
138 Fiducies, autres inst. fin. et immob.	0,51	0,09	1,59	0,37	1,09	0,28
139 Industrie de l'assurance	0,67	0,12	0,70	0,16	0,03	0,05
140 Redevances gouv. sur les ress. natur.	0,00	0,00	0,00	0,00	0,00	0,00
141 Logements occupés par leur propriétaire	0,00	0,00	0,00	0,00	0,00	0,00
142 Autres services commerciaux	0,45	0,08	4,60	1,06	4,15	0,98
143 Services profess. aux entreprises	0,94	0,16	4,03	0,93	3,10	0,77
144 Services de publicité	0,18	0,03	0,41	0,09	0,23	0,06
145 Services éducatifs	0,08	0,01	0,21	0,05	0,13	0,03
146 Hôpitaux	0,02	0,00	0,05	0,01	0,03	0,01
147 Autres services de santé	0,00	0,00	0,01	0,00	0,01	0,00
148 Hébergement et restauration	0,46	0,08	5,74	1,32	5,28	1,25
149 Films et vidéos	0,05	0,01	0,20	0,05	0,15	0,04
150 Autres serv. de divertissement et loisir	0,03	0,01	0,59	0,14	0,56	0,13

Tableau A.3A (suite)

	1961		1992		Variation 1961–1992	
	Emploi lié à l'exportation en % de l'emploi total lié à l'exportation	Emploi lié à l'exportation en % de l'emploi total	Emploi lié à l'exportation en % de l'emploi total lié à l'exportation	Emploi lié à l'exportation en % de l'emploi total	Emploi lié à l'exportation en % de l'emploi total lié à l'exportation	Emploi lié à l'exportation en % de l'emploi total
151 Buanderies et nettoyeurs	0,04	0,01	0,09	0,02	0,04	0,01
152 Autres services personnels	0,00	0,00	0,01	0,00	0,01	0,00
153 Photographes	0,01	0,00	0,03	0,01	0,02	0,01
154 Services divers	0,62	0,11	3,02	0,70	2,39	0,59
TOTAL	100,00	17,20	100,00	23,07	0,00	5,87

Tableau A.3B Parts de l'emploi, 1961 et 1992, 161 industries, classement selon la taille des variations

Classement selon la taille des variations	1961		1992		Variation 1961–1992	
	Emploi lié à l'exportation en % de l'emploi total	Emploi lié à l'exportation en % de l'exportation	Emploi lié à l'exportation en % de l'emploi total	Emploi lié à l'exportation en % de l'exportation	Emploi lié à l'exportation en % de l'emploi total	Emploi lié à l'exportation en % de l'exportation
148 Hébergement et restauration	0,46	0,08	5,74	1,32	5,28	1,25
135 Commerce de gros	3,63	0,63	7,96	1,84	4,33	1,21
142 Autres services commerciaux	0,45	0,08	4,60	1,06	4,15	0,98
078 Pièces et accessoires de véh. à moteur	0,37	0,06	3,72	0,86	3,35	0,79
143 Services profes., aux entreprises	0,94	0,16	4,03	0,93	3,10	0,77
154 Services divers	0,62	0,11	3,02	0,70	2,39	0,59
076 Véhicules à moteur	0,11	0,02	2,32	0,54	2,21	0,52
085 Matériel électronique	0,40	0,07	1,82	0,42	1,42	0,35
136 Commerce de détail	2,34	0,40	3,74	0,86	1,40	0,46
137 Banq., coop. de crédit et autr. inst. dépôt	0,46	0,08	1,55	0,36	1,09	0,28
138 Fiducies, autres inst. fin. et immob.	0,51	0,09	1,59	0,37	1,09	0,28
074 Autres machines et matériel	0,65	0,11	1,70	0,39	1,05	0,28
125 Autres transports et services connexes	0,07	0,01	1,10	0,25	1,03	0,24
031 Produits en plastique	0,13	0,02	0,98	0,23	0,84	0,20
150 Autres services de divertiss. et loisir	0,03	0,01	0,59	0,14	0,56	0,13
070 Ateliers d'usinage	0,15	0,03	0,69	0,16	0,55	0,13
108 Autres industries manufacturières n.c.a.	0,54	0,09	1,04	0,24	0,50	0,15
011 Pétrole brut et gaz naturel	0,60	0,10	1,09	0,25	0,50	0,15
030 Produits en caoutchouc	0,29	0,05	0,77	0,18	0,48	0,15
118 Transport aérien et services connexes	0,16	0,03	0,62	0,14	0,46	0,11
086 Machines de bureau et de magasin	0,26	0,04	0,71	0,16	0,45	0,12
075 Aéronautique et pièces d'avion	1,17	0,20	1,62	0,37	0,44	0,17
041 Vêtement, sauf bonneterie	0,25	0,04	0,66	0,15	0,41	0,11
089 Autres prod. élect. et électroniques	0,38	0,07	0,79	0,18	0,40	0,12
013 Services connexes à l'extraction min.	0,16	0,03	0,51	0,12	0,35	0,09
066 Métal embouti, pressé et enrobé	0,29	0,05	0,59	0,14	0,31	0,09
055 Imprimerie et édition	0,65	0,11	0,93	0,22	0,29	0,10
048 Ameublement de maison	0,04	0,01	0,33	0,08	0,29	0,07
131 Services postaux	0,26	0,04	0,52	0,12	0,26	0,08
124 Industrie du taxi	0,15	0,03	0,41	0,10	0,26	0,07
144 Services de publicité	0,18	0,03	0,41	0,09	0,23	0,06
132 Systèmes d'énergie électrique	0,77	0,13	1,00	0,23	0,23	0,10

Tableau A.3B (suite)

Classement selon la taille des variations	1961		1992		Variation 1961–1992	
	Emploi lié à l'exportation en % de l'emploi total	Emploi lié à l'exportation en % de l'emploi lié à l'exportation	Emploi lié à l'exportation en % de l'emploi total	Emploi lié à l'exportation en % de l'emploi lié à l'exportation	Emploi lié à l'exportation en % de l'emploi lié à l'exportation	Emploi lié à l'exportation en % de l'emploi total
121 Camionnage	2.92	0.50	3.13	0.72	0.21	0.22
130 Entreprises de télécomm. et autres	0.53	0.09	0.74	0.17	0.21	0.08
068 Art. de quincaillerie, outils et couteaux	0.19	0.03	0.39	0.20	0.20	0.06
134 Autres services publics n.c.a.	0.05	0.01	0.25	0.06	0.20	0.05
149 Films et vidéos	0.05	0.01	0.20	0.05	0.15	0.04
002 Pêche et piégeage	1.24	0.21	1.38	0.32	0.14	0.11
057 Acier primaire	1.10	0.19	1.24	0.29	0.14	0.10
049 Ameublement de bureau	0.00	0.00	0.14	0.03	0.14	0.03
145 Services éducatifs	0.08	0.01	0.21	0.05	0.13	0.03
077 Camions, caross. d'autob. et remorques	0.04	0.01	0.16	0.04	0.12	0.03
071 Autres métaux ouvrés	0.28	0.05	0.39	0.09	0.11	0.04
094 Verre et produits en verre	0.10	0.02	0.21	0.05	0.11	0.03
054 Autres prod. de papier façonné	0.15	0.03	0.26	0.06	0.11	0.03
098 Plastiques et résines synthétiques	0.16	0.03	0.26	0.06	0.10	0.03
050 Autres mobiliers et app. d'éclairage	0.03	0.01	0.13	0.03	0.10	0.02
073 Équipement de réfrigération commercial	0.02	0.00	0.11	0.03	0.10	0.02
103 Produits chimiques	0.43	0.07	0.52	0.12	0.09	0.05
065 Prod. métall. décoratifs et architecturaux	0.06	0.01	0.15	0.04	0.09	0.05
014 Viande et prod. viande (sauf volaille)	0.28	0.05	0.37	0.09	0.09	0.04
079 Matériel ferroviaire roulant	0.11	0.02	0.20	0.05	0.09	0.03
122 Systèmes de transport urbain	0.01	0.00	0.10	0.02	0.08	0.02
105 Articles de sport et jouets	0.06	0.01	0.15	0.03	0.08	0.02
058 Canalisations et tuyaux d'acier	0.03	0.00	0.11	0.02	0.08	0.02
059 Fonderies de fer	0.16	0.03	0.23	0.05	0.08	0.03
017 Transformation des fruits et légumes	0.08	0.01	0.15	0.04	0.07	0.02
081 Matériel de transport divers	0.03	0.01	0.11	0.02	0.07	0.02
127 Transport par pipelines	0.11	0.02	0.18	0.04	0.07	0.02
045 Châssis, portes et autres ouvr. de men.	0.23	0.04	0.30	0.07	0.07	0.03
056 Clichage, composition et reliure	0.08	0.01	0.15	0.03	0.07	0.02
022 Pain et autres prod. de boulangerie	0.04	0.01	0.11	0.02	0.06	0.02
025 Boissons gazeuses	0.01	0.00	0.07	0.02	0.06	0.01

Tableau A.3B (suite)

Classement selon la taille des variations	1961		1992		Variation 1961-1992	
	Emploi lié à l'exportation en % de l'emploi total	Emploi lié à l'exportation	Emploi lié à l'exportation en % de l'emploi total	Emploi lié à l'exportation	Emploi lié à l'exportation en % de l'emploi total	Emploi lié à l'exportation
102 Produits de toilette	0,01	0,00	0,06	0,01	0,06	0,01
099 Prod. pharmaceutiques et médicaments	0,09	0,02	0,14	0,03	0,05	0,02
064 Chaudières et métaux de charpente	0,19	0,03	0,24	0,06	0,05	0,02
063 Laminage, moulage, etc. d'aut. métaux	0,15	0,03	0,20	0,05	0,05	0,02
084 Tourne-disques, radios et téléviseurs	0,05	0,01	0,09	0,02	0,05	0,02
151 Buanderies et nettoyeurs	0,04	0,01	0,09	0,02	0,04	0,01
123 Systèmes de transport interurbain et rural	0,01	0,00	0,06	0,02	0,04	0,01
040 Moquettes, paillassons et tapis	0,00	0,00	0,04	0,01	0,04	0,01
038 Autres produits textiles	0,25	0,04	0,29	0,07	0,04	0,02
106 Enseignes et étalages	0,05	0,01	0,09	0,02	0,04	0,01
039 Achèvement et teinture de tissus	0,02	0,00	0,06	0,01	0,04	0,01
146 Hôpitaux	0,02	0,00	0,05	0,01	0,03	0,01
101 Savons et prod. de nettoyage	0,07	0,01	0,10	0,02	0,03	0,01
047 Autres industries du bois	0,22	0,04	0,25	0,06	0,03	0,02
107 Carreaux de sol, linol. et tissus enduits	0,03	0,00	0,06	0,01	0,03	0,01
100 Peintures et vernis	0,11	0,02	0,13	0,03	0,03	0,01
139 Industrie de l'assurance	0,67	0,12	0,70	0,16	0,03	0,05
053 Boîtes en carton et sacs en papier	0,27	0,05	0,30	0,07	0,03	0,02
082 Petits appareils électriques	0,02	0,00	0,05	0,01	0,03	0,01
087 Fils et câbles de transm. et d'énergie	0,13	0,02	0,15	0,03	0,02	0,01
153 Photographes	0,01	0,00	0,03	0,01	0,02	0,01
015 Produits de la volaille	0,01	0,00	0,04	0,01	0,02	0,01
027 Produits brassicoles	0,04	0,01	0,06	0,01	0,02	0,01
069 Matériel de chauffage	0,03	0,01	0,05	0,01	0,02	0,01
033 Chaussure	0,07	0,01	0,09	0,02	0,02	0,01
021 Biscuits	0,02	0,00	0,04	0,01	0,02	0,01
037 Tricots	0,01	0,00	0,03	0,01	0,02	0,01
147 Autres services de santé	0,01	0,00	0,01	0,00	0,01	0,00
083 Gros app. (élect. et non électr.)	0,08	0,01	0,09	0,02	0,01	0,01
152 Autres services personnels	0,00	0,00	0,01	0,00	0,01	0,00
104 Bijouterie et métaux précieux	0,14	0,02	0,15	0,03	0,01	0,01

Tableau A.3B (suite)

Classement selon la taille des variations	1961		1992		Variation 1961-1992	
	Emploi lié à l'exportation en % de l'emploi total lié à l'exportation	Emploi lié à l'exportation en % de l'emploi total	Emploi lié à l'exportation en % de l'emploi total lié à l'exportation	Emploi lié à l'exportation en % de l'emploi total	Emploi lié à l'exportation en % de l'emploi total lié à l'exportation	Emploi lié à l'exportation en % de l'emploi total
093 Béton prémélangé	0,01	0,00	0,02	0,00	0,01	0,00
028 Vin	0,00	0,00	0,01	0,00	0,01	0,00
052 Papier-toiture asphalté	0,02	0,00	0,02	0,01	0,01	0,00
088 Batteries	0,03	0,01	0,04	0,01	0,01	0,00
092 Produits en béton	0,02	0,00	0,03	0,01	0,00	0,00
091 Ciment	0,03	0,00	0,03	0,01	0,00	0,00
117 Autres activités de construction	0,01	0,00	0,02	0,01	0,00	0,00
034 Cuir et prod. connexes divers	0,04	0,01	0,04	0,01	0,00	0,00
113 Const. d'install. gazières et pétrolières	0,00	0,00	0,00	0,00	0,00	0,00
111 Const. d'immeubles non résidentiels	0,00	0,00	0,00	0,00	0,00	0,00
112 Const. de routes, autor. et pistes d'atterr.	0,00	0,00	0,00	0,00	0,00	0,00
114 Projets de barrages et d'irrigation	0,00	0,00	0,00	0,00	0,00	0,00
141 Logements occupés par leur propriétaire	0,00	0,00	0,00	0,00	0,00	0,00
116 Autres travaux d'ingénierie	0,00	0,00	0,00	0,00	0,00	0,00
115 Const. de ch. fer et lignes tél. et télég.	0,00	0,00	0,00	0,00	0,00	0,00
110 Construction résidentielle	0,00	0,00	0,00	0,00	0,00	0,00
067 Tréfilage et produits tréfilés	0,31	0,05	0,30	0,07	-0,00	0,02
096 Prod. du pétrole et du charbon raffinés	0,21	0,04	0,21	0,05	-0,00	0,01
140 Redevances gouv. sur les ress. natur.	0,00	0,00	0,00	0,00	0,00	0,00
023 Sucre de canne et betterave	0,02	0,00	0,01	0,00	-0,00	0,00
126 Entr. des ponts et des autoroutes	0,01	0,00	0,01	0,00	-0,00	0,00
020 Raffinage d'huile végétale (sauf maïs)	0,03	0,00	0,02	0,00	-0,01	0,00
042 Bonneterie	0,02	0,00	0,01	0,00	-0,01	-0,00
133 Systèmes de distribution du gaz	0,12	0,02	0,10	0,02	-0,02	0,00
009 Mines de sel	0,04	0,01	0,02	0,00	-0,02	-0,00
008 Min. non métall. sauf charbon et amiante	0,28	0,05	0,25	0,06	-0,03	-0,00
012 Carrières et sablières	0,13	0,02	0,09	0,02	-0,04	0,01
061 Laminage, moulage et extr. de l'alumi.	0,24	0,04	0,20	0,05	-0,04	-0,00
046 Boîtes en bois et cercueils	0,10	0,02	0,06	0,01	-0,04	0,00
062 Laminage, moulage et extr. du cuivre	0,11	0,02	0,07	0,02	-0,04	-0,00
090 Matériaux en céramique	0,06	0,01	0,01	0,00	-0,05	-0,01

Tableau A.3B (suite)

Classement selon la taille des variations	1961		1992		Variation 1961–1992	
	Emploi lié à l'exportation en % de l'emploi total lié à l'exportation	Emploi lié à l'exportation en % de l'emploi total	Emploi lié à l'exportation en % de l'emploi total lié à l'exportation	Emploi lié à l'exportation en % de l'emploi total	Emploi lié à l'exportation en % de l'emploi total lié à l'exportation	Emploi lié à l'exportation en % de l'emploi total
036 Fils de laine et textiles tissés	0,14	0,02	0,07	0,02	-0,07	-0,01
032 Tanneries de cuir	0,09	0,02	0,07	0,01	-0,07	-0,01
029 Produits du tabac	0,13	0,02	0,06	0,01	-0,07	-0,01
018 Produits laitiers	0,17	0,03	0,09	0,02	-0,08	-0,01
095 Produits min. non métalliques n.c.a.	0,38	0,07	0,27	0,06	-0,11	-0,01
080 Construction et réparation de navires	0,25	0,04	0,11	0,03	-0,14	-0,00
035 Fibres chimiques, fils et textiles tissés	0,51	0,09	0,34	0,08	-0,17	-0,02
019 Nourriture pour animaux	0,34	0,06	0,16	0,04	-0,18	-0,01
024 Industries alimentaires diverses	0,53	0,09	0,34	0,08	-0,19	-0,02
044 Plaqués et contreplaqués	0,36	0,06	0,16	0,04	-0,20	-0,01
129 Télécommunications et radiodiffusion	0,42	0,07	0,21	0,05	-0,20	-0,03
026 Produits de distillerie	0,31	0,05	0,09	0,02	-0,22	-0,02
016 Produits du poisson	1,11	0,19	0,87	0,20	-0,25	-0,03
010 Mines de charbon	0,52	0,09	0,25	0,06	-0,27	0,01
128 Stockage et entreposage	0,78	0,13	0,49	0,11	-0,29	-0,03
097 Produits chimiques industriels n.c.a.	1,05	0,18	0,63	0,15	-0,42	-0,04
072 Instruments agricoles	0,72	0,12	0,21	0,05	-0,51	-0,07
006 Mines de fer	0,79	0,14	0,22	0,05	-0,58	-0,09
007 Mines d'amiante	0,72	0,12	0,10	0,02	-0,62	-0,10
109 Réparation, construction	2,11	0,36	1,28	0,30	-0,83	-0,07
004 Mines d'or	1,81	0,31	0,35	0,08	-1,46	-0,23
120 Transport par eau et services connexes	2,10	0,36	0,62	0,14	-1,48	-0,22
043 Scieries, atel. de rabot. et us. bardeaux	3,85	0,66	1,99	0,46	-1,86	-0,20
060 Fonte et affinage métaux non-ferreux	3,18	0,55	1,20	0,28	-1,98	-0,27
005 Autres mines métalliques	3,35	0,58	0,87	0,20	-2,48	-0,38
051 Pâtes et papiers	5,92	1,02	2,64	0,61	-3,27	-0,41
119 Transport ferroviaire et services conn.	5,07	0,87	1,30	0,30	-3,77	-0,57
003 Abattage et foresterie	5,55	0,95	1,77	0,41	-3,78	-0,55
001 Agriculture et ind. connexes	26,93	4,63	8,69	2,01	-18,24	-2,63
TOTAL	100,00	17,20	100,00	23,07	0,00	5,87

Tableau A.4A Décomposition des variations des parts de l'emploi, 1961–1992, 161 industries

	1961	1992	Variation 1961–1992	Attribuable à :			
	Emploi lié à l'exportation en % de l'emploi total lié à l'exportation	Emploi lié à l'exportation en % de l'emploi total lié à l'exportation	Emploi lié à l'exportation en % de l'emploi total lié à l'exportation	Variation de la part des exportations	Variation du ratio emploi/ production des coefficients entrées-sorties	Variation des coefficients d'importation	Interaction résiduelle
001 Agriculture et ind. connexes	26,93	8,69	-18,24	-13,16	-3,23	-0,30	-2,09
002 Pêche et piégeage	1,24	1,38	0,14	-0,64	0,46	-0,14	0,24
003 Abattage et foresterie	5,55	1,77	-3,78	-1,36	-1,17	-0,21	-1,15
004 Mines d'or	1,81	0,35	-1,46	-0,31	-0,64	-0,02	-0,50
005 Autres mines métalliques	3,35	0,87	-2,48	-1,31	-0,14	-0,26	-0,72
006 Mines de fer	0,79	0,22	-0,58	-0,48	-0,04	-0,05	-0,06
007 Mines d'amiante	0,72	0,10	-0,62	-1,06	0,04	-0,03	0,41
008 Min. non mét. sauf charbon et amiante	0,28	0,25	-0,03	0,01	-0,26	-0,02	0,17
009 Mines de sel	0,04	0,02	-0,02	0,01	-0,00	-0,00	0,05
010 Mines de charbon	0,52	0,25	-0,27	0,18	-0,89	-0,01	-0,00
011 Pétrole brut et gaz naturel	0,60	1,09	0,50	0,47	-0,25	-0,05	0,47
012 Carrières et sablières	0,13	0,09	-0,04	-0,06	0,00	0,01	0,03
013 Services connexes à l'extraction min.	0,16	0,51	0,35	0,04	0,24	0,06	-0,21
014 Viande et pr. de la viande (sauf volaille)	0,28	0,37	0,09	0,02	0,09	0,01	0,03
015 Produits de la volaille	0,01	0,04	0,02	0,01	0,01	0,00	-0,00
016 Produits du poisson	1,11	0,87	-0,25	-0,31	0,07	0,05	0,04
017 Transformation des fruits et légumes	0,08	0,15	0,07	0,08	-0,01	0,01	0,02
018 Produits laitiers	0,17	0,09	-0,08	-0,05	-0,01	0,00	0,00
019 Nourriture pour animaux	0,34	0,16	-0,18	-0,16	-0,02	-0,01	0,00
020 Raffinage d'huile végétale (sauf maïs)	0,03	0,02	-0,01	-0,01	-0,00	-0,00	0,00
021 Biscuits	0,02	0,04	0,02	0,02	-0,01	0,00	0,00
022 Pain et autres prod. de boulangerie	0,04	0,11	0,06	0,07	-0,01	0,00	0,01
023 Sucre de canne et betterave	0,02	0,01	-0,00	0,00	0,00	0,00	0,00
024 Industries alimentaires diverses	0,53	0,34	-0,19	-0,20	0,04	-0,06	0,01
025 Boissons gazeuses	0,01	0,07	0,06	0,05	-0,05	0,01	0,05
026 Produits de distillerie	0,31	0,09	-0,22	-0,25	0,01	0,01	0,02
027 Produits brassicoles	0,04	0,06	0,02	0,02	-0,00	0,01	0,00
028 Vin	0,00	0,01	0,01	0,01	-0,00	-0,00	-0,00
029 Produits du tabac	0,13	0,06	-0,07	-0,02	-0,03	-0,00	-0,02
030 Produits en caoutchouc	0,29	0,77	0,48	0,55	0,13	-0,15	0,08

Tableau A.4A (suite)

	1961	1992	Variation 1961–1992	Attribuable à :				
	Emploi lié à l'exportation en % de l'emploi total lié à l'exportation	Emploi lié à l'exportation en % de l'emploi total lié à l'exportation	Emploi lié à l'exportation en % de l'emploi total lié à l'exportation	Variation de la part des exportations	Variation du ratio emploi/production	Variation des coefficients entrées-sorties	Variation des coefficients d'importation	Interaction résiduelle
031 Produits en plastique	0,13	0,98	0,84	0,59	0,06	0,21	-0,04	0,03
032 Tanneries de cuir	0,09	0,02	-0,07	-0,07	0,00	0,00	-0,02	0,02
033 Chaussure	0,07	0,09	0,02	0,02	0,01	-0,01	-0,01	0,01
034 Cuir et prod. connexes divers	0,04	0,04	0,00	0,01	0,01	-0,00	-0,01	0,00
035 Fibres chimiques, fils et textiles tissés	0,51	0,34	-0,17	0,05	-0,05	-0,14	-0,06	0,03
036 Fils de laine et textiles tissés	0,14	0,07	-0,07	-0,03	0,00	-0,04	-0,02	0,02
037 Tricots	0,01	0,03	0,02	0,02	-0,00	0,01	-0,02	-0,00
038 Autres produits textiles	0,25	0,29	0,04	0,06	0,05	-0,05	-0,02	-0,00
039 Achèvement et teinture de tissus	0,02	0,06	0,04	0,04	0,01	0,01	-0,01	0,00
040 Moquettes, paillassons et tapis	0,00	0,04	0,04	0,04	-0,01	-0,00	-0,00	-0,02
041 Vêtement, sauf bonneterie	0,25	0,66	0,41	0,45	0,05	-0,07	-0,01	-0,01
042 Bonneterie	0,02	0,01	-0,01	-0,01	0,00	-0,00	0,00	0,00
043 Scieries, atel. rabot. et usines bardeaux	3,85	1,99	-1,86	-0,98	-0,98	-0,08	0,17	0,02
044 Plaqués et contreplaqués	0,36	0,16	-0,20	-0,17	-0,02	-0,03	0,01	0,01
045 Châssis, portes et autr. ouvr. de menuis.	0,23	0,30	0,07	0,06	0,04	-0,05	0,02	-0,00
046 Boîtes en bois et cercueils	0,10	0,06	-0,04	-0,01	-0,01	-0,01	-0,01	-0,00
047 Autres industries du bois	0,22	0,25	0,03	0,12	-0,15	-0,03	0,02	0,07
048 Ameublement de maison	0,04	0,33	0,29	0,30	0,03	-0,03	0,01	-0,02
049 Ameublement de bureau	0,00	0,14	0,13	0,13	0,00	-0,01	0,01	0,00
050 Autres mobiliers et app. d'éclairage	0,03	0,13	0,10	0,09	0,03	-0,01	0,00	-0,01
051 Pâtes et papiers	5,92	2,64	-3,27	-3,27	0,02	-0,33	0,14	0,17
052 Papier-toiture asphalté	0,02	0,02	0,01	0,01	-0,01	-0,01	0,00	0,01
053 Boîtes en carton et sacs en papier	0,27	0,30	0,03	0,06	0,03	-0,11	-0,02	0,06
054 Autres prod. de papier façonné	0,15	0,26	0,11	0,11	0,03	-0,08	-0,01	0,05
055 Imprimerie et édition	0,65	0,93	0,29	0,33	-0,01	-0,23	-0,04	0,23
056 Clichage, composition et reliure	0,08	0,15	0,07	0,06	0,02	-0,04	-0,00	0,02
057 Acier primaire	1,10	1,24	0,14	0,30	-0,03	-0,15	-0,19	0,21
058 Canalisations et tuyaux d'acier	0,03	0,11	0,08	0,05	0,04	-0,01	-0,00	0,00
059 Fonderies de fer	0,16	0,23	0,08	0,08	-0,05	-0,00	-0,02	0,08

Tableau A.4A (suite)

	1961	1992	Variation 1961-1992	Attribuable à :				
	Emploi lié à l'exportation en % de l'emploi total lié à l'exportation	Emploi lié à l'exportation en % de l'emploi total lié à l'exportation	Emploi lié à l'exportation en % de l'emploi total lié à l'exportation	Variation de la part des exportations	Variation du ratio emploi/ production	Variation des coefficients entrées-sorties	Variation des coefficients d'importation	Interaction résiduelle
060 Fonte et affinage métaux non-ferreux	3.18	1.20	-1.98	-1.79	-0.04	-0.10	-0.02	-0.03
061 Laminage, moulage et extr. de l'alum.	0.24	0.20	-0.04	0.04	-0.13	0.03	-0.08	0.10
062 Laminage, moulage et extr. du cuivre	0.11	0.07	-0.04	-0.07	0.03	-0.06	-0.04	0.10
063 Laminage, moulage, etc. d'aut. métaux	0.15	0.20	0.05	-0.02	0.07	-0.05	-0.02	0.07
064 Chaudières et métaux de charpente	0.19	0.24	0.05	0.07	0.04	-0.10	0.01	0.04
065 Prod. métall. décoratifs et architecturaux	0.06	0.15	0.09	0.08	0.01	0.00	0.00	-0.01
066 Métal embouti, pressé et enrobé	0.29	0.59	0.31	0.30	0.09	-0.09	-0.07	0.06
067 Tréfilage et produits tréfilés	0.31	0.30	-0.00	0.16	0.04	-0.23	-0.07	0.09
068 Art. de quincaillerie, outils et couteaux	0.19	0.39	0.20	0.17	0.10	-0.04	-0.02	-0.00
069 Matériel de chauffage	0.03	0.05	0.02	0.02	0.01	-0.01	-0.00	-0.00
070 Ateliers d'usinage	0.15	0.69	0.55	0.49	0.16	0.05	-0.16	-0.00
071 Autres métaux ouvrés	0.28	0.39	0.11	0.15	0.03	-0.08	-0.06	0.07
072 Instruments agricoles	0.72	0.21	-0.51	-0.57	0.02	-0.04	0.02	0.06
073 Équipement de réfrigération commercial	0.02	0.11	0.10	0.09	0.02	0.03	-0.04	-0.00
074 Autres machines et matériel	0.65	1.70	1.05	1.05	0.11	0.03	-0.05	0.05
075 Aéronautique et pièces d'avion	1.17	1.62	0.44	0.56	-0.10	-0.14	0.04	0.09
076 Véhicules à moteur	0.11	2.32	2.21	2.26	-1.56	-0.28	0.18	1.59
077 Camions, carross. d'autob. et remorques	0.04	0.16	0.12	0.12	0.02	0.01	-0.00	-0.02
078 Pièces et accessoires de véh. à moteur	0.37	3.72	3.35	3.47	-0.31	-0.03	-1.06	1.27
079 Matériel ferroviaire roulant	0.11	0.20	0.09	0.14	-0.06	-0.02	-0.01	0.03
080 Construction et réparation de navires	0.25	0.11	-0.14	-0.14	-0.02	-0.00	0.01	0.01
081 Matériel de transport divers	0.03	0.11	0.07	0.08	-0.06	-0.00	0.01	0.05
082 Petits appareils électriques	0.02	0.05	0.03	0.03	0.01	-0.01	0.01	0.00
083 Gros app. (élect. et non électr.)	0.08	0.09	0.01	0.02	-0.00	-0.01	-0.00	0.00
084 Tourne-disques, radios et téléviseurs	0.05	0.09	0.05	0.07	-0.03	-0.01	-0.05	0.07
085 Matériel électronique	0.40	1.82	1.42	1.58	-1.62	0.09	-0.39	1.75
086 Machines de bureau et de magasin	0.26	0.71	0.45	0.55	-0.16	-0.07	-0.16	0.29
087 Fils et câbles de transm. et d'énergie	0.13	0.15	0.02	0.03	0.01	-0.03	-0.02	0.03
088 Batteries	0.03	0.04	0.01	0.01	0.01	-0.01	-0.01	0.01

Tableau A-4A (suite)

	1961	1992	Variation 1961-1992	Attribuable à :				
	Emploi lié à l'exportation en % de l'emploi total	Emploi lié à l'exportation en % de l'emploi total	Emploi lié à l'exportation en % de l'emploi total	Variation de la part des exportations	Variation du ratio emploi/production	Variation des coefficients entrées-sorties	Variation des coefficients d'importation	Interaction résiduelle
089 Autres prod. élect. et électroniques	0,38	0,79	0,40	0,40	0,07	-0,06	-0,16	0,16
090 Matériaux en céramique	0,06	0,01	-0,05	-0,02	-0,00	-0,01	-0,00	-0,01
091 Ciment	0,03	0,03	0,00	0,01	0,00	-0,01	0,00	-0,00
092 Produits en béton	0,02	0,03	0,00	0,01	0,00	-0,01	0,00	0,00
093 Béton prémélangé	0,01	0,02	0,01	-0,00	0,01	-0,01	0,00	0,00
094 Verre et produits en verre	0,10	0,21	0,11	0,13	0,01	0,00	0,00	-0,03
095 Produits minéraux non métall. n.c.a.	0,38	0,27	-0,11	-0,08	-0,02	-0,11	-0,01	0,12
096 Prod. du pétrole et du charbon raffinés	0,21	0,21	-0,00	0,00	0,01	-0,06	-0,03	0,06
097 Produits chimiques industriels n.c.a.	1,05	0,63	-0,42	-0,09	-0,37	0,03	-0,00	0,05
098 Plastiques et résines synthétiques	0,16	0,26	0,10	0,13	-0,08	0,01	-0,03	0,07
099 Prod. pharmaceutiques et médicaments	0,09	0,14	0,05	0,06	-0,04	0,01	0,00	0,03
100 Peintures et vernis	0,11	0,13	0,03	0,05	-0,01	-0,00	-0,03	0,02
101 Savons et prod. de nettoyage	0,07	0,10	0,03	0,05	0,03	-0,00	-0,01	0,01
102 Produits de toilette	0,01	0,06	0,06	0,02	0,03	-0,02	-0,01	0,01
103 Produits chimiques	0,43	0,52	0,09	0,05	0,01	0,03	-0,07	0,07
104 Bijouterie et métaux précieux	0,14	0,15	0,01	0,08	0,01	-0,02	-0,00	-0,07
105 Articles de sport et jouets	0,06	0,15	0,08	0,09	0,09	-0,02	0,00	0,01
106 Enseignes et étalages	0,05	0,09	0,04	0,03	0,03	-0,03	-0,00	0,01
107 Carreaux, linoléum et tissus enduits	0,03	0,06	0,03	0,04	0,03	-0,01	-0,01	0,01
108 Autres industries manufacturières n.c.a.	0,54	1,04	0,50	0,52	0,12	-0,10	-0,09	0,06
109 Réparation, construction	2,11	1,28	-0,83	-0,41	-0,19	-0,43	0,02	0,19
110 Construction résidentielle	0,00	0,00	0,00	0,00	0,00	0,00	0,00	0,00
111 Const. d'immeubles non résidentiels	0,00	0,00	0,00	0,00	0,00	0,00	0,00	0,00
112 Const. de routes, autor. et pistes d'atter.	0,00	0,00	0,00	0,00	0,00	0,00	0,00	0,00
113 Const. d'install. gazières et pétrolières	0,00	0,00	0,00	0,00	0,00	0,00	0,00	0,00
114 Projets de barrages et d'irrigation	0,00	0,00	0,00	0,00	0,00	0,00	0,00	0,00
115 Const. de ch. fer et lignes tél. et télég.	0,00	0,00	0,00	0,00	0,00	0,00	0,00	0,00
116 Autres travaux d'ingénierie	0,00	0,00	0,00	0,00	0,00	0,00	0,00	0,00
117 Autres activités de construction	0,01	0,02	0,00	0,00	0,01	-0,01	-0,00	0,01
118 Transport aérien et services connexes	0,16	0,62	0,46	0,41	-0,04	0,03	-0,04	0,11

Tableau A.4A (suite)

	1961	1992	Variation 1961-1992	Attribuable à :				
	Emploi lié à l'exportation en % de l'emploi total lié à l'exportation	Emploi lié à l'exportation en % de l'emploi total lié à l'exportation	Emploi lié à l'exportation en % de l'emploi total lié à l'exportation	Variation de la part des exportations	Variation du ratio emploi/ production	Variation des coefficients entrées-sorties	Variation des coefficients d'importation	Interaction résiduelle
119 Transport ferroviaire et services conn.	5,07	1,30	-3,77	-0,66	-0,37	-1,80	0,01	-0,94
120 Transport par eau et services connexes	2,10	0,62	-1,48	-0,79	-0,18	-0,23	0,03	-0,30
121 Camionnage	2,92	3,13	0,21	-0,95	-0,56	0,99	0,10	0,64
122 Systèmes de transport urbain	0,01	0,10	0,08	0,07	0,05	-0,01	0,00	-0,03
123 Syst. de transport interurbain et rural	0,01	0,06	0,04	0,05	-0,01	-0,01	-0,00	0,02
124 Industrie du taxi	0,15	0,41	0,26	0,17	0,08	0,04	-0,04	0,01
125 Autres transports et services connexes	0,07	1,10	1,03	0,13	0,56	0,66	0,03	-0,35
126 Entr. des ponts et des autoroutes	0,01	0,01	-0,01	-0,00	-0,00	-0,00	0,00	0,00
127 Transport par pipelines	0,11	0,18	0,07	0,01	0,04	-0,01	0,01	0,01
128 Stockage et entreposage	0,78	0,49	-0,29	-0,56	0,17	-0,19	0,03	0,26
129 Télécommunications et radiodiffusion	0,42	0,21	-0,20	-0,08	-0,19	-0,19	-0,00	0,01
130 Entreprises de télécomm. et autres	0,53	0,74	0,21	0,20	-0,21	0,04	-0,01	0,19
131 Services postaux	0,26	0,52	0,26	0,17	0,01	0,03	0,01	0,05
132 Systèmes d'énergie électrique	0,77	1,00	0,23	-0,33	-0,21	0,39	0,00	0,38
133 Systèmes de distribution du gaz	0,12	0,10	-0,02	-0,00	-0,05	0,01	0,00	0,02
134 Autres services publics n.c.a.	0,05	0,25	0,20	-0,00	0,01	0,19	-0,00	0,01
135 Commerce de gros	3,63	7,96	4,33	1,37	1,95	0,66	0,11	0,23
136 Commerce de détail	2,34	3,74	1,40	-0,03	1,22	-0,79	0,03	0,96
137 Banq., coop. de crédit et autr. inst. dépôt	0,46	1,55	1,09	0,15	-0,01	0,80	-0,00	0,16
138 Fiducies, autres inst. fin. et immob.	0,51	1,59	1,09	0,22	0,62	0,25	0,02	-0,03
139 Industrie de l'assurance	0,67	0,70	0,03	0,17	-0,10	-0,11	0,01	0,05
140 Redevances gouv. sur les ress. natur.	0,00	0,00	0,00	0,00	0,00	0,00	0,00	0,00
141 Logements occupés par leur propriétaire	0,00	0,00	0,00	0,00	0,00	0,00	0,00	0,00
142 Autres services commerciaux	0,45	4,60	4,15	2,15	1,68	1,85	0,91	-2,45
143 Services profess. aux entreprises	0,94	4,03	3,10	1,98	0,94	1,15	0,18	-1,15
144 Services de publicité	0,18	0,41	0,23	0,01	0,07	0,17	0,01	-0,02
145 Services éducatifs	0,08	0,21	0,13	0,11	0,03	-0,02	0,02	-0,01
146 Hôpitaux	0,02	0,05	0,03	0,04	-0,01	-0,01	0,00	-0,01
147 Autres services de santé	0,00	0,01	0,01	0,00	0,00	0,01	0,00	-0,01
148 Hébergement et restauration	0,46	5,74	5,28	4,73	2,95	-0,42	0,03	-2,01

Tableau A.4A (suite)

| | 1961 | 1992 | Variation 1961-1992 | Attribuable à : | | | | |
	Emploi lié à l'exportation en % de l'emploi total lié à l'exportation	Emploi lié à l'exportation en % de l'emploi total lié à l'exportation	Emploi lié à l'exportation en % de l'emploi total lié à l'exportation	Variation de la part des exportations	Variation du ratio emploi/ production	Variation des coefficients entrées-sorties	Variation des coefficients d'importation	Interaction résiduelle
149 Films et vidéos	0,05	0,20	0,15	0,10	0,01	0,02	0,01	0,01
150 Autres services de divertiss. et loisir	0,03	0,59	0,56	0,56	0,16	-0,06	0,04	-0,14
151 Buanderies et nettoyeurs	0,04	0,09	0,04	0,02	0,02	-0,01	-0,00	0,02
152 Autres services personnels	0,00	0,01	0,01	0,00	0,00	-0,00	0,00	0,00
153 Photographes	0,01	0,03	0,02	0,01	0,02	0,01	0,00	0,00
154 Services divers	0,62	3,02	2,39	-0,02	1,77	1,03	0,07	-0,46

Tableau A.4B Décomposition des variations des parts de l'emploi, 1961-1992, 161 industries

Classement selon la taille des variations	1961 Emploi lié à l'exportation en % de l'emploi total lié à l'exportation	1992 Emploi lié à l'exportation en % de l'emploi total lié à l'exportation	Variation 1961-1992 Emploi lié à l'exportation en % de l'emploi total lié à l'exportation	Variation de la part des exportations	Attribuable à : Variation du ratio emploi/ production	Variation des coefficients entrées-sorties	Variation des coefficients d'importation	Interaction résiduelle
148 Hébergement et restauration	0,46	5,74	5,28	4,73	2,95	-0,42	0,03	-2,01
135 Commerce de gros	3,63	7,96	4,33	1,37	1,95	0,66	0,11	0,23
142 Autres services commerciaux	0,45	4,60	4,15	2,15	1,68	1,85	0,91	-2,45
078 Pièces et accessoires de véh. à moteur	0,37	3,72	3,35	3,47	-0,31	-0,03	-1,06	1,27
143 Services profess. aux entreprises	0,94	4,03	3,10	1,98	0,94	0,18	0,18	-1,15
154 Services divers	0,62	3,02	2,39	-0,02	1,77	1,03	0,07	-0,46
076 Véhicules à moteur	0,11	2,32	2,21	2,26	-1,56	-0,28	0,18	1,59
085 Matériel électronique	0,40	1,82	1,42	1,58	-1,62	0,09	-0,39	1,75
136 Commerce de détail	2,34	3,74	1,40	-0,03	1,22	-0,79	0,03	0,96
137 Banq., coop. de crédit et autr. inst. dépôt	0,46	1,55	1,09	-0,03	-0,01	0,80	-0,00	0,16
138 Fiducies, autres inst. fin. et immob.	0,51	1,59	1,09	0,22	0,62	0,25	0,02	-0,03
074 Autres machines et matériel	0,65	1,70	1,05	1,05	0,11	-0,12	-0,05	0,05
125 Autres transports et services connexes	0,07	1,10	1,03	0,13	0,56	0,66	0,03	-0,35
031 Produits en plastique	0,13	0,98	0,84	0,59	0,06	0,21	-0,04	0,03
150 Autres serv. de divertissement et loisir	0,03	0,59	0,56	0,56	0,16	-0,06	0,04	0,03
070 Ateliers d'usinage	0,15	0,69	0,55	0,49	0,16	0,05	-0,16	-0,14
108 Autres industries manufacturières n.c.a.	0,54	1,04	0,50	0,52	0,12	-0,06	-0,09	-0,06
011 Pétrole brut et gaz naturel	0,60	1,09	0,50	0,47	-0,25	-0,01	0,14	0,14
030 Produits en caoutchouc	0,29	0,77	0,48	0,55	0,13	-0,13	-0,15	0,08
118 Transport aérien et services connexes	0,16	0,62	0,46	0,41	-0,04	0,03	-0,04	0,11
086 Machines de bureau et de magasin	0,26	0,71	0,45	0,55	-0,16	-0,07	-0,16	0,29
075 Aéronautique et pièces d'avion	1,17	1,62	0,44	0,56	-0,10	-0,14	0,04	0,09
041 Vêtement, sauf bonneterie	0,25	0,66	0,41	0,41	0,05	-0,07	-0,01	-0,01
089 Autres prod. élect. et électroniques	0,38	0,79	0,40	0,40	0,07	-0,06	-0,16	0,16
013 Services connexes à l'extraction min.	0,16	0,51	0,35	0,04	0,24	0,22	0,06	-0,21
066 Métal embouti, pressé et enrobé	0,29	0,59	0,31	0,30	0,09	-0,09	-0,07	0,06
055 Imprimerie et édition	0,65	0,93	0,29	0,30	-0,01	-0,23	-0,04	0,23
048 Ameublement de maison	0,04	0,33	0,29	0,33	0,03	-0,03	0,01	-0,02
131 Services postaux	0,26	0,52	0,26	0,17	0,01	0,03	0,01	0,05

Tableau A.4B (suite)

Classement selon la taille des variations	1961 Emploi lié à l'exportation en % de l'emploi total / l'exportation lié à l'exportation	1992 Emploi lié à l'exportation en % de l'emploi total / l'exportation lié à l'exportation	Variation 1961–1992 Emploi lié à l'exportation en % de l'emploi total / l'exportation lié à l'exportation	Variation de la part des exportations	Attribuable à : Variation du ratio emploi/production	Variation des coefficients entrées-sorties	Variation des coefficients d'importation	Interaction résiduelle
124 Industrie du taxi	0,15	0,41	0,26	0,17	0,08	0,04	-0,04	0,01
144 Services de publicité	0,18	0,41	0,23	0,01	0,07	0,17	0,01	-0,02
132 Systèmes d'énergie électrique	0,77	1,00	0,23	-0,33	-0,21	0,39	0,00	0,38
121 Camionnage	2,92	3,13	0,21	-0,95	-0,56	0,99	0,10	0,64
130 Entreprises de télécomm. et autres	0,53	0,74	0,21	0,20	-0,21	0,04	-0,01	0,19
068 Art. de quincaillerie, outils et couteaux	0,19	0,39	0,20	0,17	0,10	-0,04	-0,02	-0,00
134 Autres services publics n.c.a.	0,05	0,25	0,20	-0,00	0,01	0,19	-0,02	-0,00
149 Films et vidéos	0,05	0,20	0,15	0,10	0,01	0,02	-0,00	0,01
002 Pêche et piégeage	1,24	1,38	0,14	-0,64	0,46	-0,14	0,22	0,24
057 Acier primaire	1,10	1,24	0,14	0,30	-0,03	-0,15	-0,19	0,21
049 Ameublement de bureau	0,00	0,14	0,13	0,13	0,00	-0,01	0,01	0,00
145 Services éducatifs	0,08	0,21	0,13	0,11	0,03	-0,02	0,02	-0,01
077 Camions, carross. d'autobus et remorques	0,04	0,16	0,12	0,12	0,02	0,01	-0,00	-0,02
071 Autres métaux ouvrés	0,28	0,39	0,11	0,15	0,03	-0,08	-0,06	0,07
094 Verre et produits en verre	0,10	0,21	0,11	0,13	-0,02	-0,11	-0,01	0,12
054 Autres prod. de papier façonné	0,15	0,26	0,11	0,11	0,03	-0,08	-0,01	0,05
098 Plastiques et résines synthétiques	0,16	0,26	0,10	0,13	-0,08	-0,08	-0,03	0,07
050 Autres mobiliers et app. d'éclairage	0,03	0,13	0,10	0,09	0,03	-0,01	0,00	-0,01
073 Équipement de réfrigération commercial	0,02	0,11	0,09	0,09	0,02	0,03	-0,04	-0,00
103 Produits chimiques	0,43	0,52	0,09	0,08	-0,07	0,03	-0,07	0,12
065 Prod. métall. décoratifs et architecturaux	0,06	0,15	0,09	0,08	0,01	0,00	0,00	-0,01
014 Viande et pr. de la viande (sauf volaille)	0,28	0,37	0,09	0,02	0,09	-0,06	0,01	0,03
079 Matériel ferroviaire roulant	0,11	0,20	0,09	0,14	-0,06	-0,02	-0,01	0,03
122 Systèmes de transport urbain	0,01	0,10	0,08	0,07	0,05	-0,01	0,00	-0,03
105 Articles de sport et jouets	0,06	0,15	0,08	0,09	-0,01	-0,02	0,00	0,01
058 Canalisations et tuyaux d'acier	0,03	0,11	0,08	0,05	0,04	-0,01	-0,01	0,00
059 Fonderies de fer	0,16	0,23	0,08	0,08	-0,05	-0,00	-0,02	0,08
017 Transformation des fruits et légumes	0,08	0,15	0,07	0,08	-0,01	-0,01	-0,00	0,02
081 Matériel de transport divers	0,03	0,11	0,07	0,08	-0,06	0,01	0,01	0,05

Tableau A-4B (suite)

Classement selon la taille des variations	1961	1992	Variation 1961-1992	Variation de la part des exportations	Attribuable à :			
	Emploi lié à l'exportation en % de l'emploi total lié à l'exportation	Emploi lié à l'exportation en % de l'emploi total lié à l'exportation	Emploi lié à l'exportation en % de l'emploi total lié à l'exportation		Variation du ratio emploi/production	Variation des coefficients entrées-sorties	Variation des coefficients d'importation	Interaction résiduelle
127 Transport par pipelines	0,11	0,18	0,07	0,01	0,04	-0,01	0,01	0,01
045 Châssis, portes et autres ouvr. de menuis.	0,23	0,30	0,07	0,06	0,04	-0,05	0,02	-0,00
056 Clichage, composition et reliure	0,08	0,15	0,07	0,06	0,02	-0,04	-0,00	0,02
022 Pain et autres prod. de boulangerie	0,04	0,11	0,06	0,07	0,00	-0,01	0,00	0,01
025 Boissons gazeuses	0,01	0,07	0,06	0,05	0,01	0,01	0,00	0,05
102 Produits de toilette	0,01	0,06	0,06	0,05	0,01	-0,00	-0,00	-0,01
099 Prod. pharmaceutiques et médicaments	0,09	0,14	0,05	0,06	0,01	-0,00	-0,00	0,03
064 Chaudières et métaux de charpente	0,19	0,24	0,05	0,06	-0,04	0,01	0,00	0,03
063 Laminage, moulage, etc. d'autres métaux	0,15	0,20	0,05	-0,02	0,07	0,01	0,01	0,04
084 Tourne-disques, radios et téléviseurs	0,05	0,09	0,05	0,07	-0,03	-0,05	-0,02	0,07
151 Buanderies et nettoyeurs	0,04	0,09	0,05	0,02	0,02	-0,00	-0,05	0,07
123 Systèmes de transport interurbain et rural	0,05	0,09	0,05	0,07	-0,01	-0,01	-0,01	0,07
040 Moquettes, paillassons et tapis	0,00	0,04	0,04	0,04	-0,01	-0,00	-0,00	0,01
038 Autres produits textiles	0,25	0,29	0,04	0,06	-0,01	-0,02	-0,02	0,00
106 Enseignes et étalages	0,05	0,09	0,04	0,03	0,05	-0,05	0,01	0,01
039 Achèvement et teinture de tissus	0,02	0,06	0,04	0,04	0,03	-0,03	-0,00	-0,01
146 Hôpitaux	0,02	0,06	0,04	0,04	0,01	0,01	-0,01	-0,02
101 Savons et prod. de nettoyage	0,07	0,10	0,03	0,02	0,03	0,01	0,00	0,01
047 Autres industries du bois	0,22	0,25	0,03	0,12	-0,15	-0,03	-0,01	0,07
107 Carreaux, linoléum et tissus enduits	0,03	0,06	0,03	0,04	0,00	-0,01	0,02	0,01
100 Peintures et vernis	0,11	0,13	0,03	0,05	-0,01	-0,00	0,01	0,02
139 Industrie de l'assurance	0,67	0,70	0,03	0,17	-0,10	-0,11	0,01	0,05
053 Boîtes en carton et sacs en papier	0,27	0,30	0,03	0,06	0,03	-0,11	-0,02	0,06
082 Petits appareils électriques	0,02	0,05	0,03	0,03	0,01	-0,01	-0,00	0,03
087 Fils et câbles de transm. et d'énergie	0,13	0,15	0,02	0,03	0,01	-0,03	-0,02	0,03
153 Photographes	0,01	0,03	0,02	0,01	0,02	0,01	0,00	-0,00
015 Produits de la volaille	0,01	0,04	0,02	0,01	0,01	0,00	0,00	-0,00
027 Produits brassicoles	0,04	0,06	0,02	0,02	0,01	-0,01	0,00	-0,00
069 Matériel de chauffage	0,03	0,05	0,02	0,02	0,01	-0,01	-0,00	-0,00
033 Chaussure	0,07	0,09	0,02	0,02	0,01	-0,01	-0,01	0,01

Tableau A.4B (suite)

Classement selon la taille des variations	1961 Emploi lié à l'exportation en % de l'emploi total lié à l'exportation	1992 Emploi lié à l'exportation en % de l'emploi total lié à l'exportation	Variation 1961-1992 Emploi lié à l'exportation en % de l'emploi total lié à l'exportation	Attribuable à : Variation de la part des exportations	Variation du ratio emploi/ production	Variation des coefficients entrées-sorties	Variation des coefficients d'importation	Interaction résiduelle
021 Biscuits	0,02	0,04	0,02	0,02	-0,01	0,00	0,00	0,00
037 Tricots	0,01	0,03	0,02	0,02	-0,00	0,01	-0,00	-0,00
147 Autres services de santé	0,00	0,01	0,01	0,02	0,00	0,01	0,00	-0,01
083 Gros app. (élect. et non électr.)	0,08	0,09	0,01	0,00	-0,00	0,01	-0,01	0,00
152 Autres services personnels	0,00	0,01	0,01	0,02	0,00	-0,01	0,00	0,00
104 Bijouterie et métaux précieux	0,14	0,15	0,01	0,01	0,00	-0,00	-0,00	0,00
093 Béton prémélangé	0,01	0,02	0,01	-0,00	0,01	0,00	0,00	0,00
028 Vin	0,00	0,01	0,01	0,01	0,00	-0,00	-0,00	-0,00
052 Papier-toiture asphalté	0,02	0,02	0,01	0,01	-0,01	-0,01	0,00	0,01
088 Batteries	0,03	0,04	0,01	0,01	0,01	-0,01	-0,01	0,01
092 Produits en béton	0,02	0,03	0,00	0,00	0,00	-0,01	0,00	0,00
091 Ciment	0,03	0,03	0,00	0,01	0,00	-0,01	0,00	-0,00
117 Autres activités de construction	0,01	0,02	0,00	0,00	0,01	-0,01	0,00	0,01
034 Cuir et prod. connexes	0,04	0,04	0,00	0,01	0,01	-0,00	-0,01	0,00
113 Const. d'install. gazières et pétrolières	0,00	0,00	0,00	0,00	0,00	0,00	0,00	0,00
111 Constr. d'immeubles non résidentiels	0,00	0,00	0,00	0,00	0,00	0,00	0,00	0,00
112 Const. de routes, autor. et pistes d'atterr.	0,00	0,00	0,00	0,00	0,00	0,00	0,00	0,00
114 Projets de barrages et d'irrigation	0,00	0,00	0,00	0,00	0,00	0,00	0,00	0,00
141 Logements occupés par leur propriétaire	0,00	0,00	0,00	0,00	0,00	0,00	0,00	0,00
116 Autres travaux d'ingénierie	0,00	0,00	0,00	0,00	0,00	0,00	0,00	0,00
115 Const. de ch. fer et lignes tél. et télég.	0,00	0,00	0,00	0,00	0,00	0,00	0,00	0,00
110 Construction résidentielle	0,00	0,00	0,00	0,00	0,00	0,00	0,00	0,00
140 Redevances gouv. sur les ress. natur.	0,00	0,00	0,00	0,00	0,00	0,00	0,00	0,00
096 Produits du pétrole et du charbon raffinés	0,21	0,21	-0,00	0,05	-0,10	0,00	-0,00	0,05
067 Tréfilage et produits tréfilés	0,31	0,30	-0,00	0,16	0,04	-0,23	-0,07	0,09
023 Sucre de canne et betterave	0,02	0,01	-0,00	0,00	0,00	-0,01	0,00	0,00
126 Entr. des ponts et des autoroutes	0,01	0,01	-0,01	-0,00	-0,00	-0,00	-0,00	0,00
020 Raffinage d'huile végétale (sauf maïs)	0,03	0,02	-0,01	-0,01	-0,00	-0,00	-0,00	0,00
042 Bonneterie	0,02	0,01	-0,01	-0,01	0,00	-0,00	0,00	0,00
133 Systèmes de distribution du gaz	0,12	0,10	-0,02	-0,02	-0,05	0,01	0,00	0,02

Tableau A.4B (suite)

Classement selon la taille des variations	1961 Emploi lié à l'exportation en % de l'emploi total lié à l'exportation	1992 Emploi lié à l'exportation en % de l'emploi total lié à l'exportation	Variation 1961-1992 Emploi lié à l'exportation en % de l'emploi total lié à l'exportation	Attribuable à : Variation de la part des exportations	Variation du ratio emploi/ production	Variation des coefficients entrées-sorties	Variation des coefficients d'importation	Interaction résiduelle
009 Mines de sel	0,04	0,02	-0,02	-0,01	-0,00	-0,01	0,00	-0,00
008 Min. non métall. sauf charbon et amiante	0,28	0,25	-0,03	0,01	-0,26	-0,00	0,05	0,17
012 Carrières et sablières	0,13	0,09	-0,04	-0,06	0,00	-0,01	0,00	0,03
061 Laminage, moulage et extr. de l'alum.	0,24	0,20	-0,04	0,04	-0,13	0,03	-0,08	0,10
046 Boîtes en bois et cercueils	0,10	0,06	-0,04	-0,07	0,03	-0,06	-0,04	0,10
062 Laminage, moulage et extr. du cuivre	0,11	0,07	-0,04	-0,01	-0,01	-0,01	-0,01	-0,00
090 Matériaux en céramique	0,06	0,01	-0,05	-0,05	0,03	-0,06	-0,00	0,03
036 Fils de laine et textiles tissés	0,14	0,07	-0,07	-0,03	-0,00	-0,01	-0,00	-0,01
032 Tanneries de cuir	0,09	0,02	-0,07	-0,07	0,00	0,00	-0,02	0,02
029 Produits du tabac	0,13	0,06	-0,07	-0,02	-0,00	-0,02	0,00	-0,02
018 Produits laitiers	0,17	0,09	-0,08	-0,05	-0,02	-0,01	0,00	-0,00
095 Produits minéraux non métalliques n.c.a.	0,38	0,27	-0,11	-0,08	0,00	-0,06	-0,03	0,06
080 Construction et réparation de navires	0,25	0,11	-0,14	-0,14	-0,02	-0,00	0,01	0,01
035 Fibres chimiques, fils et textiles tissés	0,51	0,34	-0,17	0,05	-0,05	-0,14	-0,06	0,03
019 Nourriture pour animaux	0,34	0,16	-0,18	-0,16	-0,00	-0,01	0,00	0,00
024 Industries alimentaires diverses	0,53	0,34	-0,19	-0,20	0,04	-0,06	0,01	0,01
044 Plaqués et contreplaqués	0,36	0,16	-0,20	-0,17	-0,02	-0,03	0,01	0,01
129 Télécommunications et radiodiffusion	0,42	0,21	-0,20	-0,08	-0,19	-0,03	-0,00	0,01
026 Produits de distillerie	0,31	0,09	-0,22	-0,25	0,01	-0,01	0,01	0,01
016 Produits du poisson	1,11	0,87	-0,25	-0,31	0,07	-0,08	0,05	0,02
010 Mines de charbon	0,52	0,25	-0,27	0,18	-0,89	-0,05	0,01	0,04
128 Stockage et entreposage	0,78	0,49	-0,29	-0,56	0,17	-0,19	0,03	0,26
097 Produits chimiques industriels n.c.a.	1,05	0,63	-0,42	-0,09	-0,37	0,03	-0,05	0,06
072 Instruments agricoles	0,72	0,21	-0,51	-0,57	0,02	-0,04	0,02	0,05
006 Mines de fer	0,79	0,22	-0,58	-0,48	-0,04	-0,03	0,03	-0,06
007 Mines d'amiante	0,72	0,10	-0,62	-1,06	0,04	-0,02	0,01	0,41
109 Réparation, construction	2,11	1,28	-0,83	-0,41	-0,19	-0,43	0,02	0,19
004 Mines d'or	1,81	0,35	-1,46	-0,31	-0,64	-0,02	0,02	-0,50
120 Transport par eau et services connexes	2,10	0,62	-1,48	-0,79	-0,18	-0,23	0,03	-0,30
043 Scieries, atel. rabot. et usines bardeaux	3,85	1,99	-1,86	-0,98	-0,98	-0,08	0,17	0,02

Tableau A-4B (suite)

Classement selon la taille des variations	1961 Emploi lié à l'exportation en % de l'emploi total	1992 Emploi lié à l'exportation en % de l'emploi total	Variation 1961-1992 Emploi lié à l'exportation en % de l'emploi total	Attribuable à : Variation de la part des exportations	Variation du ratio emploi/production	Variation des coefficients entrées-sorties	Variation des coefficients d'importation	Interaction résiduelle
060 Fonte et affinage métaux non-ferreux	3,18	1,20	-1,98	-1,79	-0,04	-0,10	-0,02	-0,03
005 Autres mines métalliques	3,35	0,87	-2,48	-1,31	-0,14	-0,26	-0,05	-0,72
051 Pâtes et papiers	5,92	2,64	-3,27	-3,27	0,02	-0,33	0,14	0,17
119 Transport ferroviaire et services connexes	5,07	1,30	-3,77	-0,66	-0,37	-1,80	0,01	-0,94
003 Abattage et foresterie	5,55	1,77	-3,78	-1,36	-1,17	-0,21	0,11	-1,15
001 Agriculture et ind. connexes	26,93	8,69	-18,24	-13,16	-3,23	-0,30	0,55	-2,09

APPENDICE 5
ÉVOLUTION DE LA COMPOSITION INDUSTRIELLE DES IMPORTATIONS : AGRÉGATION AU NIVEAU DE 161 INDUSTRIES

Les tableaux A.5A et A.5B font voir les résultats détaillés qui sous-tendent les agrégats présentés dans les tableaux 13A et 13B, à la section 5.3, issus des calculs effectués pour l'ensemble des 161 industries. Ces tableaux font voir les résultats pour les années 1961 et 1992, qui bornent l'intervalle complet de nos données entrées-sorties. Au tableau A.5A, les industries sont classées selon l'ordre numérique habituel, allant de la production primaire aux industries manufacturières et aux services. Au tableau A.5B, les industries sont classées par ordre décroissant de l'augmentation de la part de l'emploi lié aux exportations.

Les industries qui font voir l'augmentation la plus importante de la part de l'emploi lié aux importations sont principalement des industries de services de tous genres, y compris l'hébergement, les services alimentaires, les services aux entreprises, les services professionnels, le commerce de gros, les services bancaires et les autres services financiers. Pour la plupart, ces mêmes industries se retrouvent en tête de liste du côté des exportations (voir le tableau A.3B). Les industries des pièces et accessoires de véhicules à moteur se retrouvent aussi au haut du classement étant donné que les importations dans ce secteur ont augmenté massivement depuis 1961 en raison de l'intégration de l'industrie automobile nord-américaine, le Canada important principalement des pièces et exportant des véhicules montés. Les industries du vêtement, des produits en plastique, des machines de bureau et du matériel électronique ont également vu augmenter sensiblement leur part de l'emploi « remplacé » par des importations.

Au bas du tableau, on retrouve les industries qui ont enregistré les baisses les plus importantes de la part de l'emploi lié aux importations. Comme on peut le voir, celles-ci englobent des industries de production primaire comme l'agriculture et les mines de charbon, certaines industries manufacturières comme les machines agricoles, les avions et pièces et, en particulier, des services tels que le transport par rail et le transport maritime.

Enfin, nous présentons dans cet appendice, aux tableaux A.6A et A.6B, les résultats de la décomposition des changements observés dans les parts de l'emploi attribuable aux importations entre 1961 et 1992, pour l'ensemble des 161 industries. Le tableau A.6A renferme les résultats de la décomposition pour les années 1961 et 1992, présentés par ordre numérique, tandis qu'au tableau A.6B, les mêmes données sont classées en allant de l'augmentation la plus importante à la baisse la plus importante.

Tableau A.5A Parts de l'emploi, 1961 et 1992, 161 industries

	1961		1992		Variation 1961–1992	
	Emploi lié à l'importation en % de l'emploi total lié à l'importation	Emploi lié à l'importation en % de l'emploi total	Emploi lié à l'importation en % de l'emploi total lié à l'importation	Emploi lié à l'importation en % de l'emploi total	Emploi lié à l'importation en % de l'emploi total lié à l'importation	Emploi lié à l'importation en % de l'emploi total
001 Agriculture et ind. connexes	12.42	2.04	4.77	1.24	-7.64	-0.80
002 Pêche et piégeage	0.44	0.07	0.36	0.09	-0.08	-0.02
003 Abattage et foresterie	1.06	0.17	0.38	0.10	-0.69	-0.08
004 Mines d'or	0.13	0.02	0.13	0.03	-0.00	0.01
005 Autres mines métalliques	0.58	0.10	0.28	0.07	-0.30	-0.02
006 Mines de fer	0.39	0.06	0.10	0.03	-0.29	-0.04
007 Mines d'amiante	0.03	0.00	0.00	0.00	-0.03	-0.04
008 Min. non métall. sauf charbon et amiante	0.41	0.07	0.10	0.03	-0.30	-0.04
009 Mines de sel	0.02	0.00	0.02	0.00	-0.01	0.00
010 Mines de charbon	3.23	0.53	0.19	0.05	-3.04	-0.48
011 Pétrole brut et gaz naturel	1.12	0.18	0.57	0.15	-0.56	-0.04
012 Carrières et sablières	0.23	0.04	0.09	0.02	-0.14	-0.01
013 Services connexes à l'extraction min.	0.15	0.03	0.27	0.07	0.12	0.04
014 Viande et pr. de la viande (sauf volaille)	0.31	0.05	0.31	0.08	0.00	0.03
015 Produits de la volaille	0.04	0.01	0.08	0.02	0.04	0.01
016 Produits du poisson	0.22	0.04	0.34	0.09	0.12	0.05
017 Transformation des fruits et légumes	0.70	0.11	0.30	0.08	-0.40	-0.04
018 Produits laitiers	0.12	0.02	0.12	0.03	-0.00	0.01
019 Nourriture pour animaux	0.16	0.03	0.13	0.03	-0.03	0.01
020 Raffinage d'huile végétale (sauf maïs)	0.06	0.01	0.02	0.00	-0.04	-0.00
021 Biscuits	0.10	0.02	0.05	0.01	-0.04	-0.00
022 Pain et autres prod. de boulangerie	0.04	0.01	0.11	0.03	0.07	0.02
023 Sucre de canne et betterave	0.05	0.01	0.02	0.01	-0.03	-0.00
024 Industries alimentaires diverses	0.70	0.12	0.50	0.13	-0.21	0.01
025 Boissons gazeuses	0.04	0.01	0.04	0.01	0.01	0.01
026 Produits de distillerie	0.18	0.03	0.07	0.02	-0.11	-0.01
027 Produits brassicoles	0.02	0.00	0.04	0.01	0.03	0.01
028 Vin	0.05	0.01	0.09	0.02	0.04	0.01
029 Produits du tabac	0.05	0.01	0.11	0.03	0.06	0.02
030 Produits en caoutchouc	0.77	0.13	0.81	0.21	0.04	0.02
031 Produits en plastique	0.67	0.11	1.51	0.39	0.84	0.28

Tableau A.5A (suite)

	1961		1992		Variation 1961–1992	
	Emploi lié à l'importation en % de l'emploi total lié à l'importation	Emploi lié à l'importation en % de l'emploi total	Emploi lié à l'importation en % de l'emploi total lié à l'importation	Emploi lié à l'importation en % de l'emploi total	Emploi lié à l'importation en % de l'emploi total lié à l'importation	Emploi lié à l'importation en % de l'emploi total
032 Tanneries de cuir	0,14	0,02	0,11	0,03	-0,03	0,00
033 Chaussure	0,45	0,07	0,79	0,21	0,34	0,13
034 Cuir et produits connexes	0,28	0,05	0,25	0,07	-0,03	0,02
035 Fibres chimiques, fils et text. tissés	3,14	0,52	0,76	0,20	-2,38	-0,32
036 Fils de laine et textiles tissés	0,59	0,10	0,16	0,04	-0,43	-0,06
037 Tricots	0,24	0,04	0,11	0,03	-0,13	-0,01
038 Autres produits textiles	1,26	0,21	0,69	0,18	-0,57	-0,03
039 Achèvement et teinture de tissus	0,11	0,02	0,15	0,04	0,04	0,02
040 Moquettes, paillassons et tapis	0,09	0,01	0,11	0,03	0,02	0,01
041 Vêtement, sauf bonneterie	1,53	0,25	2,71	0,70	1,18	0,45
042 Bonneterie	0,06	0,01	0,05	0,01	-0,00	0,00
043 Scieries, atel. rabot. et usines bardeaux	0,65	0,11	0,24	0,06	-0,41	-0,04
044 Plaqués et contreplaqués	0,21	0,04	0,07	0,02	-0,14	-0,02
045 Châssis, portes et autres ouvr. de menuis.	0,10	0,02	0,21	0,06	0,11	0,04
046 Boîtes en bois et cercueils	0,11	0,02	0,07	0,02	-0,04	-0,00
047 Autres industries du bois	0,15	0,03	0,06	0,02	-0,09	-0,01
048 Ameublement de maison	0,33	0,06	0,58	0,15	0,24	0,10
049 Ameublement de bureau	0,06	0,01	0,07	0,02	0,02	0,01
050 Autres mobiliers et app. d'éclairage	0,16	0,03	0,25	0,07	0,09	0,04
051 Pâtes et papiers	0,86	0,14	0,58	0,15	-0,28	0,01
052 Papier-toiture asphalté	0,04	0,01	0,01	0,00	-0,02	-0,00
053 Boîtes en carton et sacs en papier	0,51	0,08	0,36	0,09	-0,15	0,01
054 Autres prod. de papier façonné	0,34	0,06	0,33	0,09	-0,01	0,03
055 Imprimerie et édition	2,35	0,39	1,94	0,51	-0,41	0,12
056 Clichage, composition et reliure	0,35	0,06	0,33	0,09	-0,02	0,03
057 Acier primaire	2,44	0,40	1,48	0,39	-0,95	-0,01
058 Canalisations et tuyaux d'acier	0,18	0,03	0,14	0,04	-0,04	0,01
059 Fonderies de fer	0,58	0,10	0,36	0,09	-0,23	-0,00
060 Fonte et affinage métaux non-ferreux	0,67	0,11	0,42	0,11	-0,25	-0,00
061 Laminage, moulage et extr. de l'alum.	0,30	0,05	0,23	0,06	-0,07	0,01
062 Laminage, moulage et extr. du cuivre	0,16	0,03	0,11	0,03	-0,05	0,00

Tableau A.5A (suite)

	1961		1992		Variation 1961–1992	
	Emploi lié à l'importation en % de l'emploi total lié à l'importation	Emploi lié à l'importation en % de l'emploi total	Emploi lié à l'importation en % de l'emploi total lié à l'importation	Emploi lié à l'importation en % de l'emploi total	Emploi lié à l'importation en % de l'emploi total lié à l'importation	Emploi lié à l'importation en % de l'emploi total
063 Laminage, moulage, etc. d'autres métaux	0,21	0,03	0,18	0,05	-0,03	0,01
064 Chaudières et métaux de charpente	0,69	0,11	0,26	0,07	-0,43	-0,05
065 Prod. métall. décoratifs et architecturaux	0,19	0,03	0,17	0,04	-0,02	0,01
066 Métal embouti, pressé et enrobé	1,19	0,20	0,83	0,22	-0,36	0,02
067 Tréfilage et produits tréfilés	0,75	0,12	0,44	0,11	-0,30	-0,01
068 Art. de quincaillerie, outils et couteaux	0,95	0,16	0,94	0,25	-0,01	0,09
069 Matériel de chauffage	0,19	0,03	0,12	0,03	-0,07	0,00
070 Ateliers d'usinage	0,72	0,12	1,01	0,26	0,29	0,14
071 Autres métaux ouvrés	1,28	0,21	0,71	0,18	-0,57	-0,03
072 Instruments agricoles	2,01	0,33	0,42	0,11	-1,58	-0,22
073 Équipement de réfrigération commercial	0,18	0,03	0,30	0,08	0,11	0,05
074 Autres machines et matériel	4,12	0,68	3,36	0,87	-0,76	0,20
075 Aéronautique et pièces d'avion	2,34	0,38	0,96	0,25	-1,38	-0,14
076 Véhicules à moteur	0,91	0,15	1,14	0,30	0,23	0,15
077 Camions, carross. d'autobus et remorques	0,21	0,03	0,33	0,09	0,12	0,05
078 Pièces et accessoires de véh. à moteur	3,55	0,58	5,34	1,39	1,80	0,81
079 Matériel ferroviaire roulant	0,18	0,03	0,17	0,04	-0,01	0,02
080 Construction et réparation de navires	0,46	0,08	0,11	0,03	-0,35	-0,05
081 Matériel de transport divers	0,17	0,03	0,15	0,04	-0,02	0,01
082 Petits appareils électriques	0,26	0,04	0,29	0,08	0,03	0,03
083 Gros app. (élect. et non élect.)	0,73	0,12	0,33	0,09	-0,40	-0,03
084 Tourne-disques, radios et téléviseurs	0,34	0,06	0,39	0,10	0,04	0,04
085 Matériel électronique	1,89	0,31	2,51	0,65	0,63	0,34
086 Machines de bureau et de magasin	0,74	0,12	1,64	0,43	0,90	0,30
087 Fils et câbles de transm. et d'énergie	0,19	0,03	0,18	0,05	-0,01	0,02
088 Batteries	0,07	0,01	0,08	0,02	0,01	0,01
089 Autres prod. élect. et électroniques	1,80	0,30	1,69	0,44	-0,11	0,14
090 Matériaux en céramique	0,53	0,09	0,19	0,05	-0,34	-0,04
091 Ciment	0,02	0,00	0,02	0,00	-0,01	0,00
092 Produits en béton	0,04	0,01	0,02	0,01	-0,02	-0,00
093 Béton prémélangé	0,01	0,00	0,01	0,00	0,00	0,00

Tableau A.5A (suite)

	1961		1992		Variation 1961–1992	
	Emploi lié à l'importation en % de l'emploi total lié à l'importation	Emploi lié à l'importation en % de l'emploi total	Emploi lié à l'importation en % de l'emploi total lié à l'importation	Emploi lié à l'importation en % de l'emploi total	Emploi lié à l'importation en % de l'emploi total lié à l'importation	Emploi lié à l'importation en % de l'emploi total
094 Verre et produits en verre	0,92	0,15	0,40	0,11	-0,52	-0,05
095 Produits minéraux non métalliques n.c.a.	0,57	0,09	0,32	0,08	-0,25	-0,01
096 Produits du pétrole et du charbon raffinés	0,29	0,05	0,16	0,04	-0,13	-0,01
097 Produits chimiques industriels n.c.a.	1,22	0,20	0,62	0,16	-0,61	-0,04
098 Plastiques et résines synthétiques	0,39	0,06	0,33	0,09	-0,05	0,02
099 Prod. pharmaceutiques et médicaments	0,29	0,06	0,39	0,10	0,10	0,05
100 Peintures et vernis	0,21	0,05	0,20	0,05	-0,01	0,02
101 Savons et prod. de nettoyage	0,16	0,03	0,18	0,05	0,03	0,02
102 Produits de toilette	0,03	0,01	0,18	0,05	0,15	0,04
103 Produits chimiques	0,92	0,15	0,67	0,17	-0,24	0,02
104 Bijouterie et métaux précieux	0,38	0,06	0,31	0,08	-0,06	0,02
105 Articles de sport et jouets	0,50	0,08	0,67	0,17	0,09	0,09
106 Enseignes et étalages	0,10	0,02	0,14	0,04	0,03	0,02
107 Carreaux, linoléum et tissus enduits	0,22	0,04	0,11	0,03	-0,11	-0,01
108 Autres industries manufacturières n.c.a.	2,74	0,45	2,58	0,67	-0,16	0,22
109 Réparation, construction	1,46	0,24	0,89	0,23	-0,57	-0,01
110 Construction résidentielle	0,00	0,00	0,00	0,00	0,00	0,00
111 Construction d'immeubles non résidentiels	0,00	0,00	0,00	0,00	0,00	0,00
112 Const. de routes, autor. et pistes d'atterr.	0,00	0,00	0,00	0,00	0,00	0,00
113 Const. d'install. gazières et pétrolières	0,00	0,00	0,00	0,00	0,00	0,00
114 Projets de barrages et d'irrigation	0,00	0,00	0,00	0,00	0,00	0,00
115 Const. de ch. fer et lignes tél. et télég.	0,00	0,00	0,00	0,00	0,00	0,00
116 Autres travaux d'ingénierie	0,00	0,00	0,00	0,00	0,00	0,00
117 Autres activités de construction	0,01	0,00	0,02	0,00	0,01	0,00
118 Transport aérien et services connexes	0,23	0,04	0,80	0,21	0,57	0,17
119 Transport ferroviaire et services connexes	1,63	0,27	0,48	0,13	-1,14	-0,14
120 Transport par eau et services connexes	1,00	0,17	0,30	0,08	-0,70	-0,09
121 Camionnage	1,22	0,20	1,10	0,29	-0,12	0,09
122 Systèmes de transport urbain	0,02	0,00	0,18	0,05	0,16	0,04
123 Systèmes de transport interurbain et rural	0,02	0,00	0,09	0,02	0,07	0,02
124 Industrie du taxi	0,26	0,04	0,61	0,16	0,35	0,12

Tableau A.5A (suite)

	1961		1992		Variation 1961–1992	
	Emploi lié à l'importation en % de l'emploi total lié à l'importation	Emploi lié à l'importation en % de l'emploi total	Emploi lié à l'importation en % de l'emploi total lié à l'importation	Emploi lié à l'importation en % de l'emploi total	Emploi lié à l'importation en % de l'emploi total lié à l'importation	Emploi lié à l'importation en % de l'emploi total
125 Autres transports et services connexes	0,04	0,01	0,51	0,13	0,47	0,13
126 Entr. des ponts et des autoroutes	0,01	0,00	0,00	0,00	-0,00	-0,00
127 Transport par pipelines	0,08	0,01	0,07	0,02	-0,01	0,01
128 Stockage et entreposage	0,17	0,03	0,11	0,03	-0,06	0,00
129 Télécommunications et radiodiffusion	0,27	0,04	0,27	0,07	-0,00	0,02
130 Entreprises de télécomm. et autres	0,72	0,12	0,77	0,20	0,06	0,08
131 Services postaux	0,38	0,06	0,45	0,12	0,07	0,05
132 Systèmes d'énergie électrique	0,52	0,08	0,64	0,17	0,13	0,08
133 Systèmes de distribution du gaz	0,13	0,02	0,08	0,02	-0,06	-0,00
134 Autres services publics n.c.a.	0,05	0,01	0,23	0,06	0,18	0,05
135 Commerce de gros	3,26	0,54	5,08	1,32	1,83	0,79
136 Commerce de détail	2,59	0,43	3,14	0,82	0,55	0,39
137 Banq., coop. de crédit et autr. inst. dépôt	0,73	0,12	1,83	0,48	1,11	0,36
138 Fiducies, autres inst. fin. et immob.	0,79	0,13	1,83	0,47	1,04	0,34
139 Industrie de l'assurance	0,51	0,08	0,62	0,16	0,11	0,08
140 Redevances gouv. sur les ress. natur.	0,00	0,00	0,00	0,00	0,00	0,00
141 Logements occupés par leur propriétaire	0,00	0,00	0,00	0,00	0,00	0,00
142 Autres services commerciaux	1,19	0,20	5,23	1,36	4,04	1,16
143 Services profess. aux entreprises	1,70	0,28	3,65	0,95	1,95	0,67
144 Services de publicité	0,24	0,04	0,56	0,15	0,32	0,11
145 Services éducatifs	0,04	0,01	0,12	0,03	0,08	0,02
146 Hôpitaux	0,03	0,01	0,08	0,02	0,04	0,01
147 Autres services de santé	0,00	0,00	0,04	0,01	0,04	0,01
148 Hébergement et restauration	0,75	0,12	8,89	2,31	8,14	2,19
149 Films et vidéos	0,25	0,04	0,24	0,06	-0,01	0,02
150 Autres serv. de divertissement et loisir	0,03	0,00	0,89	0,23	0,87	0,23
151 Buanderies et nettoyeurs	0,06	0,01	0,10	0,03	0,04	0,02
152 Autres services personnels	0,00	0,00	0,01	0,00	0,01	0,01
153 Photographes	0,01	0,00	0,04	0,01	0,02	0,01
154 Services divers	0,80	0,13	2,80	0,73	2,00	0,60
TOTAL	100,00	16,44	100,00	25,99	0,00	9,55

Tableau A.5B Parts de l'emploi, 1961 et 1992, 161 industries

Classement selon la taille des variations	1961		1992		Variation 1961–1992	
	Emploi lié à l'importation en % de l'emploi total lié à l'importation	Emploi lié à l'importation en % de l'emploi total	Emploi lié à l'importation en % de l'emploi total lié à l'importation	Emploi lié à l'importation en % de l'emploi total	Emploi lié à l'importation en % de l'emploi total lié à l'importation	Emploi lié à l'importation en % de l'emploi total
148 Hébergement et restauration	0,75	0,12	8,89	2,31	8,14	2,19
142 Autres services commerciaux	1,19	0,20	5,23	1,36	4,04	1,16
154 Services divers	0,80	0,13	2,80	0,73	2,00	0,60
143 Services profess. aux entreprises	1,70	0,28	3,65	0,95	1,95	0,67
135 Commerce de gros	3,26	0,54	5,08	1,32	1,83	0,79
078 Pièces et accessoires de véh. à moteur	3,55	0,58	5,34	1,39	1,83	0,81
041 Vêtement, sauf bonneterie	1,53	0,25	2,71	0,70	1,18	0,45
137 Banq., coop. de crédit et autr. inst. dépôt	0,73	0,12	1,83	0,48	1,11	0,36
138 Fiducies, autres inst. fin. et immob.	0,79	0,13	1,83	0,47	1,04	0,34
086 Machines de bureau et de magasin	0,74	0,12	1,64	0,43	0,90	0,30
150 Autres serv. de divertissement et loisir	0,03	0,00	0,89	0,23	0,87	0,23
031 Produits en plastique	0,67	0,11	1,51	0,39	0,84	0,28
085 Matériel électronique	1,89	0,31	2,51	0,65	0,63	0,34
118 Transport aérien et services connexes	0,23	0,04	0,80	0,21	0,57	0,17
136 Commerce de détail	2,59	0,43	3,14	0,82	0,55	0,39
125 Autres transports et services connexes	0,04	0,01	0,51	0,13	0,47	0,13
124 Industrie du taxi	0,26	0,04	0,61	0,16	0,35	0,12
033 Chaussure	0,45	0,07	0,79	0,21	0,34	0,13
144 Services de publicité	0,24	0,04	0,56	0,15	0,32	0,11
070 Ateliers d'usinage	0,72	0,12	1,01	0,26	0,29	0,14
048 Ameublement de maison	0,33	0,06	0,58	0,15	0,24	0,10
076 Véhicules à moteur	0,91	0,15	1,14	0,30	0,23	0,15
134 Autres services publics n.c.a.	0,05	0,01	0,23	0,06	0,18	0,05
105 Articles de sport et jouets	0,50	0,08	0,67	0,17	0,17	0,09
122 Systèmes de transport urbain	0,02	0,00	0,18	0,05	0,16	0,04
102 Produits de toilette	0,03	0,01	0,18	0,05	0,15	0,04
132 Systèmes d'énergie électrique	0,52	0,08	0,64	0,17	0,13	0,08
077 Camions, carross. d'autobus et remorques	0,21	0,03	0,33	0,09	0,12	0,05
016 Produits du poisson	0,22	0,04	0,34	0,09	0,12	0,05
013 Services connexes à l'extraction min.	0,15	0,03	0,27	0,07	0,12	0,04
045 Châssis, portes et autres ouvr. de menuiserie	0,10	0,02	0,21	0,06	0,11	0,04

Tableau A.5B (suite)

Classement selon la taille des variations	1961		1992		Variation 1961–1992	
	Emploi lié à l'importation en % de l'emploi total lié à l'importation	Emploi lié à l'importation en % de l'emploi total	Emploi lié à l'importation en % de l'emploi total lié à l'importation	Emploi lié à l'importation en % de l'emploi total	Emploi lié à l'importation en % de l'emploi total lié à l'importation	Emploi lié à l'importation en % de l'emploi total
073 Équipement de réfrigération commercial	0,18	0,03	0,30	0,08	0,11	0,05
139 Industrie de l'assurance	0,51	0,08	0,62	0,16	0,11	0,08
099 Prod. pharmaceutiques et médicaments	0,29	0,05	0,39	0,10	0,10	0,05
050 Autres mobiliers et app. d'éclairage	0,16	0,03	0,25	0,07	0,09	0,04
145 Services éducatifs	0,04	0,01	0,12	0,03	0,08	0,02
131 Services postaux	0,38	0,06	0,45	0,12	0,07	0,05
022 Pain et autres prod. de boulangerie	0,04	0,01	0,11	0,03	0,07	0,02
123 Systèmes de transport interurbain et rural	0,02	0,00	0,09	0,02	0,07	0,02
130 Entreprises de télécomm. et autres	0,72	0,12	0,77	0,20	0,06	0,08
029 Produits du tabac	0,05	0,01	0,11	0,03	0,06	0,02
084 Tourne-disques, radios et téléviseurs	0,34	0,06	0,39	0,10	0,04	0,04
151 Buanderies et nettoyeurs	0,06	0,01	0,10	0,03	0,04	0,02
039 Achèvement et teinture de tissus	0,11	0,02	0,15	0,04	0,04	0,02
146 Hôpitaux	0,03	0,01	0,08	0,02	0,04	0,01
028 Vin	0,05	0,01	0,09	0,02	0,04	0,02
147 Autres services de santé	0,00	0,00	0,04	0,01	0,04	0,01
030 Produits en caoutchouc	0,77	0,13	0,81	0,21	0,04	0,08
015 Produits de la volaille	0,04	0,01	0,08	0,02	0,04	0,01
106 Enseignes et étalages	0,10	0,02	0,14	0,04	0,03	0,02
082 Petits appareils électriques	0,26	0,04	0,29	0,08	0,03	0,03
101 Savons et prod. de nettoyage	0,16	0,03	0,18	0,05	0,03	0,02
027 Produits brassicoles	0,02	0,00	0,04	0,01	0,03	0,01
153 Photographes	0,01	0,00	0,04	0,01	0,02	0,01
040 Moquettes, paillassons et tapis	0,09	0,01	0,11	0,02	0,02	0,01
049 Ameublement de bureau	0,06	0,01	0,07	0,02	0,02	0,01
088 Batteries	0,07	0,01	0,08	0,02	0,01	0,01
152 Autres services personnels	0,00	0,00	0,01	0,00	0,01	0,00
025 Boissons gazeuses	0,04	0,01	0,01	0,01	0,01	0,01
117 Autres activités de construction	0,01	0,00	0,02	0,00	0,01	0,01
093 Béton prémélangé	0,01	0,00	0,01	0,00	0,00	0,00
014 Viande et pr. de la viande (sauf volaille)	0,31	0,05	0,31	0,08	0,03	0,03

Tableau A.5B (suite)

Classement selon la taille des variations	1961		1992		Variation 1961–1992	
	Emploi lié à l'importation en % de l'emploi total lié à l'importation	Emploi lié à l'importation en % de l'emploi total	Emploi lié à l'importation en % de l'emploi total lié à l'importation	Emploi lié à l'importation en % de l'emploi total	Emploi lié à l'importation en % de l'emploi total lié à l'importation	Emploi lié à l'importation en % de l'emploi total
111 Construction d'immeubles non résidentiels	0,00	0,00	0,00	0,00	0,00	0,00
110 Construction résidentielle	0,00	0,00	0,00	0,00	0,00	0,00
140 Redevances gouv. sur les ress. natur.	0,00	0,00	0,00	0,00	0,00	0,00
116 Autres travaux d'ingénierie	0,00	0,00	0,00	0,00	0,00	0,00
141 Logements occupés par leur propriétaire	0,00	0,00	0,00	0,00	0,00	0,00
115 Const. de ch. fer et lignes tél. et télég.	0,00	0,00	0,00	0,00	0,00	0,00
112 Const. de routes, autor. et pistes d'atterr.	0,00	0,00	0,00	0,00	0,00	0,00
113 Const. d'install. gazières et pétrolières	0,00	0,00	0,00	0,00	0,00	0,00
114 Projets de barrages et d'irrigation	0,00	0,00	0,00	0,00	0,00	0,00
018 Produits laitiers	0,12	0,02	0,12	0,03	-0,00	0,01
042 Bonneterie	0,06	0,01	0,05	0,01	-0,00	0,00
126 Entretien de ponts et autoroutes	0,01	0,00	0,00	0,01	-0,00	-0,00
129 Télécommunications et radiodiffusion	0,27	0,04	0,27	0,07	-0,00	0,02
004 Mines d'or	0,13	0,02	0,13	0,03	-0,00	0,01
068 Art. de quincaillerie, outils et couteaux	0,95	0,16	0,94	0,25	-0,01	0,09
091 Ciment	0,02	0,00	0,02	0,00	-0,01	0,00
079 Matériel ferroviaire roulant	0,18	0,03	0,17	0,04	-0,01	0,02
149 Films et vidéos	0,25	0,04	0,24	0,06	-0,01	0,02
087 Fils et câbles de transm. et d'énergie	0,19	0,03	0,18	0,05	-0,01	0,02
127 Transport par pipelines	0,08	0,01	0,07	0,02	-0,01	0,01
009 Mines de sel	0,02	0,00	0,02	0,00	-0,01	0,00
054 Autres prod. de papier façonné	0,34	0,06	0,33	0,09	-0,01	0,03
100 Peintures et vernis	0,21	0,03	0,20	0,05	-0,01	0,02
065 Prod. métall. décoratifs et architecturaux	0,19	0,03	0,17	0,04	-0,02	0,01
092 Produits en béton	0,04	0,01	0,02	0,01	-0,02	-0,00
056 Clichage, composition et reliure	0,35	0,06	0,33	0,09	-0,02	0,03
081 Matériel de transport divers	0,17	0,03	0,15	0,04	-0,02	0,01
052 Papier-toiture asphalté	0,04	0,01	0,01	0,00	-0,02	-0,00
023 Sucre de canne et betterave	0,05	0,01	0,02	0,01	-0,03	-0,00
007 Mines d'amiante	0,03	0,00	0,00	0,00	-0,03	-0,00
034 Cuir et prod. connexes divers	0,28	0,05	0,25	0,07	-0,03	0,02

Tableau A.5B (suite)

Classement selon la taille des variations	1961		1992		Variation 1961-1992	
	Emploi lié à l'importation en % de l'emploi total lié à l'importation	Emploi lié à l'importation en % de l'emploi total	Emploi lié à l'importation en % de l'emploi total lié à l'importation	Emploi lié à l'importation en % de l'emploi total	Emploi lié à l'importation en % de l'importation total lié à l'importation	Emploi lié à l'importation en % de l'emploi total
019 Nourriture pour animaux	0.16	0.03	0.13	0.03	-0.03	0.01
032 Tanneries de cuir	0.14	0.02	0.11	0.03	-0.03	0.00
063 Laminage, moulage, etc. d'autres métaux	0.21	0.03	0.18	0.05	-0.03	0.01
020 Raffinage d'huile végétale (sauf maïs)	0.06	0.01	0.02	0.00	-0.04	-0.00
058 Canalisations et tuyaux d'acier	0.18	0.03	0.14	0.04	-0.04	0.01
046 Boîtes en bois et cercueils	0.11	0.02	0.07	0.02	-0.04	-0.00
021 Biscuits	0.10	0.02	0.05	0.01	-0.04	-0.00
062 Laminage, moulage et extr. du cuivre	0.16	0.03	0.11	0.03	-0.05	0.00
098 Plastiques et résines synthétiques	0.39	0.06	0.33	0.09	-0.05	0.02
133 Systèmes de distribution du gaz	0.13	0.02	0.08	0.02	-0.06	-0.00
128 Stockage et entreposage	0.17	0.03	0.11	0.03	-0.06	0.00
104 Bijouterie et métaux précieux	0.38	0.06	0.31	0.08	-0.06	0.02
069 Matériel de chauffage	0.19	0.03	0.12	0.03	-0.07	0.00
061 Laminage, moulage et extr. de l'alum.	0.30	0.05	0.23	0.06	-0.07	0.01
002 Pêche et piégeage	0.44	0.07	0.36	0.09	-0.08	0.02
047 Autres industries du bois	0.15	0.03	0.06	0.02	-0.09	-0.01
089 Autres prod. élect. et électroniques	1.80	0.30	1.69	0.44	-0.11	0.14
107 Carreaux, linoléum et tissus enduits	0.22	0.04	0.11	0.03	-0.11	-0.01
026 Produits de distillerie	0.18	0.03	0.07	0.02	-0.11	-0.01
121 Camionnage	1.22	0.20	1.10	0.29	-0.12	0.09
037 Tricots	0.24	0.04	0.11	0.03	-0.13	-0.01
096 Produits du pétrole et du charbon raffinés	0.29	0.05	0.16	0.04	-0.13	-0.01
012 Carrières et sablières	0.23	0.04	0.09	0.02	-0.14	-0.01
044 Plaqués et contreplaqués	0.21	0.04	0.07	0.02	-0.14	-0.02
053 Boîtes en carton et sacs en papier	0.51	0.08	0.36	0.09	-0.15	0.01
108 Autres industries manufacturières n.c.a.	2.74	0.45	2.58	0.67	-0.16	0.22
024 Industries alimentaires diverses	0.70	0.12	0.50	0.13	-0.21	0.01
059 Fonderies de fer	0.58	0.10	0.36	0.09	-0.23	-0.00
103 Produits chimiques	0.92	0.15	0.67	0.17	-0.24	0.02
095 Produits minéraux non métalliques n.c.a.	0.57	0.09	0.32	0.08	-0.25	-0.01
060 Fonte et affinage métaux non-ferreux	0.67	0.11	0.42	0.11	-0.25	-0.00

Tableau A.5B (suite)

Classement selon la taille des variations	1961		1992		Variation 1961-1992	
	Emploi lié à l'importation en % de l'emploi total lié à l'importation	Emploi lié à l'importation en % de l'emploi total	Emploi lié à l'importation en % de l'emploi total lié à l'importation	Emploi lié à l'importation en % de l'emploi total	Emploi lié à l'importation en % de l'emploi total lié à l'importation	Emploi lié à l'importation en % de l'emploi total
051 Pâtes et papiers	0.86	0.14	0.58	0.15	-0.28	0.01
006 Mines de fer	0.39	0.06	0.10	0.03	-0.29	-0.04
005 Autres mines métalliques	0.58	0.10	0.28	0.07	-0.30	-0.02
008 Min. non métall. sauf charbon et amiante	0.41	0.07	0.10	0.03	-0.30	-0.04
067 Tréfilage et produits tréfilés	0.75	0.12	0.44	0.11	-0.30	-0.01
090 Matériaux en céramique	0.53	0.09	0.19	0.05	-0.34	-0.04
080 Construction et réparation de navires	0.46	0.08	0.11	0.03	-0.35	-0.05
066 Métal embout, pressé et enrobé	1.19	0.20	0.83	0.22	-0.36	0.02
083 Gros app. (élect. et non électr.)	0.73	0.12	0.33	0.09	-0.40	-0.03
017 Transformation des fruits et légumes	0.70	0.11	0.30	0.08	-0.40	-0.04
043 Scieries, atel. rabot. et usines bardeaux	0.65	0.11	0.24	0.06	-0.41	-0.04
055 Imprimerie et édition	2.35	0.39	1.94	0.51	-0.41	0.12
064 Chaudières et métaux de charpente	0.69	0.11	0.26	0.07	-0.43	-0.05
036 Fils de laine et textiles tissés	0.59	0.10	0.16	0.04	-0.43	-0.06
094 Verre et produits en verre	0.92	0.15	0.40	0.11	-0.52	-0.05
011 Pétrole brut et gaz naturel	1.12	0.18	0.57	0.15	-0.56	-0.04
109 Réparation, construction	1.46	0.24	0.89	0.23	-0.57	-0.01
071 Autres métaux ouvrés	1.28	0.21	0.71	0.18	-0.57	-0.03
038 Autres produits textiles	1.26	0.21	0.69	0.18	-0.57	-0.03
097 Produits chimiques industriels n.c.a.	1.22	0.20	0.62	0.16	-0.61	-0.04
003 Abattage et foresterie	1.06	0.17	0.38	0.10	-0.69	-0.08
120 Transport par eau et services connexes	1.00	0.17	0.30	0.08	-0.70	-0.09
074 Autres machines et matériel	4.12	0.68	3.36	0.87	-0.76	0.20
057 Acier primaire	2.44	0.40	1.48	0.39	-0.95	-0.01
119 Transport ferroviaire et services connexes	1.63	0.27	0.48	0.13	-1.14	-0.14
075 Aéronautique et pièces d'avion	2.34	0.38	0.96	0.25	-1.38	-0.14
072 Instruments agricoles	2.01	0.33	0.42	0.11	-1.58	-0.22
035 Fibres chimiques, fils et text. tissés	3.14	0.52	0.76	0.20	-2.38	-0.32
010 Mines de charbon	3.23	0.53	0.19	0.05	-3.04	-0.48
001 Agriculture et ind. connexes	12.42	2.04	4.77	1.24	-7.64	-0.80
TOTAL	100.00	17.20	100.00	23.07	0.00	5.87

Tableau A.6A Décomposition des variations des parts de l'emploi, 1961-1992, 161 industries

	1961	1992	Variation 1961-1992	Attribuable à :				
	Emploi lié à l'importation en % de l'emploi total lié à l'importation	Emploi lié à l'importation en % de l'emploi total lié à l'importation	Emploi lié à l'importation en % de l'emploi total lié à l'importation	Variation de la part des importations	Variation du ratio emploi/ production	Variation des coefficients entrées-sorties	Variation des coefficients d'importation	Interaction résiduelle
001 Agriculture et ind. connexes	12,42	4,77	-7,64	-4,68	-2,19	-0,58	0,23	-0,42
002 Pêche et piégeage	0,44	0,36	-0,08	-0,32	0,10	-0,07	0,06	0,14
003 Abattage et foresterie	1,06	0,38	-0,69	-0,18	-0,29	-0,10	0,00	-0,12
004 Mines d'or	0,13	0,13	-0,00	0,06	-0,25	0,01	-0,00	0,18
005 Autres mines métalliques	0,58	0,28	-0,30	-0,04	-0,07	-0,07	-0,06	-0,06
006 Mines de fer	0,39	0,10	-0,29	-0,24	-0,03	-0,02	0,02	-0,01
007 Mines d'amiante	0,03	0,00	-0,03	-0,03	0,00	-0,01	-0,00	0,01
008 Min. non métall. sauf charbon et amiante	0,41	0,10	-0,30	-0,15	-0,12	-0,01	0,03	-0,06
009 Mines de sel	0,02	0,02	-0,01	-0,00	-0,00	-0,00	-0,00	0,00
010 Mines de charbon	3,23	0,19	-3,04	-0,49	-0,73	-0,03	0,01	-1,79
011 Pétrole brut et gaz naturel	1,12	0,57	-0,56	-0,51	-0,17	0,08	0,08	-0,00
012 Carrières et sablières	0,23	0,09	-0,14	-0,15	-0,00	-0,01	0,00	0,02
013 Services connexes à l'extraction min.	0,15	0,27	0,12	-0,26	0,12	0,12	0,03	0,11
014 Viande et pr. de la viande (sauf volaille)	0,31	0,31	0,00	-0,08	0,06	-0,06	-0,00	0,08
015 Produits de la volaille	0,04	0,08	0,04	0,02	0,02	0,00	0,00	-0,01
016 Produits du poisson	0,22	0,34	0,12	0,10	0,01	-0,00	0,01	0,01
017 Transformation des fruits et légumes	0,70	0,30	-0,40	-0,38	-0,05	-0,01	0,02	0,02
018 Produits laitiers	0,12	0,12	-0,00	0,02	-0,04	-0,01	0,00	0,02
019 Nourriture pour animaux	0,16	0,13	-0,03	-0,02	-0,01	-0,01	0,00	0,01
020 Raffinage d'huile végétale (sauf maïs)	0,06	0,02	-0,04	-0,04	-0,00	-0,01	0,00	0,00
021 Biscuits	0,10	0,05	-0,04	-0,04	-0,01	0,00	0,00	0,00
022 Pain et autres prod. de boulangerie	0,04	0,11	0,07	0,07	-0,01	-0,01	0,00	0,01
023 Sucre de canne et betterave	0,05	0,02	-0,03	-0,02	0,00	-0,01	0,00	0,00
024 Industries alimentaires diverses	0,70	0,50	-0,21	-0,29	0,03	-0,01	0,03	0,00
025 Boissons gazeuses	0,04	0,04	0,01	0,00	-0,04	-0,04	0,00	0,07
026 Produits de distillerie	0,18	0,07	-0,11	-0,13	0,01	-0,01	0,00	0,02
027 Produits brassicoles	0,02	0,04	0,03	0,03	-0,00	-0,01	0,00	0,00
028 Vin	0,05	0,09	0,04	0,03	0,01	-0,00	0,00	0,00
029 Produits du tabac	0,05	0,11	0,06	0,08	-0,05	-0,01	0,00	0,04
030 Produits en caoutchouc	0,77	0,81	0,04	0,13	0,10	-0,11	-0,10	0,02

Tableau A.6A (suite)

	1961 Emploi lié à l'importation en % de l'emploi total lié à l'importation	1992 Emploi lié à l'importation en % de l'emploi total lié à l'importation	Variation 1961-1992 Emploi lié à l'importation en % de l'emploi total lié à l'importation	Variation de la part des importations	Attribuable à : Variation du ratio emploi/ production	Variation des coefficients entrées-sorties	Variation des coefficients d'importation	Interaction résiduelle
031 Produits en plastique	0,67	1,51	0,84	0,45	-0,00	0,27	0,00	0,12
032 Tanneries de cuir	0,14	0,11	-0,03	-0,01	0,00	0,00	-0,06	0,03
033 Chaussure	0,45	0,79	0,34	0,30	0,02	-0,04	0,05	0,02
034 Cuir et produits connexes	0,28	0,25	-0,03	-0,06	0,02	-0,02	-0,01	0,03
035 Fibres chimiques, fils et textiles tissés	3,14	0,76	-2,38	-1,46	-0,16	-0,20	-0,11	-0,45
036 Fils de laine et textiles tissés	0,59	0,16	-0,43	-0,33	-0,00	-0,10	-0,01	0,01
037 Tricots	0,24	0,11	-0,13	-0,12	-0,02	0,02	-0,01	-0,01
038 Autres produits textiles	1,26	0,69	-0,57	-0,65	0,09	-0,12	0,01	0,09
039 Achèvement et teinture de tissus	0,11	0,15	0,04	0,02	0,02	0,07	-0,01	-0,06
040 Moquettes, paillassons et tapis	0,09	0,11	0,02	0,02	0,02	0,00	0,01	0,02
041 Vêtement, sauf bonneterie	1,53	2,71	1,18	1,12	0,04	-0,13	0,13	0,02
042 Bonneterie	0,06	0,05	-0,00	-0,01	0,01	-0,01	0,00	0,00
043 Scieries, atel. rabot. et us. de bardeaux	0,65	0,24	-0,41	-0,17	-0,14	-0,05	0,01	-0,06
044 Plaqués et contreplaqués	0,21	0,07	-0,14	-0,11	-0,01	-0,03	0,00	0,00
045 Châssis, portes et aut. ouvr. de menuiserie	0,10	0,21	0,11	0,10	0,02	-0,01	0,01	-0,01
046 Boîtes en bois et cercueils	0,11	0,07	-0,04	-0,01	-0,02	-0,01	-0,01	0,00
047 Autres industries du bois	0,15	0,06	-0,09	-0,03	-0,04	-0,01	0,00	-0,02
048 Ameublement de maison	0,33	0,58	0,24	0,22	0,02	-0,03	0,03	0,01
049 Ameublement de bureau	0,06	0,07	0,02	0,02	-0,00	-0,00	0,01	0,00
050 Autres mobiliers et app. d'éclairage	0,16	0,25	0,09	0,06	0,04	-0,02	0,02	-0,01
051 Pâtes et papiers	0,86	0,58	-0,28	-0,06	-0,03	-0,16	-0,03	0,01
052 Papier-toiture asphalté	0,04	0,01	-0,02	-0,01	-0,01	-0,01	-0,00	-0,00
053 Boîtes en carton et sacs en papier	0,51	0,36	-0,15	-0,03	-0,01	-0,13	-0,02	0,01
054 Autres prod. de papier façonné	0,34	0,33	-0,01	0,02	0,01	-0,07	-0,00	0,03
055 Imprimerie et édition	2,35	1,94	-0,41	-0,17	-0,15	-0,31	0,05	0,16
056 Clichage, composition et reliure	0,35	0,33	-0,02	-0,07	0,03	-0,05	0,01	0,05
057 Acier primaire	2,44	1,48	-0,95	-0,60	-0,13	-0,09	-0,17	0,04

Tableau A.6A (suite)

	1961	1992	Variation 1961-1992	Variation de la part des importations	Variation du ratio emploi/production	Attribuable à :		
	Emploi lié à l'importation en % de l'emploi total lié à l'importation	Emploi lié à l'importation en % de l'emploi total lié à l'importation	Emploi lié à l'importation en % de l'emploi total lié à l'importation			Variation des coefficients entrées-sorties	Variation des coefficients d'importation	Interaction résiduelle
058 Canalisations et tuyaux d'acier	0,18	0,14	-0,04	-0,20	0,05	0,00	0,00	0,11
059 Fonderies de fer	0,58	0,36	-0,23	-0,18	-0,11	0,03	0,01	0,02
060 Fonte et affinage métaux non-ferreux	0,67	0,42	-0,25	-0,15	-0,04	-0,01	-0,09	0,03
061 Laminage, moulage et extr. de l'alum.	0,30	0,23	-0,07	0,05	-0,17	0,04	-0,09	0,11
062 Laminage, moulage et extr. du cuivre	0,16	0,11	-0,05	0,01	0,05	-0,08	-0,05	0,03
063 Lamin., moulage, etc. d'autres métaux	0,21	0,18	-0,03	-0,10	0,06	-0,04	-0,03	0,07
064 Chaudières et métaux de charpente	0,69	0,26	-0,43	-0,38	0,03	-0,14	-0,03	0,06
065 Prod. métall. décoratifs et architecturaux	0,19	0,17	-0,02	-0,02	0,01	-0,00	0,01	0,06
066 Métal embouti, pressé et enrobé	1,19	0,83	-0,36	-0,34	0,09	0,00	0,00	-0,00
067 Tréfilage et produits tréfilés	0,75	0,44	-0,30	-0,16	0,04	-0,14	-0,05	0,08
068 Art. de quincaillerie, outils et couteaux	0,95	0,94	-0,01	-0,30	0,19	-0,17	0,04	0,13
069 Matériel de chauffage	0,19	0,12	-0,07	-0,10	0,02	-0,06	0,03	0,03
070 Ateliers d'usinage	0,72	1,01	0,29	0,12	0,19	-0,02	-0,09	0,08
071 Autres métaux ouvrés	1,28	0,71	-0,57	-0,51	0,01	-0,01	-0,04	0,05
072 Instruments agricoles	2,01	0,42	-1,58	-1,86	0,02	-0,09	0,04	0,25
073 Équipement de réfrigération commercial	0,18	0,30	0,11	0,07	0,04	0,01	-0,01	0,01
074 Autres machines et matériel	4,12	3,36	-0,76	-1,08	0,02	0,01	0,10	0,33
075 Aéronautique et pièces d'avion	2,34	0,96	-1,38	-1,21	-0,13	-0,02	0,01	-0,02
076 Véhicules à moteur	0,91	1,14	0,23	0,61	-0,88	-0,08	0,09	0,49
077 Camions, carross. d'autobus et remorques	0,21	0,33	0,12	0,08	0,02	-0,01	0,02	0,09
078 Pièces et accessoires de véh. à moteur	3,55	5,34	1,80	2,28	-0,81	-0,11	-0,37	0,80
079 Matériel ferroviaire roulant	0,18	0,17	-0,01	0,05	-0,07	-0,01	-0,00	0,00
080 Construction et réparation de navires	0,46	0,11	-0,35	-0,28	-0,03	-0,01	0,01	-0,04
081 Matériel de transport divers	0,17	0,15	-0,02	0,03	-0,10	-0,00	0,01	0,04
082 Petits appareils électriques	0,26	0,29	0,03	-0,01	0,06	-0,03	0,01	0,00
083 Gros app. (élect. et non élect.)	0,73	0,33	-0,40	-0,39	-0,02	-0,02	0,01	0,02
084 Tourne-disques, radios et téléviseurs	0,34	0,39	0,04	0,16	-0,17	-0,02	-0,04	0,11
085 Matériel électronique	1,89	2,51	0,63	1,48	-2,55	0,25	-0,60	2,04
086 Machines de bureau et de magasin	0,74	1,64	0,90	1,12	-0,50	-0,08	-0,30	0,65
087 Fils et câbles de transm. et d'énergie	0,19	0,18	-0,01	0,04	0,00	-0,04	-0,02	0,02

Tableau A.6A (suite)

	1961	1992	Variation 1961–1992	Attribuable à :				
	Emploi lié à l'importation en % de l'emploi total lié à l'importation	Emploi lié à l'importation en % de l'emploi total lié à l'importation	Emploi lié à l'importation en % de l'emploi total lié à l'importation	Variation de la part des importations	Variation du ratio emploi/ production	Variation des coefficients entrées- sorties	Variation des coefficients d'importation	Interaction résiduelle
088 Batteries	0.07	0.08	0.01	0.01	0.01	-0.01	-0.00	0.00
089 Autres prod. élect. et électroniques	1.80	1.69	-0.11	-0.06	0.05	-0.12	-0.12	0.14
090 Matériaux en céramique	0.53	0.19	-0.34	-0.26	-0.03	-0.03	0.01	-0.03
091 Ciment	0.02	0.02	-0.01	-0.00	0.00	-0.00	0.00	0.00
092 Produits en béton	0.04	0.02	-0.02	-0.02	0.00	-0.01	0.00	0.00
093 Béton prémélangé	0.01	0.01	0.00	-0.00	0.01	0.00	0.00	0.00
094 Verre et produits en verre	0.92	0.40	-0.52	-0.37	-0.07	-0.10	0.00	0.01
095 Produits minéraux non métall. n.c.a.	0.57	0.32	-0.25	-0.17	-0.02	-0.09	0.00	0.04
096 Prod. du pétrole et du charbon raffinés	0.29	0.16	-0.13	-0.04	-0.02	-0.09	-0.02	0.04
097 Produits chimiques industriels n.c.a.	1.22	0.62	-0.61	-0.18	-0.42	0.05	-0.05	0.00
098 Plastiques et résines synthétiques	0.39	0.33	-0.05	0.01	-0.14	0.03	-0.03	0.07
099 Prod. pharmaceutiques et médicaments	0.29	0.39	0.10	0.14	-0.15	0.02	-0.03	0.07
100 Peintures et vernis	0.21	0.20	-0.01	0.03	-0.04	-0.01	-0.02	0.01
101 Savons et prod. de nettoyage	0.16	0.18	0.03	-0.00	0.04	-0.02	-0.00	0.01
102 Produits de toilette	0.03	0.18	0.15	0.13	0.03	-0.00	0.01	-0.02
103 Produits chimiques	0.92	0.67	-0.24	-0.15	-0.14	0.02	-0.05	0.07
104 Bijouterie et métaux précieux	0.38	0.31	-0.06	-0.08	0.02	-0.02	0.00	0.02
105 Articles de sport et jouets	0.50	0.67	0.17	0.18	-0.07	-0.03	0.04	0.06
106 Enseignes et étalages	0.10	0.14	0.03	0.02	0.04	-0.03	-0.00	0.01
107 Carreaux, linoléum et tissus enduits	0.22	0.11	-0.11	-0.09	0.00	-0.02	-0.01	0.01
108 Autres industries manufacturières n.c.a.	2.74	2.58	-0.16	-0.43	0.14	-0.10	-0.02	0.24
109 Réparation, construction	1.46	0.89	-0.57	-0.15	-0.20	-0.28	-0.01	0.06
110 Construction résidentielle	0.00	0.00	0.00	0.00	0.00	0.00	0.00	0.00
111 Construction d'immeubles non résidentiels	0.00	0.00	0.00	0.00	0.00	0.00	0.00	0.00
112 Const. de routes, autor. et pistes d'atterr.	0.00	0.00	0.00	0.00	0.00	0.00	0.00	0.00
113 Const. d'install. gazières et pétrolières	0.00	0.00	0.00	0.00	0.00	0.00	0.00	0.00
114 Projets de barrages et d'irrigation	0.00	0.00	0.00	0.00	0.00	0.00	0.00	0.00
115 Const. de ch. fer et lignes tél. et télég.	0.00	0.00	0.00	0.00	0.00	0.00	0.00	0.00
116 Autres travaux d'ingénierie	0.00	0.00	0.00	0.00	0.00	0.00	0.00	0.00
117 Autres activités de construction	0.01	0.02	0.01	0.01	0.01	-0.01	-0.00	0.00

Tableau A.6A (suite)

	1961	1992	Variation 1961-1992	Attribuable à :			
	Emploi lié à l'importation en % de l'emploi total lié à l'importation	Emploi lié à l'importation en % de l'emploi total lié à l'importation	Emploi lié à l'importation en % de l'emploi total lié à l'importation	Variation de la part des importations	Variation du ratio emploi/ production	Variation des coefficients entrées-sorties	Variation des coefficients d'importation	Interaction résiduelle
118 Transport aérien et services connexes	0,23	0,80	0,57	0,59	-0,11	-0,00	-0,01	0,11
119 Transport ferroviaire et serv. connexes	1,63	0,48	-1,14	0,04	-0,18	-0,69	-0,02	-0,29
120 Transport par eau et services connexes	1,00	0,30	-0,70	-0,35	-0,12	-0,12	0,01	-0,12
121 Camionnage	1,22	1,10	-0,12	-0,10	-0,28	0,11	-0,03	0,18
122 Systèmes de transport urbain	0,02	0,18	0,16	0,15	0,08	-0,01	0,01	-0,07
123 Systèmes de transport interurbain et rural	0,02	0,09	0,07	0,08	-0,03	-0,01	0,00	0,02
124 Industrie du taxi	0,26	0,61	0,35	0,31	0,09	-0,00	0,00	0,02
125 Autres transports et services connexes	0,04	0,51	0,47	0,18	0,25	0,27	-0,01	-0,22
126 Ent. des ponts et des autoroutes	0,01	0,00	-0,00	0,00	-0,00	-0,00	-0,03	-0,02
127 Transport par pipelines	0,08	0,07	-0,00	-0,05	0,01	0,00	-0,00	0,02
128 Stockage et entreposage	0,17	0,11	-0,06	-0,03	0,03	-0,11	0,00	0,05
129 Télécommunications et radiodiffusion	0,27	0,27	-0,00	0,05	-0,27	0,07	0,00	0,14
130 Entreprises de télécomm. et autres	0,72	0,77	0,06	0,17	-0,29	0,02	-0,01	0,16
131 Services postaux	0,38	0,45	0,07	0,07	-0,02	0,05	-0,00	0,04
132 Systèmes d'énergie électrique	0,52	0,64	0,13	-0,14	-0,19	0,29	-0,02	0,18
133 Systèmes de distribution du gaz	0,13	0,08	-0,06	-0,04	-0,04	0,01	-0,00	0,01
134 Autres services publics n.c.a.	0,05	0,23	0,18	-0,02	-0,00	0,17	-0,00	0,03
135 Commerce de gros	3,26	5,08	1,83	-0,24	1,00	0,82	-0,15	0,40
136 Commerce de détail	2,59	3,14	0,55	-0,21	0,90	-0,79	-0,00	0,66
137 Banq., coop. de crédit et autr. inst. dépôt	0,73	1,83	1,11	0,25	-0,13	0,71	0,03	0,26
138 Fiducies, autres inst. fin. et immob.	0,79	1,83	1,04	0,26	0,64	0,19	0,04	-0,10
139 Industrie de l'assurance	0,51	0,62	0,11	0,23	-0,13	-0,04	0,01	0,04
140 Redevances gouv. sur les ress. natur.	0,00	0,00	0,00	0,00	0,00	0,00	0,00	0,00
141 Logements occupés par leur propriétaire	0,00	0,00	0,00	0,00	0,00	0,00	0,00	0,00
142 Autres services commerciaux	1,19	5,23	4,04	1,50	1,70	1,64	0,92	-1,73
143 Services profess. aux entreprises	1,70	3,65	1,95	0,48	0,67	1,00	0,15	-0,35
144 Services de publicité	0,24	0,56	0,32	0,05	0,06	0,20	0,02	-0,02
145 Services éducatifs	0,04	0,12	0,08	0,07	0,01	-0,01	0,01	-0,01

Tableau A.6A (suite)

	1961	1992	Variation 1961-1992		Attribuable à :			
	Emploi lié à l'importation en % de l'emploi total lié à l'importation	Emploi lié à l'importation en % de l'emploi total lié à l'importation	Emploi lié à l'importation en % de l'emploi total lié à l'importation	Variation de la part des importations	Variation du ratio emploi/ production	Variation des coefficients entrées-sorties	Variation des coefficients d'importation	Interaction résiduelle
146 Hôpitaux	0,03	0,08	0,04	0,05	-0,01	-0,00	0,01	0,01
147 Autres services de santé	0,00	0,04	0,04	0,03	0,02	0,01	0,00	-0,02
148 Hébergement et restauration	0,75	8,89	8,14	7,66	4,29	-0,51	0,32	-3,63
149 Films et vidéos	0,25	0,24	-0,01	-0,08	-0,00	0,03	0,01	0,03
150 Autres services de divertissement et loisir	0,03	0,89	0,87	0,86	0,20	-0,05	0,06	-0,20
151 Buanderies et nettoyeurs	0,06	0,10	0,04	0,02	0,02	-0,02	0,00	0,02
152 Autres services personnels	0,00	0,01	0,01	0,01	0,02	-0,00	0,00	-0,00
153 Photographes	0,01	0,01	0,00	0,00	0,02	0,01	0,00	-0,00
154 Services divers	0,80	2,80	2,00	-0,10	1,57	0,80	0,06	-0,33

Tableau A.6B Décomposition des variations des parts de l'emploi, 1961-1992, 161 industries

Classement selon la taille des variations	1961 — Emploi lié à l'importation en % de l'emploi total lié à l'importation	1992 — Emploi lié à l'importation en % de l'emploi total lié à l'importation	Variation 1961-1992 — Emploi lié à l'importation en % de l'emploi total lié à l'importation	Variation de la part des importations	Attribuable à : Variation du ratio emploi/production	Attribuable à : Variation des coefficients entrées-sorties	Attribuable à : Variation des coefficients d'importation	Attribuable à : Interaction résiduelle
148 Hébergement et restauration	0,75	8,89	8,14	7,66	4,29	-0,51	0,32	-3,63
142 Autres services commerciaux	1,19	5,23	4,04	1,50	1,70	1,64	0,92	-1,73
154 Services divers	0,80	2,80	2,00	-0,10	1,57	0,80	0,06	-0,33
143 Services profess. aux entreprises	1,70	3,65	1,95	0,48	0,67	1,00	0,15	-0,35
135 Commerce de gros	3,26	5,08	1,83	-0,24	1,00	0,82	-0,15	0,40
078 Pièces et accessoires de véh. à moteur	3,55	5,34	1,80	2,28	-0,81	-0,11	-0,37	0,80
041 Vêtement, sauf bonneterie	1,53	2,71	1,18	1,12	0,04	-0,13	0,13	0,02
137 Banq., coop. de crédit et autr. inst. dépôt	0,73	1,83	1,11	0,25	-0,13	0,71	0,03	0,26
138 Fiducies, autres inst. fin. et immob.	0,79	1,83	1,04	0,26	0,64	0,19	0,04	-0,10
086 Machines de bureau et de magasin	0,74	1,64	0,90	1,12	-0,50	-0,08	-0,30	0,65
150 Autres services de divertissement et loisir	0,03	0,89	0,87	0,86	0,20	-0,05	0,06	-0,20
031 Produits en plastique	0,67	1,51	0,84	0,45	-0,00	0,27	0,00	0,12
085 Matériel électronique	1,89	2,51	0,63	1,48	-2,55	0,25	-0,60	2,04
118 Transport aérien et services connexes	0,23	0,80	0,57	0,59	-0,11	-0,00	-0,01	0,11
136 Commerce de détail	2,59	3,14	0,55	-0,21	0,90	-0,79	-0,00	0,66
125 Autres transports et services connexes	0,04	0,51	0,47	0,18	0,25	0,27	-0,01	-0,22
124 Industrie du taxi	0,26	0,61	0,35	0,31	0,09	-0,00	-0,01	-0,02
033 Chaussure	0,45	0,79	0,34	0,30	0,02	-0,00	-0,03	-0,02
144 Services de publicité	0,24	0,56	0,32	0,05	0,06	-0,04	0,05	-0,02
070 Ateliers d'usinage	0,72	1,01	0,29	0,05	0,06	0,20	0,02	-0,02
048 Ameublement de maison	0,33	0,58	0,24	0,12	0,19	-0,01	0,02	0,08
076 Véhicules à moteur	0,91	1,14	0,23	0,22	0,02	-0,01	-0,09	0,01
134 Autres services publics n.c.a.	0,05	0,23	0,18	0,61	-0,88	-0,08	0,09	0,49
105 Articles de sport et jouets	0,50	0,67	0,17	-0,02	-0,00	-0,03	0,04	0,06
122 Systèmes de transport urbain	0,02	0,18	0,16	0,18	-0,07	0,17	0,01	0,06
102 Produits de toilette	0,03	0,18	0,15	0,18	-0,07	-0,03	0,01	-0,07
132 Systèmes d'énergie électrique	0,03	0,18	0,15	0,15	0,08	-0,01	0,01	-0,02
077 Camions, carr. d'autobus et remorques	0,52	0,64	0,13	0,13	0,03	-0,00	0,01	0,18
016 Produits du poisson	0,21	0,33	0,12	0,08	0,02	0,29	-0,02	0,00
	0,22	0,34	0,12	0,10	0,01	-0,01	0,01	0,01

Tableau A.6B (suite)

Classement selon la taille des variations	1961 Emploi lié à l'importation en % de l'emploi total lié à l'importation	1992 Emploi lié à l'importation en % de l'emploi total lié à l'importation	Variation 1961-1992 Emploi lié à l'importation en % de l'emploi total lié à l'importation	Attribuable à : Variation de la part des importations	Variation du ratio emploi/ production	Variation des coefficients entrées-sorties d'importation	Variation des coefficients d'importation	Interaction résiduelle
013 Services connexes à l'extraction min.	0.15	0.27	0.12	-0.26	0.12	0.12	0.03	0.11
045 Châssis, portes et autres ouvr. de men.	0.10	0.21	0.11	0.10	0.02	-0.01	0.01	-0.01
073 Équipement de réfrigération commercial	0.18	0.30	0.11	0.07	0.04	0.01	-0.01	0.01
139 Industrie de l'assurance	0.51	0.62	0.11	0.23	-0.13	-0.04	0.01	0.04
099 Prod. pharmaceutique et médicaments	0.29	0.39	0.10	0.14	-0.15	0.02	0.02	0.07
050 Autres mobiliers et app. d'éclairage	0.16	0.25	0.09	0.06	0.04	-0.02	0.02	-0.01
145 Services éducatifs	0.04	0.12	0.08	0.07	0.01	-0.02	-0.01	-0.01
131 Services postaux	0.38	0.45	0.07	0.00	0.00	0.01	-0.00	0.04
022 Pain et autres prod. de boulangerie	0.04	0.11	0.07	0.07	-0.01	0.05	-0.00	0.01
123 Systèmes de transport interurbain et rural	0.02	0.09	0.07	0.08	-0.01	-0.01	0.00	0.01
130 Entreprises de télécomm. et autres	0.72	0.77	0.06	0.17	-0.29	-0.02	-0.01	0.16
029 Produits du tabac	0.05	0.11	0.06	0.08	-0.05	-0.01	0.00	0.04
084 Tourne-disques, radios et téléviseurs	0.34	0.39	0.04	0.16	-0.17	-0.02	-0.04	0.11
151 Buanderies et nettoyeurs	0.06	0.10	0.04	0.02	-0.01	0.00	0.00	0.04
039 Achèvement et teinture de tissus	0.11	0.15	0.04	0.02	0.02	0.07	-0.01	-0.06
146 Hôpitaux	0.03	0.08	0.04	0.05	-0.01	-0.00	0.01	0.01
028 Vin	0.05	0.09	0.04	0.03	0.01	-0.00	0.01	0.01
147 Autres services de santé	0.00	0.04	0.04	0.03	0.02	0.01	0.00	-0.02
030 Produits en caoutchouc	0.77	0.81	0.04	0.13	0.10	-0.11	-0.10	0.02
015 Produits de la volaille	0.04	0.08	0.04	0.02	0.02	-0.00	0.00	-0.01
106 Enseignes et étalages	0.10	0.14	0.03	0.02	0.04	-0.03	-0.00	0.01
082 Petits appareils électriques	0.26	0.29	0.03	-0.01	0.06	-0.03	-0.00	0.00
101 Indust. des savons et prod. de nettoyage	0.16	0.18	0.03	-0.00	0.04	-0.02	0.01	0.00
027 Produits brassicoles	0.02	0.04	0.03	0.03	-0.00	-0.01	-0.00	0.01
153 Photographes	0.01	0.04	0.02	0.00	0.02	-0.01	0.00	0.00
040 Moquettes, paillassons et tapis	0.09	0.11	0.02	0.03	-0.03	0.00	0.01	-0.00
049 Ameublement de bureau	0.06	0.07	0.02	0.02	-0.03	-0.00	0.01	0.02
088 Batteries	0.07	0.08	0.01	0.01	0.01	0.00	-0.00	0.00
152 Autres services personnels	0.00	0.01	0.01	0.01	0.00	-0.00	-0.00	-0.00

Tableau A.6B (suite)

Classement selon la taille des variations	1961 Emploi lié à l'importation en % de l'emploi total lié à l'importation	1992 Emploi lié à l'importation en % de l'emploi total lié à l'importation	Variation 1961-1992 Emploi lié à l'importation en % de l'emploi total lié à l'importation	Attribuable à : Variation de la part des importations	Variation du ratio emploi/ production	Variation des coefficients entrées-sorties	Variation des coefficients d'importation	Interaction résiduelle
025 Boissons gazeuses	0.04	0.04	0.01	0.00	-0.04	0.02	0.00	0.02
117 Autres activités de construction	0.01	0.02	0.01	0.00	0.01	-0.01	-0.00	0.00
093 Béton prémélangé	0.01	0.01	0.00	-0.00	0.01	0.00	0.00	0.00
014 Viande et pr. de la viande (sauf volaille)	0.31	0.31	0.00	-0.08	0.06	-0.06	-0.00	0.08
111 Construction d'immeubles non résidentiels	0.00	0.00	0.00	0.00	0.00	0.00	0.00	0.00
110 Construction résidentielle	0.00	0.00	0.00	0.00	0.00	0.00	0.00	0.00
140 Redevances gouv. sur les ress. natur.	0.00	0.00	0.00	0.00	0.00	0.00	0.00	0.00
116 Autres travaux d'ingénierie	0.00	0.00	0.00	0.00	0.00	0.00	0.00	0.00
141 Logements occupés par leur propriétaire	0.00	0.00	0.00	0.00	0.00	0.00	0.00	0.00
115 Const. de ch. fer et lignes tél. et télég.	0.00	0.00	0.00	0.00	0.00	0.00	0.00	0.00
112 Const. de routes, autor. et pistes d'atterr.	0.00	0.00	0.00	0.00	0.00	0.00	0.00	0.00
113 Const. d'install. gazières et pétrolières	0.00	0.00	0.00	0.00	0.00	0.00	0.00	0.00
114 Projets de barrages et d'irrigation	0.00	0.00	0.00	0.00	0.00	0.00	0.00	0.00
018 Produits laitiers	0.12	0.12	-0.00	0.02	-0.04	-0.01	0.00	0.02
042 Bonneterie	0.06	0.05	-0.00	-0.01	0.01	-0.01	0.00	0.00
126 Entr. des ponts et des autoroutes	0.01	0.00	-0.00	0.00	-0.00	-0.00	0.00	0.00
129 Télécommunications et radiodiffusion	0.27	0.27	-0.00	0.05	-0.27	0.07	0.00	0.14
004 Mines d'or	0.13	0.13	-0.00	0.06	-0.25	0.01	-0.00	0.18
068 Art. de quincaillerie, outils et couteaux	0.95	0.94	-0.01	-0.30	0.19	-0.06	0.03	0.13
091 Ciment	0.02	0.02	-0.01	-0.00	0.00	-0.00	0.00	0.00
079 Matériel ferroviaire roulant	0.18	0.17	-0.01	-0.05	-0.07	-0.01	-0.00	0.02
149 Films et vidéos	0.25	0.24	-0.01	-0.08	-0.00	0.03	0.01	0.03
087 Fils et câbles de transm. et d'énergie	0.19	0.18	-0.01	0.04	0.00	-0.04	-0.02	0.02
127 Transport par pipelines	0.08	0.07	-0.01	-0.05	0.01	0.01	0.00	0.02
009 Mines de sel	0.02	0.02	-0.00	-0.00	-0.00	-0.00	-0.00	0.00
054 Autres prod. de papier façonné	0.34	0.33	-0.01	0.02	0.01	-0.07	-0.00	0.03
100 Peintures et vernis	0.21	0.20	-0.01	0.03	-0.04	-0.01	-0.02	0.01
065 Prod. métall. décoratifs et architecturaux	0.19	0.17	-0.02	-0.02	0.01	-0.00	0.00	0.01
092 Produits en béton	0.04	0.02	-0.02	-0.02	0.00	-0.01	0.00	0.00

Tableau A.6B (suite)

Classement selon la taille des variations	1961 Emploi lié à l'importation en % de l'emploi total lié à l'importation	1992 Emploi lié à l'importation en % de l'emploi total lié à l'importation	Variation 1961-1992 Emploi lié à l'importation en % de l'emploi total lié à l'importation	Variation de la part des importations	Variation du ratio emploi/production	Attribuable à : Variation des coefficients entrées-sorties	Variation des coefficients d'importation	Interaction résiduelle
056 Clichage, composition et reliure	0,35	0,33	-0,02	-0,07	0,03	-0,05	0,01	0,05
081 Matériel de transport divers	0,17	0,15	-0,02	0,03	-0,10	-0,00	0,01	0,04
052 Papier-toiture asphalté	0,04	0,01	-0,02	-0,01	-0,01	-0,00	-0,00	-0,00
023 Sucre de canne et betterave	0,05	0,02	-0,03	-0,02	0,00	-0,01	0,00	0,00
007 Mines d'amiante	0,03	0,00	-0,03	-0,03	0,00	-0,01	-0,00	0,01
034 Cuir et prod. connexes divers	0,28	0,25	-0,03	-0,06	0,02	-0,02	-0,01	0,03
019 Nourriture pour animaux	0,16	0,13	-0,03	-0,02	-0,01	-0,01	-0,01	0,01
032 Tanneries de cuir	0,14	0,11	-0,03	-0,01	0,00	0,00	-0,00	0,03
063 Laminage, moulage, etc. d'autres métaux	0,21	0,18	-0,03	-0,10	0,06	-0,04	0,00	0,07
020 Raffinage d'huile végétale (sauf maïs)	0,06	0,02	-0,04	-0,04	-0,00	-0,00	0,00	0,00
058 Canalisations et tuyaux d'acier	0,18	0,14	-0,04	-0,20	0,05	0,00	0,00	0,11
046 Boîtes en bois et cercueils	0,11	0,07	-0,04	-0,01	-0,02	-0,01	-0,01	0,00
021 Biscuits	0,10	0,05	-0,04	-0,04	-0,01	0,00	0,00	0,00
062 Laminage, moulage et extrusion du cuivre	0,16	0,11	-0,05	-0,04	0,05	-0,08	-0,05	0,03
098 Plastiques et résines synthétiques	0,39	0,33	-0,05	0,01	-0,14	0,03	-0,03	0,07
133 Systèmes de distribution du gaz	0,13	0,08	-0,06	-0,03	-0,04	0,01	-0,00	0,01
128 Stockage et entreposage	0,17	0,11	-0,06	-0,03	0,03	0,01	-0,00	0,05
104 Bijouterie et métaux précieux	0,38	0,31	-0,07	-0,08	0,02	-0,11	0,00	0,02
069 Matériel de chauffage	0,19	0,12	-0,07	-0,10	0,02	-0,02	0,00	0,03
061 Laminage, moulage et extr. de l'aluminium	0,30	0,23	-0,07	0,05	-0,17	0,04	-0,09	0,11
002 Pêche et piégeage	0,44	0,36	-0,08	-0,32	0,10	-0,07	0,06	0,14
047 Autres industries du bois	0,15	0,06	-0,09	-0,03	-0,04	-0,01	0,00	-0,02
089 Autres prod. élect. et électroniques	1,80	1,69	-0,11	-0,06	0,05	-0,12	-0,12	0,14
107 Carreaux de sol, linol. et tissus enduits	0,22	0,11	-0,11	-0,09	0,00	-0,02	-0,01	0,01
026 Produits de distillerie	0,18	0,07	-0,12	-0,13	0,01	0,00	0,00	0,02
121 Camionnage	1,22	1,10	-0,12	-0,10	-0,28	0,11	-0,03	0,18
037 Tricots	0,24	0,11	-0,13	-0,12	-0,02	0,02	0,00	-0,01
096 Prod. du pétrole et du charbon raffinés	0,29	0,16	-0,13	-0,04	-0,09	-0,00	-0,00	0,00
012 Carrières et sablières	0,23	0,09	-0,14	-0,15	-0,00	-0,01	0,00	0,02

Tableau A.6B (suite)

Classement selon la taille des variations	1961 Emploi lié à l'importation en % de l'emploi total lié à l'importation	1992 Emploi lié à l'importation en % de l'emploi total lié à l'importation	Variation 1961–1992 Emploi lié à l'importation en % de l'emploi total lié à l'importation	Attribuable à : Variation de la part des importations	Variation du ratio emploi/ production	Variation des coefficients entrées-sorties d'importation	Variation des coefficients d'importation	Interaction résiduelle
044 Plaqués et contreplaqués	0,21	0,07	-0,14	-0,11	-0,01	-0,03	0,00	0,00
053 Boîtes en carton et sacs en papier	0,51	0,36	-0,15	-0,03	0,02	-0,13	-0,02	0,01
108 Autres industries manufacturières n.c.a.	2,74	2,58	-0,16	-0,43	0,14	-0,10	-0,02	0,24
024 Industries alimentaires diverses	0,70	0,50	-0,21	-0,29	0,03	-0,04	0,03	0,07
059 Fonderies de fer	0,58	0,36	-0,23	-0,18	-0,11	0,03	0,01	0,02
103 Produits chimiques	0,92	0,67	-0,24	-0,15	-0,14	0,02	-0,05	0,07
095 Produits minéraux non métall. n.c.a.	0,57	0,32	-0,25	-0,17	-0,02	-0,09	-0,02	0,04
060 Fonte et affinage métaux non-ferreux	0,67	0,42	-0,25	-0,15	-0,04	-0,01	-0,09	0,03
051 Pâtes et papiers	0,86	0,58	-0,28	-0,06	-0,03	-0,16	-0,03	0,01
006 Mines de fer	0,39	0,10	-0,29	-0,24	-0,03	-0,02	0,02	-0,01
005 Autres mines métalliques	0,58	0,28	-0,30	-0,04	-0,07	-0,07	-0,06	-0,06
008 Mines non mét. sauf charbon et amiante	0,41	0,10	-0,30	-0,15	-0,12	-0,00	0,03	-0,06
067 Tréfilage et produits tréfilés	0,75	0,44	-0,30	-0,16	0,04	-0,17	-0,05	0,04
090 Matériaux en céramique	0,53	0,19	-0,34	-0,26	-0,03	-0,03	0,01	-0,03
080 Construction et réparation de navires	0,46	0,11	-0,35	-0,28	-0,03	-0,01	0,01	-0,04
066 Métal embouti, pressé et enrobé	1,19	0,83	-0,36	-0,34	0,09	-0,14	-0,05	0,08
083 Gros app. (élect. et non électr.)	0,73	0,33	-0,40	-0,39	-0,02	-0,02	0,01	0,02
017 Transformation des fruits et légumes	0,70	0,30	-0,40	-0,38	-0,05	-0,01	0,02	0,02
043 Scieries, at. rabot. et usines de bardeaux	0,65	0,24	-0,41	-0,17	-0,14	-0,05	0,01	-0,06
055 Imprimerie et édition	2,35	1,94	-0,41	-0,17	-0,15	-0,31	0,05	0,16
064 Chaudières et métaux de charpente	0,69	0,26	-0,43	-0,38	0,03	-0,14	0,01	0,06
036 Fils de laine et textiles tissés	0,59	0,16	-0,43	-0,33	-0,00	-0,10	-0,01	0,01
094 Verre et produits en verre	0,92	0,40	-0,52	-0,37	-0,07	-0,10	0,00	0,01
011 Pétrole brut et gaz naturel	1,12	0,57	-0,56	-0,51	-0,17	0,05	0,08	-0,00
109 Réparation, construction	1,46	0,89	-0,57	-0,15	-0,20	-0,28	-0,01	0,06
071 Autres métaux ouvrés	1,28	0,71	-0,57	-0,51	0,01	-0,09	-0,04	0,05
038 Autres produits textiles	1,26	0,69	-0,57	-0,65	0,09	-0,12	0,01	0,09
097 Produits chimiques industriels n.c.a.	1,22	0,62	-0,61	-0,18	-0,42	0,05	-0,05	0,00
003 Abattage et foresterie	1,06	0,38	-0,69	-0,18	-0,29	-0,10	0,00	-0,12

Tableau A.6B (suite)

Classement selon la taille des variations	1961 Emploi lié à l'importation en % de l'emploi total lié à l'importation	1992 Emploi lié à l'importation en % de l'emploi total lié à l'importation	Variation 1961-1992 Emploi lié à l'importation en % de l'emploi total lié à l'importation	Variation de la part des importations	Attribuable à : Variation du ratio emploi/production	Variation des coefficients entrées-sorties d'importation	Variation des coefficients d'importation	Interaction résiduelle
120 Transport par eau et services connexes	1,00	0,30	-0,70	-0,35	-0,12	-0,12	0,01	-0,12
074 Autres machines et matériel	4,12	3,36	-0,76	-1,08	0,02	-0,13	0,10	0,33
057 Acier primaire	2,44	1,48	-0,95	-0,60	-0,13	-0,09	-0,17	0,04
119 Transp. ferroviaire et services connexes	1,63	0,48	-1,14	0,04	-0,18	-0,69	-0,02	-0,29
075 Aéronautique et pièces d'avion	2,34	0,96	-1,38	-1,21	-0,13	-0,02	0,01	-0,02
072 Instruments agricoles	2,01	0,42	-1,58	-1,86	0,02	-0,04	0,04	0,25
010 Mines de charbon	3,23	0,19	-3,04	-0,49	-0,73	-0,03	0,01	-1,79
001 Agriculture et ind. connexes	12,42	4,77	-7,64	-4,68	-2,19	-0,58	0,23	-0,42

PUBLICATIONS DE RECHERCHE D'INDUSTRIE CANADA

COLLECTION DOCUMENTS DE TRAVAIL

N° 1   **L'intégration économique de l'Amérique du Nord : les tendances de l'investissement étranger direct et les 1 000 entreprises les plus grandes**, Industrie Canada, personnel de la Direction de l'analyse de la politique micro-économique, notamment John Knubley, Marc Legault et P.Someshwar Rao, 1994.

N° 2   **Les multinationales canadiennes : analyse de leurs activités et résultats**, Industrie Canada, personnel de la Direction de l'analyse de la politique micro-économique, notamment P. Someshwar Rao, Marc Legault et Ashfaq Ahmad, 1994.

N° 3   **Débordements transfrontaliers de R-D entre les industries du Canada et des États-Unis**, Jeffrey I. Bernstein, Université Carleton et National Bureau of Economic Research, dans le cadre d'un contrat avec Industrie Canada, 1994.

N° 4   **L'impact économique des activités de fusion et d'acquisition sur les entreprises**, Gilles Mcdougall, Direction de l'analyse de la politique micro-économique, Industrie Canada, 1995.

N° 5   **La transition de l'université au monde du travail : analyse du cheminement de diplômés récents**, Ross Finnie, École d'administration publique, Université Carleton et Statistique Canada, 1995.

N° 6   **La mesure du coût d'observation lié aux dépenses fiscales : les stimulants à la recherche-développement**, Sally Gunz, Université de Waterloo, Alan Macnaughton, Université de Waterloo, et Karen Wensley, Ernst & Young, Toronto, dans le cadre d'un contrat avec Industrie Canada, 1996.

N° 7   **Les structures de régie, la prise de décision et le rendement des entreprises en Amérique du Nord**, P. Someshwar Rao et Clifton R. Lee-Sing, Direction de l'analyse de la politique micro-économique, Industrie Canada, 1996.

N° 8   **L'investissement étranger direct et l'intégration économique de la zone APEC**, Ashfaq Ahmad, P. Someshwar Rao et Colleen Barnes, Direction de l'analyse de la politique micro-économique, Industrie Canada, 1996.

N° 9   **Les stratégies de mandat mondial des filiales canadiennes**, Julian Birkinshaw, Institute of International Business, Stockholm School of Economics, dans le cadre d'un contrat avec Industrie Canada, 1996.

N° 10   **R-D et croissance de la productivité dans le secteur manufacturier et l'industrie du matériel de communications au Canada**, Jeffrey I. Bernstein, Université Carleton et National Bureau of Economic Research, dans le cadre d'un contrat avec Industrie Canada, 1996.

N° 11   **Évolution à long terme de la convergence régionale au Canada**, Serge Coulombe, Département de sciences économiques, Université d'Ottawa, et Frank C. Lee, Industrie Canada, 1996.

N° 12   **Les répercussions de la technologie et des importations sur l'emploi et les salaires au Canada**, Frank C. Lee, Industrie Canada, 1996.

N° 13   **La formation d'alliances stratégiques dans les industries canadiennes : une analyse microéconomique**, Sunder Magun, Applied International Economics, 1996.

N° 14   **Performance de l'emploi dans l'économie du savoir**, Surendra Gera, Industrie Canada, et Philippe Massé, Développement des ressources humaines Canada, 1997.

N° 15　**L'économie du savoir et l'évolution de la production industrielle**, Surendra Gera, Industrie Canada, et Kurt Mang, ministère des Finances, 1997.

N° 16　**Stratégies commerciales des PME et des grandes entreprises au Canada**, Gilles Mcdougall et David Swimmer, Direction de l'analyse de la politique micro-économique, Industrie Canada, 1997.

N° 17　**Incidence sur l'économie mondiale des réformes en matière d'investissement étranger et de commerce mises en oeuvre en Chine**, Winnie Lam, Direction de l'analyse de la politique micro-économique, Industrie Canada, 1997.

N° 18　**Les disparités régionales au Canada : diagnostic, tendances et leçons pour la politique économique**, Serge Coulombe, Département de sciences économiques, Université d'Ottawa, 1997.

N° 19　**Retombées de la R-D entre industries et en provenance des États-Unis, production industrielle et croissance de la productivité au Canada**, Jeffrey I. Bernstein, Université Carleton et National Bureau of Economic Research, dans le cadre d'un contrat avec Industrie Canada, 1998.

N° 20　**Technologie de l'information et croissance de la productivité du travail : analyse empirique de la situation au Canada et aux États-Unis**, Surendra Gera, Wulong Gu et Frank C. Lee, Direction de l'analyse de la politique micro-économique, Industrie Canada, 1998.

N° 21　**Progrès technique incorporé au capital et ralentissement de la croissance de la productivité au Canada**, Surendra Gera, Wulong Gu et Frank C. Lee, Direction de l'analyse de la politique micro-économique, Industrie Canada, 1998.

N° 23　**La restructuration de l'industrie canadienne : analyse micro-économique**, Sunder Magun, Applied International Economics, dans le cadre d'un contrat avec Industrie Canada, 1998.

N° 24　**Les politiques du gouvernement canadien à l'égard de l'investissement étranger direct au Canada**, Steven Globerman, Université Simon Fraser et Université Western Washington, et Daniel Shapiro, Université Simon Fraser, dans le cadre d'un contrat avec Industrie Canada, 1998.

N° 25　**Une évaluation structuraliste des politiques technologiques – Pertinence du modèle schumpétérien**, Richard G. Lipsey et Kenneth Carlaw, Université Simon Fraser, avec la collaboration de Davit D. Akman, chercheur associé, dans le cadre d'un contrat avec Industrie Canada, 1998.

N° 26　**Commerce intrasociété des entreprises transnationales étrangères au Canada**, Richard A. Cameron, Direction de l'analyse de la politique micro-économique, Industrie Canada, 1998.

N° 27　**La hausse récente des demandes de brevets et la performance des principaux pays industrialisés sur le plan de l'innovation – Tendances et explications**, Mohammed Rafiquzzaman et Lori Whewell, Direction de l'analyse de la politique micro-économique, Industrie Canada, 1998.

N° 28　**Technologie et demande de compétences : une analyse au niveau de l'industrie**, Surendra Gera et Wulong Gu, Industrie Canada, et Zhengxi Lin, Statistique Canada, 1999.

N° 29　**L'écart de productivité entre les entreprises canadiennes et américaines**, Frank C. Lee et Jianmin Tang, Direction de l'analyse de la politique micro-économique, Industrie Canada, 1999.

N° 30　**Investissement étranger direct et croissance de la productivité : l'expérience du Canada comme pays d'accueil**, Surendra Gera, Wulong Gu et Frank C. Lee, Direction de l'analyse de la politique micro-économique, Industrie Canada, 1999.

COLLECTION DOCUMENTS DE DISCUSSION

N° 1   **Les multinationales comme agents du changement : définition d'une nouvelle politique canadienne en matière d'investissement étranger direct,** Lorraine Eden, Université Carleton, 1994.

N° 2   **Le changement technologique et les institutions économiques internationales,** Sylvia Ostry, Centre for International Studies, Université de Toronto, dans le cadre d'un contrat avec Industrie Canada, 1995.

N° 3   **La régie des sociétés au Canada et les choix sur le plan des politiques,** Ronald J. Daniels, Faculté de droit, Université de Toronto, et Randall Morck, Faculté d'administration des affaires, Université de l'Alberta, 1996.

N° 4   **L'investissement étranger direct et les politiques d'encadrement du marché : réduire les frictions dans les politiques axées sur la concurrence et la propriété intellectuelle au sein de l'APEC,** Ronald Hirshhorn, 1996.

N° 5   **La recherche d'Industrie Canada sur l'investissement étranger : enseignements et incidence sur les politiques,** Ronald Hirshhorn, 1997.

N° 6   **Rivalité sur les marchés internationaux et nouveaux enjeux pour l'Organisation mondiale du commerce,** Edward M. Graham, Institute for International Economics, Washington (DC), dans le cadre d'un contrat avec Industrie Canada, 1998.

N° 7   **Conséquences des restrictions à la propriété étrangère pour l'économie canadienne – Une analyse sectorielle,** Steven Globerman, Université Western Washington, dans le cadre d'un contrat avec Industrie Canada, 1999.

COLLECTION DOCUMENTS HORS SÉRIE

N° 1   **Obstacles officiels et officieux à l'investissement dans les pays du G-7 : analyse par pays,** Industrie Canada, personnel de la Direction de l'analyse de la politique micro-économique, notamment Ashfaq Ahmad, Colleen Barnes, John Knubley, Rosemary D. MacDonald et Christopher Wilkie, 1994.

       Obstacles officiels et officieux à l'investissement dans les pays du G-7 : résumé et conclusions, Industrie Canada, personnel de la Direction de l'analyse de la politique micro-économique, notamment Ashfaq Ahmad, Colleen Barnes et John Knubley, 1994.

N° 2   **Les initiatives d'expansion commerciale dans les filiales de multinationales au Canada,** Julian Birkinshaw, Université Western Ontario, dans le cadre d'un contrat avec Industrie Canada, 1995.

N° 3   **Le rôle des consortiums de R-D dans le développement de la technologie,** Vinod Kumar, Research Centre for Technology Management, Université Carleton, et Sunder Magun, Centre de droit et de politique commerciale, Université d'Ottawa et Université Carleton, dans le cadre d'un contrat avec Industrie Canada, 1995.

N° 4   **Écarts hommes/femmes dans les programmes universitaires,** Sid Gilbert, Université de Guelph, et Alan Pomfret, King's College, Université Western Ontario, 1995.

N° 5   **La compétitivité : notions et mesures,** Donald G. McFetridge, Département d'économique, Université Carleton, 1995.

N° 6   **Aspects institutionnels des stimulants fiscaux à la R-D : le crédit d'impôt à la RS&DE**, G. Bruce Doern, École d'administration publique, Université Carleton, 1995.

N° 7   **La politique de concurrence en tant que dimension de la politique économique : une analyse comparative**, Robert D. Anderson et S. Dev Khosla, Direction de l'économique et des affaires internationales, Bureau de la politique de concurrence, Industrie Canada, 1995.

N° 8   **Mécanismes et pratiques d'évaluation des répercussions sociales et culturelles des sciences et de la technologie**, Liora Salter, Osgoode Hall Law School, Université de Toronto, dans le cadre d'un contrat avec Industrie Canada, 1995.

N° 9   **Sciences et technologie : perspectives sur les politiques publiques**, Donald G.McFetridge, Département d'économique, Université Carleton, dans le cadre d'un contrat avec Industrie Canada, 1995.

N° 10   **Innovation endogène et croissance : conséquences du point de vue canadien**, Pierre Fortin, Université du Québec à Montréal et Institut canadien de recherches avancées, et Elhanan Helpman, Université de Tel-Aviv et Institut canadien de recherches avancées, dans le cadre d'un contrat avec Industrie Canada, 1995.

N° 11   **Les rapports université-industrie en sciences et technologie**, Jérôme Doutriaux, Université d'Ottawa, et Margaret Barker, Meg Barker Consulting, dans le cadre d'un contrat avec Industrie Canada, 1995.

N° 12   **Technologie et économie : examen de certaines relations critiques**, Michael Gibbons, Université de Sussex, dans le cadre d'un contrat avec Industrie Canada, 1995.

N° 13   **Le perfectionnement des compétences des cadres au Canada**, Keith Newton, Industrie Canada, 1995.

N° 14   **Le facteur humain dans le rendement des entreprises : stratégies de gestion axées sur la productivité et la compétitivité dans l'économie du savoir**, Keith Newton, Industrie Canada, 1996.

.N° 15   **Les charges sociales et l'emploi : un examen de la documentation**, Joni Baran, Industrie Canada, 1996.

N° 16   **Le développement durable : concepts, mesures et déficiences des marchés et des politiques au niveau de l'économie ouverte, de l'industrie et de l'entreprise**, Philippe Crabbé, Institut de recherche sur l'environnement et l'économie, Université d'Ottawa, 1997.

N° 17   **La mesure du développement durable : étude des pratiques en vigueur**, Peter Hardi et Stephan Barg, avec la collaboration de Tony Hodge et Laszlo Pinter, Institut international du développement durable, 1997.

N° 18   **Réduction des obstacles réglementaires au commerce : leçons à tirer de l'expérience européenne pour le Canada**, Ramesh Chaitoo et Michael Hart, Centre de droit et de politique commerciale, Université Carleton, 1997.

N° 19   **Analyse des mécanismes de règlement des différends commerciaux internationaux et conséquences pour l'Accord canadien sur le commerce intérieur**, E. Wayne Clendenning et Robert J. Clendenning, E. Wayne Clendenning & Associates Inc., dans le cadre d'un contrat avec Industrie Canada, 1997.

N° 20   **Les entreprises autochtones : caractéristiques et stratégies de croissance**, David Caldwell et Pamela Hunt, Centre de conseils en gestion, dans le cadre d'un contrat avec Entreprise autochtone Canada, 1998.

COLLECTION LE CANADA AU 21ᵉ SIÈCLE

Nᵒ 1   **Tendances mondiales : 1980-2015 et au delà**, J. Bradford De Long, Université de la Californie, Berkeley, dans le cadre d'un contrat avec Industrie Canada, 1998.

Nᵒ 2   **Libéralisation étendue axée sur les aspects fondamentaux : un cadre pour la politique commerciale canadienne**, Randy Wigle, Université Wilfrid Laurier, dans le cadre d'un contrat avec Industrie Canada, 1998.

Nᵒ 3   **L'intégration économique de l'Amérique du Nord : les 25 dernières années et les 25 prochaines années**, Gary C. Hufbauer et Jeffrey J. Schott, Institute for International Economics, Washington (DC), dans le cadre d'un contrat avec Industrie Canada, 1998.

Nᵒ 4   **Les tendances démographiques au Canada, 1996-2006 : les répercussions sur les secteurs public et privé**, David K. Foot, Richard A. Loreto et Thomas W. McCormack, Madison Avenue Demographics Group, dans le cadre d'un contrat avec Industrie Canada, 1998.

Nᵒ 5   **Investissement : les défis à relever au Canada**, Ronald P. M. Giammarino, Université de la Colombie-Britannique, dans le cadre d'un contrat avec Industrie Canada, 1998.

Nᵒ 6   **Visualiser le 21e siècle – Investissements en infrastructure pour la croissance économique, le bien-être et le mieux-être des Canadiens**, Christian DeBresson, Université du Québec à Montréal, et Stéphanie Barker, Université de Montréal, dans le cadre d'un contrat avec Industrie Canada, 1998.

Nᵒ 7   **Les conséquences du changement technologique pour les politiques de main-d'oeuvre**, Julian R. Betts, Université de la Californie à San Diego, dans le cadre d'un contrat avec Industrie Canada, 1998.

Nᵒ 8   **L'économie et l'environnement : l'expérience récente du Canada et les perspectives d'avenir**, Brian R. Copeland, Université de la Colombie-Britannique, dans le cadre d'un contrat avec Industrie Canada, 1998.

Nᵒ 9   **Réactions individuelles à l'évolution du marché du travail au Canada**, Paul Beaudry et David A. Green, Université de la Colombie-Britannique, dans le cadre d'un contrat avec Industrie Canada, 1998.

Nᵒ 10   **La réaction des entreprises – L'innovation à l'ère de l'information**, Randall Morck, Université de l'Alberta, et Bernard Yeung, Université du Michigan, dans le cadre d'un contrat avec Industrie Canada, 1998.

Nᵒ 11   **Institutions et croissance – Les politiques-cadres en tant qu'instrument de compétitivité**, Ronald J. Daniels, Université de Toronto, dans le cadre d'un contrat avec Industrie Canada, 1998.

COLLECTION PERSPECTIVES SUR LE LIBRE-ÉCHANGE NORD-AMÉRICAIN

Nᵒ 1   **La fabrication dans les pays de petite taille peut-elle survivre à la libéralisation du commerce? L'expérience de l'Accord de libre-échange Canada-États-Unis**, Keith Head et John Ries, Université de la Colombie-Britannique, dans le cadre d'un contrat avec Industrie Canada, 1999.

Nᵒ 2   **Modélisation des liens entre le commerce et l'investissement étranger direct au Canada**, Walid Hejazi et A. Edward Safarian, Université de Toronto, dans le cadre d'un contrat avec Industrie Canada, 1999.

N° 3   **Libéralisation des échanges et migration de travailleurs qualifiés**, Steven Globerman, Université
        Western Washington et Université Simon Fraser, dans le cadre d'un contrat avec Industrie Canada, 1999.

N° 4   **Évolution du profil sectoriel et professionnel du commerce international du Canada**, Peter Dungan et
        Steve Murphy, Institute for Policy Analysis, Université de Toronto, dans le cadre d'un contrat avec
        Industrie Canada, 1999.

PUBLICATIONS CONJOINTES

Capital Budgeting in the Public Sector, en collaboration avec l'Institut John Deutsch, sous la direction
de Jack Mintz et Ross S. Preston, 1994.

Infrastructure and Competitiveness, en collaboration avec l'Institut John Deutsch, sous la direction de
Jack Mintz et Ross S. Preston, 1994.

Getting the Green Light: Environmental Regulation and Investment in Canada, en collaboration avec
l'Institut C. D. Howe, sous la direction de Jamie Benidickson, G. Bruce Doern et Nancy Olewiler, 1994.

Pour obtenir des exemplaires de l'un des documents publiés dans le cadre du Programme des publications de
recherche, veuillez communiquer avec le :

Responsable des publications
Analyse de la politique micro-économique
Industrie Canada
5ᵉ étage, tour ouest
235, rue Queen
Ottawa (Ontario) K1A 0H5

Tél. : (613) 952-5704
Fax : (613) 991-1261
Courriel : mepa.apme@ic.gc.ca